The Hellenistic West

Although the Hellenistic period has become increasingly popular in research and teaching in recent years, the western Mediterranean is rarely considered part of the 'Hellenistic world'; instead the cities, peoples and kingdoms of the West are usually only discussed insofar as they relate to Rome. This book contends that the rift between the 'Greek East' and the 'Roman West' is more a product of the traditional separation of Roman and Greek history than a reflection of the Hellenistic-period Mediterranean, which was a strongly interconnected cultural and economic zone, with the rising Roman Republic just one among many powers in the region, East and West. The contributors argue for a dynamic reading of the economy, politics and history of the central and western Mediterranean beyond Rome, and in doing so problematise the concepts of 'East', 'West' and 'Hellenistic' itself.

JONATHAN R. W. PRAG is University Lecturer in Ancient History at the University of Oxford and Fellow and Tutor of Merton College, Oxford. He has published articles on ancient Sicily, Punic identity, Greek and Roman epigraphy and Roman Republican history, with a particular interest in Roman Republican imperialism. He has edited volumes on Cicero and Petronius and is currently writing a monograph on the use of non-Italian soldiers by the Roman Republican army, collaborating on a commentary on Cicero's *Verrines* and working on a new digital corpus of Sicilian inscriptions.

JOSEPHINE CRAWLEY QUINN is University Lecturer in Ancient History at the University of Oxford and Fellow and Tutor of Worcester College, Oxford. She has published articles on a range of topics in Mediterranean history and archaeology, with particular interests in ancient North Africa and the Phoenicians. She has also co-edited a volume of essays on the Punic Mediterranean with Nicholas Vella, served as editor of the *Papers of the British School at Rome* 2008–11, and co-directs the Tunisian–British excavations at Utica with Andrew Wilson and Elizabeth Fentress.

The Hellenistic West

Rethinking the Ancient Mediterranean

Edited by

JONATHAN R. W. PRAG

AND

JOSEPHINE CRAWLEY QUINN

CAMBRIDGE
UNIVERSITY PRESS

CAMBRIDGE
UNIVERSITY PRESS

University Printing House, Cambridge CB2 8BS, United Kingdom

Cambridge University Press is part of the University of Cambridge.

It furthers the University's mission by disseminating knowledge in the pursuit of education, learning and research at the highest international levels of excellence.

www.cambridge.org
Information on this title: www.cambridge.org/9781316625705

© Cambridge University Press 2013

This publication is in copyright. Subject to statutory exception and to the provisions of relevant collective licensing agreements, no reproduction of any part may take place without the written permission of Cambridge University Press.

First published 2013
Reprinted 2014
First paperback edition 2016

A catalogue record for this publication is available from the British Library

Library of Congress Cataloguing in Publication data
The Hellenistic West : rethinking the ancient Mediterranean / edited by Jonathan R.W. Prag and Josephine Crawley Quinn.
pages cm
Includes bibliographical references and index.
ISBN 978-1-107-03242-2
1. Mediterranean Region – Civilization – Greek influences. 2. Mediterranean Region – History – To 476. 3. Hellenism – History. 4. Greeks – Mediterranean Region – History. 5. Greeks – Colonization – Mediterranean Region. I. Prag, J. R. W., author, editor of compilation. II. Quinn, Josephine Crawley, author, editor of compilation.
DF235.H45 2013
937.00481–dc23

2013013369

ISBN 978-1-107-03242-2 Hardback
ISBN 978-1-316-62570-5 Paperback

Cambridge University Press has no responsibility for the persistence or accuracy of URLs for external or third-party internet websites referred to in this publication, and does not guarantee that any content on such websites is, or will remain, accurate or appropriate.

Contents

Figures

Colour plates

Contributors

EDWARD BISPHAM is Lecturer in Ancient History in the Faculty of Classics at the University of Oxford and a Fellow of Brasenose College, Oxford.

ANDREW ERSKINE is Professor of Ancient History in the School of History, Classics and Archaeology at the University of Edinburgh.

ELIZABETH FENTRESS is an independent scholar and President of the International Association of Classical Archaeology (AIAC).

SIMON KEAY is Professor of Roman Archaeology in the Department of Archaeology at the University of Southampton and Research Professor at the British School at Rome.

ANN KUTTNER is Associate Professor in the Department of History of Art at the University of Pennsylvania.

MIREIA LÓPEZ-BERTRAN is a postdoctoral fellow of the Spanish Ministry of Education and Culture/Fundación Española para la Ciencia y Tecnología (FECYT) in the School of Humanities at the University of Glasgow.

JONATHAN R. W. PRAG is Lecturer in Ancient History in the Faculty of Classics at the University of Oxford and a Fellow of Merton College, Oxford.

NICHOLAS PURCELL is Camden Professor of Ancient History in the Faculty of Classics at the University of Oxford and a Fellow of Brasenose College, Oxford.

JOSEPHINE CRAWLEY QUINN is Lecturer in Ancient History in the Faculty of Classics at the University of Oxford and a Fellow of Worcester College, Oxford.

PETER VAN DOMMELEN is Joukowsky Family Professor of Archaeology and Professor of Anthropology at the Joukowsky Institute for Archaeology and the Ancient World, Brown University.

ANDREW WALLACE-HADRILL is Professor of Roman Studies and Director of Research in the Faculty of Classics, University of Cambridge.

ANDREW WILSON is Professor of the Archaeology of the Roman Empire and Head of the School of Archaeology at the University of Oxford, and a Fellow of All Souls College, Oxford.

R. J. A. WILSON is Professor of the Archaeology of the Roman Empire in the Department of Classical, Near Eastern and Religious Studies at the University of British Columbia.

LIV MARIAH YARROW is Associate Professor in the Classics Department at Brooklyn College, The City University of New York.

Acknowledgements

First and foremost we wish to thank the contributors to this volume for their enthusiasm, hard work, practical help and in particular for their patience, as the book's gestation has been longer than we would have wished. We are no less grateful to Jean-Louis Ferrary for his lively participation in both the Oxford and Rome seminars, and warmly direct readers to the now-published version of his paper (Ferrary 2011). In addition to the individual contributors, and the participants at the different meetings, we would like to thank the staff at the Oxford Faculty of Classics and at the British School at Rome for their hospitality and, for their help and support at various stages along the way, Boris Chrubasik, John Ma, Bert Smith, Nicola Terrenato, Chris Brooke and Gaia Scerif. We also owe a major debt of gratitude to Michael Sharp for his advice and support from the beginning of the project.

We are grateful for the financial support of the Arts and Humanities Research Council (AHRC), the Faculty of Classics at the University of Oxford, the Classics Faculty's Craven Committee, the British School at Rome, The Warden and Scholars of Merton College and The Provost and Fellows of Worcester College.

Peter Derow introduced us to each other in 2000 and was a great supporter of this project. He died in December 2006, and we dedicate this volume to his memory.

Abbreviations

Journal titles are abbreviated after the fashion of *L'Année philologique*. Ancient authors and their works are abbreviated after Hornblower, S. and Spawforth, A. (eds.) (2003) *The Oxford Classical Dictionary*, 3rd edn revised, Oxford. The other abbreviations employed in the volume are detailed below.

AE	*L'Année épigraphique. Revue des publications épigraphiques relatives à l'antiquité romaine*. Paris. 1888–.
BE	*Bulletin épigraphique*, published annually in *Revue des Études Grecques*. 1888–.
CCAG	Cumont, F. *et al.* (eds.) (1898–1953). *Catalogus Codicum Astrologorum Graecorum* (12 vols.). Brussels.
CIL	*Corpus Inscriptionum Latinarum, consilio et auctoritate Academiae litterarum regiae Borussicae editum*. Berlin. 1863–.
CILA	*Corpus de inscripciones latinas de Andalucía*. Seville. 1989–.
CIS	*Corpus Inscriptionum Semiticarum, ab Academia Inscriptionum et Litterarum Humaniorum conditum atque digestum*. Paris. 1881–.
FGrH	Jacoby, F. (1923–). *Die Fragmente der griechischen Historiker*. Berlin, Leiden.
I. Lamp.	Frisch, P. (1978). *Die Inschriften von Lampsakos*. Bonn.
I. Magnesia	Kern, O. (1900). *Die Inschriften von Magnesia am Maeander*. Berlin.
ICO	Amadasi Guzzo, M. G. (1967). *Le Iscrizioni fenicie e puniche delle colonie in Occidente*. Studi Semitici 28. Rome.
ID	*Inscriptions de Délos* (7 vols.). Paris. 1926–72.
IG	*Inscriptiones Graecae*. Berlin. 1903–. (Note that *IG* XIV was published prior to this series and subsequently

	integrated into it: Kaibel, G. (1890). *Inscriptiones Graecae Italiae et Siciliae*. Berlin.)
LTUR	Steinby, E. M. (ed.) (1993–9). *Lexicon topographicum urbis Romae* (6 vols.). Rome.
OGIS	Dittenberger, W. (1903–5). *Orientis Graeci Inscriptiones Selectae. Supplementum Sylloges Inscriptionum Graecarum* (2 vols.). Leipzig.
RDGE	Sherk, R. K. (1969). *Roman Documents from the Greek East: Senatus Consulta and Epistulae to the Age of Augustus*. Baltimore.
RIL	Chabot, J.-B. (1940–1). *Recueil des inscriptions libyques*. Paris.
RPC	Burnett, A., Amandry, M. and Ripollès, P. P. (1992). *Roman Provincial Coinage*, Vol. I. London and Paris.
RRC	Crawford, M. H. (1974). *Roman Republican Coinage* (2 vols.). Cambridge.
SEG	*Supplementum Epigraphicum Graecum*. Leiden. 1923–.
SNG ANS	*Sylloge Nummorum Graecorum. The Collection of the American Numismatic Society*. New York. 1961–.
SNG München	*Sylloge Nummorum Graecorum Deutschland. Staatliche Münzsammlung München*. Berlin. 1968–.
Syll.^{3}	Dittenberger, W. (1915–24). *Sylloge Inscriptionum Graecarum* (4 vols.), 3rd edn. Leipzig.
Ve.	Vetter, E. (1953). *Handbuch der italischen Dialekte*. Heidelberg.

Introduction

JONATHAN R. W. PRAG AND JOSEPHINE CRAWLEY QUINN

The Hellenistic West: provocation, posturing or, as we will argue, a useful paradox? We are not trying to create a new sub-discipline or regional history, and it will become clear that we would not be entirely happy to see the term embedded in academic discourse. Crucially, this is not a volume about the Hellenisation of the western Mediterranean. Instead, the overriding motivation for instituting the seminar, workshop and conference panels which underlie this set of papers was our disquiet at the persistence of the historiographical tradition of the 'Greek East and Roman West', and the negative effect this has had on attempts to write history both of and in the Mediterranean. It is this binary tradition which creates our paradoxical title for a volume concerned, loosely, with the western half of the Mediterranean in the last four centuries BC, in deliberate contrast to work on the western Mediterranean under Rome, or the eastern Mediterranean under the Hellenistic kingdoms. We wanted to decentralise Greek and Roman narratives in the study of the ancient Mediterranean – without deemphasising them. The absence of such a study seemed to us to call for redress; it also raised questions about the categories we think in, including 'Hellenistic' and 'West'. Before briefly advertising our collective response, we shall examine the problems of these particular categorisations in more depth.

East and West

In general terms, the gap between the Greek East and the Roman West that concerned us is easily illustrated in the latest companions and handbooks. Works on the Hellenistic world rarely extend westwards of the Adriatic or Cyrenaica.[1] Works on the Roman Republic are only concerned with a

[1] Examples of limited engagement: Shipley 2000: 51–2 on Agathocles, 368–99 on Rome and Greece; Erskine 2003a has one chapter (E. Dench 'Beyond Greeks and Barbarians: Italy and Sicily in the Hellenistic Age') and cf. Fig. 2.1 for a map that stops at the Adriatic and Fig. 4.1 for a map of 'Italy and the West' in which Italy is in fact 'the West'; Bugh 2006a has no map that extends beyond the Adriatic and no specific section on anything west of Greece.

region once it comes under Roman rule and, outside of specialised studies of a region such as the Iberian peninsula, the general narrative of Rome and the West is itself narrowly focused upon the clash with Carthage as precursor to the clash between Rome and the eastern Greek world (as indeed already in Polybius).[2] The second edition of the *Cambridge Ancient History* demonstrates the point perfectly: vol. VI, *The Fourth Century BC*, ranges extremely widely indeed; but with vol. VII a split occurs. VII.i, *The Hellenistic World*, has a chapter on 'Agathocles', but otherwise nothing west of mainland Greece or Ptolemaic Egypt; VII.ii, *The Rise of Rome to 220 BC*, is focused entirely upon Rome and Italy with the very limited exception of chapters on 'Pyrrhus' and 'Carthage and Rome'. The world outside of the Hellenistic kingdoms and the Roman Republic essentially ceases to exist in the course of the fourth century, until or unless it comes into contact with the Macedonian spear or Roman sword.

Of course, one should not criticise histories of *x* for not being histories of *y*. But it remains curious that in a post-colonial, post-modern world, in which the concepts of both Romanisation and Hellenisation have been challenged for several decades, a world in which the broader division between East and West – conveniently labelled 'Orientalism' – has been undermined and the prioritisation of Greco–Roman culture repeatedly called into question, this particular strait-jacket remains. Attempts to overcome it are not new, and our title consciously echoes the now-classic conference volume of 1976, *Hellenismus in Mittelitalien*.[3] But even the increasingly sophisticated approaches to 'Hellenism' in Italy inspired by that work ultimately served to perpetuate the Greek East/Roman West dichotomy and to prioritise eastern Hellenism.[4] More recent work has extended that particular vision and placed greater emphasis upon local

[2] The chapters in Flower 2004 offer a typical sequence: expansion in Italy, the wars with Carthage, and 'Rome and Greek world'; the same narrative can be found also in Eckstein 2006 (esp. 118–80, Italy and Carthage) whose aims are in principle grander. J. Richardson 1986 is a fine example of a regional Romano-centric study. Van Dommelen and Gómez Bellard 2008 are almost unique in offering a non-Romano-centric study of the western Mediterranean basin in this period.

[3] Zanker 1976a. The same problem is implicit in the provocative observation of Pollitt 1993: 103: 'This symposium has provoked a number of interesting reflections on the role of frontiers in the Hellenistic world. The chief fountain of inspiration for the artists of the Hellenistic period was understandably old Greece, but to the extent that they were affected by frontiers, I think it can be asserted that the most influential one was not the Sudan or the Hindu Kush; it was the Tiber.'

[4] Bilde *et al.* 1993 is perhaps the closest in spirit to our enterprise: the editors note (p. 10), after the work of Champion, that 'there is no such thing as simple polarity and distinction between a centre and a periphery', and that there is a need 'to accommodate not only the dynamics of change, but also the differing views, past as well as present, on the presumed centres and peripheries'.

cultures in response to Hellenisation and/or Romanisation.[5] Indeed, the increased emphasis upon local and material culture studies has resulted in an increasing deconstruction of the pre- and post-Rome narratives at the local level.[6] The recent focus upon Carthage and the Punic world has likewise had a decentralising effect (below, n. 24). However, it is not obvious to us that the overarching model has altered, nor the dichotomy weakened, and one of our explicit aims has been to challenge the pervasive meta-narrative of ancient history which separates Mediterranean history into East and (then) West, and presents Rome as a successor to the eastern Hellenistic kingdoms.[7]

Hellenistics

Our other major aim was to use the western context to investigate the ambiguities and ultimately the value of the term 'Hellenistic', traditionally and variously used in a chronological, politico-institutional or socio-cultural sense. The adjective has its ultimate origins in the noun ἑλληνισμός (*hellenismos*), famously first deployed in 2 *Maccabees* 4.13 (of which the subsequently epitomised original is generally thought to be later second century BC), and already there carrying the sense of

[5] So, for example, Torelli 1995 prioritises the responses of local cultures in Italy in response to Rome, building explicitly on Zanker 1976a and others, but the papers collected in *Pallas* 70 (2006) mark in many respects a repeat of the model of Zanker's *Hellenismus* colloquium: the subject matter is narrowly 'Hellenisation', rather than the broader questions of interaction, regionalism and periodisation; the focus is chronologically very limited, and the principal extension is the increased reference to Carthage in tandem with Rome. Further recent work in the same general direction can be found in Osanna and Torelli 2006. Colivicchi 2011 shifts the focus slightly, albeit in an ultimately Romano-centric fashion and with a narrow concentration on Italy (plus two papers on Sicily). Curti *et al.* 1996: 181–8 (esp. the final paragraph of 188) still offers one of the most nuanced responses to the issues. For an up-to-date treatment of Italy in this period, both in terms of evidence and conceptual approaches, see now Wallace-Hadrill 2008.

[6] Although 'Romanisation' has undergone very extensive deconstruction in the last two decades, volumes such as Keay and Terrenato 2001 maintain the underlying model of the (post-conquest) 'Roman West'. Van Dommelen and Terrenato 2007 has more in common with our aims and approach, but it is still couched in terms of 'the differences between the ways in which both different regions became part of the Roman Republic and how different social and economic groups within these regional communities were incorporated in the new Republican setting' (introduction, p. 7). There is a convenient overview of historiographical issues associated with Italy in this period in Dench 2003: 295–8; cf. Campagna 2003c on Sicily.

[7] Firmly maintained and so reinforced, whether intentionally or not, by e.g. Scheidel *et al.* 2007: the only chapter specifically on the 'western Mediterranean' is 'The Iron Age in the western Mediterranean', thereafter sections examine 'Classical Greece', 'The Hellenistic States', 'Early Italy and the Roman Republic', etc. (cf. Archibald *et al.* 2011: 12).

'the Greek way of life', rather than the narrower language-based signification which was primary in the earlier use of ἑλληνίζειν (*hellénizein*, e.g. Thucydides 2.68).[8] 'Hellenism' thus in broad terms designates the Greek way of life, and that meaning, at least in English, has never been lost. However, famously, the nineteenth-century German scholar Johann Gustav Droysen gave the German equivalent *Hellenismus* a rather more particular focus, both in terms of content and chronology. Droysen developed an idea of *Hellenismus* as fusion between Greek and non-Greek, principally in the period between Alexander the Great and Jesus Christ, which led to the increasing formalisation of the 'Hellenistic' period as the period of *Hellenismus*.[9] But Droysen himself was unclear about the chronological and geographical limits of the concept, even if he was clear on the particular significance of the period between Alexander and Christ (for geographical reasons as much as anything else, of which more below). The terminology of Hellenism has the potential to extend forwards and backwards so far as elements of Greek-speaking civilisation are involved.[10] This is perhaps more obvious in English, where there is a real reluctance to treat 'Hellenism' as equivalent to (Droysen's) *Hellenismus* and so to limit its significance to the period traditionally known as Hellenistic.[11] By denying the potential equivalence, however, one also denies the ambiguity present in both the terms Hellenism and *Hellenismus*, in Droysen no less than elsewhere, and by extension in the term Hellenistic. After all, no claim about Hellenism or about Hellenising, whether linguistic or cultural, makes much sense except in relation to something which can be described by someone as more or less non-Greek.

In the face of such ambiguities, and the general trend for deconstruction of which this volume is but another example, historians of the Hellenistic period seem increasingly content to adopt 'an honest definition of the hellenistic world in plain language . . . [in terms of its primary constituant

[8] For the date of 2 Maccabees, e.g. Habicht 1976: 170–5.

[9] Trenchant summaries of the topic by Walter Eder, s.v. 'Hellenism', in *Brill's New Pauly, Antiquity*, Leiden, 2005, VI, cols. 85–6 and Simon Hornblower, s.v. 'Hellenism, Hellenization', in *The Oxford Classical Dictionary* (3rd edn revised), Oxford, 2003, 677–9. See also Wallace-Hadrill and Bispham's Chapters 2 and 3 (this volume), on Droysen and Hellenism, as well as, classically, Momigliano 1970 and Bichler 1983.

[10] Noted already, e.g., by Préaux 1978: 5–6.

[11] Typical example of rejection, without further explanation, in Bugh 2006b: 1; contrast the earlier reverse approach in Tarn and Griffith 1952: 1, n. 1, claiming that 'Hellenism' is the mis-formed noun from 'Hellenistic' (rather than the unwieldy 'Hellenisticism'). There is an instructive parallel here in the absence from modern English usage of the noun 'Punics', from the adjective 'Punic', which has similarly led to considerable terminological confusion (cf. Aubet 2001: 12–13; Prag 2006: 4–7).

element] namely the highly distinctive group of inter-marrying and warring dynasts that presided over it, both directly and indirectly'.[12] Nothing wrong with that, but if so narrowly defined then Hellenistic history indeed runs in parallel to Roman Republican history (and Romanisation), and everything else is left out. However, Hellenistic historians tend to want to have their cake and to eat it, since the period is often presented as distinctive culturally, socially and economically as well as politically; here Droysen's *Hellenismus* – and Hellenism – resurface, and this is where the difference with Roman Republican history is most apparent. Tellingly, in the chapters which cover these other elements in works on the Hellenistic world, the geographical focus tends to be much broader than in the rest of the volume.[13]

Yet Droysen, who gets blamed for so much, did not intend a narrow geographical limitation to his Hellenistic world: the opening pages of volume three of his paradigm-shifting history make this abundantly clear.[14] For Droysen, the 'West' was the Mediterranean, all the way to the bounds of Ocean; the 'East' was the Iranian plateau, from the Syrian, Asia Minor and Caucasus mountains all the way to the Indus. The reason why the period from Alexander to Christ was so important, culturally, was because it was for Droysen the crucial period when the boundary between this East and West was broken down, only to be re-formed as the opposition between Rome and Parthia established itself.[15] This indeed resulted in a model where the important boundary between East and West shifted westwards into the Mediterranean: 'the old opposition between Asia and Europe' was overturned – in fact reversed – with the developing cultural

[12] Ogden 2002b: x–xi, echoed approvingly by Lane Fox 2011: 4; cf. Shipley 2000: 3, 'an investigation of the effects of Macedonian conquest upon Greece and the Near East'.

[13] So to take two of the more narrowly defined recent works: in Bugh 2006a, John Davies on economies summarises the '"main lines" of Mediterranean exchange' with a list of routes that goes from the Black Sea to the far western Mediterranean, including Carthage and Etruria, and looks wholly at odds with the volume as a whole (p. 78); Peter Stewart on art puts the houses of Sicilian Morgantina alongside those of Delos (p. 166, 178), although Sicily barely features in the volume otherwise; and in Ogden 2002a, Westgate on mosaics devotes considerable space to e.g. Morgantina, while ranging from Spain to Afghanistan. In similar vein, it is rather striking that the cover illustration of Flower 2004 (*Companion to the Roman Republic*) should be the famous Nilotic mosaic from Praeneste (baldly described in the cover note as 'Roman' and only picked up in any meaningful way in Ann Kuttner's chapter on art; Egypt otherwise warrants about two paragraphs).

[14] In the following reference is made to and quotations taken from the three-volume German second edition of 1877–8, which united Droysen's original history of Alexander (1833) with his two-volume history of the period 323–220 BC (1836 and 1843).

[15] See the concluding chapter in this volume by Purcell for a much more detailed reconsideration of history in the period in these geographical terms.

divide for Droysen being first that between Punic West and Greek/ Hellenistic East, followed by a three-way division as Rome rises between Punic West and Hellenistic East.[16] Droysen nevertheless went on to devote more pages to the western Mediterranean than we have found in any later history of the so-called Hellenistic world, as part of a vision which was concerned to map the evolution of both East and West (in his broad definition) in relation to and under the influence of Hellenism. Pyrrhus' expedition into Italy and Sicily requires a chapter by itself, precisely because 'with the war against Pyrrhus, Rome entered the sphere of major political relationships, which, bound up with the Punic name and that of *Hellenismus*, extended from the Pillars of Hercules to the Ganges'.[17] Very strikingly, it is Polybius 1.3.3–4 that Droysen chooses to quote in full in the course of a set of remarks concluding the introductory chapter to volume III, which range from Rome and Carthage, through Lagid and Seleucid actions, and the formation of Parthian and Greek Bactrian empires, to the Pergamene and northern dynasties:

> Previously the doings of the world had been, so to say, dispersed, as they were held together by no unity of initiative, results, or locality; but ever since this date history has been an organic whole, and the affairs of Italy and Libya have been interlinked with those of Greece and Asia, all leading up to one end.

Droysen follows this up by noting again that '. . . a great coherence embraces political relations from the Pillars of Hercules to the Indus . . .'[18] Droysen, like Polybius, and in contrast to most subsequent Hellenistic history, had space for Rome, Carthage and further west still, in a vision of the *oikoumene* that was explicitly greater than that of the Macedonian conquests alone:

> . . . they [the Macedonians] still left the greater part of the inhabited world in the hands of others. For not once did they attempt to lay claim to Sicily, Sardinia or Libya, and as to Europe, if one is to be blunt about it, they did not even know of the most warlike peoples of the West.[19]

It would of course be wholly futile to deny that within this grand historical vision Hellenism still has pride of place: Droysen's view of Rome is more explicit than Polybius', with the ensuing narrative ultimately couched in

[16] Droysen 1877–8: III, 6: 'Rome drove itself like a wedge between Punic West and Hellenistic East'.

[17] Droysen 1877–8: III, 183.

[18] Droysen 1877–8: III, 114–15; note moreover that Droysen's *symploke* (to use the Polybian term) is on display a whole century earlier than Polybius'. See Erskine (Chapter 1 in this volume) and Quinn 2013 for a fuller discussion of the Polybian presentation.

[19] Polyb. 1.2.5–6 (trans. Erskine, and see further Erskine in Chapter 1).

terms of the struggle of Hellenism against, *inter alia*, the 'demonic force of the Roman people'.[20] Nevertheless, the broader vision is undeniable.

Why, then, has the history of the Mediterranean world in this period, since Droysen, become ever more compartmentalised and subordinated to these grand narratives of Greece and Rome rather than less?[21] This is hardly a question we can answer in full here, but we pick out several trends and themes.

Firstly, Droysen belonged to an age when one could write entirely positively of Carthage, on a par with Rome, for instance comparing Punic policy (favourably) with the model of English imperialism in the eighteenth century.[22] As is now well-documented, the shifting fortunes of Phoenicio-Punic studies, in particular from the later nineteenth century onwards, have had consequences for how we write the history of the western Mediterranean.[23] The recent flourishing of Punic studies has so far done little to alter the broader Greek East/Roman West dichotomy, since the Punic world is itself most often constructed as a discrete Western phenomenon, focused upon Carthage and viewed in opposition to both the Greek East and the developing Roman West (as indeed it was by Droysen), while also perceived as lacking in significance, other than as one part of the Roman West, by the second century BC.[24] The continued relative isolation of Punic studies is also symptomatic of the broader problem not simply of the prioritisation of Greco-Roman culture (and in particular Greco-Roman texts), but of the more general prioritisation of textual evidence over material culture, as well as the oft-bemoaned trend towards academic specialisation and in particular the historical divisions between classical ancient history and (non-classical) archaeology. 'When no . . . texts are available it can even be hard to acknowledge that a culture

[20] Droysen 1877–8: III, 185.

[21] The striking exception, although still couched firmly in terms of Hellenism and Rome, is Grimal *et al.* 1968.

[22] Droysen 1877–8: III, 292: In the period between Pyrrhus and the First Punic War, 'the prudent and cautiously calculating [Carthaginian] government demonstrated an energy, prudence, maintenance of material resources, and ruthless sacrifice of its immense treasury, such as would subsequently only be seen in English policy of the eighteenth century'. In this respect Hornblower (n. 9 above) is a little harsh on Droysen when he places him alongside all those later writers who were Bernal's target for undervaluing the Semitic Mediterranean.

[23] See e.g. Bernal 1987: cc. 8–9; Vella 1996; Liverani 1998; Bonnet 2005.

[24] This growth in Punic studies has been marked by the rise in manuals such as Lipiński 1992, Krings 1995 or Bondì 2009a; exhibition volumes such as *I Fenici* (1988), *Hannibal ad Portas* (2004), *La Méditerranée des Phéniciens* (2007); the major quinquennial *Congresso internazionale di studi fenici e punici* (begun in Rome in 1979); and research volumes such as Van Dommelen and Gómez Bellard 2008 or Quinn and Vella (forthcoming).

exists at all in any but the anthropological sense. Yet it hardly needs pointing out that such an intellectual framework is basically colonialist.'[25] If this is a problem for Punic studies, it is an even greater problem for the study of regions such as Numidia, Iberia, Gaul or Sardinia.

Secondly, we identify a more specific historiographic trend. Arthur Eckstein has recently taken up the banner of Maurice Holleaux's powerful and hugely influential attempt to demolish the evidence for Roman political engagement with the Greek East prior to the very end of the third century BC. This is a view which takes as one of its central tenets the idea of a 'sudden emergence of deep Roman involvement in the Greek Mediterranean' – 'Rome enters the Greek East'.[26] Although Holleaux himself did not deny the existence of contact between Rome and the Greek world in general, his powerful polemic levelled against any evidence for early Roman imperial engagement with the Greek East seems to have had this as its (unintended?) consequence. Holleaux's target was the idea that Rome had a preconceived intention to extend the conquest of Italy eastwards into the Greek world.[27] To achieve this end, he began by systematically rejecting each of the supposed instances of political contact between Rome and the Greek East in the period between Pyrrhus and the First Illyrian War, beginning with the accounts of an embassy between Rome and Apollonia (on the east coast of the Adriatic) in 266 BC. The scholarly genealogy presented by Holleaux for criticism as 'les historiens modernes', 'gens d'imagination' who had accepted that and other such incidents, begins with Droysen and continues through Mommsen and Hirschfeld to 'autres encores'.[28] Droysen, in line with his pan-Mediterranean approach, regularly accepted and discussed this and many other such episodes – but he is visibly alone in the list as a non-Roman historian and, after Holleaux, it seems, that door was firmly closed.[29] Ernst Badian subsequently made a serious plea for Sicily's importance in the development of Roman imperial practices, but the

[25] Davies 1984: 263; the general refrain is common in Hellenistic handbooks (e.g. Bugh 2006b: 3), but only with reference to how to treat the East.

[26] Eckstein 2008: 6 where he makes explicit that he offers 'a view similar to Holleaux'; cf. Holleaux 1921: esp. 1–24.

[27] This is not the place to discuss the merits of Holleaux's specific arguments (see 1921: i–iv for the statement of aims); but one might note that Pyrrhus and the 'Greek' world of southern Italy, Sicily and the Gallo-Iberian litoral are spectacularly ignored. Pyrrhus, defender of 'l'hellénisme contre la barbarie', is explicitly left out of consideration because he and his predecessors 'are not relevant to the history of the Republic's foreign policy' (1921: i).

[28] Holleaux 1921: 2 at nn. 4–7.

[29] Droysen 1877–8: III, 183–4 for Apollonia; cf. e.g. III, 183 for the Ptolemaic alliance in 273 BC; III, 303–6 on East–West political relations in the context of the First Punic War; III, 387 n.1 for the Seleucid alliance with Rome at the end of the First Punic War; and III, 439–40 on Roman

failure of that particular effort may have served merely to reinforce the East-West division in analysis of Roman imperialism.[30] What is so striking in Eckstein and other such formulations, is the apparent equation of the Mediterranean world east of the Adriatic with the 'Greek Mediterranean' or the 'Hellenic world', as well as the sweeping nature of the claim, not merely political in focus (as it was in Holleaux), but seemingly absolute.[31] This division, at least in relation to Roman political history, seems to have grown stronger with time and, as we have seen, it is the grand narratives of political history which tend to set the overall framework.

Thirdly, we emphasise geography. This theme is explored more fully by Nicholas Purcell later in this volume, but it is perhaps worth highlighting the contrast between Droysen's pan-Mediterranean 'West' and the much greater emphasis in more recent work upon a Mediterranean of two halves. In the geographical sketch with which his third volume opens, Droysen contrasted the Mediterranean North and South geographically, rather than East and West.[32] In discussion of both Asian East and Mediterranean West, these grand regions are also subdivided into multiple basins – in the case of the Mediterranean, the familiar East and West.[33] But given the shifting influence of Carthage, Rome and the Hellenistic states in Droysen's subsequent account, these basins are rarely if ever rigidly defined or to be found at the centre of the analysis. By contrast, Fernand Braudel, notwithstanding his assertion of the unity of the Mediterranean region, set out 'the narrow seas, home of history' early in his work, and in particular urged very strongly the idea of a sharp geographical East–West division, formed by the Ionian Sea and the Libyan desert, a 'double zone of emptiness, maritime and continental, separating East from West'. He goes on to assert that:

relations generally in 240 BC. Note that Holleaux was invited to contribute to the first edition of the *Cambridge Ancient History*.

30 Badian 1958: 33–43, arguing in particular for Sicily's role in the development of the concept of the *ciuitas libera*, rather than leaving all the emphasis upon T. Quinctius Flamininus and the Second Macedonian War; see especially the corrective of Ferrary 1988: 5–23.

31 Cf. Gruen 1984: 1, examining 'The earliest stages of intercourse between Roman West and Hellenic East'. Gruen of course set out to decentralise the role of Rome in an analysis of Roman imperialism and e.g. Gruen 1990 and 1992 offer sophisticated discussions of the relationship between Hellenism and Roman cultural evolution that belong in the post-*Hellenismus in Mittelitalien* tradition noted above. But the Roman West/Greek East model is not challenged, and the rest of the West remains outside the discussion (cf. 1984: 8).

32 See esp. Droysen 1877–8: III, 4; concluding p. 6 that 'These are the geographical conditions in general overview which form the foundation for the whole course of ancient history.'

33 Droysen 1877–8: III, 1–6, with the two Mediterranean basins mentioned (but not explicitly defined) on p. 6.

> To claim that the considerable obstacles between the two halves of the Mediterranean effectively separated them from each other would be to profess a form of geographical determinism, extreme, but not altogether mistaken ... The two halves of the sea, in spite of trading links and cultural exchanges, maintained their autonomy and their own spheres of influence. Genuine intermingling of populations was to be found only inside each region, and within these limits it defied all barriers of race, culture, or religion. All human links between different ends of the Mediterranean, by contrast, remained an adventure or at least a gamble.[34]

The occasional exceptions noted, but described as 'either short-lived or followed by the severing of connections' are Phoenician Carthage, Greek Marseilles, the Byzantines and the Arabs (Rome is conspicuous by its absence from this list). At this point Braudel's rapid historical examples are offered as a proof of the principle: history repeats itself, and is additionally confirmed by the reverse example of the crusades. But this only holds true if the underlying historical narratives are true. Braudel may have opened a new door on Mediterranean studies and may have argued for the study of the Mediterranean as a unity, but he simultaneously reinforced the narrative of Mediterranean East and West. Here too, the direction of travel has been altering in recent years: Mediterranean studies are now flourishing, and in *The Corrupting Sea* we have a significant attempt to reappraise the place of the Mediterranean in history.[35] The influence of that work will be apparent in a number of the contributions below, to which we now turn.

Papers

The papers in this volume derive from a series of meetings in Oxford, Rome and Vancouver over 2006 and 2007, followed up by a lengthy period of

[34] Braudel 1972: I, 103 and 133–5 for the various quotations; cf. 103 'The Mediterranean is not a single sea but a succession of small seas that communicate by means of wider or narrower entrances. In the two great east and west basins of the Mediterranean there is a series of highly individual narrow seas ...'; also Fig. 10 on p. 115. The first edition in French was published in 1949. Compare in general Horden and Purcell 2000: 9–25, and for a more recent micro-study, Quinn 2011a.

[35] Horden and Purcell 2000: esp. 123–72 (building on, e.g. the work of Shlomo Dov Goitein). For Mediterranean studies, see e.g: Harris 2005a; Malkin 2005; Van Dommelen and Knapp 2010; also the journal *Mediterranean Historical Review*, founded in 1986, which began with a survey of the work of Goitein.

circulation and revision of drafts.[36] Although all of the contributors address in some sense the historiography and definition of Hellenism and the Hellenistic they are not primarily concerned with tracing modern historiographical trends. What these chapters instead present is a set of explorations of regions and interactions, which by their very existence call into question currently perceived dichotomies, regional boundaries and cultural definitions. Part of the point of the chapters, in the light of the above-noted problems of specialisation and Greco-Roman prioritisation, is to bring to a wider audience some of the lesser-known cultures, case-studies and datasets from across the western Mediterranean.

After opening with a discussion of ancient historiographical and ideological assessments of the western Mediterranean, the chapters proceed in a loosely clockwise direction around the western Mediterranean, beginning with central Italy and proceeding thence to Sicily, Cyrenaica, North Africa, the Mediterrranean islands, the Iberian peninsula and southern Gaul. Two more wide-ranging papers on numismatic and epigraphic culture follow, and the volume concludes with a reappraisal of the place of the western Mediterranean in our attempts to conceptualise the Mediterranean in history.

The individual chapters are deliberately extremely diverse in their geographical range and the types of materials which they employ. All the contributors are keenly aware of the questions and problems which we have posed, but they have not been required to adopt a single methodology or type of approach. Neither have we asked them to sign up to or agree on a single definition of 'Hellenistic' in these chapters, though we have encouraged authors to be clear about the definitions they have in mind – a process which, tellingly, has resulted frequently in the avoidance of the term entirely, or else its strict limitation to serving as a chronological term (see further below).

We have not sought comprehensive coverage of either the western Mediterranean, or any particular aspect of ancient culture. A comprehensive study would in any case be beyond the scope of a single volume, and would risk recreating the East/West division that it was our aim to challenge; instead, it is our expectation that by tackling the questions and

[36] Eight seminars in Oxford (April–June 2006), followed by a workshop at the British School at Rome (July 2006), and a panel at the *Regionalism and Globalism in Antiquity* conference at the University of British Columbia, Vancouver (March 2007), were funded by an Arts and Humanities Research Council (AHRC) Research Networks Grant, with further support from the British School at Rome and the Classics Faculty of the University of Oxford. The paper delivered at Oxford by Jean-Louis Ferrary (13 June 2006), under the title 'The Geography of Hellenism and the Roman Hegemony', has now been published separately as Ferrary 2011.

problems of the 'Hellenistic West' from multiple angles, levels and regions, we can offer a clearer sense of why these problems exist, and open up some possible ways forward. The diversity of the subject matter discussed here reflects the current concern with how to bridge the local, regional and global levels of historical study. By including such a diverse range of specialists and interests we hope also to overcome the common problem of disciplinary specialisation and narrowness of focus that is one source of the scholarly division of the Mediterranean which we are hoping to confront.

We do not here include summaries of the individual chapters, preferring to let the authors speak for themselves. However, in line with the concerns set out in the first part of this introduction, we conclude by drawing out two principal themes that we see emerging from the contributions which follow.

Virtually all our contributors more or less explicitly accept the traditional chronological 'Hellenistic' period as being in some way meaningful for the western Mediterranean as well. The precise chronological boundaries are by no means clear – certainly 323 BC lacks any real meaning in western contexts – but whether they see an increase in the movement of people, an increase in trading relationships or, most commonly, a significant increase in the diversity and extent of cultural interaction and (re)interpretation, most note what could very loosely be tagged as increased connectivity, to be located broadly between the fourth and second centuries BC. As Ed Bispham puts it in his discussion of an Abruzzo necropolis, Fossa 'begins to talk' in the later third century BC, and it is a metaphor which could be widely extended, albeit with varying chronology.

However, there is an important corollary. Most are very unwilling to call this phenomenon 'Hellenisation'. What they see taking place in conjunction with increased connectivity is increasing dissemination and homogenisation of the available cultural language(s) (it is notable that linguistic metaphors abound in these discussions). As Simon Keay expresses it in his discussion of the Iberian peninsula between the fourth and second centuries BC, there is a 'creeping cultural convergence ... traditionally known as Hellenisation'. A typical example can be seen in the spread of *opus signinum* across the western Mediterranean basin, noted from different angles in half-a-dozen of the chapters which follow. As Liv Yarrow suggests, the emerging use of coin iconography in the region is a perfect example of the generation of the 'Hellenistic', which she (echoing other contributors) glosses as the formation of a Mediterranean cultural *koine* in action.[37] Most of the

[37] It is of course at once ironic and a direct consequence of the earlier prioritisation of the Hellenic world in modern Western culture that the term to describe the common form of Greek that

contributors are also quick to deny a single origin or one lead culture in the process.

The picture which emerges from our contributors is of a world in which the level of variety, of available cultural elements, increases significantly (something familiar from the 'Hellenistic' East). At the same time, this is a variety that, paradoxically, looks ever more similar as it repeats across the Mediterranean (and beyond). The point, then, of the 'Hellenistic West' is the paradox: looking at the West shows us that the period we usually call 'Hellenistic' is indeed important, but that it is important precisely for the cross-pollination between regions and categories that have traditionally been kept separate across the Mediterranean, across East and West; it is hard to avoid the conclusion that the term Hellenistic, despite – or indeed because of – its complex and ambiguous history, is inappropriate to use of either East or West.

emerges in the Hellenistic period (and in the Bible), should be the one that has become also that for 'a set of cultural or other attributes common to various groups' (*The New Shorter Oxford English Dictionary*, Oxford, 1993, s.v. 'koine', §3); recent discussion of Greek linguistic *koine* (and the term's broader polysemy) in Colvin 2011.

1 | The view from the East

ANDREW ERSKINE

A major catalyst for the 'Hellenistic West' project was the fact that the West does not feature very prominently in studies of the Hellenistic world, at least not until the arrival of the Romans (see Introduction). This is not the case with earlier Greek history, where colonisation and Athens' imperialist ventures in Sicily guarantee the West a reasonable representation in any book on Greek history before Alexander. This in itself is revealing. Alexander re-orientates the Greek world and our conception of it towards the East. Scholars may now stress the interconnectedness of the Mediterranean, Hellenistic or otherwise, but scholarly categories such as the Roman West and the Greek East have tended to militate against an understanding of that unity. Such categories, however, may well have their origins in the Hellenistic period itself; the Hellenistic West may not so much have slipped off the conceptual map of the Hellenistic world as never been properly attached in the first place.

My focus in this chapter will be on the eastern Greek view of the West, both Greek and non-Greek, though with an emphasis on the former. From an eastern perspective the West was different and its characterisation far from simple. By the East I mean anything to the east of Italy and Sicily, the region that might traditionally be described as the Hellenistic World. The view from Megalopolis may be distinct from the view from Alexandria or from Magnesia-on-the-Maeander, but cumulatively they give us a sense of an eastern perspective.

Polybius and the clouds from the West

Polybius offers important contemporary evidence, albeit written in Rome for the most part rather than Megalopolis and contemporary to the second century rather than the third. Polybius takes as the starting point of his history the 140th Olympiad, chosen because he believed that it was at this time that the affairs of the inhabited world came together and thus one unified history became possible (220–216 BC). As he put it in the introduction to his history:

In earlier times the affairs of the inhabited world (οἰκουμένη) had been, so to speak, scattered, on account of their being separated by origins, results and place. From this point onwards, however, history becomes an organic whole, and Italian and Libyan affairs are interlinked with Asian and Greek affairs (ταῖς Ἑλληνικαῖς), all leading up to one end.[1]

Four regions are listed but they are conceived as two halves, on the one hand Italy and Libya, on the other Greece and Asia, the former in the accusative, the latter in the dative.[2] One might suggest that Polybius has in mind Greeks more generally and his use of Ἑλληνικαῖς might extend to the Greeks of Sicily or even Italy but it is quite clear from the context and from subsequent remarks that he is using the word in a geographical sense. Two sentences later he explains how victory in the Second Punic War, the Italian and Libyan part of the equation, encouraged the Romans 'to stretch out their hands to grasp the rest and to cross with armed forces to Hellas and the region of Asia'. In his fifth book Polybius recounts the conference and peace of Naupactus in 217 BC. Here Philip V of Macedon made peace with the Aetolians in anticipation of events in the West, an occasion which Polybius believed to be crucial to the merging of the separate strands of Mediterranean history. It was this, he says, that first bound the affairs of Hellas (αἱ κατὰ τὴν Ἑλλάδα πράξεις) together with those of Italy and Libya.[3]

Underlying this division for Polybius was political power and its distribution in the Mediterranean world. The Macedonian empire at one stage covered the whole East but stopped at the Adriatic, never reaching Sicily, Sardinia or Libya. As Polybius puts it at 1.2.4–6:

In Europe the Macedonians ruled from the lands along the Adriatic as far as the Danube, which would appear to be a fairly small part of that continent. Later they also gained mastery of Asia when they overthrew the Persian empire. But, although they were reckoned to have become rulers of a greater number of places and states than any people had ever done before, they still left the greater part of the inhabited world in the hands of others. For not once did they attempt to lay claim to Sicily, Sardinia or Libya, and as to Europe, if one is to be blunt about it, they did not even know of the most warlike peoples of the West (τὰ μαχιμώτατα γένη τῶν προσεσπερίων ἐθνῶν).[4] But the Romans have made not merely certain parts of the world subject to themselves but the whole world.

1 Polyb. 1.3.3–6.

2 Combination of Greece and Asia might be surprising for those for whom Europe and Asia is the established polarity (cf. Cobet 1996 on the latter).

3 Polyb. 5.105.4–10 with Walbank 1975 and Pédech 1964: 505–9 on Polybian *symploke.*

4 Rather obscured in Paton's Loeb translation: 'the most warlike nations of Western Europe' (unchanged in Walbank and Habicht's revision).

Here is a world divided; Macedon is the defining element of the East while the West is something of a mix, the islands, North Africa and parts of continental Europe. It is noticeable also that Polybius writes not of Alexander but of the Macedonians and their empire, so it might be tempting to think he has in mind at this point not the Macedonian kingdom but some broader Macedonian East that resulted from Alexander's conquests. Generally, however, when writing of Macedon and the Macedonians he means the Macedonian kingdom, which for him is a continuous entity from Philip II to Perseus despite the upheaval of the early Hellenistic years.[5] Macedon under Philip V and Perseus may not have been the ruler of the East but Polybius seems to see Rome's overthrow of Macedon as equivalent to Macedon's overthrow of the Persian empire, thus suggesting a fairly wide-ranging conception of Macedonian power right up until the time of its destruction.[6] The Peloponnesian background of Polybius may be relevant here; Macedon was the Hellenistic kingdom that impinged most directly upon him and this proximity may have helped to shape his conception of Macedonian power.

What distinguished East from West was Macedonian conquest. It was, he notes elsewhere, the Macedonian phalanx that conquered Asia and Greece, while the Roman legion conquered Africa and Europe.[7] The peoples around the Adriatic and the Ionian seas may have shared their sea and been closer to their maritime neighbours than to some of those sharing the same land-mass with them, but for Polybius the Adriatic and the Ionian seas combined to make a significant boundary, separating West from East. It was the crossing of that boundary by the Romans at the outbreak of the First Illyrian War in 229 BC that was a turning point, one that merited serious attention and Polybius duly gave it. Not only was this the first time that the Romans had made this crossing with an army, it was also, he said, the first time they had been diplomatically involved in Greece.[8]

229 BC may have been a turning point but Polybius places most emphasis on the 140th Olympiad, which marks the beginning of the fifty-three years in which the Romans acquired worldwide rule; in particular he highlights the transforming character of 217 BC and the peace of Naupactus. There are

[5] Walbank 1993.

[6] Polyb. 29.21, Walbank 1993: 1729–30, cf. also Polyb. 38.22 (=App. *Pun.* 132).

[7] Polyb. 18.28.2.

[8] Polyb. 2.2.1–2, 2.12.7–8. This latter passage does appear to contradict Polyb. 30.5.6–8, a controversial passage that suggests a longstanding connection between Rome and Rhodes: Walbank 1957–79: III, 423–6 and Berthold 1984: 233–7. For possible diplomatic relations before the First Illyrian War, not mentioned by Polybius, see n. 12 below. Later Polybius (18.12.5) notes that Flamininus was the first Roman to cross with an army to Hellas (as opposed to Illyria).

two reasons for this emphasis; firstly, it shows how Fortune brought everything together at this time, but secondly, it also demonstrates Polybius' own originality in making this date the starting point for a unified view of Mediterranean history, something which no one had yet attempted.[9] This stress on emerging unity, however, may also have led to an exaggerated conception of the Mediterranean before 217 as being deeply divided. It is noticeable that Pyrrhus' campaigns in Italy and Sicily, which had been treated by the Sicilian Timaeus, fall just outside the scope of Polybius' history, which begins the background narrative of the first two books at the point where Timaeus ended.[10] In his writings Timaeus seems to have been concerned to assert the standing of the Greek West in relation to the mainland, a stance that may itself have indirectly helped to promote a separation of the West from the East by giving the West a separate identity.[11] Polybius, by beginning where Timaeus left off, would be uniting western and eastern historiography just as Fortune united world events.

A divided Mediterranean served to emphasise the significance and novelty of what had happened and of what Polybius himself was doing. This may lie behind the considerable scholarly controversy about the historicity and significance of a number of incidents in the third century recorded by other writers but not mentioned by Polybius. Thus Appian, Dio, Eutropius and the *Periochae* of Livy all tell of an agreement between Ptolemy II and Rome in the 270s BC but Polybius is silent. An Apollonian embassy to Rome in the 260s is reported by Dio, Eutropius, the *Periochae* of Livy and Valerius Maximus but again not by Polybius. Nor does Polybius have anything to say of an Acarnanian appeal to Rome for help against the Aetolians in the 230s, which is narrated at some length in Justin's epitome of Pompeius Trogus.[12] Then there is the First Punic War, which takes up much of Polybius' first book. The war had a major effect on the Greeks of Sicily, where most of the fighting took place, yet in Polybius' account it seems strangely disconnected from the rest of the Greek world.

[9] Walbank 1972: 66–71 suggests that Polybius may have overstressed unity for literary effect.

[10] Polyb. 1.5–6, Timaeus *FGrH* 566 T9.

[11] For this tendency in Timaeus, Feeney 2007: 47–52; for the presentation of the West in Timaeus' writings, see Baron 2013: 89–112.

[12] Ptolemy: App. *Sik.* 1, Dio Cass. Frag. 41 (Zonar. 8.6.11), Eutr. 2.15, Livy, *Per.* 14; Apollonia: Dio Cass. Frag. 42 (Zonar. 8.7), Livy, *Per.* 15, Val. Max. 6.6.5; Acarnania: Just. *Epit.* 28.1–2. For the scholarly controversy, note in particular Holleaux 1921: 1–22, 60–83, Gruen 1984: 62–4, Errington 1989: 83–5, with Corsten 1992, Dany 1999: 98–119 on the Acarnanian appeal. Holleaux looks to Polybius and questions the historicity or significance of these incidents, but for Holleaux, who has been fundamental to this debate, the turning point is not 229 or 217 but 200 BC. See also n. 8 above.

This sense of disconnection is again evident in a series of speeches that Polybius attributes to speakers on the Greek mainland in the late third century as they look with some anxiety across the sea to the war between Carthage and Rome. Agelaos of Naupactus, speaking before the Macedonian king at the conference at Naupactus, may talk of Italy and Sicily but he also talks more vaguely of the West, culminating in the vividly expressed fear that 'the clouds that are now gathering in the West' will settle on Greece. The phrase is picked up by another Polybian speaker, the Acarnanian Lyciscus, who attacks the Aetolians for allying with Rome and thus having 'invoked such a great cloud from the West, which for the present will probably cast its shadow first over the Macedonians, but will move on to be the cause of great evils for all the Greeks'.[13] The lack of precision is rhetorical but it also conveys an impression of distance and remoteness not evident when a speaker uses more precise geographical terms and fits with Polybius' representation of two rather separate halves. Nor would one imagine from this that the West is a place where Greeks live: the cloud from the West, says Lyciscus, will hit first Macedon, then all Greeks.

Polybius thus posits quite a gulf between West and East. It is difficult to say how widely shared this conception was among his contemporaries; I am not suggesting that it was unique to Polybius or even that it began with him, although it did suit Polybius' general thesis especially well. This way of dividing the world may have had a significant subliminal influence on modern scholarship and the separation of the West from the rest of the Hellenistic world. Nonetheless, there may be something to be said for this division. What unites the 'Hellenistic' is on some views Macedonian conquest and it is this that seems to underlie Polybius' position: the Macedonians, he says, never conquered Sicily, Sardinia or Libya, nor did they even know of the most warlike peoples of the West. So, although Polybius may have been unaware of Johann Gustav Droysen and his conception of the Hellenistic world, there is some common ground between the two, and perhaps not coincidentally.[14] With Macedonian conquest goes the dominance of what might be loosely described as Greco-Macedonian culture. Its interaction with the cultures of the peoples in the East is complex and varied, as much recent scholarship has shown, but at the centre is a Hellenistic king whose primary mode of expressing power is in Greek idioms, which are then imitated by

[13] Polyb. 5.104.10, 9.37.10.

[14] Droysen 1877–78, cf. Bichler 1983 on the concept of *Hellenismus*, the Introduction to this volume, and the chapter by Andrew Wallace-Hadrill. Also note Lane Fox 2011.

the smaller non-Greek kingdoms of the region.[15] This is something different from what is happening in the West where there is no one dominant group and Carthaginians, Romans, Greeks and others are competing, as third century Sicily demonstrates.

The Panhellenic approach

There is, however, another way of looking at the West, or at least at the western Greeks. Polybius may present us with a divided Mediterranean but if attention is focused on Greek cities it is possible to observe a sense of community, a sense of shared Greekness that transcends West and East. Here the epigraphic evidence offers a far more integrated picture of the Greek world than the Polybian narrative implies. Cities naturally look first to their own region but when they move beyond that there is no indication that the Adriatic Sea marks some kind of dividing line. A Panhellenic festival, for instance, would be expected to attract Greeks from all over the Mediterranean and would do so. Kinship, historical or mythical, could play an active part in linking cities from the Iberian peninsula to Asia Minor.[16] Greekness was not constrained by geography. Cities interact in numerous different ways with other cities across the Mediterranean, engaged as much in international partnership and community as in the more familiar activities of war and aggression.[17]

This conception of a Greek world that embraces both West and East comes across vividly in a document from its traditional centre, Delphi. The well-known list of *theorodokoi*, extensive but nonetheless incomplete, records the names of the hosts of Delphic *theoroi* in each of over two hundred Greek cities that would have been visited by the *theoroi* as they travelled to make announcements on behalf of the sanctuary.[18] In the West their itinerary extended as far as Massalia and included a tour of Sicilian cities such as Camarina and Tauromenion and Italian ones such as Tarentum and Rhegium.[19] In the East they visited not only older cities but also the newer ones such as Laodicea-by-the-sea in Syria and various Ptolemaic foundations, acknowledgement of Alexander's new world order but an acknowledgement

[15] Ma 2003a: 187–8; at the same time Polybius may have had reservations about seeing these kingdoms as properly Greek, Erskine 2013.

[16] C. Jones 1999, Erskine 2002, Patterson 2010.

[17] Giovannini 1993, Ma 2003b.

[18] Plassart 1921 for the text with discussion; it is also the subject of Jacques Ouhlen's unpublished 1992 doctorate, which offers a number of new readings.

[19] Plassart 1921, column IV, line 83–117; on the Sicilian cities Manganaro 1964 and 1996.

that does not extend far beyond the coast.[20] This is the Greek world as viewed from Delphi. The dating of the inscription has proved to be controversial, a circumstance not helped by indications that it was composed over time; some favour the 220s BC, some the following decade and others the early second century.[21] The document, however, is in no way unusual in the picture it presents of a network of Greek cities spanning the Mediterranean, whether in the fourth century, as found in a *theorodokoi* list from Epidaurus, or later. Evidence for Panhellenic festivals from Cos and Magnesia-on-the-Maeander demonstrates a similarly broad vision of the Greek world but one underpinned, as will be seen, by a different perspective.[22]

Delphi's inviolable and Panhellenic status was long-standing and widely recognised, but the third century also saw a rise in the number of claims to inviolability (*asylia*) by other states on behalf of their chief sanctuary or their city and sanctuary if the sanctuary was located within the city.[23] Frequently these occurred in parallel with the establishment of a Panhellenic festival. It was no easy matter to set these up. A claim to inviolability and a Panhellenic festival was only plausible if it could be seen to have been accepted by the community of Greeks. This, therefore, led to a significant campaign by the city to obtain recognition from their fellow Greeks. Groups of sacred ambassadors, *theoroi*, would travel round the Greek world, making their city's case; they would address the assemblies of cities they visited, produce documents in support of the claim and look to receive an affirmative decree to take home with them.[24] In the third century BC the phenomenon appears to have been restricted to the Aegean area and western Asia Minor, spreading in a somewhat different form in the second century BC further round the eastern Mediterranean coast to Syria and Palestine.[25]

Although Polybius may have seen the West as politically divided from the East, these decrees make clear the strong feeling of shared ethnicity that there was among all Greeks wherever in the Mediterranean they were located. The *theoroi* travelled widely and the resulting decrees form an image of the perceived extent of the Greek world. No doubt too, the more widely dispersed the Greeks who acknowledged the *asylia* and the Panhellenic status of the festival, the more authoritative was the claim.

[20] Laodicea: column IV, line 78; Ptolemaic foundations: column IV, lines 17–19, on which Plassart 1921: 62, Cohen 2006: 390; on coastal preference, cf. Ma 2003b: 26, Parker 2004: 16.

[21] For example, 220s BC: Daux 1949, Hatzopoulos 1991 with *BE* 1994.432; 210s BC: Knoepfler 1993; early second century: Plassart 1921, Manganaro 1996. See also *SEG* 43.221 and 46.555.

[22] For Epidaurus, *IG* IV.1.94–5 on which Perlman 2000: 67–98; for Cos and Magnesia see below; on the institution of *theorodokia* in general, Dillon 1997: 9–18, Perlman 2000.

[23] Collected in Rigsby 1996. [24] Cf. Erskine 2002. [25] Rigsby 1996: 25–8.

The first substantially documented claim is that of Cos on behalf of its temple of Asclepius in the late 240s BC. More than forty decrees survive in various states of incompleteness, collected by the roving ambassadors and subsequently inscribed in the sanctuary as confirmation.[26] What survives is accidental; there are replies from Hellenistic kings, most probably Ptolemaic and Seleucid, one from the Bithynian king Ziaelas, a large number from cities of northern Greece and Macedon, such as Amphipolis, Cassandreia and Pella, several from Peloponnesian cities such as Sparta and Elis, some Cretan cities and, significantly, four from cities in the West. Two are from South Italy, Naples and Elea, both visited by a team of three Coan ambassadors, who in the case of Naples 'renew *oikeiotes* and *eunoia* (goodwill)'; whether *oikeiotes* here was as strong as kinship or merely some form of relationship is unclear.[27] Certainly it was not uncommon for ambassadors to draw attention to kinship based on shared mythical genealogy.[28] At least one of the ambassadors then went on to Sicily. In the case of the two Sicilian cities for which records survive, Camarina and Gela, the *theoroi* did claim kinship or *syngeneia*, a claim made on the grounds that Cos was the joint founder of the cities. This most likely means that Cos participated in Timoleon's refoundation of these cities in the mid-fourth century BC.[29] In these decrees shared Greekness binds cities together across the Mediterranean and in the two Sicilian examples it is the stronger bond of *syngeneia* that links the cities to Cos. The response of the Bithynian king Ziaelas is of interest here too. Written in a Greek that has not impressed the scholars who have studied it, the response highlights his family's goodwill to all Greeks. The Coans, by approaching a king somewhat on the margins of the Greek world, were recognising his desire to participate in the community of Greeks, a community which stretched well into the West. His descendants would later build up strong links with a western city in a manner that would meet with Polybius' strong disapproval.[30]

A similarly illuminating *asylia* dossier comes from late third-century Magnesia-on-the-Maeander in western Asia Minor.[31] In 208 BC, while Philip V of Macedon was tackling Roman interference in mainland Greece and

[26] Rigsby 1996: 106–53; Herzog and Klaffenbach 1952.

[27] Naples: Rigsby 1996: no. 46 (lines 4–5, 8 for renewal); Elea: Rigsby 1996: no. 47.

[28] Erskine 2002.

[29] Camerina and Gela: Rigsby 1996: nos. 48–9; on Cos and Timoleon's refoundation, Sherwin-White 1978: 80–1, Curty 1995: 50–1.

[30] Rigsby 1996: no. 11, Welles 1934: no. 25, both of whom comment negatively on the Greek. For Polybius' critical comments on Ziaelas' descendant Prusias, Polyb. 30.18, 36.15.

[31] *I.Magnesia*, nos. 16–87; Rigsby 1996: 179–279 gives the text of all the responses, together with commentary.

Hannibal was losing his way in Italy, Magnesia was planning an extensive diplomatic campaign. The Magnesians had established a Panhellenic festival in honour of Artemis Leukophryene and sent ambassadors throughout the Greek world to obtain recognition for this festival and also for the inviolability of their city and territory. About twenty groups of ambassadors travelled thousands of miles, covering an area from Sicily to Iran, making the Magnesian case and gathering together the responses of cities, leagues and kings. This was an extraordinarily wide-ranging and thorough campaign. Approximately ninety replies were inscribed, of which over sixty survive and a further one hundred cities are listed only by name.[32] In Sicily the ambassadors are known to have visited Syracuse and, if the reconstruction of the text is correct, it looks as if their appeal there was based on *syngeneia*.[33] What is particularly striking about this decree is its date. These *theoroi* were travelling in the West at a time of tremendous turbulence; the Second Punic War had been going for around ten years and Syracuse itself would have been recovering from its devastating sack by the Roman commander M. Claudius Marcellus only three years earlier.[34] Travel was dangerous at the best of times and it would have been easy for these ambassadors to feel that crossing the Adriatic in the present circumstances was beyond the call of local patriotism. This is a telling reflection on the strength of shared Greek identity across the Mediterranean and perhaps a statement of support from one Greek city to another at time of crisis, even if it would be another fifteen years or so before that crisis reached Magnesia.[35]

The decrees from Cos and Magnesia are revealing too of the changes that have taken place in the Greek world. These cities, which for so long existed in the marginal territory between Greek and Persian, can now look upon themselves as the centre of a Greek world that extends far into the east, south to Egypt and as far west as Sicily or even Massalia. Whereas the Delphic *theorodokoi* list reflects the view from the traditional centre of the Greek world, a different perspective emerges in the texts from Cos and Magnesia, one that moves beyond the Mediterranean while still incorporating the West.[36] Magnesian *theoroi* are thus to be found not only in Sicily but also travelling deep into the Seleucid kingdom to Antioch-in-Persis, while Coan *theoroi* venture into Bithynia. Centrality no doubt conferred a sense of

[32] Rigsby 1996: 180; on the campaign, Gehrke 2000: 287–97, Erskine 2002: 98–100, Sammartano 2008–9.

[33] Rigsby 1996: no. 120, Curty 1995: 116, 123, with Sammartano 2008–9, esp. 127–39.

[34] Polyb. 8.3–7, 9.10, Livy 25.31. [35] Cf. Derow 2003: 57.

[36] Cf. Parker 2004: 16, who notes of the (albeit incomplete) Delphic *theorodokia* inscription that it 'still looks like the Greek world of the 4th century or even earlier'.

importance upon these cities and left the Greeks of the West in their turn aspiring to be like their eastern counterparts. Hieron II of Syracuse would surely have liked to be a king on the Ptolemaic model, a sentiment that may lie behind his building of a ship so grotesquely over-sized that there were few harbours it could dock in. Originally called Syrakosia he renamed it Alexandris and gave it as a gift to Ptolemy II.[37] Similarly, together with his son Gelon, he can be seen competing with the kings of the East in the extravagance of his gifts following the Rhodian earthquake of 227–226 BC; the link between the two cities reinforced by a gift of a statue group in which the *demos* of Syracuse crowns the *demos* of Rhodes. This is, however, no one-way relationship; as with Cos and Magnesia the initiative appears to have come from the Rhodians, who would have included the Sicilian Greeks in their fund-raising campaign.[38]

It was not uncommon in these exchanges for the initial approach to be based on an appeal to kinship. Such ties of kinship, whether rooted in the historical past or some mythical genealogy, were a feature of shared Greekness and linked communities together across the Mediterranean. Together they formed invisible networks that could be drawn upon and developed where necessary.[39] As the Coan and Magnesian decrees reveal, their ambassadors sometimes resorted to kinship arguments and the Rhodians too may have done so after their earthquake.[40] This was not something limited to widespread campaigns such as these major Panhellenic enterprises; it can also be seen at work on a smaller scale. In the 190s when Lampsacus in the Troad was threatened by Antiochus III, it sent an embassy to the Romans with the aim of securing Roman protection and in particular inclusion in the treaty that was being made with Philip V of Macedon. In order to approach Rome, a state that they had no direct experience of, they turned for assistance to another Greek city but not to one close at hand; instead it was to the city of Massalia on the coast of southern Gaul. They chose Massalia, not merely because of the western city's long familiarity with Rome, but because they could claim kinship with it. The two cities shared the same mother city, dating from the time of Phocaean colonisation some four hundred years previously. In the inscription honouring the Lampsacene ambassadors the two peoples

37 Ath. 5.206d–209e; Bugh 2006c: 276–7; cf. Roger Wilson, this volume, on Hieron II. For the influence of Hellenistic kingship on Hieron and earlier on Agathocles, see Zambon 2008, especially 217–19 with summary of argument at 267–9.

38 Polyb. 5.88–90, Diod. Sic. 26.8; Walbank 1957–79: I, 616–19; cf. *Lind. Temp. Chron.* 41.

39 Cf. Erskine 2005: 131–2.

40 While the arguments used by the Rhodians at the time of their earthquake are not known, the mythological stories attributed to Zenon of Rhodes by Diodorus (5.55–6) are suggestive of the form that any kinship arguments may have taken.

are 'brothers' (ἀδελφοί). The long and arduous journey from one end of the Mediterranean to the other may be in part a consequence of international pressures but it is also revealing testimony to the strength and extent of common Greek identity. Not only do the Lampsacenes go to Massalia but the Massaliotes welcomed them and duly accompanied them to Rome.[41]

Underpinning all this activity was a sense of shared Greekness and, when it was felt appropriate, fellow-feeling across the Mediterranean, West and East. This is an image rather at odds with that observed in Polybius, where the West is strangely remote. These two images, pulling in different directions, may have helped to shape the way that the West was characterised by the Greeks of the East, a theme that will be explored in the second half of this chapter. However much the western Greeks may have had in common with the wider Greek community, they came to be seen as belonging to the West. As such their Greek identity was increasingly infused, in the minds of their more easterly counterparts at least, with the barbarian character that was so much part of the West.

The barbarian West

An important way in which the West was construed was as a region of barbarians, an image that dates back to the Classical period. The basic distinction Greeks such as Aristotle made at that time was between European and Asiatic barbarians; European ones tended to be tribal, warlike, but not too bright, while Asiatic ones were cleverer, but cowardly and self-indulgent. The Greeks were somewhere in the middle, combining courage and intelligence. This classification seems to have been directed more at northern Europeans than those of the western Mediterranean coast, to judge at least from the importance of weather conditions in determining the developed character.[42] Nonetheless it is Greece that comes out of it most favourably. The shift in the centre of the Greek world eastwards, however, may have tended to push the western Greeks towards the margins, which they inhabited with an array of non-Greek peoples, and thus to change the way in which they themselves were

[41] *I.Lamp.* 4 (*Syll.*[3] 591); bibliography here tends to focus on the Roman aspect, in particular the Lampsacene use of kinship arguments in their dealings with Rome, cf. Bickermann 1932, Ferrary 1988: 133–41, Erskine 2001: 169–72. For Lampsacus as Phocaean colony: Charon *FGrH* 262 F7, Ephorus *FGrH* 70 F46, Pomponius Mela 1.97, Steph. Byz. s.v. Λάμψακος, Magie 1950: 903 n. 118; Massalia as Phocaean colony: Thuc. 1.13.6, Isoc. *Arch.* 84, Paus. 10.8.6, cf. Momigliano 1975: 51–2. For Phocaean colonisation generally, Domínguez Monedero 2004.

[42] Arist. *Pol.* 1327b23–33, Hippoc. *Aer.* 16–18; on such environmental theories, Sassi 2001: 105–39.

perceived, a process that will be considered in the next section of this chapter. First it is necessary to explore the barbarian character of the West.

Some of the most vivid accounts of non-Greek tribes come from Polybius in his description of the Celts of northern Italy, who seem to be the very model of a European barbarian. Yet by focussing on them to the exclusion of others the barbarianness of the West in the imagination of the East can easily be underestimated. The Celts certainly did fulfil most of the requirements for a well-rounded barbarian but there were also others, both tribal and fully urbanised, who should not be overlooked. These others may not have been represented in such an extreme fashion but they nonetheless were perceived as barbarians, albeit not necessarily consistently so. Among these would be the mountain peoples of Italy and the natives of Sicily, but most importantly the Carthaginians and Romans.[43] This did not escape Greek observers in the East who tended to see their western counterparts as corrupted by association. In the East too, of course, Greeks lived among people who were not Greek but here they could reassure themselves that they were in the ascendancy.

Polybius' representation of the Celts in the second book of his history is very revealing of his ideas not only about the Celts but also about the Romans. He begins with some ethnography: the Celts live in unwalled villages, they sleep on leaves, they have only moveable possessions, hence their preference for wealth in cattle and gold, and they have two interests – war and farming (γεωργία), in which respect they are rather reminiscent of the Romans themselves. Their lives are therefore simple, far removed from that of the Greek *polis*. This is not a wholly consistent picture; Polybius' Celts manage to be both farmers and nomadic, an unusual combination.[44] He then moves on to the conflict between the Celts and the Romans in the 220s BC, giving a very powerful evocation of the Celts in battle and the Roman response to them. The Celts in this passage are stereotypical barbarian warriors that Aristotle would easily have recognised, warlike, spirited,

[43] Celts: Williams, 2001, esp. 68–99, Mitchell 2003; mountain peoples: Dench 1995; native Sicilians: Domínguez Monedero 2006a: 324–42 offers a useful survey of Greek-native interaction but more work needs to be done on Greek perceptions of native Sicilians; Carthaginians: see below; Romans: Erskine 2000, Champion 2004: esp. 47–57, 193–202; in general: Champion 2004: 30–63.

[44] Polyb. 2.17.8–12; in 2.17.9 Polybius notes that the Celts are τῆς λοιπῆς κατασκευῆς ἄμοιροι which Walbank 1957–79: I, 184 translates (rejecting Paton's translation) as 'without knowledge of the other arts of civilization' (though not appearing in his and Habicht's revision of Paton, but adopted by Manuela Mari in her Italian translation), cf. Eckstein 1995: 123–4. Williams 2001: 80–2 points out the inconsistency between the primitive way of life depicted here and the references to Celtic towns later in the narrative.

but short on reason. They advance into battle noisy, terrifying, impassioned, naked:

The Romans were on the one hand encouraged by having surrounded the enemy on all sides but on the other they were alarmed by the ornaments and clamour of the Celtic force. For the mass of horn-blowers and trumpeters was beyond reckoning and together with the army shouting its battle-cry at the same time, the tremendous din was such that not only the trumpets and soldiers but also the whole countryside, echoing with their sound, seemed to possess a voice. Equally terrifying was the appearance and movements of the naked men in the front, striking in both their strength and physique. All those in the front ranks were richly adorned with gold torques and armlets. The Romans were at once frightened by what they saw but at the same time, spurred on by hope of profit, they became twice as eager for battle.[45]

Finally Polybius sums up this war:

Thus ended the war against the Celts, a war which, if judged by the desperation and daring of those who fought and by the battles and the number who died and took part in them, is second to none recorded in history, but which in terms of plans and the lack of sense shown in executing them was utterly contemptible. This was because not most of what the Celts did but absolutely everything they did was directed by impulse (θυμός) rather than by calculation (λογισμός).[46]

The Celts are barbarians: they lack the rationality of the Greek and are guided by θυμός, and the dramatic descriptions of their performance in battle demonstrate this. Nevertheless, there is a curious omission in this section of Polybius covering Rome's war with the Celts.

In the nineteen chapters on this conflict not once does Polybius call the Celts 'barbarians', even though everything about them conforms to a Greek stereotype of the barbarian. This is not discretion or restraint on his part. The account of the war immediately prompts a digression about sudden and unexpected 'barbarian' invasions in which significantly the term 'barbarian' is used but Polybius is now thinking of Greeks being faced with such invasions.[47] The term 'barbarian' makes sense when Celts are encountering Greeks in a way that it does not when they are opposed to Romans. This is revealing about Polybius' conception of the Romans and suggests that his picture of them is more ambiguous than it at first appears. The Celts, as observed above, behave exactly as Celts would be expected to behave but it is worth looking again at how Polybius has chosen to represent the Romans. They are frightened at the spectacle of the Celtic army in front of them

[45] Polyb. 2.29.5–9. [46] Polyb. 2.35.2–3, on which see especially Champion 2004: 114–17.
[47] Polyb. 2.35.6.

but the sight of all the gold decorating the bodies of their enemy drives them onwards into battle, their desire for profit overcoming their fear. Consequently it is as much *thumos* as *logismos* in the case of the Romans too.[48] Indeed, in this display of greed they are demonstrating a very typical barbarian trait, one often ascribed to the Romans. Already in the 190s BC T. Quinctius Flamininus is found trying to rebut suggestions that the Romans are money-loving (φιλαργύροι) in a letter he writes to the city of Chyretiae.[49]

Romans themselves from Cato to Livy were conscious that to the Greeks they were barbarians, but no extant Greek author explicitly refers to them as such, tending instead to attribute the idea to others.[50] Polybius, for example, only uses the term 'barbarian' of the Romans when he is employing direct speech. At the battle of Cynoscephalae in 197 BC messengers come to Philip V with a rather premature report on the Roman movements: 'the barbarians are fleeing'. In a series of speeches by leading Greek politicians, including those of Agelaos and Lyciscus referred to in the first section above, the Romans are the new barbarian menace that needs to be kept out of Greece. Their treatment of captured towns is savage (ὠμός) and characteristic of a barbarian (βαρβαρικός); they are the exponents of *hubris* and lawlessness (παρανομία).[51] The speakers here are voicing common criticisms of barbarians who do not conform to accepted standards of behaviour. Polybius himself may not call the Romans 'barbarians' in his own voice, but he does ascribe characteristics to them which are often associated with barbarians; they are brutal, greedy and excessively religious.[52] Elsewhere Plutarch records Pyrrhus' surprise that the Roman forces are organised, and not the disorderly barbarians he had anticipated.[53] Even in the late first century BC Dionysius of Halicarnassus can report that it is a generally held but mistaken belief that the Romans are barbarians – whereas in fact they are Greeks.[54]

Carthage comes in for very similar treatment in Greek sources. It had little in common with the Celtic tribes. It was urban, ruled by an élite, powerful in

[48] Champion 2004: 117 would see a parallel between Romans fighting Celts and Greeks fighting Celts, both displaying λογισμός to defeat the irrational barbarian Celts but the depiction of the Roman vs. Celt conflict seems more complex than this allows.

[49] *RDGE* 33; on Greek perceptions of Romans as 'money-loving', Erskine 1996.

[50] Roman authors: Cato in Plin. *HN* 29.14, Plaut. *Asin.* 11, *Trin.* prolog. 19, *Mil.* 211, Livy 31.34.8.

[51] Messengers: Polyb. 18.22.8; speeches: 5.104, 9.32.3–39 (esp. 9.37.6, 38.5), 11.4–6 (esp. 11.5.6–8 on sacking of cities, cf. 10.15). Note in 9.37.7–8, 39.3 the Romans are ἀλλόφυλοι.

[52] Brutality: 10.15 (sack of New Carthage); greed: 2.29.7–9, 11.24.11, 18.34–35; excessive religiosity: 3.112.6–9, 6.56; for a full discussion of the barbarian characteristics of the Romans, Erskine 2000, cf. also Champion 2004; for a different interpretation, Schmitt 1957–8.

[53] Plut. *Pyrrh.* 16, cf. *Flam.* 5.

[54] Dion. Hal. *Ant. Rom.* 1.5, 4.26.5, 7.70, 7.72.18.

the Mediterranean, and it had long had close links with the Greek world; Aristotle includes a description of the Carthaginian constitution in his *Politics* and compares it with the Spartan and Cretan constitutions.[55] Yet, the Carthaginians could be termed 'barbarians', and much of the Greek characterisation of the Carthaginians is just what we would expect of a barbarian.[56] Sometimes the evidence dates from after the final destruction of Carthage in 146 BC, but it nonetheless reflects long-standing Greek ideas about this neighbouring people.

The notorious cruelty of the Carthaginians is evoked by Diodorus in his violent description of the sack of Selinunte in 409 BC. Indiscriminately burning and slaughtering the inhabitants, the victorious Carthaginians made their way round the city, severed hands strung round their bodies, severed heads skewered onto their spears. These men were barbarians with 'incomprehensible speech and animal behaviour'.[57] Diodorus of course was a Sicilian, so hardly representing an eastern perspective, and may here reflect a strong Sicilian anti-Carthaginian feeling, but the general sentiments appear to have been shared in some form among other Greeks. The Carthaginians are represented as no more generous to their own people; unsuccessful generals were widely reported to risk crucifixion; the reader only has to wait until the eleventh chapter to meet the first crucifixion in Polybius' history.[58] In common with other barbarian peoples the Carthaginians are described as intensely religious, to the point that they will sacrifice their own children. A crisis in 310 BC is said to have led to the sacrifice of two hundred aristocratic boys.[59] Cannibalism is another custom alien to the Greeks and found associated in their minds with barbarians; there is no suggestion that Carthaginians practised cannibalism but, significantly perhaps, Polybius does report a council meeting where an adviser to Hannibal suggests that the only way that the army would be able to reach Italy would be if the soldiers were to be trained to eat human flesh.[60]

[55] Arist. *Pol.* 2.1272b24–1273b25.

[56] Termed 'barbarians': Hdt. 7.158, [Plato] *Ep.* 7.333a, 8.353a, Diod. Sic. 13.57–8, Plut. *Tim.* 11.2, 24.4, 37.5; for Greek (and Roman) perceptions of the Phoenicians and Carthaginians, see Isaac 2004: 324–35; Barceló 1994 argues that the classical view was more positive. Published after this chapter was completed there are now Prag 2010a and Gruen 2011: 115–40.

[57] Diod. Sic. 13.57–8; ὠμότης: 13.57.5, 58.2; ἀσύνετον μὲν τὴν φωνήν, θηριώδη δὲ τὸν τρόπον ἔχοντας: 13.58.2. For cruelty, see also Diod. Sic. 14.46.2, Plut. *Mor.* 799d.

[58] Polyb. 1.11.5 (cf. 1.24, 1.86), App. *Pun.* 24, Zonar. 8.11, 8.17.

[59] Diod. Sic. 20.14, cf. [Plato] *Minos* 315bc, Kleitarchos *FGrH* 137F9 (Schol. Pl. *Rep.* 337a). For the problem of child sacrifice in Carthage, Lancel 1995: 227–56, esp. 248–56.

[60] Polyb. 24.6–9, cf. Hdt. 4.18.3, Arist. *Eth. Nic.* 7.1148b19–24, Strabo 4.5.4 for cannibalism among barbarians. Cannibalism was also said to have occurred among the mercenaries in the Carthaginian Mercenary War, Polyb. 1.84.9–85.2.

The Carthaginians are also prone to passion; it is the anger and resentment of Hamilcar Barca and the Carthaginian people that is said to have been responsible for the Second Punic War.[61] They are unscrupulous and greedy, so much so that greed is one of the few restraints on their cruelty. Thus at the sack of Selinunte they refrain from a more extensive massacre for fear that despairing suppliants would set fire to the temples and all the wealth deposited there.[62] Hannibal's character faults were said to have been his excessive cruelty and love of money, the latter the very same charge and term (φιλάργυρος) that was levelled against the Romans. Polybius acquits Hannibal of excessive cruelty but finds him guilty on the charge of greed.[63] Across a range of texts the Carthaginians turn out to be cruel, greedy, passionate and overly religious. There may be some truth in this, but it must also be remembered that this is a Greek image that conforms to a stereotype of what a barbarian is expected to be like.

Being Greek in the West

Viewed from the East then, the West would have seemed to be a place where barbarians were a little out of hand. In the fifth century, Euripides had presented Iphigeneia as saying to her mother, 'It is right that Greeks should rule barbarians, mother, but not that barbarians should rule Greeks. For they are slaves, but Greeks are free.' The first line was later quoted with approval by Aristotle in support of his claim that barbarians are incapable of ruling and that barbarians and slaves are identical.[64] The Greeks of the East had got it right. They had subjugated the barbarian, as Alexander and his successors proved, or they fought him off as the defence of Delphi against the invading Celts showed. The Greeks of the West, however, living alongside Celts, Carthaginians, Romans, Samnites, Bruttians and so on, are represented as having a more troubled and compromised relationship with the barbarian. Significantly they are presented as losing their Greekness and becoming 'barbarised', in other words as taking on the dominant characteristics of the West. The sharp separation between West and East that can be observed in the writings of Polybius may be one of the factors that made such a shift in perception easier.

[61] Polyb. 3.9.6–9, 3.10.5; the role of emotion here is explored in detail by Eckstein 1989.

[62] Arist. *Pol.* 1273a26–b8, Polyb. 6.56.1–5, 9.25.4, with Diod. Sic. 13.57.4–6 on Selinunte. Note that it also takes a Greek to bring order to the disorderly Carthaginians in the First Punic War, Polyb. 1.32–6.

[63] Polyb. 9.22.8, 24–5, Walbank 1957–79: II, 153.

[64] Eur. *IA* 1400–1; Arist. *Pol.* 1.1252b6–9.

The proximity of the barbarian to the Greek is inescapable if uncomfortable. When Polybius recounts Hieron of Syracuse's conflict against the Mamertines, Campanian mercenaries who had seized control of nearby Messana in an episode that would lead the Romans to make their first intervention in Sicily, it is drawn very starkly as a struggle against 'barbarians', a point overlooked in Paton's translation. The terminology asserts distance, the geography proximity.[65] The kings of the East present themselves as protectors of things Greek and celebrate their defeat of the barbarian, for which the Celts provided a very useful object lesson: Antiochus I and his elephant battle, Antigonus Gonatas at Lysimacheia, and the Attalids whose enthusiasm for making this point may have been in part a consequence of their own questionable background.[66] These kings demonstrate that the barbarian is under control and that power is Greek. Hieron may be attempting something very similar, and that is how he is presented in Theocritus' sixteenth *Idyll*, but ultimately he only succeeds by compromising; he makes an agreement with the Romans.[67]

Whatever the truth of Greek cultural identity in the West, it was perceived in antiquity as being subject to erosion, a consequence of their association with non-Greek neighbours, who were too many and increasingly too powerful. In particular from the perspective of an East where a dominant class of Greeks and Macedonians could keep the idea of being Greek secure and even extend it, those in the West, lacking this form of protection, could easily be viewed, both by others and by themselves, as being too close and too vulnerable to the barbarian.

There are repeated mentions of the failure of Greek cities to hold onto their Greek identity in the face of barbarian pressure. Polybius, for instance, is impressed at the way that Greek cities of southern Italy in the late fifth century formed a league together which was modelled on the Achaean League (which for Polybius would be the best model for good Greek government). But this would not last. Ultimately, he says, they were forced against their will to abandon this constitution, partly because of the intervention of Dionysius of Syracuse but also significantly due to the surrounding 'barbarians'.[68] Strabo in the late first century BC is much quoted for his verdict on the Greek cities of South Italy:

> Beginning from the time of the Trojan War, the Greeks seized for themselves much of the interior country and increased in power to such an extent that this region

[65] Polyb. 1.9, 1.11.7, Erskine 2000: 173; note that it is unchanged in the revised Loeb translation of Walbank and Habicht.

[66] Mitchell 2003: 283–4. [67] Theoc. *Id.* 16.76–104, Polyb. 1.16–17. [68] Polyb. 2.39.

together with Sicily was called Great Greece (Magna Graecia). Now, however, with the exception of Tarentum, Rhegium, and Naples, the whole area has become utterly barbarised (ἐκβεβαρβαρῶσθαι); part of it is in the hands of the Lucanians and the Bruttii, and part held by the Campanians and these are really Romans, since they have become Romans.[69]

Naples was one of the places that Cos had sent an embassy to back in the mid-third century but so too was Elea (Velia) which does not appear in this list of Greek survivors. Should its absence be interpreted as a sign of barbarisation or merely as a consequence of relative insignificance? Certainly epigraphic evidence would suggest that Elea did maintain its Greek character until at least Strabo's day.[70] My concern in this chapter, however, is not so much with any change that took place among the Greeks of southern Italy, but with how these Greeks were perceived. What our sources present is a failure of political superiority leading not merely to a failure of cultural superiority but also to the loss of Greek identity, encapsulated in the word ἐκβεβαρβαρῶσθαι, an exceptionally strong word to be using.

The word recurs in a passage of the *Deipnosophists*, written by Athenaeus from Naucratis in Egypt a couple of centuries later. Again it is used of a town of southern Italy, on this occasion Poseidonia (or Paestum as it comes to be known). The subject in the *Deipnosophists* at this point is the degeneration of the art of music and Athenaeus turns to Aristoxenus of Tarentum, who wrote extensively on music:

But musicians nowadays consider the goal of their art to be theatrical success. Hence, says Aristoxenus in his *Miscellaneous Table Talk*, we are doing the same as the people of Poseidonia who live on the Tyrrhenian Gulf. It happened that although they were Greek in origin they were utterly barbarised (ἐκβεβαρβαρῶσθαι), becoming Tyrrhenians or Romans, and they changed their language and the rest of their way of life, but nonetheless they celebrate one of the Greek festivals even to this day, in which they come together and remember their ancient names and customs and after they have lamented to each other and wept they go home. In this way then, he says, since the theatres have been utterly barbarised and the art of music has become vulgar and totally ruined, we likewise, although we are now few, can remember among ourselves what the art of music used to be. This is what Aristoxenus says.[71]

Aristoxenus spent time in Athens during the fourth century BC and he was even considered, certainly by himself, as a possible successor to Aristotle, but he was also a native of Tarentum. The negative image of Poseidonia presented here may be a consequence of this Tarentine perspective and may

[69] Strabo 6.1.2. [70] Lomas 1993: 103. [71] Ath. 14.632a.

even reflect a desire to shore up Tarentum's sense of Greek identity in a threatening environment by emphasising the failings of its neighbours.[72] Nevertheless, the passage should be approached cautiously; Athenaeus can elaborate his sources without clearly signalling it, so the dividing line between Aristoxenus and Athenaeus might not be so clear as is often assumed. The third sentence in the passage quoted above may be, in part at least, explanatory material from Athenaeus himself, thus the description of the festival as ἔτι καὶ νῦν and the reference to the Romans, which would seem to overstate Roman influence in fourth-century Poseidonia.[73] It is noteworthy too that for one or both of these two authors 'becoming Roman' could be equated with being barbarised. It is important, however, to remember that Athenaeus is citing Aristoxenus not for the barbarisation of the Greeks of southern Italy but for his views on the degeneration of music and the remarks need to be understood within that context.[74] The passage gives a sense of the way in which the Greeks of the West were troubled by their relationship with their non-Greek neighbours, but it also shows how readily that discomfort was picked up by other Greeks.

A frequently reported characteristic of the western Greeks is a tendency towards luxury and indolence. It would be easy to mistake them for the eastern barbarians of Greek tradition, almost Persian in their decadence. This image may have two main causes. Firstly, it may result from the strong association between the West and barbarianness; thus the Greeks of the West are tainted by their surroundings and so are depicted in a manner more commonly used to depict barbarians. Secondly, such decadence helped to explain their failure in the face of the rise of other powers, both the inland peoples such as Lucanians and Bruttians and subsequently the Romans.[75] When, for instance, Syracuse is captured by the Romans in spite of all the skills of Archimedes, it is because the inhabitants are drunk.[76]

Luxury might seem to have been associated with the West long before the Hellenistic period. Sybaris in particular was synonymous with luxury and, although the city had ceased to exist by the time of Alexander, it may well have given encouragement to this perception of the West.[77] Subsequently,

[72] Herring 2007, cf. Fraschetti 1981a with Pedley 1990 and Wonder 2002 on the material background.

[73] For Athenaeus' far from straightforward method of citation, Gorman 2007, cf. Pelling 2000. It would have been much easier to talk of Poseidonia/Paestum as Roman after the introduction of a Latin colony in 273 BC, Cornell 1995: 364.

[74] For musical context, Gibson 2004: 113.

[75] Cf. Dench 2003: 302.

[76] Polyb. 8.37; cf. Thuc. 7.73 for drunkenness at a Syracusan festival in 413 BC at the time of the Athenian campaign, although on that occasion it followed victory rather than preceded defeat.

[77] T. Dunbabin 1948: 75–83 for a lively depiction of the excesses of Sybaris.

Thurii was founded on the site of Sybaris and already in the late fifth century the Athenian playwright Metagenes had entitled one of his comedies the *Thurio-Persians*, a title that would seem to build on the Sybarite reputation for luxury to suggest some kind of equivalence between South Italians and Persians.[78] Initially this reputation appears to have been attached to one especially wealthy and extravagant citizen of Sybaris, Smindyrides, who is even said to have given his name to a woman's shoe, an association between luxury and effeminacy also evident in Athenian images of the Persian.[79] It may, however, have taken the Hellenistic period to establish firmly the cliché of Sybarite luxury. It is the focus of many pages in the twelfth book of Athenaeus' *Deipnosophists* which is devoted to luxury. Much of Athenaeus' material on this derives in some form from Timaeus, but whether the emphasis on luxury belongs to the Hellenistic Timaeus or the third-century AD Athenaeus is far from clear. It has recently been argued that scholars have underestimated Athenaeus' role in shaping his source material and that Timaeus was less concerned with luxury than has often been believed.[80] If so, it shows Athenaeus from his eastern and Egyptian perspective finding material in the West that supported his own prejudices. For Athenaeus the Sybarites were the epitome of self-indulgent luxury that eventually brought about their own ruin.

Tarentum became a prime example of luxurious living, a contemporary Sybaris. When Pyrrhus arrived to assist the city against the Romans, he found a city obsessed with self-indulgence, an image which pervades the literature on Tarentum.[81] Athenaeus, on this occasion citing the third-century BC writer Clearchus of Soli, says that the Tarentines were 'so far advanced in luxury that they used to make their whole body smooth and introduced this form of shaving to everybody else'; in their dress, he continues, they adopted a style that would later be associated with women's fashions.[82] This abandonment of masculinity would go along with the suggestion of Persian-style luxury; no wonder they could not cope with the Romans.

The widely told story of their insulting treatment of the visiting Roman embassy shortly before the war with Pyrrhus captures their failure to stand up against Rome while at the same time calling into question their very assertion of Greekness. Dionysius of Halicarnassus' telling of the events is revealing. When the Roman ambassador addresses the Tarentine assembly

[78] P. Ceccarelli 1996: 129–30, cf. also Diod. Sic. 13.83–4 on Agrigentum.

[79] Hdt. 6.127, Diod. Sic. 8.19, Ath. 6.273b–c, 12.511c, 12.541b, Ael. *VH* 9.24, 12.24; woman's shoe, Poll. 7.89, Hesychius *s.v.* σμυνδαρίδια; effeminacy and Persians: E. Hall 1993.

[80] Gorman 2007, which takes Athenaeus' treatment of Sybaris as a case-study.

[81] Plut. *Pyrrh.* 16, App. *Sam.* 8; Lomas 1997; Walbank 1957–79: II, 101.

[82] Ath. 12.522d.

in Greek, he is met with jeering as the Tarentines watch out for errors in his Greek and call him barbarous. Dionysius here highlights the Greek/barbarian opposition, but the story itself undermines it, not least when a drunken member of the audience somehow manages to relieve himself on the ambassador's sacred robe. The Tarentines are behaving like barbarians and the dignified Greek-speaking Romans come across as more like Greeks; but then Dionysius did think the Romans were Greek in origin.[83]

Greek writers seem very ready to observe and report a decline into barbarism on the part of the Greeks beyond the Adriatic. Some explanation of this is needed. The distancing of the West that we have noticed in Polybius may have been part of this, encouraging a more negative view of the western Greeks in spite of the continuing strong sense of shared ethnicity evident in epigraphic texts such as the *asylia* decrees. These represent two different ways of conceiving the world, the one underpinned by geopolitics, the other by ethnicity. They are not, however, unrelated. Separating West from East allowed the Greeks of the West to become in the imagination of the East more closely associated with the barbarian. This made it all the easier to observe a form of cultural degeneration going on, one that could explain the Greek failure to respond adequately to the increasingly successful non-Greek populations around them.[84]

[83] Dion. Hal. *Ant. Rom.* 19.5, cf. App. *Sam.* 7, Dio Cass. 9.39.5–9, Zonar. 8.2. For the Greek origin of the Romans, Dion. Hal. *Ant. Rom.* 1.5.1, 7.72.14–16.

[84] I am grateful to the Leverhulme Trust for the Research Fellowship that gave the time to complete this chapter.

2 | Hellenistic Pompeii: between Oscan, Greek, Roman and Punic

ANDREW WALLACE-HADRILL

Pompeii looks at once East and West. Culturally, it embodies the contradictions of the 'Hellenistic West'. Undoubtedly a wave of influence from the eastern Mediterranean makes a profound impact on Pompeii in the second century BCE. Yet Pompeii had no need to turn to the East to access the Hellenic. Embedded in Magna Graecia, with the influence of the Greek colonies from Pithecoussae to Neapolis close to hand from its earliest history, it enjoyed easy contact with Sicily, with its double Greek and Punic heritage. The picture of a culturally virgin Italy transformed by Hellenistic influence in the wake of conquest works no better for Pompeii than for Latium.[1] In an earlier paper, I have suggested that already for the Pompeii of the archaic period, it does not help to separate the layers of influence, Greek, Etruscan and local: the identity of Pompeii lies not in one or other layer, but in its ability to bring them into communication with each other.[2] In looking now at Pompeii of the 'Hellenistic' period, I shall suggest again that the complexity of the layering has been underestimated. Dazzled by the glamour of the Hellenistic East, we have overlooked the importance of the western contacts, including those with the Punic world.

Hellenistic Pompeii

The period that stretches from the third century to the early first has long enjoyed a sort of double characterisation: from the ethnic point of view, it is seen as Samnite or Oscan, from the art-historical as 'Hellenistic'. The term *Hellenismus* seems to have been used first in this context by Augustus Mau in 1908:

This chapter is a companion piece to my contribution to the Getty collection on Cultural Identities which focuses on the archaic period (Wallace-Hadrill 2011). Both papers develop in greater detail ideas offered in Wallace-Hadrill 2008: 129–37. Both publications have benefited from the stimulating discussion at the conferences in Rome and Los Angeles; my particular gratitude goes to Jo Quinn, without whose persistence this contribution would have fallen by the wayside.

[1] Wallace-Hadrill 2008: 73–143. [2] Wallace-Hadrill 2011.

It definitely belongs in terms of steps of development to the Hellenistic period, that from Alexander the Great onwards. The tufo period is in terms of art history that of Hellenism in Pompeii, in political terms that of the Samnites since their Hellenisation; it ends with the founding of the Roman colony.[3]

The 1920s and 1930s saw the three monumental volumes of *Die Hellenistiche Kunst in Pompeji* by Erich Pernice, examining successively bronze vessels, marble furniture and pavements and mosaics.[4] One of the most influential, if briefest, contributions along these lines was Hans Lauter's essay entitled, 'Zur Siedlungsstruktur Pompejis in samnitischer Zeit', which rightly underlined the building boom of this period and its importance in shaping the town. From the outset, he identifies Samnite as Hellenistic: 'Pompeii's Samnite period, which essentially coincides with the Hellenistic age . . .'[5] This characterisation of third- and second-century Pompeii as 'Hellenistic' reached its fullest expression with Paul Zanker, whose collection of essays on *Hellenismus in Mittelitalien* offered the most wide-ranging study of the phenomenon in Italy; he discussed Hellenistic Pompeii in his influential essay, 'Pompeji: Stadtbilder als Spiegel von Gesellschaft und Herrschaftsform', subsequently translated and transformed into a book in Italian and English, each with interesting variants.[6] Dividing the changing urban image of the town into a series of time-slices, he entitled our period in the original German, 'die Hellenistiche Stadt der zweiten Jahrhunderts v. Chr.', though the English translation restores a bit of ethnicity by calling the chapter, 'The Hellenistic City of the Oscans'.[7]

'Hellenistic' is one of those categories that is particularly risky to invoke if you are not aware of its ideological presuppositions. Johann Gustav Droysen coined the term to characterise a particular epoch, from Alexander to (more or less) Augustus on the premise that there was a broad cultural movement which gave some sort of Mediterranean-wide coherence to the period, a *Verschmelzung* or fusion of Greek with

[3] Mau 1908: 39: 'Er gehört seiner Entwicklungsstufe nach entschieden dem Hellenismus, der Zeit nach Alexander d.Gr. an. Die Tuffperiode ist kunstgeschichtlich der Hellenismus in Pompeji, politisch die Zeit der Samniten seit ihrer Hellenisierung; sie endet mit der Gründung der römischen Kolonie.' The reference to *Hellenismus* occurs only in the second edition of 1908, not in the first of 1900 or the translation by F.W. Kelsey. The change is perhaps due to the recent publication of the first volume of Delbrück's *Hellenistische Bauten in Latium* (Delbrück 1907–12).

[4] Pernice 1925–38.

[5] Lauter 1975: 147, 'Pompejis samnitische Zeit, die im wesentlichen mit der hellenistischen Epoche zusammenfällt . . .'.

[6] Zanker 1976a, 1988b, Italian translation 1993a, English translation 1998.

[7] Zanker 1988b: 5, 1998: 32, where the words 'of the Oscans' are taken from the first words of the section.

Oriental culture.[8] He was, as Luciano Canfora (1987) showed, influenced by Niebuhr, who in turn was influenced by the Danish ethnographer Father Carsten, who studied cultural fusion in the colonialist situation of the West Indies, and specifically Creole languages and cultures. Droysen's *Hellenismus* is a sort of creolisation of Greek culture, fused with the Oriental. The most perverse thing about this construct is the violence it does to the Greek usage of *hellenismos* and *hellenizein*, which invariably refer to the insistence on pure Greek in foreign contexts: the anxiety of the grammarian is that Jews, Egyptians, Syrians or Carthaginians should speak an uncontaminated language, the very opposite of the fusion which Droysen posited.[9]

It may seem safe to speak of 'Hellenism' in a neutral sort of way simply to refer to the cultural *koine* that we can recognise both in the Greek eastern Mediterranean and in the Roman West: yet that is the product not of Greek/Oriental fusion, but of Roman conquest. Unconsciously, Orientalism lurks in the background. Take Zanker's discussion of the figured capitals from the Casa dei Capitelli Figurati. One shows the owner and his wife, while a second capital shows a drunken satyr (or Silenus) and a maenad.[10]

> The men are naked to the waist, the women swathed in the usual modest robes, but their expressions and embrace make it clear that here, too, they are enjoying wine and an amorous encounter. Through this juxtaposition the owner announces in the most explicit manner his identification with the Dionysiac, hedonistic lifestyle celebrated by Oriental monarchs ('Könige des Ostens') and characteristic of contemporary Greek cities. The portal thus proclaims his adoption of a specific form of Greek culture. (Zanker 1998: 37)

The discussion is closely linked to his analysis of the contrasting styles of Octavian and Antony, and the attempt to discredit Antony by association with the 'oriental luxury' of the Hellenistic kingdoms: the rhetoric of Asiatic luxury and excess, with its roots in fifth-century Athenian writing, and cheerfully recycled by the Romans of Cicero's generation, underpins the characterisation of the 'Hellenistic'.[11] Yet the image of the drunken Silenus was familiar in the West from the archaic period onwards, on Etruscan sarcophagi and mirrors, on terracotta antefixes, on the coinage of Sicilian Naxos, on the decorative plaques of bronze beds and so many contexts: why

[8] Droysen 1836, 1843, 1877–8. See Momigliano 1970, Bichler 1983.

[9] See my discussion in Wallace-Hadrill 2008: 20–2.

[10] Staub Gierow 1994: 48 describes it as Silenus and maenad; p.73 gives a date of *c.* 120 BCE and questions Zanker's association with the Bacchanalia of 186.

[11] On the links between Asiatic style, Dionysus and Orientalism, Zanker 1988a: 64.

should this image now evoke the kingdoms of the East? It is remarkable how tenacious is the assumption that the Dionysiac is somehow 'Oriental', when it is a persistent characteristic of Greek art and culture at all periods.[12]

For Zanker, the Oscans are enthusiastic newcomers to Hellenistic culture:

> In the case of the palatial tufa houses of the second century B.C., by contrast, the proportions had been correct. The Oscan landowners and merchants who built them were newcomers to Hellenistic culture, but nonetheless full participants in it, indistinguishable from the Greeks of the mother country and Asia Minor except perhaps for a slight degree of excess. When their successors began taking the great Roman aristocrats' villas as their point of orientation, however, Pompeii lapsed into cultural provincialism. (Zanker 1998: 75)

That is to say, the Oscans of the second century were discovering Greek culture for the first time, despite living in a city which for a good five centuries had been in close contact with the Greek cities of the Bay of Naples; and their contact with the Hellenistic East was unmediated by contact with the Romans, in spite of the fact that it was with Roman armies that they went East to fight as *socii*, and in the wake of Roman conquest that they operated as *negotiatores*. I suggest we might replace this picture of unmediated Hellenisation restricted to a single moment with a picture of a Pompeian cultural negotiation: just as in the archaic period it is difficult to distinguish Greek from Etruscan influence, in this later period we should beware of separating the Hellenistic from the Roman.

Cultural identity is not just about who you are, but who you do business with: the Pompeian necessarily did business with the Greek world of south Italy, with the Oscan-speaking world of central Italy and Samnium, and the Latin-speaking world of Rome. We could ask for no better symbol of this triangulation than the dedication to Mummius in the temple of Apollo that was revealed from its plaster by Andrea Martelli (Martelli 2002, cf. Yarrow 2006). The Oscan lettering and name forms are coherent with the overwhelming use of Oscan in public inscriptions in Pompeii in the second century, and with an implicit association with the Oscan speakers of the interior. The celebration of the conqueror of Achaea spells out Pompeii's role as an ally of Rome in the eastern campaigns, from whose booty they were benefiting; while the location of the temple of Apollo, which is rebuilt at this time in the finely cut tufo of the Hellenistic *Tuffperiode*, decorated with bronze statues of Apollo and Artemis that might themselves be part of the loot of Corinth, point not to a first encounter with Hellenistic culture

[12] On supposed 'Oriental' cults, see Beard *et al.* 1998: 246–8, and 92–6 on the cult of Bacchus.

(Achaea, after all, is scarcely eastern), but to the potential of war booty to update and embellish a sanctuary that had from the outset made an engagement with the Greeks explicit.[13]

In thinking of the Hellenistic in Italy, we should wean ourselves from the Droysenian obsession with the Oriental, and focus more on the western Mediterranean, and in particular on its Punic cultural background. For a snapshot of what Pompeii's Mediterranean-wide links looked like in the pre-imperial period, you need look no further than its coinage. Clive Stannard, who started by analysing the 180 or so coins found in the British School at Rome (BSR)/University of Reading excavations in Region I insula 9, then compared our sample to other finds in Pompeii, Gragnano and large numbers of finds by metal detector from the Liri river around Minturno (Stannard 2005). The distribution pattern that comes out, subsequently confirmed by Richard Abdy's study of the larger sample from the Anglo-American project, is strikingly consistent: a good number of local Campanian mintages, especially Naples itself; a certain number of South Italian, Sicilian and Punic issues; a substantial presence from Massalia; a massive presence of the extraordinary small bronze pieces of Ebusus (Ibiza), with the type of the Punic god Bes; and a tiny handful from the eastern Mediterranean. That is to say, not surprisingly, that Pompeii looks West more than East, and links to the Greek cities of Neapolis and Massalia, and the once-Punic Panormus, more strongly than to central Greece, let alone Asia. And it is in this western Mediterranean context that the Punic is a more potent player than the Hellenisation model is ever prepared to admit. Piero Guzzo (2007: 76) has recently suggested that Ebusus might have played a role analogous to Delos for trade with the western Mediterranean. If so, that increases the chances of a cultural engagement with the Punic.

From this point of view, it is worth thinking again about the typical *facies* of the domestic building of the third and second centuries, what Mau called the *Kalksteinperiode*. Its characterising feature was the use of local Sarno travertine ('limestone' is technically a misnomer), both in ashlar blocks and in the arrangement of chains of alternating vertical and horizontal elements referred to as *opus africanum*. Despite its Vitruvian ring, the term is not Roman but modern, and rightly points to its frequency in Punic North Africa.[14] There is a close association between this building technique

[13] Cf. Wallace-Hadrill 2008: 131–3.

[14] Adam 1999: 120–1. Peterse 1999 is the fullest analysis of the use of this building technique in Pompeii.

and plasterwork in the *faux marbre* of the first style, and flooring in *cocciopesto*, with a red background of crushed ceramics, and decoration in its simplest form of rows of white marble chips. The BSR/Reading project met this combination in the house of Amarantus (I.9.12), excavating half a metre below the remodelled *tablinum* with its fourth-style decoration (Wallace-Hadrill 2005: 105). Subsequently, the pattern has been found repeatedly in Filippo Coarelli's ambitious series of excavations focused in the north-west quarter of the town (Region VI). As his recently published volume, *Rileggere Pompei*, shows in detail, there are two major phases of development (Coarelli and Pesando 2005). The first, broadly in the third century, defines the layout of the house plots, and creates a series of solidly built atrium houses in Sarno stone, with so-called *opus signinum* floors of red *cocciopesto* with white marble chips, and walls decorated in first- or masonry-style plaster, typically with yellow socles. The second phase, in the second century, transforms several of the houses, raising them by as much as half a metre, but still uses travertine, *cocciopesto* and first-style plasterwork. The House of the Centaur is a particularly clear example.[15]

Coarelli's team, in a total of over eighty trenches, have repeatedly found situations in which third- or early second-century structures are buried beneath raised floors with this repetitive typology. This suggests we might think again about the use of this highly characteristic construction style, which is so widespread in Pompeii, and has such a limited distribution pattern in the Mediterranean, in Punic and Roman North Africa (as its name suggests), in Punic Sicily (Mozia from the fourth century, Punic Selinunte and, perhaps above all, Solunto), and in Sardinia (e.g. Nora).[16] *Opus africanum* is a rarity in mainland Italy beyond Campania, and far from being a standard Italic building technique. The distribution pattern has been provisionally mapped by Lisa Fentress, and the association of *opus africanum* with areas of Punic domination or Punic contact is so strong that she has suggested that the use of the technique in Campania might be attributed to Carthaginian prisoners of war.[17] That must remain at the level of speculation, but the fundamental point is that the links between Campania and the Punic world, whether direct or mediated through the Sicilian Greeks, reflect the continued cultural complexity of the area.

It is therefore with particular interest that I have learnt from Will Wootton, who has studied the flooring of Euesperides under Andrew

[15] See in detail Pesando 2008. [16] On Solunto see Wolf 2003.

[17] I am grateful to Lisa Fentress for allowing me to refer to an unpublished paper delivered at the British School at Rome; see also Fentress (Chapter 6) in this volume.

Wilson, the importance of Punic flooring in the technology of *cocciopesto* technique as practised in Italy. Part of the story seems to be a Punic obsession with bathing: *cocciopesto* flooring has water-resistant properties, and was much used for bathing facilities, especially at Kerkouane. The route for transmission of these very specific technologies, of wall-construction and flooring, is presumably through Sicily, with surely Panormus as the key point of contact.[18] The link between the Bay of Naples and Palermo has remained historically tenacious, and it makes sense that Pompeii looked in this direction too. If there is a Hellenistic fusion that is reaching Pompeii in the third and early second centuries, it is that of Greek and Punic which characterises Sicily, not the supposed Greek and Oriental of the eastern Mediterranean.

This is not to deny eastern contact, but rather to downdate it. The sack of Corinth does seem to mark a change. The tufo period at Pompeii does seem to belong to one quite specific episode. The distribution of ashlar tufo façades is quite localised. They chase down the via dell'Abbondanza as far as the Stabian baths, chase uphill up the via Stabiana, then head back to the Forum along the via della Fortuna.[19] It is hard to explain such a distribution in terms of mere fashion, and it looks strongly like an act of communal will to renew façades in certain streets to embellish the city. The tufo façades are not integral to the construction of the houses behind them, but stuck on. They climaxed at the top of the via dell'Abbondanza with a monumental gateway of tufo, right opposite the temple of Apollo. It seems that we are looking at a major urban renewal in the wake of the sack of Corinth.

This timing nicely suits the chronology of the most famous 'Hellenistic' house of Pompeii, the House of the Faun. Its tufo façade ties it into this phase of urban embellishment. Its spectacular mosaics point explicitly to the East, to Alexander's campaigns, and to Egypt as represented by the Nilotica which in their turn tie in so closely to the late second-century monumentalisation of Praeneste. In this context, we may welcome the suggestion, made simultaneously by Fabrizio Pesando (1996) studying the House of the Faun, and by Meyboom (1995) studying the Palestrina mosaic, that the owners of the house were the Satrii, a well-attested family in Oscan areas, and that the choice of the Faun, or rather Satyr, to decorate both their

[18] On so-called *opus signinum* paving in Sicily, see Palmieri 1983, Tsakirgis 1990 and the contributions to the Palermo conference of 1996 by Camerata Scovazzo 1997, C. Greco 1997, Isler 1997 and Joly 1997. See further the chapters by Lisa Fentress (Chapter 6), Andrew Wilson (Chapter 5), and Roger Wilson (Chapter 4) in this volume.

[19] See Wallace-Hadrill 2008: 134.

atrium and their master-bedroom, was a play on their name. It is not difficult to imagine a Satrius leading the Pompeian *socii* into some eastern engagement, sacking some innocent centre, and coming back fancying himself a proper Alexander triumphant over the East.

At the entrance to the House of the Faun is a stretch of *cocciopesto* flooring with white marble chips spelling out the Latin greeting, *HAVE*. This has caused some concern to those who want Oscan to be the only visible language in pre-colonial Pompeii, and Latin to be the exclusive language of the Roman colony. But, as Zevi has argued (1998), there is no need to downdate the inscription to after 80 BCE. Latin, of necessity, was the *lingua franca* of the Roman and allied armies; the local élites must have mastered it, and so too might their troops. Public inscriptions were put up in Oscan in Pompeii not for ignorance of Latin, but in awareness of a separate cultural identity that is marked throughout central Italy in the second century. But to infer from this that they were culturally out of contact with Rome is absurd. Consider only Lisa Fentress's demonstration (2003a) that the early second-century House of Diana at Cosa was built to exactly the same ground plan, down to quite small details, as the House of Sallust at Pompeii. We can add that there are many similarities between the row-houses of Cosa and those studied by Nappo (1997) at Pompeii. It is no coincidence that Pompeii is the type-site for the Roman atrium house. The Pompeians were building their houses on models familiar in Roman colonies long before they themselves became one, even if they were using building technologies that pointed to the Punic world.

I have underlined the ambivalence of the cultural affinities met in Pompeii. For a final example of how difficult the boundaries are, we may consider the small theatre or Odeion at Pompeii. As is well known, it is extraordinarily close in design to the theatre at the sanctuary site of Pietrabbondante, that ultimate symbol of Samnite separatism. But it was erected, according to its dedication, by C. Quinctius Valgus and M. Porcius, the same Sullan colonial magistrates who built the amphitheatre, that ultimate symbol of the Roman. The same theatre design, then, might be Samnite in Pietrabbondante, and Roman in Pompeii. But of course it was also potentially Samnite in Pompeii – we cannot exclude that it had been projected before the Social War, and only finished off by the Sullan *duoviri*. And on the other hand, it was also Hellenistic, with its elegant sphinx finials and Atlas supports. The design could come from the East, although as Roger Wilson shows (Chapter 4, this volume), there are plenty of parallels to find in Sicily too. But since the same design was also found at Sarno, the model might be more local, even Capua.

Conclusion

'Hellenistic' Pompeii, as it emerges from this discussion, is a great deal less coherent, culturally, than imagined. Far from being a simple Italic city that experiences a single acculturating transformation from the eastern Mediterranean, it enters the period with a long history of influences, from its Greek and Samnite neighbours, and from the dominant powers of central Italy, Etruscan or Roman. The third and second centuries see the material prosperity and urban fabric of the city transformed. But we can distinguish, it would appear, separate waves of influence. In the third century, Pompeii belongs in the ambit of Magna Graecia, with features of material culture that point to Sicily and, beyond that, to the zone of Punic influence. 146 BCE, with the simultaneous destructions of Carthage and Corinth, may mark a real turning point: a western cultural *koine* that emerged from a dialogue between western Greek and Punic is finally displaced by an eastern Mediterranean *koine*. It marks a quantum leap in material culture, what the Romans called *luxuria* and the Greeks *tryphe*. It coincides with what the Romans described as the end of *metus hostilis*, once Carthage was no longer there to be a bogey man. It is the direct result of Roman imperialism. The Pompeians, like the Romans themselves, looked for a new expression of cultural identity in the larger Mediterranean they now together controlled.

3 The 'Hellenistics of death' in Adriatic central Italy

EDWARD BISPHAM

Introduction

This chapter examines burial and death ritual between the late fourth and late first centuries BC (the period broadly categorised as 'Hellenistic' in scholarship on Italy) within the Vestinian *ethnos*.[1] It looks in particular at data from the recent excavations of the cemetery at Fossa, near L'Aquila, in the modern *regione* of Abruzzo (see Figure 3.4 for a map of sites mentioned); in drawing conclusions, evidence from neighbouring cemeteries will be briefly discussed.[2] I will avoid an excessively culture-historical approach, not allowing wider ethnic ascription of the Fossan mortuary population to be a major determining factor in analysis; rather, I will look out for nuances beneath the broad carapace of ethnic identity.[3] Nevertheless, I hope to avoid throwing the baby out with the bath water: the Vestini formed a state entity with a discrete identity. The Vestini, rather than constituent Vestinian polities,

I dedicate this chapter to the memory of Domenico Fossataro; among his many acts of kindness to me was an introduction to Fossa. I am grateful to the editors for inviting me to participate in the Hellenistic West network, and for subsequent comments, both patient and probing; to the reader for Cambridge University Press for some acute suggestions; to Silvano Agostini, Vincenzo D'Ercole, Amalia Faustoferri, Lisa Bligh, Beatrice Fidelibus, Susan Kane, Archer Martin, Annalisa Marzano, Christopher Noon, Maria Stamatopoulou and Keith Swift, all of whom have allowed me to pick their brains. Earlier versions were read to the Hellenistic West conference in Rome in 2006, and subsequently in Vancouver, Oberlin and Leicester – I am grateful to the organisers of all these meetings, and to all those who offered comments, especially Neil Christie, Jean-Louis Ferrary, Lin Foxhall, David Mattingly, Graham Shipley, Martin Sterry and Andrew Wilson. All remaining inadequacies are my own. In what follows, IA = Iron Age; BG = black gloss; t. = tomb, tt. = tombs. All dates BC unless otherwise indicated.

[1] Definition and subdivision of this period, in the absence of relevant 'watershed moments' in Italy itself, are not standardised, however: 'republican', 'Vestinian', 'Italic' etc. are used beside 'Hellenistic'. See Copersino and D'Ercole (2003: 335), who use the labels 'italico-ellenistica' (mid-fourth to late third century) and 'ellenistico-romana' (late third to late first century) to articulate the period. These terms are at least grounded in an important shift in burial practices at Fossa, and highlight changing cultural dynamics.

[2] Only adult burials are considered in what follows. I hope to discuss the Hellenistic mortuary data from Abruzzo in greater depth elsewhere.

[3] The work of Copersino and D'Ercole 2003, a study fundamental to this chapter, is more strongly culture-historical in tone.

fielded armies against the Romans; Roman records preserve the memory of triumphs over the Vestini, in turn followed by a peace treaty (*foedus*) with the Vestini as a unit; this was the level at which 'international relations' operated until the Social War.[4] 'Vestinian' will thus serve here as one heuristic category among others.

I shall review the burials from Fossa, consider what behaviours and values they may imply, and then ask 'what, if anything, was Hellenistic about them?' The influence on Italy of cultural idioms from the Greek East in this period has been much studied, not only in terms of myth, literature, art and architecture, urbanism and new cults, but also of the *mentalités* which such influence (however acquired, however mediated) presupposed.[5] Recent work has concentrated on the processes of interaction, and the formulation of cultural discourses, rather than pointing to an object and saying 'this is Greek', or evoking a binary opposition in material culture between autochthonous and allochthonous.[6] Overall, however, little attention has been paid to burial and death ritual in the context of cultural interaction, especially in central Apennine Italy. Yet everyone who lived in the Hellenistic period had one thing in common: sooner or later they all died, and most of those who died were buried, if not always in ways visible to the archaeologist. And burials, and what they allow us to infer about death ritual, are informative about societies, their tensions and their preoccupations: 'Ritual fashions are the stuff social structure is made of.'[7] The omission of burial and death ritual from general overviews is thus, to put it mildly, surprising.[8] It then seems worth asking, as Italy became much

[4] For the narrative of the Roman conquest, see Cornell 1989: 372–7, and 363–4, Table 7 for triumphs; Cornell 1995: 355–8.

[5] Papers in Zanker 1976a (including two important studies which addressed themselves to central Apennine Italy: La Regina (1976) on Samnium and Mercando (1976) on Picenum, focussing in part on funerary assemblages from the Greek city of Ancona; for a reassessment of the Ancona tombs, see now Colivicchi 2008); Gruen 1992; Dench 2005. Note also Momigliano 1970: 139, 'the word Hellenism is often associated with the cultures of Carthage and Rome'.

[6] Wallace-Hadrill 2008. [7] Morris 1992: 33.

[8] A standard work on Greek burial (Kurtz and Boardman 1971), in part reflecting a bias in contemporary published material, gives only two chapters (of 18) and thirty-four pages (of 380) to specific discussion of the Hellenistic situation (Hellenistic examples do appear by way of illustration elsewhere in the second half of the book). The splendid *Blackwell Companion to the Hellenistic World* has only two chapters offering anything substantial on burial: Dench 2003 (Italy) and Mitchell 2003 (Galatians). Only in the cases of those who were in some sense 'marginal' to the Hellenistic enterprise, or left no written records, does it seem proper to examine burial and death ritual. Susan Rotroff's chapter in *The Cambridge Companion to the Hellenistic World* does discuss grave goods, but death is oddly absent from her otherwise exhaustive list of areas of behaviour which can be illuminated by studies of material culture (Rotroff 2006a: 153–4; 136–7 (list)); solitary passing reference to miniature statuettes in graves: Stewart 2006: 174; to burial clubs: Mikalson 2006: 211. There is a brief survey of types of funerary monument in

more seriously integrated into the economic and cultural networks of the Hellenistic East, what light burial and death ritual shed on that integration and its reception.

In what follows, elements of burial or death ritual which suggest the cultural interaction of the mortuary population of Fossa (those buried, and by proxy those burying) with wider 'Hellenistic' ideas and practices will be assessed, and set against other exogenous influences, and the persistence of local custom. The extent to which we can identify elements of the *corredi* (grave goods), or elements of funerary ritual, as 'Hellenistic', will be shown to vary considerably. More importantly, it will be argued that this variety, by contrast with a high level of homogeneity in the burials of the archaic period, is itself fundamentally 'Hellenistic'. It is a variety, moreover, which is not only mirrored by almost systemic variation in burial practice across the Greek East, but which also allows us to begin to understand how the West could be considered 'Hellenistic', and what that might mean.

The protean Hellenistic – problems of definition

It is trite, but true, to observe that we need to consider first what, if anything, Hellenistic is, before asking what, if anything, makes the West, or any aspect of it, 'Hellenistic'.[9] This is an undertaking fraught with difficulty.[10] Hellenistic is a modern coinage from the Greek verb *hellēnizein*, which normally means 'to speak Greek' (and by extension, within a more restricted context, to read and write Greek), but can sometimes have the further sense 'to act like a Greek' (a behavioural package for which there could be no zero-focalised manual).[11]

At one end of the spectrum of Greekness we are perhaps most familiar with a Hellenistic world seen through the eyes of a dominant Graeco-Macedonian elite who were able to *hellēnizein* both linguistically and culturally. But such a view excludes many others who were, or made themselves, able to *hellēnizein* in either sense. Or in both senses: it is wrong to keep

Chamoux 2003: 348–51 (cf. 175 for the funerary *stēlai* of Demetrias, also Kurtz and Boardman 1971: 235 and Pl. 62). Note too Zanker 1993b on Smyrna.

9 The same question could be asked of the 'Hellenistic South', or the 'Hellenistic North' (for the latter, Braund 2002: 200, 205).

10 See the contributions of Yarrow and Erskine (Chapters 1 and 12 in this volume).

11 Préaux 1978: 5 (cultural *and* linguistic); Ogden 2002b: ix, Wallace-Hadrill 2008: 4–6, 21–2, 57–8 (basically linguistic, with other behavioural connotations; importantly something the subject repeatedly practises on him/herself); Davies 2006: 75–6: Greek inscriptions 'define our period chronologically and geographically' (76), but note also Bodel 2001: 13–15 for diversity of Greek epigraphic cultures after Alexander.

speaking and behaving apart, as if they denote two separate modes which can be clearly differentiated. For the Egyptian who seriously aspired to the tax-status of *Hellēn*, proficiency in Greek, in the mouth of someone who also possessed a Greek name, was clearly essential. This, however, was a part – albeit the most significant and hard-to-acquire part – of a grammar of 'Greekness', which also embraced diet, dress, the use (if not exclusive) of Greek forms of legal instrument and arbitration, frequentation of the *gumnasion*, family structure and households built on slave-owning, *inter alia.*[12] Any of these could in theory be learnt, acquired, usurped or adopted in isolation from the others, but mastery of the 'grammar' of the dominant power, as opposed to a functional literacy or the stumbling sloppiness of the tourist, was essential for social and political advancement. Finally, no sensible definition of the Hellenistic world can rule out of court interactions between either (or both) of these two groups and others who did not want, or were unable, to *hellēnizein* in either sense. These might be conservative Jewish opponents of 'Hellenisation' in second-century Jerusalem;[13] down-trodden natives, like the camel driver whose complaint, that he has not been paid because he is *barbaros* and does not know how to *hellēnizein*, is preserved (in Greek, ironically) in the Zenon papyrus archive;[14] or even ordinary peasants whose lives were nonetheless changed by the advent of new settlements, settlers and ideas about agricultural production and agrarian relations.[15]

But one must start, as the Hellenistic started, with Droysen. His extremely influential conception, itself shaped by Hegel, was of an age where Greek culture (*Hellenismus*), spread under absolute monarchy, was adopted by non-Greeks, resulting in a cultural fusion (*Mischkultur*) and thus a levelling (*Verschmelzung*).[16] This encouraged henotheism and the syncretism of the Hellenic and the Jewish, and thus enabled the rise of a new monotheistic religion, Christianity.[17] The nature of this contact between Greeks and natives

[12] This list is largely based on Thompson 2001: 307–12, 2006: 105. See also *OGIS* 737, a Greek-style honorific decree set up by the Idumaian *politeuma* in Memphis: Thompson 1984: 1071–3.

[13] II *Maccabees* 13 for *hellēnizein* used of the changes attempted in Jerusalem.

[14] *P. Columbia Zenon* 66, ll. 19–21 = Austin 2006: no. 307 = Bagnall and Derow 2004: no. 137 and Pl. 9.

[15] Alcock 1994: 175.

[16] Cf. Plut. *Mor.* 328c-e ('On the Fortune or Courage of Alexander the Great'), a passage crucial for Droysen: Bosworth 2006: 16–17.

[17] Droysen 1833, 1836, 1843, 1877–8; Momigliano 1970; Préaux 1978: 5–9; Bichler 1983; Bosworth 2003; Erskine 2003b: 2; Bugh 2006b: 1; Bosworth 2006: 9–10, 14, 19; Thompson 2006: 107; Errington 2008: 8; Wallace-Hadrill 2008: 20–3, Wallace-Hadrill, Chapter 2 of this volume; note Will 1984: 61 for a very Droysenesque formulation, cf. Walbank 1992: 226, 251, for Christianity as 'the product of a mixed Jewish and Hellenistic environment'.

has remained a central concern of scholars, although presuppositions and methodologies have changed over time. In the two generations after Alexander many men left the older Greek *poleis* (high-volume mobility over long distances is surely a characteristic of the period) as settlers, mercenaries or even prisoners of war, often for new lives in the Diadochs' city foundations;[18] this in turn encouraged more flexible conceptions of citizenship.[19] Mobility and settlement in turn led to a series of developing encounters within and across the boundaries of the new Greek kingdoms between Greeks and natives.[20] Some scholars have placed weight on the constructive nature and consequences of these interactions, cultural, economic or both. There was, for example, very considerable demand for objects or foodstuffs, not least wine and oil, which were valued because they evoked unambiguously Greek behaviours and mentalities, whether on the part of Greek *émigrés*, or of non-Greeks 'going Greek' (such as the notable consumption of Rhodian wine in Jerusalem until just after the middle of the second century, or the imitation of the ubiquitous mould-made or 'Megarian' bowls in Sardeis)[21] – a

[18] I give a small selection from the vast bibliography on city-foundation and mobility in this period, and one biased towards more recent items. Walbank 1992: 14, 60–78, 108–9, 117–18, 125–6, 133–40 (city-foundation drives 'Hellenisation' of East, noting resettlement of orientals as well as Greeks), 159, 163–4, 181–4, 250; Billows 1995; Cohen 1995; Fraser 1996; Mileta 2002: 164–7; La'da 2002 (origins of Greek immigrants to Egypt); Bosworth 2006: 17–18; W. Adams 2006: 36, 43–5; Shipley and Hansen 2006: 54–6, 60; Davies 2006: 83–6; Thompson 2006: 98, 100–2, 104; Stewart 2006: 162–3; Krevans and Sens 2006: 187–8 (mobility and the *koinē*); Errington 2008: 6, 28, 40, 57, 61, 68–74, 113, 151; *SEG* 42.661 (Seuthes and Seuthopolis). Mikalson 2006: 210, on the ubiquity of the *gumnasion* and its culture (note for example *Syll.*[3] 578, 691; *SEG* 27.261, 47.890 = Bagnall and Derow 2004: no. 78); Alcock 1994: 188, on the implications for the rural hinterland of new foundations, cf. Davies 2006: 83.

[19] *OGIS* 229 = Bagnall and Derow 2004: no. 29; Walbank 1992: 68, 131–2, 136–7, 149–52, 166–7; Davies 1984: 262–3; Savalli 1985; Davies 2002: 8–10; Buraselis 2003; Shipley and Hansen 2006: 61–3, 68; Davies 2006: 79, 90; Thompson 2006: 94, 99–100, 107–8 (linked to need for manpower); Errington 2008: 74–5 (more fluid forms taken by citizenship, and other forms of status, voluntary or imposed).

[20] Polyb. 34.14.1–5, Livy 38.17: Alexandria; Préaux 1978: 9; Walbank 1992: 14–15, 28, 63–4, 67 (decisive unifying role for the Mediterranean), 78, 110, 184–5 (scientific advance and broader cultural horizons), 198–208, 250 (exploration); Burstein 1993: 38; Holt 1993: 54: the concept of the 'frontier society' as central to the Hellenistic experience; Gruen 1993: 239 (and P. Green 1993b: 6 on the 'Tiber-frontier', alluded to tantalisingly by discussants at the Austin symposium, but not the subject of a paper); papers in Bilde *et al.* 1993; Erskine 2003b: 3; for the 'Black Sea frontier': Walbank 1984a: 12, 19; Will 1984: 35; Braund 2002; Errington 2008: 54. There is also a religious frontier, often crossed, where new gods were met: Walbank 1992: 121, 210, 220–2; 222–6 on the Jews; Bruneau 1970: 460, 469; Shipley and Hansen 2006: 61–2; Mikalson 2006: 208–12, 217–20 (Alexandria, Delos, cf. Rotroff 2006a: 145); Davies 2006: 83 (immigration into Greece); Krevans and Sens 2006 (the Hellenistic novel and the wider world).

[21] Rotroff 2006a: 143 with further references, 149 (noting also the absence of these bowls in Mesopotamia and the upper satrapies).

major factor underpinning the explosion of seaborne trade in this period.[22] Others have stressed the degree to which Greek and indigenous cultures remained aloof from, or even hostile to, one another, with an (initially) closed Graeco-Macedonian ruling elite exploiting the natives.[23] There were of course Greeks living in the West, but in Italy they formed by the Hellenistic period not a ruling elite but a series of enclaves with highly porous borders, across which men, money, behaviours and their manifestations moved with relative facility. What is harder to gauge, as we shall see, is how far non-Greeks in Italy were engaged in dialogues with the Hellenistic Greek world in its widest sense, and how far any such engagement was (self-)conscious and directed.

Under eastern eyes?

It has not proved easy for scholars to isolate even individual elements which can be agreed to be fundamentally 'Hellenistic'. If one were to compare any 'obvious' checklist of the diagnostic features against manifestations of the same phenomena in Italy, there would perhaps be little to tick off in the Italian column (in contrast, we may note, to Sicily).[24] Thus one could

22 Some out of very many examples: Errington 2008: 42–3, 65, 70–1 (indigenous survivals in royal practice); Colledge 1987; Roueché and Sherwin-White 1985; Walbank 1992: 64–5 (relative permeability of organisations like *eranoi* and *thiasoi* to non-Hellenes), 117 (intermarriage of Greek men with local women in Egypt; cf. Thompson 2002: 153, 2006: 104–5, 118–20, 214); A. Lloyd 2002 (native militia and office-holding by native elites in Ptolemaic Egypt); Clarysse 1992 (Egyptian onomastic practice), cf. Thompson 2002: 138–9, 2006: 104–6. Greek adoption of Egyptian adoration of deities (*proskynēmata*): Parca 2001: 62; dossier from Tyriaion: Jonnes and Ricl 1998; Braund 2002: 206 ('cultural osmosis' between Scythians and Bosporans), cf. 208, 210–13. Achaimenid texture of the Seleukid kingdom: Briant 1982a; Kuhrt and Sherwin-White 1987; Errington 2008: 38–9, 112, 128–9; *contra* Mileta 2002: 160–1; Greek and Asiatic features at Aï Khanoum: Bernard 1967; economic aspects: Davies 2006: 84, 89; 'hybridisation' of Greek shapes and Lydian finish for pottery: Rotroff 2006a: 147–50, cf. Hannestad 1983: 83–120 (the differential adoption of Greek shapes into local repertoires explained by the varying density of Greek settlement).

23 Polyb. 4.45.1–46.6: Byzantion's ongoing war with Thracians and Gauls in its hinterland; Theoc. *Id.* 15.44–55 (disdain for Egyptians). Selected discussions: Momigliano 1975; P. Green 1990: ch. 19, cf. 1993b: 9; Walbank 1992: 63–5, 114–17, 159, 161, 249; Thompson 2002: 140, 142–4, 149–50, 152–3 (particular characteristics of Greek families and households, cf. 2006: 102–6, noting *inter alia* how separate socio-legal systems eventually show some degree of cross-over in favour of the Greek), 107–8 (importance of free Greek status in grants of *epigamia*); Bosworth 2006: 16–19; Errington 2008: 6, 70–1, 113 ('Hellenisation' of Sardeis, but see Rotroff 2006a: 148–9); Davies 2006: 76 (economic power of Greek elites), 83.

24 As Jonathan Prag points out to me, noting *inter alia* the presence of Dionysiac *technitai* in Syracuse (pers. comm.).

ask: where are the *gumnasia*? Where are the *thiasoi*? Which Italian communities seek *asulia* for their shrines, or grant it to the sanctuaries or cities of Anatolia?[25] Where are the egregious civic benefactors and their honours, crowns and decrees, where are the Samnite or Vestinian equivalents of Protogenes of Olbia?[26] Where are the analogues of the Library and Mouseion of Alexandria? Where is the high-volume exchange of the countless embassies[27] which criss-crossed the Aegean and the Near East with their cargoes of dialogue, requests for and recognition of arbitration, privilege and benefaction, advertisements for games and festivals, claims of *sungeneia*, proposals for *sumpoliteia* or *isopoliteia*, promotion of mysteries and oracles and the ubiquitous *technitai* of Dionysos?[28] Where are the literary figures, Italian equivalents of Aristodama of Smyrna, or the *proxenia* granted to her?[29] Where are the kings, where the *koinē*?[30]

Yet the common denominator underlying such diagnostic features is that, for all the care taken to side-step Hellenocentric assumptions, and look at interaction across frontiers, they are essentially framed in terms of what has been observed between the Aegean and the Iranian plateau. To tick off (or fail to tick off) the elements of our eastern 'Greek' model against what we find in Italy, runs the risk of telling us no more than that Italy cannot have lain anywhere in the area between the Aegean and Iran (which we knew anyway). It further suggests a hierarchical relationship: the East is packed with these 'Hellenistic' features, and therefore culturally sophisticated, whereas Italy has far fewer, more widely scattered, and is therefore a rather miserable place, getting by on a few dodgy imitations rather than proper designer labels.

Instead, we need an approach which allows the Italian 'Hellenistic' to speak in its own voice, and to be understood in its own terms, using comparisons

[25] Musti 1963; Walbank 1992: 141–2, 145–8, 151; Rigsby 1996; Erskine 2002: 98–9; Shipley and Hansen 2006: 63.

[26] *Euergēsia*: Walbank 1984a: 12; 1992: 142, 164–5; Ma 2000a: 182–94; Erskine 2002: 105; Errington 2008: 67–8, 107; for the nexus between the weakness of *polis* finance and private benefaction, which often enabled major items of civic expenditure: Préaux 1978: 489–524; Davies 1984: 311; Shipley 2000: 96–103; Braund 2002: 205; Davies 2006: 76, 87–8; Errington 2008: 108.

[27] See on embassies, Erskine, Chapter 1, this volume; some of the papers in Eilers 2009 consider embassies in the context of the Roman west.

[28] Polyb. 28.19.2–5 for the *locus classicus*, Alexandria in 169 BC; Walbank 1984a: 10–12, 1992: 62–3, 68–9, 73, 86, 136–7, 141–50; Erskine 2002; Davies 2002: 9 for the main forms of interaction; Shipley and Hansen 2006: 63, 68; Errington 2008: 5–7. Arbitration: Ager 1996; *technitai* of Dionysos: Le Guen 2001; Lightfoot 2002; Aneziri 2003.

[29] Aristodama: *Syll.*[3] 532 (218/7 BC), Walbank 1992: 73, 148; *proxenia* in general: Walbank 1992: 148–9.

[30] *Koinē* as a defining feature of the Hellenistic world: Walbank 1992: 14, 62; W. Adams 2006: 45; Krevans and Sens 2006: 186–9; see the discussion above on *hellēnizein*.

with the Greek East to analyse, and not denigrate, the West. There were varying forms and levels of engagement with Hellenistic modes in Italy, and they cannot be assessed properly by being read off quickly against an eastern yardstick.[31] I turn now to examine in more detail what can be said of Italian engagement with Hellenistic ritual or social practices in the sphere of burial.

Burial and death ritual among the Vestini

The *necropolis* of Fossa was one of the places where the Vestinian community of Aveia buried its dead.[32] Most of the Vestini, including those of Aveia, were incorporated into the Roman citizenship in 290 BC, following their defeat; at some subsequent point in the third century a *praefectura* was established for the administration of the area.[33] Fossa is the only Abruzzese cemetery from this period to have been the object of both high-quality systematic excavation (of enough tombs to constitute a statistically significant sample) and full, timely publication.[34] This material will allow us to form a good impression of the evolution of burial practices over the period, and the values which those practices symbolise. Brief reference will be made for comparative purposes to the Vestinian *necropolis* of Bazzano, just upstream from Fossa in the Aterno valley.[35] The following presentation

[31] Note also that there are ideas which travel from West to East: the phenomenon of stamping fineware with the name of the producer prior to firing appears on Calene BG, for example, well before it is taken up by the Greek manufacturers of 'Megarian bowls' (Pucci 2001: 143, with further references).

[32] In 2005 another cemetery probably serving Aveia was discovered at Varranone – Poggio Picenze; so far some 250 tombs have been excavated, but only a preliminary summary has been published: D'Ercole and Martellone 2008: 63–4; consideration of this material is beyond the scope of the present chapter.

[33] *CIL* IX.3627 for a 'praef(ectus?)'; on the incorporation of the Vestini: La Regina 1968; Humbert 1978: 226–33. About Aveia itself we know little.

[34] Copersino and D'Ercole 2003. Other volumes in this excellent series deal with the early Iron Age and Orientalising/Archaic phases of the cemetery; a fourth, presenting the synthetic analysis of the material for the latter, is awaited. On the importance of the excavations: Letta 2003a: 7. Publication was indeed timely – the chamber tombs, as well as many of the surrounding modern villages, were reduced to rubble in the earthquake of April 2009.

[35] Bazzano is perhaps the most thoroughly excavated cemetery in Abruzzo, but has yet to see proper publication; there are about 500 Hellenistic graves apparently concentrated in the centre of the plain, perhaps covering an area of up to 6 hectares (ha). Copersino and D'Ercole 2003: 372–3: the burial area seems to be subdivided by a network of major and minor roads. See also D'Ercole 1998; Copersino and D'Ercole 2003: 365 (covering only two of the eight zones excavated), and Fig. 33 for a schematic map of the excavations. The possible extent of the entire

of the evidence makes no claims to originality, but it will bring it to the attention of a wider Anglophone audience.

In this section I take it as axiomatic that the mortuary population of any given cemetery is not to be taken as a straightforward proxy for the living community. Mortuary populations can provide distorting pictures of local societies, either over- or under-representing certain groups, whether defined by age, gender or socio-economic status. They also tend to construct an idealising picture of how the dead wished to be seen, or how their surviving family, or the community, wished to see them. Nevertheless, the ideologies surrounding mortuary practice do provide insights into the values of the living society; they are shaped by them, and in turn shape them.

Fossa

The cemetery was excavated between 1992 and 2000 (Figure 3.1). The site lies on gently sloping ground just outside the modern village of Fossa and less than 0.5 km from the Aterno river.[36] A total of 575 tombs were excavated, although the full extent of the *necropolis* was not explored.[37]

The cemetery was used between the late ninth century BC and the Roman imperial period.[38] The phase with which we will be concerned follows on in the stratigraphic sequence from a period of marked alluvial deposition, which may have seen an interruption in the use of the site after the end of the archaic period. There are some 150 tombs dated to this period: the period of greatest use falls in the fourth to third centuries, followed by a marked decline in numbers of tombs (but not of depositions) in the second.[39]

cemetery is about 30 ha, of which 35,000 m^2 had been excavated by 2003 (Copersino and D'Ercole 2003: 365–6), with 1,662 burials of all periods found by 2005 (Reggiani 2008: 30).

36 On the site, the wider area, and the state of territorial study: Cosentino and Mieli 2003: 12–24.

37 Reggiani 2008: 30. There are also groups of tombs on the low spur of Colle Restoppia, a few hundred metres to the SW: Cosentino and Mieli 2003: 17–19, Foto 2–3, Fig. 5; some of these *might* be Hellenistic in date, but dating is impossible in the absence of associated stratified deposits.

38 Cosentino and Mieli 2003: 12, with further bibliography. The last *a fossa* burials date to the early first century BC, while chamber tombs continued to be built into the first half of the first century BC, and used into the Augustan period: Rizzitelli 2003d: 328, 2003e: 331, 2003f: 331; Copersino 2004: 249.

39 Copersino 2003: 308, 309, grafico 1. Alluvial deposition: Cosentino and Mieli 2003: 12–13; *contra* Letta 2003a: 7.

Figure 3.1 Fossa, general view with chamber tomb.

Fossan tomb types

There are eight chamber tombs;[40] of these, five contained funerary beds, whose frame, head-rest and legs were decorated with bone appliqués, sometimes of considerable artistic quality.[41] The first chamber tombs are datable to the first half of the second century.[42] Most are laid out along the road(s) that ran past (or through) the cemetery.[43] They are rectangular in plan; earlier tombs have walls of large roughly squared blocks laid in courses, later examples use smaller stones mortared together; the tombs are roofed with either a

[40] Copersino 2003: 308, and n. 8 for evidence for a ninth chamber tomb, destroyed in antiquity.

[41] Copersino 2003: 307–8 (the others probably had simpler wooden beds, *cf.* Rizzitelli 2003e: 331); t.430 contained two beds; two others are represented by sporadic finds of fragments (D'Ercole and Martellone 2008: 61); reconstructed example: D'Ercole and Martellone 2008: Fig. 6.

[42] Cosentino and Mieli 2003: 13; Letta 2003a: 7; Copersino 2003: 308; Rizzitelli 2003e: 331. Further chamber tombs were built in the middle of the second century, and again at the end of that century/beginning of the next, possibly marking the emergence of new families within the elite (Copersino 2003: 308); Copersino 2004: 249 reviews the chronology of the tombs' construction, with a suggestive hypothesis on plot size.

[43] Rizzitelli 2003c: Tav. 2 (chamber tombs in orange); two roads: Rizzitelli 2003d: 331, 2003c: Tav. 2, 2003e: 331. Many later *a fossa* tombs are governed by the same orientations, representing a major change from previous use of space, and leading to intercutting of older and newer tombs.

single large slab, or three or four smaller ones.[44] Access was through a *dromos* (filled in after burial) passing through (generally) a trilithon doorway in one of the short sides of the tomb, formed of well-cut blocks, and closed by one or two stone slabs set vertically.[45] The chambers probably originally formed the innermost part of a *tumulus* of heaped earth, recalling Iron Age *tumuli*.[46] Internal walls were plastered; floors were of gravel, sand or beaten earth, into which one or more pits could be cut for the re-deposition of earlier burials of the same family.[47] t.63, one of the earliest chamber tombs, was placed squarely within the largest surviving Iron Age *tumulus*, distinct from other contemporary burials and away from the road: a clear claim for links with earlier generations, and attachment to the landscape.[48]

The rest of the tombs are individual 'flat' graves cut straight into the subsoil (*a fossa*), with the deceased laid supine and fully extended. Until the end of the third century most used various combinations of wooden boards and hollowed tree-trunks to provide a simple lining, and thereafter wooden coffins; the presence of shrouds is suggested by the disposition of the limbs and the presence of a single *fibula* in the centre of the thorax.[49] Grave goods become increasingly standardised over the course of the second century (although the last such graves can contain prestige objects – a mirror, a stylus – emulating the wealthier grave goods), and are generally less rich and varied than those of the chamber tombs. Despite this standardisation, the *disposition* of the grave goods within the grave becomes essentially 'decentralised', to the point that if arrangement of grave goods within the burial is indeed determined by the funerary ritual, there is then no standard ritual.[50]

Developments to the mid-third century

The burials which concern us can be divided into three sub-phases: (1) last half of the fourth century; (2) end of the fourth to the late third century; and

[44] Rizzitelli 2003e: 331, but see the important corrections of Copersino 2004.

[45] Copersino 2004: 247–9 (noting that the blocking of the doorway of t. 520 with small stones, mortared together, suggests permanent closure; on t.520 see also Martellone 2008a).

[46] Copersino 2004: 249 and Fig. 7. [47] Copersino 2003: 308; Rizzitelli 2003e: 331.

[48] Copersino 2003: 308, most of the chamber tombs overlie earlier *a fossa* burials, whose contents were generally treated with respect; Rizzitelli 2003e: 331, cf. tt.1 and 124 which also appropriated IA *tumuli*.

[49] Rizzitelli 2003c: 327, 2003d: 329–30 (rare exceptions probably denote lower social status). The shroud became less common in later *a cassone* tombs (see below): *ead.* 2003d: 330.

[50] Rizzitelli 2003d: 328.

(3) late third onwards.[51] The grave assemblages of the first period (as far as they can be attributed with any confidence) share some characteristics with those of the preceding century.[52] Female graves as a rule contained glass-paste bead necklaces, which recur as late as the start of the third century; some metal personal ornaments known from the archaic period (or earlier) also continue through and beyond this phase. This very restricted range of grave goods, indeed in some cases the almost complete disappearance of the *corredo*, is paralleled outside Vestinian territory at Campovalano and at Alfedena.[53] In male graves there is a marked discontinuity with respect to Iron Age and archaic practice, with the disappearance of offensive weaponry (and in at least one case drastic restriction of other grave goods).[54] We may suspect that social norms were already operating by the mid-fourth century across Apennine Italy to limit outlay on funerals, perhaps connected with the transformation of gentilicial aristocracies at the end of the archaic period and the ongoing process of state-formation.[55] Such norms would explain changes in funerary ritual and in the types of objects suitable for constructing the status of the deceased.[56]

Five early tombs post-dating the middle of the fourth century are characterised by the presence of over-painted BG *skyphoi*, or in one case a 'Gnathian' vessel.[57] These imported, fashionable, vessels are nevertheless used in a very traditional way, placed inside an *olla* (a globular or ovoid storage jar), normally at the feet of the deceased.[58] The placing of a drinking vessel inside the *olla* was a feature of the earliest burials at Fossa, although initially a one-handled cup fulfilled this role; now new, cosmopolitan shapes are deployed in fresh contexts to serve traditional roles.[59] The *skyphos* + *olla* pairing is not the standard one, however: more frequently *ollae* contain miniature *ollae* or *pocula* in a coarseware fabric.[60] It seems probable, then, that the adoption of

[51] Phases (defined on the basis of changes in the *corredi*): first phase: Benelli 2003; second and third: Copersino 2003: 308 (roughly co-extensive with the period of greatest use of the *necropolis*).

[52] For the difficulties of dating to the fifth and fourth centuries see Benelli 2003: 322.

[53] Benelli 2003: 322 with further references. [54] Benelli 2003: 322.

[55] Bispham 2007: 191–4 for these changes in Samnium. [56] Benelli 2003: 322–3.

[57] Rizzitelli 2003b: 323–4.

[58] Placement of the *olla*: Copersino 2003: 308. On *ollae* (and other similar productions): Rizzitelli 2003a: 293–305. Some are made in an *impasto* fabric (effectively a crude coarseware fabric), but thrown on the wheel, not made by hand (Rizzitelli 2003a: 293–4). Similarity of Fossan *pocula* to examples from Bazzano: Rizzitelli 2003a: 302.

[59] Rizzitelli 2003b: 324. For the earlier pairing (not however attested between *c.* 500 and *c.* 350 BC: Rizzitelli 2003b) see Cosentino *et al.* 2001 (early IA), and D'Ercole and Benelli 2004: e.g. 52–3 (t.121), 97–8 (t.245) (Orientalising and archaic periods, when *kantharoi*, *anforette* and dippers join the cups); the association is common but not ubiquitous.

[60] Rizzitelli 2003b: 324.

the *skyphos* for this traditional role points to an attempt on the part of the deceased or his/her family to use imported goods to project status within a traditional context. The personal ornament in these graves is limited to *fibulae*, bracelets, necklaces and rings (bronze for women, iron for men). Objects concerned with bodily cleanliness are rarer: tweezers are exclusively found in male graves, whereas utensils for cleaning fingernails and ears seem to belong to the female sphere. Three female tombs have spindle-whorls.[61]

The second sub-phase sees no major changes: *pocula* and one-handled cups in *impasto* continue to predominate over imported BG *skyphoi* inside *ollae* as the dipping/drinking vessel; other BG vessels, especially bowls, some imported, do, however, join the repertoire.[62] The earlier tendency for limited personal ornament in *corredi* now becomes exaggerated. For example there are only two necklaces in female graves; both denote higher status individuals, at least one being an imported item with representations of human heads in glass paste (t. 351, which also produced a fine pair of bracelets).[63] Other than these items, we find a single spindle whorl in a female grave (the last of its kind to be deposited), and a pair of tweezers in a male grave. Otherwise ornament consists of unremarkable *fibulae* and finger-rings.[64] The pairing of *olla* + drinking vessel/dipper, placed by the feet, continues in this period. In some graves a stone barrier is constructed around this pair, a feature which goes back to the early Iron Age, and underlines the traditional nature of the combination; additional BG cups, continuing a practice current from the archaic period, are placed by the lower legs.[65]

Status differentiation from the late third century

Fossa's third sub-phase begins in the late third century, with the start of a bifurcation in burial practice. A status differential becomes apparent, expressed through tomb size as well as contents, which will lead in two or

[61] Rizzitelli 2003b: 325. Some of these earlier assemblages recall those of Campovalano, where imported *skyphoi* and *fibulae* with simple bows and glass-paste bead necklaces recur in the Picene VI phase (*c.* 385–270 BC): M. Guidobaldi 1995: 54, Tavv. 5–6; the presence at Campovalano of objects associated with weaving is similarly slight in female graves (only in five tombs): M. Guidobaldi 1996: 199.

[62] Rizzitelli 2003c: 325 for more detailed analysis.

[63] Rizzitelli 2003c: 326, 325, Fig. 1; it is very similar to one from t. 833 at Bazzano; for further parallels, Negroni Catacchio 1989: 680.

[64] Rizzitelli 2003c: 326.

[65] Rizzitelli 2003c: 327; early IA *ripostiglio* around the *olla*: Cosentino *et al.* 2001; *kylix*/chalice placed by the lower legs in archaic depositions: D'Ercole and Benelli 2004.

Figure 3.2 Fossa, *a cassone* tomb t. 401.

three generations to the chamber tomb. At the end of the third century about a dozen rather large *a fossa* graves were carefully fitted with a wooden lining; these are termed by the excavators tombs *a cassone* (Figure 3.2).[66] Their assemblages include new items, anticipating the richer *corredi* of the chamber tombs.[67] The transition between the third- and second-century situations is best appreciated in four tombs: tt. 406, 224 (female); 333, 328 (male). In these the traditional set of *olla* + drinking/dipping vessel at the feet of the deceased is augmented (or sometimes replaced) by increasing numbers of BG vases (and imitations), arranged by the lower legs and feet of the corpse.[68] There are also 'new' forms (new in this position in the grave): *skyphoi* and plates, and the pair of BG *pyxides* of different sizes, probably

[66] Copersino 2003: 311 suggests that these tombs are characteristic of a 'ceto . . . medio', but since these tombs also precede the appearance of chamber tombs, one might rather say that they *became* characteristic of such a group, however defined; Rizzitelli 2003d: 329 on the correlation between this type of tomb and significant *corredi*.

[67] Copersino 2003: 307; also D'Ercole and Copersino 2003: 281, Foto 3 (t. 401); Rizzitelli 2003d: 328.

[68] Sometimes turned upside down: Rizzitelli 2003d: 328, 327 Foto 4.

locally produced, which now become typical of male Fossan graves.[69] The 'liberation' of the *skyphos* (and the *poculum* – seen for the last time in these graves) from their previous association with the *olla*, and their arrangement with other vessels for eating and drinking, indicate a break with previous ideological schemes, and a new emphasis on more highly articulated (that is, sophisticated) contexts of consumption, as well as perhaps libatory practices in the funerary ritual (upside-down vases). Some of these graves also contain banqueting utensils. In t. 224 we can see how a new 'grammar' of the symbolic language of death ritual is being 'learnt' at this stage: this female grave has the pair of *pyxides* and the soon-to-be-classic Fossan three-piece banquet set of bowl + knife + *kreagrai*[70] both hereafter characteristic of *male* depositions.[71] This female deposition, together with t.333, is also the earliest *a cassone* tomb at Fossa (*a cassone* burials themselves become largely the preserve of males). The ways in which the proper intersection of status, family and gender are to be expressed in death are at this stage still being explored.[72]

These four tombs announce a new 'language' of burial at Fossa: the experimentation of the transitional period hardens into a recognisable 'grammar', with the new, wider repertoire allowing the expression of a more elaborate symbolic language in the funerary ritual, perhaps engaging functionally specific items within a more articulated performance. The number and variety of objects deposited in almost all tombs now increase. BG *paterae*, *pyxides* and lamps enter the repertoire. These are followed in the middle of the second century by *unguentaria* (often two, sometimes as many as four) in a regional fineware fabric;[73] while the number of imported vessels falls.[74] *Ollae* (full size

[69] On the variety of shapes among Adriatic *pyxides*, some of which diverge from canonical Etruscan/Campana B form, and the possibility of influence, direct or indirect, from Athens and the Greek East: Rizzitelli 2003a: 290–2.

[70] *Kreagrai* are tongs, almost certainly used for handling freshly cooked meat (Rizzitelli 2003a: 292).

[71] By contrast a single *pyxis* becomes characteristic of female graves: Rizzitelli 2003d: 328.

[72] Rizzitelli 2003d: 328, 330.

[73] This denotes a fine fabric largely without inclusions, used for a range of table wares or storage vessels; it is often referred to in English as 'buff ware', and in Italian as *argilla depurata*. Vessels of this type can be over-painted/slipped (although often they retain such coatings poorly) in whole or part, or left unpainted.

[74] On the Fossan BG assemblage and imitations: Rizzitelli 2003a: 285–92, noting (285–7) the existence of at least two local fabrics, and similarities with the BG assemblage from Bazzano; cf. also Benelli 2003: 322. Most of the BG vessels are local products (i.e. produced at an unknown centre or centres nearby for short- or medium-range distribution); the imports, principally of *petites estampilles* and related wares, and Campana B products, are mostly from Etruria or Latium, sometimes Apulia, but not Campania. These imports appear in male and female tombs as prestige objects. A broadly 'Tyrrhenian' influence also manifests itself in a preference for cups and plates, and to a lesser degree for *skyphoi* and *pyxides* (forms also imitated in the earlier phases in coarseware fabrics).

and miniature)[75] remain from earlier practice, but considerable importance is now invested in the pairs plate + cup, placed, like the *ollae*, near the feet of the deceased, but linked to an ideology of banqueting,[76] and *unguentarium* (piriform or fusiform) + *pyxis*, connected to the care of the body.[77] A similar story can be told for metal utensils.[78] In particular, the set knife + spit + *kreagrai* becomes standard; at the same time personal ornament disappears, with the exception of rings, found exclusively in male tombs;[79] two *a cassone* tombs (the later second century) contain strigils.[80]

Within a couple of generations the first chamber tombs appear. These display the 'set' of grave goods already standardised in *a fossa* graves, but add to it as conspicuously as they monumentalised the form of the *a cassone* burials. Beside the standard metal objects, strigils, lamp-stands and mirrors are almost invariably found; other objects include a casket with metal and bone fittings, hair pins and a bone fitting for a distaff.[81] *Skyphoi* are often replaced by two-handled cups; entirely or largely exclusive to chamber tombs are table and transport amphorae, and *lagynoi*.[82] Some of these elements clearly flesh out existing ritual practices: lamps are provided with lamp stands, transport amphorae supply the wine whose consumption was previously symbolised by the drinking vessels; other objects reflect ideologies of leisure and physical prowess.[83]

Individual classes of object themselves repay attention. *Kreagrai* are almost exclusively an attribute of male graves. Only iron examples are known, perhaps suggesting that they were intrinsically more valuable than other items, which could be substituted with lead copies. Interestingly (with

[75] The *olla* now begins to shrink, and the *olletta*, which replaces the *poculum*, becomes more common, often deposited in multiple examples: Rizzitelli 2003a: 294, 2003d: 327–9.

[76] Vases like the *skyphoi*, more common in *a cassone* tombs, and the single *lagynos* (a one-handled decanter), belong in the same conceptual sphere; the *lagynos* becomes fashionable as a banqueting vessel in the Aegean over the second century, and forms part of a change in the sympotic repertoire consistent with a shift in emphasis from the communal towards the individual in banqueting (Rotroff 2006a: 145–6).

[77] Copersino 2003: 310. The 'fusiform' shape is symmetrical, with a long thin foot and neck tapering from an ovoid central body, like a spindle wrapped in wool (example in t. 516: D'Ercole and Copersino 2003: 239, Tav. 165, 30); the 'piriform' type is shorter, and has a globular body rising directly from a flat base, and a short neck (example in t. 430: D'Ercole and Copersino 2003: 224, Tav. 155, 22 and 23). *Pyxides* were probably used to contain cosmetics.

[78] Rizzitelli 2003a: 285–6, 290 (finewares), 292 (metal objects); Rizzitelli 2003d: 327–8.

[79] Copersino 2003: 309; Rizzitelli 2003d: 327, 329.

[80] Copersino 2003: 310 (these are also found in pits for 'reduction' reburials, for which see below); Rizzitelli 2003a: 292, 2003d: 329.

[81] Copersino 2003: 310; Rizzitelli 2003e: 331.

[82] Rizzitelli 2003a: 287, 2003e: 331.

[83] Rizzitelli 2003e: 331.

one possible exception) the examples from the chamber tombs all have six teeth, and those from *a fossa* graves four.[84] 'Sets' relating to feasting, and in particular to the consumption of meat (spits, *kreagrai*, knives), aim to construct a particular status for the deceased, to evoke a manner of living which presupposes considerable disposable income, as well as the leisure to enjoy it. As at Bazzano, these 'sets', with the exception of the knives, sometimes appear in reduced dimensions, and thus seem to have a symbolic value.[85] The emphasis on meat is interesting: at the Aequian *tumulus* of Corvaro di Borgorose, meat, having been a central part of the archaic diet, becomes rare in the Hellenistic period.[86] This may of course suggest that at Corvaro we are dealing with a different social group, or a broader cross-section of society; but *if* in the world of upland central Italy at this period regular access to meat in the diet was becoming increasingly the prerogative of a few, the use of *kreagrai* in the construction of status for the deceased makes sense.

Lamp-stands appear in *a fossa* graves in the middle of the second century, both male and female; these recall lived, domestic contexts, and may also have some sort of symbolic purpose relating to the 'illumination' of the afterlife; but as at Bazzano, their presence is mainly restricted to chamber tombs, suggesting that they are a marker of status.[87] All types of tomb contain lamps, but only chamber tombs boast iron *thymiatēria*;[88] comparing the number of lamps with the number of depositions in each chamber tomb, it becomes clear that burial was normally accompanied by the deposition of a single lamp.[89]

More complicated is the case of the strigil. Those at Fossa are of the so-called 'Greek type' (or type B), found in Etruria from the fourth century onwards, and common in central Italy until the end of the second century.[90] Strigils spread from Etruscan and Latial contexts northwards (e.g. Monte Bibele)[91] and southwards (e.g. Samnite Caudium).[92] Deposition in graves (late fourth century onwards) originally occurs in elite male contexts; the strigil is a luxury object associated with male athletic prowess, *aretē* and bodily perfection. In

[84] Rizzitelli 2003a: 292. As at Bazzano, knives are found in male and female tombs.

[85] Rizzitelli 2003a: 292 and n. 20 (cf. the use of lead substitutes), 2003d: 327–8, 2003e: 331 (noting that the lead versions seem to be characteristic of later depositions).

[86] Catalano 1996.

[87] Rizzitelli 2003a: 292 (only two examples from tombs *a fossa*), 2003d: 329.

[88] On this class of objects (and on lamp stands), see Testa 1989.

[89] Copersino 2003: 310, t. 124 contained five burials but three lamps. It is probable that the *thymiatēria* were left *in situ* in the tomb, and re-used with each subsequent deposition.

[90] Rizzitelli 2003a: 292–3 (with further bibliography).

[91] Vitali 1987.

[92] Tagliamonte 1996: 204.

some cemeteries strigils continue to appear exclusively in male tombs.[93] Very soon, however, starting again in Etruria and Latium, strigils appear in female tombs in some *necropoleis*; at Fossa they are deposited with both sexes.

Their significance in female tombs is unclear: do they connote leisure and care of the body, or are they shorthand for a more general set of cultural values?[94] The former seems more plausible; but in any case the presence of strigils in female, and even non-elite, graves in some *necropoleis*, shows that certain communities/families/groups were engaged in transvaluing the strigil, making of it an object capable of expressing aspirations to status for a variety of agents. Significantly, a similar development is seen in Athens. From the early fourth century the presence of strigils and mirrors in graves suddenly became extremely common. Yet at the same time, the strongly gendered context of the strigil, at least as familiar from classical Attic vase-painting as an attribute of the young male, was being weakened, as they began to appear in the graves of older men and of women. This, too, has been understood as a transvaluation, from accessory of the young man in the *palaistra* to a more general signifier of personal hygiene. This suggests that females stake a claim to be understood in terms of more than marriage and motherhood, namely as desirable, and as autonomous in controlling their image as consumed by others.[95] It seems hard to believe that these processes, in Athens and in Italy, developed entirely independently; we shall return to some possible implications.

In the distribution of some objects connoting personal hygiene at Fossa, however, there is clearly a marked (and long-standing) gender distinction: nail-cleaners are confined to female tombs, tweezers to male.[96] The majority of these objects is found in chamber tombs: mirrors and hair pins also belong to the feminine toilet set (as does a wooden 'vanity box' containing cosmetic items). Chamber tombs are also distinguished by the presence of gaming pieces, often in stone but also in glass paste of various colours, and bone dice, found near the hand or upper limbs of the deceased, as if to show

[93] For example, at Bazzano; also Corvaro di Borgorose (Alvino 1996), Caudium and Monte Bibele.

[94] For Rizzitelli (2003a: 293) strigils bespeak matrimonial status, and women's 'winning' of domestic excellence, analogous to male physical prowess; cf. *ead.* 2003d: 329; Massa Pairault 1991. For Copersino (2003: 310), however, the strigil was used by women in everyday life to remove excess oil before putting on clothes; she hypothesises a set of strigils of different sizes and shapes differentiated functionally (not unlike the selection of blades on a Swiss Army knife). Finds of 'female' objects in 'male' graves are rare: in some instances, such as ash-chests from around Asciano in N. Etruria, the explanation may be that women were buried (unrecorded) with husbands who had predeceased them: Nielsen 1989.

[95] Houby-Nielsen 1997; Rotroff 2006a: 153–4.

[96] Copersino 2003: 308–9.

Figure 3.3 Reconstruction of the funerary bed from chamber tomb t. 520 (Fossa), with the *corredo* in the foreground. For colour version see plate section.

them at leisure.[97] The chamber tombs are thus rich in finds connoting high status; moreover, the finds specific to them tend to be of better quality and higher value than those in other contemporary graves.[98] This is most conspicuously illustrated by the funerary iron and wood beds fitted with carved appliqués in bone found in five of the chamber tombs; the earliest dates from the early first century BC (Figure 3.3).[99]

Funerary beds of this sort are in fact more common in northern Abruzzo than any other region of Italy, known from a number of sites besides Fossa.

[97] Copersino 2003: 310 (some seventy-five gaming pieces and twenty dice; both may have been integral to the same game), and Foto 4; Rizzitelli 2003e: 331.

[98] Copersino 2003: 310–11. It is, however, worth noting that the only inscribed epitaph from the cemetery is from a tomb *a fossa* of the late second/early first century BC (t. 469; possibly just antedating the appearance of chamber tombs). Here an individual is concerned to memorialise himself, and to lay claim to the cultural capital of both literacy and a permanent monument. The onomastic formula is Latin, but the *praenomen* of the deceased (Te = *Tertis = Lat. *Tertius*) and of the father (Pompo) have a Vestinian flavour; see Letta 2003b. The tomb is otherwise notable for the presence of a bone stylus, flagging claims to literacy which reinforce those of the epitaph and of graffiti on pots in the tomb; note also the bones of young animals, perhaps sacrificed during the ritual, a rare find at Fossa: D'Ercole and Copersino 2003: 125–8; Rizzitelli 2003d: 329. Only one other tomb contains any writing, the chamber tomb t. 430, with graffiti on vases: Rizzitelli 2003e: 331 n. 23.

[99] Letta 2003a: 8; Copersino 2003: 308, 317 (raising the accepted date for the introduction of such beds in this area by half a century); Rizzitelli 2003e: 331; Copersino 2004: 247 for their precise location within the tomb.

Among the Vestini we may cite Bazzano, Capestrano (Capo d'Acqua), Varranone (Poggio Picenze), Fossa Lago Santo (Navelli (Incerulae)), Calascio (Pesatro), L'Aquila (S. Gregorio), Pinne and Pianello (all from chamber tombs); then Marsic Gioia dei Marsi, Pescina (Venere), Collelongo (Amplero and Aielli); Paelignian Corfinium; Praetuttian Interamnia (La Cona); and Sabine Foruli and Amiternum among others.[100] There are also examples from elsewhere in Italy (Rome, Ancona, Norcia, sites in Latium and Cisalpina and, found in 2005, a very well preserved example from the newly discovered Western *necropolis* at Aquinum in southern Lazio);[101] and from a number of transalpine contexts.[102] They first appear at the very end of the third or the start of the second century BC; the latest examples belong to the late first century AD.[103] Three of the five Fossan examples (those in tt. 2, 430 and 520) were for males, the other for two females; cumulatively the evidence for central Italian practice suggests that such beds were more characteristic of female depositions.[104]

Only those from Bazzano, Fossa and Aquinum, however, have been recovered during rigorous modern scientific excavations *and* been the object of careful post-excavation analysis. The beds contributed to the funerary ritual through both their intrinsic value[105] and their figurative decoration, exalting the dead individuals and allowing a more compelling construction of their status,[106] whether in the context of immediate family, a wider gentilician entity, or in the presence of the whole community.[107] Given their form

[100] Ghedini 2008: 19; Reggiani 2008: 30–2, 35; D'Ercole and Martellone 2008: 59–61, 63–5; Martellone 2008c.

[101] Full discussion in Sapelli Ragni 2008b; Ghedini 2008: 15, 24–5; Bellini 2008; Pracchia and Carcieri 2008; Carcieri and Montanelli 2008;Trigona 2008; Aureli 2008.

[102] Key studies: Nicholls 1979; Letta 1984; Nicholls 1991; D'Ercole and Martellone 2005; overview of distribution: Bianchi 2000: Figs. 23–33; Ghedini 2008: 17–18; Cisalpina: Bianchi 2000; see also the catalogue entries in Sapelli Ragni 2008a: 102–11.

[103] Chronology: Letta 1984; Sapelli Ragni 2008b: 11–12; Ghedini 2008: 15, 17–18, 23; Reggiani 2008: 35; D'Ercole and Martellone 2008: 66.

[104] D'Ercole and Martellone 2007; Sapelli Ragni 2008b: 13; Reggiani 2008: 36; D'Ercole and Martellone 2008: 62, 64 n. 18, 66.

[105] On the growing opulence of high-class beds in this period: Copersino 2003: 311; Sapelli Ragni 2008b: 12; Talamo 2008: 72.

[106] D'Ercole and Martellone 2008: 66. In the case of the seven chamber tombs with multiple depositions, the funerary bed can sometimes be attributed to a particular deposition, as in the case of t. 430, where the remains of both beds clearly belong with the bones of earlier occupants, re-deposited in 'reduction pits' cut in the tomb floor (D'Ercole and Martellone 2008: 62 and Fig. 5, 66). For similar problems in attributing elements of *corredi* in multiple-use tombs: Copersino 2003: 311, 317–18; for fuller discussion of the issue: Rizzitelli 2003e: 331.

[107] Copersino 2003: 311 suggests the last, noting that beds in Roman culture could have a public, symbolic function as well as a private one; cf. Reggiani 2008: 35, citing the Amiternum relief; D'Ercole and Martellone 2008: 66.

and decoration, it seems likely that the Fossan beds were made exclusively for funerary use, rather than being part of the possessions of the deceased.[108]

Greek couches for dining are said to have first arrived in Rome as war booty in March 186 BC.[109] Beds are said to have become a part of Roman funerary ritual (the *feretrum*, Isid. *Etym.* 20.11.7) in the second century. They were used both for the laying out of the body during mourning, and for carrying it to and placing it in the tomb (the second is famously depicted in a first-century BC relief from Amiternum, where the form of the *klinē* recalls the Fossan examples).[110] The second century also seems to be the date of the earliest archaeologically attested funerary *klinai* of this type (with decoration in bone or ivory) in Italy. While to identify Manlius Vulso's triumph of 186 as giving the impetus to this fashion may be misleadingly precise, both the general chronology and the geographical origin of the object copied (the Hellenistic East rather than specifically Galatia) seem right. This means that we will end up discounting a *substantial* influence on central Italic practice by Etruscan mortuary ritual (to say nothing of possible Egyptian or Phrygian antecedents). The bed has considerable antiquity as a part of the *corredo* in Etruscan tombs from the Orientalising period onwards, with the Regolini Galassi tomb (*c.* 650 BC) at Caere offering a famous example.[111] Representation of the deceased, whether individuals or a married couple (as in the late sixth-century sarcophagus from the Banditaccia cemetery at Caere, now in the Louvre),[112] reclining on a *klinē* as if at banquet, becomes a central motif in the decoration of the lids of Etruscan sarcophagi and cinerary urns.[113] These evoke a nexus of aristocratic settings *par excellence*, the *sumposion*, the afterlife as everlasting banquet (the *Totenmahl*), and the banquet within the funerary ritual. The banquet also figures in the world constructed by many Fossan *corredi*.[114] In Etruria funerary *klinai* carved in relief within tombs appear from the later seventh century, such

[108] Copersino 2003: 311, 313.

[109] Livy 39.6.7; Plin. *HN* 34.114, cf. 37.12; Copersino 2003: 312–14 with further bibliography; Reggiani 2008: 34; Talamo 2008: 71. Note also the 'small and humble' Punic beds, which came to Rome from Carthage, presumably as war booty: Isid. *Etym.* 20.11.3–4.

[110] Scholars often refer to these two elements of the ritual by their Greek names: *prothesis* and *ekphora*. Amiternum relief: F. Kleiner 2007: Figs. 6–10.

[111] Haynes 2000: Fig. 59 (a variant on rock-cut beds common in Etruscan tombs, on which see also Barker and Rasmussen 1998: 249, noting possible Phrygian antecedents); probably earlier is an iron bed-frame from a high-status female tomb from Marsiliana d'Albegna (Haynes 2000: 129–30; first quarter of the seventh century).

[112] Haynes 2000: Fig. 176.

[113] The earliest example is on the lid to the ash urn of a male from Tolle (t. 23), near Castelluccio di Pienza, from the third quarter of the seventh century: Haynes 2000: 107–8.

[114] Copersino 2003: 312, 314.

as those in the Tomb of the Ship 1, in the Banditaccia cemetery at Caere.[115] But, importantly, Etruscan mortuary ritual favours cremation over the normal central Italic rite of inhumation, and the design of the beds, and the nature of the overall ritual, looks different.[116]

More important as a precedent is Macedonia, from the time of Philip II onwards.[117] Part of the Macedonian legacy, however diluted, may be the fashion for the chamber tomb itself across large swathes of the Mediterranean. A number of Macedonian chambered *tumulus*-burials contained *klinai*. Some were in stone but stuccoed and painted to resemble the real thing, others in wood with fittings and decorative panels in ivory, sometimes gilded (most famously in the Vergina *tumulus* attributed to Philip II). These features were copied in other Greek (and Magna Graecian) contexts.[118] Nevertheless the Macedonian material does not always offer a direct provenance for the stylistic detail of the Fossan beds; and, importantly there are significant differences, above all in the manufacture of the legs and the S-shaped *fulcra* or head-rests.[119] How the elements of the final package (most or all of which must derive from the East) reached Italy is still unclear. Some influences were doubtless mediated by Delos, which was famous for bronze-working, including the feet and frames of *klinai*; indeed Pliny claims that it was after Delos became known as a production centre for such dining couches that bronze came to be used for making statues of gods, men and animals (*HN* 34.9). Alexandria was another production centre, and later funerary beds were probably imported from its workshops, or made by its immigrant craftsmen (and such influence seems clear on the 'Esquiline bed' from Rome), but the evidence for its products or artistic output being a major influence on Italic *klinai* at the point where they first appear is not convincing.[120]

115 Haynes 2000: 72, Fig. 48, and 91 for differences between male and female *klinai* at Caere; cf. the Campana tomb 1, at Monte Abetone, Caere (Haynes 2000: 87 and Fig. 69).

116 Sapelli Ragni 2008b: 13. At some urban *necropoleis*, such as Corfinium and Interamna Praetuttiorum (La Cona), cremation is used, becoming more common in the Roman period (D'Ercole and Martellone 2008: 59–61).

117 Macedonian and other Hellenistic precedents: Sapelli Ragni 2008b: 12; Ghedini 2008: 17, 23–4 (opening the possibility of trans-Adriatic mediation independent of Rome); Reggiani 2008: 34–5. Funerary *klinai* are of course known earlier: for example from Südhügel in the Kerameikos in Athens (*c.* 530 BC), wood, decorated with amber and ivory: Garland 1982: 131 n. 30 and references there.

118 For a brief but informative survey, Kurtz and Boardman 1971: 274–7, 279 (north Greek predecessors), 280 (Eretria), Pls. 80–2 (noting esp. 81, from Taras); Stewart 2006: 161.

119 Letta 1984; Ghedini 2008: 18.

120 Cf. Coarelli 1996a; Ghedini 2008: 22–4. More weight attached to Alexandrian influence: Copersino 2003: 311, 316, with further bibliography; Esquiline bed: Talamo 2008: 69–71 with further bibliography.

The remains of the Fossan beds (and the similar but not identical examples from Bazzano) as studied by Copersino, seem to draw, rather eclectically, on a wide repertoire of stylistic elements, and on models produced both in ebony/ivory and in bronze.[121] Or rather, the craftsmen who made these beds and those from Bazzano, probably operating from one or more regional centres, as she argues, drew on a variety of influences, which they made their own, making up in vivacity for the lack of the high-quality artistic finish of eastern or even central Italian bronze examples.[122] Dionysiac themes such as the *thiasos* appear not only on Hellenistic dining *klinai*, but also commonly in Roman funerary art.[123] There Dionysos has an eschatological or soteriological function, representing the hope of life after death, and hence the presence of Dionysos (both bearded and beardless) on the Fossan (and other Italian) beds, with his animal companions such as panthers, his *thyrsus*, the maenads and so on.[124]

The Fossan Hellenistic

The Fossan mortuary population gives the impression of conservatism and traditionalism in burial practice, both of which may have their origins in presumptive restrictions on funerary practice at the end of the archaic period, but last through almost to the end of the third century, during which time, whatever Aveian society was like (or that section of it buried at Fossa), there was almost no attempt to construct social ranking or hierarchy

[121] Note the female figures on the bed from t. 430, rendered in the classic Greek dress of *chitōn* and *himation*: D'Ercole and Copersino 2003: 232–3, Tav. 160, 161; Copersino 2003: 315; on the wide range and varied combinations of iconographic themes drawn on, from the banal to the original, see Ghedini 2008: 19–25; the variety of Fossan decorative solutions: D'Ercole and Martellone 2008: 62–3, cf. 63–6 (Poggio Picenze, Bazzano and Incerulae).

[122] Copersino 2003: 316–18; the beds show evidence of being made in different sections by different craftsmen, and then assembled, probably all in the same place; her Fig. 11 is evocative of the concentration of examples of beds with bone appliqués in Vestinian, Marsic and Paelignian territory, and in itself argues strongly against the derivation of all these products from a single centre (such as Ancona); Ghedini 2008: 22–3; Reggiani 2008: 35; D'Ercole and Martellone 2008: 63.

[123] Sapelli Ragni 2008b: 12; Ghedini 2008: 17, 22; Talamo 2008: 71. Note also the popularity of Dionysiac scenes and motifs in Hellenistic mosaics: Westgate 2002: 238; cf. Stewart 2006: 161–2; for private dining-clubs devoted to Dionysos: Mikalson 2006: 211; importance of Dionysiac worship in Alexandria: Fraser 1972: I, 203–4.

[124] Copersino 2003: 313–16, with further bibliography (note 315 for a cult site of Dionysos at Aveia, and *CIL* IX.3606); Sapelli Ragni 2008b: 12; Ghedini 2008: 21–2, 24; Reggiani 2008: 32; D'Ercole and Martellone 2008: 63 and Fig. 7, 65–6; Talamo 2008: 69–71; Martellone 2008a, 2008c; Apolline, Herculean and other imagery is also employed (Ghedini 2008: 19–21; Reggiani 2008: 35–6; Bellini 2008: 40; D'Ercole and Martellone 2008: 64–5; Martellone 2008b).

through death ritual.[125] The late third and early second centuries see a striking change, with the arrival of new goods to articulate old rituals, and the adoption, over perhaps a single generation, of much richer sets of grave goods, evoking an ideology of banqueting, and specifically of meat-eating.[126] Construction of the status connoted by these items seems not to be restricted to elites; but now mortuary society allows more expression of differential status in death, with the appearance of *a cassone* tombs. Two or three generations later, a handful of elite families began to take extraordinary steps to distinguish their dead from all others, building chamber tombs, and continuing the expansion of the repertoire of grave goods already present in the *a cassone* tombs. Care of the body, a theme already given expression in death ritual through the deposition of *pyxides*, becomes more prominent across the second century with the addition of first *unguentaria* and then strigils to the repertoire; the world of leisure is evoked by dice and gaming pieces. Finally, a world of Dionysiac wealth (and eschatology) and international sophistication is alluded to, as funerary *klinai* appear at the start of the first century.

It is not certain which is more striking, the late date at which this relatively isolated mountain society of the dead throws off its post-archaic sobriety, or the suddenness of the change, with the influx over a few generations of elements of funerary society which are commonly found across and indeed outside the rest of the region: BG finewares (predominantly open shapes), mirrors, *unguentaria*, strigils, banqueting sets etc. The stubbornness of Fossan funerary practice in ignoring exogenous influences over most of the third century is striking, as is the persistence of traditional forms, not least the longevity of the *olla* in its traditional Iron Age position, despite its diminishing dimensions. Even some modifications of the funerary ritual could have come to seem conservative: the survival of the *skyphos* into the first century is a case in point, with this shape persisting here, albeit in small numbers, later than anywhere else in central Apennine or even Tyrrhenian Italy.[127] In other aspects of the ritual, not least in the apparent distaste for

[125] Cf. Rizzitelli 2003f: 331, noting that imported objects are used to construct status.

[126] The adoption of a new ritual seems less likely.

[127] The last *skyphoi* were deposited in late second- and early first-century graves, e.g. t. 469, late second century (D'Ercole and Copersino 2003: 125–8); t. 123, first half first century – miniature example in infant tomb (D'Ercole and Copersino 2003: 40–3). Elsewhere the *skyphos* had been abandoned at the end of the third century (Rizzitelli 2003a: 287), although second-century use is possible in a couple of sites (Campochiaro: Capini 1984; Fonte San Nicola (San Buono): Faustoferri 1997: 111, schede 81–5). Some Fossan *skyphoi* closely resemble those from Bazzano, and probably derive from the same workshop; occasionally, from *c.* 150 BC onwards in elite tombs, we find a two-handled cup rather than the *skyphos*.

burial with weapons, we see a significant rupture with the traditions of the Iron Age, perhaps exaggerated by the austerity of the fourth and third centuries. Even more significant is the way in which, after the Hannibalic War, Fossa becomes much more like other cemeteries in the region and, to a lesser extent, across the peninsula.

How is the largely static, parochial nature of mortuary ritual prior to the Hannibalic War, and the rapid shift towards more widely shared practices thereafter, to be understood? One possibility is to appeal to a familiar antinomy, that between 'resistance' on the one hand and 'Romanisation' on the other. This is the line taken by Rizzitelli, for example; here again strigils are to the fore: she cites their presence at Corvaro di Borgorose from the early third century to show how Fossa lagged behind.[128] Rizzitelli sees the late adoption of such elements as 'resistance to Romanisation', as a 'superficial' veneer added to a sound base of local tradition.[129] Thus they, and the changes they represent, become acculturative window-dressing rather than a fundamental determinant of the Fossan cultural matrix. Similarly, she characterises the developments from the late third century onwards as cultural 'homogenisation' on the basis of 'urban' patterns of burial, as 'auto-Romanisation' by those burying and being buried.[130] Such an explanatory model is rather tired-looking, though, and unappealingly binary. Corvaro is *sui generis* in a poorly known area, and the extent of possible influence from Latin colonies at Carseoli and Alba Fucens adds a variable not in play at Fossa; it is not perhaps the best yardstick for measuring (lack of) change. As for Romanisation, its most significant problem is that it is a very blunt descriptor, it does not *explain* very much. This is ironic, inasmuch as Romanisation, like Hellenisation, is, to quote Andrew Wallace-Hadrill, part of 'our own interpretative framework'; it is not what was, but how we try to make sense of what was.[131] In the present context, to invoke Romanisation tells us nothing about what the dead of Fossa (and their families) thought they were 'resisting', and still less about why they 'gave up' over a couple of generations.

In looking for explanations I propose to leave Rome and Romanisation aside, and think in terms of neighbouring settlements and their cultural *praxeis* in dialogue over time. The ongoing needs of local elites to distinguish themselves from subaltern groups, and to 'keep up' with the neighbours by adding new elements to the ritual and the *corredo*, will also be significant. A local or regional perspective, to set beside wider ones which embrace the

[128] Alvino 1996; 2004: 63; Rizzitelli 2003f: 332. [129] Rizzitelli 2003f: 332; Torelli 1996: 42.

[130] Rizzitelli 2003f: 332; Torelli 1996: 41 for the latter term; and for important reservations about the concept, Stek 2009: 9–10, 12–16.

[131] Wallace-Hadrill 2008: 78; see also Dench 2003, 2005.

peninsula or even the Mediterranean, can be of some analytical value. To return briefly to strigils: there was no overriding need for Fossans to bury males *and* females with them. To do so was to make a choice, one which had been embraced in some communities and rejected in others. To choose one way or the other involved not anxiety or aspiration directed at Rome, or even a woollier sense of Roman-ness, but rather formed part of a more regional cultural conversation, one which also addressed the place of women in local social structures. For what it is worth, Fossa went the same way as Athens, not neighbouring Bazzano. But questions about Fossa and Rome, if they have any meaning, must be secondary to questions about Fossa and Bazzano, Fossa and Capestrano, and so on. The same is true for possible 'Hellenistic' influences.

I wrote in the introduction of a 'grammar of Greekness', the mastery by non-Greeks of various Greek behavioural modes. I wish here to pursue the metaphor of grammar, building on the approach of Wallace-Hadrill, who has recently used the linguistic metaphors of bilingualism and code-switching in order to advance the debate on cultural change.[132] I shall use the metaphor differently in what follows, and indeed not in the context in which I first invoked 'grammar', that of a direct interaction between non-Greeks and Greeks in positions of political, economic or social power. Instead I shall suggest that the changes in the burial rite which we have considered at Fossa constitute the adoption of a 'grammar' which is also that of other local centres, or which at least underpins the mutual intelligibility of a number of cultural 'dialects'. Fossa, after generations of 'silence', starts to 'talk' to her neighbours, whether under the pressures of the Hannibalic War and growing elite confidence derived from mutual support between Rome and allied Italian aristocracies, or under the stimulus of the opening up of the Aegean to Roman/Italian conquest and trade. Over time her ability to 'talk' thus is sustained by the addition of new elements to the 'grammar' (*unguentaria*, strigils, gaming paraphernalia), and the resulting enlarged 'conversation' is most eagerly sustained by the elites of Aveia. The shared grammar is constructed of building blocks or cultural 'lexemes' which have been circulating in Italy for some time, and are themselves derived from a wider Hellenistic matrix of social behaviours.

Brief comparison of the situation at Fossa with what is known from Bazzano and Capestrano in the Navelli plain, may suggest elements of burial practice unique to the inland Vestini, such as *a cassone* tombs and stone-built chamber tombs, or the absence of both offensive weapons (with the exception

[132] Wallace-Hadrill 2008: ch. 3.

of a few spearheads from Bazzano) and of armour from male graves.[133] Personal ornament is also limited, with some rings in iron, bronze and silver, a few *fibulae*, always in bronze, and very few bracelets; the rarity of necklaces is underlined by the fact that both known examples are exotic imports: one in glass paste, with pendants in the form of women's heads, the other a glass paste example with a fine multi-coloured head of Punic manufacture.[134] Care of the body is mainly represented by iron strigils, which are used for male depositions only at Capestrano and Bazzano, but are deposited – as we saw – with both sexes at Fossa; other objects for cleaning, shaving or depilating the body are present less systematically. Vessels for cosmetic products are more common: *unguentaria*, glass bottles and BG *pyxides*, which are a particular feature of female graves (except at Fossa).[135] BG vessels, above all in open shapes, are common: especially plates, *paterae*, bowls and cups. Coarseware *ollae*, large and miniature, are normal at Fossa, less prevalent elsewhere. Metal vases are very rare.[136] Lamps are fairly common in the tombs of this region, especially in chamber tombs, where, whatever their symbolic value, the interior needed to be illuminated for the funerary ritual for each deposition, especially where the 'reduction' of the previous incumbent had to be effected; *thymiatēria*, found at both Fossa and Bazzano, could act as either incense burners or support for lamps or candles.[137] The deposition of knives, spits and *kreagrai* recalled banqueting in life and in the funerary ritual. But despite the broad similarities presented by these three *necropoleis*, and the features unique to their corner of Italy, the differences between them are equally revealing. Bazzano adopts the strigil earlier than Fossa, only to restrict it to the male sphere, and does not bury men with *pyxides*. At Bazzano there are some cases of burial with weapons, but much less interest in maintaining the traditional *olla* + drinking/dipping vessel as a central part of the burial ritual than at Fossa. High-end grave sets are not restricted to the occupants of chamber tombs, as they are at Fossa and probably Capestrano. All in all, local variations emerge as strongly as shared practices.[138]

[133] Copersino and D'Ercole 2003: 374 and n. 43.

[134] Copersino and D'Ercole 2003: 374; for the necklaces Figs. 54 and 55. t. 833 from Bazzano, which contained the Punic glass-paste bead necklace, was an infant tomb, and also contained a bronze pan and an iron bracelet; the pendant in the form of a head is closely paralleled by that from t. 8 at Monte Giove/Penna S. Andrea (Copersino and D'Ercole 2003: 374 n. 45).

[135] Copersino and D'Ercole 2003: 374 and n. 46.

[136] Copersino and D'Ercole 2003: 374–5.

[137] Copersino and D'Ercole 2003: 375.

[138] Cf. perhaps the way that Etruscan cinerary urns in this period display an iconographic repertoire which is characterised both by the sharing of some motifs between centres and the restriction of others to particular local productions: Barker and Rasmussen 1998: 289–90.

The Hellenistic in Italy, and the 'Hellenistics' of death

Having reviewed the evidence, we may address the big question posed at the outset: what, if anything, is Hellenistic about it? Very striking, not only at Fossa but across Abruzzo, are the subtle diversities within an overarching broad unity of practice, diversities which distinguish region from region, and site from adjacent site. In discussing Fossa I had recourse to the metaphor of a new 'grammar' of burial practices developed over the course of the late third and second centuries. I also alluded to 'conversations' with other local centres which this grammar permitted, because it was shared and thus mutually intelligible, even though not identical in each community.[139] Using this basic grammar, each community of the dead constructed its own 'dialect', privileging some items, ignoring others, and seeking subtle variations in areas such as – to continue the metaphor – word order. Each is comprehensible to outsiders but distinctive, and permeable to exogenous influences; each is dynamic, and changes from generation to generation in response to internal and external stimuli. This diversity within unity is, I believe, central to understanding the nature and development of the Hellenistic in Italy, and to the elaboration and interaction of its local variants, which I would like to call *Hellenistics*.

As we have seen, assessing the significance of Italian material against a Greek yardstick is problematic; indeed it is largely futile in the case of individual objects.[140] Thus, noting the prevalence after a certain date of fusiform *unguentaria* at Fossa and elsewhere, we might invoke the proliferation of the same vessels in Hellenistic Athens, where cremation was the norm.[141] But what does that tell us? Does it reveal more or less than the absence from Fossa of another staple of Athenian Hellenistic grave goods, the gold-leaf wreath or headband?[142] These items are also common in Magna Graecia, with fine examples also from Daunia, the Greek city of Ancona, and even in an early third-century Senonian Gallic grave at Montefortino.[143] To ask 'which is more Greek, the

[139] This concept could be applied to the study of *intra*-community discourse as well, in cases where more than one cemetery serving a community has been studied.

[140] See Stek 2009: 13–14 on the inability of objects to carry intrinsic meaning for identity.

[141] Kurtz and Boardman 1971: 164–5. [142] Kurtz and Boardman 1971: 163, 165.

[143] Mercando 1976: 160–1, Fig. 3, cf. Fig. 14 for an example from Ancona. One may wonder whether the popularity of diadems in southern Italian grave goods does not in some measure represent a trickle-down from eastern royal self-fashioning (on the diadem and Hellenistic kingship: Polyb. 30.2.4; Ritter 1965; Walbank 1984b: 67; Walbank *et al.* 1984: Plates 22b and esp. 65b) – but such an association must be secondary to Dionysiac and funerary ones.

graves with *unguentaria* or those with wreaths?' is pointless. Analysis must proceed contextually, at the level of assemblages. No Fossan assemblage could be mistaken for a *corredo* from Ancona, where high-quality Greek grave goods are interred with bodies marked by Greek *stēlai*.[144] Yet the two are clearly using the same basic elements (vases, strigils, mirrors, other cosmetic items) to formulate similar sorts of claims about the dead. Of course there are differences, and these prohibit confusion of the two assemblages; but they are mutually intelligible, because the two draw on the same individual items and use them as symbols to express similar ideas through a similar grammar. I would argue that neither is more Hellenistic than the other: both are examples of *Hellenistics*, the local formulation of cultural practices drawing on the same pool of behaviours and objects associated with them.

A useful – and vivid – parallel for the concept of the Italian Hellenistic which I am trying to advance may be found in the later Middle Ages. Of travel within Italy in this period John Larner wrote:

> To move from one town to another less than 30 miles away called for sharp revision of attitudes and knowledge. Weights, measures, currencies, could all be different. So varied, for instance, were the towns' calculations on when the year began that a traveller, leaving Lucca on the 20 March 1300 and taking a day for his journey, would arrive at Florence on 21 March 1299. From there, after a leisurely week's trip, he would enter Pisa on the 29 March 1301. If he then took ship to Naples he would have had to discover on what day Easter fell before knowing in which century he would arrive.[145]

The fluidity of this world can in turn be instructively contrasted with that which prevailed later in western-central Italy under Florentine hegemony: Florence adopted a rather heavy-handed attitude towards its subject communities in the later fourteenth and fifteenth centuries: representatives had to be present in Florence on St John's Day, when candles and sometimes a *pallium* were offered to the saint; Arezzo and Pistoia were obliged to observe the same religious festivals as Florence, and Pisa to supply a monthly tribute

[144] See Mercando 1976 for these. It does not matter for the purposes of this argument whether these are middle Hellenistic, or the product of late republican/early Augustan nostalgia (Colivicchi 2008) – they are very Greek.

[145] Quotations from Larner 1980: 1, 3. Jonathan Prag points out to me that in Sicily in the late Hellenistic period considerable variation manifested in local calendars co-existed with taxation structures which were uniform across the island; diversity in one field is not necessarily a proxy for diversity everywhere. On variation between local calendars in the Greek *poleis*, and their importance in structuring local time and local history and identity, see the illuminating remarks of Clarke 2008: 33–56, 215–17.

to the cathedral, and its guilds to adopt the same patron saints as their Florentine counterparts.[146]

The Italian Hellenistic, I contend, is like Larner's Italian later Middle Ages: rather sharp differences existed from place to place, locally treasured no doubt, but mutually comprehensible because they were all variations on the same theme, local twists on the same basic dataset, on one level mutually incompatible, but co-existing nevertheless, and not obviously deterring connectivity. Medieval Italian elites *were* linked by trade, by literature, by a shared classical culture, by a consciousness, when they travelled abroad, of greater difference between themselves and Catalans, Frenchmen or Englishmen, than those they noted between each other.

The imagined community of the Hellenistic was, for its participants, cultural. It was, like all cultural systems, open – note how the kinship diplomacy which was a notable feature of its interaction not only used myth to permit access to the 'community' for outsiders, but seems to have used myth *particularly* as the interface between Greeks and non-Greeks.[147] It had to be able to deal with variety – and variety is one of the fundamentals of the Hellenistic in the East: the sheer diversity of forms of burial across the Greek East is further evidence of this, were any needed. There was no prescribed cultural orthodoxy, but a set of social and cultural norms (e.g. forms of bathing or banqueting) was endorsed through practice, together with a range of material objects, styles and settings through which these practices might be expressed *and* manipulated (*andrōnes*, theatres, mirrors, strigils). Arguably, its content was nothing more or less than the sum of elite behaviours, political, religious, social and economic, and their contexts and physical attributes, mediated by their trickle-down into the social world of the urban *bourgeoisies* of the kingdoms and cities of Greece and the East.[148] Very importantly though, this 'package' was accessible to, and used by, those outside the Aegean and the near East, and quickly became integrated into other cultures, Punic and Italic for example, which added to and developed the whole. Elites within these local cultures, like local cultures in the East, were attracted by the cachet of the Hellenistic package, whether or not they were specifically aware of its (largely)

146 Hay and Law give a balanced survey of the nature of Florentine rule, more interventionist than its Venetian counterpart, but less brutally imperialist than sometimes thought (1989: 117–19). Note also the Florentine *catasto* of 1427–30 AD, a unique attempt to create a single tax assessment embracing both Florence and the subject cities.

147 Erskine 2002.

148 In trying to enunciate the cultural content of the Hellenistic behavioural world, I refer the reader back to my earlier attempt to distinguish between diagnosis of 'Hellenistic' on the basis of isolated or co-extensive symptoms, and embedded modes of behaviour which constituted the experience of the 'Hellenistic' for contemporaries.

Greek roots, or that it was driven by the power, wealth and prestige of the late Argead and subsequently the Successor kingdoms. But this attraction was not fatal: rather it was constructive, and allowed living cultural systems to engage with the new package, and draw on it in different measure in each case.

There is, of course, a difference between buying an amphora of Knidian wine, because it is reputed to taste good, and having one's house rebuilt with a decorated *andrōn* and *klinai* and buying a range of fine over-painted or BG tablewares ready for a *sumposion*, or something like it. Some adoptions of the Hellenistic package were doubtless (to Greek eyes) clumsy and partial. Yet, as in the case of the New Zealand Maori who, banned by the British colonial authorities from the practice of leaving the dead out for long periods of mourning, co-opted the European technology of the photograph in order to have the dead with them for the requisite time and satisfy the authorities, these engagements were almost all knowing.[149] Whether they served a short-term tactical aim, or a wider strategic goal, to figure new expressions of the drunken evening or of an entire social life, they were the result of conscious agency on the part of local communities.

Motivations for adopting any or all parts of the Hellenistic package, for deciding how to arrange the individual items once adopted, and how to manipulate the 'grammar' of the Hellenistic in the local context, all lay at local level. Certainly intra- and intercommunity competition would affect the 'thickness' or 'thinness' of the result, but we may broadly distinguish two layers of engagement beyond the very short-term. We may illustrate them by comparing the *Greek*-style pebble mosaics in the *local* Daunian tradition of the late fourth/early third centuries, with the later Hellenistic situation in Italy (or at least at Pompeii).[150] In the former case there is clearly a knowledge of a range of Greek motifs, and of how the Greeks combined them to decorate the pavements of particular rooms for particular social purposes; both patron and artist knew what they were doing, and that they were drawing on the Greek repertoire because it represented sophistication and served to underline status; and at the least, whether they associated the style with Taras, Phoinike or Pella, probably identified it as Greek. In later Hellenistic Pompeii, by contrast, there is a preference for plain mosaics surrounding *emblēmata* or figured panels. These copy famous paintings (or mosaic copies of paintings) or genre scenes which evoke the standard themes of shared Hellenistic *paideia*: myth, drama, especially comedy, philosophy

[149] King 2003: 253–4, cf. 516; photographic portraits began to be placed in meeting-houses at the same time, extending the traditional idea of such houses embodying and expressing – literally through decorative carving – the genealogy of the *hapu* (tribal sub-group).

[150] On mosaics, see also R. and A. Wilson, Chapters 4 and 5 in this volume.

and sometimes historical episodes, as with the Alexander mosaic.[151] The difference then is between, on the one hand, the conscious exploitation of well-known elements of a decorative repertoire to underpin particular social strategies, and on the other a more knowing and allusive taste for the specifically pictorial, used as a shorthand to express belonging to a self-referencing *koinē*.[152] Our Apennine burials belong in the first category.

Participation in the (imagined) Hellenistic community was enabled though elite connectivity – indeed, it was elite connectivity which spread, developed and sustained the Hellenistic, and without which it would have been unthinkable.[153] In the process new elements were added and old ones reconfigured, as we have noted. Connectivity allowed Central Apennine elites access to a developing world of Hellenistic elite values *and* to the wider Mediterranean which, like the Vestinian homeland, increasingly felt the impact of this world. It is thus highly suggestive of the nature of the networks exploited by these elites that, for example, Punic necklaces were placed in graves as prestige items at Fossa, Bazzano and elsewhere; elite connectivity in the West was not simply about Rhodian amphorae or Corinthian bronzes.[154] The Hellenistic package was spread by the Hellenistic economic boom, by migration and pilgrimage, diplomatic missions and marriage ties, mercenary service and political ambition, whether the Adriatic policy of Dionysios II of Syracuse, the invasion of Pyrrhos, or the Roman conquest and the first two Punic Wars.[155] One aspect of elite connectivity is especially pertinent: local elites intermarried, and marriage partners were exchanged between, as well as within, neighbouring cities, as has been well demonstrated *à propos* of Cicero's *Pro Cluentio* by Philippe Moreau.[156] Both weddings and funerals then brought together elites from neighbouring cities, and allowed observation of marriage and death rituals, of similarity and difference: if Larinum in the age of Cluentius is anything to go by, both such opportunities for interaction were rather frequent.

151 Westgate 2002: 244–5, with further references.

152 Cf. the self-conscious bookishness of much Hellenistic literature: Bing 1988; Krevans and Sens 2006: 194–5. For the importance in elite self-construction of collection and display of Hellenistic art, esp. sculpture, see Kreeb 1988: 155–60, 200–15, 242–3 (Delos); Hales 2002: 258–9.

153 Rotroff 2006a: 147–8.

154 Copersino and D'Ercole 2003: 376; D'Ercole and Martellone 2004.

155 For the relationships which embodied this policy as potentially forming part of the diplomatic grammar which might have informed international relations as developed in the Hellenistic period: Davies 2002: 3.

156 Moreau 1983; Cicero alludes to a *mos Larinatium* for wedding feasts (*Clu.* 166), a reference his audience was expected to understand as being to a distinctive practice, but one which nevertheless needed no explanation.

We noted above Andrew Wallace-Hadrill's conception of the relationship between cultures as a *dialogue*, and of the product as a dynamic form of bilingualism.[157] I have tried to develop this notion by using the metaphor of learning and extending 'grammar' to describe Vestinian (and by extension other local) access to and absorption of the Hellenistic cultural package. The new 'grammar' certainly made it possible to 'say' new things, but it did not overwrite existing means of communication. Its interaction with traditional ways of expressing values might provoke anxieties, but these arose within a dialogue, not a monologue. Indeed, as we can see in the case of the development of the *olla* at Fossa, access to the new Hellenistic grammar allowed (some) people the possibility not simply to say new things, but to say old-fashioned but important things in new and more sophisticated ways; others chose not to take the option.

Indeed the whole picture for our period is conditioned at the outset by the upheavals which marked the end of the archaic period, and the emergence of state entities such as the Vestini. As we have seen, there is some reason to think that these changes are reflected in the austerity, and even in some cases the temporary elimination, of some Central Apennine *corredi* in the fourth and earlier third centuries.[158] Some strands of traditional ideology emerged into the third century beside new ones, different in intensity from place to place:[159] two are important, the survival (or rejection) of the old warrior ethos, as reflected (or not) in offensive and/or defensive elements in the funerary assemblage; and the (very old) association of the *olla* with one or two smaller vessels, to be conceived of as dipping/drinking vessels for what the *olla* contained.[160] The precise interaction between local cultural expression and the possibilities offered by each successive 'upgrade' to the Hellenistic cultural package was affected in each community by a number of constraining or enabling variables: existing traditions, including

[157] See Wallace-Hadrill 2008: ch. 3; see also ch. 1 for a critique of, *inter alia*, hybridisation as a model for understanding cultural interaction and change; 'hybridisation' has proven popular in some quarters as a tool for 'analysing' these processes in the Hellenistic: so Colledge 1987; Rotroff 2006a: 149; and Van Dommelen and López-Bertran, Chapter 9, this volume.

[158] Benelli 2003: 323, who notes that a similar phenomenon in burial morphology is encountered in fifth-century Latium (Colonna 1977). On state-formation in this area, see Letta 1994.

[159] Some idealologies were not so new – grave goods tied to banqueting (from *kantharoi* to spits) and to care of the body (razors and shears) are found in the Central Apennine burial repertoire in the Iron Age.

[160] The constraints imposed on manipulation of material culture by existing cultural patterns are not to be confused with 'resistance', for all that natives may 'bolster cultural solidarity through material culture' (Rotroff 2006a: 148); on re-reading 'resistance' see now Jiménez Díez 2008a.

the perceived or endorsed values of the deceased, of his or her immediate family, of the community, or even of the *ethnos*; and the precise weight to be given to wealth, cultural and economic contacts, social status, observance of religious rituals and gender roles. An example of the last is whether or not it was acceptable for women to begin to articulate their aspirations to cultivation of the body beautiful, and to individualism, through appropriation of the male symbol of the strigil, as they had started doing, as it might be, in the community further down the valley.

The availability of new 'upgrades' (themselves the result of on-going dialogue), and the series of decisions made within families and communities over previous generations, conditioned how the dialogue went on: thus new items entered the mortuary repertoire and others vanished, although there was a general tendency to regional and then peninsula-wide convergence as connectivity intensified. The latter stages of the dialogue reveal a fairly widespread, but not universal, standardisation in poorer burials, and the adoption by the rich of chamber tombs, in which as well as wealth, the

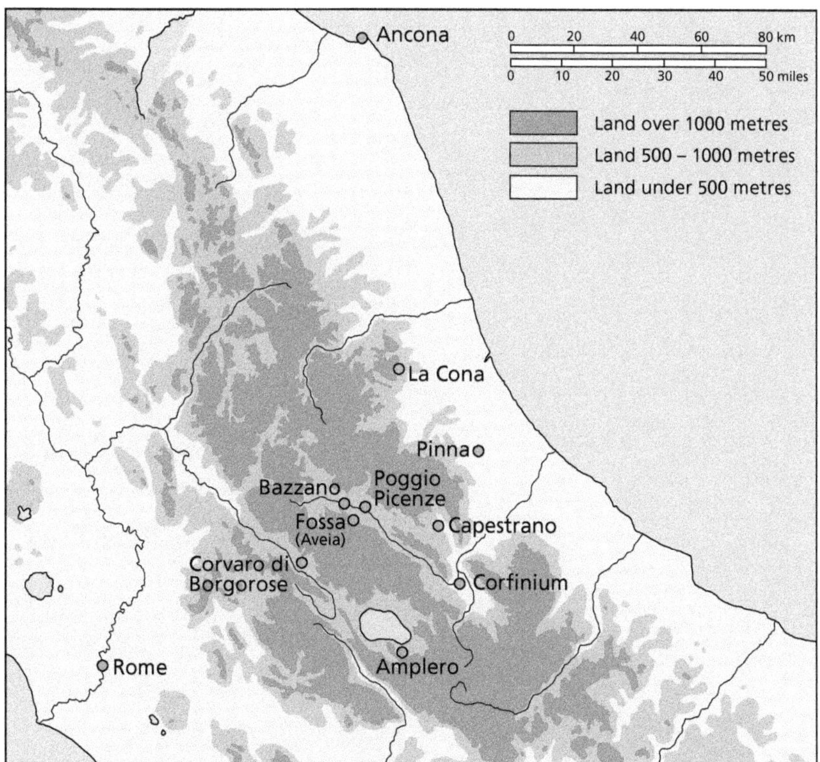

Figure 3.4 Map of sites mentioned in the text.

ideologies of care of the body and of leisure are strongly promoted. What I want to add to Wallace-Hadrill's dialogue is the idea of the regional 'conversation', conducted on the basis of a broad shared repertoire of traditional and new objects, within which a grammar is elaborated which underpins a series of differing but mutually intelligible dialects. The conversation is many-sided, conducted between Fossa and Bazzano, Fossa and Capestrano, Bazzano and Capestrano, and so on, eventually, indirectly through all other interlocutors, and at times directly, with Greece (and for that matter Rome). Cemeteries leave us not just the evidence of dialogue, then, but the different parts in a conversation in which different Hellenistics communicated and developed their own versions of the common cultural matrix.

In what way, then, are our cemeteries Hellenistic? They show us how difference and co-identification, both expressed through the same symbolic grammar, were at the heart of the interactions which underpinned the Hellenistic in Italy. They are thus quintessentially Hellenistic.

4 | Hellenistic Sicily, *c.* 270–100 BC

R. J. A. WILSON

Introduction

Hellenistic Sicily is a paradox. On the one hand, this 'miniature continent', as Braudel called it, can be seen to be part of a broader Mediterranean 'Greek' *koine* during the third and second centuries BC; on the other hand, the island forged its own distinctive identity with its own idiosyncracies and regional differences.[1] There is not just 'one' Hellenistic Sicily, but several: this was a region where, uniquely, Greek, Carthaginian and Roman culture met and intermingled, but with differing emphases in different regions and at different times. The result was a place very distinct from anywhere else in the Hellenistic West. Defining it is not straightforward. There is no clear starting parameter – culturally and politically, Sicily in the early decades of the third century BC was not much different from 'late classical' Sicily in the fourth. Agathocles of Syracuse may be seen as a 'Hellenistic' king because he post-dates the death of Alexander, but there was no seismic shift in Sicilian politics at that time as there was in the Greek East. Only the political and military upheavals which accompanied the First Punic War (264–241 BC) and then the Second (218–211 BC) led to irrevocable change, but even then Sicily was a land of contrasts. The difference in fortune between war-ravaged central and western Sicily after the First Punic War, incorporated under Rome's sway after 241 BC, and the stability and prosperity of the flourishing eastern part of the island, which formed Hieron's independent kingdom, was stark.

Hellenistic Sicily is therefore a complex and multi-faceted phenomenon, and space precludes detailed analysis here. This chapter, with a focus on the material rather than the historical evidence, will concentrate on the third and second centuries BC (rather than before or after), and will examine three contrasting

[1] Braudel 1972: I, 148. My grateful thanks go to Jonathan Prag for his acute editorial comments on an earlier draft of this chapter, and for kindly drawing my attention to some appropriate bibliographical addenda. I use the term Hellenistic throughout this chapter in a chronological sense, referring broadly to any time within the period between the death of Alexander the Great (323 BC) and the battle of Actium (31 BC), as customary when discussing the Greek East. That the label should serve likewise for discussion of Sicily at this period, however, is also an indicator of the limited cultural impact made by Rome after its incorporation of most of Sicily after 241 BC (and all of the island after 211 BC) down into the late first century BC.

Figure 4.1 Map of Sicily, showing places mentioned in the text.

geographical areas (Figure 4.1): south-east and eastern Sicily, especially in the third century BC; central Sicily after its incorporation into the sphere of Rome after 241 BC; and the far west, where the influence of Carthaginian culture, even after the demise of Carthage in 146 BC, remained strong.

The Syracusan kingdom of Hieron II: eastern Sicily

Hieron's long reign, which lasted from *c.* 270 until his death in 215 BC, saw a remarkable period of peace and prosperity under his benevolent rule.[2] His opportunistic politics removed Syracuse from the fray: for having flirted with Carthage he firmly sided with Rome as a trusted and dependable ally in a treaty of *philia*, 'friendship', and therefore escaped the incorporation of his kingdom into the orbit of Rome.[3] This was no petty small-minded Sicilian tyrant: Hieron deployed the central geographical position of his

[2] For the historical background, De Sensi Sestito 1977; for recent accounts, Zambon 2006 and 2008: 179–221; for a cultural perspective, Campagna 2004; Lehmler 2005: 120–87; Veit 2009; and now Lyons *et al.* 2012, especially 31–6.

[3] Cf. Polyb. 1.16.10–11: 'King Hieron, having placed himself under the protection of the Romans, continued to furnish them with the resources of which they stood in urgent need, and ruled over Syracuse henceforth in security, treating the Greeks in such a way as to win from them crowns and other honours. We may, indeed, regard him as the most illustrious of princes and the one who reaped longest the fruits of his own wisdom in particular cases and in general policy'

Figure 4.2 Bronze coin of Hieron II, after 263 BC. Obverse: head of Hieron II wearing royal diadem, facing left; reverse: mounted horseman with helmet and lance, facing right; legend in the exergue: ΙΕΡΩΝΟΣ.

Figure 4.3 Silver coin (tetradrachm) of Philistis, wife of Hieron II, after 263 BC. Obverse: veiled head of Queen Philistis, to left; reverse: Nike drives a galloping quadriga, with legend above and below, ΒΑΣΙΛΙΣΣΑΣ ΦΙΛΙΣΤΙΔΟΣ.

independent Sicilian kingdom to maximum advantage, and saw himself as a major player on the ancient world's global stage. Not only does his coinage (the first in Sicily to portray the living ruler) depict him in the manner of a Hellenistic king, wearing the royal diadem (Figure 4.2); but his queen Philistis also features on separate and much more plentiful issues, inspired no doubt by Ptolemaic coins featuring queens Berenice and Arsinoe II (Figure 4.3).[4] Even the weight of the Syracusan coinage series was switched in favour of the lighter Ptolemaic standard, a further clear sign of the influence of Ptolemaic coinage on Hieron's. Hieron's links with Egypt are demonstrable in other ways. His great ship, the *Syrakosia*, built *c.* 240 BC and intended to make a grand propaganda tour of the Hellenistic world, bestowing largesse as a sign of Hieron's bounty and wealth, was given away as a present to Ptolemy in Alexandria when Hieron realised that its designer, Archimedes, got one thing wrong: it was too big for most Mediterranean ports in its day.[5] In Alexandria it inspired contemporary imitations: the sumptuous Nile yacht, the *Thalamegos*, for example, which belonged to

(transl. W. R. Paton, Leob edn). On the treaty of 263 BC between Rome and Syracuse (and the later agreement of 248 BC), Eckstein 1980 and 1987: 115–31.

[4] For the coinage in full, Caccamo Caltabiano *et al.* 1997.

[5] Ath. 5.206d–209b; MacIntosh Turfa and Steinmayer 1999; and now Castagnino Berlinghieri 2010.

Ptolemy IV Philopater (221–205 BC), and which is described at length by Kallixeinos in an account preserved in Athenaeus, was a direct descendant.[6] It is also tempting to wonder just how and when it was that the papyrus plant reached Sicily: it grows in profusion along the banks of the Ciane river just south of Syracuse, and it also occurs along the Fiumefreddo river near Taormina (Tauromenium), also within Hieron's kingdom. Was this plant, native to the Nile Valley, just possibly a gift to Hieron from Ptolemy III Euergetes (246–221 BC) or Ptolemy IV Philopator? Documentary evidence is, however, completely absent before AD 972/3, when it is reported as growing near Palermo; so an introduction 1200 years earlier remains pure, unsupported speculation.[7] The papyrus in the Fountain of Arethusa at Syracuse is a modern introduction: eighteenth- and early nineteenth-century engravings and watercolours of the fountain show no trace of it.[8]

Peter Green has suggested that Hieron II cannot be regarded as a genuine Hellenistic king because he was too dependent on Rome.[9] Hieron would not have seen it that way. He was pragmatic in his dealings with Rome, for sure, but he was well liked and respected by Hellenistic monarchs in the East; and although with the hindsight of history modern commentators might call him an early example of a 'client king', the inevitability of the absorption of his kingdom by Rome after his death was by no means obvious at the time.[10] Indeed on Hieron's death it did pass initially to his grandson, and not directly to Rome. Hieron had every reason to think, therefore, that his kingdom would remain intact and that he had merely done some astute political gambling in switching sides and backing as his principal ally a winner, Rome, and not a loser, Carthage.

Throughout his reign Hieron acted with an assured self-confidence on the Mediterranean stage, never slow to seize an opportunity for self-publicity in the wider world. In addition to his close relations with Ptolemaic Egypt, he was prominent in pan-Hellenic festivals: his actions included the erection of statues of himself and his family at Olympia and Delphi, and the prompting of

[6] Ath. 5.203e–204b, after 221 BC. Its length (104 m) is two-thirds bigger again than the estimated length of the *Syrakosia* (*c.* 62 m); for a reconstruction, Pfrommer 1999: 93–117.

[7] Lewis 1974: 19, who (n. 24) refers to suggestions of a Hieronian introduction as 'a perennial ghost refusing to be laid'. If the *massa papirianensis* named in a letter of Gregory the Great (*Ep.* 9.170) took its name from papyrus growing on the estate, the plant is attested in Sicily from at least the sixth century AD.

[8] Gringeri Pantano 2003: Pl. 49–50 (and 159 for Houel's account of papyrus flourishing at the Fonte Ciane in his day); Beneventano del Bosco 1995: 147, 159 and 198.

[9] P. Green 1990: 226.

[10] E.g. Serrati 2000: 118 and 2007: 478; contrast, however, Burton 2003: 352–3, who suggests that the relationship was one of *amicitia* rather than a formal *clientela*.

dedications there by other Sicilian city-states in his kingdom, such as Taormina; and when an earthquake struck Rhodes in 227 BC, he gave 100 silver talents in aid to the stricken city.[11] Other political and/or commercial contacts are attested with Cyrenaica and Asia Minor in the East, and with Rome of course in the West: this was a king with a pan-Mediterranean political, social and economic network.[12] His euergetism is not known, however, to have extended to building work outside his own kingdom.[13]

At home, all the signs are that the reign of Hieron was one of exceptional artistic and cultural creativity. It was at the court of Hieron's Syracuse, for example, that Theocritus composed his *Idylls*, and it was in third-century Syracuse that one of the greatest mathematical and scientific geniuses of all time, Archimedes, lived, worked and died. But what of the material culture of Hieron's kingdom? Did it share a general *koine* in the Hellenistic period, making its artifacts and buildings indistinguishable from those elsewhere in the third-century Hellenistic world? Or was there an individualism suggestive of a genuine originality and creativity which is distinctively Sicilian, or indeed Hieronian? The answer is probably both. Take metalworking, for example. We know from literary evidence that Hieron's Syracuse had goldsmiths and silversmiths working there, but few items have actually survived.[14] One magnificent exception is the eclectic hoard of silver tableware recently (2009) transferred back to Sicily from the Metropolitan Museum in New York, which is known to have been illicitly excavated in a house in Morgantina, where it had been concealed during the Roman attack on that city in 211 BC: it is now in the museum at Aidone (Figure 4.4).[15] Guzzo, in his full publication of this hoard, has drawn attention to certain parallels from Asia Minor for the buckets with theatre-mask feet, and reckons that Alexandria might have been the home of the craftsmen who made the stunning Scylla medallion.[16] That might be right; but equally it is by no

[11] Paus. 6.12.2–5 (Olympia, Delphi); Polyb. 5.88 (Rhodes) and *Lind. Temp. Chron.* 122–6. On Hieron's overseas contacts, see especially Portale 2004.

[12] For Hieron's 'internationalism', both political and commercial, De Sensi Sestito 1977: 165–78.

[13] Portale 2002 draws attention to a Sicilian-Corinthian capital and an architrave of 'Hieronian' type at Gortyn; while these demonstrate cultural contact with Sicily, they cannot be taken as proof of an intervention by Hieron himself with the gift of a building.

[14] E.g. Vitr. 9. *Praef.* 9–10 for the story of the gold crown and Archimedes (the goldsmith was Syracusan); Polyb. 5.88.5 for silver cauldrons presented to Rhodes, presumably of Syracusan manufacture. For gold and silver items of possibly or certainly Hieronian date, see R. Wilson 2013: nos. 126 and 133, with full bibliography.

[15] M. Bell 2000.

[16] Guzzo 2003. For other bibliography, R. Wilson 2013: no. 133; and for the Scylla medallion reintegrated (photographically) in the bowl from which it came, see M. Bell 2011a: 3 (also 2011b: Fig. 47a).

Figure 4.4 Morgantina, a hoard of fifteen gilt-silver pieces of tableware. It was illicitly excavated in *c.* 1980/1, smuggled out of Italy, and after over twenty-five years in the Metropolitan Museum of New York, was returned to Italy in 2009. Its original find-spot was identified by excavation in 1997/8. The hoard consists of two buckets with feet in the form of theatrical masks; four bowls, three of which have appliqué leaf decoration in the centre of their interiors; a *phiale* libation plate with star-burst decoration and the usual central *omphalos*; two small *pyxides* from the same workshop, of which one features on its lid Demeter with cornucopia and the child Ploutos on her knee, and the other shows Eros; a miniature altar decorated with garlands in relief (supported by *bucrania*); a drinking-cup (*skyphos*) with projecting horizontal handles folded back on themselves; a ladle; a small jug; a pair of horns; and a superb medallion, belonging to the centre of a bowl, featuring the monster Scylla. Inscriptions on three items indicate that at least these were 'sacred to the gods', and presumably therefore originally belonged to a sanctuary. Whatever its original home or homes (the group is not homogeneous), the silverware was buried in a Morgantina house in 211 BC, no doubt during the Roman siege of the town prior to its capture that year, and was never recovered.

Figure 4.5 Morgantina, House of the Ganymede (for its position, see Figure 4.10). Mosaic in the *tessera* technique showing Ganymede being swept up to Mount Olympus by Zeus in the form of an eagle, whose tail feathers and the tips of the outspread wings are visible at bottom left and bottom right; second half of the third century BC, perhaps *c.* 225 BC. Size of figured panel including border: 1.05 m by 1.30 m. *In situ.*

means impossible that these were created in a Syracusan workshop, producing pieces in a style and of an artistic standard which matched those of workshops elsewhere in the contemporary Hellenistic world. The same might be said of the intricate early *tessera* mosaics which survive at Morgantina, such as that depicting Ganymede being taken to heaven by Zeus in the form of an eagle, laid sometime between the middle of the third century BC and the destruction of Morgantina in 211 BC (Figure 4.5). When uncovered in the 1950s there were heady suggestions that Sicilians might have actually invented this new mosaic technique, which in time superseded the more limited pebble technique; but discoveries in the last fifty years in Egypt and neighbouring areas show that similar experiments with chip and *tessera* pavements were going on there at around the same time.[17] It may well therefore prove to be the case that it was Alexandria which first tried out the *tessera* technique in the first half of the third century BC, and that the Hieronian kingdom in Sicily was one of the first areas

[17] Phillips 1960; Tsakirgis 1989: 395–400. For the House of the Ganymede, see most recently M. Bell in Minà 2005: 157, and for both house and mosaics, see now especially M. Bell 2011b.

Figure 4.6 Morgantina, 'House of Arched Cistern', showing the voussoir arch over the entrance to a cistern, and one of the house's two peristyles beyond; about the middle of the third century BC.

to catch on to its advantages over pebble and other types of floor composition.[18] The Ganymede floor and other less ambitious third-century pavements at Morgantina show Hieronian craftsmen as capable of providing the latest up-to-date novelties in lavish interior décor.

Morgantina also displays, in the House of the Arched Cistern of *c.* 250 BC, what may be the earliest true voussoir arch in Sicily, and among the earliest anywhere in the West, albeit on a small scale (Figure 4.6).[19] Whether larger examples of the voussoir arch were being employed in Syracuse at this time, we do not know; but it would not be surprising if they were. The principle of the voussoir arch had already been understood by Democritus in the fifth century BC, and it had reached southern Italy in monumental form by about the end of the fourth century BC; but it was not to enjoy

[18] Cf., more cautiously, Westgate 2002: 225–31 ('it is not clear exactly when it [*tessera* mosaic] was invented, or where, or how . . . [the idea that it might be Alexandria] is based on a hypothetical model of gradual stylistic and technical development which is not underpinned by dates from external evidence'). I take the mosaic from the 'villa' at Capo Soprano, Gela, seen by some as an early example of tessellation, to post-date the destruction of that city in 282 BC (so Pilo 2006: 163, second half of the third century BC at the earliest).

[19] Sjöqvist 1962: 138–40; specifically on the date, 140 with Fig. 21. There is nothing in this or the previous preliminary report (Stillwell 1961: 279–80) to suggest that the cistern is other than primary to the house. The mosaics here (Tsakirgis 1989: 401–03) are also likely to be third-century.

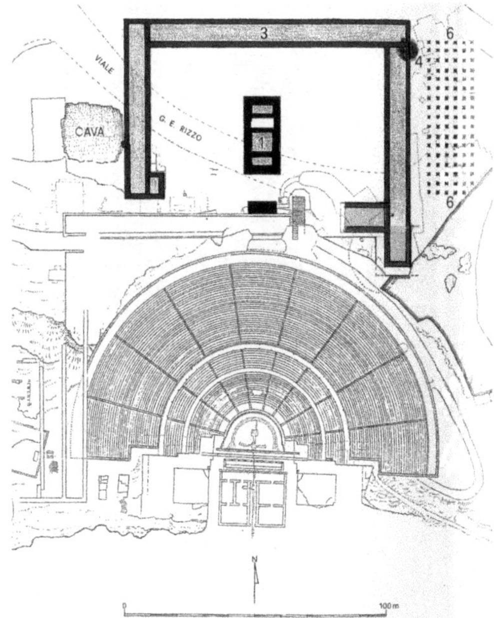

Figure 4.7 Syracuse, plan of the theatre of Hieron II (after 238 BC). There is an L-shaped stoa framing the theatre at the top level of seating (the nymphaeum mentioned in the text, not marked here, opens off the centre of its north wing). A staircase at the east end of this stoa gave access to an additional, more imposing, *pi*-shaped stoa (3), also Hieronian, on a terrace at a higher level to the north. The pi-shaped stoa, 110 m by 90 m, itself frames a small temple-tomb (1), believed by its excavator to be pre-Hieronian.

widespread currency in southern Italy and Sicily until much later in the Hellenistic period.[20] Hieron's kingdom once more shows itself as being abreast of the latest technological advances.

In contrast, another side of Hieronian architecture is displayed by those structures which are not just slavish copies of what is found in the wider Hellenistic world, but which rather demonstrate genuine originality and creativity. The vast showpiece theatre at Syracuse (238 BC or later: Figure 4.7) with its diameter of 138 m, and its rock-cut inscriptions in honour of Hieron and members of his family (Figure 4.8), shows a near semi-circular form which not only set the tone for all later theatres in Sicily (as we shall see), but also, more significantly, for those of the Italian mainland in the Hellenistic period as well;[21] and it was on these Sicilian and south Italian models, not on

[20] Posidonius *apud* Sen. *Ep*. 90.32. The earliest large-scale arch in Italy is probably the Porta Rosa at Elea, now thought to date 'to the end of the fourth century BC, if not to the beginning of the third, rather than to the fourth century more generally' (Vecchio 2003: 22).

[21] Rizzo 1923; Polacco and Anti 1981; Lehmler 2005: 122–35.

Figure 4.8 Syracuse, theatre of Hieron, part of a rock-cut inscription on the wall of the upper *diazoma*, an annular corridor which separates two sections of seating. Legible in this photograph is (ΒΑΣΙΛΙΣ)ΣΑΣ ΦΙΛΙΣΤΙΔΟΣ, 'of Queen Philistis' (the queen's name is visible in its entirety here). There were nine inscriptions in all, one facing each of the 'wedges' (*kerkides*) of seating into which the rows of seats below this *diazoma* are divided. Zeus Olympios was invoked at the centre, with the names of four additional divinities or heroes to the East (only one survives, fragmentarily; it refers to Herakles). The four to the west of Zeus cited Hieron, whose name is only partly preserved; Philistis; their daughter-in-law Nereis; and their son Gelon (the last is lost). It was the marriage of the last two in 238 BC which provides the *terminus post quem* for the date of the theatre (assuming that the inscriptions were primary: they do seem likely to have been integral to its expression of dynastic ambitions); the *terminus post quem non* for it is Gelon's death *c.* 216 BC (he predeceased his father by a few months).

the theatres of mainland Greece, that the Romans based their own theatres, when finally they got around to building them in the first century BC.[22] Syracuse may not have been the first theatre to favour the semi-circular or near semi-circular form (at present Metaponto's of *c.* 300 BC has that distinction, if Mertens' and De Siena's dating for it is right), but it was certainly a catalyst for the diffusion of the new form.[23] Also striking is the monumental pi-shaped stoa, uncovered on the upper terrace above the theatre at Syracuse,

22 Polacco 1977, but with the *caveat* of Sear 2006a: 49; cf. also R. Wilson 1990b: 68–72; Lehmler 2005: 172–6; Sear 2006a: 48–50. The exact D-shape of the Syracuse theatre may be a Hieronian feature or a reflection of later (Roman) re-cutting of the rock: Morgantina's theatre has the *analemmata* on the same alignment, but Acrae's Hieronian theatre probably does not (although its plan is damaged). Later copies elsewhere in Sicily (see below) have either near-converging *analemmata* (Solunto, Tindari) or the strict D-shape (Segesta, Monte Iato, Montagna di Marzo).

23 Mertens and De Siena 1982; Sear 2006a: 48.

enclosing an earlier heroon: perhaps Hieron was here imitating new multi-level building complexes known from elsewhere, such as at the sanctuaries of Asclepios on Kos and of Athena Lindia at Rhodes.[24]

Despite the futility of attempts to reconstruct the form of the Hieronian *skene* of the Syracuse theatre from the mass of multi-period rock-cut holes on the site which defy reliable interpretation, we know that this scene building was decorated with satyrs and maenads in the *telamon* pose, a striking innovation in Greek theatre architecture.[25] This motif, clearly inspired by the famous temple of Zeus at Agrigento (Acragas/Agrigentum) of over two centuries before, was much favoured by Hieron, who incorporated *telamon* figures also into his Great Altar, as well as into the decoration of his ship, the *Syrakosia*; in a domestic context it also occurs in a house at Centuripe.[26] Hieron's gigantic altar itself is also another example of a breath of fresh air in the interpretation of a well-known architectural type (Figure 4.9). No other Greek altar had ever been so big – big enough (or so it was claimed) to slaughter 1,000 oxen simultaneously.[27] While it had, as far as we know, no direct imitators on such a gigantic scale, the Great Altar of Hieron is typical of the architectural output of his age: vast, showy and different. They are hallmarks of a ruler with a limitless purse who used large and extravagant architectural monuments as a potent visual symbol of his power, prestige and wealth.[28]

It is hard to visualise Hieron's showpiece capital from the other fragments that survive (its Temple of Olympian Zeus on the agora in Achradina, for example, was much admired, even if we do not know the details[29]), and there are uncertainties of dating which bedevil the study of *disiecta membra*, such as statue fragments and pieces of architectural ornament, ripped from their original contexts.[30] However, an upland outpost in the far western reaches of

[24] For a plan, cf. conveniently Voza 1999: 103, Fig. 81.

[25] Rizzo 1923: 97–101; Lehmler 2005: 128–30; striking new photograph in Ciurcina 2006: 19, Fig. 9.

[26] Cf. R. Wilson 1990b: 70–1 with Figs. 5.5–6 (Centuripe). *Syrakosia*: Ath. 5.208b. For another example in a domestic context, but outside the kingdom of Hieron (at Segesta), see n. 68 below.

[27] On the Altar, see most recently Karlsson 1996; Parisi Presicce 2004; and Lehmler 2005: 135–45.

[28] Among comparatively recent discoveries is a large excavation area near Piazza Adda which includes a circular monument of apparently Hieronian date: Voza 1999: 106, Fig. 83. For two temples of 'early' Hieronian date elsewhere in his kingdom (at Taormina and Megara Hyblaea), cf. Correa Morales 2000: 209–14 (although a later Hieronian date has been plausibly argued by Campagna 2004: 162–4).

[29] Cic. *Verr.* 4.119 describes it as 'superb' (*templum egregium*); Diod. Sic. 16.83.2 (Hieronian date; situated on the agora); Campagna 2004: 157–61. Another example of Hieronian architectural originality is the extraordinary underground chamber tomb at Helorus, marked on the surface by a striking column ('La Pizzuta') still over 10 m high, a unique funerary monument anywhere in the Hellenistic world: Lauter 1986: 96–7 with Abb. 16b; R. Wilson 2013: no. 134.

[30] On architectural ornament von Sydow 1984 remains fundamental, but the chronology of some pieces has rightly been challenged (e.g. by Campagna 2004: 153–5 and 162–4; Portale 2002: 285–6, n. 20 and 294, n. 47). On Hieronian ornament, see also Correa Morales 2000: 214–9.

Figure 4.9 Syracuse, Altar of Hieron seen from the north-west; dedicated to Zeus Eleutherios, it measured exactly a *stadion* in length (600 Doric feet or 195.84 m). Only the rock-cut structures survive *in situ*, the superstructure in cut stone having been robbed, mainly in the sixteenth century; however some pieces of the Doric frieze and a few sima blocks decorated with lions' heads have been found, fallen from the superstructure. The Altar's original height has been calculated as nearly 11 m. In the foreground, entrance steps are visible which led the worshipper, after turning right, to a long upward-sloping ramp. The doorway was flanked by carved figures, probably Atlas figures, of which the lower part of one remains *in situ*. For colour version see plate section.

his kingdom, the city of Morgantina, does provide us with a substantial picture of what Hieronian building programmes may have looked like elsewhere, albeit that they were, no doubt, a pale and provincial reflection of the magnificence of his capital (Figure 4.10).[31] The current excavator of Morgantina, Malcolm Bell III, dates many of the monuments of the central sector, including the great stoas which frame the agora, and the theatre (also of D-shaped plan with *analemmata* on the same alignment), to around the middle or to the third quarter of the third century BC.[32] The two public granaries, one of them at least claimed as a gift of Hieron himself but perhaps more likely just a practical response to the needs to conform to the king's tax-in-kind policy (the *lex Hieronica*), are the

[31] Campagna 2004: 155–7 has disputed whether Hieron's kingdom extended as far as Morgantina, but although proof is lacking (such is the nature of archaeology if epigraphic support is absent), it seems to me to be beyond reasonable doubt.

[32] M. Bell 1993, 1999, 2007a, 2007b. For an excellent overview of what is known about Morgantina, see Tsakirgis 1995, and now M. Bell 2010. For the theatre, see now Sposito 2011, who however opts (129), I think wrongly, for a slightly earlier date, *c.* 300 BC.

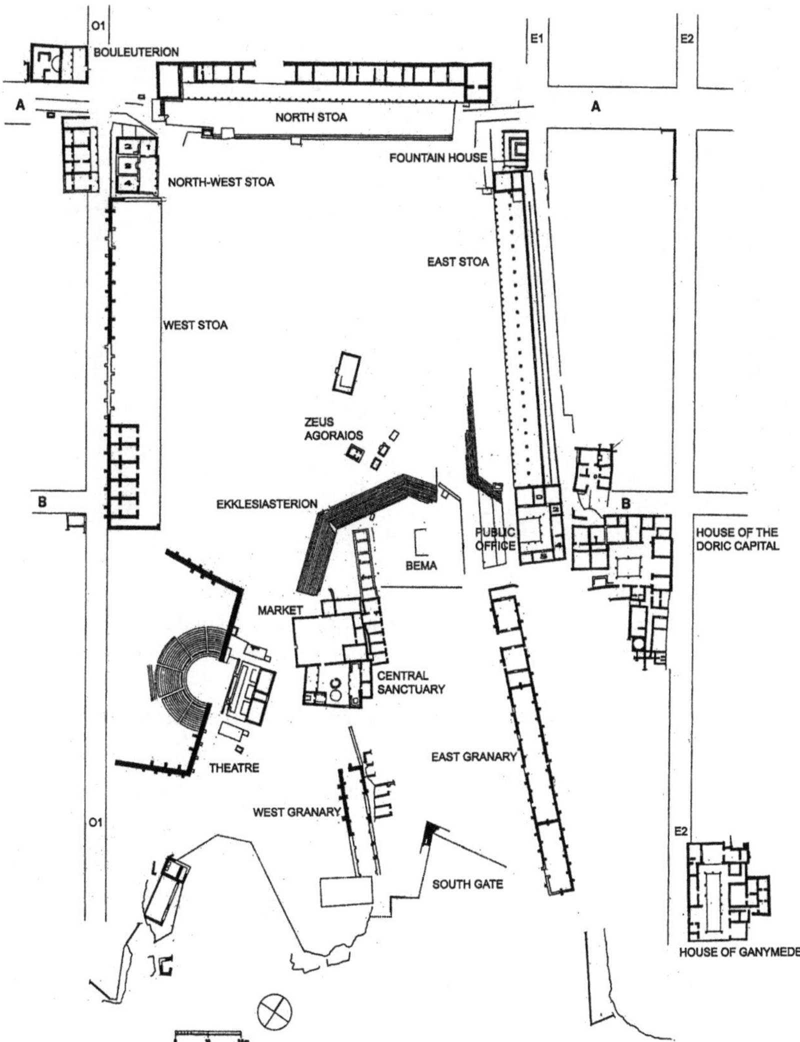

Figure 4.10 Morgantina, plan of central area of the excavated town, including the agora, as it was in the second half of the third century BC. Neither the north-west nor west stoas were ever completed.

earliest such buildings in the Graeco-Roman world to show a feature commonplace in their later Roman counterparts – external buttresses to take the strain of the grain stored within (Figure 4.11).[33]

[33] For the structures (and the idea that one is Hieron's gift): Deussen 1994; M. Bell 1984–5: 506–10; M. Bell 2007b: 124; also Lehmler 2005: 176–7; R. Wilson 2013: no. 129. The smaller (which has just four surviving external buttresses, as opposed to a full series on the second larger one) used to be thought Agathoclean on coin evidence, but the coins give only a *terminus ante quem non* and it is not impossible that it is Hieronian in date: so too now M. Bell 2007a: 187.

Figure 4.11 Morgantina, the east granary, seen from the south, provided with projecting buttresses both externally and internally; around the middle of the third century BC. The building is an impressive 93 m long and about 7.70 m wide.

In stoa-building, too, there is much at Morgantina of interest. Three of the stoas there show the unusual feature of a framing room at either end, a feature also present in the north-west stoa of the Agrigento Asclepieion; it also occurs (in a later variant) in a second-century stoa at Helorus.[34] Whether projecting in front of the stoa's main façade or not, these side rooms appear to have been a Sicilian (and later a south Italian) peculiarity.[35] One of the Morgantina stoas, the West, was also intended to be two-storied,

It would be no surprise if the impressive public granaries of Syracuse (Livy 24.21.11) were also buttressed. Buttressed granaries are known in earlier civilisations, e.g. at Harappa in the Indus valley, third millennium BC (but a building of uncertain function), and in Babylon under Nebuchadnezzar (604–561 BC): Rickman 1971: 151 and 253.

[34] Morgantina, the North Stoa, the East Stoa (exactly 300 Doric feet long, or half a *stadion*) and the aborted North-West Stoa: M. Bell 1993: 331–4; Sposito 1995: 51–9. Agrigento, Asclepieion: De Miro 2003: 50–3 and 298, plan ('third century BC'). Helorus: Coulton 1976: 242; Voza 1999: 118, Fig. 92. The vast stoa underlying the Naumachia reservoir at Taormina, probably late Hieronian, has 'avancorpi' at either end, which might possibly represent slightly projecting end rooms (Campagna and La Torre 2008: 123 and 126, Figs. 13, 15 and 18; Campagna, forthcoming; see also R. Wilson 2012: 248), but this is not certain. The stoa is of uncertain length (perhaps 400 Doric feet?), but is longer than the East Stoa at Morgantina.

[35] On Sicilian stoas in general (and the unusual nature of this feature), Lehmler 2005: 163–8, at 168; cf. also M. Bell 2005: 159–62, at 159 (where the agora's north stoa at Camarina and the north stoa above the Syracuse theatre are also said to be examples of this type, but neither appear so on published plans). Side rooms also occur in a stoa on the island of Poros in the Saronic Gulf (Kalauria Stoa F: Coulton 1976: 243, Fig. 69), where, however, the colonnade continues round the front of the slightly projecting side rooms, an arrangement not paralleled in Sicily (at Morgantina

although the project was never completed. The two-storied stoa is not unique to Sicily – the earliest may have been the late fourth-century example in the Asclepieion at Athens – but most of the Hellenistic-period stoas of mainland Greece are single-storey structures.[36] Attalos' stoa in Athens (whose capital at Pergamon had several), and Philip V of Macedon's stoa on Delos are among the exceptions – and it is symptomatic in connection with the example in Sicily (once no doubt matched by others at Syracuse) that these stoas in Greece were also built by publicity-seeking kings wanting to make their mark on the wider Hellenistic scene.

Three further examples of Hieronian originality only serve to emphasise the diversity of the architectural and technical creativity of the age. One is the invention of new varieties of both the Corinthian and the Ionic capital, which, while an accurate chronology is impossible on the strength of our present evidence, were almost certainly first invented and introduced during his reign. Sicilian Corinthian was taller than the classic Hellenistic version of the order, with spiky acanthus leaves, smooth *cauliculus* and often the inclusion of a flower in the middle of each side (Figure 4.12).[37] Sicilian Ionic was a diagonal version of the capital, in which the volutes appear on all four sides, not just on back and front as on the classic Ionic capital, and there are usually palmettes added at 45-degree angles as well (Figure 4.13).[38] Both varieties came in time to be used all over Sicily; but what is interesting is that the types also spread to the Italian mainland and North Africa during the second and first centuries BC, as well as as far east as Crete – an example of a Sicilian regional architectural idiosyncracy enjoying in addition ultra-regional circulation.[39] New types of Sicilian entablature are also likely to have been products of the Hieronian age.[40]

A second further aspect of third-century BC Syracusan originality is in its waterworks. The rock-cut aqueduct serving the nymphaeum behind

the front wall of each side room is flush with the end of the façade colonnade; at Eloro the side rooms are separately colonnaded, but not continuously with the stoa's façade).

36 M. Bell 1993: 333. Elsewhere: Coulton 1976: 124–9 (the small L-shaped stoa at Perachora is another early two-storied example). The inspiration was probably provided by Macedonian royal architecture, such as Philip II's palace at Vergina (before 336 BC), where the entrance was flanked by 'impressive two-storied stoas – the first in the history of Greek architecture' (Kottaridi 2011: 233 with Fig. 268).

37 Lauter-Bufe 1987; on chronology (a probable Hieronian origin): R. Wilson 1990b: 72–3 with n. 18 on 87; Campagna 2003a.

38 Villa 1988; R. Wilson 1990b: 73. As Campagna 2003b: 177, n. 40, rightly points out (discussing an idiosyncratic example in Messina best paralleled in Punic contexts in Tunisia), the Hieronian date of the invention of this type of Ionic capital, while likely, is hypothetical at present, pending further detailed evidence from Syracuse itself.

39 R. Wilson 1990b: 74, Figs. 5.8–9 (which needs updating); R. Wilson 2013: nos. 127 and 154b. Crete: Portale 2002.

40 Von Sydow 1984: 335–9.

Figure 4.12 Syracuse, limestone Corinthian capital of Sicilian Hellenistic type, from the area of the ancient agora ('Foro Siracusano'), but without a precise context. The generally tall shape, the heavy central flower, the smooth rounded helices (which stem not from the back of the volutes but independently), and above all the spiky, pointed acanthus leaves, are among the distinguishing characteristics of this type of capital. Late third century BC (?). Height: 42.5 cm.

Figure 4.13 Monte Iato, Ionic capital of Sicilian Hellenistic type, from Peristyle House 1. The distinguishing feature of such capitals is above all the presence on the inner side of the volutes of two palmettes, which vary in position from an angle of 45° (as here) to one of near verticality. Probably second quarter of the second century BC. Height: 31 cm.

the theatre, an integral part of the Hieronian project, has the curious and ill-understood feature of an additional 'service' channel above the water-bearing one.[41] This feature helps to date to the same period the other rock-cut aqueducts serving Syracuse, because the idiosyncracy, hardly found elsewhere, looks like being a local and probably short-lived phenomenon, possibly the work of a single designer.[42] Most intriguingly of all, the course of one of these Hellenistic twin-level aqueducts, the deepest of all, aims not for the city but for a precipice on the southern slopes of Epipolae. The implication is that use was made of the power of water unleashed by the sudden drop in height, and that a water mill was situated there.[43] If that is right, the location would be the site of the ancient world's oldest known water-driven mill.[44]

A third invention concerns roofing. A circular room in a public bath at Morgantina (the so-called northern baths), and another in a bath building in Hieronian Syracuse (and possibly also the circular room in contemporary baths at Megara Hyblaea) was domed with a structure using interlocking hollow tubular tiles (Figure 4.14).[45] These were larger versions of a type of roofing very widespread from the second century AD onwards, especially in North Africa but also, in time, at many other places across the Mediterranean world. There is no clear evidence for a continuity of use of this bold, precocious and highly original roofing method through the four centuries which separate third-century BC Sicily from second-century AD North Africa, although there is now a second-century BC instance of its use in Spain, and vaulting of this type is also attested (rarely) at Pompeii.[46] Once again one wonders whether it is not too fanciful to suggest (although direct proof is lacking) that its invention in Sicily might be due to the creative brilliance of Archimedes, that ancient Sicilian Leonardo da Vinci. Something similar was probably

41 R. Wilson 2000a: 12–15.

42 A short stretch in Athens shows this feature: Tölle-Kastenbein 1994: 32–8 with Abb. 32; discussion in R. Wilson 2000a: 32, n. 65.

43 R. Wilson 2000a: 13–14.

44 For an up-to-date account of the origin of the water-mill, see O. Wikander in Oleson 2008: 141–2.

45 Morgantina: H. Allen 1974: 376–9; new excavations in Lucore 2009. In addition Lucore 2011 draws attention to the remarkable discovery in 2010 of an opening in the side of a pool immediately above the hypocaust, which must have served for the insertion of a metal water-tank, what Vitruvius (5.10.1) calls the *testudines alveorum* ('the tortoises of the pools'); they were so known because of their semi-circular shape and their metal plating. Usually thought of as peculiar to Roman baths, the '*testudo*' at Morgantina is a unique discovery from the Hellenistic world, the earliest example of its type known. Megara Hyblaea: Vallet *et al.* 1983: 56 ('couverte probablement par une sorte de voûte'). Syracuse: Cultrera 1938. On circular rooms in Sicilian bath-buildings (both public and private), cf. Bürge 2001.

46 R. Wilson 1992; Storz 1994; for the Spanish example, Lucore 2009: 54, n. 17, with reference.

Figure 4.14 Morgantina, North Baths, vaulting tubes from the roofing as found in its collapsed state; probably third quarter of the third century BC. In addition to the domed room (5.75 m in diameter: top left in this photograph), two other rooms in this small bathing complex had barrel vaults made of the same material, one 5 m wide (foreground) and the other 5.5 m wide (top right). The tubes are made of terracotta and narrow to a point at one end so that they can interlock with one another; in construction, each tube was set at a slight angle to its neighbour in order to achieve the curve of the dome or vault. Lime mortar was the binding agent throughout, and was used also to cover the tubes both on the inner and outer surfaces; when the structure was complete, therefore, the tubes were invisible. At Morgantina they are generally about 60–70 cm in length (and 12–15 cm in diameter), much larger than later examples in Roman North Africa and elsewhere, which are rarely more than 20 cm long. For colour version see plate section.

going on in a circular room uncovered on the edge of the agora at Acrae, where the extant remains of brick ribbing (here embedded into the rock-cut part of the chamber) clearly formed the basic framework for another dome. One wonders whether in this case square, slightly curved pantiles filled the gaps between the ribs, a system attested in the second-century BC baths at Fregellae in central Italy;[47] but in the absence of publication, both the chronology and the materials which composed the rest of this dome, of which presumably traces remained in the collapsed fill, is unknown, and speculation is therefore premature.[48] These are

[47] Tsiolis 2006: 246–7, with Fig. 6.

[48] Its plan can be made out in Voza 1999: 131, Fig. 101 but it is not mentioned in the accompanying account of Acrae (*ibid.* 129–39).

regional examples of experiments in roofing which, while they had no immediate, lasting impact elsewhere, were clearly bold and precociously early attempts at covering a circular space with something other than a conventional timber roof. Early forerunners of the Roman concrete dome of two centuries later, these domed structures, for their sheer ingenuity and daring originality, deserve more than a footnote in the history of the evolution of architectural thought.

What happened in eastern Sicily in the second century, after the Hieronian era had come to an end, is a chapter in the history of Hellenistic Sicily still to be written. It has been customary in Sicilian historiography to see the fall of Syracuse in 212 BC as a cultural and economic watershed, and its aftermath as discontinuous with what had gone before; but although chronological problems remain until the typology and dating of Hellenistic pottery in the island is refined, the general impression gradually emerging is one of cultural continuity.[49] A case in point is the remarkable Hellenistic terracotta production of Centuripe, renowned for its large, showy painted vessels with polychrome figured scenes, sometimes with additional plastic ornamental details in moulded terracotta.[50] Often claimed on insufficient evidence to be an exclusively third-century production, one that died with the fall of Hieron's kingdom, these vessels were very probably still being made in the second century,[51] while the flourishing industry manufacturing small-scale terracotta figurines (earning Centuripe the soubriquet of the 'Sicilian Tanagra') certainly continued into the second and also the first centuries BC.[52] It would also not be surprising if the most recent stratified finds from Syracuse were to demonstrate that

[49] Cf. my remarks in R. Wilson 1990a: 27.

[50] Libertini 1926 (pottery on 143–86) is a starting-point for all things Centuripan, supplemented by Rizza 2002, the essays by M. Frasca and R. Patanè in Osanna and Torelli 2006: 193–210, and now Biondi 2010. None of the recent work seems to have shed light on the period of production of the polychrome vases (cf. in brief Malfitana 2011: 193).

[51] Cf. Wintermeyer 1975: 137–8 and 152–3 for the view (partly because of associated terracottas in graves) that the pottery was produced in both the third and the second centuries BC; also E. Joly in Bonacasa and Joly 1985: 352–3, at 352. For a recent discussion of the chronology, supporting Wintermeyer, cf. Portale 2001–2: 44–54, and for a wide-ranging new discussion of Centuripe pottery, see now Portale 2011. Also very important is the recent publication and detailed catalogue of both pottery and terracottas from the contrada Cassino necropolis, with the clear demonstration from the contemporaneity of material in recorded grave groups that both pottery and terracotta production at Centuripe continued into and throughout much of the second century BC (Musomeci 2010).

[52] Cf. Higgins 1967: 124 ('the entire Hellenistic period'); cf. (e.g.) Langlotz and Himer 1965: nos. 144, 148 right, 150, 160 (all second/first centuries BC).

terracotta production there also continued well into the period under Roman rule, rather than that it ceased in 212 BC as is presently assumed.[53]

The cultural impact of Rome on eastern Sicily in the century after 212 BC is hard to assess. An influx of 'Romans' in the island, not least in Syracuse itself, must have had some effect, but its impact is rarely traceable in the material record. The Roman governor, the *praetor*, presumably moved into the palace of Hieron on the southern tip of Ortygia – with what alterations we do not know.[54] Greek continued to be the ubiquitous language – Cicero later had to remind his audience that the Syracusans called their *curia* the *bouleuterion* – and this is reflected in the epigraphic record.[55] A rare tombstone of this period in Latin, decorated with a plough carved in low relief, was set up in memory of Cn. Marcius – perhaps an *arator* from Italy, lured to Sicily by the promise of material gain from agriculture – but this perhaps belongs to the first century BC rather than to the second; C. Norbanus' record of road building, also in Latin and from Syracuse, is another, belonging to the 80s BC.[56] Study of unpublished material in Syracuse and elsewhere, an urgent desideratum, should in the future dramatically enrich our understanding of the Roman element in eastern Sicily's late Hellenistic cultural make-up.

One part of eastern Sicily, Messina and its hinterland, was exposed in the third century to a different cultural element. When it was captured by Mamertine mercenaries in 288 BC, an event which precipitated the first Punic War, *Messana* became the 'city of the Mamertines', but the coinage, apart from two issues using the Oscan form 'Mamertinoum', continued to be minted with the ethnic in Greek.[57] There are a handful of Oscan inscriptions

[53] E.g. M. Bell 1981: 74–9, noting, however, a revival in the production of terracottas at Morgantina in the later first century BC (and probably also at Catania), and second-century production at Centuripe.

[54] Lehmler 2005: 101–2 with Abb. 40 places the palace in central Ortygia on the basis of *AE* 1946.207, a late Roman inscription referring to the *praetorium*; but the stone was not found *in situ* (it and another had been 'reused as building material': Cultrera 1940: 219). The place of choice *par excellence* for the premier residence in Syracuse was surely the southern tip of Ortygia (under the present Castello Maniace), which enjoys the most majestic view over both the Great Harbour and Plemmyrion (so R. Wilson 1990a: 345). For a completely different view, that the palace was situated on the 'acropolis' on Achradina overlooking Ortygia, cf. Polacco and Mirisola 1998–9; but that Sicily's governor (*praetor*) resided in what had been Hieron's palace, and that the latter was situated on Ortygia ('*Insula*'), is clear from Cic. *Verr.* 4.118.

[55] Cic. *Verr.* 2.50.

[56] Cn. Marcius: R. Wilson 1990a: 356, n. 97 with reference. Norbanus: *CIL* I^2.2951 (the *praetor* of 89 and 88/7 BC). Cf. also, for both inscriptions, Prag 2007a: 259–60 with nn. 69–70.

[57] Mastelloni 2005; Crawford 2006. Cf. in general for Messina at this period, Pinzone 2002. On Oscan, cf. also Orioles 1992 and Sironen 1995.

on stone, as well as some brick stamps and graffiti, but the gods continued to be worshipped under their Greek names. With the exception of a couple of 'Italic'-style chamber tombs, one containing a pot inscribed with the name of what sounds like an Oscan lady, Pakia Pomptia, written in Greek, Messina has not produced material assemblages any different from those elsewhere in north-east Sicily.[58] Mamertine influence therefore appears (on the present, admittedly limited, evidence) to have been superficial and short-lived. A plastic vase in the form of a wolf, of *c.* 200–150 BC, on the other hand, with the twins depicted in relief beneath it, is perhaps a local product making a nod in the direction of Rome; certainly the lupercal is otherwise unknown in Sicilian Hellenistic iconography.[59]

Central Sicily

By contrast with the comparative stability and wealth of eastern Sicily, there is little in the way of major public building which can be dated with certainty to the third century BC in central or western Sicily, or any hint that this part of the island shared the same prosperity as that enjoyed in Hieron's kingdom. That is not surprising. It is difficult to assess the precise impact that fighting had on the physical fabric and the economy of this western part of the province in the course of two bloody Punic wars, but the hints that we have from the sources, to which can be added an increasing body of archaeological evidence, suggest that it was not inconsiderable. Camarina, taken by Rome in 258 BC when most of its population is said to have been sold into slavery, has been demonstrated archaeologically to have been a shadow of its former self thereafter, and places like Agrigento, another city where part of the population was sold into slavery, or Myttistraton, sacked also in 258, although both recovered, may have taken time to regain their former prosperity.[60] The reduction by as much as a third between the end of the fourth century BC and the end of the third century in the total number of hill towns that still continued to be inhabited, although not every abandonment was the result of the Punic Wars, is also significant, and another signal of relative urban decline.[61]

[58] Mastelloni 2004a; Crawford 2006: 525. [59] Mastelloni 2004b: 51, Fig. 6.

[60] Camarina: Polyb. 1.24.12; Diod. Sic. 23.9.4; for the post-258 BC city ('fase IV'), G. Di Stefano 2006: 157–60. Agrigento: Polyb. 1.19.14–15; Diod. Sic. 23.9.1. Myttistraton: Polyb. 1.24.11.

[61] R. Wilson 1985: 314–9; discussed also by Perkins 2007: 50–1 (cf. also 40, for results from the Monreale survey which suggest a slight reduction in settlement after the First Punic War

A century later, however, we have a different story. In the course of the second century BC, renewed prosperity shows itself in the extensive rebuilding programmes that many of the still surviving towns seem to have undergone, starting perhaps about 180 BC or 170 BC, but gathering pace in the second half of the second century. The explanation comes from the economic fall-out that resulted from their incorporation into Rome's fledgling new *provincia*. The profundity of this change cannot be over-emphasised. Sicilians had to alter focus, from belonging to small, nominally independent and, in many cases self-sufficient, city-states, to one where they had demands from a new, external master – a master moreover who imposed taxation-in-kind in the form of a corn tithe. The Sicilian communities apparently responded to this new challenge with enthusiasm: perhaps it was the economic stimulus of being able to sell the equivalent of a second corn tithe on the open market that spurred them on to greater efforts in the hope of increasing wealth. The likelihood is that there was an explosion in Sicilian agriculture, with more land probably coming under cultivation than ever before. Far from being oppressed by excessive taxation, the Sicilian communities began to flourish, with beneficial effects on the building programmes, public and private, which were financed by the extra cash generated.[62]

The notion that Sicilian urbanism flourished in the second century BC was controversial when first mooted twenty years ago,[63] but fresh excavations and fuller publication of older ones over the past two decades have only served to emphasise just how many Sicilian towns were engaged in considerable rebuilding programmes at this time, at places such as Agrigento, Pantelleria, Segesta, Licata, Monte Iato (Ietas), Solunto, Halaesa and Tindari (Tyndaris), to list only some of the better documented examples.[64]

but an increase throughout the second century BC). The pattern has been detected also in coin-circulation patterns: Frey-Kupper 2006: 44 notes the 'general impoverishment' of western Sicily after the mid-third century BC and 'a serious lack of coin'; she contrasts that situation with the flourishing state of the monetary economy of western Sicily by the late second century BC.

[62] Cf. Campagna 2007: 110, who refers to a 'vero e proprio *boom* dell'attività edilizia' between the second half of the second century BC and the beginning of the first; cf. also Campagna 2006: 15–16 and *passim*.

[63] In R. Wilson 1990a: 20–8, reiterated in R. Wilson 2000b: 140–50; see the discussion in Campagna 2003c, especially 23–7, and, more generally, Prag 2009a. The excellent reassessment by Campagna (2011b) of the nature of urban landscapes in northern and western Sicily in, above all, the second century BC, reached me after the completion of my manuscript.

[64] Agrigento: cf. most recently De Miro 2009 (e.g. 57, late Hellenistic, second/first century BC, Hellenistic-Roman quarter). Pantelleria: Osanna 2006. Segesta: see notes 65 and 66. Licata: La Torre 2005. Monte Iato: Isler 2000a is a useful summary (although his dating, e.g. a claim on pp. 21–2 that Ietas and Solunto 'and probably . . . other cities, such as Segesta', were entirely reconstructed *c.* 300 BC, is controversial: see note 68 below). Solunto: see note 67. Halaesa: cf. most recently Scibona and Tigano 2009 (e.g. 27, stoa on agora datable to the end of the second

At Segesta, for example, the famous ancient theatre, so long believed to belong to *c.* 300 BC, has now been dated on both archaeological and architectural grounds to the second half of the second century BC (Figure 4.15).[65] At Segesta, too, the impressive reshaping of the agora and its surrounds, which included a showy two-storey stoa (Figure 4.16), and a *bouleuterion* nearby, is also datable to the later second century BC.[66] A similar rebuilding of the civic centre happened around the same time at Solunto, another place with theatre, *bouleuterion* and imposing two-storey stoa (the last fronting the paved piazza of the market-place: Figure 4.17), all part of a more or less contemporary building programme designed to remodel the very heart of the town.[67]

Such two-storey stoas, as we have already seen, are not a commonplace in mainland Greece, and the question that inevitably arises about this Sicilian second-century BC architecture in general is whether it is part of a wider pattern in the Greek world of the Hellenistic period, or whether it follows rules of its own – and, if the latter, whether the inspiration for it should be sought once again in the buildings of Hieronian Syracuse a century earlier. The pattern of theatre-building in the second century BC suggests very strongly the latter. Not only is the near semi-circular shape of the theatre, seen on the grand scale at Syracuse, almost universally adopted, but so too are decorative details – satyrs and maenads decorating the stage building at Monte Iato (Figure 4.18), further *telamon* figures (if only on a small scale) in the theatres at Solunto and Segesta, and in the *bouleuterion* as well, it seems,

century BC). Tindari: Spigo 2005 (e.g. 47 and 63, Casa C and theatre in present form, both second half of second century BC); La Torre 2004: 122 and 137 (late second century for Casa B); Leone and Spigo 2008 (e.g. 105, but there the main phase of urban layout is thought to date rather earlier, to the second half of the third century BC).

65 D'Andria 1997; Campagna 1997 (and more recently 2006: 17). For the persuasive view that *IG* XIV.288, a pair of honorific inscriptions commemorating Phalakros and his wife Phalakria, might have come from the scene building of the theatre and record its benefactors, cf. Campagna 2007: 121–5.

66 Parra 2006; Ampolo 2010: 3–49 (seven papers by various scholars); and four papers in Ampolo 2012: 271–326. On Sicilian Hellenistic *agorai* and stoas, cf. most helpfully Campagna 2006: 21–5; also R. Wilson 2012.

67 Cutroni Tusa *et al.* 1994; for its significance within the wider picture of Hellenistic Sicily, and for discussion of chronology (rejecting the hitherto prevailing 'fourth-century BC' emphasis): Portale 2006; cf. also Portale 2007a. On the date of the Solunto theatre (second century BC), Wiegand 1997: 29 and 54–5. Solunto agora/stoa, *c.* 130/20 BC: von Sydow 1984: 355–6. Street-paving with inscription of donor: Wiegand 1991: 126 (late second century BC), discussed also in the context of Sicilian euergetism at this period by Campagna 2007: 113 and 2011b: 168–71. What appears to have been a north Sicilian peculiarity of stoas (at Solunto, Termini Imerese and Halaesa) is the use of at least some of the rear rooms for a religious function (as shrines, sometimes with central altars) rather than as shops: R. Wilson 2012: 252–5.

Figure 4.15 Segesta, the Hellenistic theatre, second half of the second century BC. The view from the auditorium would not have been as dramatic as it is today, since most of it will have been blocked by the two-storey stage-building, now reduced to foundations. The latter employed Doric columns in the lower storey and Ionic above, as at Solunto, Tindari and elsewhere. The small projecting 'wings' (*paraskenia*) of this stage building are another Sicilian idiosyncrasy, and the relief figures decorating them (satyrs?) were probably inspired by similar decoration in the Hieronian theatre at Syracuse (Figure 4.7). Statue bases found here name Phalakros and his wife Phalakria, the former set up by the 'people' (*damos*) of Segesta; they were perhaps the theatre's benefactors. For colour version see plate section.

at the latter.[68] Another distinctively Sicilian aspect of these theatres is the presence of small projecting wings (*paraskenia*) on either side of the stage building, usually with their front walls set at an oblique angle in order not to interfere with the sight lines of spectators in the *cavea*. Whether this feature too had its origins in Hieronian Syracuse we cannot

[68] Monte Iato: Isler Kerenyi 1976; for the theatre in general, cf. Isler 2000a: 46–62 and 2000b. For comments on the chronology, cf. (e.g.) R. Wilson 1990b: 69–71; Wiegand 1997: 48–51; D'Andria 2005: 184; Sear 2006a: 48–9; Campagna 2006: 20–1. In support of the high dating (defended most recently by Isler 2011), Nicola Bonacasa has been a consistent proponent, e.g. Bonacasa 1996: 423–4; 1999: 261–3; and most recently 2008: 58. Solunto: Wiegand 1997: 32 and 60–1 with Taf. 25–6. Segesta, Pan figures: Wiegand 1997: 44–7 (cf. also maenad and satyr in bas-relief decorating a pilaster at Segesta in a private context: Camerata Scovazzo 1997: 112). Segesta, *bouleuterion*: Parra 2006: 109–112 with Fig. 8 (end of the second century BC). For the possibility that the first phase of the Taormina theatre is second-century rather than Hieronian, cf. Dimartino 2009. The most recently discovered Sicilian theatre, that of Montagna di Marzo, is also ascribed to the second century (Guzzardi 2004: 544–7 with Tav. LV, Fig. 1). On Sicilian Hellenistic theatre-building, see most usefully Campagna 2006: 16–21. See also note 22 above.

Figure 4.16 Segesta, the limestone stoa bordering the east side of the agora, reconstruction view looking south-east. This imposing two-storey stoa, using Doric in the lower and Ionic in the upper, was constructed in the last quarter of the second century BC. The building is *pi*-shaped, with short projecting wings at either end which are not quite parallel to one other (probably for reasons of topography; only the south-east wing appears here). There were 35 columns along the main façade of a building just over an impressive 100 m in length. For colour version see plate section.

Figure 4.17 Solunto, remains of the stoa and the agora onto which it opened, from the south-west; second century BC. The remains are not well preserved (the shops, shrines or offices which lined the back of the stoa's ground floor are the most conspicuous feature here), but scattered remains of architectural ornament are sufficient to document a two-storey structure, like the stoa on the agora at Segesta (Figure 4.16). On the terrace above it to the left, just off photograph, lie the town's theatre and *bouleuterion*.

Figure 4.18 Monte Iato (Ietas), limestone relief statue of a maenad in the *telamon* pose, one of a pair which, together with two satyrs, decorated the stage building of the theatre. The dress of the maenad here, with high belt and swallow-tail folds in the drapery hems, is paralleled in other late Hellenistic sculpture in the island, especially in eastern Sicily. Probably first half of the second century BC. Height: 1.99 m.

tell – the form of the third-century stage-building there is not, as we have seen, now ascertainable – but it had an influence on the shaping of Campanian theatres such as the first theatre at Pompeii and that at Sarno in the second century BC, where the scene buildings take the same form. This is an indication of the importance of Hellenistic Sicily as a conduit for new ideas which (as noted above) helped shape the development of Roman theatre design in Italy.[69] Of course outside influences in turn no doubt played their part in shaping late second-century BC Sicilian architecture – the *bouleuterion* with semi-circular seating rows might owe something to Asia Minor models such as that at Miletus, for example – but by and large Sicilian patrons and their architects were capable of forging a distinctive identity of their own, with widespread use of their homegrown varieties of the 'Sicilian' Ionic and the 'Sicilian' Corinthian orders discussed above.[70]

Another Sicilian idiosyncracy was a fondness for architectural rule-breaking, witnessed above all by a flagrant intermingling of Ionic and Doric elements. The tomb of *c.* 100 BC (the misnamed 'Tomb of Theron'), for example, outside the south gate of Agrigento (Figure 4.19), has a tall false door with its quadripartite division that is ultimately inspired by Macedonian tomb architecture, but which by the later second century BC was so hackneyed and commonplace that it had passed into the general Hellenistic *koine* in the West – seen in Second-style wall paintings in Pompeii, for example, or in the architecture of Numidian tombs – but alongside it and above it are Sicilian Ionic capitals associated with a Doric frieze of metopes and triglyphs.[71] Other examples include the nearby temple, the 'Oratory of Phalaris', at Agrigento, of *c.* 100 BC, also with Ionic columns supporting a Doric frieze, a combination seen in smaller pieces as well, such as on a Hellenistic-period sarcophagus from Cefalù (Cephaloedium; Figure 4.20); the stage building of the theatre at Tindari on the north coast, also perhaps *c.* 100 BC, which has an entablature featuring Ionic dentils above Doric capitals; and, to give another small-scale example, the extraordinary

[69] Cf. especially Wiegand 1997: 31–2 and 43–51 and Sear 2006a: 49–50. Winter (2006: 189; cf. also 109–10) calls the Segesta theatre 'Italo-Hellenistic'.

[70] This is in contrast to the majority of known *bouleuteria* elsewhere, which prefer the *pi*-shaped arrangement of seating, from Glanon in the far West to Priene in the East. Miletus: Lauter 1986: 164–6. Sicilian *bouleuteria*: Iannello 1994; Isler 2003; M. Bell 2005: 163; and Campagna 2006: 25–8. The semi-circular arrangement of the seating as early as 415 BC in the New Bouleuterion at Athens is entirely conjectural (Camp 1986: 90–1); nor do I accept that the early *bouleuterion* at Ietas is likely to be as early as the late fourth century BC (see also Campagna 2006: 27–8).

[71] P. Marconi 1929: 124–7; R. Wilson 1990b: 83, with Fig. 5.22. Winter 2006: 188 plausibly sees it as influenced by Punic tower tombs in North Africa. I do not accept the second-century AD date proposed for this tomb by De Miro (e.g. 1996a: 165), by which time the use in Sicily of a mixed Doric/Ionic style had long since vanished.

Figure 4.19 Agrigento, tomb still standing outside the south gate, curiously spared by post-antique stone robbers; height 7.64 m. Dubbed erroneously the 'Tomb of Theron', after Akragas' tyrant in the early fifth century BC, the monument belongs in all likelihood 400 years later (*c.* 100 BC). On a two-step stylobate rises a plain lower storey 4.81 m square surmounted by an upper one decorated in relief with a false door in the middle of each side; at the corners are engaged columns in the Ionic order supporting a Doric frieze. The original form of the tomb's now-lost summit is uncertain.

pair of bronze tablets recently published from Halaesa, with in this instance rudimentary Corinthian capitals supporting a Doric frieze.[72]

With private dwellings – and Sicily is rich in examples of houses of Hellenistic date – the vast majority belong to the standard courtyard type, with rooms ranged around a central columnar peristyle, a type ubiquitous around the Mediterranean from the mid-third century BC.[73] While the use

[72] Agrigento: P. Marconi 1929: 123–4, with reconstruction, Fig. 78. Cefalù: Tullio 1984: 600–2. Tindari: von Sydow 1984: 327–32; Wiegand 1997: 48–9 with Abb. 14. Halaesa: G. Scibona in Scibona and Tigano 2009: 97–112, with Figs. 6–7 (perhaps first-century BC rather than second). For some Italian examples of mixed orders, cf. Zanker 1976a: 208, Fig. 70; Winter 2006: 195–6.

[73] De Miro 1980 and 1996b; Isler and Käch 1997; Wolf 2003, especially 79–110; Tsakirgis 2009, with earlier bibliography; in brief also Isler 2005.

Figure 4.20 Cefalù, fragmentary sarcophagus of limestone, from a necropolis in the Spinito district on the south-west side of the town. The sarcophagus is decorated in relief with columns in the Ionic order; they support a Doric entablature including a frieze of triglyphs and metopes. Probably second century BC. Width of the short side seen here: 69.8 cm; height including lid: 77.8 cm.

of the stone-columned peristyle in a domestic setting can probably be seen as ultimately deriving from Hellenistic-period palace architecture of the later fourth and early third century BC, it is misleading to see the direct influence of Macedon on such houses as the two-storeyed 'Peristyle House 1' at Monte Iato, with its superimposed orders of Doric and Ionic, its rich stucco mouldings, and its mosaic pavements in fine tessellated technique as well as *opus signinum*.[74] A more probable and more direct source of

[74] E.g. Isler 1996, reinforced by a belief that the house dates to *c.* 300 BC (so also Dalcher 1994) rather than to the second century BC. For a rejection of this high dating, cf. (e.g.) R. Wilson 1990b: 75–6, and 2000b: 149–50; Portale 2001–2: 64–75; 2006: 80–1; Campagna 2003c: 10; Campagna 2011b: 164–5; Campagna 2011a: 189–93 (and 193–210 for a detailed re-examination of the moulded stucco cornices of this house in the wider context of the Mediterranean, with the conclusion than none is earlier than *c.* 200 BC: the house dates to the first half of the second century BC, and probably to its second quarter; cf. also *ibid.* 208–10 for the dating of Peristyle

inspiration is likely to have been the wealthy houses of Hieronian Syracuse, but sadly these are almost entirely lost.

What does seem to be clear is that the influence of the Italian peninsula, in both public and private architecture, appears to have been minimal. In domestic building only two houses out of hundreds of examples, one at Agrigento and one at Marsala (Lilybaeum), appear to be of the atrium-and-peristyle type so familiar from the Italian mainland, and even these, at least in the form in which they survive, lack true *impluvia*.[75] It is tempting to think that the finest second-century mosaics from the province of Sicilia (both still *in situ*), one in Palermo (the damaged Hunt mosaic), and the other in Rabat (Malta), which have richly festooned borders incorporating theatrical masks, might represent a borrowing from Campania, where such borders are familiar.[76] But survival rates of mosaic material, with the overwhelming preponderance in favour of the Vesuvian cities for obvious reasons (a freak natural catastrophe), might hide the possibility that the 'influence' went rather in the opposite direction – that Sicily, whether directly or indirectly, was a purveyor of visual motifs originating in the eastern Mediterranean to southern Italy, rather than the other way round. Certainly there is evidence for the survival in Sicily of the habit, absent in Campania, of using lead strips in at least some tessellated mosaics of the second century, which suggests an independence of practice on the part of Sicilian mosaicists. Their use might, in fact, be under the influence of Alexandria, if fragments using such lead strips at Segesta, immediately adjacent to a floor signed by an Alexandrian mosaicist, Dionysios, are anything to go by.[77]

House 2). In support of the high dating, see Isler 2011 and the works by Bonacasa cited in n. 68 above. For a summary of this and other peristyle houses at Monte Iato, Isler 2000a: 66–93, 2001 and 2005. For the notion that such influence is likely to have reached the rest of Sicily via the Hellenistic kingdom of Hieron II in Syracuse, cf. Tsakirgis 2009: 118–19.

[75] R. Wilson 1990a: 115 and 123, with Figs. 103 and 111 (Agrigento, Casa del Atrio Tetrastilio; and Marsala, house at Capo Boeo); Hollegaard Olsen *et al.* 1995: 218–23 and 226–8. For the former, see now De Miro 2009: 47–51, House I B, now called the 'Casa atrio e peristilio'. I do not accept as true *atria* (although they are often so called) any small four-columned courts at the centre of houses, where they serve the same function as (small) peristyles (e.g. Marsala, via Sibilla: R. Wilson 1990a: 124; Hollegaard Olsen *et al.* 1995: 229–30; Solunto, Casa di Leda, etc.: *ibid.* 240–1). For an example of such a tetrastyle court in a house at Heraclea Minoa, cf. the sensible discussion of Campagna 1996: 119–20.

[76] Palermo: Wootton 2002, with earlier bibliography; for recent work on this house, C. Di Stefano 1997; Spatafora 2005: 42–5; and F. Spatafora and G. Montali in Osanna and Torelli 2006: 133–51. Rabat: Bonanno 1992: Pls. 47–9, and ill. on 45; 2005: 166. Pompeian examples include those from the Casa delle Colombe, the Casa del Fauno and the 'Plato and the philosophers' mosaic: Andreae 2003: 164–5 (details on 240), 194–5 and 248. Cf. in general, von Boeselager 1983: 47–8.

[77] Dionysios: *SEG* 41.833; for the date, K. Dunbabin 1999: 273 with n. 23. Use of lead strips in Sicily: von Boeselager 1983: 53–5; at Segesta, Camerata Scovazzo 1997: 109 and 112, with Figs. 5–6 and 10.

Figure 4.21 Monte Iato, reconstruction drawing by P. Omahen of the junction between the North Stoa (right) and the West Stoa; the paving of the agora is visible in the foreground. The West Stoa is dated by its excavators to the late second century BC; the North Stoa which it abuts is earlier, but probably also belongs to the second century. In the far north-west corner of the latter is a *tribunal*, a platform probably intended to take the chair of a presiding magistrate; if so, the North Stoa presumably had also a judicial function. The moulding of its front edge bears the name, unusually for this period in Latin, of Cn. Host(ilius), clearly not a Sicilian, but this may have been inscribed in a secondary period and does not necessarily imply that he was the *tribunal*'s donor; unfortunately the rest of the inscription is lost.

In public building there is much the same story. Capitals of Sicilian type, both Corinthian and Ionic diagonal capitals, get adopted in Campania, for example, and *telamon* decoration, perhaps ultimately of Hieronian inspiration, are used for minor decoration at Pompeii, for example, in the odeum and in the Forum baths, in baths at Fregellae, and in the theatre at Pietrabbondante.[78] In the opposite direction there is no sign of the basilica as an architectural type reaching Sicily – rather, as in the Greek East, Hellenistic Sicily seems to have continued to use the stoa for the hearing of judicial cases, if the *podia* for presiding officials, in the East Stoa at Morgantina and the North Stoa at Monte Iato (Figure 4.21), are correctly so interpreted; but whether that is also the case at Halaesa, where a pair of Greek inscriptions as well as a Latin one refer to its *basilica*, is still uncertain, since we cannot be sure if the word refers to a stoa used for basilical purposes, a *stoa basilike*, or to a separate dedicated building of Italian type.[79]

78 *Telamones* in Pompeii and Pietrabbondante: Sear 2006a: 50; in baths at Pompeii and Fregellae: Tsiolis 2006: 247–8, with Fig. 7. Cf. also discussion of the motif in La Torre 2004: 131–2.

79 Isler 2000a: 37, Fig. 5. Morgantina: M. Bell 1993: 332, with Fig. 9. Halaesa: Scibona and Tigano 2009: 102–3 and 106 with n. 37; discussed in R. Wilson 2012: 254–5.

Figure 4.22 Agrigento, late Hellenistic temple known as the 'Oratory of Phalaris', probably *c.* 100 BC; it measures 12.40 by 8.85 m. The temple was prostyle with four columns along the façade, and was erected on a platform (*podium*) in the Italic manner; its access staircase at the front has been robbed out. The pointed arch dates to the period of reuse of the structure as a Christian chapel in late medieval times. Antiquarians report that the temple had Ionic capitals; some fragments of Doric metopes and trigylphs from its entablature can be seen on the ground. The temple faced onto a paved square, now largely vanished, on which lay the temple's altar (left foreground) and a semi-circular *exedra* seat (bottom right). The piazza covered the superseded remains of a rock-cut *ekklesiasterion*, the seats of which are also visible.

The one category of building which does make a limited appearance in Sicily is the Italic-style *podium* temple, of which there are Hellenistic examples on the west side of the agora at Monte Iato, and on a lesser piazza (the 'Oratory of Phalaris') at Agrigento (Figure 4.22); furthermore there is numismatic evidence that the famous temple of Astarte Venus at Eryx also took the same form.[80] The last is no surprise: traditionally visited by Aeneas on the way to his destiny in Italy (one Roman version even claimed he was its founder), the cult was well known at Rome, where the alleged Trojan ancestry of the Elymians who cared for the Sicilian temple was also noted,

[80] Monte Iato: Daehn 1991. Agrigento: see notes 72 and 83. Erice: *RRC* 424 (57 BC). For discussion, cf. also R. Wilson 1990b: 74–5. The recent discovery, however, that the small Temple B at Selinus of *c.* 300 BC was also raised on a *podium* with frontal access (Marconi 2012: 279–82) raises the possibility of even earlier Italic influence on Sicily, or alternatively of a Hellenico-Punic Sicilian architect experimenting with an alternative temple form independent of Italian models.

and Diodorus reports on the latter's popularity with visiting Romans.[81] Whether the Romano-Italic form of the other two temples also betokens interventionist activity by Italian donors or merely the gradual absorption by local benefactors of new and different architectural ideas, coming to Sicily from outside, is harder to assess. It has been suggested on the basis of tile stamps that the Monte Iato temple might have been the gift of a Latin-speaking Roman magistrate, but this seems improbable.[82] The Agrigento temple, on the other hand, is a more likely candidate for outside benefaction, in that its ruins produced a Latin inscription.[83] This is itself a rarity in a city which, even when it became a *municipium* under Augustus, was capable of erecting inscriptions which translated into Greek the very Roman title of its chief magistracy (*duoviri*).[84] Yet for all the Roman form of these temples at Monte Iato and Agrigento, they use rubble fill rather than concrete in their *podia*, and the latter resorts to large-scale block technique in its construction, the same time-honoured building technique that Agrigentine architects had been using for centuries. It is in fact symptomatic of the continuing Hellenism of Hellenistic Sicily that Latin inscriptions until Augustan times are rare.[85]

[81] Diod. Sic. 4.83.6. On the Roman version, cf. Wiseman 2004: 165 ('since the Eryx cult had been founded by Aeneas for his goddess mother, she was really an ancestress of Rome'). A shrine of Venus Erycina was dedicated on the Capitoline in 215 BC (Livy 23.30.13–14; 23.31.9), and a temple allegedly copying the Sicilian one was dedicated in front of the Porta Collina in 181 BC (Livy 40.34.4). On the importance of the Trojan ancestry of the Elymians, cf. Sammartano 2003; Battistoni 2010: 117–27; and Prag 2011a.

[82] The tiles, used to roof the West Stoa (not *sensu stricto* the temple: Daehn 1991: 45), were stamped (in Latin, not Greek) *P I R* (the reading is completely clear: Müller 1976: 64–5 with Taf. 35–6). This has been taken to indicate that they were issued by P(ublius) R(upilius), consular governor of Sicily in 132/1 BC (Isler 2000a: 37, who reads the stamp as *P R*). *Pace* R. Wilson 1990b: 75, not only is the identification with the magistrate entirely conjectural, and in view of the presence of the letter 'I', implausible (cf. Daehn 1991: 135, n. 55: 'the connection with Publius Rupilius remains a conjecture'; see also Campagna 2007: 120, and Prag 2007a: 252, n. 28), but also it might be questioned whether a consul would have invested in tile-making facilities (stamping his own name, rather than 'official issue') during the short tenure of a Sicilian command concerned largely with quelling a slave revolt.

[83] *CIL* I^2.2649: [– – –]*ius M. f. Ter. Pius* | [– – –] *matrem suam*; P. Marconi 1929: 123, Fig. 77 (interpreting it as a *heroon*). De Miro 1988: 67–9, takes it as private and disassociates it from the temple (in the museum display it is treated as funerary). The inscription is certainly honorific (but the shape of the block excludes a statue base, unless it was set in masonry), and it might well therefore be associated with the temple (*pace* Campagna 2007: 119); Prag 2010b: 307 believes the man is 'presumably a resident Italian' (his tribe is the Teretina), and perhaps a *negotiator* in Agrigento. On the role of Italians in Sicily during the late Republic, cf. R. Wilson 1990a: 28–30 with references.

[84] *AE* 1966.168*bis*; *SEG* 46.1252 = *AE* 1996.809, with Fiorentini 2009: 85.

[85] Prag 2007a: 257–60 with earlier bibliography.

Figure 4.23 Marsala, part of the necropolis in via Fante on the north side of ancient Lilybaeum, with *epitymbia* marking the site of cremation burials. *Epitymbia* are grave monuments built in a stepped formation, on the uppermost level of which was set a vertical grave slab or some more elaborate form of grave marker (such as a stuccoed and painted *aedicula*). No such markers remain *in situ* in this photograph. Second century BC.

Another aspect of the island's Hellenism is the continuing vitality of that quintessentially Greek institution, the *gymnasium*, to which Jonathan Prag and Elena Mango have recently drawn attention.[86] So far from being in decline in Hellenistic Sicily, the *gymnasium* was flourishing, with over twenty examples attested on archaeological, literary and/or epigraphic grounds.[87] In addition to their traditional role as places of relaxation and exercise for the local elite, Prag has demonstrated that they also served in Sicily as recruiting and training grounds for citizen soldiery, a regular function also performed by *gymnasia* in the Greek East.[88] The case of the *gymnasium* reflects an important aspect of Rome's attitude towards its first province – a policy wherever possible of leaving long-hallowed institutions and practices well alone. *Gymnasia* in addition fulfilled a role in the service of Rome, by providing a pool of locally trained Sicilian militias to maintain law and order, so obviating the need (exceptional circumstances apart) for Roman garrisons.

Space precludes here a detailed appraisal of Sicilian burial customs in the third and second centuries BC, but one aspect of them which has clearly emerged from recent excavations is the near-ubiquity of the so-called *eptymbion* grave-marker (Figure 4.23). This term applies to a burial,

86 Prag 2007b: 87–96; Mango 2009. Cf. also, for a specifically Hieronian perspective, Ferruti 2004.

87 Prag 2007b: 89, n. 114 collects the evidence, to which add now, for the Agrigento gymnasium, Fiorentini 2009; cf. also the overview of Campagna 2006: 29–31.

88 Especially Prag 2007b: 90–3; cf. also Ma 2000b for a wider discussion of the importance of military activity for civic identity.

whether cremation or inhumation, marked on the surface by a square or rectangular base, on top of which is what is best described as a stepped pyramid; it comes in a number of slightly differing variants. Their use starts in the first half of the third century BC and continues into the first century BC. Extensive *epitymbia* necropoleis have been published in exemplary detail in recent years from places as far apart as Marsala on the westernmost point of Sicily, Cefalù in the middle of the north coast and Tripi (Abacaenum) in the north-east corner: it is clear, in fact, that they occur all over the island, from Hieron's kingdom in the East to the Carthaginian *epikrateia* in the West.[89] The form is usually seen as Alexandrian in inspiration, perhaps through the medium once again of Hieronian Syracuse (although some may predate his reign), and the type certainly occurs, although only in small numbers, in Alexandrian cemeteries such as El-Shabti and Khadrâ.[90] It is, however, so common and so universal in Hellenistic Sicily that it became something of a defining insular speciality in the funerary fashions of the middle class.

It would be wrong, however, to suggest that, with few exceptions, Hellenistic Sicily turned its back on the outside world and followed its own instincts; the true nature of the fabric of the island's cultural and artistic life at this period is probably far more nuanced than present evidence allows us to detect. We are, for example, very largely ignorant about major sculpture in the island during Hellenistic times – how much of it was carved locally and how much imported.[91] Certainly the island was in a key geographical position to take full advantage of pan-Mediterranean contacts, as on the small scale its material culture clearly demonstrates. To take just one example, imported artifacts from a single rubbish deposit of the second century BC at a low-status agricultural village at Campanaio (AG), just inland from Heraclea Minoa on the south coast, included wine amphorae from Rhodes, fragments of a brazier with Silenus heads from Cyrenaica and parts of a multi-stamped *mortarium* from North Africa, as

89 Marsala: Bechtold 1999, especially 37–47. Cefalù: Tullio 2009. Tripi (Abacaenum): Bacci and Coppolino 2009. They are also attested in Sicily at Syracuse, Lentini, Camarina, Butera, Centuripe, Morgantina, Lipari, Selinus, Entella, Monte Saraceno (Ravanusa) and Monte Riparato (Caltavuturo); Diod. Sic. (16.83.3) appears to mention them (bigger examples?) also at Agyrium (Agira).

90 Adriani 1966: 117–20 (no. 69), with Figs. K–M on 119; Tav. 39, Figs. 145–6 and Tav. 40, Fig. 149.

91 Overall surveys in (e.g.) Bonacasa 1996, 1999, 2008: 57–61; Bonacasa and Joly 1985: 277–332; Portale 2001–2; Portale *et al.* 2005: 110–14. For some fine photographs of relevant material in Syracuse Museum, Ciurcina 2006. For the general 'Greekness' of cultural horizons in Roman Republican Sicily, cf. Portale 2007b: 158–61.

well as oil amphorae made in Carthage;[92] while a distinctive decorated Spanish-made pottery, detected in an increasing number of Sicilian coastal towns, is a reminder of another important trade route about which we know little at this period, that between Sicily and the Iberian peninsula.[93]

Western Sicily

In the far west of the island, in the area of the former Carthaginian *epikrateia*, a further strand in the cultural make-up after 241 BC is detectable, namely the lingering influence of Phoenicio-Carthaginian culture.[94] The three key sites are Palermo (Panormus), Solunto (Soloeis/Soluntum) and Marsala (Lilybaeum), the last founded by Carthage after the destruction of Motya in 397 BC. The overall impression of Solunto, for example, is of a 'typical' Hellenistic 'Greek' town, with its agora, stoa, theatre, *bouleuterion* and peristyle houses; yet its inhabitants continued to bury their dead in Phoenicio-Carthaginian-style chamber tombs, approached down a staircase, as they had from the archaic period.[95] Solunto also contains, on the terrace behind the theatre, a striking example of what is almost certainly a Carthaginian-style sanctuary (Figure 4.24). It consists of a number of elongated individual cells (four in two pairs and one on its own), each with a rear area for the worship of separate divinities, and all set entirely at ground level – an arrangement so utterly different from both Greek and Roman cult practice; yet within one of these shrines was found a statue of a seated Zeus in rough provincial style which stylistically and culturally belongs to the Hellenistic 'Greek' world. The statue was carved *c.* 150 BC, probably contemporary with the building it adorned.[96] Also

[92] R. Wilson 2000c: 342–5 with Fig. 7. For trade links between western Sicily and North Africa at this period, cf. Bechtold 2007, especially 65–7; more generally Perkins 2007: 43–5 and 49. For an overview of pottery production and trade in Sicily in the third to first centuries BC, see now Malfitana 2011.

[93] Muscolino 2006; examples are known from Heraclea Minoa, Marsala, Tindari, Lipari and Taormina (the last in a second-century BC cistern deposit), and now also Pantelleria (Osanna *et al.* 2003: 93, Fig. 51 = Badisches Landesmuseum Karlsruhe 2004: 223, no. 9). On the relationship between Sicily and Iberia in general, although without reference to material culture of this date, see Anello and Martínez-Pinna 2006.

[94] For a fuller treatment of this topic, R. Wilson 2005. For an attempt to assess the rather elusive Punic character of rural settlement in western Sicily, see Spanò Giammellaro *et al.* 2008.

[95] Late Hellenistic tombs: Pace 1945: 713–14, with Fig. 196. Town in general: see note 67 above.

[96] R. Wilson 2005: 914–17; for the statue, R. Wilson 1990a: 26, Fig. 21, with earlier bibliography; R. Wilson 2013: no. 140 (no. 139 for the temple). For a rather different interpretation of the statue, cf. Tusa 2001. For a very different reading of this monument, cf. C. Albanese in Osanna and Torelli 2006: 177–92. Other late Punic temples are known in Sicily on Monte

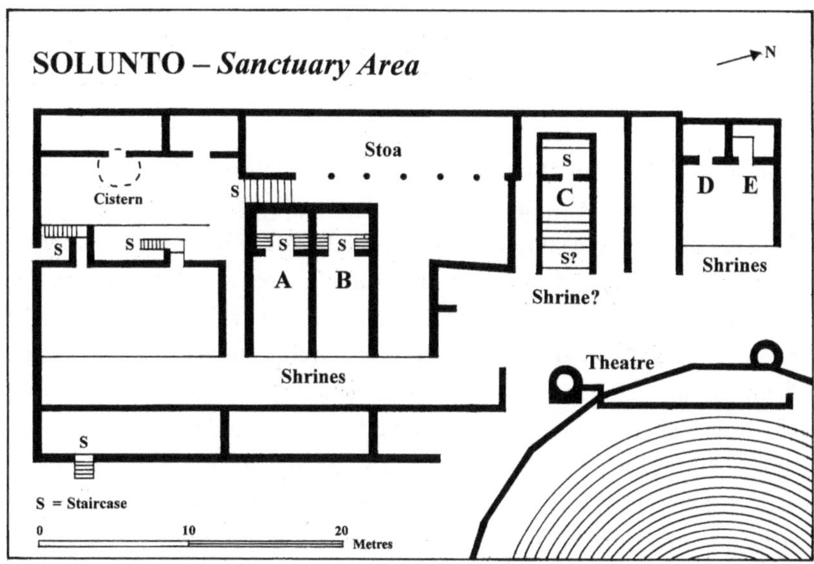

Figure 4.24 Solunto, plan of a Carthaginian-style sanctuary immediately west of the ancient theatre (which appears to encroach on the precinct's north-east corner, and so is later). It was first partly uncovered in the mid-nineteenth century and then completely in the 1960s. Within the complex are five elongated shrines (A–E), four arranged in pairs. All have a compartment at the far end in which a cult statue or statues were housed, usually on a raised shelf (in A and B reached by steps). Shrine A contained the statue of Zeus now in Palermo's Museo Archeologico Regionale, D produced a figure of Mercury, and E yielded a sixth-century BC statue of a seated and now headless female deity, clearly brought from the archaic city which lay on the plain by the sea below. Probably mid-second century BC.

at Solunto is a distinctive type of stone altar with three upright slabs, partitioning the horizontal main surface into two parts – closely paralleled by another example in Selinus during its period under Carthaginian control (pre-250 BC).[97] Other discoveries at Solunto further hint at its Phoenicio-Carthaginian origins – the use of *opus africanum* walling,

Adranone, a probable Carthaginian military fortress destroyed during the First Punic War: Fiorentini 1995, 1998; R. Wilson 2013: no. 142.

97 Tusa 1966. It is called the 'altar of the three betyls', but this is a misleading name: the uprights are not 'betyls' at all. The parallel with the Selinus altar appears valid, but altars normally stand in front of shrines, and given the topography (there is steeply rising ground to the west), it is hard to see what the original arrangement was. The surrounding wall contains reused material (including a new inscription honouring Sextus Peducaeus as *propraetor*: Calascibetta and Di Leonardo 2012) and so cannot be earlier than 76/5 BC, the date of his praetorship; so an earlier lay-out may have been substantially different. Doubt has, however, been expressed to me as to whether this is a religious structure at all.

consisting of orthostats at intervals that separate coursed rubble walling;[98] the so-called symbol of Tanit on a pair of Hellenistic-period altars, a symbol which also occurs frequently in contemporary Lilybaeum and is attested in Sicily at least until the late first century BC, on the city coinage of Cossyra (Pantelleria);[99] the use of the typically Carthaginian round-ended cistern, for example under the Casa di Leda at Solunto (Figure 4.25), and now also attested in numerous examples (of the second century BC) on the acropolis at Pantelleria;[100] the indirect route into some houses at Solunto where the principal rooms are out of sight from the street, reflecting a typically 'private' Carthaginian approach to domestic architecture;[101] and most significant of all, perhaps, the countless pavements, both here and all over Hellenistic Sicily, of *opus signinum*, with or without inlaid *tessera* decoration (Figure 4.26). This style of flooring, Cato's *pavimenta punica*, was almost certainly invented in Carthage in the late fourth century BC; it is present at Carthaginian-controlled Selinus by the first half of the third century, and then rapidly spreads to the rest of Hellenistic Sicily, whence to Campania and eventually Rome and elsewhere in central Italy.[102] This is a further example of Hellenistic Sicily acting as an important conduit for the dissemination of new ideas, albeit in this case one not of Sicilian origin.

Another legacy of Carthaginian domination in western Sicily was language. Punic inscriptions continue into the second century BC, and to a lesser extent later too, and Punic was spoken, in the countryside at least, into the second century AD, if Apuleius is to be believed.[103] But at Lilybaeum, for example, Greek had replaced Punic epigraphically by 150/100 BC, even if

[98] R. Wilson 2005: 913–14, with Fig. 9; cf. also Fentress, Chapter 6, this volume (for the use of *opus africanum* in general in the Hellenistic West).

[99] R. Wilson 2005: 909–11, with references. One of the altars is Badisches Landesmuseum Karlsruhe 2004: 205, no. 61. Cossura coin: *RPC* I, no. 675.

[100] Solunto: Cutroni Tusa *et al.* 1994: Tav. 10, 16 and 31 (also in the 'Casa delle due cisterne' and the 'Bottega artigianale con abitazione'); for other Sicilian examples of this type of Hellenistic date at Marsala and Mozia, R. Wilson 2000a: 12 and 2005: 913, with references. Pantelleria: Osanna *et al.* 2003: 69, Fig. 13; 70, Fig. 16; and 81, Fig. 31; Osanna 2006: 38–40, with Figs. 7–9. On the close commercial links between Pantelleria and Carthage, hardly surprising for an island physically closer to North Africa than to Sicily, see Cerasetti 2000.

[101] E.g. in the 'Casa del Cerchio in Mosaico' (R. Wilson 2005: 913, Fig. 7), 'Casa del vano circolare', 'Casa del deposito a volta', and the 'Casa delle ghirlande': Cutroni Tusa *et al.* 1994: Tav. 12, 13, 24 and 35. For the notion of privacy in Punic houses, Daniels 1995.

[102] K. Dunbabin 1999: 20 and 101–3; Cato *apud* Festus, *De verb. sig.* 282 L. On *opus signinum* pavements in Sicily, see Joly 1997; (for Solunto) C. Greco 1997; (for Morgantina) Tsakirgis 1990; cf. also the comments of Tsakirgis 2009: 117–18, Wolf 2003: 60, and Fentress, Chapter 6, this volume.

[103] Cf. Prag, this volume. Punic inscriptions in Sicily: Amadasi Guzzo 1967. *Trilingues*: Apul. *Met.* 11.5 (the third language after Greek and Latin must surely be intended here as Punic, since Elymian, Sikan, Sikel, etc. had disappeared long before the Hellenistic period, let alone the Empire).

Figure 4.25 Solunto, House of the Leda, round-ended water cistern originally underlying the east side of the house's peristyle, from the south. It is 3 m wide and 12 m long. Second century BC.

Punic nomenclature lingers on for a while in some Greek texts. Documents of late Hellenistic date such as a *tessera hospitalis* naming Imulch Inibalos Chloros, or a lead *defixio* mentioning Agbor Bouki(os?), husband of Barbara Lollia (Figure 4.27), are witnesses of an essentially mixed Helleno-Punic population which had also by *c.* 100 BC (?) adopted a range of Latin or Italic names as well;[104] while a funerary marker of the same date has a painted text recording Achilles, son of Prothymos, accompanied by a pair of open hands, a well-known attribute of Carthaginian *stelai* in Carthage (but only occasionally elsewhere in North Africa) prior to 146 BC.[105] There is also a

[104] *IG* XIV.279 = C. Di Stefano 1984: 124, no. 153 with Fig. 70 (*tessera*); *SEG* 34.953 = C. Di Stefano 1984: 163–4, no. 185, here Fig. 4.27 (*defixio*), republished in Curbera 1997; cf. also Curbera 1999: 181, no. 49, with further references.

[105] *SEG* 34.955 = 39.1005 = C. Di Stefano 1984: 175, no. 191, with Fig. 95; cf. R. Wilson 2005: 911, with Fig. 6. For examples of Punic *stelai* in Carthage decorated with a single hand, cf. Brown 1991: 96, with Figs. 11, 14–17, 20–4, 26–35, 37, 39, 42; examples with a pair of hands: Brown 1991: Fig. 39.564; Moscati 1988a: 615–16, nos. 185 and 192.

Figure 4.26 Solunto, House of the Harpocrates, *opus signinum* floor with inlaid decoration in white *tesserae*. The room, which measures 3.55 m by 3.75 m, opens directly onto a small peristyle court at the heart of the house. Probably second or early first century BC. *In situ.*

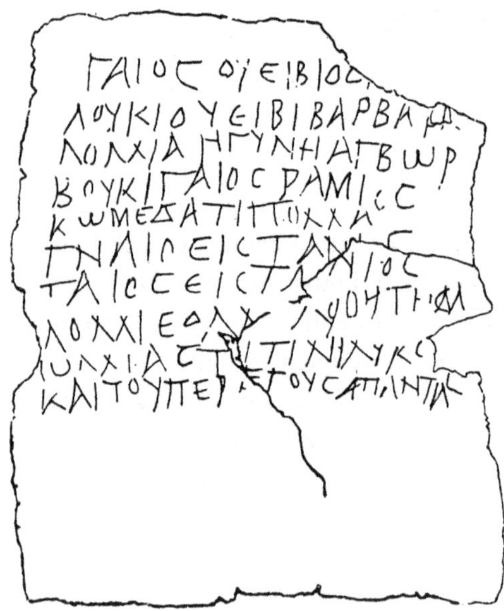

Figure 4.27 Marsala, lead *defixio* (curse tablet) found in a tomb, *c.* 100 BC (or later?). It reads 'Gaios Vibios (son of?) Loukios Vibi(os), Barbara Lollia, wife of Agbor Bouki(os?), Gaios Ramios, Komedia Tittolla (?), Gnaio(s) Eistanios, Gaios Eistanios, Lollia Allia (mother of?) Lollia, Titini(os?) Luko[. . .] and all those in addition to them.' The names listed appear to be the inscriber's opponents (and so to be cursed), possibly in a case of litigation. The final line, reading *autous* for *etous*, is a 'catch-all' formula, known from other *defixiones*, to ensure that no-one is omitted. Height: 11 cm; width: 9 cm.

hint that the Punic cubit as a basic unit of measurement continued to be used in western Sicily for some time after 241 BC, presumably because that is what local architects and their forebears had been used to employing for centuries, and saw no reason to change.[106] All these instances and many more are reminders that three and a half centuries of Phoenician and then Carthaginian culture were not obliterated at a stroke by the island's political transfer to Roman hegemony.

Hellenistic Sicily, then, is a fascinating, eclectic melting-pot of cultures, hardly surprising in view of its central geographical position in the Graeco-Roman world. There is little sign of a pan-Sicilian identity emerging at this time under the aegis of Rome; the mentality of an island made up of individual city-states was not changed overnight.[107] Sicily undoubtedly drew its cultural diversity from its multifarious contacts around the Mediterranean, but such was its strength of character and its ability to innovate during the Hellenistic period that it rarely copied slavishly from elsewhere, forging instead its own distinctive, regional and sub-regional identities.

[106] E.g. the second-century BC rebuilding of Solunto continued to use the Punic cubit in the layout of the *insulae*: C. Greco 2005: 18. For the use of the Punic cubit in the layout of Lilybaeum, Caruso 2003: 177; 2005: especially 777–82.

[107] Cf. especially Prag 2009b; also Perkins 2007: 34–6 and 49–52.

5 Trading across the Syrtes: Euesperides and the Punic world

ANDREW WILSON

Introduction

Interaction between the Greek and Punic worlds is usually treated along the axis of contact between Sicily and Carthage; accounts of contact between the Punic sphere and the Greek world of the eastern Mediterranean are few.[1] I review here the evidence from recent excavations at Euesperides in Libya that indicate a considerable degree of contact, both in terms of trade and the transmission of technologies, between Greek-speaking Cyrenaica and the central and western Mediterranean, and in particular between Cyrenaica and Punic-speaking North Africa. Euesperides is an important case-study for contacts between the eastern and western Mediterranean in the Hellenistic period because the excavations have focused on reconstructing trading relations by provenancing the pottery (transport amphorae, fine painted pottery and cooking wares) found at the site and analysing the relative proportions of different kinds of imports and local wares. This approach, while common in other periods of archaeology, has almost never been applied to Classical or Hellenistic Greek sites in the eastern Mediterranean, with the result that our understanding of long-distance trading relations and contacts in the Hellenistic world often rests on poor foundations. Euesperides may be unique in the degree of attention paid to what its ceramic assemblage can tell us about trading links, but this chapter argues that the pattern of contacts it shows is unlikely to be unique for the Hellenistic Mediterranean.

Euesperides was the most westerly of the Greek settlements in Cyrenaica, and now lies within the suburbs of the modern town of Benghazi (Figure 5.1). It stood on the edge of a lagoon, now filled in, which formerly connected with the sea. The ancient nucleus of the city is a low artificial tell mound over a slight rise in bedrock, with an extension onto low-lying ground to the south (Figure 5.2). In antiquity the city was associated with the Gardens of the Hesperides, which were identified by authors from Pseudo-Scylax onwards

[1] Though see Wolff 1986 for imported Greek amphorae in Punic Carthage, Zimmerman Munn 2003 for Punic imports to Corinth from the western Mediterranean and Wolff 2004 for a first survey of Punic amphorae in the eastern Mediterranean.

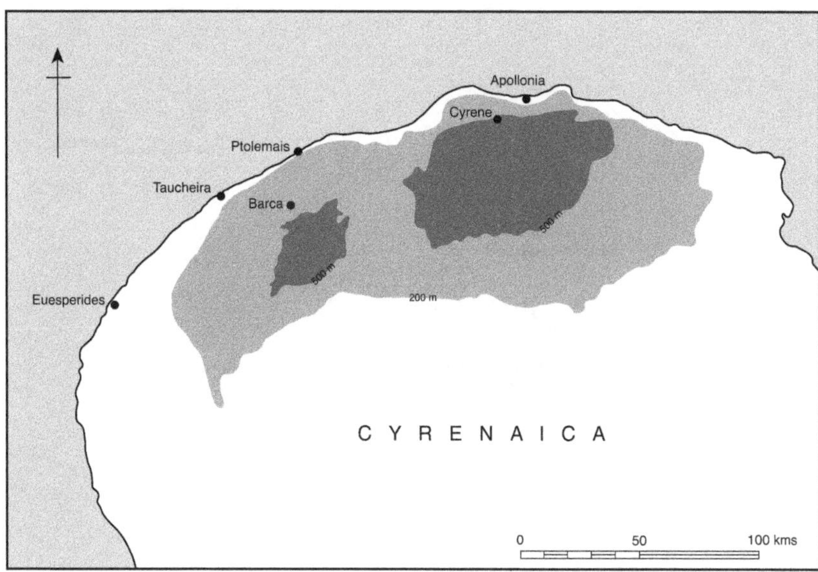

Figure 5.1 The location of Euesperides.

with a series of natural features just to the east: the drab monotony of the Benghazi coastal plain, with its thin scattering of terra rossa soil barely covering the limestone bedrock, is punctuated by a series of large sinkholes or dolines, sunk some 10 m into the limestone bedrock, in which vegetation grows lushly.[2] Together with the chain of coastal lagoons at Benghazi which offered a natural anchorage, the Gardens must have been a principal factor in attracting the Greek colonists who settled at Euesperides, somewhere around 580 BC, to this particular part of the Cyrenaican coast.

The earliest pottery from the site is dated *c*. 580–560 BC, consistent perhaps with Herodotus' account of a second wave of Cyrenaican colonisation at this period.[3] Euesperides is mentioned occasionally in ancient sources, often in the context of power struggles with Cyrene or conflict with the local Nasamones tribe.[4] Gylippus and a Spartan fleet passed by Euesperides after being blown off course in 414 BC on their way to Sicily, and helped to lift a siege by the Nasamones.[5] The city sided with Thibron against Cyrene when he invaded Cyrenaica in 323 BC, and found itself on the losing side in the following year.[6] The site was abandoned in the middle of the third century – the abundant coin record abruptly stops with the

[2] Stucchi 1976. [3] Hdt. 4.159.1–4, which seems to refer principally to Cyrene.

[4] For summaries of the literary, epigraphic and numismatic evidence for the history of Euesperides, see Vickers *et al.* 1994; J. Lloyd *et al.* 1995; A. Wilson *et al.* 1999; Göransson 2007: 32–5.

[5] Thuc. 7.50. [6] Diod. Sic. 18.19-21; cf. Laronde 1987: 41–84.

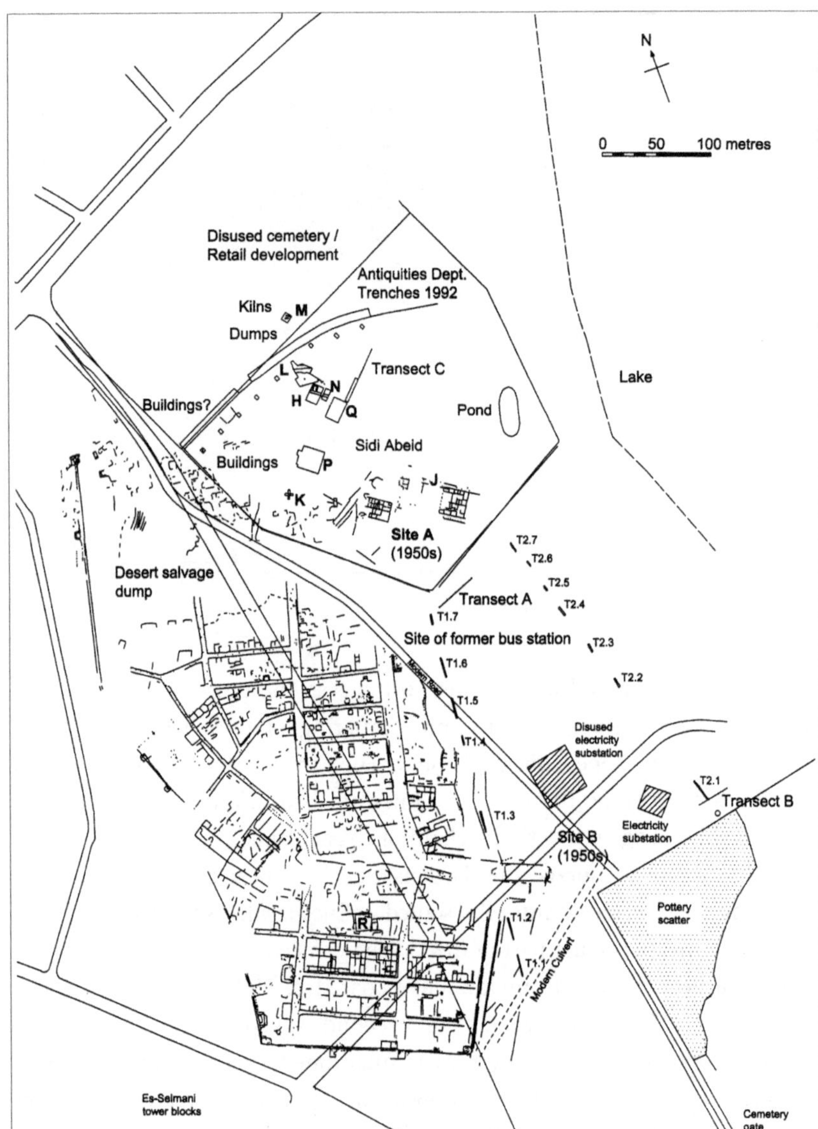

Figure 5.2 Plan of Euesperides, showing location of excavated trenches.

death of Magas, governor of Ptolemaic Cyrenaica, variously dated 258 or 250 BC – and the population was transferred to a new city just 2.5 km away, named Berenice.[7] A combination of historical and archaeological evidence suggests that this move may have been a reprisal against the city by Queen Berenice (Magas' daughter, and eventually the wife of Ptolemy II) for

[7] Bond and Swales 1965; Laronde 1987: 390–4, 405–6; Buttrey 1994.

opposing her during the power struggles which followed the death of Magas.[8] There was no subsequent ancient occupation of Euesperides, and all the material thus pre-dates the mid-third century. It is a rare example of a site where one can investigate Classical and Hellenistic deposits without an overburden of Roman and medieval levels.

The site of Euesperides was identified in 1948 from an RAF air photo which showed the ancient street grid in the Lower City.[9] Various investigations were made in the 1950s and 1960s, including excavations by the Ashmolean Museum and Barri Jones, which are unpublished except for brief preliminary reports.[10] Euesperides had already suffered badly in the twentieth century from stone-robbing in the late Ottoman period and the expansion of an Islamic cemetery over the tell mound in the 1930s; in 1951 the Municipality of Benghazi bulldozed away part of the tell to fill in the salt lagoons. Later a makeshift bus station occupied part of the site, and workshops were built on the north-west part of the city, while rubbish is dumped and burned on the Lower City to this day. In the 1990s an illegal attempt to build a shopping centre on the northern part of the site led to the Libyan Department of Antiquities inviting the Society for Libyan Studies to undertake work at the site; the Society organised a survey of the site in 1994, followed by a programme of excavations directed by John Lloyd from 1995–8 to prove the extent and significance of the archaeology there.[11] A large amount of pottery was recovered, and this and other evidence raised further questions about the city's economy.[12] Accordingly, after John Lloyd's project was completed in 1998, Paul Bennett of Canterbury Archaeological Trust and I, together with Ahmed Buzaian of Gar Younis University, put together a proposal for new work. Our principal aims included the investigation of living conditions, diet and urban infrastructure, and the examination of evidence for the city's economy and trading links, which will be my focus in this chapter.[13]

Our excavations, which ran from 1999 until 2006,[14] focused on three trenches (P, Q and R), including areas of domestic housing, urban defences, part of a set of Hellenistic public baths and areas devoted to purple dye production using *Murex trunculus* shellfish.[15] The excavations were

[8] Laronde 1987: 395–6; A. Wilson 2005. [9] Goodchild 1952.
[10] Vickers *et al.* 1994; G. Jones 1983, 1985. [11] Hayes and Mattingly 1995.
[12] J. Lloyd *et al.* 1995; Buzaian and Lloyd 1996; J. Lloyd *et al.*1998.
[13] Interim reports each year in *Libyan Studies* from 1999 to 2006.
[14] The excavations were funded by the Society for Libyan Studies and the Craven Committee of the University of Oxford, with a grant towards the 2000 season from the Oppenheim Foundation, and support in kind from the Department of Antiquities of Libya and from Gar Younis University, Benghazi.
[15] *Murex* processing: A. Wilson *et al.* 2004: 165–9; A. Wilson and Tébar Megías 2008.

supplemented by a programme of surface investigation across the remainder of the site, and some environmental coring work. Since a particular focus of the project was the investigation of the city's economy and trading contacts, the pottery was provenanced by petrological analysis of the clays used and quantified to assess the relative proportions of different types of ceramic goods and containers coming from different regions of the Mediterranean in different periods.

Euesperides and trading contact with the wider world

Prior to our excavations, knowledge of Cyrenaica's contacts with the central and western Mediterranean in the Hellenistic period was scant; indeed, this was true generally of relations between the eastern and western Mediterranean. One inscription from Euesperides known since the 1920s and published by Peter Fraser in 1951 is a decree of the city's *boule* honouring two *proxenoi* from Syracuse, Eubios son of Eubios, and Hagestratos son of Moschion (both otherwise unknown).[16] Fraser, who dated it to the second half of the fourth century BC on grounds of lettering and the simplicity of the honorific formula, comments: 'Our proxeny-decree testifies to contacts between the city and the outside world, though a picture of political relations (into which it would be tempting to introduce Agathocles) between Euesperides and Syracuse cannot be built on a single proxeny-decree.'[17]

Strabo reports that the Greeks used to exchange silphium juice mixed with bran for Punic wine at Charax, a station half-way along the coast of the Syrtic gulf.[18] But a study by André Laronde in 1990 of the material evidence then available for trade between Cyrenaica and Punic Tripolitania or Tunisia concluded that any such exchange must have been comparatively unimportant as there was little or no archaeological evidence for trading contact between the two regions across the Syrtic Gulf.[19] Fulford's study of trade in the late Hellenistic and Roman period also concluded that there was little direct interchange of goods between Cyrenaica and Tripolitania.[20] The material from our recent excavations, however, changes this picture radically, and it is to that material that I now turn.

[16] Fraser 1951; *SEG* 18.772: Ἐφόρων καὶ γερόντων | ἐπαγόντων, ἅδε τᾶι βωλᾶι | Εὔβιον Εὐβιότω, Ἁγέστ-|ρατον Μοσχίωνος, Συρ-|ρακοσίος, Εὐσπεριτᾶν | προξένος ἦμεν αὐτὸς | καὶ ἐκγόνος. Fraser refers to the inscription's whereabouts as unknown; we have located it in a Cyrene storeroom.

[17] Fraser 1951: 133–5, 140; cf. also *SEG* 40.1594 on numismatic and epigraphic evidence for contacts between Cyrene and Sicily.

[18] Strabo 17.3.20. [19] Laronde 1990. [20] Fulford 1989.

Coins

Coinage is not generally a good indicator of long-distance trade; merchants will typically use the cash they receive for one cargo to buy another in the same port, so the coins themselves need not travel far. This is especially true of the Ptolemaic empire, which seems to have operated as a closed-currency zone with foreign coin being exchanged at the ports. Even within the Ptolemaic empire, Cyrenaica seems to have been a separate currency area; at Euesperides and other cities of the Pentapolis, Ptolemaic coins from Egypt are absent, and almost all the coins are local, Cyrenaican issues. Foreign coin must have been exchanged and remelted to produce local coinage.[21]

It is perhaps significant therefore that of 362 catalogued ancient coins predating the city's abandonment, five Carthaginian coins are found which have slipped through the moneychangers' net; this compares with one of Aegina, one of Athens, one of Croton and two from unidentified non-Cyrenaican mints.[22] All the remaining 352 coins are Cyrenaican.[23] Two of the Carthaginian coins are dated 370–340 BC, and the other three date from the late fourth or early third century BC. They are certainly suggestive of contact with the Punic world, and the single coin of Croton hints at links with Magna Graecia, but they are too few to allow conclusions to be drawn. We need to turn instead to other categories of evidence.

Pottery

Pottery of course has considerable potential for illustrating trade; it is not biodegradable and so survives well, even if broken, and the geographical origin can frequently be indicated or pinpointed by petrological study of the mineral inclusions in the clay. Despite this, its potential for illuminating Classical and Hellenistic trade remains underdeveloped; most attention has been paid to typological studies of fineware shapes, attempts to attribute decorated vases to particular painters, and a long-running debate over the value of Greek painted pottery ('fineware') in antiquity.[24] While it is widely recognised that Attic pottery achieved a widespread distribution, there is no

[21] Cf. A. Wilson *et al.* 2002: 116; A. Wilson *et al.* 2004: 187.

[22] The total of 362 coins combines the coins from the surface collection by Bond and Swales in the 1960s (Bond and Swales 1965) and the excavations between 1994 and 2005.

[23] The coins have been studied by T. Buttrey, who has prepared reports for the final publication.

[24] E.g. Vickers 1985; Boardman 1988a, 1988b; Gill 1988, 1991.

comprehensive study of that distribution, nor has the phenomenon been coherently integrated into larger attempts at analysing Classical or Hellenistic economies. The position one takes on the debate over the value of Attic finewares is important here; is this a luxury trade, and so of minor overall significance? Alternatively, what are the implications for the scale and importance of trade if such pottery is not thought to be very valuable? It seems that many scholars would now accept some version of the position which downplays the value of Attic pottery – and especially black glaze pottery – in antiquity; but the corollary does not seem to have been followed through: if relatively low-value pottery is so widespread, it will hardly have been traded as entire shiploads for its own sake. Rather, it is more likely that it travelled as part-cargoes with other goods, and could thus act as a proxy indicator of the movement of much larger and economically more important trade flows of goods which are not usually traceable in the archaeological record, such as textiles, hides, grain, timber and slaves. Abundant finds of imported pottery should therefore indicate abundant shipping. Some light may be shed on this by examining fineware distributions in the context of the distribution of other kinds of pottery.

But if the potential contribution of fineware studies to the understanding of the economy of the Greek world has not been fully realised, this is all the more true of studies of amphorae and coarsewares (unpainted pottery, including plain table wares and cooking vessels), which have been comparatively neglected for the Classical and Hellenistic periods. The state of Greek amphora studies in the second decade of the twenty-first century resembles that of Roman amphora studies in the early 1970s before the publication of John Riley's work on the amphorae from Berenice/Benghazi, while the situation for Classical and Hellenistic Greek coarsewares is perhaps closer to that of Roman coarse pottery studies in the 1950s.[25] It is impossible to find a publication of a site of Classical or early Hellenistic date in the eastern Mediterranean where the finewares, coarsewares and transport amphorae have been published as quantified and provenanced assemblages. Instead, one finds purely typological studies, such as the Athenian Agora reports, in which selected finewares (selected on no clear principle) are presented.[26] Amphora stamps, or complete amphorae, may also be published, but not the fragmentary rims, handles and bases which are nevertheless diagnostic of particular types or forms. Coarsewares or cooking

[25] Riley 1979.

[26] E.g. Athenian Agora: Sparkes and Talcott 1970; Rotroff 1997. Cyrene: Schaus 1985: xxi–xxii, 1–2 (sherds selected on basis of preservation; test quantification conducted on 4,014 sherds from just 1 m^3 of excavated deposit).

wares are usually ignored. Although Martin Millett in 1979 wrote that quantification was 'what should be expected in any pottery report as a minimum standard', none of the pottery reports available for eastern Mediterranean sites of this period that I have seen satisfies this basic criterion.[27] Put another way, no research excavation on a Classical or early Hellenistic site in the eastern Mediterranean has yet published its pottery in a manner that would meet even the most elementary requirements of a report on a rescue excavation conducted on a Romano-British site in the last twenty years. This regrettable state of affairs means that one can gain no clear picture of the proportions of local to imported wares, and hence of the importance of trade in any of these categories of ceramic materials, at any eastern Mediterranean site other than Euesperides and its successor Berenice. I labour this point because it is important to understand the limitations of the currently published archaeological material for constructing wider historical pictures; the regionally bounded models of Hellenistic economies currently in vogue among many ancient historians have been developed without an awareness of how much of the material evidence for long-distance exchange has not been properly studied or published.[28] If the study of the ancient Greek economy is ever to make any real progress, there is an urgent need for archaeologists working on the Classical Greek and Hellenistic periods to acquaint themselves with what their colleagues in other periods and regions do with pottery assemblages.

One of the aims of the excavations at Euesperides was therefore to analyse the pottery as a quantified set of assemblages that could inform us about the nature and characteristics of the city's trading relations over time. Our analysis relied heavily on petrological studies of pottery fabrics that examined the composition of the clay used to discriminate between local production and imports. The geology of Cyrenaica is characterised by limestones and coastal dune sandstones, overlain by terra rossa and marl clays rich in microfossils. There are no volcanic elements in the local rocks, and gold mica and ferrous particles are lacking; pottery containing such inclusions must therefore be imported. Pottery may be quantified in several different ways: by count or weight of all pieces (rims, bases, handles and sherds – RBHS), or just of diagnostic pieces (rims, bases, handles – RBH); by estimated vessel equivalents (EVEs) based on the proportion of rim diameters present, or minimum numbers of individual vessels (MNI).[29] Typically, RBH counts will have

[27] Millett 1979.

[28] E.g. Reger 1994; Archibald 2001: 259 notes the paucity of studies of long-distance contacts in the Hellenistic period.

[29] Orton and Tyers 1990; Orton 1993; Orton *et al.* 1993; Swift 2006: 61–3.

fewer unidentified pieces, but, especially in relatively small samples, RBHS counts may give a better idea of the full range of wares present, as they may include body sherds in fabrics not represented in the diagnostic rims, bases and handles. Test analyses on the coarseware assemblages suggested that the coarsewares showed broadly consistent relationships between the different quantification indices, and this may be more generally true within individual ceramic categories (finewares, coarsewares and amphorae), though not of course when comparing amphorae with finewares, where for example the much greater thickness of amphora sherds than finewares would create a bias when measuring by weight.[30] For this reason, and because they may have had different trading patterns, finewares, amphorae and coarsewares are analysed separately. In advance of the final publication of the material, my discussion here draws heavily on the work of the project's pottery specialists: Eleni Zimi (fine pottery), Kristian Göransson (amphorae) and Keith Swift (coarsewares), and predominantly reports quantification by count of all sherds and of diagnostic pieces (RBHS and RBH).[31]

Finewares

Eleni Zimi's preliminary analysis suggests that during the fifth century BC and into the fourth century Attic black glaze wares account for some 80 per cent of the total finewares at Euesperides (by count of RBHS). Local production accounts for less than 10 per cent, whether measured by total sherd count or weight. By the last quarter of the fourth century the number of non-Attic imports rises, especially from Corinth and, increasingly, from southern and central Italy.

The changes in the proportions of imports from Athens and other areas in the early Hellenistic period, however, remain difficult to track in chronological detail, owing to problems with the dating of Attic black glazed wares. The importance of Athens in fineware production, coupled with the longevity of excavations (since 1931) at the Athenian Agora, has lent the publications of the Agora excavations an extraordinary influence in studies of ancient Greek pottery. The chronology for Hellenistic Attic black glaze

[30] Swift 2006: 62–3.

[31] Annual reports on the pottery have appeared in the interim reports on the project in *Libyan Studies* between 1999 and 2006; the amphorae from the excavations up until 2005 are published in preliminary form in Kristian Göransson's doctoral thesis at Lund University (Göransson 2007; cf. also Göransson 2004), while a preliminary treatment of the coarsewares is given in Keith Swift's unpublished Oxford doctoral thesis (Swift 2006). Volumes on the different classes of pottery are in preparation.

proposed by Susan Rotroff in *Agora* XXIX is widely – and often uncritically – used, but has serious flaws. Not only does it rely on the inherently implausible assumption that all shapes evolved at a uniform rate (e.g. from short and fat to tall and thin),[32] but many of the key contexts from outside the Agora used as supposedly fixed points to establish the chronology are not secure.[33] Furthermore, the use of the Agora contexts themselves to provide a chronological framework is suspect.[34] Rotroff tends to date a context by assigning dates on stylistic grounds to the bulk of the material in it, but often treats the latest material as intrusive, rather than as providing a *terminus post quem* for the formation of the deposit as one would normally do. Worryingly, most deposits she lists contain material she regards as intrusive.[35] If the material is really intrusive, this would be an alarming comment on the quality of the Agora excavations, or on errors made in mixing the material from contexts during processing; it would vitiate the stratigraphic integrity of most contexts excavated at the Agora. Alternatively, if the late material is not in fact intrusive, it serves to give a *terminus post quem* for the context, and Rotroff has probably dated the material too early, unless one wishes to regard the bulk of each context as heavily residual (i.e. containing a lot of material redeposited from earlier layers). The upshot of all this is that pottery forms that she dates as 325–300 BC could well go down to 250 BC – and indeed, at Euesperides, Attic black glaze in such forms commonly occurs in stratified contexts dated by coins minted between 280–250 BC, although black glaze forms that would be dated after 300 on the *Agora* XXIX chronology are rare.

It is undeniable, however, that in the third century BC southern Italy had become increasingly important as a supplier of fineware. The south Italian imports include red figure pottery, a number of examples of 'Gnathia' ware, the Italian version of Attic West Slope technique painted pottery, and pre-Campana black glaze vessels such as a ribbed small bowl from the fill of a well in Area Q that was probably filled when the site was abandoned (Figure 5.3). There are also central Italian black glaze pots from the *petits*

32 Rotroff 1997: 8–9, 24–5; deposit summaries: 431–73.

33 E.g. Rotroff wishes to consider all material from Olynthos as dating before the sack of the city by Philip II in 348 BC, and attempts to ignore later occupation which might take some of the pottery there down to 316 BC; and she considers material from phase III of the Pnyx in Athens as a closed deposit dating to the fourth century BC, ignoring the Roman pottery which either dates the phase to the third century AD or indicates extensive disturbance vitiating the material's utility as dating evidence from a sealed context: Rotroff 1997: 18–23.

34 For an extraordinary discussion of the manner in which the excavators of the Agora have sometimes rewritten their stratigraphy, inventing or removing layers based on preconceived views of pottery dates, see Rotroff 2005.

35 Some examples from many: D–E 8–9:1; E 3:1; E 14:1, lower fill; H 16:3 north chamber; J 5:1, V.

Figure 5.3 Pre-Campana Italian black glaze small bowl with inturned rim and ribbing on exterior, found in a well in Area Q filled when the site was abandoned in the mid-third century BC. For colour version see plate section.

estampilles workshop near Rome (Figure 5.4). The fineware picture thus suggests an opening up of trade contacts towards the central Mediterranean in the late fourth and early third centuries BC. This is consonant with the recognised distribution of red figure and Gnathia wares to Greece and the Aegean in the early Hellenistic period, and the demise in the importance of Attic black glaze exports; but further work is needed on quantification and chronology to gauge the extent and rate of this shift.[36]

Transport amphorae

The evidence of transport amphorae helps here. Much still remains to be done on Greek amphorae; we have only a fairly basic understanding of regional typologies, many common classes of material are poorly studied, and Whitbread's excellent book remains the only serious work on fabric petrology, though it deals only with some of the more common types.[37] Moreover, since little residue analysis has been done, the contents of particular amphora types tend to be identified via a simplistic equation in which a type is identified with a region, that region is said by one or two literary sources to be renowned for wine, *ergo* that amphora type is a wine amphora. In the case of Koan, Knidian, Rhodian and Thasian amphorae this is probably correct, but in other cases one might wish for more evidence. The result is also a surprisingly low incidence of recognised olive-oil amphorae (Corinthian A; Samos); and

[36] Distribution is impressionistic, owing to the lack of proper distribution studies, but includes a very limited amount of Gnathia ware and Campanian black glaze at Athens: Rotroff 1997: 221.

[37] Whitbread 1995.

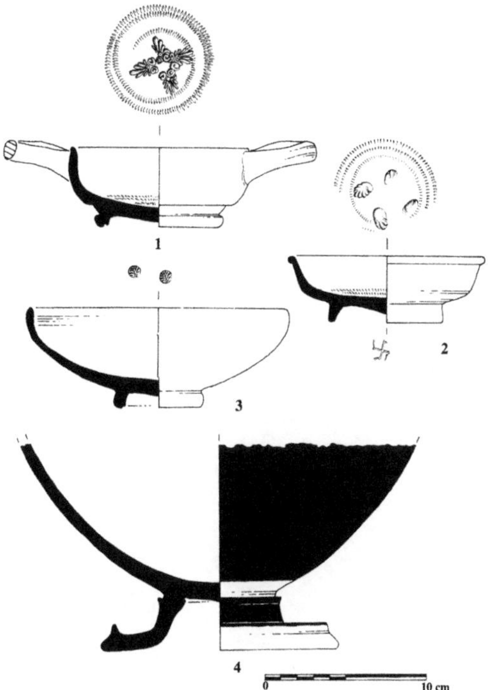

Figure 5.4 Italian black glazed pottery from the assemblage lying on the floor of Room 5, Area P, sealed by the mud brick collapse of the penultimate phase between 261 and 250 BC. Nos 1–3 from the *petits estampilles* workshop near Rome:
(1) Bolsal cup with four stamped palmettes within rouletting on interior.
(2) Shallow bowl with four palmettes within rouletting on interior.
(3) Echinus deep bowl with narrow foot and four free palmettes on interior.
(4) South Italian bolster or lug-handled krater with moulded foot.

despite the identification of fish remains in a Black Sea amphora, no Greek amphora type from the Aegean has yet been identified as carrying salted fish.[38] This can hardly represent the full picture.

Despite these uncertainties, we can still make a lot of progress. Like the other pottery, most of our amphorae come from occupation deposits in houses, levelling or make-up layers in construction deposits, street refuse deposits, or the rubbish dump in the quarry in Area Q. The vast majority are therefore represented by broken sherds – in most cases, not even the diagnostic sherds of rims, bases or handles that can be assigned to known forms. We have to proceed therefore by using the fabric of stamped handles or distinctive bases or rims from forms whose origin is known to create control groups that we know came from particular regions, against which,

[38] Lund and Gabrielsen 2005: 164.

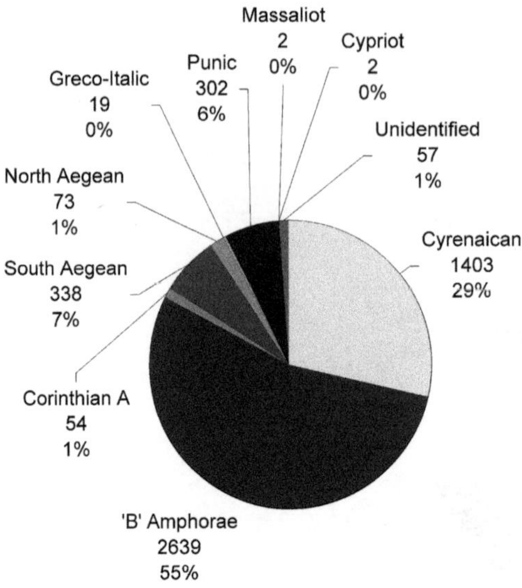

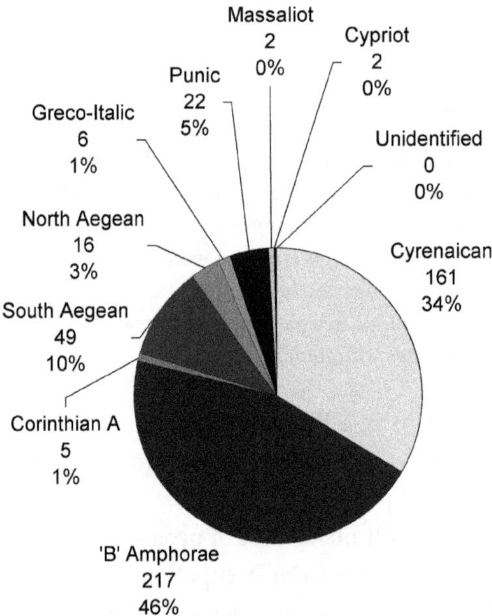

Figure 5.5 Relative proportions of amphorae from different regions in selected fully quantified early Hellenistic contexts (*c.* 325–250 BC) from Areas P and Q at Euesperides: (a) all sherds (RBHS; total = 4889); (b) diagnostic sherds only (RBH; total = 480).

and in combination with Whitbread's descriptions, fabrics from non-diagnostic body sherds can be matched. The relative proportions of amphorae from different regions, from selected well-stratified contexts of early Hellenistic date in Areas P and Q, are shown in Figure 5.5 both by total sherd count (RBHS) and by diagnostic pieces (RBH). The two different quantification indices show broadly similar pictures, the main differences being caused by the difficulty of assigning some body sherds to North Aegean, South Aegean or Greco-Italic groups.

Imports outnumber Cyrenaican amphorae. We have many of the expected types from the Aegean – the assemblage is dominated by the so-called 'Corinthian B' type amphorae (55 per cent by RBHS count; 48 per cent by RBH), which were not in fact made in Corinth at all, but on Corcyra, and also in Sicily, although we have not as yet identified any definitely Sicilian variants at Euesperides. There are also numerous wine amphorae from the south-west Aegean – Chian, Knidian and Koan, but only one Rhodian example. Such southern Aegean forms constitute 7–10 per cent of the Hellenistic assemblages (by count of RBHS and RBH respectively). They are notably more common than northern Aegean forms, which amount to only 1–3 per cent of the total; no Black Sea amphorae have been identified at the site.

Western imports to Euesperides include Greco-Italic wine amphorae produced in southern Italy and Sicily; these total about 1 per cent of the Hellenistic amphorae. Sicilian examples of the so-called MGS IV-V Greco-Italic types have been recognised in the early Hellenistic levels, with sinuous handles, outflared rims and pointed or stub toes (Figure 5.6). Sicilian fabrics are pretty homogeneous, and we cannot as yet assign these to a particular production centre, but the regional attribution is in itself significant.

More readily distinguishable in general terms are Punic amphorae, which make up 5 per cent by RBH count (6 per cent by RBHS) of the amphorae found at the site – several times as much as the Sicilian or Italian material.[39] Western Phoenician and Punic amphorae retained a distinctive morphology derived from their Levantine predecessors, which persisted as an aesthetic totally alien to the classic Graeco-Roman amphora tradition, with an elongated body and small ear handles attached below the shoulder. The so-called torpedo or hole-mouthed jars, which make up 18 per cent of the Punic amphorae at the site, are wholly unsuitable for the pouring of liquids.[40] Indeed, examples from shipwrecks in the western Mediterranean have been found containing joints of salted meat preserved in wine, or salted fish, and fish-bones and scales of tunny

[39] Göransson 2007: 220. For Punic amphorae at Euesperides generally: A. Wilson *et al.* 2002: 109–13; A. Wilson *et al.* 2004: 175–8; Göransson 2007: 174–88.

[40] I.e. thirteen rims, bases and handles catalogued in Göransson 2007: 178–9, from a total of seventy-two Punic amphora rims, bases and handles of all periods.

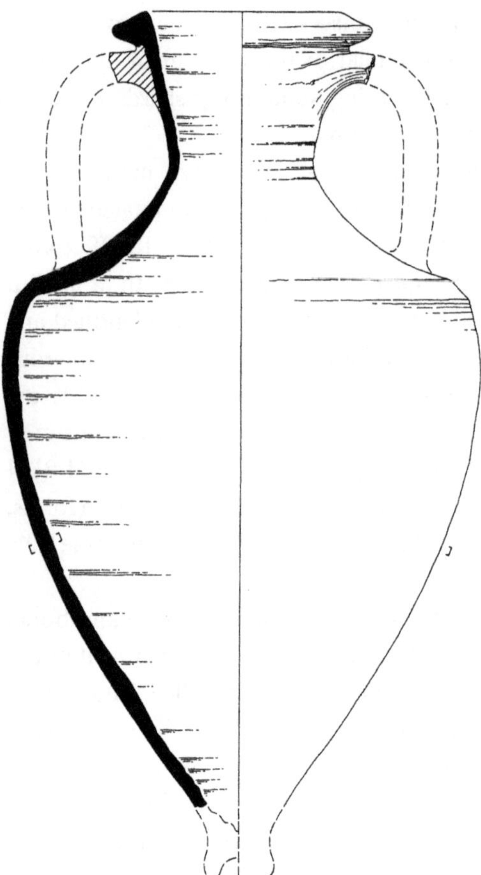

Figure 5.6 Greco-Italic amphora of type MGS V, from the refuse dump in the quarry in Area Q (899). Inv. no. CP 4032.

and sea-bream were found in association with the numerous Punic amphora sherds from the 'Punic Amphora Building' at Corinth.[41]

At Euesperides evidence for Punic contact perhaps as early as the late fifth or fourth century BC is provided by a flared body sherd that should belong to one of the extreme western Punic types of that period, perhaps made near Kouass on the Atlantic coast of Morocco.[42] Other sherds and bases, common in late fourth- and third-century contexts, clearly belong to hole-mouthed jar types produced in Tunisia (Figure 5.7), and so we can probably infer the import of salted meat and fish from Carthaginian territory in the

[41] Ramón Torres 1995; Zimmerman Munn 2003: 201–2.

[42] A. Wilson *et al.* 2002: 109–10; cf. Ramón Torres 1995, sub-group 11.2.1.0. Cf. Zimmerman Munn 2003, for trade in similar amphorae from the Straits of Gibraltar to Corinth in the fifth century BC.

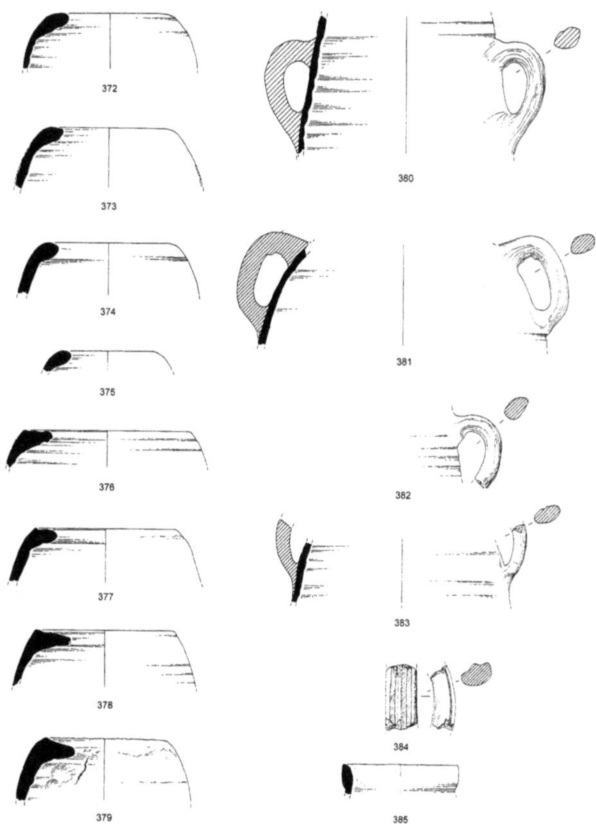

Figure 5.7 Punic hole-mouthed or 'torpedo' jars from Euesperides. Nos. 372–5 (mid-third century BC): Ramón type T-4.2.1.2. Nos. 376–9 (generally 350–250 BC): Ramón type T-4.2.1.5. Nos. 383–4 (generally 325–250 BC): Ramón series S-4.0.0.0.

early Hellenistic period. Other forms with outflared rims and 'trumpet-shaped' mouths are also represented, probably belonging to Tunisian or Tripolitanian oil or wine jars (Figure 5.8).[43]

One distinctively ridged body sherd probably belongs to Ramón's late fourth- or third-century type 8.1.1.1, from Ibiza. Examples of this type from a wreck off Menorca have been found to have a pitched lining, which would be consistent with carrying either wine or salted products – interestingly, amphorae of this kind excavated at the Iberian settlement of Ullastret contained rabbit bones.[44] So the import of preserved meats from the Balearics is a possibility.

The Punic fabrics are as distinctive as the forms; while their quartz-rich clays are typical of the entire North African littoral (and similar to Cyrenaican clays),

[43] Göransson 2007: 181–5; cf. Ramón Torres 1995, types T–2.2.1.2, T–6.1.1.2, T–7.1.2.1 and T–7.2.1.1.

[44] Ramón Torres 1995: 220–2, 264–5.

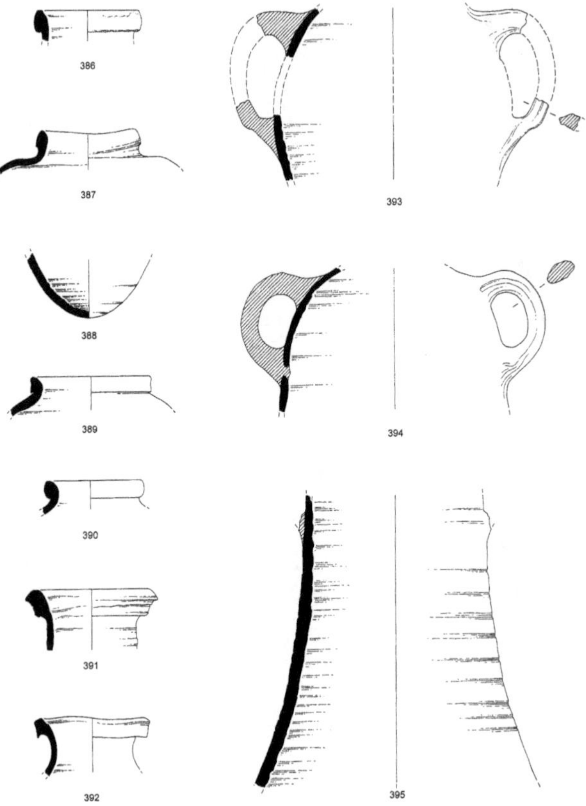

Figure 5.8 Punic amphorae from Euesperides, perhaps for olive oil or wine. Nos. 386–8 (mid-third century BC): Ramón type T-2.2.1.2 or T-7.1.2.1. No. 389 (325–250 BC): Berenice D91/Cintas 314. No. 390 (*c.* 325–250 BC): Ramón type T-6.1.1.2. Nos. 391–4 (*c.* 325–250 BC): Ramón type T-7.2.1.1. No. 395 (fifth/early fourth century BC): Ramón series SG-11.2.1.0.

they are fired at a much higher temperature and have either a whitish exterior as a result of applying a saline wash before firing, or a blackened surface caused by smudging – deliberately adding carbon-rich organic matter (e.g. dung) to the kiln fuel to create a reducing atmosphere in which the kiln is deprived of oxygen. These characteristics make it possible also to identify a number of Greek shapes made in Punic fabrics, including a Greco-Italic amphora, among the material imported to Euesperides.[45] In other words, the Greco-Italic wine amphora shape was being copied in Punic North Africa, which is an interesting comment on cultural borrowings between the Greek and Punic worlds.[46] So far as I am aware, Punic Greco-Italics have not been recognised prior to our work,

[45] Göransson 2007: 188.

[46] Cf. Fentress, Chapter 6 this volume, for other cultural borrowings in agriculture and architecture.

although there seems to be a local example at Lepcis Magna,[47] and the amphorae from Punic tombs at Mellita in Tripolitania, on display in the Punic Museum at Sabratha, include Greco-Italic forms in what look like Punic North African fabrics.[48]

Although the coarsewares (below) show evidence for trading contact between Euesperides and the Punic world already from the fifth century BC, it is only in the Hellenistic period that the import of Punic amphorae becomes really significant. In fills of pits belonging to the early or mid-fourth century BC in Area P, only seven Punic sherds were noted out of a total of *c.* 220 amphora sherds. But they are considerably more abundant in contexts of *c.* 325 BC onwards, down to the end of the site in 250 BC. The archaeological evidence thus tallies well with what little can be reconstructed from written sources: around 380 BC Barce and Carthage went to war over control of the Syrtic Gulf (the Greater Syrtis); Cyrene intervened *c.* 375–360 BC, and then was at war with Carthage from *c.* 360 to 340 BC.[49] The settlement limited Cyrene's area of influence to points east of the Arae Philaenorum, roughly midway along the Syrtic Gulf. Given the poor agricultural potential of the regions bordering the Syrtic Gulf, this war must have been about trade, reflecting the growing importance of commercial exchange between Cyrenaica and Punic Africa; but it is after the resolution of this conflict that the archaeological evidence for Cyrenaican trade with the Punic world becomes abundant. However, the limited quantity of excavated deposits which date to before the introduction of bronze coinage in Cyrenaica in 325 BC, coupled with the inevitable lack of close dating from ceramics when there is no coinage as an external control for the date, means that we cannot as yet determine how quickly this increase occurred after 340 BC, or whether it is primarily a phenomenon of the later 320s.

As well as identifying imported amphorae, our project distinguished five classes of local amphorae – four main classes of Cyrenaican amphorae, and locally made examples of the so-called Corinthian B type (Figure 5.9).[50] Classes 1 and 2 are essentially earlier versions of Riley's Hellenistic amphorae types 1 and 2 identified at Berenice.[51] Class 1 (an earlier form of Riley 1) is similar to Chian amphorae; Class 3 is distinguished by an out-turned rim and

[47] Göransson 2007: 128.

[48] Personal observation 2004; cf. Göransson 2007: 128. For the publication of the amphorae, see Bisi and Di Vita 1969–70; Bisi 1983.

[49] Sallust, *Iug.* 79.4–5; Laronde 1987: 28, 487; Göransson 2007: 28 and 221.

[50] Göransson 2007: 51–82.

[51] Riley 1979: 119–22 and Fig. 68; Swift and Göransson in A. Wilson *et al.* 2005: 166–71; Göransson 2007: 51, 57.

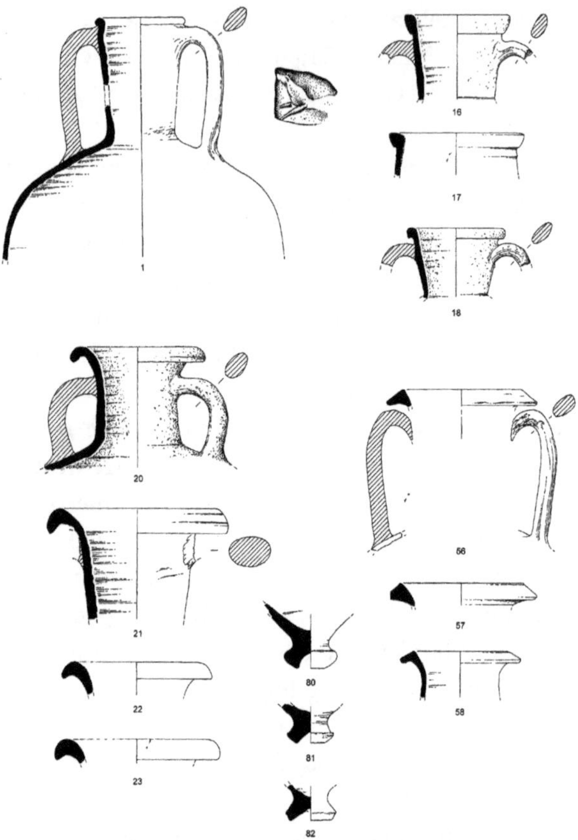

Figure 5.9 Cyrenaican amphorae. 1: Cyrenaican Class 1. 16–18: Cyrenaican Class 2. 20–4: Cyrenaican Class 3. 56–8: Cyrenaican Class 4. 80–2: Cyrenaican amphora toes, not currently attributable to amphorae class.

shorter handles; Class 4 has a splayed neck and triangular rim cross-section and seems to be a local version of Greco-Italic forms. We can begin to distinguish, on the grounds of fossil fragments included in the clays, between production of the Benghazi plain, and of the region around Cyrene; the various classes were made in more than one area within Cyrenaica. We do not yet know what these amphorae contained: among the possible available products one might think of wine, olive oil, silphium derivatives and salted fish. Tempting as it might be to associate each of these four possibilities with one of our four classes, that would doubtless be over-simplistic; and amphorae might also carry other goods, such as nuts, or grain. Morphologically, the similarity between Class 1 and Chian amphorae, and between Class 4 and Greco-Italic amphorae, suggests wine as a probable content for these forms, while Class 3 echoes Corinthian A forms, thought to have held olive oil; but those indicators can at best only be hints in the absence of residue analysis.

The identification of these Cyrenaican amphora classes, hitherto unknown, allows us to begin to hunt for Cyrenaican exports. Given the morphological resemblance between Class 1 and Chian amphorae, it is possible that some Cyrenaican exports may have been published as Chian amphorae at other sites – one could only know by looking at the fabrics, which are rarely described in Greek amphora publications. But we can at least now identify two rim sherds of Cyrenaican Class 3 among the unclassified material published from Sabratha, in a fabric whose description is consistent with Cyrenaican fabrics.[52] This provides welcome confirmation of the reciprocal trade of Cyrenaican exports to Punic North Africa that one would expect from the discovery of numerous Punic imports at Euesperides.

Coarse pottery

Little previous work had been done on Greek cooking and coarsewares when we started excavating at Euesperides. Apart from some very good petrological work by Marie Farnsworth on coarsewares from excavations at Athens and Corinth,[53] and an unsatisfactory study by Edwards of some of the other Corinth material,[54] there is a somewhat cursory study of the Agora material by Sparkes and Talcott in *Agora* XII; this paid almost no attention to fabrics beyond the jejune statement that 'Cooking ware is the term adopted here for the gritty brown to red fabric used in all times and places for pots meant to be set over the fire'.[55] Rotroff's study of the Hellenistic plain wares from the Athenian Agora (*Agora* XXXIII) appeared in 2006, and while this represents a step in the right direction and does pay more attention to fabric classification, it lacks both macroscopic and thin-section fabric photographs, and attempts at quantification are once again seriously hampered by the Agora excavation's unsystematic collection and retention policies and the extensive weeding of the collections that has taken place since excavation. Keith Swift therefore had to build form and fabric typologies for the Euesperides coarsewares almost from scratch. His work constitutes an impressive piece of petrological research, and one of the most startling conclusions was that between a quarter and a third (25 per cent by RBH; 32 per cent by RBHS) of the cooking and coarsewares used at Euesperides in the period 350–325 BC were imports from outside Cyrenaica

[52] Dore and Keay 1989: 82 (Fabric 5a) and Fig. 10, no. 163. [53] Farnsworth 1964.

[54] Edwards 1975: 104–43, unquantified and with little detail in fabric descriptions.

[55] Sparkes and Talcott 1970: 84.

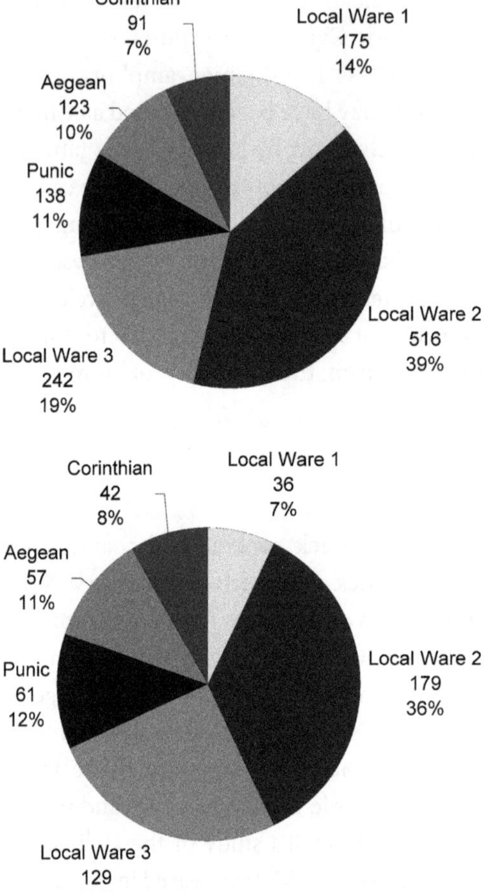

Figure 5.10 Relative proportions of coarsewares from different regions in the fully quantified early Hellenistic contexts (*c.* 325–250 BC) from Euesperides: (a) all sherds (RBHS; total = 1285); (b) diagnostic sherds only (RBH; total = 504).

(Figure 5.10).[56] If these relatively low-value goods were appearing at the site in large quantities, this suggests regular and intensive long-distance maritime trade with the regions of supply. Moreover, since it is unlikely that ships will have sailed fully laden with cooking vessels and little else, the cooking wares must have arrived as part-cargoes, and thus provide a proxy indicator for larger trade flows in other goods. As is the case in the Roman Mediterranean, the widespread distribution of certain types of

[56] Swift 2006; cf. also interim contributions by Swift in A. Wilson *et al.* 2001: 170–2; A. Wilson *et al.* 2002: 113–5; A. Wilson *et al.* 2003: 214–21; A. Wilson *et al.* 2004: 175; A. Wilson *et al.* 2005: 161–5; A. Wilson *et al.* 2006: 152–3.

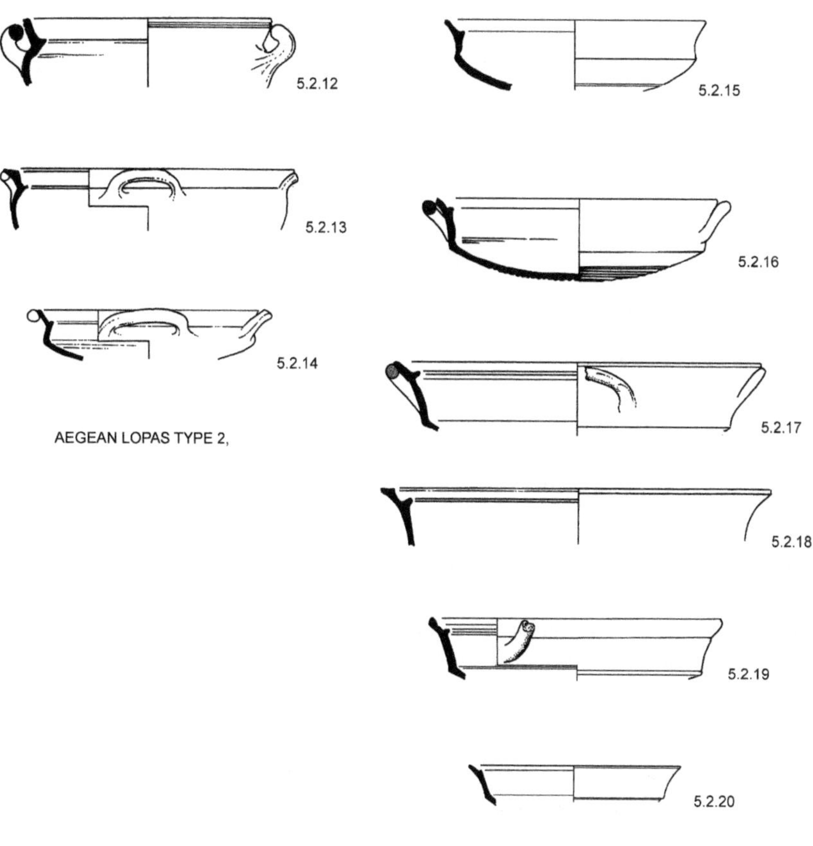

Figure 5.11 Aegean cooking wares, probably made on Aegina – *lopas* Types 2 and 3. Cf. Figure. 5.12.

cooking wares around the Hellenistic Mediterranean is indicative of a well-connected trading world. Subsequently, important new work on the trade in mortaria confirms this picture.[57]

Certain imports were easy enough to recognise by volcanic inclusions in the clay – these include a distinctive group whose origin can be located in the Cycladic arc, probably on Aegina. These include *lopades* and *chytrai* (saucepans and cooking pots), the former often with distinctive lid seats (Figure 5.11). These Aegean wares accounted for 10–11 per cent of the total Hellenistic coarse pottery.

Pottery in a greenish-yellow fabric apparently matching known examples from Corinth, and definitely not Cyrenaican, constitutes 7–8 per cent of the

[57] Spataro and Villing 2009; Villing and Pemberton 2010.

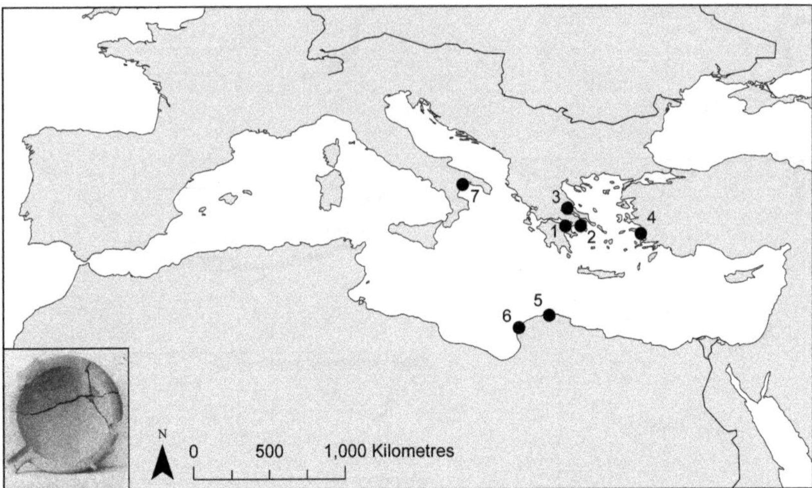

Figure 5.12 Distribution map of Corinthian mortaria. This map is indicative only; it shows sites from which published examples have been identified (though not always by their excavators), and further systematic research would undoubtedly reveal many more sites. The inset photograph is a mortarium from Cyrene, published as a 'libation bowl' (Rowe and Healy 1959: Plate 34 c). 1 = Corinth; 2 = Athens; 3 = Nea Halos; 4 = Miletos; 5 = Cyrene; 6 = Euesperides; 7 = Ponte Fabrizio.

Hellenistic coarsewares. Bowl mortaria and mouldmade mortaria are especially common in this fabric, and the forms, spouts and bolster-shaped handles are highly distinctive. Mortaria are shallow bowls with a wide pouring spout, usually thought to be for pounding and grinding herbs and spices.[58] The quantity in which Corinthian wares, especially mortaria, appear at Euesperides suggests that they should occur elsewhere too. Their distinctive shape allows them to be recognised from publications, even where the authors did not attribute them; and we can attempt a preliminary distribution map (Figure 5.12).[59] Published identified examples are known from Corinth; Athens;[60] and Nea Halos in Thessaly;[61] there are also examples from Miletos.[62] Alan Rowe published a photo of what he thought was a 'libation vessel' from a tomb at Cyrene, but is clearly a Corinthian mortarium (Figure 5.12, inset).[63] The distribution is predominantly eastern but a

[58] Villing and Pemberton 2010: 557–9, 602–20; see Cool 2006: 42–6 in relation to Roman mortaria and their function.

[59] For greater detail on the emerging picture of production and distribution of Corinthian mortaria, see now the important study of Villing and Pemberton 2010.

[60] Rotroff 2006b: 101–2.

[61] Beestman-Kruyshaar 2003: 264 no. P271.

[62] Alexandra Villing, pers. comm.

[63] Rowe and Healy 1959: Plate 34 c.

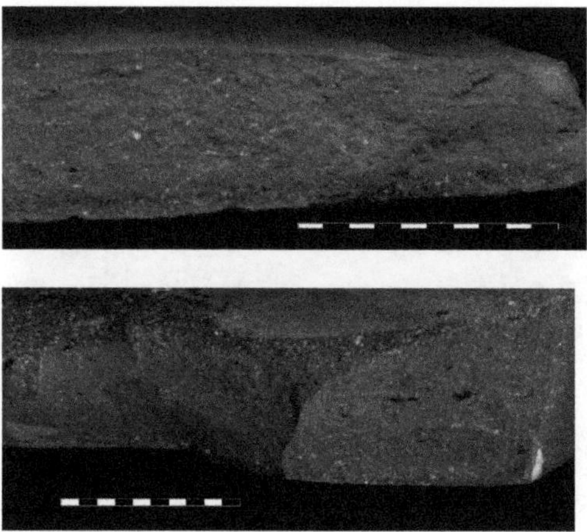

Figure 5.13 Punic fabrics. Top: Punic amphora fabric Group 1. Bottom: Punic coarseware fabric Group 1. Scales in mm. For colour version see plate section.

photograph of excavations at the farmstead of Ponte Fabrizio near Metaponto clearly shows a central Mediterranean example.[64]

The real surprise was the Punic coarsewares. Among the bewildering variety of coarse pottery from the site were large quantities of pots in reddish fabrics which bore some similarities to Cyrenaican clay. North African clays are pretty homogeneous, but the quartz inclusions range along a scale from sparse to frequent. Cyrenaican clays have a sparse quartz content, but discriminating them from other North African clays on this basis alone is very difficult. However, when the sherds with medium to high quartz contents were grouped according to other criteria – such as firing temperature, or shapes and forming techniques – distinctive patterns were apparent. Demonstrably local wares had finger-smoothed rims, thumb impressions where the handles were attached, and were fired at relatively low temperatures. The more quartz-rich fabrics were higher-fired, with clean, angular lines and extensive use of tools for knife-trimming edges and rims. This suggested that these wares formed a distinct, non-Cyrenaican group produced somewhere else in North Africa.

Confirmation that they were Punic coarsewares came via co-identification with Punic amphora fabrics, which showed not only a similar range of clays and quartz inclusions, but also identical firing techniques (Figure 5.13). The forms included almost the full range of coarse pottery – *lopades*, *chytrai*, *lekanai*, bowls, jugs and table amphorae (Figure 5.14). These

[64] Carter 1980.

Figure 5.14 Punic cooking wares.

Punic coarsewares fell into two main groups: one in a reddish, oxidised fabric, and the other in a dark, reduced fabric, created by smudging the kiln atmosphere. This is a deliberate effect, and requires considerable skill in controlling the firing conditions of the kiln. Similar wares of both types have been found at Sabratha and Carthage, although at the moment we do not know whether the two types represent different regional productions – e.g. in Tripolitania, central or northern Tunisia – or were contemporary productions in the same regions.

The Punic cooking wares display considerable command of pottery production techniques and particularly of firing technology – the Punic potters were evidently way ahead of their Cyrenaican Greek counterparts in this respect. Features of the Punic wares, including the high firing temperatures creating hard fabrics, and the smudging of surface treatment, foreshadow the African cookware tradition that produced a widely exported class of cooking pots in the Roman period.

In total, the Punic wares represent 11–12 per cent of the total coarse pottery at Euesperides, the largest imported ware group. This is a surprising figure, and fleshes out the picture given by the amphorae. Evidently, despite the feared reputation of the Syrtic Gulf, there was plenty of shipping contact

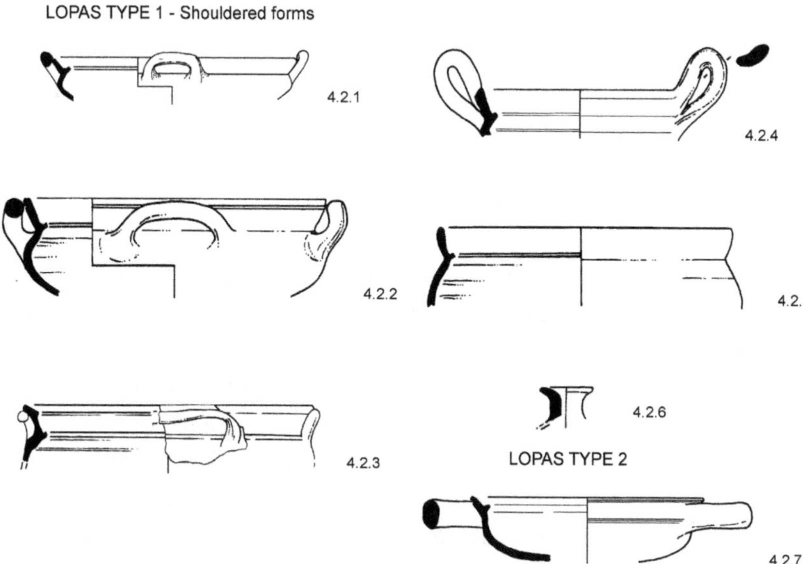

Figure 5.15 Punic *lopas* Types 1 and 2. Cf. Figure 5.8.

across it in the early Hellenistic period.[65] Again, the presence of these distinctive wares in quantity at Euesperides suggests that they ought to be recognisable among the coarse pottery assemblages at other sites. One might expect distribution to southern Italy, and it would be worth examining assemblages from the Aegean to see if they reached there too.

A further observation: the Punic *lopas* and *chytra* forms imitate those of the Aegean or Aeginetan cooking wares (Figure 5.15).[66] This provides a hint that the Aeginetan group was also traded to the Punic world. The coarsewares suggest a picture of interconnected trade flows and cultural borrowing between the eastern Mediterranean and Punic North Africa, although more research on other sites is needed to develop this.

In any event, if glazed and even painted pottery is not thought to have been especially expensive, the coarsewares and cooking wares must have been low-value items. They should have travelled as part-cargoes with other, more valuable goods, including the amphora-borne commodities, but also perishables – textiles, grain, nuts, lentils, pulses and beans carried in sacks.

[65] On the dangers of the Syrtes, e.g. Sall. *Iug.* 78; Strabo 17.3.20; Pomponius Mela 1.30, 32; Plin. *HN* 5.3.26.

[66] Swift 2006: 180–3.

And if they are sufficiently common to account for a third of the total of cooking wares at Euesperides, that argues for a considerable degree of maritime trade. And much of this connectivity was evidently with the Punic West.

Mosaic technology and *pavimenta punica*

These contacts go beyond simple trade and are reflected also in technological affinities with the Punic world shown by the mosaic floors from Euesperides. The mosaic floors include two floors in irregular white limestone tesserae excavated by Barri Jones in 1968–9 and several plain pebble and mixed pebble and tessellated floors from the recent excavations; in addition, fragments of pebble mosaic from various points across the site have been collected by surface survey. My discussion here draws heavily on research by Will Wootton, who examined the floors from our excavations in Area P as one of the case-studies included in his doctoral thesis.[67]

In one property of the penultimate phase in Area P, whose construction is dated to 282 BC or later by coins of Magas in Revolt found in the construction levels, a room with a floor of plain greyish pebbles and a threshold inscription picked out in blue pebbles, restorable as ΕΥΚ[ΑΙΡΙ]Α ΕΡΓ[ΟΙΣ] ('Good fortune in your deeds'), may be the *andron* since the mosaic floor, inscription and wine amphora in a pot-stand near the door suggest a function for receiving guests and perhaps dining. Next to it a larger room with an earth floor was found to have a large collection of pottery vessels (for food preparation and cosmetics) and a cluster of seventy-two loomweights marking the site of a loom; this was probably the *gynaikon*. These materials were all found lying on the floors, covered by a half-metre thick layer of mud-brick demolition. The pottery was completely reconstructable and numerous coins were also found on the floor; we have what looks like a usage assemblage of the house at the moment of its sudden destruction. There is no sign of a great conflagration, and earthquake must be a likely possibility. This event is securely dated by three coins of Magas Reconciled with Ptolemy II, struck in or after 261 BC, found lying on the floors.[68]

Reconstruction followed immediately, and apparently on a more lavish scale. The construction, use and abandonment of this final phase must all fall in the tight bracket 261–250 BC at the outside. The walls had been almost

[67] Wootton 2006; A. Wilson *et al.* 2003: 193–5, 197–200; A. Wilson *et al.* 2004: 154–8.

[68] A. Wilson *et al.* 2003: 193–7, 224 Fig. 18.

Figure 5.16 General view of final phase floors in Area P, facing SW. In the foreground, a room (antechamber?) in plain pebble mosaic; behind to the right, the room with wave-crest mosaic, and to the left the site of a destroyed mosaic, found in pieces in the robber trenches and modern graves that cut the ancient layers. Scale: 1 m. For colour version see plate section.

entirely robbed out following the city's abandonment, and most of the floor levels were destroyed by modern graves and by surface erosion. However, parts of three mosaic-floored rooms were discovered initially by John Lloyd's project in 1998, and further investigated between 1999 and 2006: an anteroom floored with small plain pebbles set in cement, giving onto a room with a blue threshold panel and a wave-crest motif in split pebbles framing a central white panel in irregular limestone tesserae (Figures 5.16 and 5.17). To the left in Figure 5.16, other floors have been completely lost, deeply cut about by ancient robber trenches along the wall lines, and by modern graves – except for a small patch of *opus signinum* flooring still *in situ*. This room, however, had clearly had another mosaic floor, as the spatial distribution of mosaic fragments from robber trenches and grave fills showed.

The wide variety of different types and patterns represented in the fragments from the completely destroyed floor suggests a more elaborate design in this room; they include another wave crest, in blue-black split pebbles, but also motifs with pebbles set on edge, and green, white and red elements. Part of the design can be reconstructed as a dolphin, in split pebbles, with its eye made from a red terracotta sherd. The tail, which in Figure 5.18 appears

Figure 5.17 Detail of the wave-crest mosaic floor found in Area P in 1998. Scale: 20 cm in 10 cm units.

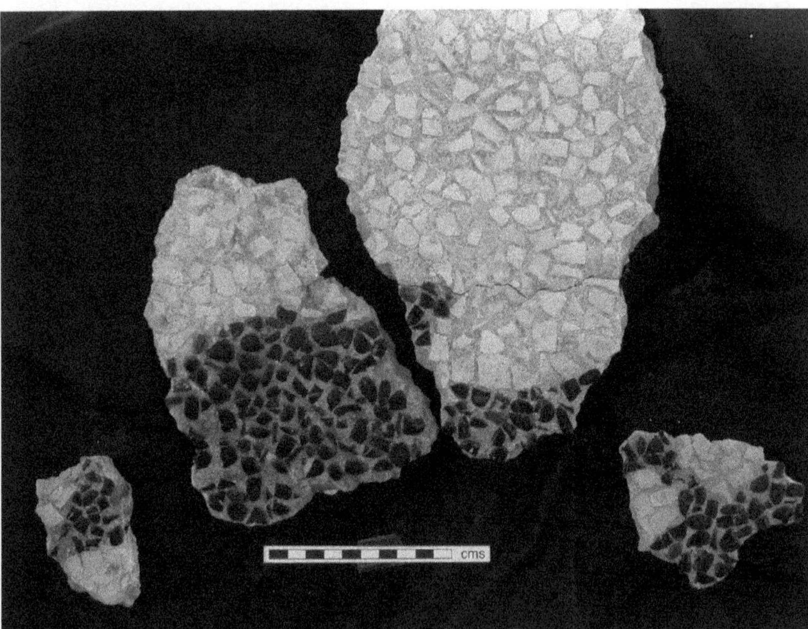

Figure 5.18 Pebble mosaic fragments representing two dolphins (the tail belongs to a second dolphin), from the destroyed mosaic floor of the final phase in Area P. For colour version see plate section.

the wrong way up, should belong in fact to another dolphin, facing the other way. At least two dolphins, therefore, probably formed part of the central design, with other non-geometrical elements – perhaps floral or marine – and surrounded within a wave-crest border. At the edges of the room was a surround of *opus signinum*, a pinkish cement with crushed terracotta, as shown by the find of fragments *in situ* and by other fragments in the robber trenches. Belonging to an earlier floor, stratified below the final phase mosaics, and which must belong to the penultimate phase, were fragments of terracotta sherds set in cement. We therefore have mosaics made variously from irregular limestone tesserae, split pebbles, whole pebbles, whole pebbles set on edge and *opus signinum*, not only in the same suite of rooms, but in many cases actually in the same floor, all dated to 261–250 BC. This is important new material for the debate about the origins of tessellation.

Greek mosaics of the fourth century BC are pebble mosaics, such as the well-known ones from Pella, Alexandria or Paphos. Mixed technique floors including both pebbles and irregular tesserae are known from Alexandria and Lebena in the third century BC, while third-century floors from Morgantina and Megara Hyblaea employ a mixture of tesserae and *opus signinum*; none of these, however, is dated more closely within the third century.[69] Mosaic floors on Delos and at Pergamon use a combination of pebbles and irregular stone chips. By the second century tessellation had largely replaced these older techniques. Some have thought that tessellation evolved out of pebble mosaics, to enable more precise pictorial representations.[70] The obstacle to the simple evolutionary view has been that the mixed technique mosaics are not well dated, and that they co-existed with pebble floors and floors of pure tessellation, while some mixed technique floors with large stone chips continued to be laid in the second and even first centuries BC.[71] Complicating the picture further is the possibility of some Punic influence, since some fourth-century BC floors at Carthage (earlier than the first dated tessellated floors in the eastern Mediterranean), and fourth- or third-century BC floors at Kerkouane in Tunisia are made of pinkish *opus signinum*, with a scattering of white tesserae as a random pattern, or occasionally forming very simple outline motifs, such as the Tanit symbol.[72]

[69] Alexandria: Daszewski 1985: Cat. nos. 3 and 4; Guimier-Sorbets 2001: 282–5; K. Dunbabin 1999: 22–4. Lebena: K. Dunbabin 1999: 18–19. Morgantina and Megara Hyblaea: K. Dunbabin 1994: 28–9, 32. See Wootton 2006 for discussion.

[70] E.g. Levi 1947: 4; Robertson 1965: 77–8; summarised by Dunbabin 1979: 266.

[71] Dunbabin 1979, 1994, 1999: 18–37. [72] Cf. Fentress, this volume (Chapter 6).

The Euesperides mosaics from the final phase contribute to the debate in two ways. Firstly, they provide a fixed point for some mixed technique floors – exactly where one would expect it on the evolutionary view, in the mid-third century (261–250 BC), and succeeding the plain pebble mosaic of the penultimate phase (*c.* 282–260 BC). Rounding out the picture slightly are the floors excavated by Barri Jones at the site in 1968–9, which consist of irregular white limestone tesserae, one floor with a black border made of terracotta sherds (which we can now, incidentally, identify as the reduced-fabric Punic coarsewares). These floors are undated, but belong to the last stages of the city at some point in the first half of the third century BC; they should be broadly contemporary with (and can hardly be much later than) the mixed technique floors in Area P. They suggest not an absolutely straightforward developmental sequence, but rather a period of experimentation in which mixed technique and irregular tesserae floors might exist contemporaneously.

Yet, at the same time, the Euesperides floors also support the idea of some Punic influence. They include surrounds of *opus signinum* – originally a Punic technique, found in Carthage in the fourth and even the fifth century BC. It is found in Sicily in the third century BC, but Euesperides to my knowledge represents the earliest attested use of this technique in the eastern Mediterranean.[73] There can be little doubt that it was introduced to Euesperides from Punic North Africa or Sicily.

Opus signinum floors at both Euesperides and Punic Kerkouane have terracotta aggregate, with a fine upper layer of pink cement containing crushed terracotta. Moreover, Will Wootton's work on the technical composition of these floors shows closer affinities, in the processes by which they were laid, with Punic floors in North Africa than with Greek pebble mosaic floors from the eastern Mediterranean.[74] All the pavements at Euesperides have foundations constructed in two layers: a bed of fist-sized pebbles, and then a thick layer of mortar, into which the tesserae or pebbles are set directly (Figure 5.19). This contrasts with all known comparative examples of Greek pebble mosaics, as at Olynthos and Eretria, which have three layers of foundations.[75] The first two layers correspond to the two at Euesperides, but on top of these is a finer layer of mortar into which the surface materials are set. Because the upper layer of mortar could only be laid when the first two bedding layers had set, its thinness stops the surface materials sinking into the mortar.

[73] Dunbabin 1999: 20; cf. discussion in Fentress (Chapter 6), and Roger Wilson (Chapter 4), this volume.

[74] A. Wilson *et al.* 2004: 157; Wootton 2006. [75] Salzmann 1982: 42–3.

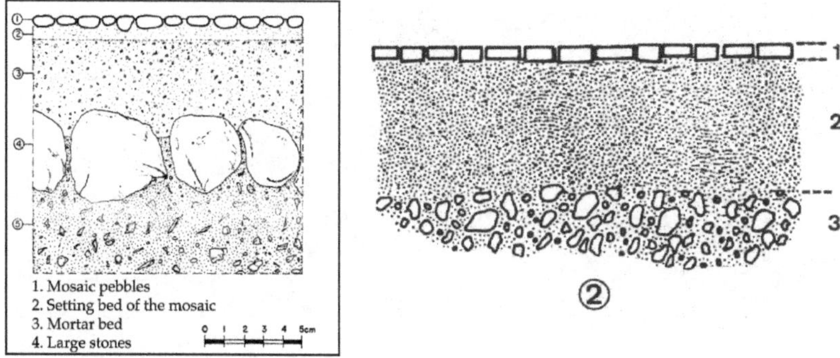

Figure 5.19 Two- and three-layer construction technique for mosaic floors.

The two-layer technique found at Euesperides is, however, paralleled in the central Mediterranean, in *opus signinum* floors at Kerkouane and Morgantina, and in Punic tessellated floors at Carthage.[76] This looks like a Western tradition. The disadvantage of this technique is that the layer into which the surface materials must be set when wet is so thick that the pebbles or tesserae can sink into it, as at both Euesperides and Carthage. The terracotta and mosaic floors therefore show a cultural interplay of technologies: while their aesthetic designs – either plain, or with a plain or simple central field surrounded by a border – owe more to eastern Mediterranean influences, the technology of their composition, with two-layer foundations and the use of *opus signinum*, reveals strong influences from the Punic world and Sicily.

In the context of Western borrowings, the discovery in 2006 in Area Q of a set of public baths with a circular room with a floor of terracotta sherds set in cement is intriguing (Figure 5.20).[77] The floor contains areas of sherds set on edge, and has been patched in later repairs, but mainly consists of terracotta sherds laid flat, as in Punic pavements (Figure 5.21). It too has only two layers of foundation. The building probably dates within the third century BC; it post-dates a phase of rubbish dumping in an extra-mural quarry ditch during the second half of the fourth century, when it appears that the city wall was moved further out and this area became intramural. Towards the end of the city's life the building was heavily altered and may have changed function – the bath tubs inside the circular wall were robbed out and a series of tanks built over the infilled robber trench. Flooring technologies, *opus signinum* waterproofing and baths form part of a cultural and technological *koine* that was spread around the Mediterranean in the Hellenistic period. Indeed, this is a considerable part

[76] Wootton in A. Wilson *et al.* 2004: 157. [77] A. Wilson *et al.* 2006: 134–44.

Figure 5.20 The Hellenistic baths in Area Q, with a floor of terracotta sherds set in cement. The bathtubs around the inside of the circular room's walls have been robbed out. Scale: 0.5 m in 10 cm units. For colour version see plate section.

Figure 5.21 Detail of floor of terracotta sherds set in cement, from the Hellenistic baths, Euesperides. Scale: 10 cm in cm units. For colour version see plate section.

of the Punic architectural package discussed elsewhere in this volume in the chapters by Andrew Wallace-Hadrill (Chapter 2), Roger Wilson (Chapter 4) and Elizabeth Fentress (Chapter 6).

Conclusion

The pottery from Euesperides provides evidence for extensive trade between Cyrenaica and the Punic world, and also with southern Italy and Sicily, which seems to have intensified greatly in the early Hellenistic period; and the mosaic and *opus signinum* floors show us that it was not just goods, but also ideas, technologies and fashions that were exchanged. We now have a much richer economic context in which to insert the Euesperides/Syracuse proxeny decree that also illustrates the kind of élite trading contacts discussed in Elizabeth Fentress' chapter in this volume (Chapter 6). Was Euesperides typical? Sadly, the state of publication of pottery assemblages elsewhere in the eastern Mediterranean does not yet allow us to answer that question definitively. There are Punic amphorae from underwater excavations at Apollonia near Cyrene, but quantified assemblages are required to assess whether there is a significant difference in this regard between eastern and western Cyrenaica.[78] Much more work is required on amphorae and coarsewares, but the identification of major traded groups of Corinthian, Aegean and Punic coarsewares at Euesperides gives hope that these should be identified at other sites too; and the imitation of Aegean coarseware forms by Punic potters hints at trade in Aegean coarsewares to Punic North Africa as well.

We seem to see, in these pottery assemblages of the early Hellenistic period, a foreshadowing of the long-distance trade flows that are characteristic of the Roman world. As noted above, the conflict from *c.* 380–340 BC between Barce and Cyrene on the one hand, and Carthage on the other, must represent the growing importance of trade across the Syrtic Gulf or along its shores; and the resolution of this conflict on terms which settled the frontier between Greek and Punic territories should have created more favourable conditions for this trade. Indeed, it is striking that Euesperides' trading contacts as represented by the pottery appear both to intensify and extend westwards after the mid-fourth century BC. The exact point at which this happened remains imprecise, because of the problems of dating Greek pottery using typologies derived from the Agora excavations, but it appears

[78] Laronde, pers. comm.

broadly contemporary with the first issues of bronze coinage in Cyrenaica, struck in 325 BC. This suggests two further possible factors that may have contributed to the intensification of trading activity. The first is precisely the introduction of bronze coinage, of small change, which transformed the way coinage could be used. In a bimetallic system of gold and silver, the function of coinage was partly as a portable store of wealth, and the extent to which it could function as money for everyday small-scale transactions was limited by the lowest denomination threshold, below which transactions must have been carried out by barter. Although it is now increasingly recognised that many Greek city states did issue small change as tiny silver coins[79] – and both silver obols and coin moulds for them are known from Euesperides[80] – the addition of low-value bronze coins to the system allowed the issuing of a wider range of small denominations in a format that was easier to handle and less easy to lose than tiny silver obols. This increase in the usability of small change enabled the coinage to function more effectively as money for a wider range of everyday, small-scale purchases. This must have facilitated commerce at every level; bronze coinage reduced transaction costs for small-scale everyday purchases, and thus stimulated exchange, not only at this lowest level but right up through the monetary system. Importantly, the excavations suggest that the economy of Euesperides became rapidly and apparently quite thoroughly monetised in the wake of the introduction of bronze coinage: the last three phases of occupation in Area P have produced numerous bronze coins, all dating between 325 and 250 BC, thirty-one of which were casual losses in the construction levels of the penultimate phase (282–262 BC) over an area of just 200 m^2. Seven coins were found lying on the floor of Room 5 in the destruction assemblage of the penultimate phase of Area P (262–250 BC), and if this room is correctly identified as the *gynaikon* this suggests that such monetisation extended to the women of the household.

The second factor is geo-political – the resolution of the mid-fourth-century war between Carthage and the Cyrenaican cities provided more stable conditions in which to conduct trade across the Syrtes, but a further stimulus may also have been provided in the immediate wake of Alexander's conquest of Persia. The economically inward-looking Achaemenid empire was broken up and reorientated towards the Mediterranean, while simultaneously the release of booty from Alexander's conquests into the Mediterranean world considerably increased the money supply and the size of available consumption funds. These processes created larger markets

[79] Kim 2002. [80] A. Wilson *et al.* 2001: 173–4.

for Mediterranean trade that may in turn be expected to have drawn the central and western Mediterranean into closer contact with the eastern. Indeed, the very introduction of bronze coinage in Cyrenaica in 325 BC, two years before Alexander's death, may be a part of this process.

In addition to these general economic developments, the particular episode of Thibron's invasion of Cyrenaica in 323 BC may also play a part in this story of increasing interplay between regions of the Mediterranean in the immediate aftermath of Alexander's death and the break-up of his short-lived empire into the Successor States. Alexander's treasurer Harpalus fled with Alexander's war-chest, but was murdered by his supposed friend, Thibron, who used the money to invade Cyrenaica with 7,000 mercenaries, intending to carve out for himself a kingdom there.[81] Euesperides and Barce allied with him and he struck coin at Euesperides.[82] He never managed to gain permanent control of Cyrene, however, and by 321 he had been captured and executed. Despite the brevity of his activity in Cyrenaica (a little more than a year), his bronze coins with the head of Heracles on the obverse and a club and quiver on the reverse are common among the finds from Euesperides, and were still circulating at the time of the city's abandonment.[83] I suspect that the influx of coin that Thibron's invasion entailed may have played a part in ensuring the rapid monetisation of the urban economy of Euesperides that created favourable conditions for trade in the early Hellenistic period.

The sudden end of occupation at Euesperides *c.* 250 BC cuts off the story abruptly; the excavations at its successor site, Berenice, were not able to investigate the earliest deposits there on any large scale. But by the later second century BC at Berenice there is a markedly reduced proportion of Punic imports by comparison with the picture from Euesperides over a century earlier, reflecting the increasing orientation of North African trade towards Italy and the western Mediterranean in the aftermath of the Punic Wars, and Rome's emergence as the dominant power in the central Mediterranean.[84]

Both Carthage's war with Barce and Cyrene, and its wars with Rome, were fought primarily for control of trade in particular regions of the Mediterranean. Far from implying a separation and lack of contact between

[81] Diod. Sic. 18.19.

[82] Diod. Sic. 18.20.3. A. Wilson 2005: 1650–2. Thibron's coinage at Euesperides: Buttrey in A. Wilson *et al.* 2002: 117–19.

[83] For the identification of these issues with Thibron, see Buttrey in A. Wilson *et al.* 2002: 117–19.

[84] Swift in A. Wilson *et al.* 2005: 165.

the warring parties, such wars actually attest considerable prior trading contacts; and the archaeological evidence from Euesperides supports this at least with regard to contact between Cyrenaica and the Punic world in the late fourth and first half of the third centuries BC. In both cases trade intensified after the conclusion of the wars. The archaeology also allows us to see that these contacts included a degree of cultural exchange as well. For the early Hellenistic period, before the Punic Wars, the imitation of Greco-Italic amphorae and of Aeginetan cooking wares in Punic North Africa deepens our appreciation of Punic cultural borrowings from the Greek world. But the Punic imports to Euesperides – of amphorae containing perhaps salted meat, fish, wine and oil, of cooking wares and coarsewares, and of flooring technologies – suggest that parts of the Greek world were not averse to importing and learning from the Punic world too.

6 Strangers in the city: élite communication in the Hellenistic central Mediterranean

ELIZABETH FENTRESS

We owe to Nicholas Purcell and Peregrine Horden a new attention to the role of the merchant in the Mediterranean economy.[1] Not only have they put the word 'cabotage' onto everyone's lips, but they have made us concentrate on the differences in circulation at any given time, and on the attention individual cities pay to their trade and traders. What I want to do here is to look at the role, not of cabotage, but of élite merchants in a specific area of the Mediterranean, roughly the north–south axis between Etruria, Rome, Sicily and the Carthaginian territories and, in particular, at the interaction between Punic, Greek, Etruscan and finally Roman traders there. This is an axis and an area on which I have worked for other periods, and one that I feel is crucial for understanding the western Mediterranean at any time.[2] These economic interactions are of course most visible in their surviving material residue, pottery, but on this occasion I want to examine the effects of the networks created by the merchants in this area, linking them, rather paradoxically, to agricultural and architectural forms, which are usually seen in opposition to trade as an economic choice.

Expatriates and merchant networks

The obvious place to start is in Sicily, the heart of these networks, at a moment of almost idyllic peace for the merchant, the end of the fifth century BC. Diodorus Siculus shows the Agrigentines busily selling wine and oil to Carthage,[3] while there was clearly a colony of Greeks in Carthage itself.[4] A famous passage from Diodorus demonstrates that a number of Carthaginians had set up large and expensive establishments in Syracuse by 406 BC. The

[1] Horden and Purcell 2000. I am grateful to Josephine Crawley Quinn, Phil Perkins, Andrew Wilson and Jonathan Prag for their many comments and suggestions.

[2] See Keay (Chapter 10) and van Dommelen/López-Bertran (Chapter 9) in this volume for investigations of regions further to the West.

[3] Diod. Sic. 13.81.4; Hans 1983: 52; Anello 2002: 345 suggests a treaty between Syracuse and Carthage in 480 BC which would have kept Carthage neutral for the next seventy-five years.

[4] Diod. Sic. 14.77.5.

passage is worth quoting in full, not least because it also illustrates the precarious nature of their relationships with their hosts:

After the assembly the Syracusans, with the permission of Dionysius, sacked the goods of the Phoenicians. For quite a few Carthaginians lived in Syracuse with great properties, and many merchants had ships in the port, charged with merchandise, that were all sacked by the Syracusans. Other Sicilians crushed in the same manner the Phoenicians that lived with them.[5]

The passage makes it clear that Syracuse was not the only city that harboured such a settlement. What we seem to be seeing is the sort of trading networks we know so well for the late Middle Ages in the Mediterranean or the Near East, with trading houses establishing antennae in cities in which they dealt, their expatriate representatives able to handle customs, docking, storage and general relationships with the ports and the other merchants. These groups, for which the term trading enclave is preferable to that of colony, constituted foreign groups within the cities of the host country, whose contacts with their home cities remained strong.[6] Such *fonduqs* would have created links with the local traders at the port, and a substantial community of interests would then join the merchants of different nationalities, despite the episodic hostility of the general populace, as in 406. Marriage ties would have strengthened such relationships – we know, for instance, that the Hamilcar who commanded the Carthaginian forces at the battle of Himera in the early fifth century was the son of a Syracusan woman.[7]

The result of such relationships is seen in treaties such as that of 405–404 BC in which the Greek cities of Sicily that came into the Carthaginian dominion were forced to destroy their fortifications, but were allowed to keep their magistrates – those very oligarchs with whom Carthaginian merchants had been trading a few years earlier.[8] The Carthaginians were doing well by doing good, and maintaining their friends in power. Another result of this interaction was the construction of Greek sanctuaries within Punic towns – those on Motya, where Dionysius urged the inhabitants to take shelter to protect them from slaughter by his soldiers (and to preserve them as a commodity for later sale as slaves),[9] or the sanctuary of Demeter and Kore constructed at

[5] Diod. Sic. 14.46.1.

[6] For discussion of the use of the word 'colony' see Stein (ed.) 2005 *passim*; Dietler 1998: 297.

[7] Hdt. 7.165. Later on, Hippocrates and Epicydes, lieutenants of Hannibal, were the children of a Carthaginian and grandchildren of a Syracusan exile, refugee in Africa (Polyb. 7.2.4).

[8] Diod. Sic. 13.114. See Sordi 1980; Anello 2002: 353.

[9] Diod. Sic. 14.53.2. On the three Greek funerary inscriptions of the sixth and fifth centuries BC from Motya, Jeffery 1990: 272.

Carthage in 396 BC to atone for the pillage of the Syracusan city. This was instituted by Greeks already in the city, whose help was requested to establish the cult and whose leading members served as priests.[10] Note that these, again, were not just any Greeks, but reasonable interlocutors and potential priests, literate and élite. Although there are no tombs of specifically Greek type at Carthage, a number of inscriptions have been recovered from Punic-style chamber tombs, indicating, among other evidence for Greek presence, the burial of a man from Heraclea Minoa.[11]

The easy and familiar interaction on the level of the major oligarchs and merchants would have increased the tendency of the Carthaginians to support the minor Greek cities against Dionysius, tyrant of Syracuse, which in turn may have been one of the reasons he turned on them. The slaughter of the Punic traders was, of course, the beginning of a bad fourth century, which would see the sack and destruction of Agrigento, Motya, Selinunte and a host of lesser towns, while firming up the division of the island between a Carthaginian *eparchia* in the West, now including Selinunte, and a Greek East under the hegemony of Syracuse. However, on the model of Horden and Purcell's useful formula that piracy is commerce carried on by other means, we may argue that the wars created massive potential for communication between the political and ethnic groupings that took part in them, broadening and deepening the networks of relationships between the protagonists.[12] The first aspect of this is that the wars engaged not only the allied armies but also large numbers of mercenaries from elsewhere. These mercenaries thus enjoyed, if they survived, the benefits of foreign travel. Diodorus shows us Dionysius calling mercenaries in to the city to help with his fortifications, including inhabitants of other cities transplanted to Syracuse, *liberti*, exiles, workmen and specialists from all over the Greek and Punic world.[13] Meanwhile the Carthaginians regularly fought alongside Campanian troops, an axis that would be of major importance in the subsequent period.[14]

The Carthaginian reaction to Syracusan aggression was quite clearly a hardening of positions, resulting in an eparchy in which there were certainly subaltern Greek cities, but very little in the way of friendly commerce:

10 Diod. Sic. 14.77.4–5; Xella 1969; Bonnet 2006b.

11 On the Punic tombs of Carthage, Bénichou-Safar 1982. She does not mention the Heraclea text, which is found instead in Fantar 2004, citing Chabot in *CRAI*, séance du 19 février 1926, 41, who cites Delattre. For further epigraphic traces of Greeks in Carthaginian tombs Fantar 2002: 230.

12 Horden and Purcell 2000: 158. Note the Etruscan pirate Postumius, who put in at Syracuse as a friendly city only to be seized and executed by Timoleon: Diod. Sic. 16.82.3.

13 Diod. Sic. 13.95.4-96.

14 Tagliamonte 2002.

indeed, the Carthaginian senate at the beginning of the fourth century BC debated a ban on the teaching of the Greek language.[15] There seems to be little doubt that contacts with eastern Sicily declined, and the new centres that rose on Selinunte and Akragas seem far more heavily Punic than we would expect if their populations consisted of survivors rather than new settlers. Houses with Punic forms, *opus africanum* walls and *opus signinum* pavements marked with the sign of Tanit replaced Greek-style buildings, while Punic sanctuaries are built inside earlier ones.[16]

Other interactions are very difficult to demonstrate archaeologically, and recourse to stylistic considerations is hardly useful, although often appealed to. Supposedly Hellenic traits in terracottas, pottery forms or column capitals may be transmitted by objects as much as by people: what we are looking for are genuine foreign enclaves. Ida Tamburello has argued that at Palermo the necropolis contains both Punic and Greek burials, indicating a mixed population.[17] However, her suggestion is based on the fact that some burials contained a lot of Greek pottery while others contained only local Punic forms. A moment's reflection would suggest that this could just as easily be explained by relative differences in wealth, with the Greek pottery acquired by those who could afford it, and the local Punic pottery the default purchase for those who could not. More convincing Punic burials are found at Cefalù, where a group of fourth- or third-century burials are found in amphorae, a typical Punic practice.[18] At Agrigento, there are walls in *opus africanum* dating to the fifth century, although this is hardly certain evidence for a Punic enclave there.[19] The great sanctuaries such as Erice (Eryx) probably served as neutral places for contact and exchange between Greeks, Elymians, Sicilians and Punic traders.[20] Herodotus shows Greek merchants trading freely in Punic emporia.[21] Other evidence for strangers in the Punic cities of Sicily is wanting, unless you count the splendidly ambiguous Motya Charioteer. He may simply have been a statue looted from Agrigento, as Malcolm Bell and others have suggested, but he may, at the limit, have been a charioteer for a Motyan owner who participated in Greek chariot races.[22]

In central Italy the situation before the fourth century BC is similar. On the one hand, contacts with Greeks were present from an early date: in Etruria, small groups of Greek craftsmen can be found in Caere, in Veii and

[15] Just. *Epit.* 20.5.13.

[16] See most recently D'Andria and Campagna 2002 and in general Mertens 1997 with previous bibliography.

[17] Tamburello 1966. [18] Tullio 2005. [19] Fiorentini 2002: 157. [20] Bonnet 2006a: 216.

[21] Hdt. 7.157–8. On the identification of these, Gras 2000.

[22] E.g. Tusa 1983. An affirmation of Greek origins with a full bibliography in M. Bell 1995.

in Tarquinia at the beginning of the sixth century BC or even earlier.[23] The emporia of the Tuscan coast were prime centres of interaction: the settlement at Gravisca clearly housed a number of Greeks, at least periodically, as the large number of sixth-century dedications in the shrines to Hera and Aphrodite show.[24] These, however, diminish in number in the fifth century, when the sanctuary appears to have lost much of its international character. In Campania, of course, such contacts were intense, with settlements of Etruscans and Greeks built side by side, and sanctuaries such as that at Pontecagnano where we find dedications both in Etruscan and Greek.[25]

Etruscan traders, too, established trading enclaves. Although much of the Etruscan commerce with Liguria and Gaul has been assumed to have been 'floating', archaeological evidence for a permanent settlement in an indigenous context comes from the site of Lattes, on the coast west of the Rhône. Here two houses were found dating from the earliest levels of the walled settlement, around the end of the sixth century BC. Their construction technique, in plastered mud-brick on stone foundations, is unusual for the site, as are the very large quantities of Etruscan ceramics, with a deposit of wine amphorae in one of the rooms. Some of the sherds also carried Etruscan graffiti, carved onto cooking pots of Etruscan type.[26]

Contacts between Etruria and Carthage were also longstanding, with bucchero being imported to Carthage from the middle of the seventh century BC, and in large quantities from the beginning of the sixth through the first quarter of the fifth.[27] A later example of the relationship between an Etruscan town, Caere, and Phoenician traders is provided by the well-known dedication of gifts in the sanctuary of Uni-Astarte at its port city of Pyrgi, probably to be identified as the settlement called Punicum on the Tuscan coast known from the Peutinger Table. Again, the site was clearly a flourishing emporium in the sixth century. The sanctuary appears to date from the early fifth century and was probably used for sacred prostitution,

[23] Colonna 2004; see also the sanctuary at Gravisca: Torelli (2004) who concludes that, like the Etruscans, the Greeks who frequented the sanctuary were fairly lower class. On Caere, Lulof 2005; on Veio, Camporeale 2004. For Tarquinia we have the well-known myth of Demaratus, who is said to have arrived with a substantial Greek escort of craftsmen towards the middle of the seventh century: Dion. Hal. *Ant. Rom.* 3.46.3. On this myth and its archaeological correlates e.g. Ridgway and Ridgway 1994. On Greco-Etruscan relations in general Pallottino 1979 [1966].

[24] Torelli 1977, 1982. Only twenty inscriptions at Gravisca are later than 530 BC, compared to sixty in the previous quarter century; he suggests that the *emporion* was transferred to Tarquinia itself in the fifth century. See also Leighton 2004: 128–31. For the suggestion that the founder of the François tomb at Vulci was married to a woman of Punic origin, Coarelli 1983: 58–60.

[25] For Campania see D'Agostino and Cerchiai 2004.

[26] Dietler 2010: 97; Py 1995.

[27] Von Hase 1993.

although Cristofani has suggested that the chambers were used for the housing of passing sailors.[28]

What is interesting, however, is what happens after the decline of the emporia, in that both Gravisca and Pyrgi appear to have lost that function by the middle of the fifth century BC. That Punic–Etruscan relationships nonetheless persisted in the fourth century is demonstrated by a singular sarcophagus from Tarquinia of the middle of the century, containing the remains of an Etruscan aristocrat, Larth Partunu, wearing an earring which suggests Punic dress (we know of their penchant for earrings from the *Poenulus*),[29] and holding a *pyxis* in his hand which should indicate a priestly function (Figure 6.1).[30] Of Parian marble, the sarcophagus was clearly created in Carthage, where two very similar sarcophagi are found.[31] Its sides were subsequently decorated with Etruscan paintings. The anthropomorphic sarcophagus is a type diffused throughout the Phoenicio-Punic world,

Figure 6.1 Detail of sarcophagus of Larth Partunu, from Tarquinia.

[28] Cristofani 1989.

[29] Plaut. *Poen.* 983. His long, loose *chiton* may be the sort of costume referred to in lines 1299 and 1304.

[30] Herbig 1952: no. 121; Blanck 1983; Cataldi Dini 1988.

[31] Torelli 1993: Pl. XIV, 1.

deriving, ultimately, from Egypt – but in this case it was imported to Etruria, presumably by its eventual occupant. Sandrine Crouzet, who is currently studying this and related objects, suggests that the deceased was a mercenary.[32] It has even been suggested that Partunu was not the figure depicted, because of his Punic earring.[33] These interpretations seem far-fetched: the figure, with its priestly reference and Punic earring, is far too specific; we cannot imagine an Etruscan aristocrat choosing a second-hand figure to represent him on his sarcophagus. It seems more probable that it does indeed represent Partunu, a merchant whose style when in Carthage would have fitted in with that of his hosts, and have advertised his fluency with foreign cultures at home. Only such a merchant would have had the ability to command the shipping for this expensive and above all heavy souvenir.

The existence of Etruscans living in Carthage is also suggested by the well-known sixth-century *tessera hospitalis* found in a Carthaginian tomb, inscribed in Etruscan on a small ivory plaque, which would have given its owner an introduction into some central Etruscan city. The name inscribed there, Puinel, is attested otherwise only at Volterrae.[34] This *tessera*, like the second-century ivory of clasped hands known from Lilybaeum inscribed with a Greek text which names one *Imulch Inibalos Chlōros*, implies that the post-emporial trading arrangements involved stays inside the host cities that were based on personal relationships.[35] Messineo suggests that the plaques with two gentile names, like the inscribed ivory lion from S. Omobono[36] or the bronze ram's head found near Fucino and inscribed in Latin,[37] could confirm *hospes* relationships between two families. Indeed there would be little point in creating the elaborate *tesserae* to confirm pacts between two individuals already known to each other.[38] We thus seem to be seeing a gradual shift from the emporia, where foreign traders were kept firmly outside the cities, towards an interpenetration of the élites, with foreign enclaves and networks of relationships between

[32] Crouzet 2004: 15.

[33] Leighton 2004: 157. Massa Pairault believes even less plausibly that the sarcophagus was manufactured in Etruria for a Carthaginian client and suggests that the paintings, of Greeks battling with Amazons, refer to the struggle between Syracusan Greeks and Carthage, then the ally of Tarquinia (1997: 130–3).

[34] Delattre 1890: 192–3, nn. 4–5. For the text Pallottino 1979 and Rix 1991: Af. 3.1; for a discussion with previous bibliography Prag 2006: 8–9. See also the cippus of Caeretan type identified by Pallottino in the tophet of Salammbo: Pallottino 1979 [1966]: 393, and Pl. VIII, 1.

[35] *IG* XIV.279; C. Di Stefano 1993: 47 and Pl. L, with previous bibliography.

[36] Messineo 1983: 3–4, with previous bibliography.

[37] Bernabei 1895: 85–6.

[38] Note that the exchange goes on for generations: Hanno in Plautus' *Poenulus* plans to show his *tessera* to the *son* of his old friend (955); he then cites past hospitality at Carthage, both his own and that of his father. On *tesserae* see also Jonathan Prag, Chapter 11 in this volume.

members of the merchant classes. The trading settlements had economic consequences – those settled in them would have had better knowledge of the local market, and have been able to communicate with merchants from their own countries – but also social ones, in the middle ground between the external traders and their native hosts. The privileged relationship between these small groups of merchants and the indigenous culture will have left a stamp on the tastes, and the customs, of each party.[39]

By the time we reach the fully Hellenistic period, however, the picture has changed again, and the sparring partner, both in war and in trade, is Rome. Rome had, of course, been dealing with individual Sicilian cities such as Gela as early as the beginning of the fifth century BC.[40] The wars are not an issue here, although we should, again, remember how much Hannibal's officers and troops learned of Italy, or how much those of Scipio learned of the hinterland of Carthage. But the wars were hardly the first contacts between the two powers; R. E. A. Palmer has reviewed the peaceful, and above all commercial, relationships between Rome and Carthage.[41] The first treaty between the two was made in 509 BC, the second around 348.[42] The studies of Barbara Scardigli show that both of these treaties establish trade relations between the two towns, with no restrictions on their use of each other's major ports, although the Romans were forbidden to trade in the Sahel, or anywhere beyond Cap Bon.[43] The second treaty was initiated by the Carthaginians, whose envoys had come seeking friendship and alliance and, according to Livy, was renewed in 306 BC.[44] The first treaty specifies that trade was to be overseen by heralds, or clerks, in North Africa and Sardinia. Such trade as there was must have stopped during the First Punic War, which concluded in 241 BC, but in the period which followed there was certainly a vast increase in dealings with Carthage and the African towns.[45] Palmer suggests that there may have been enclaves of Punic traders in Rome, centred in the Vicus Africus or the Vicus Sobrius, the latter dedicated to the very African god Mercurius Sobrius, to whom dedications are common in Roman-period Africa, and whose shrines, I have argued elsewhere, were commonly the sites of *nundinae*.[46] Palmer also makes much of Plautus' *Poenulus*, produced on the Roman stage around 190 BC, and

[39] On such cross-cultural trade and its implications Curtin 1984.

[40] This incident was the purchase of grain by the Romans during a famine: Livy 2.34; Dio Cass. 5.18.4. Gallo 1992 and most recently Mafodda 2004.

[41] Palmer 1997; for foreign communities in Imperial Rome see Ricci 2005.

[42] On the treaties Polyb. 3.22–5. [43] Scardigli 1991.

[44] Livy 7.27.2. I do not enter here into the long-running dispute concerning the so-called 'Philinus Treaty'; for the most recent contribution see Eckstein 2010.

[45] Polyb. 1.83.10 confirms an immediate resumption of trade. [46] Fentress 2007.

assuming a certain familiarity with Punic slang, while presenting its hero, Hanno, and his family in a favourable light. But these are the only traces we can find of a Punic community in Rome, and they are not altogether convincing.

Better evidence comes from Latium. The extramural sanctuary of Casarinaccio in Ardea has material that strongly suggests a Punic presence in the city. Two vases of local manufacture, dated to the third century BC, carry Punic inscriptions on their lids: one was inscribed by a certain Mago.[47] Votive objects include one of the familiar glass pendents of a mask of a bearded man, dating between the end of the fourth and the third century BC.[48] Parallels for the mask in Lazio are found at the sanctuary of Diana at Nemi and at Anzio. All of these seem to relate to trade in the context of the treaty of 306, and the presence of Punic traders in the cities and at the sanctuaries. In this context Ardea's refusal of support for Rome in the Second Punic War might be related to consistent Punic contacts with the city.[49]

Good parallels for the settlement of trading enclaves in cities controlled by others are found both at Vaga and at Cirta, sites of massacres of Italian citizens before the Jugurthine War at the end of the second century BC.[50] The penetration of Italian merchants this far inland does emphasise just how important the grain from these areas was, but it also shows the degree to which merchants travelled, and lived, as a group. Such groups were operating in Sicily as well during the second century: evidence from Cicero's discussion of judicial procedure in Sicily under the *lex Rupilia* shows *negotiatores*, presumably Roman or Italian citizens, who might also sit in judgement and bring cases.[51] At Syracuse we find, among many others, one L. (or T.) Herennius, a *negotiator ex Africa* and banker from Leptis Magna who was beheaded by Verres.[52] Here again, we are seeing a resident community of foreigners with constant ties to their home countries.

Another instance of such contact may come from Jerba. Here the town of Būrgū was almost submerged in black glaze pottery of predominantly Campanian origin from the end of the Second Punic War onwards.[53] Campanian, too, were the Greco-Italic and Dressel 1 amphorae found all

[47] Acconcia 2005: 126–7. I am grateful to Paolo Liverani for drawing my attention to this.

[48] L. Ceccarelli 2010: 317–9. [49] Livy 27.9. [50] Sall. *Iug.* 21.2; 26.1.

[51] E.g. Cic. *Verr.* 2.34; see Musti 1980.

[52] Cic. *Verr.* 1.14; 5.155. Cicero shows *negotiatores* throughout the ports of the island: '. . . how much was extorted from the *negotiatores* who do business at Syracuse, at Agrigentum, at Panormus, at Lilybaeum . . .' (*Verr.* 2.153). For a complete list of *negotiatores* in Sicily in the second and first century, mainly derived from Cicero, see Fraschetti 1981b.

[53] Ben Tahar 2009.

Figure 6.2 Hellenistic puteal from Būrgū, Jerba.

over the site in massive quantities.[54] This could, of course, simply be the result of the activities of Jerban or other merchants – except for one quite splendid detail, a white marble puteal discovered during the excavation of the monumental tomb on the south side of the city (Figure 6.2).[55] It is so clearly related to similar cistern heads from Pompeii that its Campanian origin is without doubt.[56] Now it may, of course, also be a trade good, but it seems far more likely that it was imported by someone who, if not a Campanian aristocrat himself, wanted to live like one, and knew how it was done.

Jerba brings us to a final case of élite communication within the central Mediterranean: the royal tombs discussed by Ann Kuttner (Chapter 8) and Josephine Crawley Quinn (Chapter 7) in this volume. The Būrgū tomb shows the Egyptianising sculpture that must represent a prince with Alexandrian pretensions (Figure 6.3), well aware of the similar tombs that were being produced in Sabratha around the same time, or, indeed, in central Numidia at Thugga or at Siga along the coast of Mauretania.[57] In

[54] Fontana 2009. [55] Ferchiou 2009a.

[56] For a good parallel see Sear 2006b: Fig. 24, from the Casa della Caccia Antica.

[57] Ferchiou 2009b.

Figure 6.3 Reconstruction of the Hellenistic 'Egyptianising' tomb at Būrgū, Jerba.

addition to the multiple messages unpacked by Josephine Crawley Quinn, these tombs signal the degree to which their occupants got around and communicated with each other, interacting along the shores of the Mediterranean through architecture, through style and through trade.

I have dwelt at length on the evidence of foreign colonies inside existing cities in the central Mediterranean in order to get beyond a simple model of diffusion of culture through contact – stopping in a port, picking up a cargo, buying a Greek vase. It is residence in, or at least profound contact with, another community that allows the *habitus* of the foreign city to be absorbed by foreigners. Élite merchants will thus have participated in the lives and styles of the local élites, while forming personal bonds with them. This brief spin around élite connectivity in the Hellenistic central Mediterranean provides the background for the specifically élite relationships that I want to discuss in the rest of this chapter: the transmission of particular agricultural and architectural forms in the fourth through second centuries BC.

Agricultural strategies and competitive gardening

The agricultural form at issue is the specialised estate producing cash crops for the market, usually depending on intensive arboriculture; I am not going to use the term villa, as it just confuses the issue. Now, the production of a surplus in grain which could solve the problems of major cities had been common for a long time – Rome and Athens' search for dependable sources of grain are early and well known. In a sense the principal interaction between Rome, Sicily and Africa was about grain. Sicily, particularly its *mesogeia*, was a source of grain from an early period.[58] The small towns that dotted the interior of Sicily, and the later dispersed settlement in the Hellenistic period, were there to produce grain, both for themselves and, for anyone able to dominate them, for tax or tribute.[59] Africa too was to become an important grain source, and before the grain of the Mejerda valley served Rome it served Carthage. But it is hard to conceive that surpluses from extensive farming of grain were the subject of juicy profits for the farmers.

The situation on the coast was very different. Here the merchant class lived, whether in Sicily, Campania or Africa. The first genuinely profitable farming we hear of in the sources for this area is that of the Agrigentines and their sale of olive oil and wine to Carthage.[60] Olives and wine are intensive crops, designed for the market, and associated with the élite merchant class who could deal in them. According to Diodorus, they had made Agrigento rich: the great temple of Zeus was built with the money deriving from this trade. Agrigento was clearly not the only city that had gone in for intensive arboriculture: Diodorus' accounts of the wars of the early fourth century BC are full of the chopping down of trees when a city is under seige.[61]

I would submit that these are not just any trees, but proper orchards, whose destruction made a fine preliminary for the massacre of the inhabitants of a town. It is not surprising that the destruction of orchards is one of the principal activities of the Israeli army in their harassment of Palestinian villages: trees and vines are always perceived as a source of wealth, whose cultivation represents a fixed capital as well as an infinitely renewable source of income.[62] There are several peculiarities of tree crops, compared with grain. Firstly, their fruits, at harvest time, are extremely vulnerable to theft, both by birds (or indeed wild boar) and by people. Secondly, if cultivated on any scale they periodically require intensive labour to harvest and process, while pruning in February or March is equally necessary. Finally, the processed product – wine, oil, dried fruit and nuts – requires storage and packaging for shipment. All of these considerations suggest that the owner of such an estate would need some sort of building there in order to oversee these operations:

[58] Above n. 40. [59] Perkins 2007: 38–41. [60] Diod. Sic. 13.81.4.

[61] E.g. Diod. Sic. 14.48.5. See also the destruction of Athens' orchards by the Spartans in 430/429 BC: Thuc. 2.54.1.

[62] Benvenisti 2000: *passim*.

in effect to manage his capital.[63] The protection of olive trees with walls is already visible in late fifth-century BC Sicily, with the walled grove of trees in which over 6,000 Athenians and their allies were defeated by the Syracusans – a story which also reveals the substantial size of the plantation.[64] It is not a coincidence that the first dispersed settlement in Etruria, in the sixth century, seems to coincide with the production of wine for export, as the numerous amphorae recorded in wrecks between Etruria and Gaul seem to show.[65]

Now, while tree crops and the raising of large cattle, which seems to have been common near Carthage, are eminently subjects for display, none of this is the case with grain, which can be more or less left to its own devices until harvest, and then carried off for storage in the city.[66] Areas devoted to grain production are notoriously empty of settlement – we may think of vast tracts of modern Puglia, or central Sicily, where there is no dispersed settlement on the wheatlands. It is thus not by chance, as I have recently argued, that the Berber inhabitants of the area of the Tunisian Tell subject to Carthage lived in villages, while the coastal areas around urban centres such as Carthage and Būrgū were marked by a dispersed settlement pattern including large villas and small farms.[67] In the Carthaginian hinterland, surplus grain produced in the villages was taxed, and we may presume that any excess crops were consumed in the villages themselves.[68] On the coast, grain production would have supported households that produced cash crops on estates owned by Carthaginians.[69]

The chronological priority of the Sicilian coastal wine-producing estates over those of Carthage seems assured: apart from Diodorus' remark about the Agrigentines,[70] we know from survey of only six rural sites in the immediate hinterland of Carthage in the fourth century BC, while the Danish team at Segermes found none.[71] By the beginning of the third century, the number of these rises to fifty. Diodorus' often-cited account of the expedition of Agathocles in 310 BC shows just such estates, with sumptuous buildings, irrigated agriculture (another measure of intensivity) and tree crops.[72] It may be that the disruption of trade with eastern Sicily

63 The point is made by Perkins 1999: 191. I am grateful to him for reminding me of the fundamental work of Sereni 1970. On tree planting as capital investment Foxhall 2007: 73–5.

64 Thuc. 7.81.1–4. I am grateful to Andrew Wilson for drawing this passage to my attention. For references to field walls (and perhaps some terraces) in Greek texts see Price and Nixon 2005.

65 See the lists in Long 2004. On Etruscan trade in general, Gras 1985.

66 Fentress and Docter 2008: 111. 67 Fentress 2006. 68 Polyb. 1.71 (240 BC).

69 Fentress 2006. 70 Diod. Sic. 13.81.4.

71 Fentress and Docter 2008: 108–9; Dietz *et al.* 1995; Dietz (ed.) 2000.

72 Diod. Sic. 20.8. On Carthaginian wine production see Lancel 1995: 278–82.

during the fourth century spurred the Carthaginian élite to create their own wine and oil plantations, but it seems more likely that the process was already stimulated by their interaction with the Greek Sicilian élite, and the competition between them. The suggestion that the practices of intensive arboriculture were transferred via Sicily is hardly new: it was discussed by Toynbee as early as 1965.[73] What I want to emphasise here, however, are extra-economic aspects of intensive agriculture, and the way in which it is a product of communication and competition between élites. Just this sort of communication and competition is visible in the parallel development of villa estates in central Italy, but that is another story. Élite agriculture and architectural practice was conditioned by interaction and competition between *all* the élites of the central Mediterranean as well as by their desire to turn a profit.[74] Rather than denying the economic importance of the intensive agriculture practised on these estates, I want to suggest that it is inseparable from questions of style and display, and that these elements are forms of communication like any other.

We are dealing, then, not simply with the sort of economic rationality touted by Andrea Carandini twenty-five years ago for Columella's vineyard,[75] but also with a form of display behaviour, competitive gardening, if you will, which shows itself not only in the creation of estates, but in the cultivation of new species and the writing of manuals.[76] Now, there is abundant evidence that peasants are averse to new crops: the story of the diffusion of the potato is a well-known example.[77] In the same way the propagation of new tree-crops passed between the élite, rather than by some mysterious diffusionary process: the almond was the *nux graeca*, the pomegranate the *malum punicum*, while a special variety of African figs was planted in Cato the Elder's time.[78] We can imagine that wealthy landowners exchanged cuttings or nursery plants as gifts, as well as acquiring them on the market. It is into this context that we must place Mago, who, as Greene and Kehoe neatly demonstrate, was part of the third-century Carthaginian élite, listed by Pliny after Xenophon among the generals who did

[73] Toynbee 1965: II, 162–4.

[74] Purcell writes: 'So closely intertwined were the cultural and ideological characteristics of the élites of the ancient Mediterranean by the Augustan period that a distinctive form of the principal vehicle for the principal economic concern of those élites would be very striking . . .' (1995: 165).

[75] Carandini 1983.

[76] On the agriculture of the Roman villa as an expression of Republican virtue see Wallace-Hadrill 1998. The first significant article on agriculture as display is Purcell 1995.

[77] Zuckerman 2000: 83, for Parmentier's ruse in which a field of potatoes was closely guarded during the day, so that the peasants would steal the potatoes at night.

[78] *Nux graeca*: Mago in Plin. *HN* 17.63; *malum punicum*: Cato, *Agr.* 7.3; African figs: *id.* 8.1.

agricultural writing.[79] As far as we know from the citations that survive, he concentrated on arboriculture, specifying the ways to plant olives and vines and, particularly relevant for our purposes, how to produce the sweet raisin wine, *passum*, that was clearly a product of Jerba and Carthage in the second and first century BC.[80]

The archaeological evidence for the intensity of Punic arboriculture comes from the territory of Jerba as well as from that of Carthage. The Jerban case is even clearer: third-century BC settlement is dense and articulated into villas and small farms, while amphorae in the Punic tradition of the second century were found in great abundance, with fully eight kilns identified in the course of a survey of the island.[81] These are enormously important because these are the only such kilns that have been published, although the great diversity of the fabrics of this sort of amphora certainly suggests that there were numerous areas of production. The type, Van der Werff forms 2 and 3, was produced in Byzacena and eastern Tripolitania.[82] Although Jerba cannot be considered the only zone in which they were produced, it must have been one of the most important, and their generally coastal distribution is evident.

The kilns are distributed along a road that appears to connect the town of Būrgū to its hinterland, in the area of the greatest density of villas. There are none to the north of the town, where we would expect to find them if their products were being exported from the port at Ghizen, so we must conclude that Meninx itself was the port that was used to ship them, perhaps together with the murex dye and fish sauce produced there. However, these kilns are certainly not producing garum amphorae, as they are almost always connected to agricultural settlements in the island's interior, and are never situated on the coast itself. This production is certainly a signal of the economic growth of the territory after the Second Punic War, and the development of these settlements must be connected to the emergence of new systems of agricultural exploitation and the bringing into production of most of the agricultural land of the island. The wine carried in the amphorae was clearly targeted at the Italian market, and that is where we find them traded. Amphorae in the Punic tradition are numerous at Ostia, at Rome, along the coast of Central Tyrrhenian Italy and even in the interior, at sites such as Privernum and Statonia in the middle Tiber Valley.[83] The fact that

[79] Greene and Kehoe 1995; Plin. *HN* 18.22. Hieron II of Syracuse figures first on the list. Varro, *Rust.* 1.1.8-10 also lists garden experts, starting with Hieron II, but concludes 'all these are surpassed in reputation by Mago of Carthage . . .'; see also Columella, *Rust.* 1.1.8.

[80] Fentress 2001. [81] Fentress 2001; Fontana 2009: 270–7. [82] Fontana 2009: 270–7.

[83] Fontana 2009: 270–7.

on wrecks they are regularly associated with Italic amphorae suggests the importance of Italian *negotiatores* in their trade, a relationship also implied by the predominance of Italian imports on the island.[84] These merchants must have had close ties to the island élites, although there is no evidence that they were directly involved with agricultural production on the island.

A final indication of the importance of the mercantile networks between Sicily, Africa and Campania in the spread of intensive agriculture in the coastal *paralia* is the *absence* of this sort of production on the Spanish coast in the second century BC. As yet there are no proven luxury villas there until the time of Augustus. Now, there is no earthly reason why local élites were not perfectly able to set themselves up in modern villas with intensive arboriculture – except, perhaps, that they were not in close communication with their peers in Sicily and, eventually, central Italy.

The network, then, was both coastal and central. It is perhaps no coincidence that the only inland olive farm we know of for the Numidian period is the Numidian royal capital of Cirta where, as we have seen, various merchants had their homes, and where the sanctuary of El Hofra shows that Greeks, Numidians and Italians were all busily inscribing in Punic.[85] The grain trade provided the engine which moved goods along, but the intensive productions of the *paralia* provided the wealth for the local élites.

Building fashions in the central Mediterranean

At this point we need to revisit the question of the buildings that went with these farms and their relationship to each other. Again, I want to place the very clear relationships between the Sicilian and Carthaginian buildings into the context of the communication between their commercial élites. Insofar as a farmer was a member of the urban élite he would invest more in the building's architecture and adornment, so that it would represent his very urban style. A striking example of this sort of architecture is that of the *bagli* in the region of Marsala, vast eighteenth-century buildings built at the height of the boom in Marsala wine, generated by British investment and demand. Deserted for eleven months out of the year, they came into their own only at harvest, when they were used not only for the processing and storage of the crop but also for a month in the country in which receptions were held by the various families, who could, thereby, admire each other's houses and vineyards. This is certainly agriculture for profit, but it is also

[84] Fontana 2009: 270–7 and Table 16.13. [85] Berthier 1980; Bertrandy 1985.

agriculture for display: I should note that even the largely abandoned *bagli* that characterise the vineyards of the Marsalese are still used at the *vendemmia*, which leads to worrying thoughts about parallels with the late Roman villas that they so closely resemble.

The importance of the farm buildings in terms of display is perfectly obvious in Cato the Elder, in spite of his moralising on Greek-derived architectural elements:

> Build your dwelling-house in accordance with your means. If you build substantially on a good farm, placing the house in a good situation, so that you can live comfortably in the country, you will like to visit it, and will do so more often; the farm will improve, there will be less wrongdoing, and you will receive greater returns. . . . Near a town it is well to have a garden planted with all manner of vegetables, and all manner of flowers for garlands – Megarian bulbs, conjugulan myrtle, white and black myrtle, Delphian, Cyprian, and wild laurel, smooth nuts, such as Abellan, Praenestine, and Greek filberts. The suburban farm, and especially if it be the only one, should be laid out and planted as ingeniously as possible.[86]

This is as good a description of the agriculture of display as Pliny's of the oasis of Tacape: in both, the planting is complex and ingenious, showing the style and investment of the owner.[87] *A fortiori* the farm building should be urban and complex. Now, I am not going to linger on the peristyle villas of Africa and Sicily: I have done this elsewhere.[88] It is not necessary to do more than mention that the early peristyle villa of Motya, for example, is highly unlikely to have been an urban *domus*, but was apparently an isolated building on an island whose city was destroyed a hundred years previously.[89] I suggest that the excavated portion is part of an early villa. It seems now to date to the end of the fourth century BC, when all but a few traces of occupation elsewhere on the island had disappeared. The mosaics are classically Hellenistic, related to the pebble mosaics of Pella and Alexandria.[90] The owner, however, was almost certainly Punic, insofar as the island, on which the original Punic town was located before its destruction, is firmly sited in the *eparchia* of Carthage, close to the refounded capital of Lilybaeum. But he was clearly in touch with the sort of élite that was commissioning pebble mosaics elsewhere in the Mediterranean, and through them could find the workshop of artisans who would produce them.

[86] Cato, *Agr.* 4.1 and 8.2 (trans. W. D. Hooper and H. B. Ash, Loeb Classical Library).
[87] Plin. *HN* 18.188. [88] Fentress 2001: 255–60.
[89] Tusa 1997; Famà 1997 has the most recent plan of the building and previous bibliography.
[90] See Andrew Wilson, Chapter 5 in this volume.

A more characteristic Punic technique is *signinum* floors decorated with marble tesserae. In Kerkouane and the area of Carthage, these were in production well before we find them in central Italy, although not long before their appearance at Morgantina.[91] The principal rooms in the houses of Kerkouane have *signinum* floors decorated with marble tesserae, sometimes with a meander at the threshold, and the occasional sign of Tanit.[92] These date to the middle of the fourth century – a date which might be applied to those of the Punic houses of Selinunte, as well as the Punic sanctuaries built into the Greek temples there.[93] The same paving was also used in villas such as that of Gammarth, near Carthage, excavated by Fantar.[94] This is an extremely interesting building, of which it would have been good to know more – what we can see includes some proportion of a large courtyard, with an oil press in its corner, and private baths inside the residential area. It was decorated with *signinum* floors with marble tesserae, and stone cornices covered with white stucco. The passage of *pavimentum punicum* from Africa into Sicily and thence central Italy is well known, and various means of transmission have been suggested.[95] Gaggiotti's suggestion that the technique was transmitted from Carthage to central Italy, and specifically to the town of Signia, by gangs of Carthaginian prisoners and hostages is certainly plausible.[96]

An even more elaborate architectural form is that of the small domestic bath, of which we have numerous fourth-century examples from Kerkouane. These are often lavishly decorated with tesselated *signinum* floors, with the walls and benches covered with the same material.[97] The baths were raised above floor-level, generally with a step to sit on. Now, Kerkouane was destroyed at the latest in 256 BC, but seems to have suffered badly already at the hands of Agathocles, and there seems little doubt that these baths, as well as the peristyles of the houses, date to the fourth century. They should relate to the Greek baths in the form known from elsewhere in the Mediterranean,[98] developed at Kerkouane with specifically Punic traits,

[91] Tsakirgis 1990 and Andrew Wilson (Chapter 5) and Roger Wilson (Chapter 4) in this volume.

[92] Tsakirgis 1990: Pl. XIV. It is argued by F. Guidobaldi (1995: 2–3) and Grandi Carletti (2001) that the use of the term *signinum* for pavements in cement with pounded tile is philologically incorrect. However, as *cocciopesto* or cement do not form acceptable, universally understood terms in English, I shall continue to use *signinum* for pavements with pounded tile, alternating with *pavimenta punica*. See most recently Vassal 2006: 24–6.

[93] On the dating and plan of the Punic sanctuary in temples A and O see most recently D'Andria and Campagna 2002.

[94] Fantar 1985: 14–23 and Pl. XIII, b. [95] Joly 1997. [96] Gaggiotti 1987: 215–21.

[97] Fantar 1985: 305–58.

[98] Note, however, the large number of private baths at Olynthus: Robinson and Graham 1938: 199–204.

such as the use in them of tesselated *opus signinum*.[99] Small private baths of this type are known from Sicily as well: at Megara Hyblaea,[100] Monte Iato[101] and Morgantina.[102] The bath at Megara Hyblaea, indeed, seems to have been owned by a certain C. Modius, an Italian.[103] It is thus hardly surprising to see very similar private baths turning up in Campania and the area of Rome in the early second century. The most famous of these is the private bath of Scipio Africanus at Liternum with its little, dark bathroom, so unlike those of the time of Seneca.[104] Another example from the Villa Prato at Sperlonga, whose excavators would date it to the middle of the second century, might give us some idea of what the baths at Liternum were like (Figure 6.4).[105] A similar ensemble is said to come from Ciampino and is clearly by the same group of workmen.[106] One of the baths at Sperlonga is made with a terracotta *sabot*, for which comparisons can be found as far apart as Punic Solunto[107] and Monte Iato in Sicily, Castiglione di Paludi in Calabria (in a third-century building), second-century Cosa and a shipwreck off Marseille.[108] The form seems to derive from earlier Greek public baths, but it is notable that we also find it in Punic and Roman contexts.[109]

My point is that there must be some agent of transmission that we are missing, and that a continuity between the Campanian baths and Punic and Sicilian practice of small private baths through the third century is highly likely. The private bath, with its terracotta or masonry *sabot* and decorated *signinum* is specifically a feature of domestic architecture common among the *Punic* élite, which passes, like so much else, into 'Hellenistic' Roman practice via Sicily.

A final element in the architectural ensemble that we find here is the three-sided peristyle. Although not generalised in Kerkouane, it makes a

99 Fantar 1985: 354. 100 Megara Hyblaea: Vallet *et al.* 1983: 15.

101 Monte Iato: Dalcher 1994: 37–9 and Pl. 13.

102 Morgantina, 'House of the Arched Cistern': Tsakirgis 1984: 132–3 and, in general, 383–5. Other possible Morgantina bathrooms are identified in the 'House of the Official' and that of the 'Doric Capital'.

103 Torelli 2008. 104 Sen. *Ep.* 86. 105 Broise and Lafon 2001: 70–89.

106 Broise and Lafon 2001: 143. The negative number given there is false, but it appears to be the same site as De Rossi 1979: site 89 p. 64.

107 For Solunto, observation in the Solunto antiquarium. There has been no standard treatment of bathtubs since Cook 1959 and Ginouvès 1962.

108 For Monte Iato, Castiglione di Paludi and Marseille see Broise and Lafon 2001: 85 and n. 101, as well as Fig. 141; for Cosa, Scott 1993: Pl. 21. Note that the presence on a shipwreck of such a bath suggests that it was an article of trade.

109 An analysis of the fabric of these baths might point to a common place of manufacture.

Figure 6.4 The bathroom at the Villa Prato.

striking appearance in the large second-century houses excavated at Carthage by the German team,[110] and is evident in the villa with corner towers at Contrada Mirabile, in western Sicily, of similar date.[111] Although Vitruvius defines this feature as 'Greek', we find it in a series of buildings in which Punic and Roman elements are almost equally present.[112] And, we might note, none of the early villas of Magna Graecia have three-sided peristyles, nor do I know any from the eastern Mediterranean.[113] I have argued elsewhere that Vitruvius' knowledge of 'Greek' houses came from Sicily.[114]

We are dealing here with the formation, for farms and farm buildings, as well as urban dwellings, of a style that mixed Punic and Hellenistic elements: a style that included *signinum* floors, stuccoed stone mouldings and private baths as well, and, in particular, the use of large peristyle villas with corner towers. These seem to show a specifically central Mediterranean development of a villa style, in parallel to that based on the *atrium* which was developing in Italy during the same period, between the fourth and the second centuries. It developed out of the connectivity between the Punic and Sicilian élites, a connectivity that would eventually result in the sort of fusion between the two that we can see in the painted aediculae of

[110] Carthage: Rakob 1991a: Fig. 39. [111] Contrada Mirabile: Fentress 1998.
[112] Vitr. *De arch.* 6.7. [113] See the examples in Russo 2006. [114] Fentress 1998: 38.

first-century Lilybaeum,[115] or the tombstone with the dedication from Cefalù which reads Πομπήϊα | Ῥούφου Μέγα | Μεγάλαι χαῖρε ('Pompeia Megala, daughter of Rufus Megas, farewell' – a Greek freedwoman of a Roman family?), whose top is decorated with a sketched-out anthropomorphic figure.[116]

The building style was hardly disconnected from central Italy, which, as Andrew Wallace-Hadrill points out, picked up many of its elements.[117] This is the case with the elaborately patterned, *signinum*-decorated baths at Villa Prato, which, with its turrets, its peristyle and the segregated spaces for the family that strongly suggest the *gynacaeum*, seems to represent a northern outlier of the Sicilian-style villa.[118] Of course, this simply shows that by the mid-second century, the network was now focused on Campania as well as Rome itself. Although Gaggiotti's suggestion that the fall of Carthage had brought a number of teams of builders to Italy as slaves is engaging, and hardly impossible, I believe that the components of the style were picked up by reciprocal visits to the town houses and estates of the local élite by passing or resident foreigners.[119] The villa owners – and of course Scipio Africanus is the most obvious example – had to know what to ask for. Artisans, slave or free, could be imported – the *signinum* baths of Sperlonga and Ciampino must have been made by the same team – but someone had to want them. The *committente*, or his architect, had to be aware of what the latest Sicilian fashion actually was.

The people who were doing the communication were people who, like Larth Partunu, crossed political and ethnic borders much more than is generally supposed: I remain genuinely puzzled by the fact that the Cosan decurions of the beginning of the second century lived in houses that did not differ by a centimetre from those of their Samnite peers in Pompeii.[120] Here, of course, we can explain the similarities by the rôle of Rome and its great families as style-setters, and describe the provinces as fashion victims. That this was not the case everywhere is shown by Sicily and Punic North Africa,

115 Lilybaeum: Vento 2000.

116 *SEG* 42.849, reporting Tullio 1988–9: 680 and Pl. 114. Tullio describes the figure as aniconic and thus in relationship to Punic practice: the deceased is represented as a flat, roughly shaped relief, prone on the top of the stone, a distant cousin of the sarcophagi of the type of the tomb of the priest discussed above.

117 Wallace Hadrill, Chapter 2 in this volume; see now Torelli 2011, for the origins of the Roman villa in Magna Graecia.

118 Broise and Lafon 2001. For further discussion, Fentress 2003b.

119 Gaggiotti 1987: 219–20. On the hostages see J. Allen 2006: 49–52. Note that this may also explain the very localised spread of *opus africanum* in second-century Pompeii.

120 The measurements of the House of Diana at Cosa are almost identical to that of Sallust at Pompeii: Fentress 2003a: 19–21.

where the élite evolved their own style and *koine*. How Magna Graecia connects is another problem altogether: sites like the early third-century villa at Moltone del Tolve[121] seem to be built along the *atrium* pattern, with an external tower, while a whole new crop of third-century villas is awaiting study as a class.[122] But I will leave this to someone else, and finish by encouraging more serious archaeological investigation of the ones we know of from field survey: magnetometry is now a given, and Sicily is ideal for it. I have felt a number of times when writing this chapter that I was attempting to get a crop off a field that is overworked, and needs, not fallow, but manure, in the form of new and better information.

Conclusions

The interaction of élites, even – and particularly – from states that our sources would see as opposed to each other, is seen in this paper as central to the circulation of economic and architectural practice as well as goods. Here the distinction between merchants and political élites has been, to some extent, fudged, with the activities of the latter as soldiers seen as almost equally important from the point of view of the transmission of style and ideas. How communication took place, whether through interpreters or through a common language, above all Greek, is not immediately clear. Probably many of the traders were bi- or trilingual, as were members of the élite, from the Numidian kings on downwards.[123] Competition, even with the enemy, was evidently an important element in this interaction. There is also a level of straightforward exchange of ideas, of farming or flooring techniques, that shows the élites as much united as separated. They moved in a *koine* of similar styles and ideas, which in the subsequent centuries became perceived as a *Roman koine*.[124] Here, however, we can see the development of an intensive interplay, what Dietler would call 'entanglement,' between the quite distinct political and linguistic communities of the central Mediterranean that preceded, and to some extent formed, the closer integration of the Roman world.[125]

[121] Moltone del Tolve: Tocco 1992.

[122] New material is examined in Russo 2006; I am grateful to Helga di Giuseppe for bringing this to my attention.

[123] On bilingualism in the next period see Wallace-Hadrill 2008: 3–36. [124] *Ibid.*

[125] Dietler 2010: *passim*.

7 Monumental power: 'Numidian Royal Architecture' in context

JOSEPHINE CRAWLEY QUINN

Numidian Royal Architecture

In 1842 the British consul-general at Tunis, Colonel Sir Thomas Reade, acquired an intriguing bilingual Libyan and Punic inscription (Figure 7.1) from a mausoleum just outside ancient Thugga in the Tunisian Tell.[1] The square-based tower tomb, originally about 21 m high, was still standing to its third storey at the time; Reade had it dismantled for his purpose (Figure 7.2), and had the inscription cut from its stone and then cut in half for easier transportation to England, where the two parts passed to the British Museum.[2]

The tomb itself was reconstructed by French archaeologists between 1908 and 1910,[3] and is striking both for its beauty and its eclecticism (Figure 7.3).[4] Above a six-step stylobate, the first storey has corner pilasters with aeolic capitals (Figure 7.4), an archaic style originating in the Levant and reasonably widespread in Carthage and the surrounding region in the Hellenistic period.[5] The second storey, by contrast, has an engaged ionic colonnade recalling classical Greek architecture. Above this is a cavetto cornice (Figure 7.5), a moulding pioneered in Dynastic Egypt architecture, though long popular in the Levant as well as the Maghreb.[6] The third storey again has aeolic pilasters at its corners; between them relief panels on every side depict two people (the

This paper was written in response to and in dialogue with Ann Kuttner; I also owe thanks for comments, questions and answers to Christopher Brooke, Maria Brosius, Luca Cherstich, Lisa Fentress, Erich Gruen, Benjamin Isaac, Dorothy King, Judith McKenzie, Margaret Miller, Emanuele Papi, Jonathan Prag, Bert Smith, Andrew Stewart, David Stone, Susan Walker, John Wilkes, Andrew Wilson and Roger Wilson. All dates after this introductory section are BCE.

1 *RIL* 1. See Figure 7.23 for a map of many of the sites discussed in the text.

2 Poinssot and Salomonson 1959 [1960]: 146 n. 3; see also P. Février 1989: I, 28 on earlier debate over the fate of the inscription.

3 L. Poinssot 1910.

4 On the Thugga mausoleum, see in particular C. Poinssot 1958: 58–61; Poinssot and Salomonson 1959 [1960]; Rakob 1979: 156–8.

5 Lézine 1959: 59–62; Poinssot and Salomonson 1963: 82–8; Ferchiou 1989: 83–8. Betancourt 1977: 27–49 gives eastern Mediterranean examples.

6 Lézine 1959: 97–101; Ferchiou 1989: 291–9; Winter 2006: 228–9 on the eastern Mediterranean versions.

Figure 7.1 The Libyco-Punic inscription from the Thugga mausoleum (*RIL* 1): (a) Libyan; (b) Punic.

Figure 7.2 The Thugga mausoleum between 1842 and 1908.

Figure 7.3 The Thugga mausoleum (from South). For colour version see plate section.

deceased? a god?), riding in a quadriga with a high box, large wheels and a driver (Figure 7.5). The latter image is close in terms of the figures depicted in the chariot to a common scene in Persian iconography and on the coinage of Sidon in the period of the Persian domination of Phoenicia (Figure 7.6a)[7] – but even closer in terms of the form of the wheel and the depiction of the horses to images of Jupiter on a quadriga on Roman coinage of the late third century (Figure 7.6b).[8] Horses with riders stand on pedestals at all four corners.

[7] For a full discussion of the 'chariot scene' which appears on fourth-century double shekels from Sidon, see Elayi and Elayi 2004: 493–524. Their 'Groupe III' coins provide particularly close parallels for the Thugga relief, with the horses depicted at a gallop. More distant parallels from Persia itself include seals of King Darius hunting lion-related beasts (e.g. BM WA 89132), an agate cylinder from Egyptian Thebes labelled 'Darius, the Great King' in Old Persian, Elamite, and Babylonian (Boston MFA 21.1193), and one of the Apadana reliefs from Persepolis (BM ANE 118843: top register of east wing of north staircase).

[8] *RRC* 28/3–4 (225–212 BCE); 29/3–4; 30/1; 31/1; 32/1; 33/1; 34/1 (all 225–214 BCE). Cf. also Figure 4.3, this volume.

Figure 7.4 Detail from the Thugga mausoleum: aeolic pilaster.

Figure 7.5 Detail from the Thugga mausoleum: lower cavetto cornice and quadriga relief.

Figure 7.6 (a) Coin featuring quadriga from Sidon: Betlyon 1982: no. 40, reverse only, 342–339 BCE (25.64 g); (b) Coin featuring quadriga from Rome: *RRC* 28/3, reverse only, 225–212 BCE (6.63 g).

Above another cavetto cornice is a terminal pyramid with sirens carved in the round at its corners. Finally, a small lion – an age-old symbol of royal power in the Near East – was probably perched on top.[9]

The monument can be plausibly dated to the third/second century BCE, on the basis of the style of the architectural decoration and in particular of the Punic script, which the general consensus would put around the end of the third century.[10] We do not know who occupied or built it. The text of the bilingual inscription, originally placed to the right of an access window on the east face of the first storey, names an 'Atban', followed by the names of the various artisans, masons and labourers involved in the construction of the monument, which has therefore become known as the Mausoleum of Atban.[11] But since the discovery in the notes of the early nineteenth-century visitor Comte Borgia that there was originally a second inscription on the mausoleum[12] – already largely effaced in Borgia's time and presumably of no interest to Reade – there has been debate as to whether the mausoleum was built for or by this Atban; if the latter, the true funerary inscription would be the missing one.[13]

The Thugga mausoleum is just one of a series of large-scale, Hellenistic-period monuments that still dot the landscape of the Maghreb. These have

[9] The lion was found at the foot of the monument during the restoration, so the placement is not secure: C. Poinssot 1958: 58. Of many Near Eastern parallels perhaps the closest is the probably fourth-century dynastic 'Lion tomb' at Knidos where a (larger) lion sat on a base atop the stepped pyramid that is the upper element of the tomb: I. Jenkins 2006: 228–31.

[10] *RIL* p. 2. [11] Poinssot and Salomonson 1959 [1960]: 146.

[12] Comte Borgia: Poinssot and Salomonson 1959 [1960]: 146–7.

[13] J. Février 1959 and Ferron 1969–70 argue for the latter interpretation. The fact that a son of Atban is listed among the builders of the monument is often cited as a point in favour of this interpretation, though the category into which he falls is disputed, and it need not of course be the same Atban. For doubts about this reading, see Ghaki 1997: 27–8; in addition, the fact that the first line of the inscription, which names Atban, is separated by a considerable space from the list of builders might be thought to argue for him as the honorand. The first characters of both the Punic and Libyan texts, which would clarify this point, are missing.

Figure 7.7 Reconstructions of tower tombs; (left to right) Beni Rhénane, Es Soumaa, Sabratha Mausoleum B, Thugga Mausoleum.

been studied in detail by Friedrich Rakob, who coined the now-canonical term 'Numidian Royal Architecture' for the group (Figure 7.7).[14] As well as another quadrilateral mausoleum over 30 m in height, Es Soumaa at El Khroub in Northern Algeria,[15] there are four tower monuments built in a distinctive hexagonal form with concave sides: the tomb of Beni Rhénane near the ancient city of Siga in western Algeria;[16] Mausolea A and B at the port of Sabratha on the Libyan coast;[17] and a tomb at Henchir Būrgū on the Tunisian island of Jerba.[18] There are also two tumulus tombs: the

[14] Rakob 1979, 1983; for a more recent survey of the turriform monuments, which also discusses the other types, see Prados Martínez 2008.

[15] Bonnell 1915 [1916]. Es Soumaa had not been robbed when it was excavated, and the grave goods (pottery, weapons and silver) suggest a date in the mid-late second century BCE: for a report of the finds, see *Die Numider* 1979: 285–382.

[16] Vuillemot 1964; Bouchenaki 1991. This monument, also *c.* 30 m high, has been dated to *c.* 200 BCE on the evidence of pottery found nearby as well as style.

[17] These are not in fact true mausolea, as there is no evidence for burial chambers. Mausoleum B, almost 24 m high, has been meticulously reconstructed (Di Vita 1976) and has a clear stratigraphy and associated pottery which place its initial construction in the first decades of the second century BCE or possibly a little earlier (Bessi 2003).

[18] Weriemmi-Akkari 1985; Ferchiou 2009b. The state of preservation of this monument makes it extremely difficult to reconstruct (the figure that Fentress reproduces in Chapter 6 in this volume (Figure 6.3) is openly speculative), but the architectural style and the pottery found in a foundation deposit suggest a date in the second quarter of the second century BCE (Ferchiou 2009b: 111).

Figure 7.8 The Medracen. For colour version see plate section.

Figure 7.9 The Kbor er Roumia. For colour version see plate section.

Medracen in the Aurès mountains of Northern Algeria (Figure 7.8);[19] and the monument near Tipasa on the Algerian coast known as Kbor er Roumia, or 'La Tombe de la Chrétienne', on account of the 'Macedonian crosses' carved on its false doors (Figure 7.9).[20] Finally, there are the 'altars' with striking weapons-friezes at Simitthus and Kbor Klib that Ann Kuttner discusses in Chapter 8 in this volume.[21]

All of these monuments were built within the area ruled by the mid-second century BCE by Massinissa and his descendants, indigenous kings that we (with the Romans) call Numidian. Nonetheless, Kbor er Roumia is the only one positively identified as royal, described by Pomponius Mela as

[19] Camps 1973, 1994. The Medracen, 58.86 m in diameter by 18.5 m high, is usually put first in the sequence of tombs on the basis of style as well as carbon dating undertaken in the early 1970s, which suggested a date not later than 200 BCE (Camps 1973: 510–12); Camps considers a fourth-century date most likely.

[20] Bouchenaki 1991. Coarelli and Thébert date this (63 x 32.4 m) tomb to the late second or perhaps early first century BCE on stylistic grounds (1988: 766).

[21] A likely third 'altar' near Althiburos is signaled at Kallala *et al.* 2008: 98–100.

'the common tomb of the royal family'.[22] Even then precisely which royal family is difficult to say; most likely this is one of the later examples in the set, and should in fact be connected with the Mauretanian kings based further to the west.[23] We do not know who occupied or commissioned any of the other monuments, and I will suggest here that to assume that they are all 'Royal', or even 'Numidian', elides the local identities and leaders involved. Nonetheless, their locations and approximate dating suggest that this genre of architecture should be associated with the emergence of the Numidian states.[24]

Although these monuments have varied forms and functions, they all share the Thugga mausoleum's grand scale and its cosmopolitan approach to architectural decoration, and in the context of this project they provide a useful opportunity to investigate non-Roman cultures and connections in the 'Hellenistic West'. On the rare occasions that they have attracted scholarly attention in the past, discussion has usually focused on assigning them to one or another artistic tradition, and in particular on the question of whether they were influenced by 'Punic' or 'Hellenistic' models. But these attempts to classify the monuments as part of a particular cultural group or tradition under-interpret them, not least because they remove them from their local contexts and builders. After outlining this traditional debate, and those local contexts, I will suggest here that the forms and motifs that the monuments' architects borrow from elsewhere are not passive markers of external 'influence', nor of participation in any single 'cultural tradition', but instead invited a multiplicity of possible readings, with deliberate references to a variety of specific places and sources of power, local and further afield, past and present, and were used by their authors to articulate and reinforce their own power within new social and political structures in the region.

Culture wars

The 'Hellenistic' interpretation of Numidian Royal Architecture is most associated with Filippo Coarelli and Yvon Thébert, who argued in a classic

[22] Pomponius Mela 1.31: 'ultra monumentum commune regiae gentis, deinde Icosium Ruthisia urbes . . .'

[23] Coarelli and Thébert 1988: 766.

[24] Attempts to associate the tombs with particular kings are legion. For the suggestion, for instance, that the Thugga mausoleum is the (symbolic) tomb of Massinissa: Ferron 1969–70: 95–7. Coarelli and Thébert suggest that he was actually buried in the Medracen (1988: 805). For scepticism about specifically royal associations: Moore 2007: 77–80.

survey that these monuments borrowed from a solely eastern Mediterranean architectural tradition which exploited artistic elements and techniques from the Greek world.[25] For them, this tradition started in Persia with the sixth-century tomb of Cyrus at Pasargadae and continued in Asia Minor through the Monument of the Nereids at Xanthos (*c.* 400) and the fourth-century Mausoleum of Halicarnassus, to the early third-century Mausoleum of Belevi and the articulated tumulus in the Hellenistic Asklepeion at Pergamon. They denied any significant reference to Carthage in the architecture, emphasising instead the evidence for direct contacts between the Numidian kings and the cities and rulers of the eastern Mediterranean, and apparent local familiarity with Hellenistic iconographic 'codes', such as the significance of the diadem on royal coin-portraits.[26] By participating in and reinforcing this 'Numidian Hellenism', they suggested, the builders of the tombs (whom they took to be members of the royal dynasty) demonstrated their links with the eastern Mediterranean world, and compared themselves to eastern Mediterranean kings with their notionally absolute power, a message which would be particularly inappropriate in a Carthaginian context since that city was strongly against monarchy in this period.[27]

There is a great deal to be said for this argument, and one could add further examples of parallels and models in the eastern Mediterranean: in the case of the tumulus tombs, for instance, the early Hellenistic tomb near Pella in Macedon discussed by Kuttner in Chapter 8 of this volume. Other scholars have argued, however, and equally forcefully, that it was in fact the 'Punic' or more broadly Phoenician world that provided the inspiration for this African architecture.[28] Gabriel Camps argued that the 'Numidian' monuments refer primarily to Punic and Phoenician traditions, and that this phenomenon illustrates the high levels of acculturation between the Carthaginian and Numidian elites in the Hellenistic period.[29] For other

[25] Coarelli and Thébert 1988: 811.

[26] Coarelli and Thébert 1988: 812, 815, though cf. 808 where they are prepared to countenance some kind of mediating role for Carthage, and even the possible involvement of Punic architects. For an interesting argument in the opposite direction, that the 'Hellenistic' architecture of Sicily and thus Italy and Rome was communicated from the East via Carthage, see Martin 1970.

[27] Coarelli and Thébert 1988: 811; cf. Rakob 1983: 330, on 'the self-fashioning of the Numidian kings . . . who considered themselves the equals of the Hellenistic kings.'

[28] The label 'Punic' has traditionally been used to refer to the world of the western Phoenicians, especially from the sixth century onwards. For more on the definition and problems of this word, see the introduction to Quinn and Vella forthcoming.

[29] Most recently, Camps 1995, strongly supported by Shaw 2005: 125 n. 69. The main vehicle for cultural interchange in Camps' view was intermarriage with Carthaginian women 'avec leurs parfums et leurs bijoux' (1995: 236).

scholars, it is the tower-form monuments in particular that are associated with Punic architecture and influence.[30] For Serge Lancel, for instance, the Thugga Mausoleum is 'the only great monument of Punic architecture still standing on Tunisian soil', inheriting the 'Egypto-Greek' elements of its decoration via a lost world of monumental Punic architecture.[31] In his opinion, reflections of this architecture have survived for us in the stelai with winged solar disks, aeolic capitals, ionic columns and cavetto cornices found in the tophets at Carthage, Hadrumetum and other western Phoenician colonies in Sicily and Sardinia, as well as an aeolic pilaster depicted on an architectural fragment from Medjez-el-Bab, and the cavetto cornice and aeolic pilasters of a small *naiskos* found at Thuburbo Maius.[32] One could add to this list some larger-scale fragments of cavetto cornice and aeolic pilaster capitals found in Carthage, Utica and the wider Maghreb,[33] as well as the aeolic capital found at the Phoenician colony of Motya on Sicily, and the larger-scale 'Ma'abed' shrine at the Phoenician colony of Nora on Sardinia with its *uraeus* and winged sun-disk.[34]

Other evidence offered for the 'Punic' origin of the form of the pyramid-topped tower-tombs includes the existence of a series of similar but smaller-scale mausolea found within the *fossa regia*[35] (traditionally taken to be the dividing line between Numidian and Carthaginian territory in this period[36]), as well as the graffiti representations of tower-tombs in Hellenistic-period, 'Punic'-style, shaft-tombs in necropoleis on Carthaginian Cap Bon and in the Sahel (Figure 7.10).[37] Further east, potential Phoenician models for the form are found in the Levant, at Amrit in Syria, for instance, and in the Kidron Valley in Jerusalem.[38]

Some scholars have also argued for local elements: for Stéphane Gsell, the articulated circular form of the Medracen went back to the *bazina* tomb-type, a tumulus with some architectural articulation found all over North Africa in the pre-Islamic period (Figure 7.11), and the Medracen and Kbor

[30] The most recent example is Prados Martínez 2008.

[31] Lancel 1995: 307, following C. Poinssot 1958: 59.

[32] Lancel 1995: 305–14; on the Carthage stelai see Quinn 2011b.

[33] Ferchiou 1989: 83–8, 291–9; Rakob 1991b: 71–3; 1998: 30–1.

[34] Whitaker 1921: 281, Fig. 61; Pesce 1952–4.

[35] Poinssot and Salomonson 1959 [1960] for an example; Quinn 2003: 20–1 for a brief survey with earlier bibliography; most recently Ferchiou 2008. The relative chronology of these 'Punic' tombs and the larger 'Numidian' ones is unclear.

[36] For misgivings on that score, see Quinn 2004 – although the straightforward equation of Carthaginian political power and 'Punic' culture is the greater problem here.

[37] Rakob 1979: 145–6.

[38] Poinssot and Salomonson 1963: 80; Rakob 1983: 332–3; see Fedak 1990: 140–50 for examples and images.

Figure 7.10 Graffiti from Jebel Mlezza shaft tombs (Cap Bon, third/second century).

Figure 7.11 *Bazina* tomb at Tiddis.

er Roumia were therefore 'indigenous monuments dressed in a cloak of foreign extraction', that is to say, 'a Greco-Oriental or Greek architectural façade'.[39] Like Gsell, Camps suggests that the Medracen 'responds to ahistorical indigenous traditions, which owe to the outside world only an architectural *mise-en-page*', though in his interpretation this *mise-en-page* is Punic rather than Greek: 'an interweaving of African elements and Phoenician contributions'.[40] For Coarelli and Thébert, however, these *bazinas* were of an entirely inappropriate scale and level of sophistication to

[39] Gsell 1914–28: VI, 262 (my transl.).

[40] Camps 1961b: 200; 1995: 247 (my transl.); followed by Krandel-Ben Younès 2002: 100–2. For the incorporation of prestige elements into native substructures in another context, see Millett 1990: 74.

serve as models for the 'Royal Architecture', which for them signified a positive rupture with earlier African traditions.[41]

However, the various parallels that have been suggested only demonstrate the basic problem with any approach based on a dichotomy between 'Punic' and 'Hellenistic' cultural traditions. It is certainly possible to distinguish in general between the architectural fashions and emphases of the Greek-speaking and Phoenician-speaking areas of the Mediterranean in the Hellenistic period: just as a 'Hellenistic' set of overlapping styles can be identified,[42] in some respects the western and eastern Phoenician worlds could be said to constitute a cultural *koine* in the Classical and Hellenistic periods.[43] Nonetheless, it is not possible to pin down two clear, distinct and bounded traditions, and the eclecticism sometimes seen as distinctively 'Hellenistic' is a central element in all Mediterranean architecture in this period. The Levantine tower-tombs, for instance, draw on various regional traditions including those first found in Egypt and Greece, and it is striking that elements that Coarelli and Thébert list as 'Egyptianising' on the monument at Simitthus – cavetto cornices, architraves with winged sun-disks, *uraei* and Egyptianising figures and sphinx iconography – are also found at the Hellenistic-period Phoenician temple at Umm el-Amed.[44] Cavetto cornices and aeolic capitals are also found in Italy.[45] This eclecticism characterises all major Mediterranean cities of the Hellenistic period, from Alexandria and Pergamon to Rome and Carthage itself, whose art and architecture draw heavily on a great variety of models, including features originally associated not only with the Levant (aeolic capitals), and Egypt (cavetto cornices), but also Greece (ionic columns).[46] 'Punic' and

[41] Instead, they followed Thiersch 1910 in positing a glamorous predecessor for the Medracen: the now-lost tomb of Alexander the Great, built by Ptolemy IV Philopater at Alexandria between 221 and 205, and which would then serve as a model for Augustus' mausoleum in Rome as well: Coarelli and Thébert 1988: 791–3. Ancient references to the physical appearance of Alexander's mausoleum (Zenobius, *Proverbia* 3.94; Lucan 8.694, 10.19) are extremely vague, but Venit has suggested that it may be identified with the Alabaster tomb, which lay under a tumulus (2002: 7–8 with n. 51).

[42] Surveys include Lauter 1986; Pollitt 1986; Smith 1991.

[43] See for instance Quinn 2011b: 394–8 on borrowings and shared trends in small-scale sculpture between Carthage and the Levant. Note however Bondì forthcoming on the differences between different 'Punicities' in the Hellenistic period.

[44] Coarelli and Thébert 1988: 804–6. On Umm el-Amed see Vella 2001, who also discusses the particularly Phoenician religious significance of the winged sun-disks found in this context (39).

[45] Cavetto: Arnold 2003: 46. Interestingly for us, the aeolic capital found in Rome on the fifth-century Columna Minucia (for which see Plin. *HN* 18.15; 34.21), is represented on later second-century coinage (*RRC* 242/1: 135 BCE).

[46] Quinn 2003, 2011b; for another example of this phenomenon, see R. Wilson, Chapter 4 of this volume, on the Sicilian 'Corinthian' capital.

'Hellenistic' are not two separate cultural worlds in this period, and there is no evidence that ancients saw them that way.

Nor can a 'Punic' tradition be clearly demarcated from a local or 'Libyan' world in Africa: graffiti of mausolea similar to those found in supposedly 'Punic' shaft-tombs on Cap Bon are also found, for instance, in above-ground 'Libyan' rock-cut tombs (*haouanet*) in northern Tunisia.[47] The 'Punic' label traditionally assigned to shaft-tombs does not necessarily relate to the people who used them in any case: Libyan script and Libyan names are sometimes found in tombs of this type,[48] just as 'Punic' decorative motifs (including the so-called 'sign of Tanit') are found in the *haouanet* tombs.[49] More generally, as Coarelli and Thébert point out, to single the *bazinas* out as a peculiarly Libyan or African phenomenon is to create a cultural barrier where one does not exist, since tumulus tombs at all scales are found all over the Mediterranean and neighbouring regions.[50]

This brings me to the first of three structural problems that can be identified with the traditional approach to these monuments: the insistence on fitting them into one or another 'tradition', or even a combination of 'traditions', which depends on the dubious notion that there were monolithic and distinct 'Hellenistic', 'Punic' or indeed 'Libyan' cultural traditions.[51] This ignores the complexity of material culture in North Africa in the Hellenistic period, and in the Mediterranean as a whole for that matter, and in this sense the terms of the traditional debate are too limited. But in another way they are also too general: interpretations in terms of generalised modern culture-categories mean that the references to more specific places and models that could have been read into and off these monuments are too often ignored or skated over.

The second problem with the traditional debate is that it panders to theoretical frameworks that privilege the study of origins and 'influence': the idea implicit in so much scholarship that any human phenomenon can be explained by its antecedents. This is frequently combined (tacitly or openly) with value judgements, with 'higher' colonial civilisations such as Carthage and the Hellenistic kingdoms seen as influencing 'lower', less

[47] Longerstay 1993: 19. [48] Fantar 1978: 56.

[49] Despite the ethnic distinction traditionally made between them, shaft- and *haouanet* tombs in fact share much in terms of architecture and furnishings: Fantar 1978: 56; Ben Younès 2007: 39–41; Stone 2007a: 46.

[50] Coarelli and Thébert 1988: 769–70.

[51] For more on the problems of culture-history approaches in Africa and in general, see Quinn 2003: 26–7. Coarelli and Thébert explicitly contest the validity of an approach to the Mediterranean world based on a model of separate 'blocks', which as they note privileges interpretations based on the concepts of authenticity, influence and conquest (1988: 769).

sophisticated or 'native' ones. Too often, then, the African builders of the monuments are cast as passive receptacles of cultural influence rather than as active interpreters and manipulators of culture. But the concept of 'influence' puts analysis the wrong way round: monuments do not influence other monuments; people choose to quote, adapt or even subvert earlier imagery.[52] And so I want to look at these monuments instead from the point of view of their builders, not just at the models they are using, but at the messages they are sending; they quote stylistic details from other times and places, I will argue, primarily to say something about their own.

The third problem is that, in its emphasis on the external architectural form and decoration of the monuments, the standard debate ignores other aspects of their appearance, forms of signification that depend less on what they look like than on where they can be seen and from how far away. But there is more to these monuments than what they look like reproduced in the pages of a book.[53] Seen in their own landscapes, dominating cities and plains, built in the most dramatic settings with suitably spectacular views (Figure 7.12), they are deeply imposing, impossible to miss or ignore; they define these landscapes. A 'landscape' approach to North African funerary

Figure 7.12 The Medracen in its landscape.

[52] On the problem of 'influence', see Baxandall 1985: 58–62; Stewart and Korres 2004: 97–8. I am grateful to Andrew Stewart for the point, and the references.

[53] A point made by Rakob 1983: 326.

architecture and practices has recently been suggested by David Stone and Lea Stirling,[54] and Stone has used it in two important recent articles: one on the *haouanet*, which emphasises the importance of resistance to encroaching external power in the conceptualisation and combination of their architectural form and decoration, and the other comparing mausolea, tumuli and *haouanet* tombs and dealing explicitly with the limitations of their traditional classification into 'cultures'.[55] Although I take a somewhat different route here in my interpretation of the monumental architecture, my approach owes much to Stone's work, and I hope that my conclusions are complementary. Like him, I want to start from the local political, cultural and visual contexts.

Local contexts

The literary and epigraphic evidence from Herodotus onwards suggests a segmentary, pyramidal model of social organisation in North Africa, with the population organised in nested groups, including families, kin groups, clans and tribes, alongside the Phoenician and Greek colonies established on the coast in the first half of the millennium.[56] The Hellenistic period was a time of particular social and imperial upheaval: Roman hegemony grew from the third century onwards, and the Punic Wars that led to the destruction of Carthage in 146 coincided with the emergence of large confederations of indigenous chiefdoms in the region, partly in the face of Carthaginian aggression, but also in order to take advantage of the opportunities for mercenary service on both sides. In the aftermath of the Hannibalic War (218–202), the two largest confederations coalesced under the rule of the Massylian king and Roman ally Massinissa, who conquered almost all of the area previously subject to the rival Masaesylians and ruled over it until his death in 148.

Under Massinissa the kingdom known to the Greeks and Romans as 'Numidia' underwent a process of true state development. The king now extracted surplus from his subjects rather than redistributing the profits of war to them, and new social and economic hierarchies emerged alongside the new political order. Military force was no longer dependent on tribal structures; instead, the kings had regular standing armies, and the famous

[54] Stone and Stirling 2007: 23. [55] Stone 2007a; Stone 2007b: esp. 137–8.

[56] Mattingly 1992: 32–5 for an overview. Fentress 1979: 43–7 collects the evidence for tribal structures.

Numidian cavalry in particular was brought under state control.[57] Massinissa's descendants, including Micipsa, Jugurtha and Juba I, continued to rule in the same vein until Juba's defeat by Caesar in 46 when large parts of the Numidian kingdom became the Roman province of *Africa Nova*.[58]

It is well known, however, that the hallmarks of pre-industrial states are scarcity and poor communications, both in terms of transport and of information.[59] These conditions meant that the new kings had only weak control over their nominal subjects, and that they had to devolve much power to local agents. This gave the latter the opportunity to maintain their own wealth and power bases,[60] and to present a constant challenge to the rulers' position and to the nascent state itself.[61] At the same time, the kings were themselves subjects, of Carthage or Rome.

They counterbalanced this weak vertical authority by building strong horizontal links – diplomatic, economic and cultural – with other Mediterranean elites. Syphax and Massinissa were both at times allies of Carthage as well as Rome, both adopted Punic as their official language, and married the same Carthaginian noblewoman, Sophonisba. After the Hannibalic War, Massinissa cultivated friendships with 'Hellenistic' kings,[62] as well as participating in the rituals and practices of the eastern Mediterranean by sending offerings to the fashionable Greek sanctuary of Delos.[63] His son Mastanabal took part in chariot-racing at the Panathenaic games alongside Ptolemies, and another, Micipsa, summoned Greeks to his court.[64] These associations continued in the West as well, as a fragmentary inscription from Syracuse in honour of Masteabar, a Massylian

57 Camps 1961a: 261–5; Brett and Fentress 1996: 34.

58 For a more detailed account of social and landscape change in North Africa in the fourth to second centuries, Stone 2007a: 47–52.

59 Crone 1989: ch. 2 *passim*.

60 Crone 1989: 45: 'In principle the ruler might not share his power with anyone else . . . but in practice he co-existed with a wide variety of power holders whom he was lucky even to win over . . . The best the ruler could hope for was to secure the co-operation of the local snake, tie him to the monarchic institution and give him a strong interest in the survival of the state.'

61 There were various desertions and revolts during Massinissa's reign, as under later kings: see for instance App. *Pun.* 70 (a desertion in 152), and Camps 1961a: 214–15 and Fentress 1979: 51 for difficult relations between the king and tribal chiefs.

62 Nicomedes erected a statue to him: *ID* 1577 (149/8 BCE); Roussel and Hatzfeld 1909: 484–9. Ptolemy VIII Euergetes II of Egypt wrote about him in his memoirs: *FGrH* 234 F 7–8. Duane Roller (2002) has even suggested that the 'Berber Head' from Cyrene in the British Musem is a portrait of Massinissa's son Mastanabal, dating to the reign in Cyrene of the future Ptolemy VIII (163–148 BCE), which would be a further indication of the close association of these two rulers.

63 Offering of grain: *ID* 442A, l.102–6 (179 BCE); statue: Baslez 1981: 161–2.

64 Mastanabal: *IG* II.ii.968, ll.41–4 (c. 168/3 BCE) = *IG* II/III^2.2316. Micipsa: Diod. Sic. 34/35.35.

Figure 7.13 Coin of Massinissa or Micipsa, with prancing horse on reverse (Alexandropoulos 2000: II/11–12; 14.94 g.)

ruler of the early first century, attests.[65] The royal coinage demonstrates the eclecticism with which these links were presented for internal consumption: second-century Numidian kings depict themselves with diadems in the style of eastern Mediterranean kings alongside Ammon, a favourite deity of Ptolemy III's coinage, and the 'sign of Tanit' popular in the western Phoenician colonies, over legends written in Punic (Figure 7.13).[66]

A striking counterpart to the emergence of the Numidian kingdoms was the new level of urbanism in the region, both on the coast, including the expansion of Sabratha and Lepcis Magna, and inland, where cities like Thugga, Vaga, Bulla and Cirta date back at least to the early Hellenistic period and in several cases underwent significant second-century systematisation and expansion. Urban growth may well have been connected with the assertion of royal power in the region at the expense of Carthage.[67] Four cities in any case (Bulla, Hippo, Thimida, Zama) had the epithet *regius* in the Roman period, and the citizens of Thugga itself erected a temple to Massinissa in 138.[68] Nonetheless, 'Numidian' cities seem to have been basically independent polities. Thugga provides a particularly good example of a city looking in multiple directions: despite the temple to Massinissa, it chose its own local magistracies and, unlike the Numidian kings, used Libyan as well as Punic in its public inscriptions and funerary epigraphy.[69]

Returning to the monuments themselves, I want to argue that their location, form and decoration are best understood in relation to these changes in social and political structures across the region, both referring to and reinforcing them. I will look first at the local associations they exploit, and then at their wider references.

[65] *SEG* 39.1033; 16.535. [66] Alexandropoulos 2000: II/11–12.
[67] Polyb. 31.21; Livy 40.17.1–6; 42.23; *Per.* 47–8; App. *Pun.* 67–8. [68] *RIL* 2.
[69] *Encyclopédie Berbère* s.v. 'Dougga' (http://encyclopedieberbere.revues.org/2210), with *RIL* 2.

Local messages

The new 'Royal Architecture' marked new sources of power in a variety of ways, not least by drawing attention to the institutions, centres and resources of the developing Numidian kingdoms. Most obviously, as noted above, Kbor er Roumia is positively identified as a royal tomb, and perhaps some of the others commemorated kings as well. Certainly several of the monuments are found in the vicinity of major cities with royal connections. As well as the mausoleum right outside Thugga, the mausoleum at Beni Rhénane is just across the river from Siga, the capital of King Syphax's Masaesylian confederation in the late third century; Es Soumaa is about 15 km from Massinissa's second-century capital of Cirta (which is visible from the monument); Kbor Klib is 20 km from the 'royal city' of Zama Regia; and the 'altar' at Simitthus is a similar distance from Bulla Regia. The Medracen, by contrast, was a long way from cities with known royal connections, but in Roman times a neighbouring lake was called the *lacus regius*.[70]

As David Stone has emphasised, the monuments probably also operated as territorial or boundary markers, and this is an especially attractive argument in the context of the territorial aggression of the Numidian kings.[71] The region of the Medracen, in particular, was disputed between the Massyli and Masaesyli in the third century, and the mausolea at Sabratha and Thugga as well as the 'altar' at Simitthus are found in areas taken at least temporarily from Carthaginian hegemony by Massinissa in the first half of the second century. If the monuments are in part thought of as territory markers, it is particularly interesting that two of them were already in ruins by the late Hellenistic period. The mausoleum at Beni Rhénane was deliberately and systematically destroyed by the middle of the second century, after the fall of King Syphax's Masaesylian state,[72] and Mausoleum B at Sabratha was allowed to fall into disrepair before being pillaged for materials in a replanning of the area in the early first century; this could be related to the Massylian kings' loss of control of the region.[73] It has even been

[70] Camps 1973: 516. It may also have a connection with Ichoukane, a large but unidentified and unexcavated indigenous site of the Hellenistic period about 30 km away, with a vast cemetery and a double wall: Brett and Fentress 1996: 32.

[71] Stone 2007b: 140–1, pointing to J. Février 1957 for the Numidian inscription found near Jebel Massouge which uses a tomb (possibly the Thugga mausoleum) as an approximate marker of distance in a territorial context. Cf. Rakob 1979: 120 on how the Simitthus monument is a 'monument and landmark' of royal power after the area was taken from Carthage in 152.

[72] Camps 1995: 243. [73] Bessi 2003: 401.

suggested that the effacement of the second inscription on the Thugga mausoleum (discussed earlier) could have been a political, rather than environmental, act.[74]

Moving to the realm of architectural decoration, and to that of visual language rather than simply statement, some of these monuments participate in the construction of a highly militaristic identity for a new and militaristic state. This is clearest on the 'altars', with their dramatic friezes of shields and armour (Kuttner, Chapter 8, this volume). Weapons friezes are of course not uncommon on Hellenistic-period monuments, but the African tower-tombs and sanctuaries also have a variety of specific references to cavalry, including the cavalry shields at Simitthus, Kbor Klib, and Es Soumaa, and the horsemen at Thugga whom I have already discussed.[75] The ideological importance of this theme is also emphasised on the state coinage, which very frequently features a rearing or racing horse (Figure 7.13). As noted above, cavalry fighting, the basis of the kingdoms' international status and success, was something that the Numidians did as a whole, and as a state, and under royal supervision.

As well as making references to the kingdoms, their conquests and their armies, fragments of large statues found at Es Soumaa[76] and Jerba[77] illustrate how the monuments draw attention more generally to the distinction of new elites and the development of hierarchies in the region, royal or otherwise. In the cases of the Medracen and Beni Rhénane, oversize monuments sit in the middle of cemeteries of smaller tombs, emphasising the power of the occupant relative to the others buried around him, and the sheer amount of labour that must have been required to build these tombs makes a similar point. The tomb at Beni Rhénane demonstrates the new organisation of power in a different way, with multiple separate but interconnected underground burial chambers, suggesting that it was supposed to be dynastic (Figure 7.14).[78] It is possible that the monument at Thugga, which has three accessible chambers inside, may also have been used or intended for dynastic burial.[79]

[74] J. Février 1959: 57, though Ferron 1969–70: 94 reports petrological analyses showing that the stone used in the monument, while all from the same quarry, is of varying durability.

[75] The round cavalry shields (discussed in greater detail by Kuttner, Chapter 8 in this volume) were the standard African cavalry armour for centuries, and representations of them are found from Morocco to Libya (Laporte 1992: 393). They are of course found elsewhere in Mediterranean architecture, including the Lion Tomb at Knidos, and are frequent in Roman painting.

[76] Es Soumaa: Rakob 1983: 335. [77] Jerba: Ferchiou 2009b. [78] Rakob 1983: 334.

[79] Poinssot and Salomonson 1959 [1960]: 143–7 for this suggestion and for the internal dispositions of the monument, known only from the papers of Comte Borgia.

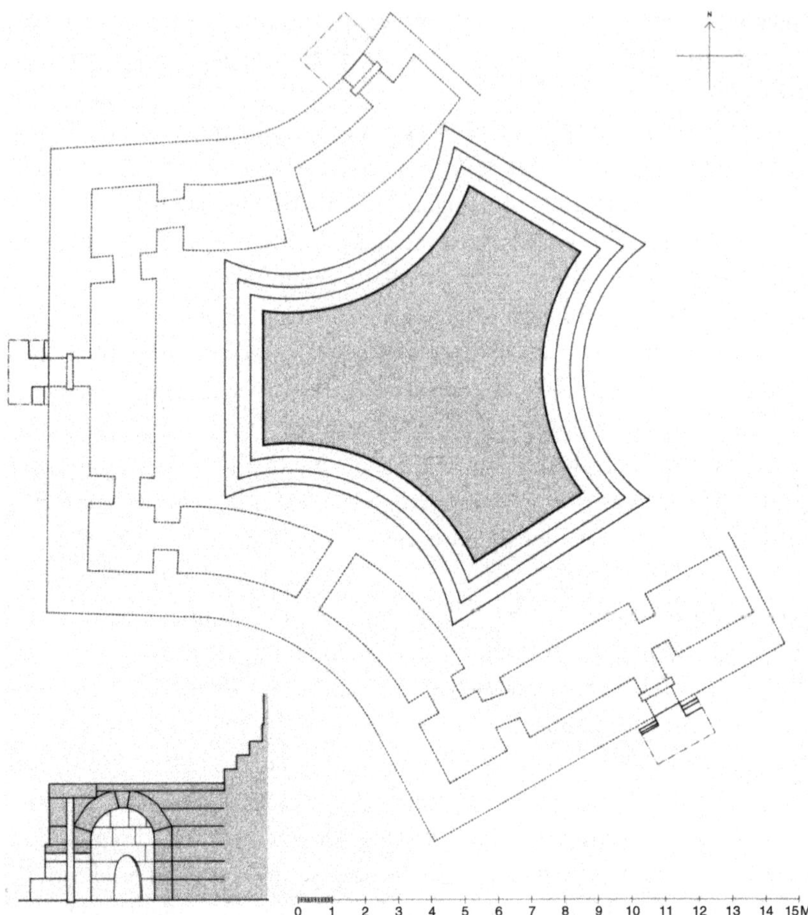

Figure 7.14 Plan of the Beni Rhénane Mausoleum (Siga, Algeria).

The monuments also define new economic centres and important economic axes in the region: just as the Simitthus 'altar' marks the crossroads of the major land routes from Carthage to Hippo Regius and from Sicca Veneria to Thabraca,[80] and marks the location of the royal marble quarries, the Medracen is on the main route south from Cirta into the Aurès,[81] the Thugga mausoleum dominates the road and river routes from the coastal port of Carthage into the heart of the grain-producing Tell, and Kbor er Roumia is clearly visible to those sailing the coastal trade-route.[82]

[80] Rakob 1983: 327. [81] Camps 1973: 515.

[82] Cf. Horden and Purcell 2000: 126: '. . . the identity of a powerful Mediterranean figure depends on how his identity is perceived from its maritime approaches.'

Figure 7.15 Kbor er Roumia seen from the forum at Tipasa.

The monuments tie in with the phenomenon of urbanisation too. Several of the tower-tombs were built beside growing cities, including those just outside the walls at Thugga and Sabratha and the mausoleum of Beni Rhénane, which overlooks Siga from just a little further away.[83] Perhaps the most striking link between the world of the city and that of the king can be seen between the Libyphoenician coastal town of Tipasa and the royal tomb of Kbor er Roumia, about eight kilometres away, which dominates the horizon looking inland from the city's forum (Figure 7.15).[84] Unless these monuments were all built by the new royal families or their representatives, they point to the growth of urban elites, and claims to power independent of the new kingdoms.

These civic claims need not have been oppositional; indeed, they could have worked with and reinforced the symbolism of the royal power which seems to have been the precondition for the new success of the cities and their elites. If the Thugga mausoleum was erected for a local leader, Atban or someone else, the horsemen could represent the personal cavalry of the defunct, guarding his tomb, which would reinforce the overall message of personal and individual power that the monument conveys. At the same time, however, the cavalry imagery would provide a connection between the royal and civic symbolic realms. If, on the other hand, it was built by or for a representative of the Massylian royal family, it could be seen as balancing the power of the city itself (Figure 7.16). Whatever the precise status of the defunct, his power and the growth of the city both depended in some sense on the emergence of the new kingdoms.

[83] Fentress has noted that these are in the 'classic position of a *heroon*' (2006: 8).

[84] Thanks to Emanuele Papi for literally pointing this out to me.

Figure 7.16 The Thugga mausoleum as a counterpoint to the city.

There is a temptation here to recall Gellner's classic description of agrarian societies, where elites seek to distinguish themselves in horizontal strata above local farming communities, doing their best to differentiate themselves from each other and in particular from the 'petty' local communities.[85] One can imagine these towers and hill-top monuments talking to each other across the landscape, high above the local cemeteries and settlements they grace with their physical presence – and, as I shall discuss shortly, reaching further to connect with the monuments of international elites. But these monuments do not just sit on top of pre-existing communities and traditions in the region, they are also engaged with them, participating in a range of local practices and significations.

As noted above, the Medracen and the tomb at Beni Rhénane are built in existing cemeteries, and so although they are distinguished vertically from the surrounding *bazina* tombs, they are also horizontally identified with them. In the case of the Medracen at least, this visual identification would have been encouraged by the replication in the larger monument of the circular form of the *bazina* and other round tombs, whether or not this was the only or primary referent of that form. At the same time the reproduction on the bigger scale 'trumps' the smaller, older tombs; the connection creates a hierarchy.

Design elements also suggest that these monuments were not simply imposed on landscapes but closely tied to existing local cult and funerary practices. Like many of the *bazina* tombs, as well as the tombs found in the Garamantian centres of the Fazzan, the entrances and corridors of the two monumental tumuli are oriented east, and they have external structures – platforms, altars or bases – also projecting east.[86] The internal corridor at

[85] Gellner 1983: 10; see further Brett and Fentress 1996: 333.

[86] Camps 1973: 479–83 for the parallels between the access routes into the Medracen and the *bazina* tombs *à degrés*, as well as for details reported in the nineteenth century of the 14 x 25 m structure attached to the eastern side of the Medracen, whose traces have since been obliterated by a local cemetery, and for the note that a similar eastern-oriented 'aire cultuelle' is found at Kbor er Roumia, as well as at the late antique *djedars*; Rakob has suggested the structure beside the Medracen carried an altar, a cult building or an incubation chamber (1983: 330). For the Garamantian tombs, Mattingly 2007: 147, 160.

Kbor er Roumia, which runs from the entrance all the way around the monument, turning in towards the burial chamber shortly before completing the full circle, recalls the internal arrangements of some of the more elaborate *bazinas*[87] and, like some 'Libyan' *haouanet* and 'Punic' shaft-tombs in the region, this deambulatory at Kbor er Roumia and the upper-level burial chambers of the Thugga mausoleum (to which access is also from the east) have niches in the walls.[88] Traces of red paint found on the cult building at the Medracen may well link to the African practice of using red ochre to mark bodies and tombs, also found locally in cemeteries from the Sahel[89] to the Sahara.[90]

Other features of the monuments imply on-going local activity at the sites, perhaps hero- or ruler-cult.[91] As well as the altars or cult buildings associated with the round tombs, Kbor Klib has an altar to the west of the monument that is contemporary with the original construction, and although there are no archaeological traces of cult buildings in the vicinity of the tower-tombs, the graffiti representations of them on the walls of contemporary rock-cut tombs in northern Tunisia associate them with flaming altars.[92] In a little-noticed passage in Suetonius' biography, Augustus, spending the last days of his life at Capri, observes that the tumulus of Masgaba, one of his favourites who had died the year before, 'was visited by a large crowd with many torches' (98.4). Masgaba must be an African name, and the dead man was presumably an itinerant Numidian nobleman.[93]

There may have been activity inside the tombs as well: Herodotus and Pomponius Mela both tell us, for instance, that some Libyans practised incubation and dream-divination in their tombs.[94] The entrances of the round tombs could be opened for re-entry after the deposition of the body, as could that of the Thugga mausoleum, and the niches at Kbor er

[87] Rakob 1983: 334, where he also compares the circular disposition of the underground funerary chambers at Beni Rhénane, and the deambulatories of the late antique *djedars*.

[88] Ferron notes this, along with the local funerary custom of burying the dead person above ground, and the way in which the double funerary chamber within the second storey of the Thugga monument 'correspond au plan de nombreuses haouânet' (1969–70: 89 n.17).

[89] Lancel 1995: 291; cf. Hdt. 4.191, 194. [90] Mattingly 2007: 157, with 144 for pyramid tombs.

[91] Coarelli and Thébert discuss the association of colonnades with heroism going back to Asia Minor (1988: 799).

[92] The Simitthus monument also has an altar (to its east) in its reincarnation as a Roman temple, but no pre-Roman phase or version has been found.

[93] Lacerenza 2002; thanks to Lisa Fentress for the reference.

[94] Hdt. 4.172; Pomponius Mela 1.8.45 (both discussing the Nasamones/Augilae). For a summary of the evidence for the African practice of worshipping at tombs, see Stone and Stirling 2007: 22–3.

Roumia and Thugga may have held lights.[95] The location of the monument at Simitthus is particularly interesting in this respect, on top of a hill covered in carvings of 'Libyan' gods and shrines, and so capitalising on pre-existing sacred associations. Overall, it is clear that these monuments were not just for looking at, but provided new venues for existing activities, and therefore useful local legitimacy for the new rulers and elites.

Social permeability is also a feature of the cavalry imagery in the monuments and on the royal coinage discussed above, which presents another challenge to Gellner's thesis of horizontal differentiation, blurring the distinctions between elite and local sources of power by co-opting much lower levels of representation. Small-scale sculptures of riders are common in Numidia in the Hellenistic period; as well as the 'Chemtou horseman' from Simitthus (Figure 7.17), there are a series of around a dozen 'chieftain stelai' found in an area of Grand Kabylie, all about a metre high and now dated on

Figure 7.17 The 'Chemtou horseman'.

[95] See Camps 1973: 496 and 502 for the closing and locking mechanisms at the Medracen, 'well known in the tombs and hypogea of the eastern tradition', which in his view 'permitted the later introduction of cremated remains'.

Figure 7.18 Abizar chieftain stele.

stylistic grounds to the third or second centuries (Figure 7.18).[96] They feature local gods or leaders, almost always on horseback, brandishing javelins and the typical African cavalry shield. In some cases their name is recorded in Libyan on the stele. Much is unclear about these stelai, including whether they are funerary or votive, whether the main figure is a man or a god, and the meaning of the small secondary figure. The relative chronology of these small-scale representations of riders and the monumental architecture is very obscure, but older stelai from the region of Constantine feature the same shield device, which suggests that the builders of the 'Numidian' monuments did have a repertoire of relevant local images to build upon. The graffiti representations of the tower-tombs in smaller rock-cut tombs elsewhere in Tunisia (Figure 7.10) suggest that this incorporation of imagery between different social strata can work from the bottom up as well as the top down, and reach across political borders: the smaller tower mausolea within the *fossa regia* may be another example of this phenomenon. It may even be that these small stelai were intended in part as a sign of difference from the new social order embodied in at least some of the larger

[96] Laporte 1992; Camps *et al.* 1996.

monuments – the use of Libyan rather than the Punic of the royal coinage and epigraphy might point in that direction. But what I want to note here is the way that the essentials of this local image, the rider and his shield, are incorporated into the signs of that new order, the royal coinage and the elite monuments, just as the Numidian state had incorporated the cavalry strength of the smaller tribes and clans.

Global references

Extending the perspective beyond the Numidian kingdoms, how and why did the builders of these monuments draw on external models and associations? Not, I think, by aligning their monuments with one or another 'cultural tradition', but by pointing to a variety of places and ideas that reinforced the local power, status and authority of the builders of the tombs. These builders had a huge range of models to draw upon in constructing these tombs, as did their viewers in interpreting them; no doubt the overlap between these perspectives was never perfect: not all possible references and referents were intended by the builders or recognised by every, even any, viewer. But it does seem to me that many of these different references point in similar directions, invoking particular associations of antiquity and of ancient power: useful associations for new leaders facing the growing threat of Rome.

In order to make this case in the space available, I will return to the Thugga mausoleum and attempt to delineate some of the content in that tomb's obvious 'connectivity'. I am building here on the work of Coarelli and Thébert, and in particular on their claim that the use of foreign models showcased the Numidian kings' links with the eastern Mediterranean world, and equivalence to the kings there, though I will extend the scope of this approach to encompass the western Mediterranean, on the principle that the same reference can have multiple referents.

As I noted in the introduction, the monument at Thugga has a set of Egyptian references. Even if these associations are not as striking at Thugga as at some of the other monuments in the series, such as Mausoleum B at Sabratha, they can provide a useful starting point for an investigation of the complex possibilities of the symbolic logic at work. As well as the cavetto cornice already mentioned, the aeolic capitals incorporate lotus flowers, and the form of a square tomb topped with a pyramid is first found in second-millennium BCE Egypt, and also features in graffiti in other Egyptian tombs (Figure 7.19). Whether or not that was known to our

Figure 7.19 Graffiti in Egyptian tombs.

builder, the terminal pyramid pointed to the famous Egyptian royal tombs at Giza and Saqqara, which were becoming at this time a focus of Mediterranean tourism.[97]

But do these associations mean that the builders were making a specific connection with the contemporary Ptolemaic kingdom in Egypt, and its capital of Alexandria?[98] The contacts between King Massinissa and Ptolemy

[97] Baines and Riggs 2001. [98] As suggested at Coarelli and Thébert 1988: 809.

VIII, who in 163 was imposed by Rome as king at Cyrene before succeeding to the main Ptolemaic throne at Alexandria after Massinissa's death, are well known. However, there is not much positive evidence for specifically Alexandrian references in the architecture. Little of that city's monumental architecture survives, and despite intriguing literary references to Cleopatra's multi-storey above-ground tomb,[99] there are few parallels with the 'Numidian' monuments to be found in the elite underground tombs that have been excavated there.[100] In addition, the Thugga mausoleum, like the other African tombs, fails to exploit the distinguishing features of Alexandrian architecture such as Alexandrian capitals and screen walls.[101]

Even if direct Alexandrian references are infrequent, however, Sandro Stucchi has shown that many of the forms and architectural features of the monuments can be found in Cyrenaican funerary architecture, most or all of which seem to date from the time of Ptolemaic hegemony there.[102] These include the only surviving large-scale Cyrenaican tower-tomb, Mausoleum 2 at Ptolemais, which is dated by Stucchi on stylistic grounds to the late third or first half of the second century (Figure 7.20). In his book on Hellenistic Cyrenaica, André Laronde describes this mausoleum, orginally at least 30 m high, as unique in terms of its architecture and its dimensions.[103] But in fact (and while bearing in mind the speculative nature of Stucchi's reconstruction) it has clear similarities of scale and form to the Thugga tomb (the square plan, stepped base and multiple stories below a terminal pyramid, albeit stepped in this case rather than smooth); these and the deployment of the Doric order and cavalry shields also link the Cyrenaican tomb to Es Soumaa. It is debatable, however, whether such visual associations with Cyrenaica would have amounted to a claim to a connection with the Ptolemies: the Cyrenaican tombs studied by Stucchi have little in common with specifically Ptolemaic architecture, and in any case Ptolemaic hegemony in Cyrenaica was by no means comprehensive.[104] The similarities might be seen instead as a reference to pre-existing communities, such as the independent cities of Cyrenaica, facing the encroaching imperial power of the Ptolemies.

One clear link that does exist between 'Numidian' and Ptolemaic architectural strategies is their shared fascination with Pharaonic Egypt. Recent underwater excavations have revealed the many Pharaonic-period sphinxes,

[99] Plut. *Ant.* 77–9, with Dio Cass. 51.10.9.

[100] On the elite tombs at Alexandria, Adriani 1966; Venit 2002.

[101] My thanks to Judith McKenzie for a useful conversation on this point.

[102] Stucchi 1987.

[103] Laronde 1987: 444 (following Stucchi).

[104] Laronde suggests that it is the tomb of a minor Ptolemy (1987: 444).

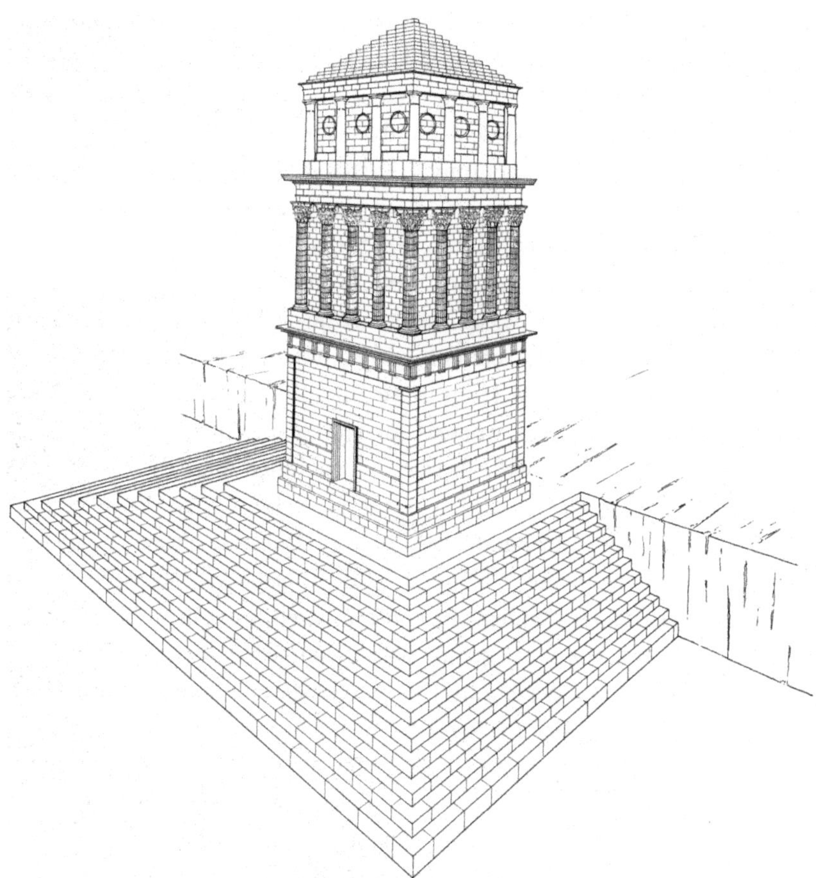

Figure 7.20 Mausoleum 2 at Ptolemais: reconstruction.

obelisks and palmette columns transplanted to Alexandria, particularly from Heliopolis.[105] This Ptolemaic 'Egyptianising' is also to some extent apparent in surviving funerary architecture at Alexandria, although the Ptolemaic temples to Egyptian gods elsewhere in Egypt, such as the temples of Amun at Karnak, Isis at Philae and Horus at Edfu, provide more impressive demonstrations of construction in the Pharaonic tradition.[106] Nonetheless, the builders of the 'Numidian' monuments adapt the art and architecture of Pharaonic Egypt in a rather different way from the Ptolemies; they do not simply reproduce or quote Ptolemaic culture.

Firstly, Ptolemaic architecture tends to be either distinctively Egyptian, or distinctively Greek – there are certainly juxtapositions such as the sphinxes

[105] McKenzie 2007: 42. [106] Venit 2002.

in the Moustapha Pasha I Tomb,[107] the Egyptian-style statues of both dynastic and Ptolemaic date alongside classical ones in the Serapeum enclosure,[108] and the obelisk in the Arsinoeion,[109] but the real mixture of Egyptian and Greek forms, orders and details in the same visual field, such as are found at Thugga, comes only in first-century or later Alexandria.[110] Secondly, Ptolemaic builders use and emphasise different aspects of Pharaonic art from those we find in the 'Numidian' architecture, and they use them in different ways. Cavetto cornices appear only on the temples to the Egyptian gods outside Alexandria, not in the city or on Ptolemaic tombs, and it seems that pyramids were not used in Ptolemaic architecture at all: it was perhaps easier for those kings to memorialise the Egyptian gods than their imperial predecessors, whereas for Numidian elites it was the connection and comparison with foreign rulers rather than their gods that mattered.[111]

So it is easier to see our builders as reinterpreting and reusing Pharaonic Egypt in parallel with the Ptolemies, rather than as simply copying the Ptolemaic version. This endeavour could in itself, of course, be a way of claiming association or even equality with the Ptolemies, and in the context of increasing Roman hegemony, the Ptolemaic monarchy could have provided a useful model for semi-independence in the face of and in co-operation with Roman power. But the references to the Pharaonic world send messages of their own too: as well as evoking the mystery and exoticism of Pharaonic Egypt, they suggest an identification with the pre-Roman and pre-Greek indigenous power of the Pharaohs.

The Thugga tomb's Egyptian associations are just some among many, of course, and similar strategies could inform the references Coarelli and Thébert find there to the form and decoration of the monuments of the pre-Hellenistic kings of the Near East. Mausolus for instance, builder of probably the best known and most expensive tomb in the Mediterranean at Halicarnassus, would have provided a good example of an independent power in the orbit of the Persian empire. It is, in fact, striking how little these monuments quote directly from contemporary 'Hellenistic' kingdoms

[107] The tomb itself is early to mid-third-century (Venit 2002: 51, dated by pottery and painting), but the sphinxes' pedestals are freestanding and so could have been added later.

[108] McKenzie 2007: 55.

[109] Plin. *HN* 36.14; McKenzie 2007: 55.

[110] For a rare exception, see the second-century Ezbet el-Makhlouf Tomb M (Venit 2002: 193). McKenzie (2007: ch. 3–4) has a full discussion of the development of Ptolemaic architecture, and various possible (and subtle) interplays of Greek and Egyptian elements within it.

[111] The Ptolemies are of course presented in Pharaonic terms in some contexts, but this practice seems to relate to Pharaonic rule as a living and incorporated institution rather than in terms of the memorialisation of individual celebrity.

as opposed to powers that went before or alongside them: the Numidians are reinterpreting the past for their own purposes, and in the process demonstrating their cultural parity with contemporary Mediterranean monarchs. These references to the powers of the past are reinforced by the archaising style of the monuments, particularly noticeable at Thugga in the stiffness and spare style of the chariot relief, with the horses' limbs presented in strict series (Figure 7.5).[112]

Similar conclusions can again be drawn from a closer examination of the 'Phoenicianising' aspects of the tomb. Aeolic capitals and cavetto cornices (though not pyramids) had long been popular in the cities of the Levant, which had faced and to some extent faced down powers including Persia, while the echo of the famous chariot scene from Sidonian coinage also evokes the much greater power of the Great King himself whose iconography underlines the Sidonian image. In the West the parallels with the art and architecture of Carthage, another famous hold-out against Greco-Roman power, could hardly be missed. Carthage was of course a political enemy of the Numidian kings in the second century, and such associations perhaps again marked not allegiance, alliance, or 'acculturation' so much as comparability. Alternatively, if the Thugga mausoleum should be seen as the monument of an individual or city in competition to a degree with the new royal power in Numidia, an association with Carthage would make a different kind of sense. Such associations can be found in other contexts in Thugga, where a sanctuary was established around this time that looks very much like a tophet (though the sacrifices are of animals rather than children), and which appears to have adopted Carthaginian-style political magistracies at some point in the later Hellenistic period; these all point to the exploitation and harnessing of the rhetorical power of Carthage, especially once it was no longer a present danger.[113]

Other possible references could of course be suggested. Nonetheless, I hope that it is now clear that the Thugga mausoleum does not simply refer to one 'tradition' to convey its message of personal power in the context of a new kingdom, but calls on multiple sources of power and authority from the East and West, sought in the past as much as or even more than in the present, and highlighting indigenous alternatives to the external powers of Greece, Carthage and Rome in the service of promoting

[112] Cf. for instance, the relief supposed to be from the Sikyonian treasury of *c.* 560 at Delphi, depicting Kastor, Polydeukes, Idas and Lynkeus stealing a herd of cattle with very similar legs. On similarly archaising aspects of the Medracen, Coarelli and Thébert 1988: 776.

[113] Quinn 2009: 270–1, 2011b: 402–3. Contrast Wallace-Hadrill's description, Chapter 2 in this volume, of how Italy becomes less Punic after 146.

the authority of the region's elites in the face of internal and external incursion. While the references may encompass the Mediterranean and even more, the audience is local, and so are the messages that these references send.

Conclusions

I have argued here that 'Numidian Royal Architecture' was built by and for people connected with, and invested in, a variety of aspects of the new social and political order in Numidia, and that it was built at least in part to stabilise and reinforce that order. The builders bolstered their prestige by co-opting global references, and their legitimacy by co-opting local ones. Through their architecture these local elites (royal or otherwise) constructed themselves as on a par with those of larger Mediterranean states and created networks of political and cultural association that reached down the local social scale and across the Mediterranean world in different directions in space as well as time. The particular connections suggested with earlier imperial powers mean that these are networks not only of association but also of memory. Or more accurately, of false memory – of associations that did not exist in a time before the coming of Rome.

None of this seems to be about exclusive cultural or ethnic identity, but rather about the exploitation of real and symbolic sources of power. These cultural connections cut across lines of conventionally understood political, ethnic or cultural identities: the builders are interested in what they share with other agents, cities and states, not in what makes them different.

Moreover, these networks of association were constructed in collaboration with Rome. Roman generals went along with the Numidian kings' self-invention as on a par with greater Mediterranean powers, for instance giving Syphax and Massinissa the same honours as Ptolemy IV during the Hannibalic War.[114] Roman art, too, may witness this collaborative construction of power, if Ann Kuttner is right in Chapter 8 in this volume to interpret the painting in the Casa di Giuseppe II at Pompeii as a

[114] Livy 27.4.8 (Syphax receives a purple toga and tunic, a golden *patera*, and a curule chair in 210); 27.4.10 (Ptolemy IV receives a purple toga and tunic and a curule chair from the same ambassadors in 210); 30.15.11 (Massinissa receives an embroidered toga, a golden wreath, a golden *patera*, a curule chair and an ivory sceptre in 203; cf. App. *Pun.* 32 for the same event with a slightly different list of gifts); Livy 31.11.12 (Massinissa receives a purple toga, a tunic decorated with palms, an ivory sceptre and a curule chair in 200; this may be a doublet). For doubts about the reliability of the 210 embassy to Syphax and Ptolemy, see Holleaux 1921: 66–8.

representation of Sophonisba committing suicide in Massinissa's arms: the couple depicted both wear diadems, a recognition or reiteration in a Roman context of their equivalence to the rulers of the Successor kingdoms. Similarly, the local celebration of the Numidian cavalry, who fought as a separate contingent in the Roman army, is paralleled in Roman art and literature.[115] This architecture forms part of a cultural negotiation between Rome and Numidia that parallels their political negotiation.

Coda

Two final monuments take us earlier and further west and then later and much further east: conscious emulation or recognition is less likely in these cases, but they provide interesting parallels for the approach to architecture in the Numidian tombs, in interestingly similar contexts. One is the mausoleum of *c.* 500 BCE found in a cemetery at Pozo Moro, near Albacete, and now in Madrid: a tower-tomb built on a stepped base with a cavetto cornice separating two storeys, and sculptures of lions built into the structure of the monument at the base of each of those storeys (Figure 7.21).[116] It may well have had a pyramid on top, but even without it the resemblance to the tower-tombs is clear.[117] It was destroyed in the mid-fourth century, when a necropolis of tumulus tombs had already begun to grow up around it.[118]

The Pozo Moro monument is only the most famous of a set of more than thirty Iberian funerary towers dating from the archaic to Hellenistic periods, and displaying a series of distinctive features including cavetto cornices, relief friezes and animals sculpted out of square blocks.[119] As with the Numidian monuments, these make a studied combination of references to local and foreign traditions, and in a Numidian re-reading, or re-writing, these Iberian references could constitute yet another appeal to memories of past indigenous power, and perhaps evoke a more general (and more contemporary) Iberian resistance to Carthage and Rome.

The phenomenon of cosmopolitan eclecticism alongside local connectivity helping to negotiate power in multiple horizontal, vertical and chronological directions was not, however, simply a western phenomenon, nor indeed a Mediterranean one. In the mid-first century, Antiochus I of Kommagene built a sanctuary at Nemrud Dagh in eastern Turkey (Figure 7.22) which provides

[115] Rostovtzeff 1946. [116] Almagro-Gorbea 1983a; López Pardo 2006.
[117] Rakob 1983: 333. [118] Almagro-Gorbea 1983a: 182. [119] Almagro-Gorbea 1983b.

Figure 7.21 Pozo Moro mausoleum: reconstruction by Almagro-Gorbea.

an interesting counterpart and comparison to the Numidian architecture.[120] Like the Numidian kings, Antiochus was an indigenous ruler operating a fair distance from the major powers of the Mediterranean, ruling a theoretically independent state which was in effect a Roman client-kingdom. Antiochus used the Roman connection to consolidate his local power, but maintained an unstable relationship with his hegemon, and intermittently worked with and for the Parthians to the east instead.

The sanctuary consists of a burial mound – an enormous mountain-top tomb, 150 x 49 m – between, among other things, two terraces of gigantic sculptures depicting Antiochus himself and a selection of other state gods seated on thrones. As with the 'Numidian' architecture, the sculpture is an artificial mixture of artistic motifs and techniques, in this case looking both west to the Hellenistic kingdoms and to regions further east, with the odd

[120] Sanders 1996.

Figure 7.22 Nemrud Dagh.

local touch such as Antiochus' Armenian tiara.[121] Antiochus' helpful inscription makes it clear that the mixture is deliberate. In it he claims descent from Darius and the Achaemenid kings through the satrapal dynasty of Armenia, and from the Seleucids and Alexander the Great through a marriage alliance, and he explains that he had the images made 'according to the ancient *logos* of the Persians and the Hellenes, most blessed roots of my family'.[122] As in Numidia, sources of past power are brought in as reinforcements for a new one.

Bert Smith is unimpressed:

We could wish to have this sort of evidence for almost any other time and place in the Hellenistic world, rather than Kommagene. The king and his monuments belong ... in a time of swift change and in a political and cultural backwater. Almost no aspects can safely be taken as typical. The monuments existed in the first place due to the megalomania of a minor potentate and survive because he ruled high in the Taurus mountain range and built them on top of hills out of limestone which few subsequently thought it was worth their while to remove. The

[121] Smith 1986: 104 describes the style as 'an artificial combination of Oriental-looking bodies with neo-classical heads which wear Oriental hats'.

[122] *OGIS* 383.

quantities of sculpture and documentation stand in about inverse proportion to their broader historical significance.[123]

This may not be entirely fair on this king and his monuments: juxtaposing the architecture of Kommagene with that of Numidia can help us make more of both, and see a sense in which both are 'typical' of wider practices outside the major Successor kingdoms. I do not want to posit here a direct connection between these regions, or conscious imitation of 'Numidian' architecture by Antiochus, nor to evoke some notion of globalised resistance to Roman imperialism. Instead, I suggest simply that the two architectural sets show interesting structural similarities at a conceptual level. In both cases the builders negotiate elite power and identity in relation to bigger states, to each other and to their local populations in non-Successor kingdoms, sandwiched vertically between different levels of imperial power and

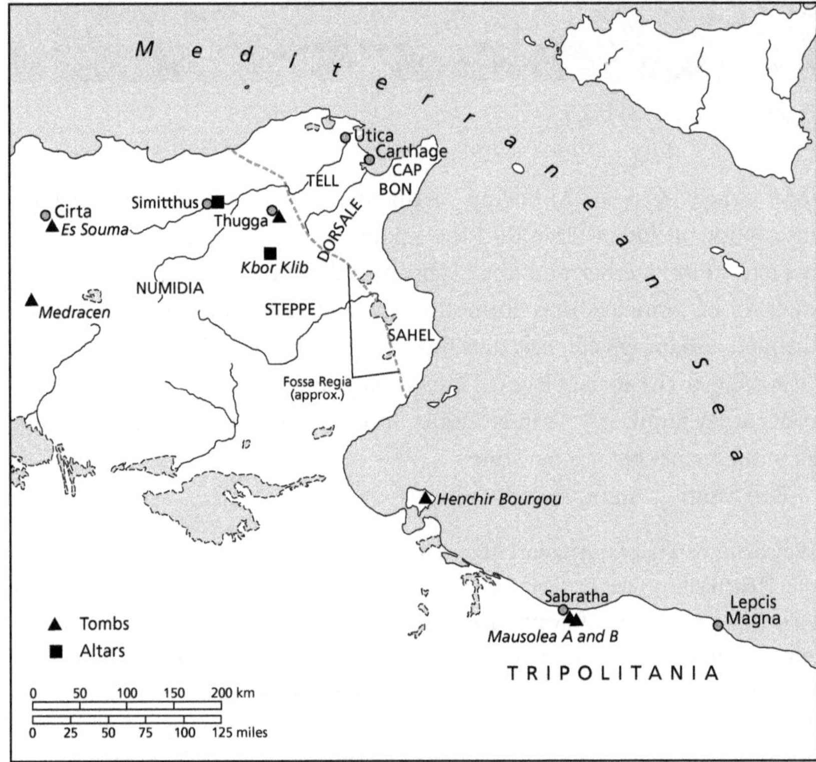

Figure 7.23 Map of sites mentioned in the text, with the exception of El Khroub and Kbour er Roumia further to the east.

123 Smith 1986: 102–3, reacting to Rostovtzeff's claims that Kommagene was typical of Seleucid ruler cult.

horizontally as well as chronologically between different imperial spaces and types of state. Like the African architecture, the sanctuaries of Kommagene such as Nemrud Dagh combine global and local references with a local function – here explicitly ruler cult – to reinforce the message about the extent of their builder's power and importance. And as with 'Numidian Royal Architecture', they might be thought to somewhat overstate the case.

8 Representing Hellenistic Numidia, in Africa and at Rome

ANN KUTTNER

This essay probes complex visual culture in and about Numidia from the second century BCE to the early first century CE, set in the contexts of the Hellenistic West Mediterranean and of the reciprocal engagement of Numidia and Rome.[1] Although the rootword 'Hellene' in 'Hellenistic' poses problems, the latter term has advantages (and no accepted synonyms) for all who are currently trying to make Mediterranean studies consider *all* that zone's peoples, and their cultural, socio-political and religious interrelations. Because my case-studies are about self-conscious visual artifice ('Hellenistic art') in the service of socio-political meanings, the term Hellenistic usefully reminds that, from at least the later fourth century onwards, splendour in an international 'look of things' cannot have been perceived as simply *Greek*, because too many peoples had been using what seem to us Greek 'styles' for far too long for that to have been the case in their impressions of one another.[2]

[1] My profound thanks for unstinting critique to our scholar-editors, Jo Quinn and Jon Prag, and my co-authors for their critical engagement in our originating conferences. I am very grateful to Bruce Hitchner for responses to several drafts. All flaws are my responsibility. Extremely synthetic but necessarily brief, this chapter cannot systematically survey nor document all its frames of reference, and bibliography is sadly abbreviated; readers should recur to 'global references' that make portals into deep scholarship; I regret omitting so much important and current work, and obvious comparanda. On the other hand, the chapter is also a project meant to suggest that synthesising even 'common knowledge' across fields and disciplines, and easily accessible primary evidence, can contribute to knowledge.

[2] To sample the 'Hellenistic' look of things (since the 1980s an enormous field of study), see, for sculpture, Smith 1991 (compactly) and (at great length) Ridgway 1990, 2000, 2002; Winter 2006 for architecture; overview across art, artifact and architecture, Pollitt 1986 and Onians 1979. We need a book on Republican art; for now, and especially for the public displays here referenced: briefly but tellingly Pollitt 1986; Strong 1988; Gruen 1992; and the exhibitions *Kaiser Augustus und die verlorene Republik* of 1988 (hereafter *Kaiser Augustus* 1988) and *L'età della conquista: il fascino dell'arte greca a Roma* of 2010 (hereafter *L'età della conquista* 2010). For Numidia, fundamental remains the 1979 exhibition *Die Numider* (hereafter *Die Numider* 1979). There are no reviews even partially systematic of fourth- to second-century west (or east) Phoenician art and architecture. For history: on realities and affairs in the Numidian and Mauretanian kingdoms, with attention to the archaeology and, where relevant, Punic contexts, Storm 2001; *Die Numider* 1979; Coltelloni-Trannoy 1997; and for the Second Punic War era, Lancel 1998; affairs in Numidia and Mauretania in the first century BCE are accessible in the global Sulla bibliography at n. 69. For the Roman Republican framework, its engagement with west and east Greeks and the Diadoch eastern kingdoms, a good basic Anglophone portal to the evidence and to models for interpreting it because of its Mediterranean overview is the work of Gruen, whether affirming or

Because the record of Republican art is limited, and the Numidian record very small, a significant initial dossier is possible. The case-studies circle temporally: from the Caesaro-Augustan period, Juba I's age and immediate aftermath, back to second-century Numidia, then forward again to just before the epoch where I started; that project aims both to destabilise some master narratives of Roman art history and expand Numidian ones. For historians querying cultural self-assertion and intracultural optics, it is good to test artifacts deliberately made to bear the weight of constructing Self and Other. The evidence admits no question that the leaders of both Rome and Numidia thus practised *Kunstpolitik*. Though Numidian monumental art was lacking until the second-century construction of the centralised kingdom (for which see Quinn, Chapter 7 of this volume), its dynasts' monuments show no clumsiness in what we can call the international, Hellenistic mode of elite visual artifice. That was also true of Carthage and the Libyo-Phoenician sphere, Numidia's mother-cultures by proximity, even if this brief essay cannot, alas, do more than evoke that cosmopolitan landscape of what I will broadly call a Punic cultural zone in western North Africa (by contrast to more easterly Greco-Libyan Cyrene and Egypt); upon that zone, since the fifth century, the Carthaginian Empire's heartland and its sophisticated capital naturally will have exerted significant force.

Painting the picture: Numidian princes and fatal banquets

It is 46 BCE, in Rome: Caesar celebrates a multiple triumph, for the campaigns in which culminated his struggle to survive and dominate other politician-generals in the penultimate Republican Civil War.[3] Romans have lived bloody civil conflict for over two generations, but this quadruple festival's images of dying Roman enemies were unique. There had been no representational delineation of that internecine strife in public *monimenta*, nor would there be again, at least in the extant corpus, until Constantine's Arch depicted the assault on Italian cities and Maxentius' Roman soldiers drowning in the Tiber. That makes Caesar's picture of a Romano-Numidian suicide pact of extreme import.

contesting models: 1984 and with a cultural optic added 1990 and 1992; see also the volumes of the *Cambridge Ancient History* for the period ('Hellenistic' and 'Republican'), and the 'companions' edited by Erskine 2003a and Bugh 2006a. For the Sullan era, see n. 69. For Caesar's, still superb and with fine documentation of art and patronage, Weinstock 1971.

[3] Caesar's triumph, diverse details: App. *B Civ.* 2.101; Flor. 2.13.88–9; Vell. Pat. 2.56; Quint. *Inst.* 6.3.61; Suet. *Iul.* 37–9, 49, 51; Plut. *Caes.* 55; Dio Cass. 43.19–21 and 40.41; Cic. *Off.* 2.28. Also Livy, *Per.* 115; Plin. *HN* 19.144; Suet. *Aug.* 8.

Two of the celebrations were for easily foreign wars, against Gauls and the Pontic kingdom. Another, however, celebrated 47 BCE's Battle of the Nile, an intervention in that Successor kingdom's civil wars, Caesar allied with his successful claimant Cleopatra VII. No such easy assignment here of the 'Other' to lesser, enemy people. This triumph tacitly engaged Roman civil conflict, too: Caesar could appear to avenge the murder by Cleopatra's brother of Roman Pompey, even though Pompey was his political enemy. But Caesar's fourth, African celebration openly discussed Roman internecine killing along with foreign war. The *simulacra* of towns taken, their very material symbolic (African ivory: Quint. *Inst.* 6.3.61; Vell. Pat. 2.56), included many sites that the Roman 'rebels' defended. Numidia was nominal enemy only because its king Juba I pledged his Roman *fides* to the wrong side. Those 'rebel' legions had entrenched in North Africa as an almost last redoubt. Now, many of their leaders were self-murdered; for the Republican Civil Wars' closing phases saw a rash of Roman honour-suicides such as Rome had never before witnessed. Caesar tried to give his Romans the chance to mourn, in order to go forward in civil *pax*, advertising strongly that he would not have had his peers die and that he would be no Sulla, Marius or Cinna, quick to savage dissenters. As a means to that, his unprecedented images honoured suiciding leaders' ends as tragic, alongside the typical exciting pictures of foreign enemies' downfall. The crowd responded as desired (and not, as many scholars posit, in disapproval):

> He ... presented in the processions ... the individuals and all their sufferings by means of statues and paintings – all except Pompey, whom alone he decided not to portray, since Pompey was still much missed by all. The crowd, although feeling intimidated, groaned at disasters to their own people, particularly when they saw Lucius Scipio, commander-in-chief, stabbing himself in the chest and throwing himself into the sea, Petreius committing suicide at his banquet, Cato rending himself like a wild animal. But they exulted over Achillas and Pothinos [evil advisors of Cleopatra's brother, responsible for Pompey's assassination], and laughed at the rout of Pharnakes [of Pontos]. (App. *B Civ.* 2.101.)[4]

Caesar's 'Petreius committing suicide at his banquet' documented a suicide pact between Numidian king Juba I and the Roman 'rebel' general Petreius, in Juba's palace. Most scholarly citation is brief, and without Juba; none appraise

[4] For the view that Caesar caricatured his enemies, and that Appian, though we know him biased against Caesar, truthfully describes crowds angry at the suicide commemoratives, see e.g. Holliday 1997: 145–6. Appian, like Livy interested in pictures, lets us compare prior images from Pompey's triumph of 61 (*Mith.* 117) – Mithridates' suicide invited gloating response, but the images of his children forced by him to die in the royal palace called for pity.

its reconstructible contours. Greek Appian, our only extant source, his Roman sources now lost, was solely concerned to denote Roman suicide. But Roman word-pictures demonstrate that that joint death's peculiar poignancy was that it was jointly undertaken. There are two textual accounts: a death-duel, or drinking poison together. It is perhaps more likely that the latter was painted, since Roman and foreigner fighting would have resembled enemies not friends. One saw then these sworn friends at a last meal in a country palace – a stage adding special melodrama – where they had fled after their rout at Thapsus. The picture begs consideration in the context of many important themes, not least late Republican Roman nobles' self-assimilation to Hellenistic kings. But it has not received the scholarly attention given to, for instance, Tiberius Gracchus' Second Punic War painting of 214 BCE (Livy 24.19), which was similarly about *amicitia* and *fides* engaging Romans with foreigners, and perhaps African ones at that, in a banquet context.[5] The latter depicted Beneventum's rejoicing Greek citizens, delivered from Carthaginian attack, giving the army a city-wide feast served and shared by rejoicing slave-soldiers (*volones*) now freed for their service. Aptly made to grace the temple of Freedom, *libertas*, the painting celebrated the value of loyalty from foreigners, whether free or freed. Gracchus' indentured forces, 8,000 strong, were enrolled from a slave population much dependent on Carthaginian slave trade to Rome, and almost certainly contained very many North Africans; if such were recognisably pictured, the Gracchan painted banquet would be especially relevant to our picture's complex evocations.[6]

Picturing Roman North African *amicitia* and *fides*, Caesar's painting consoled those of Juba's party still alive, as well as pro-Caesarian Numidians. Petreius' death was not mocked; so too the picture mourned the death of the foreign king and all his Numidians who had been loyal to Rome, even if misguidedly. For the stability of Rome's Africa Caesar needed them as well as Romans to heal communal psychological wounds. That aim is certified by the way in which Caesar re-affirmed Juba I's line. His baby son, later Juba II, was carried in the procession (Plut. *Caes.* 55, App. *B Civ.* 2.101) as captive kings ought to be, the living picture beside the father's lifeless image: but Caesar thus showed off the toddler *as* a rightful prince. Foreign hostages had been quartered well before, but it must have startled Romans, and greatly pleased Numidians, that Caesar then fostered in his own *domus* a Numidian princeling, whom Octavian later raised like an adoptive half-brother.

Caesar bested Roman armies in Africa led by a Scipio desirous of the stature of his assumed ancestors, the two Scipiones who had earlier beaten

[5] Koortbojian 2002; Feldherr 1998: 34. [6] Palmer 1997: 28–9.

Carthage. Caesar's triumphal painting, I propose, recalled another painting, about the first of those Africani, Scipio the Elder, a Numidian king as (Scipio's) bosom-friend, and suicide by poison in a palace. This was, I suggest, a historical painting made for Africanus' Carthaginian triumph of 201 BCE, now extant as replicated in two wall-paintings at Pompeii that some have called 'The Death of Sophonisba'.[7] The situation is the reverse of 'The Suicide of Petreius and Juba': replicas show this painting's appearance, but no explanatory text survives. In Scipio's triumph of 201, however, Appian knew of enough paintings 'of exploits in the war' to remark this special class of exhibits (*Punika* 66) and Polybius notes that Romans were 'reminded vividly of their previous dangers by the actually present spectacle of the procession's displays' (16.23). The 'Third Style' wall-paintings considered here (Figures 8.1 and 8.2) were made in or just after the age of Augustus. The first was the back-wall showpiece of an important room off the atrium at one of Pompeii's architecturally grandest mansions, the 'House of Giuseppe II' (henceforth *HG*).[8] Then someone of lesser means emulated that mansion's display at the 'Casa del Fabbro' (*CdF*), again as the back-wall showpiece of a special room (8) off the atrium.[9]

HG (Figure 8.1) was taken from its wall, with many lower and upper portions broken away, to the Bourbon royal collection, then moved again in the nineteenth century to Naples' Museo Nazionale Archeologico. In the early twentieth century it was removed to the basements, not much visited; after being put on show as part of the landmark *Die Numider* exhibition in Bonn in 1979, to the basements it returned, growing cobwebbed (I saw it). In 2010, however, it was restored to the galleries, conserved; a museum handbook published it for the first time in colour, if at a regrettably small scale.[10]

[7] App. *Pun.* 65: Scipio's triumph was 'more glorious than that of any of his predecessors'; 66: '. . . Trumpeters led the advance, and wagons loaded with booty. Towers representing captured cities were carried past, and pictures showing the exploits of the war . . . then [Punic war-] elephants, and all the captured Carthaginian and [pro-Carthaginian] Numidian leaders.'

[8] Naples MN inv. 8698; 'picture', H 78 x W 79 cm; total fragment with a portion of the surround, W 1.12 m. Location: VIII.2.39, room m.

[9] Location: I.10.7, room 8. The most recent description and discussion of the two paintings is M. Roller 1996: 49–61 (*HG*, 49–52 and Fig. 8; *CdF*, 55–61). The chance to study the *CdF*'s details, I owe to Matthew Roller's gift of colour high-resolution shots. House, Allison 2004: s.v. 'Casa del Fabbro'; Ling and Ling 2004: 140–1 with b/w Fig., colour plate 22 (illustrated in tiny scale), as Third Style (the first Anglophone historiography of the Death of Sophonisba replicas).

[10] Bragantini and Sampaolo 2009: cat. 97, 248. The indispensable older b/w DAI negative (D-DAI-ROM-53.631R) is reprinted at decently large scale in *Die Numider* 1979: 487, text 486; for even better resolution at upper right, consult the negative online at the Arachne DAI image web-bank, http://arachne.uni-koeln.de/item/marbilder/378407, Object 223398. The nineteenth-century archaeologist Gell (1832) supplies our only notice of the whole salon's now-lost décor (3 and plate 3 to room m); Reinach 1922: 221 no. 3 redrew the image. Ling and

Figure 8.1 'Death of Sophonisba', Third Style (later first century BCE – early first century CE); from Pompeii, Casa di Giuseppe II (VIII.2.39), now Naples, Museo Archeologico inv. 8968. For colour version see plate section.

Ironically, the now-deplored strategy of removing a 'picture' from its painted wall saved the surfaces of *HG*. *CdF*, left uncared for *in situ*, is sadly degraded, though its intact composition fills lacunae in *HG* (Figure 8.2).

Here is that primary replica (Figure 8.1): a palatial, suicidal *symposium* ironically overseen by a statue of Dionysus, a second now-blurred statue at

Ling 2004: 140–1 gives bibliography (without Gell). It was excitedly discussed as Sophonisba from the 1860s up to Elia 1934. For the architecture of the multi-storey house and gardens (ground floor level, *c.* 850 m sq.), Mazois' graphics are unsurpassed (1824–38: II, 73, pl. 74); see Allison 2004: s.v. 'Casa di Giuseppe II' for archaeology and historiography. Mau called the décor Fourth Style; consideration of Gell's drawing, and of the ornamental surround's scant remains indicates, to me, rich Third Style (Augustan).

Figure 8.2 'Death of Sophonisba', Third Style (later first century BCE – early first century CE); at Pompeii, Casa del Fabbro (I.10.7). For colour version see plate section.

far right.[11] A couch holds centre foreground; on it recline, from viewer's right to left, a markedly dark brown, fine-boned prince, his white-skinned queen nestled in his arm; purple mantle and pale diadem-like ribbon denote his status. That mantle rests along his consort's lower body, setting off her regally golden wrap and parti-coloured purple underrobe with white bodice, and some blue below. Greco-Roman painting made men brown, women and children pale. Two devices emphasise here that the prince's skin is *distinctively* dark: the contrast to the ordinary ruddy-brown skin of the males at the couch's foot, and the iteration in the deep brown skin of the

[11] Typically for Roman painted replica series of multi-figure narratives, the *CdF* secondary replica altered background architecture, while keeping figure groupings, significant furnitures, and speaking polychromies intact; out came Dionysus' statue, perhaps wall-painter's gloss in the first place.

maid huddling with a white-skinned fellow handmaid on the couch's far side. The white girl faces away from the protagonists, in profile; the dark girl peers, face in three-quarter view, to stare at her 'white' mistress' features. Thus, the pair of maids mirrors the dark/light couple, and complements the dark/light male protagonists' exchanged gaze (below).

Three other figures cluster around the couch's foot. Clad only in a kilt-like wrap, its purple-red colour befitting regal service, a tall servant (far left) attends the couple, holding the tray (on it, food untouched) with which he brought the queen's wine cup to that couch from which he now stands back. His fine-boned features and lanky physique are those of the prince, but not of the third male, who moves in from the left. This intruder, dressed like a Roman officer (red-purple *paludimentum* (commander's cloak), *caligae* (boot-sandals)), stops almost dead at the couch's foot. He locks eyes with the prince, who lifts his face towards the visitor: that confrontation *is* the pictorial action. By contrast to the idealised, fine-boned, youthful faces of the other males, the painter denoted a verist type, or even a portrait – balding, fleshy, irregularly featured, almost snub-nosed, heavily jowled. Finally, on the couch's near side squats, half-kneeling, a boy servant, face turned to us, with a large unidentifiable object: the *CdF* composition explains the *HG* trace of his wrapped derrière.

Staging matters. A tall metal candelabrum shaft, symbolically lacking a lit lamp, rises at the couch's head. *CdF* shows what leant against it in *HG*: a big round war-shield – obviously the prince's. Icon of his heroic regality, it is also a narrative marker, in conjunction with the officer shown at left: a temporal location within a war. But the shining centrepoint of the picture is a large silver handleless drinking cup (a good fourth- to second-century profile), now drained, upheld in the queen's right palm. Her right elbow is braced on her left thigh, but her head slumps, eyes closing, and her upper body begins to fall forward helplessly. The image communicates clearly: she loses consciousness because of what she drank.

The first nineteenth-century commentators excitedly recognised the grand mansion's painting as the suicide of the Carthaginian noblewoman Sophonisba, in the palace of her new-wedded husband King Massinissa of Numidia, passionate both in love for her and in friendship with Scipio Africanus the Elder, his ally against Carthage, their *amicitia* and Massinissa's *fides* exemplary in the Roman tradition. Educated on Greek and Roman texts (see below), and inheriting centuries of visual, dramatic and musical authors' fascination by the Punic princess' travails, nineteenth-/early twentieth-century commentators knew it as a setpiece of ancient historians; the story would have been obvious too to any Roman with the historical interests that cultured persons like the *HG* mansion's owner were supposed to have.[12] By the mid-twentieth century, however, only specialists remembered the painting; eventually most moved it to the category of banquet-art's generic scenes. Although the 1979 *Die Numider* exhibition retrieved its historical character, no review of Roman history-painting of at least the last fifty years mentions it.[13] Now the new Naples handbook (Bragantini and Sampaolo 2009) and Ling's and Ling's 2004 study of the *insula* of the House of Menander (reviewing the literature) at least rebroadcast the proposition that this replica series is historical, whether depicting Sophonisba or Cleopatra.[14]

Briefly, Sophonisba was betrothed to young Massinissa to bind the Numidian leader to Carthage, whose empire depended on the military support of the various Numidian states. Carthage cancelled the betrothal for what seemed a better political move, marrying her to Syphax, another Numidian prince. He broke with Rome, while irate Massinissa joined its cause. Towards the end of the Second Punic War, Sophonisba deserted Syphax for Massinissa at his palace at Cirta; he eagerly married her – without telling Scipio. When the Roman command learnt of the marriage, afraid of charismatic Sophonisba pulling Massinissa to the Carthaginian side, Scipio despatched to the palace the

[12] This curtly distills ongoing work on the Sophonisba paintings and texts, and their Roman, Hellenistic, Punic, Numidian contexts, historical and cultural. Analogies drawn here to Attalid victory art are part of ongoing work (meanwhile see Kuttner 1997) about artistic convergence and gift-exchange between Attalid Pergamon and Rome – including master-painters gifted to Africanus' brother Lucius Scipio for his triumph's paintings (Livy 39.22.9–10). Texts: Dio Cass. 17.50, App. *Pun.* 27, Zonar. 9.13, and, coeval to or older than *HG*, Livy 29.33, 30.13–15 (30.15 the dramatic crux). Relevant are lost second- and first-century sources for them all: Wiseman 1998: 2 and 4 cites nineteenth-century theories that Scipio staged a triumph history play, *toga praetexta*, incorporating the episode. The limited historical work on Sophonisba (Sophoniba, Sofoniba) focuses on Livy, and other authors, as literary constructs, with an interest in the influence of the Cleopatra *mythos* (for instance, Moscovich 1997; Haley 1989; Toppani 1977–8). Historians of Massinissa at this crux typically evade discussing Sophonisba.

[13] State of the field accessible via Holliday 1997 and 2002. For textually attested paintings superb is Feldherr 1998; handbook access, Pollitt 1986.

[14] See n. 10. Elia 1955 suggested Cleopatra, but see Ling and Ling's 2004 critique (at 141); I add, regarding 'race', that an Antony would not have been tagged relative to the image's other Roman general as dark-skinned like that 'ethnic' maid. Bragantini and Sampaolo 2009 back Elia, because (*sic*) the woman is too mature to be Sophonisba. They evidently mean her plumpness of body and face, but Roman art did not tag advancing female years with a heavy-set body; it is obvious that pulchritude suffers from this wall-painter's clumsiness at foreshortening of face and cleavage. These authors' 'Antony' is slim and youthful vs. the balding middle-aged Roman at left; yet it would make no sense that the artist make his lover look markedly older. M. Roller 1996 discusses the replica series as imaging luxurious dining, eschewing a choice between generic and historical narrative; but, noting the 'specificity' of heterodox details (somewhat as I do) he leaves to his Roman diners the option for seeing 'learned historical narration' either of Sophonisba or Cleopatra.

demand that Sophonisba be handed over and the marriage annulled. Prince and princess were desperate that she avoid the shame of imprisonment and parade in triumph. Massinissa was caught between human *pietas* to wife and to friend, *fides* to personal and (as king) political morality. Powerless to keep her physically safe, he could only help her to die – a classic Punic honour-suicide, like that of her brother Hannibal, self-poisoned *c.* 183 BCE to escape imprisonment, and of Hasdrubal's wife in 146.[15] As the painting stresses, he gave her poison to drink, as lover shares wine with beloved. Not for nothing is her dying posture the same evocative sweep of arms and slumping head, in a husband's grasp, as the ideally featured wife of the craggy-faced Gallic chieftain in the famous late third-century Attalid victory group on Pergamon's citadel, who has given his wife the gift of escape from capture by stabbing her before killing himself.[16] Massinissa, defiantly giving Sophonisba royal burial, was devastated by grief (and, surely, by wounded *dignitas*, a sense of Roman betrayal): awe-struck at the honourable extremes to which Sophonisba and Massinissa went, seeing that corpse, Scipio with senatorial approval rewarded and consoled his friend's *fides* with the unprecedented award to an alien of consular regalia.

This summary distils from the texts, which handle diversely especially the last, most intimate events. The painting is parallel discourse, which brilliantly uses familiar visual codes and ironises standard banquet groupings to convey the essence of events, identities and personae with the forced physical juxtapositions and temporal elisions we know well in Hellenistic Greek history-painting (like the fourth-century Battle of Alexander and Darius, found at the House of the Faun in Pompeii in a mosaic replica of

[15] Like Sophonisba, Hasdrubal's wife fascinated Roman imaginations: to escape capture, and shame her husband for tamely surrendering, she leapt from the roof of the burning Temple of Eshmun into the flames with her two young children (a deliberate elaboration of Punic ritual child-sacrifice); Dio Cass. 21.30, Flor. 1.31, App. *Pun.* 131, and moral *exempla* in Val. Max. 3.2. ext.8, Jer. *Adv. Iovinian.* 1.43. To Carthaginians the most potent suicide (after that of the heroised founder Dido/Elissa) was that of fifth-century Hamilcar, who threw himself into flames after losing the battle of Himera, and was heroised posthumously by Carthage, Hdt. 7.165–7. Bode 2001: 66–71 contextualises this in Punic and also west Greek practice and beliefs. There is much to be done with the fact of, and the Greco-Roman admiration for female honour-suicides, in the Hellenistic centuries – admiration often directed to non-Greek and non-Roman women.

[16] The careful copy now in the Palazzo Altemps is quickly accessible as Pollitt 1986: 84-9, Fig. 86; on Eumenes II's associated 'long base' monument on Pergamon's acropolis, Kuttner 2001: 163. For the posture of a dying/dead beloved slumping with prolapsed arm, and would-be protector whose (lunging) body strains upright, staring for whomever might seize that body: the 'Pasquino Group' replicas of a third-/second-century Pergamene paradigm (sometimes Odysseus rescuing Patroklos body at Troy, Pollitt 1986: 118, Fig. 119); replicas of Achilles with dead/dying Penthesilea, a fourth-century pictorial composition made sculptural in the second/ first centuries BCE, Ridgway 1990: 281–3, Pl. 139.

c. 150 BCE) and in Roman so-called historical relief (like the so-called 'Altar of Domitius Ahenobarbus' census relief, *c.* 125–70 BCE).

I back the first commentators: this is the 'Death of Sophonisba'. It is neither a generic banquet scene, an unspecified 'myth', nor Cleopatra's suicide. The aulic, portentous depiction is not drunken cavorting in a mediocre setting like every ordinary banquet-piece. No mythological, rather than historical, story extant in Roman art makes protagonists bald, except the occasional very old man, Silenus or philosopher; no known wall-painting of the Republic and early Empire configures mythical figures as Roman *imperatores*. No legend, history, or myth Greek or Roman accounts for a 'black', diademed prince, or for his wedded princess with a 'black' African entourage and thus also from a people prepotent in Africa. No known 'genre scene' has 'black' servants, either.

The unique emphasis upon apposition of very dark and lighter races is clearly meant to help place the story. So is the moment, clear to read: African and Roman commanders in fraught communion, the temporal crux the prince's physically cherished African consort dying by means of a significant drink. It is historiographically interesting that all who want this to be a myth, or simply about a drunk lady (to which the regal and warlike thematics ill suit), close their eyes to the pictorialisation, unparalleled in extant art, of racial difference between 'light-skinned' Greeks/Romans and darker indigenous dynasts and followers in Africa. The African heroine's 'Greco-Roman' white-skinned and ovoid face (the replicator botched the foreshortening) is a well-known convention in 'ethnic images' of (legendary) history, Punic and otherwise; in any case, Punes were not tagged as 'dark people'.[17]

The picture is likely to effectively if unrealistically show Scipio (not Laelius or a stray officer-agent) come to confront Massinissa and an inimical Sophonisba, only to meet instead a grieving husband, a bravely dying wife.[18] A triangle of national prides, and of two personal affectional bonds up against politically grounded enmity, is clear. Carthage in the body of Sophonisba dies and Rome will live (gender studies, take note), because of Massinissa's choice of which empire to make or break. The Punic enemy's

[17] Compare: in the same *insula* of the House of Menander as the *CdF* and elsewhere, Punic (white) Dido in her palace room, meditating suicide as Aeneas' ship sails away, with her sister Anna, and personified Africa – sometimes, dark-skinned, black-haired (Ling and Ling 2004: 123–4, Pl. 94, 108); Alexander encountering fair Roxanne in generic Greco-Roman dress, by contrast to her dark Sogdian bodyguard, their ethnic costume authentically configured as Iranian-style, Fourth Style painting paraphrasing an earlier Hellenistic original – House of the Golden Bracelet, Pompeii (Stewart 1993: 186–7, colour Pl. 6-7, Fig. 59–60).

[18] Many attempt to identify portraits of the Scipiones Africani in Republican-Augustan gems and sculpture; I avoid the issue.

downfall is handled sympathetically, in keeping with then 'modern' second-century Attalid-inspired modes of conquest art. Marital love, sexual morality and patriotism choosing death over dishonour: this admiring, pitying visual appraisal would have seemed as awe-inspiring as stories of early Republican heroes who honourably kill themselves and kin, often with a sexualised twist (Lucretia, Horatius ready to kill a sister, Verginia's murder by protective father). Even the pro-Sophonisbans, as it were, skipped the implications of a replica series; but if I am correct, Romanists gain the only triumphal narrative-painting we can truly glimpse. Massinissa and his entourage certainly accompanied Scipio's 201 BCE return to Rome for a triumph. Such an image would, as had the consular regalia, reward Massinissa and bolster his throne at Rome and in Numidia. First to unite the Numidian confederation, he there needed strengthening; Numidian eyes could be pleased by how Scipio tried to make Rome value their king, their people, while Massinissa gained stature with them.

The paradigm behind the replicas had little reason to be invented two centuries later. But for the 'Third-style' viewers' comprehension, it matters that Augustan Livy gave the largest, most theatrical account of the tale (30.13–15) and that Augustan-Tiberian Valerius Maximus esteemed the suicides of Punic noblewomen (like Hasdrubal's wife at Africanus the Younger's sack of Carthage, above). Many remark the shadows of Cleopatra and Antony, Vergil's Dido (Ling and Ling's bibliographic review, 2004: 140–1); for the Third-style era, add the atmosphere of Carthage's resurrection as Roman colony, Juba II's celebrity at Rome and the enduring fascination of the Scipiones Africani. It interests in this context that *CdF* put a beard on *HG*'s shaven prince, who better fits accounts of a young, ardent Massinissa; I think that the Petreius painting of the heavily bearded Juba (we have his likeness on coins, in statuary), or other accounts of him and Numidian kings' typical beards, inflected the second version.

Historical wall-painting is rare in the Campanian domestic corpus, pre-79 CE, but it exists. Never forget that we have lost 'free' painting almost entirely; history-in-the-house, contemporary and 'ancient', is documented in many media by literary texts and by remains from the second century BCE to Late Antiquity, empire-wide.[19]

[19] Synthesis lacks. Very briefly, temporally relevant are, besides examples in my text, the early second-century reliefs about contemporary wars at Fregellae (n. 62); the fourth-century 'Alexander and Darius' painting as mosaic replica at Pompeii's House of the Faun of *c.* 150–130 BCE, Pompeii's biggest house, certainly known to our owners – like the public spoliations from Dion to Rome by Metellus Macedonicus of Alexander's history art (Lysippos' 'Granikos Group'), it glosses participation/interest in the second-century Macedonian Wars; and several pieces of Augustan

HG's owner lived on a grand enough scale to aspire to imitate patrician houses, like the Tusculan villa where Sulla kept a painting of himself receiving the Grass Crown at Nola, which Cicero owned by buying that house (Pliny, *HN* 22.12)! For the many attested paintings for Republican generals our randomly preserved texts only sometimes name a subsequent dedication at a sanctuary; but those which did not last at a temple surely cannot have been destroyed. If so, then they entered generals' houses; we know well that the aristocracy displayed triumphalist tokens at vestibule and in atrium. Houses for our Scipio to show the replicas' source include his new Liternum villa visited even by Imperial tourists, the clan *horti* in Rome, or the Tivoli *domus* of the Africani (owned by Antony, then Augustus).[20] Elite Numidians, in the Scipionic *clientela* and visiting Rome after, will hardly not have known of a Scipionic 'Massinissa and Sophonisba', and at least sometimes wished to see in it how history made in Numidian palaces won Rome an empire.

Arming Numidia's heights: the dynastic panoply monuments at Chemtou and Kbor Klib

My posited painting of Massinissa giving up his wife for Rome was art about Numidia, partly for Numidians, but by foreigners. Now let us turn to royal Numidia's own visual discourse, which surfaces for us in a later, second-century era of Massinissa and his successors (below). The cryptic, sacro-political peak-monuments of Chemtou (Simitthus) (Figures 8.3–8.8) and Kbor Klib (*KK*, Figures 8.9–8.11) are spectacular centrepieces to studies of the material visual splendour of the second-century kingdom of Numidia. My target is their relief decoration, their costume of political, economic, societal vigour, stature, strength, whether real or only imputed. That magnificence induces societal aquiescence to power and useful esteem from Others was a conscious awareness in the big world of cultivated appearances into which Massinissa ushered Numidia. How successfully our monuments met the criteria of Mediterranean high culture is evident in how easily they enter

silver in the Vesuvian Boscoreale hoard, Kuttner 1995; Baratte 1986 (deeds of Augustus, Tiberius and Drusus on two cups; Augustan victory compositions on two jugs referencing Naulochos, Actium, and Armenia; its setpiece Africa dish interests here, too). The less-grand (as the *CdF* owner was) could aspire to the way that the *nobiles* kept triumphalist displays in vestibule and atrium: an early first-century BCE vestibule (I. VII.7) was clumsily painted with an equestrian charge against Spartacus (war of 73–71 BCE; inscribed in Oscan with the name Spartacus, Cooley and Cooley 2004: cat. B14a–b, 21f, Pl. 2.1; Maiuri 1939: 5 and Fig. 5b).

[20] Ideology of elite *domus* display: Wiseman 1987. Liternum: Sen. *Ep.* 95.72.3; D'Arms 2003; Bodel 1997: 1–2, with the Porta Capena *horti*. Tibur: Cic. *Phil.* 5.7.19; Suet. *Aug.* 72; briefly, Kuttner 2003: 148 n. 160.

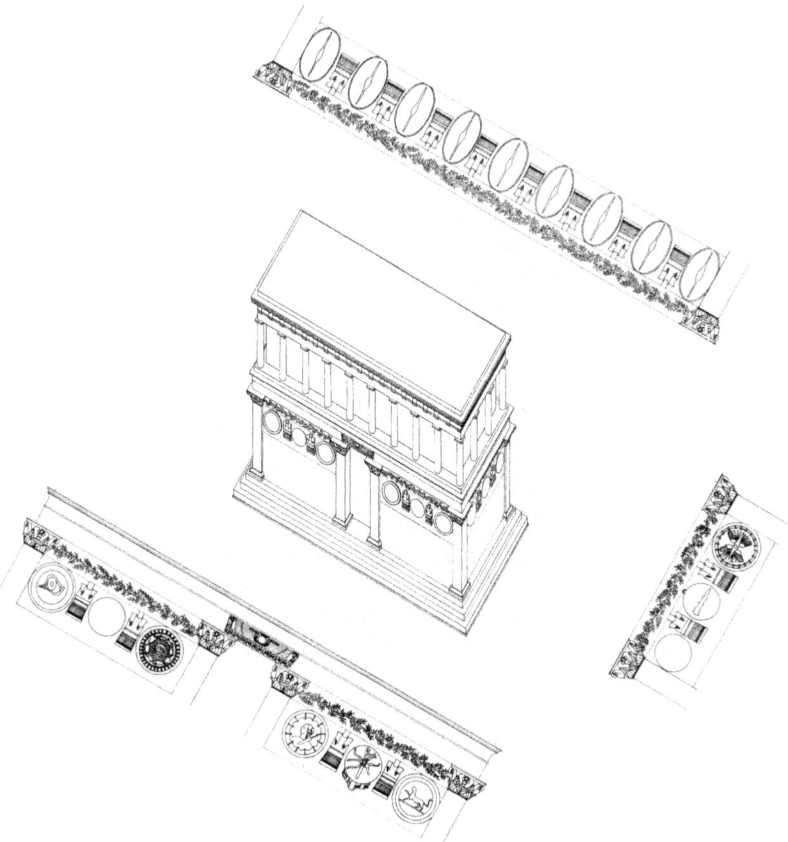

Figure 8.3 Chemtou/Simitthus, Numidian royal monument, schematic montage which illustrates the distribution of and suggests spectators' angle views for the front and side friezes of cavalrymen's round figural shields and their cuirasses, and the back frieze of infantrymen's long oval ribbed shields and their cuirasses.

our discussions of it. Only dynasts could have permitted and co-ordinated the subvention for these sites: they therefore spoke to Numidians about what kingship meant in Numidia, as well as about the collective the king ruled. Sanctuaries, palaces and civic/mercantile spaces must have been made splendid as well: but save for sparse remains from Juba II's first-century CE Cherchel, we have little beyond occasional footprints in plan, or architectural fragments, and nothing of their elaboration by *art*.[21] Intended to impress in their own time, the mountain-markers now carry an enormous burden of documentation. However my synthetic effort succeeds, I hope two things

[21] Reviewed in D. Roller 2003: 119–33, moving on from there to other cities and sites. A possible monument of the scale and type of *KK* and Chemtou at Althiburos: Kallala *et al.* 2008: 98–100, compared at 100.

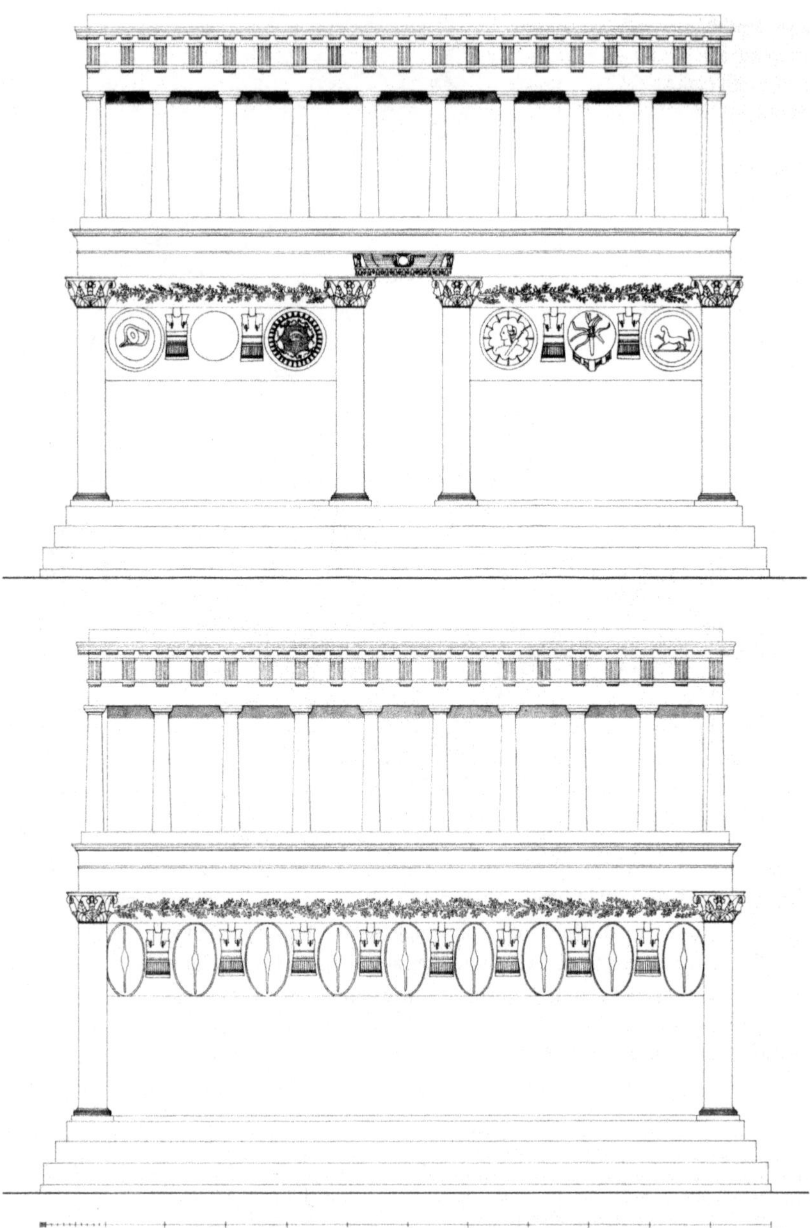

Figure 8.4 Chemtou/Simitthus, Numidian royal monument, front and back elevations.

change the discussion. One is to emphasise how these monuments address Numidians. The other is to draw us away from questions that the extant evidence will never completely answer – exactly Who, When, Why – into exploring What we can say about an artifact, a site, in despite of such ignorance.

Figure 8.5 Chemtou/Simitthus, Numidian royal monument, the extant figural shields: Hercules' club, winged thunderbolt, eye, Medusa-aegis, snake and flaming (?) torch, pacing feline. This montage (author) excerpts elevations by Rakob in *Die Numider* (in which the Artemis shield for Kbor Klib was added erroneously); the actual order of the shield slabs is unknown.

Figure 8.6 Chemtou/Simitthus, Numidian royal monument, relief fragments: figural shield with eye and fragment of the entablature's laurel-branch garland.

These wide bulks are building-sized models of buildings, articulated by fictional, relief-cut architectural members as two-story edifices with important doors. Chemtou's central portal leads nowhere; at enormously wide Kbor Klib (*KK*) there were complex arrangements for inner chambers, stairs and rooftop aediculae. Relief friezes of armour – cuirasses and

Figure 8.7 Chemtou/Simitthus, Numidian royal monument, relief fragment: shield 'covered' by *aegis* bearing a Medusa head.

shields – ringed both. Since Chemtou preserves more of an organic programme of figuration, on a structure that can be well understood, it is the focus of my primary analysis, whose propositions are to varying degrees extended to *KK*'s limited fragmentary record.

At Chemtou we see the illusion of a colonnaded gallery crowned by solid masonry, articulated with angle piers. Over the walls' high wainscoting, under an entablature frieze of laurel, circled the armours. The laurel branches' regular zig-zag was at once a novel moulding and a denotation of leaf-sprays cut for ritual, legible in both Punic-zone and Greco-Roman visual dialects: it crowns Chemtou for victory like the sacral-triumphal laurel wreaths worn by Massinissa and Micipsa on their coins.[22] The seductive visual interest, though, is that on the front and ends: round shields make an image gallery one circles the monument to see, with a different pictorial blazon on each imitating cast, carved and applied metal relief and repoussé. No other Hellenistic-era, public, sculpted armament frieze proposes such a kaleidoscopic image-within-image display but that here, at *KK*, and their cousin in Rome, the San Omobono reliefs.

[22] Fundamental: Rakob 1979: 120–9 (Chemtou-Simitthus: Figs. 30-2, drawings; 34, sphinx capital; 35, lintel detail with solar disk; 36–41, 46 (mislabeled as *KK*), armour details; 42, Doric entablature fragment); 129–32 (*KK*: esp. Fig. 44–5, elevation det. and plan; 47, cuirass relief). See also Polito 1998: 40–1; Storm 2001; and cross-references in Ferchiou's 1991 masterwork on *KK*.

Figure 8.8 (a) Chemtou/Simitthus, Numidian royal monument, relief fragment: shield with undulating serpent across flaming upright object (torch?), other details unclear. (b) Chemtou/Simitthus, Numidian royal monument, relief fragment: shield with winged thunderbolt.

Several features govern this discussion. Firstly, the front and back marshalled two parts of one force, their collaboration a significant point. Most discussion concentrates on the more 'artistically' interesting shield-reliefs, front and sides; less attention is paid to the less pictorialised back. Many illustrate the monument only with a three-quarter view (front, one short end) of the model made for the show *Die Numider*, that hides the back, as Rakob's diagrammatic scheme does not. A row of tall, narrow,

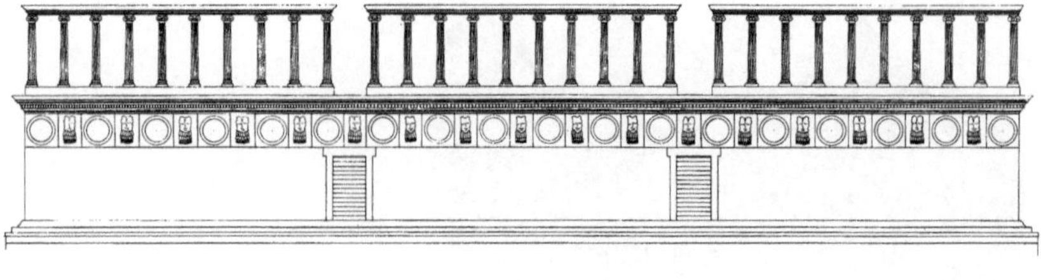

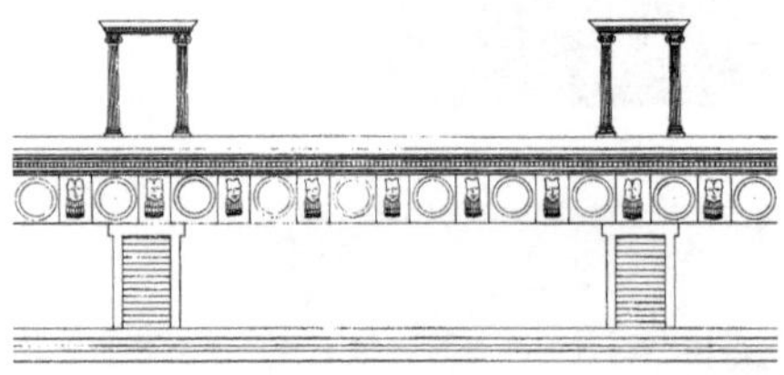

Figure 8.9 Kbor Klib, Numidian royal monument, alternative elevations.

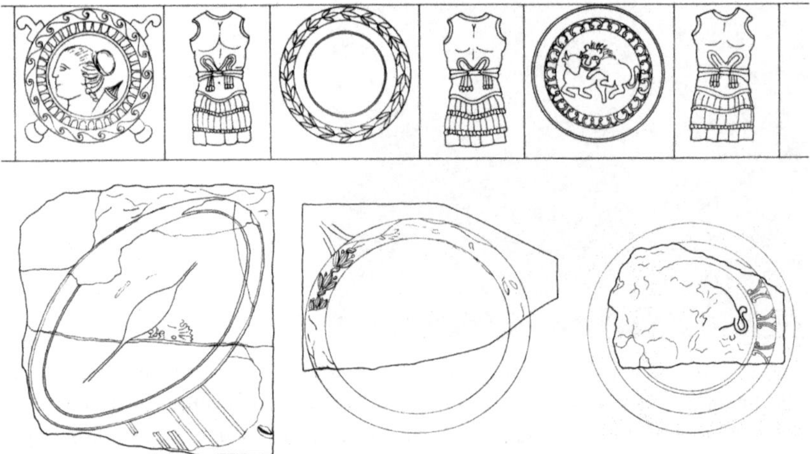

Figure 8.10 Kbor Klib, Numidian royal monument, montage (author) of figural shields using reconstructive and documentary drawings of Ferchiou 1991: Figs. 20, 14 (long shield and (?) arrows), 22 (laurel rim), 47 (lion attacking animal). The actual order of the shields is unknown. For the Artemis shield see Figure 8.11.

oval, centrally ribbed infantry body-shields guards the rear; contrasting meaningfully, in an angle view of the back and ends, round, pictorialised cavalry shields govern the other three sides (Figure 8.3). The interspersed cuirasses varied accordingly, one kind for infantry, another for cavalry. Squared neckholes are cut deep, for inserted spurs (metal has been

Figure 8.11 Kbor Klib, Numidian royal monument, relief fragment: shield with 'Artemis' bust with quiver and wave-pattern rim decoration, with sword or (as in Figure 8.10 after Ferchiou) swords behind the shield.

suggested): that may mean that helmets in metal were propped upon them, as for painted panoplies in fourth-century Macedonian burial chambers.[23]

I stress that these are Numidians' shields. They have been called booty, i.e. formal variants of Greco-Roman 'arms reliefs' in the tradition of the stunning reliefs of captured tumbled armour and all kinds of fragmented military technology from second-century Pergamon. But there was another kind of Hellenistic-era shield frieze, orderly, by our epoch inserting sometimes stake-supported cuirasses (as here) to denote the patrons' panoply (below): not booty, it showcased local power with local weaponry to local viewers. Scholars suggesting booty-display according to a genre known for verism have, indeed, been baffled by the lack of any exact match – especially for the contour of the long shields – with extant actual and imaged shields of

[23] Inserts, Rakob 1979: 125. Compare matched helmet-crowned cuirass panoply pair at Lefkadia's painted Tomb of Lyson and Kallikles in Macedon (c. 325–200 BCE), as if for the clan 'cohort' buried here. Depicted as sitting on a shelf, they flank a nailed-up Macedonian patterned shield, two greaves below, the whole framed by suspended sheathed swords and, each side, a different helmet type (Miller 1993; Polito 1998: 73–6 and Figs. 3–4).

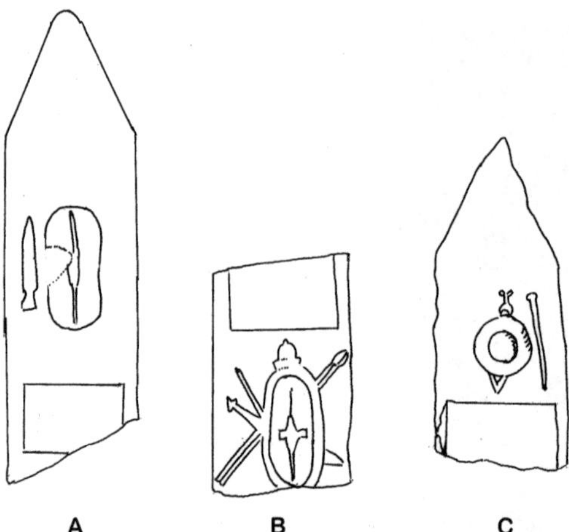

Figure 8.12 Votive stelai with arms reliefs, El Hofra sanctuary, Cirta, Constantine Museum, second century BCE: (a) 0.57 x 0.185 m, of Himilk son of Baalsillek, to Baal Ammon (sic) and Tinit – sheathed sword upright, long oval shield with central rib with slight enlargement as central boss, inscription in sunken field; (b) 0.31 x 0.185 m, of the 'commandant' Abdashtart son of Masop to [deities, names lost], sheathed sword and short spear crossed with two long lances behind long oval shield with central rib with slight enlargement with two projections as central boss and, propped atop shield, bowl-helmet with pointed upper knob and projecting rim, inscription in sunken field; (c) 0.48 x 0.19 m, of Arish son of Labi to Baal Hammon, sheathed sword with ornamental hilt behind round shield with a large round centre raised high in flattened bulge, and long staff with crowning knob (staff or sceptre) at right leaning against the shield, inscription in sunken field. Inscriptions are not shown on the drawings.

any important foe Numidia could have had. But if instead we query their *local* legibility, explanatory Numidian artifacts of the second century BCE are at hand: from the sanctuary of El Hofra, at the royal city of Cirta, arms and armour stelai depict our ribbed long oval shield;[24] and, as in contemporary 'vernacular' sandstone rider reliefs, our round shield (Figure 8.12).[25] Unknown elsewhere in the Mediterranean, its hallmark is a wide round raised central element, too large to call a 'boss', like a

[24] *Die Numider* 1979: dark limestone stelai from El Hofra (on which see 117–18, with bibl.), all Constantine Museum; 548–9 Pl. 91.1 = (a) in Figure 8.12; Pl. 91.2 = (b) in Figure 8.12; discussion of inscriptions at 109.

[25] *Die Numider* 1979: from El Hofra, 550–1 Pl. 92.1 = (c) in Figure 8.12; discussion of inscription at 109–10. The red sandstone rider stelai: 580–1, colour Pl. 107, the famous stela of Birgudul, from Abizar (Algiers, Mus. Nat.; Quinn, Chapter 7 in this volume, Fig. 7.18), mounted warrior, upper body confronting with right hand raised in prayer, left arm extended displaying our round shield, behind it (clutched) three lances; a tiny figure stands on the horse's rump, holding thick shaft with knobbed end (club or sceptre); 582–3 Pl. 108.2, as the Abizar stela but incised not relief-cut, round shield with two (clutched) lances, from Thinesouin (Algiers, Mus. du Bardo).

flattened bun with plump bulging edges – a profile demarcated at Chemtou with exaggerated care. To combine this visual data with that quality 'our arms' (not 'enemy arms') embodied in other Hellenistic Mediterranean shield and cuirass reliefs, assures that both shield types seemed veristically Numidian. Where fantasy may enter is that the cavalry shields' squashed bun-shape is much widened compared to that of the stelai, whether artistic license permitting a bigger pictorial field for the carved emblems, or perhaps veristically as a more elegant metal-version of a padded leather construction.

Shadows cast by harsh sun outlined those shapes even afar and from below, while light flashed on metal cuirass-stakes (and propped helmets?), and the marble shone like gold. The monument invited pilgrimage up a holy mountain and, once there, perambulation to see the detail. Pilgrimage honoured the army, among other things: homogenous elite footmen, holding the back of aristocratic crack cavalry with their personalised combat or parade shields. The images propose that all wear central-issue, modern cuirasses (leather and padded linen, originally Greco-Macedonian, widespread in the Hellenistic world); that message should fascinate when explaining how the second-century dynasts welded the tribes together, like the earlier Argeads of Macedon (Philip II who took over the supply of now-standardised armament to his previously self-armed forces).

Where does so much armour hang on walls, but in armouries, and aristocratic halls?[26] Where do bodyguards flank their king's door, but at palaces? (To our knowledge regional sanctuaries were not (much) hung with armour or arms; we lack evidence that it was the common practice of North African and Phoenician peoples that it was for Greeks and Italic peoples.) Guardians within architectural members cohere: sphinxes glare atop framing piers, kneeling Egyptian-prince figures gazing from the lintel's ends flank an enormous, Egyptianising winged solar disk and its rearing uraeus snakes, surely as in Egypt emblem of protector sky god, and a talisman to national or royal potency as on some Carthaginian, then Numidian coins.[27]

[26] Think of the (re-erectable) Festival Pavilion of Ptolemy II, early third century (276–270 BCE), 'Macedonian shields of gold and silver in alternation' above the interior's lower colonnade displays, which were pictorialised military costume, 'very beautiful soldiers' cloaks (*chlamydes*), woven with portraits of the kings or with stories' (Kallixeinos, *ap.* Athenaios 5.196a).

[27] Alexandropoulos 2000; Mazard 1955; convenient is Head 1887.

For *KK*, Ferchiou's reconstruction dominates.[28] The reliefs decorated the crowning courses of the tiered structure's podium (Figures 8.9–8.10). As at Chemtou, some alternate a plain body cuirass and oval shield (tilted, to fit into the squared slab format); others alternate sashed officers' cuirasses and blazoned round shields edged with 'Greek' and also not-Greek mouldings – some (i.e. laurel) iconic (Figure 8.10). Ferchiou assumed that, as at Chemtou, one class of shield took up each long face; alternative dispositions are possible. Sometimes further armament hung behind the shields, as on the stelai: a pair of sheathed swords with eagle-head hilts behind a round shield with Artemis (Figures 8.10–8.11), and, behind an oval one, something multiplex and much broken, probably a quiver of arrows denoting those Numidian archers who were to be employed as Roman auxiliaries (Figure 8.10).[29]

The column rhythm of both monuments emphasised the *taxis* of body armour, metonymic of ordered military bodies and social order. If correctly reconstructed (Figure 8.3), the Chemtou series was livened by that alignment's careful staggering: that is, vertical axes set by columns above never collide with the vertical axes, the centre-points, of the objects below, nor do they align with the centre-point of the interstice between objects. That aims at a subliminal effect of cycling tiers, as it were; it is as if we heard a vigorous backbeat rhythm, 5/7, not strict 4/4 time. This is not a mishandling of the canonic Greek symmetric alignments for stacked colonnades, where columns align between levels on vertical axes. Architectural historians know the strategy as a signal contribution of fourth- and early third-century Macedonian designers, for big multi-storey façades with galleries: Macedonians' real and imaged noble/regal dwellings, their echo in tomb façades and the wall formats of congregational sanctuary halls.[30]

[28] Ferchiou 1991 is master reference for *sondage* and structural archaeology; the late and much-regretted Naidè Ferchiou's studies have been fundamental to our understanding of the funerary monuments of Tunisia. In English, the intelligent narrative in Ross 2005 depends on Ferchiou, who still thinks of booty trophies, unfortunately equating the oval shield, as do many, with Greek or Celtic *thyreos* (though scholars cannot find a match for the Numidian images' kind of central spine and boss on an essentially plain field). Ferchiou 1991: Fig. 20 aligns the best ornamented fragments in reconstruction: one now blank with laurel rim; Artemis bust; wild feline leaping on an animal (possibly lion vs. bull). See 77–8 for catalogue and discussion. Figs.: 13 (photo) cuirass; 45 a–b (photo) cuirasses; 49 (photo, drawings) blank shield; 16 (photo) and 47 (drawing) shield with attacking feline; 14–15 (drawings) and 48 (photo) laurel-rimmed shield; 17 (drawing), 46 (photos) Artemis shield; 21 (drawing) and 51–2 (photos) oval shield with central rib and enlarged oval boss.

[29] Ferchiou 1991: 83 wonders whether these are arrows or drapery; I select weaponry in the context.

[30] Loerke 1990: 29–32 citing the Great Tomb at Lefkadia (Pollitt 1986: Fig. 20); at Samothrace, the Hieron Hall built by Arsinoe, while wife of Lysimachos, King in Macedon and Thrace (Loerke 1990: Fig.11; Pollitt 1986: Fig. 35), and her Arsinoeion rotunda (Pollitt 1986: Fig. 34); Thasos' Gate of the Sanctuary of Hera and Zeus (Pollitt 1986: Fig. 12).

Figure 8.13 Bronze coinage of Juba I (reign, 60–46 BCE), with a different building each side (see main text, n. 32). The plain building with eight-columned façade is a frequent reverse to portrait coins of Juba I, but in this rare example it is paired to a type showing a building with roof pavilions and Atlas figures for columns (arms raised and crossed over the head).

Gazing upon their land, drawing all eyes, our monuments functioned like the spectacular two-story 'loggia' wings of Hellenistic palaces, from Macedon and the eastern Successor realms to Hasdrubal's Cartagena citadel of *c.* 220 BCE (Polybios 10.10.9, visiting in 133 BCE or else talking to those who did know the site, on its regal splendour); high on its peak, it surely had (partially) two-storey peristyles.[31] This international elegance costumed a Numidian core form with Punic-canon roots – wide, relatively shallow, quadratic, flat-roofed masses with important façades. Note how Juba I's first-century BCE architecture coins, often compared to *KK* and Chemtou, will refract that module (Figure 8.13): a fantastic monolith whose flat roof carries what have been called altars but evoke much more the roof-baldachins of *KK* in Ferchiou's reconstruction, and whose porch has colossal African Atlas caryatids.[32] Its pendant type contrasts to the local building form with something in Hellenistic 'international style', a recognisable basilica-style palatial front, colonnade on high podium, over it a pedimented clerestory, so like the so-called North Oecus of Ptolemais' Palace of Columns (whose flat roof made walkways each side of the hall), Delos' Antigonid Hall of the Bulls and Roman basilicas. Our monuments'

31 Appraising the site, Lancel 1998: 39. On grand Hellenistic houses, Winter 2006: ch. 8; nb Delos' multi-storey mansions housed also a strong Phoenician mercantile community (note 'ethnic' ornament, Near Eastern style column protomes, at the House of the Trident, Webb 1996: 140–1). Palaces: Winter 2006: 165–7 (Macedon's Aigai/Vergina, important for Lefkadia, superposing a storey with solid walls and false windows, and a storey with real windows, and Pergamon); 168–78 (Seleukid, refracted in (168) the Hasmonean Palace of Hyrkanos, which syncretises with Middle Eastern palace and sanctuary features); 178 (Cyrenaic, and Ptolemaic by refraction, the 'Palace of Columns' at Ptolemais). I cannot credit that, by the time of Massinissa's *Kunstpolitik*, the palaces of the Numidian princes were exclusively one floor high.

32 Each building's function is much debated (religious? palatial?): my preferences are clear! Alexandropoulos 2000: 184–5; 401–2, no. 29, silver denarius, plain building ('octostyle temple')/ portrait; 402 no. 34, billon bronze, plain building /Atlantes building; Trell 1979; G.-C. Picard 1988.

mode of 'heterodox' assemblage is itself regional: compare Dougga's tower-tomb with its witty but also dead-serious assemblage of statuary across the range of international mimetic styles (Pharaonic included, which incorporates as at Chemtou a legacy of Phoenician (and Punic) Egyptianising design), and contours iconic regionally and internationally, all subordinate to a powerfully articulated multi-stage geometry.[33]

The reliefs only gain full meaning, as Rakob insisted for the architecture, in their landscape: armies in the sky, from their mountain-tops guarding (and warning!) all who marched the roads below. Hellenistic images of tumbled hostile weapons gloss ignominiously disordered enemy bodies. This instead is disciplined panoply art: a dignified arrangement of our own armament, carefully handled and stored, as in kindred Hellenistic panoply monuments. The Numidian stelai carefully dispose panoply elements to the same effect (Figure 8.12). For a 'national' address the ordinary and aristocratic classes collaborate en masse; if blazons speak to tribal or cohort badges, conceptual mapping glossed nation-making all the more. Contrast the self-vaunting rhetoric at the great tombs of equestrian aristocracy of *c.* 225 and 125 BCE: Dougga's small round cavalry shields, (now) blank, Sabratha's little equestrian cohort, the egoist dynastic rhetoric of the grave goods (panoply and a small army of lances) of the princely templon-tomb with colonnaded crowning *cella* of Es Soumaa (Quinn, Chapter 7, this volume).

Armament emblems are talismanic; on a building, they grace the construction with numinous protection, such that it becomes itself talismanic. Ours are, like the architecture itself, visually multilingual: mimetic representation, simple silhouettes, or abstractions (that big 'Greek' eye!); humanoid, animal, or gods' weapons that can even instantiate Numidian specialisations in war like archery. *KK*'s most elaborate shield (oddly, worked into the *Die Numider* reconstruction of Chemtou, Figures 8.4–8.5) religiously apostrophises cuirass and shield with the impenetrable Gorgon-aegis-cape (Figure 8.7), a now-unique expansion of real/imaged Greco-Roman Gorgon-boss shields. Signs of terror and violence are consistently linked to North African cultic and natural landscapes, like the club of Melqart/Hercules and a pacing desert feline (Figure 8.5);[34]

[33] See Quinn, Chapter 7 in this volume; Winter 2006: 93 and Fig. 228 (*c.* 150 BCE) noting Punic and (Punic) Egyptianising motifs; 93–4 for the 'Greco-Punic' much-decorated tower-tomb, Sabratha, Mausoleum B (Quinn, Chapter 7 this volume, Fig. 7.7; Winter 2006: Fig. 227), with bilingual inscriptions about Atban, Numidian princely patron or architect with Numidian workteams; also, 94, 298, Sicilian Akragas' 'Tomb of Theron', a Greco-Punic tower-tomb, with comparanda (R. Wilson, Chapter 4 this volume, Fig. 4.19).

[34] Club transecting shield might echo Macedonian coinage (Philip V, from 188/7 BCE on, Mørkholm 1991: 163); see below, for other Macedonian coin echoes. The pacing panther toys

KK too preserves a savage feline with an animal victim (Figure 8.10) – if, as likely, a lion, then the common regional badge of North Africa, the Libyan Lion of Carthaginian and regal Numidian coinage. Gods of fire and light matter, common theology for North Africa; besides the solar door-ornament, a thunderbolt-like blazon makes a shield-spine, whose terminals' flames meld with spread, 'orientalised' eagle/hawk wings (Figure 8.8b) – a daimon-weapon for a Baal- or Ammon-like god. For triumphalist iconicity of serpents, we have blurry but real knowledge for all northerly Africa: the lintel's Egyptianised serpents re-materialise in the snake writhing diagonally across a shield (Figure 8.8a), snake-necks of a conventional aegis become entire serpents. The Medusa suggested at least to the educated a North African potency, for she, like the indigenous goddess Greeks called Athena, was resident at Lake Tritonis. *KK*'s Artemis (Figures 8.10–8.11) *qua* warrior-goddess with her quiver, however exotic here, matches fierce protective goddesses like that African Athena and Tanit, which even the Hellenically illiterate grasped.

There are more ways to mean, than to narrate: if Chemtou and *KK* had convened gods' statues, or if these were Greco-Roman fictional assemblages, more art-historians might have dissected their signifying power. More vividly than the oft-interpreted architecture, to ancient non-art historians, the shields evoked a multi-regional, trans-historical, polyethnic domain. In that domain, the big monuments implied that the ruling Numidians' culture in all ways excelled in tradition and invention; we well understand of better-documented heterogenous realms that visual multilingualism was a tool for controlling many peoples with many pasts (e.g. fourth-century Karia, Macedonian diaspora kingdoms, Achaemenid Anatolia and the Middle East and Carthage's hegemonic sphere).[35]

Those who helped such monuments happen for the new, second-century realm were mixed too, as at any Hellenistic court: regional and international advisors, masons, carvers and architects, here Libyan, Numidian and Punic, as well as Greeks from North Africa and around the western Mediterranean. Some knew of developments in the eastern Mediterranean, especially palaces, and the tombs in Anatolia and the northern Aegean, often used to explain our markers. But to set up shield reliefs on a very big orthogonal mass, mapping the polity as a nation-in-arms, in concord across and between ranks, had an exact period analogue in one specific region: the

with Numidian coinage that appropriated the Carthaginian lion types (n. 27 for reference works).

[35] I tried this approach in Kuttner 2001: Attalids *passim*; Karia, Seleukids, Achaemenids at 137–8, 195, 186–7.

third-/second-century, people-in-arms, shield-and-cuirass panoply monuments of Antigonid Macedonian cities.[36] High up on these quadratic, building-sized piles, shield-wall façades order verist, life-scale armours. Whatever they are for (neither inscriptions nor traces of crowning statuary survive), they visibly celebrate the people-in-arms, a primal Macedonian self-conception as a cohesive citizen-body of collaborating different types (and social ranks) of cavalry and infantry, royally governed.

Sometimes, round shields of different diameter, representing cavalry and infantry, or diverse infantry corps, were ordered like a phalanx in staggered tiers (ranks), as at Antigonid palace-city Beroia;[37] at Amphipolis, relief shields hung in our kind of fictive gallery.[38] Quite soon interpolated body-armour made shield-and-cuirass rows, and long shields occurred, as at Dion, the 'national' and regal cult centre.[39] These, and (surely) other Macedonian cities with such markers, would have been sites on any itinerary of elite foreign agents and negotiators, political, military, mercantile.

The precedent was princely tomb architecture with an army of armaments: a tier of Hephaistion's Pyre of 324 BCE showed 'weapons of Macedonians and foreigners, signifying the former's courageous deeds, the latter's defeats' (Diod. Sic. 17.115.1–5); the cenotaph reliefs for Pyrrhos of Epiros at Argos in 272 BCE included 'everything . . . employed in battle' (Paus. 2.21.4). Relevant to Numidian tumuli is the colossal, third-century tumulus near the Antigonid palace-city Pella, shields ringing

[36] This selects from the enormous corpus of Macedonian shield-art, 'own-arms' panoplies, city-wall talismans, etc., of the Hellenistic and Republican world. Foundational was Markle 1999, investigating Beroia, addressing its expressive aims much as here, though without wondering what assemblage as such it imitated. By 1998 Polito's survey of arms-art could broaden Markle, with more illustrations. He highlighted that what I call panoply art was *self*-fashioning for elites and polities, in discussing the (polyethnic) Italian booty and panoply corpus of tombs (including Lucanian fourth-century with small painted blazons), gates, temples, monuments. Well-studied is the case for third-century Macedon and all its diaspora of fierce 'ethnic' self-identification by a uniquely patterned shield, in painting, coins, statuary, architectural ornament, votives, grave goods; see Liampi 1998; Kosmetatou and Waelkens 1997.

[37] For Beroia, Markle 1999: 251–3 posited Pyrrhos of Epiros, finding no Antigonid crux but Pyrrhos' repulse here of Poliorketes (288 BCE). However, see Edson 1934: 227, 232–3: Beroia was a jewel in the crown of Antigonid Macedon from 278 BCE on, when Antigonos Gonatas won here the throne; second-century Perseus crammed his court with Beroians and was often based here, enjoying palace and hunting-parks.

[38] Markle 1999: 240. On these assemblages and their aftermath, also Philipp 2004: 140 and notes.

[39] Under-published or -illustrated, though the internet hosts tourist photos. Blackman 1996: 72; Philipp 2004: 140 citing Stephanidou-Tiberiou 1998: 94, Fig. 54. Markle 1999: 141 says Pandermalis told him that 'piercings' in a cuirass indicate they are booty. If these are not for metal attachments, or much later marks (the reliefs were disassembled and remounted centuries later) they confirm the idea of 'our arms'. Greeks often dedicated battered, gashed armour in which they survived combat.

its upper socle;[40] late fourth-century elite tombs at Vergina/Aigai already sometimes flanked their portals with a pair of stucco relief-shields, and spectacular tombs everywhere, especially in Anatolia (Macedonian, Greek and indigene), quickly imitated these panoply-and-shield reliefs – and so did the monumental tower-tombs of North Africa (see above). Our cryptic monuments also honoured the collective equally with kings; as at the Tomb of Lyson and Kallikles (n. 23), design troped armoury and hall, contents hung away from damp and vermin, ready for civic defence and the king's wars. Macedon's monarch was supposed courageously to accompany aristocratic cavalry, and answer to his entire army, on whose vote rested even his power of military capital punishment. To rule Macedonians effectively meant convincing them that one enacted 'constitutional' rule, respecting the self-identity of towns, regional populations, clans. For Numidian dynasts too, nation was predicated on a warrior collective; kings fought alongside their armies, and honoured properly the leaders of clans, those below them, multiple 'Numidian tribes', and a mixed urban/rural demographic heavy with Libyans, Punes and others whom the second-century rulers had to cajole to work in harness (Quinn, Chapter 7 in this volume). So the core Macedonian visual metaphor was legible and, I strongly propose, attractive, a classic instance of convergent cultures opportunistically appropriating what seemed effective and pleasing for their own needs, to at least partly similar formal and/or rhetorical ends.

Not only these comparisons, but that some of the Numidian blazons use Macedonian coinage for compositional models guarantees a phase of attention to the Antigonid visual environment. I do not think (below) this necessarily stated 'we beat Macedon', rather than being an opportunist response, the transfer signing sophisticated Numidian agency in a very big world. Historical frames start with the Third Macedonian War (172–168 BCE). Aemilius Paullus' campaign against King Perseus of Macedon was aided by Massinissa's delivery of troops, war-elephants and food.[41] Paullus felled the

[40] Archontikos Giannitson, 250 BCE, badly published: 158.5 m perimeter, the stone socle 4.2 m high, Markle 1999: 128. Is it Antigonos Gonatas' monument for father Demetrios Poliorketes? Numidian tumuli: Quinn, Chapter 7, this volume. Fentress 2006: 11 accepted Coarelli's invented paradigm, that of Alexander's lost tomb in Alexandria as a tumulus like his predecessor Argeads at Aigai. We have no testimony to this tomb's contour. That Numidia's kings were Alexander-imitators, we do not know. It is as likely that the form was suggested by, for instance, Diadoch two-storey, templon-on-podium tombs (inflected by the Mauseoleion and extant for Lysimachos at Belevi, cf. Webb 1996: 76–9; general survey of tomb types, Fedak 1990 and 2006).

[41] Storm 2001: 307–8. That aid was 200,000 bushels of grain and pulse, 300 picked cavalry, 10 war-elephants.

kingdom of Macedon at the Battle of Pydna in 168; a Roman protectorate until 148, when the last claimant to the throne was defeated, Macedon was subsequently reduced to a province. The North African invaders must have shared in the sense of fateful achievement of Rome and its Attalid allies; by the mid-140s Numidians could bask in the knowledge that their forces had helped Rome repeatedly smash historic polities – Carthage, Macedon – on two continents. For Massinissa, and his heir, the historical iteration was personal: Massinissa helped the very Aemilius who had given Massinissa's friend Scipio a grandson (Scipio Aemilianus, Africanus the Younger).

Numidia's teams innovated on Macedonian models with shield-wall as picture-wall in an elaborate architectural setting for an allusive magnificence that the Macedonian markers, their non-Numidian offshoots, and the Attalid booty-heap genre lacked.[42] How verist are they? In Numidia's immediate world and time, in what ways were they typical or not of self-construction? And did the victors against Carthage have any Punic model, either for image-shields or armament displays? The reliefs cannot *prove* that elite Numidian shields or shield-covers (for use or spectacle) always had individuated blazons, and on this scale. Hard knowledge of Punic shields lacks; for pictorial ones, none Numidian or Punic survive in fact nor, save on our markers, in image. Still, tantalising for the Carthaginian world, and so the Numidian one in its ambit, is the notice of the fantastic silver 'Shield of Hasdrubal' bearing his portrait (head), that was wheeled about on his Punic War campaigns; but it so obviously competes with famous, personalised picture-shields for commemorative or personal use by early Hellenistic commanders, that it cannot prove a Punic habit of pictorialised shields.[43]

[42] Pictures seldom blazon weaponry in the Pergamene reliefs, none Greek, none as tondo. It tempts many to hypothesise that paint, or stucco relief, blazoned now-blank Greek relief-shields. Suggestive are: the small lion carved on one shield at Thasos' bouleuterion (Phillip 2004: 140, n. 870); the documented *drakon* relief on a marble shield on Epaminondas' tomb (d. 362 BCE; Paus. 8.11.8). Blazoned Macedonian shields make so many Hellenistic coin-types as to indicate occasional verism (not just motif for the coin), with small boss-ornaments (Gorgoneion, *kerykeion* (caduceus), thunderbolt, anchor, club, etc.) sometimes, at least, reflecting military-standard markings. The most elaborate, from Macedon, gloss, whether actually or conceptually, votive new-made shields, with kings' features syncretised to heroes and gods: Antigonos Gonatas/Pan, Markle 1977: 326, Mørkholm 1991: 134 no. 430–1; Philip V/Perseus, Mørkholm 1991: 163. (Philipp 2004: 140 articulate on the issue of iconicity for votive and use-shields.) Why Amphipolis was source for the large, votive-style Artemis Tauropolis shield-tondo on an issue of the Roman Protectorate, 158–148 BCE (Mørkholm 1991: 166–7) is unclear.

[43] Hasdrubal's 'shield', see below and n. 57. For use: shield of Epaminondas' grieving lover; on it, *tropaion* of the Battle of Leuktra where E. died (Theopompos *ap.* Athenaios 13.605A). For display: chryselephantine shield with Achilles and Penthesilea, from Vergina's 'Tomb of Philip II' (Moreno 1994: 566 Fig. 698 (colour)); its wave mouldings are the only such real shield décor known to Treister 2001: 251. Something similar may have been displayed for Alexander, actually

My view is that Numidian military elites could have them, sometimes or often, but that if so these images may have been expressionistically enlarged in the reliefs, fantasised, just as armours' relative scale was toyed with. Important to the local implication of 'succession of empires' is that the material celebration of warrior identity may be distinctively indigene – 'Numidian', Libyan, Mauretanian – not a Punic legacy. It can be hard to say what Punic art did or did not do, for so much is lost. But the lack of evidence to the contrary implies that illustrating one's persona as military in funerary and votive images and dedicated goods was rare in the West Phoenician diaspora, by stark contrast to neighbouring cultures such as Greek and Italo-Roman. Thus, sparse though they are, the Numidian rider-stelai and weapons-stelai that tap into the sub-aristocratic world, the handful of militarist tower-tombs, and their sometimes extant military grave-goods, are collectively suggestive. While only some five Numidian-era stelai show weapons (Figure 8.12), not ritual motifs, from the hundreds at the El Hofra sanctuary at the Numidian royal capital Cirta, such self-portrayals are nonexistent elsewhere in the enormous corpus of Punic sanctuary stelai! That is, Numidian-ness manifested almost certainly in the very choice of armament as real or depicted dedication.

Yet, that our reliefs signify at all has been questioned, by contrast to a supposedly obvious iconicity in Greco-Roman analogues. Or, they have been unsystematically interpreted: Polito, tagging all shields as booty, targeted a few blazons (ignoring the rest) as meaningful, in order to reconstruct a historically specific message.[44] Noting cleverly that *KK*'s designers played with emblems of second-century Macedonian coinage, and juxtaposing compositional parallels with Macedonian panoply-frieze compositions, he concluded that *KK* trumpeted Numidia's part in Paullus' conquest of Perseus of Macedon in 168 BCE. On several grounds, this is hard to credit. The weapons themselves will not suit the booty theory: Polito ignored the long shields on the back of Chemtou, that are not Macedonian (or anything else, above); like others til now, he did not notice that the round shields have not a Macedonian hoplite-shield profile but a local one (above). The assumption that the blazons legibly proclaimed to North Africa specifically that Perseus' realm had fallen is problematic. Political art wants to be understood: the designers eschewed the one thing that would have made Polito's message clear, at almost any

(or, I think, in images): Palagia 2000: 192 on Alexander's Achilles-Penthesilea shield on a Caracallan gold medallion from Aboukir, and fourth-century CE contorniates.

44 Polito 1998: 85–9 at 88–9 on *KK*. G.-C. Picard 1973: 187–8 (updating *idem* 1957 *passim*, use index) only hazards tentatively that *syntaxe*, visual grammar, enunciates something – though certain of 'Roman' S. Omobono (see below). Others are briefly sure: Philipp 2004: 140 and n. 672 takes formal blazon display seriously here as anywhere; Ferchiou 1991: 84 notes the *KK* blazons enrich their monument as much as the S. Omobono reliefs did.

Figure 8.14 Macedonian silver tetradrachm, Amphipolis mint (*c.* 158–148 BCE). Obverse: bust of Artemis Tauropolos rt. with quiver, framed as by a traditional Hellenistic Macedonian shield (half-circle series with stars and dots); reverse: Hercules' club horizontally within oak-wreath.

distance – the standard-issue decorated Macedonian shield, its patternings famous throughout the contemporary world (nested half-circles, with or without the Macedonian star as boss), just as we see it in anti-Macedonian reliefs such as Paullus' own monument at Delphi, and among the Giants' shields on the Attalid Great Altar. Indeed, even though the Artemis tondo at *KK* does paraphrase Macedonian shield-coins (Figure 8.14), the so-legible Macedonian ornament of the coin's 'rim' is omitted! Finally, Polito connects *KK*'s fictive shield-cover of a Medusa head on Athena's aegis to her slayer Perseus, dynastic hero-avatar for the eponymous Macedonian king and his father. But why would a designer intent on specifically evoking (king) Perseus, and fond of using Macedonian coins as models, not copy Philip V's actual Perseus shield-coin?[45] And it seems illogical to celebrate North Africans' defeat of a Perseus by recalling a Perseus who killed a North African being.

I have kept dating issues relative and not absolute until after exploring what is being dated. Here, the deeply thought, extensive work of Ross and Ferchiou needs address. Ross (2005: 65–7) suggested for *KK* commemoration by Massinissa (or, less probably, Micipsa) of the Battle of Zama where Massinissa helped Scipio definitively beat Carthage, placing the battlefield near the monument. His site location is likely correct: that certainly would *enrich KK*'s resonance. Insisting that archaeological evidence (citing Ferchiou whose *sondages* recovered one fragment of pottery, identifying it as third-/second-century Punic) permits even a quite early second-century date, he credited it to Massinissa any time between youth and retrospective old age, though also allowing a retrospective by Micipsa. Ross, like Ferchiou, also places *KK* before Chemtou and prefers early–mid, not mid–late, second-century dates for it.

[45] The Artemis Tauropolis tondo of the Roman Protectorate, 158–148 BCE, Mørkholm 1991: 166–7; n. 34 above for other numismatic echoes.

Several issues arise. One is that, by extension, Chemtou must then commemorate a specific battle (these authors cast around for one), and our monument genre arose in the wish to concoct something with a trophy-like function. That needs reconsideration in the light of powerful evidence that both sites accommodated ritual, which in the original period must have been as much ideological in the dynastic sense as it will have been about god X. (Ferchiou thought *KK* related to funerary ruler cult.) Did such ceremonial wait on the chance of a trophy? Ought not, then, most Numidian major sanctuaries to have had such a 'trophy'?

Second, I am not so sure *KK* predates Chemtou. They remain cousins, but different enough traits, scale and decorative choices make sequence problematic to assert. Some art histories and archaeologies always make elaborated things succeed simpler versions (i.e. the expanded panoply repertoire at *KK* – a strategy that in the East, see above, fairly clearly means 'later'); others (as in the theory just cited) say the reverse (from elaborate to simplified) is normative, or at least not eccentric, and it is certainly possible when shifting, as our markers do, from colossal to more limited scale. The Macedonian Artemis coin analogy (Figure 8.14) makes 167/6 BCE a *terminus post quem* for *KK* (Figure 8.11); since it was issued until 148, even purely formal reference to it is perhaps not to be expected more than a few years after 148. Many decades ago, excavation finds from Chemtou were assigned to the reign of Micipsa, a little after the middle of the second century; certainly those ceramics have to date to the 160s–130s BCE, but fine points of phasing need reexamination in the light of recent Hellenistic ceramic studies.[46] It would be lovely to see in either or both monuments Massinissa's patronage, referencing his campaigns from the Second Punic War up to the Third Macedonian War, but a successor's marker could be retrospective to them. So, I shall let 'mid-second century' evade the issue of date.[47] Rather I have written in such a way as to help the argument survive future archaeological discovery and passing

[46] The archaeology in *Die Numider* 1979; at *KK*, Ferchiou 1991.

[47] In any case the evidence will not support first-century BCE dates and Roman functions (e.g. that Caesar made *KK* for his 46 BCE triumph over Juba I, or entombed here Petreius and Juba I (their suicide, above) as accepted by MacKendrick 1980: 44, and by sources cited in D. Roller 2003: 38). Quinn, Chapter 7, this volume, introduces Coarelli and Thébert's date very late in the second century by reference to west Greek practice. But those comparanda do not bar an earlier second-century date. The latter ignored Punic-Phoenician architectural civilisation (Numidian mother-culture, spectacular visual environment still accessible); see, rather, Ferchiou 1991: 85–6 and 48, on *KK*'s not-Greek, Punic (and Carthaginian) ornament, structure, construction and Winter 2006 (tower-tombs' Greco-Punic modes). Fine details are here as at other Punic-zone sites too closely integrated into a different (not-Greek), sophisticated architectural canon for me to accept North African patrons waited on 'Greece' east or west as on an alarm clock. Precisely because, for instance, sculptors of Chemtou's vegetal capitals

victories in scholarly battles about purported occasions. Above all, I do not think it is necessary to say the décor means a specific battle, and instead believe that these décors evade specificity in order to vaunt Numidian perennial achievement and characterise a Numidian collective. Surely all should admit that to be at least part of their aim.

The San Omobono Reliefs ('Bocchus Monument'): a second-century BCE Numidian royal monument for the Scipiones

Beyond their internal meanings, triumphalist monuments like Chemtou and *KK* would importantly also remind Romans that Numidia was a comrade-in-arms to be cherished, as well as one not to be tampered with without severe military consequences. We know that in 167/6 BCE Massinissa would have liked to honour Aemilius Paullus at Rome itself, on the Capitol. The Senate courteously declined the king's request to visit and sacrifice, which would have given him the chance to showcase his own huge aid to that victory; instead they awarded him again the consular regalia that they and Scipio had given him in his youth.[48] But I will argue here that sometime in the mid-second century the Numidian court offered to a Roman *imperator* directly a durable gift, as part of the monumental celebration of his achievements. That general's standing allowed a monument of scale to occupy precious footage of Roman sanctuary/civic space, and an opportunity to translate the uniquely Numidian pictorialised armourial monument discussed above. It became a quadratic bulk of a different kind – an enormous statuary base surround, silvery in blue-grey limestone, by contrast to Chemtou's gold. The design team, not identical to either that of *KK* or Chemtou, though related to them, was joined now, for instance, by carvers familiar with East Aegean sculptural styles; this team added further panoply details, to work the Romans into the mix, and also to make an audience at Rome see that good (not just beaten) foreigners were included in this array, a move probably unprecedented at Rome. The Numidian monuments seem to have dedicated the patrons' armies to

deliberately made leafage, figuration, proportions, vary from west Greek acanthus capitals, these little 'sphinx trees' cannot neatly be aligned to those foreign (Greek) sequences.

48 Aid, above n. 41. Braund 1984: 55, 32 n. 23 (with kings' Capitoline dedications, such as M. perhaps wished to leave), 152–3, 159 nn. 46–9; and Storm 2001: 307–8. The turn-down was certainly not a deliberate snub: who would offend such allies? Vicious faction-war on Paullus, well-studied, maybe hobbled the vote; and though M. would live another twenty-odd years, senators could worry about destabilising Numidia should an already old king die *en route*.

numinous powers; the Roman monument dedicated also a relationship, between the two peoples who together broke empires East and West.

This is the way in which I would describe the so-called San Omobono Reliefs (Figures 8.15–8.24), six blocks and fragments in Rome, and one in Vienna, from three sides of the intermediate level of a very large quadratic base, a panoply frieze that assembled shields and cuirasses with other armaments, votive objects and 'live' Victories, and looked very like those at Chemtou and Kbor Klib.[49] The very thick, fine-grained, hard, blue-grey limestone blocks, corners secured by bolts, had a structural function; standard head-on shots obscure that these are not conventional Greco-Roman thin veneer slabs. It has been remarked that their inner faces need decipherment – it looks as if there were some projected inner spurs, i.e. for a strutwork under heavy crowning elements (Figure 8.17). The full base, often estimated *c.* 8 m x 5 m, was once eyecatching for its polychromy, with platform and crowning elements in light stones (perhaps marble) and, above, bronze or (less likely) marble statuary.

Although the frieze fragments are also sometimes known as the 'Via della Consolazione Reliefs', the label 'San Omobono Reliefs' (*SO*) tags the zone in which they were excavated in 1939 at the medieval Church of San Omobono below the SW Capitoline Hill: an important Republican sanctuary precinct, famous for its Archaic temple remains and the twin Republican temples to

[49] Those in Rome, originally in the Capitoline museums (Palazzo Conservatori), are mostly on show currently at the Centrale Montemartini (ACEA) museum; they may move back to the Capitoline museums, after the 2010 *L'età della conquista* show put them there again. Inventory numbers are Mus. Cons(ervatori) 2750 (Fig. 8.18, centre with Victories and shield), 2752 (Figs. 8.19–8.20 right front, greave, metal body-cuirass, cavalry/Dioscur shield), 2749 (Fig. 8.22, end, Minerva shield, cavalry cuirasses, *idem* on stakes with helmets propped on them), and 2749 (Fig. 8.20, horse mask, long-side corner), 3517 (Fig. 8.21, left front, cut-down fragment of Dioscur shield), 2751 (Fig. 8.24, winged-dragon shield); Vienna, Kunsthistorisches Mus. 1576 (Fig. 8.23, upper part of cuirass at right of short extant short end, with Gorgoneion, and Victory straps). For measurements, *L'età dell conquista* 2010 with massive bibliography, Fig. pl. at 203, Cat. II.19, 285–87 (Riccardo di Cesari). Also catalogued: with excavation data, Reusser 1993: 124–9; Polito 1998: 121–7; with Hölscher's canonic reconstructed plan and elevation of 1980 (cf. Fig. 8.15), in a book used more widely, *Kaiser Augustus* 1988: cat. 214, 384–6 (Hölscher), seconding his and Schäfer's Sulla-Bocchus thesis (below). Schäfer 1989: 74–83 integrated his 1979 proposals in *Die Numider* (reconstr., Fig. 134, stone-plans, Figs. 132, 133) into an excellent large Republican optic. Often only two relatively complete slabs are illustrated (central Victories, lateral Minerva and trophies, Figs. 8.18, 8.22). For Anglophone survey, easy access: Strong 1988: 48 and n., Figs. 16–17; D. Kleiner 1992: 51–2 Figs. 34-5 (correction, six fragments not four). For a set of DAI images online, including Hölscher's scheme (edited here as Fig. 8.15), see Arachne, the DAI image web-bank, s.v. Object 402592: 'Siegesmonument vom Kapitol, sog. Bocchusmonument'. Negatives are not always as sharp as desirable, but the three-quarters view of the left angle of the reconstituted base arrangement is useful, negative D-DAI-ROM-99.1617 at http://arachne.uni-koeln.de/item/marbilder/4268341.

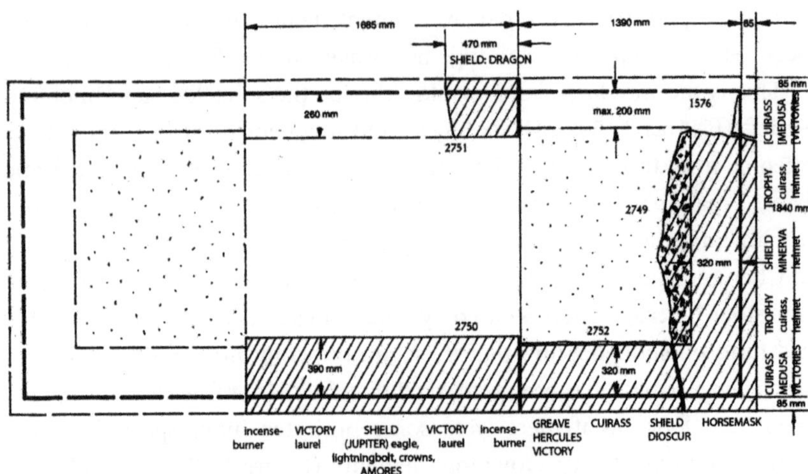

Figure 8.15 San Omobono/Via della Consolazione Republican monument base from Rome, reconstructive measured horizontal section demonstrating the mounting of the relief slabs in blue-grey stone around the now-lost core, with author's iconographic labeling.

Figure 8.16 San Omobono/Via della Consolazione Republican monument base from Rome, documentary and reconstructive drawing of the reliefs of the front of the base; missing heads and limbs on the central panel are roughly indicated; damage to the right end is not marked.

Figure 8.17 San Omobono/Via della Consolazione Republican monument base from Rome, interior view of display of slabs.

Mater Matuta and Fortuna on the perimeter of that very important sacro-political piazza, the Forum Boarium. Both were areas associated with Republican votive display (below).

The reliefs have a non-neutral label, too, however: the 'Bocchus Monument'. By the 1980s it was widely decided that the reliefs veneered the base of the otherwise lost monument, somewhere in the sanctuary compound on the Capitoline Hill, that texts attest was set up *c.* 91 BCE by King Bocchus of Mauretania (and western Numidia) about himself and Sulla; the putative locus, a Temple of Fides (below). It would now be hard to find a single discussion of Sulla, or of any Republican and Augustan *Kunstpolitik* (including my own early work) which does not exploit the *SO* reliefs. I shall talk more about Bocchus' Sullan Monument below; like a few others I strip the *SO* reliefs off it. I shall put them well back into the second century BCE, furthermore – a move which has been argued for twice in the past but with different reasoning.[50] Most new here is an attempt to think through what it meant for Numidian-Roman cultural politics that the relief-base at Rome looked like our mountain-markers.

Ever since it became possible to study them together, all note the homology in regard to the armament friezes as such, typically meditated without considering their very diverse installations. As analysed above for Chemtou and *KK*, all three fictive panoply displays diverge from that 'Hellenistic' genre pioneered at Pergamon in the parapets of the Sanctuary of Athena Polias in the second century BCE, the pictorially variegated '(booty) weapons frieze'. But our three, a so-far unique artifact class, constitute a genre too – genre meaning that composition, pictorial structure, stylistic spectrum, and key monument contours (big squared things) cohere. In visual language, in artifact typology: if X looks like a quote or a paraphrase, and can be set in a context where paradigms could be known and there were historical circumstances to make the speaking homology worthwhile, then it is a quotation; if the 'intertextual' allusion in its new frame is also intriguingly different, it is more not less likely that homologies were deliberated. Since ceramic chronologies make Chemtou, and therefore also *KK*, artifacts datable to the mid-second century BCE or just after, the *SO* base ought to date to the same period.

None, so far, however, think to date *SO* by means of the second-century artifacts it most resembles. Picard firmly assigned the monument to the first

[50] Hafner 1989 (arch of Africanus the Elder, which I critique at n. 54); H. Meyer 1991–2 (Attalid-Roman, for the Seleukid Wars). Clark 2007: 131–3 at 132, as reported also in the review by Santangelo 2008, cited my thesis with permission after hearing the original conference paper of 2006.

Figure 8.18 San Omobono/Via della Consolazione Republican monument base from Rome, front central panel: between incense burners (*thymiateria*), Victories as if living statues on bases garland with laurel a round shield. On the shield appear an eagle clutching a lightning-bolt (Jupiter's *fulmen*), with a palm over its shoulder, from which hang two military crowns, and twin Amores upholding an inscription plaque (*tabula*). Rome, Musei Capitolini, Centrale Montemartini, inv MC 2750.

century BCE, on the then seemingly impeccable grounds of that supposition 'style' (so slippery for a Hellenistic era addicted to formal syncretism), and by recourse to two premises: analogies of detail that he sought only in the eastern Mediterranean; and a formal assessment of *SO*'s 'syntax', sought in a misleading, popular conception of Roman design as more rigidly symmetrical than Greek (G.-C. Picard 1957, see n. 44). The urge to tie the reliefs to the Sulla-Bocchus Monument of 91 BCE reinforced such now outdated stylistic assessments; by contrast, I analyse below how easy it is to find Mediterranean third-/second-century generic matches for the central compositional motif, and for the formal treatment of its details.

Thus, the identification of the honorand, the date and the message are more than usually entangled. Key is the central front slab, and the focal shield, which Victories garland (Figure 8.18). The imagery and scale of the monument are so triumphalist that Romanists essentially agree a *triumphator* is honoured; though his oak-crown lacks in the little set on the shield, it is not credible such a monument went up except for a triumphing general. Scholars also agree that the two non-triumphal crowns on the central shield denote real honours, evoking the *cursus* of the man once standing above. The award of military *insignia* was governed by absolute laws; their Roman visual enumeration was not willful. Inscriptions and portrait, not the tiny relief

Figure 8.19 San Omobono/Via della Consolazione Republican monument base from Rome, front left panel: greave, with head of youthful Hercules in lionskin cap as knee-cap cover, and, on the shin, dancing Victory carrying lance and shield; plain body-cuirass; shield with one of the two Dioscuri (Castor or Pollux) with a lance upon a charging horse. Rome, Musei Capitolini, Centrale Montemartini, inv. MC 2752.

crowns, would of course have principally signified the identity of the honorand. The problem is that the crowns, all we have now, maddeningly lack visual comparanda. They are slim circlets, not made of leafage: one is a hard ring with tiny protrusions, the other's thin strands do seem vegetal. There were five Republican military crowns awarded by the Senate: *triumphalis*, of oak for triumphs (the one the triumphator wore was of gold); *ovalis*, myrtle, for *ovatio*(n) – a lesser triumph; of gold were the wall-crown, *muralis*, for the first to scale and cross a besieged wall; a modeled one called *vallaris* or *castrensis*, to the first across a fort's ditch *(vallum)* and in through breached walls; and that called grass-crown, *gramine* and siege-crown, *obsidionalis*, for saving Roman forces from imminent annihilation. The argument of Schäfer, Hölscher, *et al.* is that the crowns on *SO* are Sulla's crowns (grass-crown for textured ring, triumphal oak-leaves as the hard knobbed ring), because this is his triumphal monument and/or also somehow the monument Bocchus made for him. As that was made in the 90s BCE before Sulla had any crowns, it is proposed that the reliefs were later recut, or that the central slab was made later and inserted into the cycle, i.e. in a reassemblage by Sulla or his son after Marius took down (*sic*) that Capitoline monument, supposedly (there is in fact no evidence this happened).[51]

[51] Cf. n. 49. Those, like Reusser 1993, who balk at forcing the *SO* reliefs onto Bocchus' monument retain a reflex to give them to Sulla; I cannot agree when they tag broad Roman taste for Victories,

The central slab was never recut: I checked. The whole shield face would need rasping down, to raise new relief details without leaving a hollow in the stone surrounding them. There is no trace of either. No comparanda attest Roman commemorative relief with its historicising detailing thus reworked, save for some Imperial-era emperor heads. There is Republican evidence that political enemies could make one take back one's votives, and that they could be later reinstalled (Pliny, *HN* 34.93, on the fates of Lucullus' Hercules in the Forum); but it is extremely unlikely, and undocumented, that a base would be disassembled too, reliefs salvaged, remade. That an entire slab was later interpolated is unparalleled, and untenable because the facture is identical throughout the set; further, the hypothesis that this stone we cannot now trace was stockpiled at Rome is irrational. Bocchus' Sulla editing his later life into a *c.* 91 BCE votive is a phantom.

So if not Sulla, who? When Romans wanted to show tree-leaves, they did: it is not possible that the hard-knobbed ring is the oak-crown, *contra* the 'Sullanists'. But I commit to their identification of the circlet of strands with the crown of thin grass-blades. Parallels lack, not surprisingly – only five Republican men received the grass-crown. The occasion had to be victory snatched by one commander from 'supreme desperation' as Pliny says, in his full list of winners, saving an army from certain annihilation; only one's soldiers could vote it, right there, unanimously, plucking the battlefield's weeds to crown their saviour.[52] Only three of them were generals, whom our monument could honour (all did triumph): Sulla (grass-crown, 80 BCE, siege of Nola); Scipio Aemilianus Africanus (146 BCE, siege of Carthage); and Fabius Cunctator (203 BCE – the *SPQR*'s special vote, upon Hannibal's expulsion from Italy, for saving the *Urbs*). Lack of their only other crown, triumph-oak, in our pair, bars Sulla and Fabius. That leaves the *triumphator* Aemilianus, whose grass-crown for the assault on Carthage in 146 was perhaps his proudest honour – history was packed, after all, with triumphs – and it let him match the great Fabius of the prior Punic War. Moreover Aemilianus uniquely fits for the dyad of crowns, since for the hard object I can only think of *corona muralis* – that the protrusions splaying from the hard

Dioscuri, Jupiter signs *et al.*, as being legibly distinctively Sullan. The simplest contravention to a wish to denote Sulla is that two sign systems lack: (a) arms clearly designating a Mithridatic force (whether for his Cilician wars in the 90s, or the triumph of 81), easy with a blazon like an Amazon or griffin vs. Arimasp, even without special arms shapes at front; (b) lack of Sulla's protectors Apollo and/or Venus, at the front. The Amores, often cited for sufficiently denoting his Venus, are tiny details – there should be a big, clear Venus image, her own shield. Minerva gets called 'Roma', too: unlikely reading after seeing a front full of gods not personifications.

52 Explaining grassy siege crowns, their highest crown status, and who received them, Plin. *HN* 22.6–7, the source for my and others' overview of all the military crowns; also, Gell. *NA* 5.6.8–10; Festus 208L s.v. *obsidionalis*.

circlet gloss a turret-circuit seen head-on. The *triumphator* Scipio Aemilianus was celebrated not only for achieving the grass-crown, but for winning a mural crown as a youth. Many won the latter, but they were normally from the ranks. The high officer class very seldom went onto the first ladders at a besieged wall; it endangered one's forces if one died in that risky venture. In winning a mural crown as a *nobilis*, Scipio stood out. Singly, his non-triumphal crowns were phenomenal; as paired, unique, and celebrated so.[53]

The other traditional way to tie the reliefs to the Bocchus monument is through their putative original location on the Capitol. Reusser (1993) analysed the imprecise day-books of the rushed *scavi* of 1939 here and up the slopes; cataloguing the significant remains of sculpture and architecture, he assigned most of them to the lost Temple of Fides on the Capitolium. According to him, our reliefs had rolled down from there to their findspot – a suggestion previously made by Schäfer, to link the reliefs to a site known to be on the SW Capitoline, which Bocchus could be hypothesised as using to celebrate regal *fides* to Rome; Reusser seemed to clinch that, in so archaeological a treatise.

Let us look, however, at what the fragments' state of preservation can say about their post-installation histories. Our reliefs' tight aggregation, and the scars that they do and do not bear, indicate two or more Late Antique and/or medieval phases of reprocessing for humble and/or aesthetic ends (rubble, art-spolia), and of religiously motivated damage. Percussion breaks edge intact slabs, from whatever tools took the base apart. But smaller fragments hint someone hammered around individual pieces of armour, as may have happened for the dragon-shield (Figure 8.24). And someone sawed and squared some small 'pictures' from armour (Dioscur from shield, Figure 8.21, Gorgoneion and Victory strap from cuirass, Figure 8.23). That means a project of redisplay, the typical churchly or aristocratic post-antique wall displays of ancient *spolia*. This spoliation ceased, leaving our sawn fragments unused, but the remains uncovered. The squared fragments were broken further: slabs show the marks of deliberate defacement of 'idols', knocking off many heads, even limbs (Victories) but with relief as high or higher unmarred, probably battering at the sexy Victory on the greave, and at the devilish snake (Figure 8.24).

By contrast, non-deliberate damage to delicate carved relief edges and masses is minimal, the finish barely scratched and three big thick (nearly) whole slabs are intact of a tightly aggregated set of remains: that does not seem consonant with rolling far. The cycle, partly bolted together, had to be

53 On the inscription for his statue at Augustus' Forum among the *summi viri*, Plin. *HN* 22.13, citing Varro who saw it go up; Livy 37.2.2; Vell. Pat. 1.12.2; [Aur. Vict.] *De vir. ill.* 3.59.

Figure 8.20 San Omobono/Via della Consolazione Republican monument base from Rome, front left panel: greave, with head of youthful Hercules in lion-skin cap as knee-cap cover, and, on the shin, dancing Victory carrying lance and shield; plain body-cuirass; shield with one of the two Dioscuri (Castor or Pollux) with a lance upon a charging horse. Rome, Musei Capitolini, Centrale Montemartini, inv. MC 2752; and the adjoining horse-mask fragment from the end of the first side panel, inv. MC 2749.

laboriously disassembled from its monument. (The marble elements above and below could be burned for lime; limestone, not.) Such dilapidation as there is could have happened in Late Antiquity or after, in one assault on the traces of pagan worship, or simply in clearing after the bronze statuary got pillaged making the monument worthless. So, I would contend that the *SO* monument belongs in or not far from the *area sacra* of San Omobono, the site of its reliefs' post-antique adventures, on the principle that the heavy blocks are not likely to have been dragged very far for their reprocessing.

If correct, this would suit my proposed honorand's specific glory. The twinned temples of Mater Matuta and Fortuna Virilis bordered the Forum Boarium, crowded with third-/second-century triumphalist monuments, an important node on the triumphal procession. This forum sacred to Hercules, dominated by his Ara Maxima, often drew Punic War commemoratives, not least in cult-struggle with Carthage over whom Hercules/Melqart best liked. (The association is nice for *SO*'s greaves.)[54]

[54] See Palmer 1997: 13, 71–2, 104–12 on that cultic competition. Literature is vast on the Forum Boarium monuments – and, patronage by the Africani. Here I can but recommend *LTUR*;

Figure 8.21 San Omobono/Via della Consolazione Republican monument base from Rome, front (right) panel fragment: shield with one of the two Dioscuri (Castor or Pollux) upon a charging horse. Rome, Musei Capitolini, Centrale Montemartini, inv. MC 3517.

Several such works honoured our sanctuary. Burnt in 213 BCE, in 212 a Senate commission desperately had the twin temples reconstructed to win their goddesses' aid, in one of the worst years of Hannibal's invasion. Out front by 196 were Rome's first 'triumphal arches', and first honorific gilt-bronze images, Stertinius' twin *fornices* for his Iberian campaign (Livy 33.27.4). Mater Matuta's *cella* by 174 BCE held Tiberius Gracchus' battle-map of Sardinia, whose appended narrative emphasised, as *SO* does

Platner 1929 (still fundamental for sources, usefully online with sources hyperlinked, and not improved by L. Richardson 1992); Stamper 2005 (use the index, and plans, Figs. 27, 42); Coarelli 1988. Proposing Scipionic second-century restoration of the Ara Maxima, and attention to Hercules shrine, Coarelli, cf. *LTUR* III, s.v. 'Hercules Invictus', 'Ara Maxima'. Hafner 1989 proposes for *SO* Africanus the Elder's Capitoline arch: that is not suitable to the history of arch décor as we know it, weird as pre-third-century CE arch polychromy, and entails that disassembled slide from the Capitol which I contest.

Figure 8.22 San Omobono/Via della Consolazione Republican monument base from Rome, right end, left slab: cavalry cuirass, sashed, with Medusa head on the breastplate, a Victory on each shoulder-strap; trophy with cavalry cuirass and double-crested helmet on tree-trunk; shield with bust of Minerva; second trophy. Rome, Musei Capitolini, Centrale Montemartini, inv. MC 2749.

Figure 8.23 San Omobono/Via della Consolazione Republican monument base from Rome, right end, fragment of far right end: the fragment shows the upper portion of a cavalry cuirass with central Gorgon's head, and shoulder strap(s) with Victory. Vienna, Kunsthistorischesmuseum inv. 1576.

in my interpretation, good done by/to non-Roman allies, victims of Punic aggression (Livy 41.28.10). For novel bulk, colour, visual fascination, an *SO* monument of Scipio Aemilianus and Numidia for the taking of Carthage, could certainly compete even with Stertinius' arches, able to hold as many

Figure 8.24 San Omobono/Via della Consolazione Republican monument base from Rome, back face fragment: buckler-shaped shield with winged serpent/dragon. Rome, Musei Capitolini, Centrale Montemartini, inv. MC 2751.

gilt images as the 190 BCE arch the elder Africanus set alongside the Capitoline's slope road (seven humans, two horses; Livy 37.3.7).[55]

In this picture, homologies between *SO*, *KK* and Chemtou mean that Numidia's king (in 146 BCE Micipsa, not more than two years enthroned) collaborated to frame, even subvent or locate a commission that he may have initiated, with an *imperator* who, like Africanus the Elder, wanted to embrace his Numidian allies. What both parties gained, at home and in the other's territory, need not be spelt out, whatever the shape of the collaboration (the Roman, asking for something Numidian, or the Numidian

[55] The theory it anchored a tall, tapering plinth, like the 167 BCE Monument of Aemilius Paullus at Delphi that carried an equestrian portrait, circulates widely; see di Cesari's critique in *L'età della conquista* 2010 (above, n. 49), choosing a statue base (like me). That theory needs comparative work on scale, and structural archaeology: why were not inner faces cleaned for ashlar, instead of leaving the protruding spurs within? (An operation Schäfer thought was meant to reduce weight – sloppily done, if so.) There were no other such pillar-plinth markers at Rome, to our knowledge.

offering it; the Numidian offering and paying for the whole thing, or instead assisting a Roman 'friend' with that general's plan to put something up). In either reconstruction, there was, first, some kind of participation by sculptors who took careful notes in Numidia, whether or not they operated from a Numidian base normally; second, this general's imprimatur on *SO* paid tribute to monuments (Chemtou, *KK*, lost analogues) he could himself have seen, giving more credit to the Hellenistic Numidian cultural achievement than many moderns have done.

Aemilianus (Africanus the Younger) specially consorts with a monument that might gesture to second-century Numidian commemorative, of course; otherwise, only the elder Africanus and Paullus had such meaningful partnerships with Numidia. The Senate, it seems, barred Numidian participation in the direct assault on Carthage itself in the early 140s, but Numidia had given the pretext for the Third Punic War in the first place, and certainly aided the campaign. Scipio's ties to Numidia were tight: via Massinissa's Roman friendships *(amicitia)* Numidia had, first, helped the older Africanus, his adoptive grandfather defeat Carthage, and then helped his natural father Paullus win the Macedonian Wars (above).

For *SO*, Numidia's model (Figs. 8.3–8.11) was adapted with multiple foci to align with multiple statues, for a different kind of installation than a building frieze: the un-Greek, historicised base and podium frieze that occurs several times in the scanty Republican corpus of stone sculpture, and at large scales under Augustus, visual discourse complementing inscription and statue/superstructure.[56] The very act of depicted dedication would have caught the second-century Roman eye, too, for the central shield is (like other items) a special work of artifice like the monument it graces, a fictional donation of panoplies to a deity. Republican *imperatores* are only known to have begun dedicating precious, non-utilitarian, purpose-made votive shields with their second-century expansion into Greek territories, where sanctuaries were clustered thickly with such. The only known precedent is the dedication at the Capitolium doors by its captor Marcius of a Punic military fetish taken on campaign, a giant (137 lb) silver shield with Hasdrubal's image, seized in 211 BCE from his camp.[57] But now, Flamininus gave the Dioscuri at Delphi inscribed silver

[56] Republican and Augustan relief bases, Kuttner 1993: 228–9 and 1995: 196 and notes, adding the giant Augustan Actian basis at Nikopolis (Zachos 2003; Lange 2009: 106–11).

[57] Livy 25.39; Plin. *HN* 35.314 also notes Carthaginians taking small gold shields on campaign (Jaeger 1997: 121–4, 130–1).

shields, after smashing Philip V of Macedon in 197;[58] multiple cuirasses, helmets, ritual vessels of costliest 'Corinthian bronze', were dedicated by my *SO* candidate Scipio Aemilianus at Sicilian Enguinum, for his triumph of 146 (Cicero, *In Verrem* 4.97); in 146 also, Mummius from the sack of Corinth hung twenty-one gold purpose-made shields around Olympia's Temple of Zeus (Paus. 5.10.5).[59]

To the second century, also, belong formal and conceptual parallels for the central shield's ritual of installation by Victories at a sanctuary space, set off from the panoply series by two metallic incense burners. The only objects not in strict front or profile, their bases in three-quarters view, convey that we look into depth. Between, there pace forward on their own ground-lines facing Victories, eclectic in style: bodies of Hellenistic-era stylistic proportion (high-waisted, small breasts, long-bodied with narrow shoulders and wider hips), generically ideal heads (as in Greek statuary and in third-/second-century Latin terracotta temple sculpture extant) and, a fashion already modish in the third century, Archaistic touches to their rigid gait and to the folds of their *peploi*, thickly double-belted under the breast to fall over trailing chitons.[60] Each pulls down with her outer arm the ribbon end of a thick, tubular laurel garland just now looped across the shield's top, whose leaves splay realistically round the convex mount, and reaches the other (lost) arm to the tie-point to complete the installation. So, the shield is hung on a 'wall', at temple porch or interior: incense has been or shortly will be set ritually alight, and attendants are garlanding sacred space.[61] (Naturally, the long garland is always compared iconically to a militarist celebrant's head-wreath, the laurel *corona*.)

58 Plut. *Flam.* 12; Erskine 2001: 41–2; Sumi 2009: 170, 174–5. Note in F.'s 194 BCE triumph new-made shields, ten silver, one gold (Livy 34.52). In 101, at Rome, Marius erected shield simulacra, one at least with grimacing Cimbric/Gallic head (boss protome), Cic. *De or.* 2. 66. Republican armament display generally: Rawson 1990.

59 Romans did not normally make weapons *tropaea* on battlefields as Greeks did, nor gloss trophies for commemorative monuments until 121 BCE, in Gaul (towers by each of the two generals of the war on the Allobroges, carrying *tropaea* of enemy arms: Strabo 4.1.11; epitomising Livy, Flor. 1.37.2.6, the core text about Romans rarely making battlefield trophies).

60 'Stylistic' datings to the first century BCE often call the Victories 'Neo-Attic', adducing so-called decorative marble-relief consumed by first-century BCE Romans, much from eastern workshops. But so-called Archaising, Archaistic traits are strongly Hellenistic in Greek art itself from at least the third century. Seminal was Fullerton 1987 and 1990; for the second century use Ridgway 2000, cases throughout. The incense burners are more second-century than first-century; I know no determinative first-century match especially for the caps' profile and the acanthus type.

61 Piety in ritual structure would resonate for Numidians. Their votive corpus, like the Punic, often on stelai combines worshipper, ritual objects and furnitures, sometimes with shrine-like frames; the Punic model-shrines continue too (e.g. *Die Numider* 1979: 478–9 Pl. 50).

The relative scale of ribbon and leafage, and the tubular garland contour, match second-century depictions in mosaic, as at Pergamon's palace floors and in the vestibule of the mid-second-century BCE House of the Faun at Pompeii, and in Greco-Roman fourth- to first-century BCE relief sculpture. Most telling, this entire central composition links firmly to the early–middle second century BCE, via a class, most extant at Rhodes and Kos, of round, relief-carved funerary and votive altars with Victories and garlands.[62] Sometimes, confronting pairs, as here, arranged garlands in shallow loops, round the upper edge of the relief field, as if ritually decking temple entablatures; their costumes can be archaistic as well. Production starts in the third century: in a splendid example from Delphi, Nikai fuss with garland ribbons much as at *SO*, leafage splaying like ours.[63]

Major typological indicators, then, point to a second-century BCE *SO*. Historically and culturally, it is the joint activities of Numidia and Rome and the bonds between their leaders in the Punic Wars era that make the kind of context we want; for what is so evident from the homologies between the Numidian and Roman monuments, the transmission of deliberated design, has to have meant that some of the creators of the monument in Rome came from Numidia. The Punic Wars gave the interactions that made it possible for a large class of Roman patrons and viewers (soldiers, expatriate and commuting merchants, settlers, administrators) to make the cognitive match between the Numidian and Roman examples. Intensive visual and 'technical' exchange of the kind we have here is not usually made, in very costly political monuments of potent signification, unless there will be audiences from both sides of the transaction. Numidian audiences of elites at Rome because of military alliances, though much fewer in number than Roman audiences, help account for why it was desirable that this form and content (and perhaps material, below) pass from Africa to Rome. Romans with responsibility for setting up or permitting siting of the *SO*

62 G.-C. Picard and many after wished centralised composition specifically to be Roman, and first-century at that. However, too much adduced as parallel is subordinate ornament to something much bigger, and so given tastefully ordered structure like a frame-moulding; centralised statuary groups and ornament compositions occur in Greek traditions of all periods. Early second-century Roman heraldic imagery: the terracotta reliefs at Fregellae (House 2), *c.* 200–170 BCE, about the Seleukid Wars: Coarelli 1996b; *L'età della conquista* 2010: 294–5 Cat. III.1 (Annalisa Lo Monaco). Two compositions survive for a cuirass-on-stake, between *omphalos*-on-tripod votives, flanked by Victories, or by males in military dress.

63 Ridgway 2000: 204; Hübner 1993: 69–70 and n. 12. For Rhodes, Fraser 1977: 27–33 and cat. 85 with Fig. 84 a–d, 85 a–c; Delphi *ara*, Fig. 70, at 111 n. 145; 69 n. 12, the earliest exemplar of human figures involved with garlands, at Rhodes with third-century ceramic. Second century onwards, Rhodian and other island workshops served in Karia, for Pergamon, west Greeks and at Rome.

monument had to know that Numidians at Rome, in perennial diplomatic engagement for prospective military assistance as well as ratification of this or that Numidian claim to the Numidian throne, would take the reference as celebrating Numidia(ns); in turn there have to have been socio-political uses of this monument, for the Numidian dynasts trying to impress their own, and Romans. At the same time, no Roman shrewd enough to achieve the extreme power within the *res publica* indicated by the monument would have been so naïve as to waste the opportunity for hortatory address to his own people, in regard to core content of the reliefs.

The significant difference is what the different audiences were supposed to grasp about whom the panoplies belonged to: in Numidia, (polycultural) *us*; in Rome, (homogenous) *us and our* (other-culture) *friends* – that is to say, an intra-national *us*. All imply a third relationship, of dominance over *those others we beat* – implicitly in Numidia, overtly in Rome. The transmission-event itself was iconic of such friendship: it encoded *amicitia* as mediated by art-gift, art-kinship. That acting out of political and military alliance by states, cities and individuals exchanging monuments, designers, designs was very characteristic of Hellenistic-era courts in the Greek world, not least in their relations with Rome from the third century onwards; it was coming to be true of relations between Late Republican aristocrats themselves. These transactions, documented by texts and by the character of extant art and architecture, are much spoken-of regarding Rome and the hegemonic powers of the east Mediterranean and Sicily; this essay urges that we take seriously the possibility that *SO* is the fruit of just such art-friendship between royal Numidia and (a leader of) Rome. To do that, it is time to parse the full relief series.

The SO reliefs centre on frontally viewed panoply elements isolated in mid-frieze, blank ground around them, a stark *dignitas* of horizontal and vertical *parataxis*. Seriated were shields with big, figural relief blazons, each centring a cluster of other, evenly spaced panoply elements, sometimes but not always cuirasses. We know we have one long-side's centrepiece slab (Victories with shield details about the honorand, a small space of depth and event, Figure 8.18) of a quite long frieze, with round picture-shields, infantry metal cuirasses, pictorialised greaves, war-horse masks (Figure 8.20); the angled return to much of a short end (cuirasses, cuirass-trophies, Minerva shield, Figure 8.22); and unplaced is a biscuit-shaped shield, edges convex, from the back (Figure 8.24). This last fragment has puzzled all Greco-Romanists: on it rests all our knowledge that items in the *SO* friezes referenced the strongly foreign, the exotic (to Romans). A serpent with bird-wings and tail writhes across it, as strange to Greco-Roman artifacts as the shield shape itself (below); the sensuously stacked coils derive directly, as Meyer saw, from 'Pergamene' snake renderings, the sensuous, so-called baroque mode of the second-century Great Altar and related works of the Attalid sphere. I discuss with more detail below what is evident at first sight, the collage of mimetic style with different systems of stylisation, and make the case for its Numidianness.

Mimesis flirted all across with witty formalism: the plausibility of hard things flat against walls vs. the ground's dissolving into abstract 'air', and miniature/colossal mutation imputed to one object by its companion. The first is unusual in the comparative eastern corpus for armament art: the second, foreign there, is conveyed, less extremely, at *KK* and Chemtou. The same thematic threads as in Numidia laced the series, like the seriation of deistic emblems, and of fierce talismanic beasts (hawk-dragon, warhorses as mask or as ridden, lion as helmet, eagle). At *SO* another thread is a putative single workshop, serving two peoples, with consistently wave-bordered shields – whose only match is at *KK* (Figure 8.11), and whose only other parallel may be the subtle wave mouldings nested within the fourth-century chryselephantine shield from Vergina (n. 43)!

What differs is the degree of fantasy, the relation of armament as shown to its usage by either or any people concerned. Cuirasses apart, little on the *SO* monument has a direct match in Latium, Samnite central Italy or Etruria, Magna Graecia, Sicily, or easterly 'Greece'. Above all, no Romans used round shields, the main motif; and the reliefs' hoplite-shield profile does not tag glaringly Numidia either. The serpent-buckler (Figure 8.24) is not Roman, Greek, Celtic, German, Iranian or of any other 'ethnic' protagonist people in big Hellenistic and Roman histories whose arms or images of them are known. Whether or not Romans understood the specifics of its foreignness, the logical hypothesis is that the shield contour, in the larger context of Numidian resemblance, should be Numidian too. Our fragment was one of a pair, the extant mirroring-images on the base front prove; was there more such distinctive weaponry on the back, to give the whole honorific a foreign, Numidian signature of dedication? The cuirasses resemble Hellenistic and Republican plain metal (infantry) and padded linen (cavalry) elite cuirasses (Figures 8.19 and 8.22); the plain horse-mask (Figure 8.20) aims at verism too. But neither Roman nor Numidian armies used greaves (Figure 8.19). No known Italic and Greek greaves actually worn in battle were this much encrusted, though specialists know the luxuriant treatment of fourth-century and Hellenistic-period metal armour's figural relief, its distribution at sites in Latium and Magna Graecia, with a taste too for sexy feminine motifs as here.[64] This is art-armour, fiction: the knee-cover is the mask of young Hercules, in lion-skin cap, and the entire shin-guard is taken up by whirling Victory as if in a shield-dance, swinging a shield behind her left shoulder, lance in lowered right hand. By contrast with the sensual hyper-realism here and elsewhere, the big Minerva-head in a shield on the end is in very flat, fictive relief, with stiff hard profile; that kind of eclecticism matches well the Numidian monuments' apposition of *mimesis* with what snobbish Hellenism would call crude delineation.

Romans knew what they saw, and did not see: the interestingly real, foreign and fabulous mixed, and no recognisable booty assemblage to signify 'X lost'. I return to the central episode (Figures 8.16 and 8.18), about dedicating a 'friendly', not a booty, shield, which keyed viewers to think the other shields bearing Roman gods, and by extension the whole panoply, was 'Our (Friends')' armour too. If the side(s') tiny cuirasses on trunk-shafts (Figure 8.22) are not also friendly panoplies, then they are such abstracted, miniaturised victory emblems as to be empty of specific reference to any one Mediterranean people. The details of Roman honorific are on this central shield, fantastically arranged. The weight of relief is centred, on a functional shield, and so normally in images. Here, the largest 'metal' ornament is below – Jupiter's eagle clutching his thunderbolt, beating its wings, steadying a palm-frond from whose end dangle two crowns and a sacral ribbon. Overhead tiny Amores fly in with a now-blank *tabula* – at once a 'real' shield-relief, the *tabula* for a legionary designation attested for Roman soldiers' shield-covers and an inscription plaque one might affix to any monument.[65] Joining signs of happy festival and pleasure to signs of war is a very Hellenistic, and Republican, binary. Jove's eagle signals the Capitolium, where *triumphatores* dedicated. But the profusely evoked deities signified that this denoted-space is also anywhere in the sacral *Urbs*.

The pantheon could aid Numidian thoughts as well, of a bond by shared cult; it is interesting to match the base's icons with the Numidian monument-reliefs (above) that also denote sky-gods (i.e. like Jupiter) personified as thunderbolts, Athena/Minerva and Gorgon references, and Hercules motifs. Cavalry gods and armaments at *SO* would appeal too, to their speciality in

[64] Good for an Italian sphere are cuirass shoulder-straps from the Siris river, probably Tarentine, *c.* 390–340 BCE, British Museum, with Hercules fighting Hippolyta, and one similar from Praeneste: Grandjouan *et al.* 1989: Fig. 1 at 20–1; more third-century south-central Italian votive relief-armours with Amazons, Treister 2004: 196, 198; relief-armour, Treister 2001 (armament parallels *passim*).

[65] Miniaturist Amor schemes, sometimes triumphalist, already second-century Pergamene, Hübner 1993: 68–70, 190–1; Attalid iconicity, Kuttner 2001: 161–2.

warfare. That I can trace a match to the *SO* shields' wave-border only at *KK*, even if that is the first match made in scholarship to date (above), could be dismissed. But there does seem to be special linkage in the writhing snake on the strangely shaped buckler that none can place. With a *daimon* that is neither Greek nor Italo-Roman nor Egyptian numen or motif, this has been key to interpreting the reliefs as alien booty (snake signifying Mithridates, etc.). Look past the Pergamene surface-style of the sensuous coils, at the Numidian writhing-snake blazon, which is simply in a different formal mode; look at the particular form of wings on the winged-thunderbolt shield (Figure 8.8b) for the curling wing-tips, which, like that stiff-profile bird-tail (is it Egyptianising?) have no easy match in Hellenistic archaistic art.[66] The strange collage reminds of the mixture of culturally diverse canons of *mimesis* and outright stylisation on the North African mountain-markers and tombs discussed above. It is not possible for me to imagine a Greco-Roman Hellenistic artist conceiving such a guardian serpent without direction by someone thinking visually like a North African, and so, adding North African elements to the pantheon that the representations on the relief armours collectively present. Since the actual shield-shape has no analogue in any other context and as *SO*'s only extant formal and conceptual cousin is the Numidian monument genre, it seems a strong hypothesis that this winged-serpent buckler is meant to be 'Numidian' votive armour. In this reading the fragment strengthens the case for collaborative design between artists aware of Numidian ideas and forms, and artists trained, as many details show, elsewhere in the Mediterranean.

The stone passed over to those carvers was a foreign gift to Rome too, impressive to those who saw the unwieldy raw-materials disembarked, artists in their train. This dense, finely grained, blue-grey limestone has been key to construing Numidianness for *SO* (as 'Bocchus Monument'). It has been contentiously linked to Thala in North Africa and, although the one scientific assay yielded no match in documented Mediterranean quarries, the North African littoral and hinterland from Gibraltar to Tripolitania is rich in grey calcareous stones, some so fine-grained and partly metamorphised that, as here, it resembles marble; too few have had their isotopic profile

[66] H. Meyer sensed something was conveyed about Roman international relations, because of the monument's formal links especially to Pergamon, such that he selected Attalid co-sponsors (1991–2). But much that he cited one would now call more generically 'Hellenistic', and/or typical for the international workshops serving the Republic that used Attalid designers without necessarily making borrowing iconographic. It is dubious that an aim to look 'Pergamene' would not inflect the entire cycle's composition and rendering, starting with choosing to do Attalid-style *spolia* heaps, of verist, practical armament.

calibrated.[67] Dark limestones were much employed in North Africa from the fourth to the first century BCE for visible masonry, statuary and relief, sometimes very well made, including stelai at Carthage and in Numidian sanctuaries.[68] By contrast, in the rare regions of the central and eastern Hellenistic Mediterranean where local dark stones were used for bases and architecture, they were not (with the exception of the boat-base of the Nike of Samothrace) seen as worth elaborating sculpturally as such, let alone on the scale of *SO*. Usage counts as well as source: if we never find the right quarry, it is still the case that this is not Italian stone, and that such polychromy, for statuary bases, architectural façades and commemorative relief is unparalleled to date at Republican and early Imperial Rome. The material's artistic exploitation looked, and was, foreign. (The construction technique, discussed above, was not normative Greco-Roman either.) North African eyes could see what looked just like the dark stones of their own commemorative arts, and a compliment to their practices of polychromy in *giallo antico* marble as at Chemtou. Here, as there and at *KK*, the monument celebrates both an outstanding patron or honorand and a people-in-arms – horse and foot united under gods' protection and king or Republican constitution, a message which is reified in walls of massed panoplies, shields and cuirasses, and amplified in the seriated armaments' depicted reliefs. Those reliefs aspire to perdurable signification no matter what the future might forget, the present not grasp, of their encoding of more specific address to contemporary historical realities.

Numidia invades Rome: the victory monument for Bocchus' defeat of Jugurtha

The close of the 90s BCE saw the making of true fusion art, in this essay's terms. A highly calculated religious and political monument about Numidia and Rome was documentably invented by a North African monarch and

[67] The proposition was made by Schäfer 1979: 248–9; the thesis has tempted many, who wished to see a Bocchus bringing native stone to Rome, and has as often been set to one side. See most recently, *L'età della conquista* 2010: cat. II.19 and, deploring the lack of further assay, Polito 1998: 123, 125.

[68] The range of Numidian 'marbles', see e.g. Röder 1988. The stelai from the Salammbo Tophet: Fantar 1974 citing the Rider Stele (above n. 25), and a significant image of sacrifice; a shaft showcasing a floral (rose) emblem of Tanit/Astarte, Delcor 1976, citing the rich lode of grey-stone stelai at Numido-Punic El Hofra. Delattre 1898–9: février 1898, 10–11, Fig. 14: a finely carved stele from the last Punic/earliest Roman levels at the so-called Ceres Temple, initially a Tanit precinct zone, depicting an obelisk-like tophet, fruit and objects; *ibid.* janvier 1898, 12, Fig. 23, from the tomb of '. . . son of Hanno', a spectacular stele contoured like a horned and pedimented shrine/altar, on the shaft a voluted Ionic capital form, turned to emblem as high-relief outlines.

a Roman aristocratic politician-commander. It aimed at altering the perception of history by means of genre, site, content, design and the very fact of patronal collusion, between Sulla and North African ally, in this Mauro-Numidian art-gift at an urban peak-sanctuary.[69] It is one of the weirdest victory monuments we know for Rome and the Hellenistic world, because it was set up fifteen years after the events portrayed: the hand-over of Jugurtha by Bocchus of Mauretania to Sulla, as agent for Marius' armies, the event that effectively ended the long, bloody Jugurthine Wars of 112–105 BCE, originally an internecine struggle for the Numidian throne. Bocchus made it about Sulla's achievements at empire-building, and his own labour for that empire, foundational to his accession, both under a divine dispensation to success. The king was Mauretanian; but I am in this essay interested to meditate how his commission spoke to the new Mauretanian possession of enormous tracts of western Numidia, and his status as a king of Numidians; it could not but do so, and it is not plausible that it did so only in a threatening, rather than an also conciliatory, tone.

What we know is from Plutarch, in his Lives of Sulla and of Marius, almost identical passages: 'trophy-bearing Victories [*Sulla* 6.1: 'some images bearing trophies'] on the Capitol, and by their side gilded figures representing Jugurtha [of Numidia] surrendered by him [Bocchus of Mauretania] to Sulla' in 106 BCE, closing the Jugurthine Wars (*Marius* 32.2). In this Numidian, North African invasion of Rome's visual environment, its most sacred spaces, Bocchus may well have sought to recall to his contemporaries at home that great Massinissa himself was courteously denied a request to come to Rome to sacrifice at the Arx (and so, give a votive), to acclaim Paullus' 168 BCE defeat of Macedon at Pydna and his own huge aid to that (see above). Plutarch asserts that although the monument's construction greatly enraged Marius (below), and brought tensions between his party and Sulla's to very near open violence, the outbreak of the Social War very shortly after put a temporary stop to that competition. The Social War started in 91: the kind of short time-span Plutarch implies cannot go back before 92, at the most, or we would certainly hear of manoeuvres made openly and formally by the Marians to annul the religious and political legality of its dedication; I find it most plausible that the actual gap between dedication and war was not more than a few months.

Historians and art-historians are keen to use the Bocchus Monument to understand Sulla (but not Bocchus), and to exemplify Sulla's mastery of

[69] Sulla, see usefully Hinard 2008; Keaveney 2005; Gisborne 2005; C. Mackay 2000; special emphasis on his commemoratives, Thein 2002.

visual rhetoric. For all the expenditure of scholarly effort on the commission's 'propaganda' aspects, however, there are still thoughts to add about its materiality and visuality. Had we only the inscription but no description, as often for Roman monuments, scholars would feel no right to assert that Bocchus' portrait stood in the Capitoline precincts. Instead, we can know how North African home pride would be specially exhorted by Bocchus' mountain-marker, because no other foreign ruler's portrait is yet certified for Rome's sacred spaces until Cleopatra's collusion with Caesar to put her image in his Temple of Venus Genetrix. Nor could any sanely propose from the inscription (which would not name what was pictured) a Roman documentary figure group about contemporary historical interaction that is not military engagement or parade. As political ceremony only, Bocchus' statuary is a *unicum* in firmly known Republican commemorative, with very few Hellenistic Greek parallels. So, we should think about a Mauretanian/Numidian king's name branding something of marvellous modernity.

The political context matters, for this odd monument that, uniquely in Roman militarist commemorative, was put up years after what it depicted and in its place and genre (monumental statuary) assorted oddly from a non-triumphator. In 91 BCE, Marius' erstwhile quaestor, who had since enjoyed success as a fighting praetor in Cilicia, was jockeying with him for leadership in the impending, enormous war with Mithridates. The shiny re-enactment of his past dangerous exploit could advertise how Fortuna had endowed agency on him before to save Rome, to invite that his charisma be reenlisted. In describing the artwork Plutarch (above), and so his sources, stressed how anxious Bocchus, for his part, was to keep on his side the voting Roman *SPQR*, which held the North African regal appointments in its gift, and hoped this votive would please. How many of Bocchus' own saw his dedication of 91 BCE did not matter as much as *who* saw it (his own elites now and later present at Rome), and that many, of all social ranks knew of it (which the court, and gossip, would ensure). It flaunted his command of Roman dispensations in North Africa, as well as appealing to a sense of communal, 'national' potency in Roman affairs. ('National' is anachronistic, but I ironise deliberately: it is preferable to 'state', in signifying a collective body-politic.) If I am correct that the wall-paintings at Pompeii (Figures 8.1–8.2) transmit 'The Death of Sophonisba' from a Scipionic triumph-painting of 201 BCE still on view, it is interesting that Bocchus' visual configuration also embodied tensions between affectional, familial and political *fides*, a triangle of Numidian prince, Roman commander, transacting beside a North African noble tormented by thought of capture. Sulla and Jugurtha were roughly coeval as junior politician-officers, and must have had encounters, both serving the Roman command; Sallust emphasises how Jugurtha had a particular charm for Romans (such Numidian charms were a trope since Massinissa charmed Scipio). So, we can say, Jugurtha violated *fides* at multiple levels when he attacked his erstwhile companions and commanders. Bocchus had to choose between Rome and a marriage (to Jugurtha's daughter), when he chose to ambush Jugurtha not Sulla; his and Sulla's images self-consciously, enduringly, reminded Rome of that difficult choice, and of Bocchus' *fides*.

That Sulla claimed the real agency in beating Jugurtha was rammed home, all recognise, by the locus that only he can have helped Bocchus obtain: the *area Capitolina* (of the Temple of Jupiter Optimus Maximus, Capitoline peaks) where the new trophies challenged Marius' older Victories and trophies from the Cimbric Wars (adding narrative statuary was aesthetic one-upmanship).[70] But the commission also addressed extant Sullan pseudo-triumphalist art. Some time soon after or before Sulla returned to Rome with Marius for the latter's Numidian triumph, he commissioned a ring-stone with 'the surrender of Jugurtha to him by Bocchus'.[71] A strange seal: history narrative is so very rare in extant Hellenistic and Republican intaglios, and this visual autobiography is unique. It was as public as private, broadcasting wax-relief impressions authenticating Sulla's public written voice (even, potentially, sent to North Africans).

I still accept the wide consensus among Roman historians, numismatists and art historians that coins of Sulla's son Faustus copy these sealings thirty-five years later in 56 BCE (Figure 8.25; *RRC* 426/1); that these coins circulated in North Africa, perhaps even from traveling mints there, merits its own discussion of Numidian viewers. But I do recant the equally widespread assumption that the coin/gem illustrates the statuary of 91 BCE.[72] In the centre of the coin image sits Sulla, in magisterial toga, rigidly upright with Roman *auctoritas* upon magistrate's or commander's *sella*. Two monarchs down on one knee flank him – at his left, Jugurtha with hands chained behind, head down; at his right, Bocchus gazing up to him, offering an olive or laurel branch. But in 91, Bocchus was not likely to have offered,

[70] Documented via Caesar's restoration of them, Sulla having taken them down (and returned them to Marius' wife, Caesar's aunt): Vell. Pat. 2.33–4, Suet. *Iul.* 11, Plut. *Caes.* 6. See Spannagel 2003. I cannot consider here whether, and how, Sulla's and Bocchus' monument related to the famous 'twin trophies' at the margins of the battlefield of Chaironeia, 86 BCE; see the start of this section for general Sulla bibl., and Camp *et al.* 1992; note that one was for (and delegated for erection by) his foreign, Greek allies.

[71] Plut. *Mar.* 10.5–6; also *Sull.* 3.4, *Mor.* 806c–d.

[72] So all bibliography to Sulla, to the Bocchus Monument, and to *SO* as 'Bocchus Monument' – such typically illustrate it from Schäfer 1979 to myself in 1995: Fig. 50; *RRC* 426/1.

Figure 8.25 Denarius of Faustus Cornelius Sulla, 56 BCE (Crawford *RRC* 426/1), Rome mint. Reverse: kneeling Bocchus (r.) offers laurel to Faustus' father Sulla enthroned on magistrate's seat and wearing toga, Jugurtha kneels with bound hands; inscr. *FELIX* ('fortunate', Sulla's chosen epithet). (Obverse, not shown: bust of Diana, *lituus* and crescent moon, inscr. *FAUSTUS*.)

nor Sulla to have enforced, an image in public statuary of the ruler of Mauretania and western Numidia grovelling like one beaten – as this composition about foreigner and Roman would have seemed in the landscape of triumphalist markers.

Self-vaunting in his own ring was one thing, the advertisement of collaboration with a king who differently now mattered, another; Sulla will have treated with Bocchus for future access to auxiliaries, and (already, no doubt, to buy votes) money and grain. I propose that, for this public image, one that *Bocchus* (rather than Sulla) will have himself inscribed, Bocchus stood, dignified, whether cowed Jugurtha was marched upright or forced to kneel. (At the Capitol, the image of the 'usurper' alive mocked his horrible death down the Capitol's slopes, starved in the noisome *Carcer* after marching in Marius' triumph.) Sulla may not have wished to appear as seated magistrate in public sculpture: such portraits were rare because of the social bar against real officials remaining seated in the company of their standing peers and superiors. Better, surely, for this solicitation of further military appointment, if Sulla wore the all-purpose military costume quaestors shared with generals. We cannot know how those *tropaia* looked. But certainly in 92/91 BCE Bocchus would not let Numidian arms be depicted in any way that too much diminished solidarity, fealty in his now partly Numidian realm, however that was handled.

If I am correct that the second-century base was a regal-imperatorial collusion, then Bocchus will have felt especially empowered not to make a less proud statement about his kingship. The subject obviously admonished Bocchus' Numidians not to rebel against proper order; but he also sought to solicit fealty, discredit Jugurtha, to keep that in effect. In any design, it promised that being a Good Numidian under a king loyal to his Roman ally, despising Bad Numidian rebels, gave agency over the ally's imperial fate. As interestingly, whether Bocchus or Sulla realised it, this monument costumed in Hellenistic visual splendour could convey that good Numidians could sway the internal politics of that superior ally. If the monument survived Marius, and Juba I recalled it during his own engagement with Republican infighting, that might well have made him smile, entertaining, in happier days than Caesar had painted, Roman confederates and clients.

In so short an essay, there is much elided that could show Numidian self-fashioning, and Roman gazes exchanged. That would of course address Juba II of Mauretania as well: this essay opened with his father's death in the service of a Republic, complexly memorialised by the first Julio-Claudians.[73] He consummated, as excavated Cherchel shows, that rich Numidian dialogue with Libyo-Punic, Hellenistic and Roman complex visual culture which the Battle of Zama enabled some 200 years before. The child matured with, the man saw, the monuments here described. As classic Hellenistic, and Numidian, author-king, Juba II told back to Greeks, Romans, Punes and Numidians their own histories; this essay has succeeded if one can better believe it was not un-Numidian that he also explained to Romans their art and antiquities.

[73] D. Roller 2003, *passim*, on Juba II's formation and cultural enterprises.

9 | Hellenism as subaltern practice: rural cults in the Punic world

PETER VAN DOMMELEN AND MIREIA LÓPEZ-BERTRAN

Hellenistic culture and the Punic world

The 'Punic world' took shape in the western Mediterranean in the course of the later sixth and fifth centuries BC, when Carthage established itself as the dominant political and cultural force in central North Africa, western Sicily, southern Sardinia and Ibiza. It was in this period, too, that Carthage acquired a leading role among the existing Phoenician settlements in southern Iberia (Andalusia and southern Portugal) and the Moroccan coastlands that had been established in earlier centuries. In all these areas, Carthaginian or, more generally, Punic cultural traditions and material culture became prominent and increasingly distinct from the older Phoenician traditions in the course of the later fifth century BC, as Punic culture was widely adopted by colonial (Phoenician) and indigenous inhabitants alike. In the Punic core regions of coastal Tunisia, southern Sardinia and western Sicily, they largely replaced pre-existing local cultural traditions. By the fourth century BC, the shores of the far western Mediterranean and Atlantic were thus connected to the central Mediterranean regions of southern Sardinia, western Sicily and Cape Bon by a shared Punic culture and language (Figure 9.1).[1]

In recognition of the substantial variations in culture between these regions, it is increasingly argued that the prominent role of Carthage in the western Mediterranean should be understood not so much as that of an all-powerful coloniser but rather be seen as that of the leading player in a well-connected colonial network.[2] It is in this vein that our use of the label 'Punic world' emphasises both the cultural and economic connections between North Africa, western Sicily, southern Sardinia, Ibiza and southern Iberia without necessarily implying a commanding military or political role for Carthage.[3]

1 Despite these numerous connections, however, there are no compelling reasons to interpret these developments in ethnic terms: see discussion in Moscati 1988b and Prag 2006.

2 See e.g. Whittaker 1978; Wagner 1989; López Castro 1991; van Dommelen 2002; Domínguez Monedero 2006b.

3 See definition and discussion in van Dommelen and Gómez Bellard 2008: 2–12.

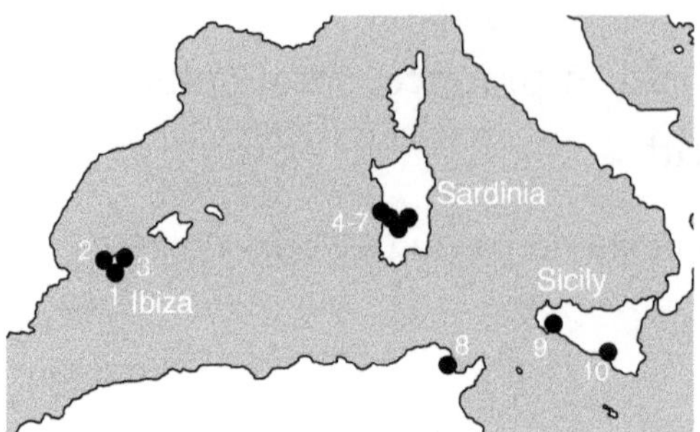

Figure 9.1 Map of the western Mediterranean showing the regions and places discussed. Key: (1) Ibiza town; (2) Sa Caleta; (3) Es Culleram; (4) Cuccuru s'Arriu; (5) *Nuraghe* Lugherras; (6) *Nuraghe* Genna Maria; (7) *Nuraghe* Su Mulinu; (8) Carthage; (9) Selinunte; (10) Gela.

Hellenic culture or, in more generic terms, Greek cultural influence was a consistent feature of the Punic world throughout its history. Greek elements in general were already prominently present in the Phoenician settlements of the eighth and seventh centuries BC. A remarkable example that dates back to the early phases of Carthage itself is the so-called '*chapelle* Cintas', which is a presumed foundation deposit in the *tophet* sanctuary of Carthage. Ranking among the earliest contexts known in Carthage and dateable to the early eighth century BC, the deposit includes notably more Greek (mostly Euboean) than Phoenician objects, despite it being part of a *tophet*, which is an otherwise typically Phoenician institution in the central Mediterranean.[4]

The consistent and ubiquitous presence of Greek pottery in Phoenician and Punic sites is widely regarded as signalling long-term contact with and, by implication, a profound impact of Greek culture on the Phoenician-Punic world. The sheer fact that by the fifth century BC the typically Phoenician red slip table ware had been replaced with Greek-style black gloss pottery only offers further support to the often-expressed view that Punic culture was profoundly Hellenised from early on in its history. While substantial quantities of black gloss pottery were always imported from Athens, the rapid emergence of production centres in Punic regions from Carthage to Sardinia, Ibiza and Morocco shows the prominence of originally Greek types.[5]

Greek influence was not limited to material culture, either. It included most famously the adoption of the Greek goddesses Demeter and Kore into

[4] As discussed by Aubet 2001: 218–26 and Lancel 1995: 28–9. See Wagner 1986 for a critical discussion.

[5] See e.g. the evidence presented by Chelbi 1992 and Kbiri Alaoui 2007 for Punic North Africa (Tunisia and Morocco respectively).

the Punic pantheon. As reported by Diodorus Siculus (14.77.4–5), the cult was officially introduced in Carthage in 396 BC. According to this account, it represented an act of repentance for the destruction by Carthaginian troops of a temple in Syracuse dedicated to Demeter (cf. Diod. Sic. 14.70.4). Ritual know-how and objects were obtained from Greeks living in Carthage and nearby Sicily to celebrate the appropriate rituals in the correct Greek way.[6] The 'success' of this cult as attested by numerous shrines dedicated to Demeter throughout the Punic world is routinely cited as evidence for the Hellenisation of the Punic world.[7]

Rural cults

Our primary aim in this chapter is to analyse critically the nature and impact of 'Greek cultural influences' in and on the Punic world. More specifically, we focus on the role and significance of the Demeter cult in rural contexts. While it is clear that Demeter cults also existed in Punic urban settings, as they did in Greek ones, the majority have been documented in the countryside, where quite different social and economic conditions may be assumed than in the towns. One major difference was that the latter were colonial foundations of Phoenician origin that had been in existence for many generations when the first Demeter shrines were installed, whereas extensive rural settlement only developed at any scale in the Punic countryside from the late fifth and early fourth century BC onwards – in other words, not much earlier than the official introduction of Demeter to Carthage. We therefore propose that rural contexts are particularly helpful for evaluating not only the complexity and variability of Hellenism in the western Mediterranean generally, but also for assessing the role of local culture in the construction of 'Greek culture'. We will accordingly scrutinise some of these 'Demeter rituals' in detail to highlight the complexity and heterogeneity of the material culture and ritual performances involved; using these case-studies, we will also suggest how cross-cultural contacts and 'Greek influence' in general may more pertinently be understood and represented in more nuanced ways.

Because this is not the place to survey all cult sites in the Punic regions that may have been dedicated to Demeter, we focus in this chapter on the two

[6] Peri 2003: 145–6; Campanella and Garbati 2008: 28–33.

[7] See e.g. C. Picard 1984 for Carthage and Marín Ceballos 2004: 319–22 for Spain, as discussed by Bonnet 2006b: 367–8.

western Mediterranean islands of Ibiza and Sardinia.[8] These are not only two core regions of the Punic world but also offer several well-documented ritual sites associated with Demeter. Despite their shared Phoenician-Punic cultural heritage, however, there existed significant cultural differences between these islands that can be ascribed to their different pre-colonial histories: while Ibiza was uninhabited prior to the establishment of the Phoenician settlements in the seventh century BC, Sardinia had already enjoyed a long and rich history of indigenous cultural developments and external contacts when the Phoenicians first set foot on the island. In the absence of indigenous inhabitants, it does not come as a surprise, therefore, that Ibiza developed cultural traditions quite close to those of Carthage, as is for instance immediately evident in the burial rites practised in the Puig des Molins cemetery of Ibiza town.[9] The Punic cultural traditions found in southern Sardinia, by contrast, display a notably distinctive character of their own, even if there is no shortage of close cultural ties with Carthage and the Cape Bon peninsula.[10]

In order to realise these goals, we have organised this paper as follows: first, we discuss the theoretical background and some implicit assumptions of the terms Hellenism and Hellenisation. Secondly, we briefly present the archaeological evidence of several 'rural shrines' in Ibiza and Sardinia before we proceed to the third part of our paper to discuss this material and to compare the situations of both islands. We eventually conclude that the presence of 'Demeter materials' does not necessarily imply the existence of a 'Demeter cult and rituals' as so often presumed and we accordingly call into question any notion of 'Hellenisation' as a straightforward and one-way process of cultural change.

Hellenism between culture and practice

What is Hellenism? At a basic level, this term – or the equivalent neologism 'Hellenicity' and the more conventional term 'Hellenisation' – centres on the appearance, presence or adoption of Greek (material) culture and traditions, regardless of time and place. Whether it is also about ethnic

[8] See Peri 2003; López-Bertran 2007 for a general discussion of the Demeter cult in the Punic world. Regionally focused studies of the cult can be found in C. Picard 1984 (Carthage); Bonet Rosado 1995 (eastern Spain); Hinz 1998 (Sicily); and Garbati 2003, 2008 (Sardinia); while López-Bertran 2007 discusses ritual sites in Punic Sardinia, Ibiza and Iberia.

[9] See evidence presented by Gómez Bellard 1996, 2002.

[10] For an overview, see Barreca 1986, while van Dommelen 2002 discusses the articulation of Punic and local cultural traditions.

identity is a matter still open to debate, since Jonathan Hall has claimed that it was only in Archaic Greece that what he calls 'Hellenicity' also served as the basis for communal and conscious self-identification in ethnic terms. In his view, it was only in the course of the fifth century BC that 'the definitional basis of Hellenic identity shifted from ethnic to broader cultural criteria'.[11]

At the same time, Hellenism, in the sense implied by Droysen's *Hellenismus*, is also commonly defined in very specific chronological and political terms as the 'Hellenistic Age' 'bounded by [the] political events' of the death of Alexander the Great and the Battle of Actium, which by implication set the chronological limits of 323–31 BC.[12] As this traditional definition has gradually been overtaken by the recognition that the implications and effects of these political events went well beyond politics and influenced not only 'the adoption or adaptation of Greek names, words and institutions, but also the reception of Greek political ideas, lifestyle and literary, artistic and architectural ideas and practices', it becomes evident that the erstwhile rather narrow conception of the Hellenistic is merging with a broader understanding of 'Hellenisation' and Greek influences in the Mediterranean and beyond.[13]

As few scholars would nowadays take issue with the assertion that 'the Hellenistic world is as much a cultural phenomenon as a political one', we wish to explore what that actually means, both in the so-called Hellenistic period and earlier. Cultural change and continuity are particularly highlighted in recent studies, because the establishment of myriad Greek communities in far-flung countries and very different cultural environments is seen as playing a significant role in the spreading of Greek culture and traditions. This approach is summed up by the claim that '[t]o understand the Hellenistic world, it is essential to grasp both [*sc.* cultural change and continuity]'.[14] Hellenism and Hellenisation are thus gradually merging and the question of how we think about cultural change accordingly comes centre stage.

[11] J. Hall 2002: 7–8, 172–228; but see Antonaccio 2005: 101–10 for a more nuanced view; on the term 'Hellenicity', see J. Hall 2002: xix; on 'Hellenisation', see Dougherty and Kurke 2003b; Antonaccio 2003; J. Hall 2002: 104–11; and J. Hall 2003.

[12] Erskine 2003b: 2.

[13] Cartledge 1997: 5. These quotations are taken from the introductions to just two of a much larger number of overviews, surveys and compendia of the Hellenistic world published in the last decade or so; see also the Introduction to this volume. See Wallace-Hadrill 2008: 17–28 for a comprehensive discussion.

[14] Erskine 2003b: 3, while concerning Italy a similar view has already been expressed by Zanker 1976b: 11.

Hellenism as a cultural category

Culture and cultural change are concepts that have long been a central concern to archaeologists and anthropologists alike and scholars from both disciplines have reflected extensively on these matters; we will therefore refrain from giving an overview of these debates.[15] Because we are certainly not the first ones to highlight the relevance of these debates for discussing Hellenism/ Hellenisation and similar terms such as Romanisation or Orientalism, we start more or less *in medias res* with the observation that discussions of Hellenism pay very little, if any, attention to these debates and tend to be based on a rather outdated concept of the notion of 'culture'.[16] Not only do hardly any of the recent publications explicitly raise this topic, it is also evident from the habitual references to Greek language, clothing and indeed politics and ritual that most contributors subscribe to a so-called essentialist concept of culture.[17] In this perspective, culture is a clearly bounded and autonomous entity that is characterised by a stable and unique series of specific traits or 'markers'. These include tangible elements such as certain types of pottery or clothing but also immaterial 'traditions' like burial customs, literary genres or political systems that in this view can be relied on to distinguish one culture from another and to trace the influence of one on others. Ticking off a number of specific features on a 'cultural checklist' is, in this view, sufficient to establish reliably that the inhabitants of a settlement or region belong(ed) to a recognised cultural group, such as Greeks or Etruscans.

As both archaeologists and anthropologists have argued, this view suffers from two fatal flaws. The first one is that it has little or no regard for the role of people in the creation and maintenance of culture and that it reduces them at best to passive on-lookers. People are endowed with a set of cultural markers in their youth, if not at birth, and are from an essentialist perspective little more than carriers of their culture throughout their lifetime. To be sure, they may be influenced by other cultures but they always remain

[15] While any archaeological or anthropological handbook will provide a good introduction, Marshall Sahlins' Huxley Lecture is a particularly perceptive discussion of how discussions of culture have fared: Sahlins 1999.

[16] See in particular the reflections of two anthropologists on Hellenism: Gallini 1973 and Friedman 1990. For Orientalism, see the volume *Debating Orientalization* (Riva and Vella 2006); concerning Romanisation the bibliography is huge: e.g. Mattingly 2004. Dougherty and Kurke 2003a and Wallace-Hadrill 2008: 17–28 offer a rare Classical perspective on these matters; see also Veyne 1979; Dougherty and Kurke 2003b; and J. Hall 2003.

[17] Notable exceptions are Cartledge 1997: 4–8; Antonaccio 2005: 109; Hodos 2006: 11; and, especially, both Dietler 2005: 55–61 and Wallace-Hadrill 2008: 28–32.

passive objects who are moved around and affected by meetings, mergers or clashes between the cultures that they are carrying. The second flaw is that the essentialist culture concept prioritises the 'authenticity' and 'pure origins' of meanings and objects: this not only depends on the essentialist assumption that the meaning of objects and traditions is inherently tied to and engrained in culture (material or otherwise) and therefore unable to be changed; but it also entails a disregard of their reuse, adaptation, appropriation and reconceptualisation; it is no coincidence that secondary usage, if recognised in the first place, is often regarded as second-rate and derivative and consequently as less important. These views are finally often imbued with preconceived ideas in Classical and Western European culture about the priority, if not superiority, of the Greek world.[18]

Hellenism in practice

As post-modern and post-colonial ideas emphasise the primacy of human agency and the contingency and constructed nature of social meanings, Hellenism and the expansion of 'Greek culture' must be reconsidered in terms of the people themselves, of Greek background or otherwise, who travelled across the Mediterranean and beyond and who met and mingled with other people in different ways and in different places. The critical point is that it is not cultures that travelled but people (as they still do).

In response to the conventional ideas of Hellenism, we therefore propose to adopt a local perspective to scrutinise in detail some of those situations in which people from different cultural backgrounds lived together and forged relationships, as part of which many different types of material culture were used and new traditions and new items were adopted or old ones reinvented for new purposes. In sum, we propose to abandon any essentialist notion of culture and meaning and to adopt instead a constructivist perspective on society and culture. As a consequence, we insist that references to 'mixing' of cultures or cultural syncretism offer an insufficient basis for understanding cultural change and the meanings of objects and practices. We emphasise instead the social processes of interaction, negotiation and indeed

[18] Friedman 1990, 1992 discusses the conceptual background of the connections between European and Western identities and the Classical past, while Dietler 2005 and van Dommelen 2006a, 2006b explore the issue in detail in relation to archaeology. Cartledge 1997 and P. Green 1993b approach these matters from a Classical perspective, which leads them to slightly different emphases.

conflict among the inhabitants of a given context as giving rise to new 'hybrid practices' and cultural customs.[19]

Demeter in the Punic western Mediterranean

Demeter was widely worshipped throughout the Greek world, even if she was rarely the main deity of a town or city-state. As befits her rural connotations and in line with the importance of agriculture in general and cereal production in particular in the ancient world, numerous small shrines and some larger sanctuaries dedicated to Demeter existed in the territories of most Greek city-states; in many cases, more than one sanctuary might be present, frequently also close to or indeed within the town itself, as for instance in Gela. Like many other Greek cult sites, most of the shrines dedicated to Demeter were located close to a spring or stream.[20]

The Demeter cult and rituals were closely associated with the cycles of the agricultural year, as is evident from her various epithets, such as *Kalligeneia* ('who brings forth beautiful offspring') or *Achaia* ('reaper'), that refer to specific activities or products. Because of the cyclical emphasis on certain times of the year and given the rural background of ancient society, Demeter was particularly worshipped at many festivals celebrated at a more or less fixed time of the year at many of the rural shrines. The *Thesmophoria* is probably the festival best known that was celebrated across the Greek world at the start of the agricultural year after the dry and hot summer.[21]

In archaeological terms, shrines dedicated to Demeter are characterised by a remarkably consistent core set of votive dedications and other finds used in ritual practices. Small figurines of animals, pigs in particular, of food, notably cakes, of vessels for carrying grain and water, and of people, almost exclusively women, make up the bulk of votives found at shrines dedicated to Demeter. They were complemented by offerings of animals, pigs in particular, and of prepared foods, in particular certain types of cakes or pastries. The latter were either offered whole and deposited in a pit or

[19] Such claims have been current since at least Zanker 1976b: 11; but see Potter 2003 for a nuanced discussion. Hybridisation is increasingly gaining ground as a concept to capture the innovative and active nature of cultural interaction: Friedman 1995; van Dommelen 2006a; 2006b; Antonaccio 2003; 2005; Knapp 2008: 57–61.

[20] See Cole 1994 and Hinz 1998: 169–237 on the Demeter cult in general; Cole 1988 and 2004: 7–65 on the location of ritual sites in Greece; see Hinz 1998: 50 for Sicily.

[21] Brumfield 1981: 70–95 discusses the *Thesmophoria* in relation to the agricultural year.

consumed as a sacrificial meal; animals were first slaughtered, butchered and cooked.[22]

Lamps and torches make up another category of objects that are consistently present at cult sites dedicated to Demeter, largely because certain rituals were performed at night. Torches are frequently depicted on vase-paintings and coins associated with Demeter and specially made multi-nozzle lamps are encountered in Demeter shrines throughout the Greek world. The latter show few signs of actual use and tend to be found as votive offerings alongside other items, which suggests that they were specifically made for a single occasion and offered afterwards. Regular lamps of the usual types commonly found in settlement contexts appear to be a later occurrence particularly common in Sicily.[23]

Sicily

The island of Sicily occupies a crucial place in our discussion, not only because it represents an important meeting-point between Punic and Greek colonial cultures in general, but also specifically because it was from this region that the Demeter cult was introduced to the Punic world. There is moreover a long tradition of associating Demeter with Sicily, as is shown for instance by Cicero's comment 'that the whole island of Sicily was consecrated to *Ceres* and *Libera*' (Cic. *Verr.* 4.106).

The earliest evidence for a Demeter cult in Sicily dates back to the second half of the seventh century BC and all early instances are closely associated with a Greek colonial town, even if in most cases the sites tend to be situated just outside rather than inside the inhabited areas. A good case in point may be found at Gela, where two ritual sites were established shortly after the mid-seventh century BC, both dedicated to Demeter: one is the well-known sanctuary at Bitalemi on a hilltop across the Gela river and the other one is the so-called Predio Sola site, which lay just beyond the (later) southern city-wall.[24] In no case, including the ones later established in the *chorai*, is there evidence of earlier non-Greek (indigenous) ritual activities. The

[22] See Clinton 2005: 100 and Detienne 1989: 134–5 in general and Hinz 1998: 28–30 for Sicily.

[23] On the ritual use of lamps and torches, see Hinz 1998: 49 and 230, Parisinou 2000: 136–47 and Hermanns 2004: 20–6 and 101–15.

[24] See Holloway 1991: 56–60 for an overview of Gela and its sanctuaries, while detailed information on the shrines is provided by Hinz 1998: 56–64.

archaeological evidence strongly suggests, in other words, that the Demeter cult was brought to Sicily by Greek settlers.[25]

By 396 BC, when the Demeter cult was officially introduced to Carthage, it was well established across Greek Sicily, with major sanctuaries just outside the major colonial settlements, including Gela, Selinunte and Syracuse. Further inland, including beyond the *chorai* of the Greek settlements, Demeter was also worshipped in indigenous contexts such as Morgantina and Sabucina. Beyond Sicily, numerous ritual sites throughout the western Mediterranean have been associated with the cult of Demeter for a variety of reasons, including several on the two islands of Ibiza and Sardinia.[26]

Ibiza

The island of Ibiza was first settled by Phoenicians in the mid-seventh century BC, when at least two small Phoenician settlements were established on the east coast of the island at Sa Caleta and Ibiza town (Es Soto). Around the end of the seventh century, Sa Caleta was abandoned and all Phoenician presence was concentrated in Ibiza town. Both Ibiza and its adjunct, Formentera, had been uninhabited for at least the previous five to six centuries and Ibiza town remained the only settlement on these islands from the sixth century BC onwards.[27]

Whereas the earliest inhabitants of Ibiza had maintained close connections with the Phoenician settlements in Andalusia, Ibiza became much more involved in the Punic world of the central Mediterranean. It developed close ties with Carthage from the mid-sixth century BC onwards, as is evident in the burial evidence. In the fifth century, the town gradually expanded and by the turn of the century a number of small rural sites first appeared elsewhere on the island.[28]

One of the earliest sites established away from Ibiza town was the cave shrine of Es Culleram, which is situated in the far north of the island, which is about as remote as possible on Ibiza (Figure 9.2). The cave is situated high up the northern slope of the narrow Sant Vicent valley that cuts through the

[25] As argued in detail and convincingly by Hinz 1998: 19–21 and 219–23.

[26] Orlandini 1968; Hinz 1998: 169–217 (including south Italy); for Greek rituals in inland Sicily, see Hodos 2006: 121–9.

[27] Costa Ribas and Fernández Gómez 2000; Gómez Bellard 2002.

[28] See van Dommelen and Gómez Bellard 2008: 5–12 for the Carthaginian influence in the central and western Mediterranean; Gómez Bellard 1993 and 2008b: 46–8, 72–4 for details of the Ibizan developments.

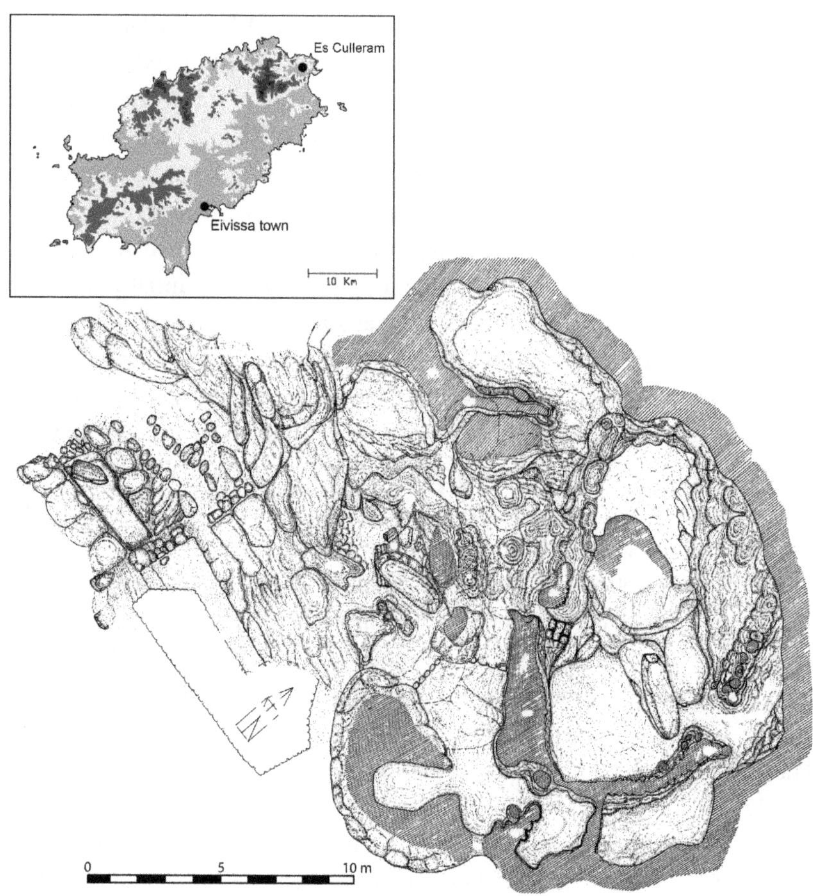

Figure 9.2 Plan of the cave of Es Culleram. Inset: map of Ibiza showing the sites discussed.

steep mountains towards the sea. It was established by the end of the fifth century BC and reached its highest point of activity during the third century BC, before being abandoned a century later. A number of small rural settlement sites (farmsteads) were built in the valley below from the late fifth century BC onwards, which coincides with the moment that the cave of Es Culleram was first used as a shrine. The main period of activity in the cave, of the third and second centuries BC, also coincides with the expansion of rural settlement in the valley from eight to fourteen sites.[29]

The cave consists of two main rooms, one of which has collapsed in the more recent past, with several smaller spaces behind them. A small cistern

[29] Gómez Bellard *et al.* 2005 and Gómez Bellard *et al.* 2011.

had been built against the rock face outside the cave. A large number of finds were recovered from the cave when it was first explored in 1907 and 1908, including more than 1,114 complete and fragmentary terracotta figurines, but unfortunately no information at all was recorded about their contexts.[30] The finds include coins, two possible *baetili*, two gold medallions and two Punic inscriptions dedicated to Tanit and Reshef-Melqart respectively. Substantial amounts of pottery were also found, in particular cooking, eating and drinking vessels and some amphorae. A substantial portion of these objects, however, are of much smaller size than usual and were clearly not intended for regular usage. Large quantities of animal bones, almost exclusively of sheep and goat, show that eating and drinking were nevertheless regular activities in or outside the cave and suggest that sacrificial meals were a significant feature of the rituals performed at Es Culleram. Careful analysis of the faunal remains has also shown that most of the animal skulls were burnt and that the animals had been butchered at the cave itself.[31]

The two inscriptions evidently show that two Punic deities were worshipped in the cave but the numerous figurines interestingly suggest a rather more complex situation. Of the five iconographical models that have been distinguished, three in particular are relevant to our discussion. These are the so-called 'winged figurines', 'plain figurines' and 'incense burners'. The first type, which is unique to the Es Culleram cave, presents a winged female figure that is usually wearing a *kalathos* (headdress) (Figure 9.3).[32] The wings, the herald's wand (*caduceus*) and the solar disc or lotus flowers also worn by the figure identify her as representing the Carthaginian goddess Tanit. The second group is characterised by obvious iconographic references to Demeter such as a *kalathos*, a veil, torches, piglets and babies. The third group, which comprises seventeen items, is made up of incense burners (*thymiateria*) in the shape of a female head that are habitually associated with the cult of Demeter and Persephone. It is unclear, however, whether any of these objects had effectively been used to burn incense or other spices; they might alternatively also represent votive offerings.[33] Several features, however, occur across the figurine categories: the *kalathos* can for instance be seen on all three figurine types – although not necessarily on every single

[30] Marín Ceballos *et al.* 2010: 137.

[31] For descriptions of the cave and its finds, in particular the figurines, see Aubet 1982 and Gómez Bellard 2008a: 122–3; Ramón Torres 1985; unfortunately, no contextual information exists for the faunal evidence: Morales Pérez 2003.

[32] The winged figurines have also been found in Carthage and it has been argued that this iconography is clearly Egyptian: Marín Ceballos *et al.* 2010: 144.

[33] For the typology and catalogue of the figurines from Es Culleram, see Aubet 1982 and Fernández *et al.* 2007; for *thymiateria* in the Punic and Iberian worlds, see Pena 2000, 2007.

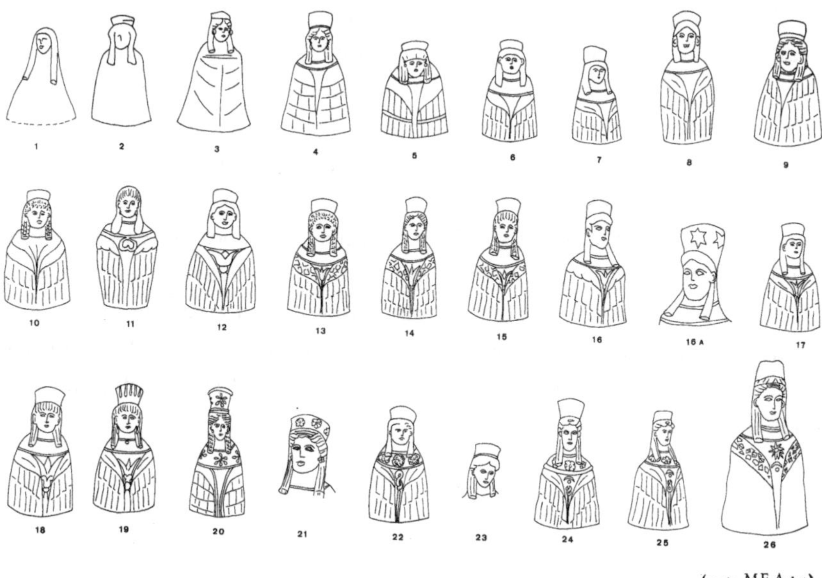

Figure 9.3 Winged terracotta figurines from the Es Culleram cave shrine representing the iconographic types discussed.

specimen – while the second and third groups share a close association with Demeter.

Es Culleram has been interpreted as a rural shrine devoted to Tanit because of the deity's chthonic and fertility connotations and the use of a cave well matches the underworld association. The other two groups of figurines, however, suggest that Demeter also played a significant role in the rituals performed there. Because the oldest figurines, at least in typological terms, are those associated with Tanit, it may be reasonable to assume that the cave was originally dedicated to Tanit. But it is also quite clear that at some point in time, probably during the fourth century BC, at least some of the rituals underwent changes and that new practices and votive offerings were introduced that elsewhere are more commonly associated with Demeter. Because the latter became quite prominent, it is generally proposed that Demeter joined Tanit at Es Culleram in the course of the late fourth or third century BC and that the Greek cult eventually replaced the traditional Carthaginian deity altogether.[34]

[34] On Demeter and Tanit, see San Nicolás Pedraz 2000: 680–1. Because the cave also looks out eastward over the open sea, a maritime connection involving Melqart has been proposed by Gómez Bellard and Vidal González 2000: 122–3.

The problem with this interpretation, however, is that it treats the two cults as autonomous cultural phenomena that move independently and that always and everywhere hold the same meanings. As we argued above, this view relies on the essentialist presumption that the Demeter figurines and incense burners had the same significance in Punic Ibiza as in the Greek world. We also insist that it is simply meaningless to claim that Demeter 'moved' to Ibiza and 'replaced Tanit', because that does not consider how and why these cult practices were passed on from Sicily or North Africa. Neither does it address what the combination of ritual practices might have meant in rural Ibiza, as the combination of features on many of the figurines and the introduction of new ritual activities suggest that the situation was rather complex.

Sardinia

The island of Sardinia was first settled by Phoenicians as early as the mid- to late eighth century BC, when a number of permanent settlements were established on the western and southern coasts, of which Sulcis, Tharros and Nora were the most important. Not only did all of these remain occupied throughout the Phoenician period into the Punic (and indeed Roman) periods but in their vicinity a dozen or so new and mostly smaller sites were subsequently also established. One of these was Karales (Cagliari) which eventually became the largest and most prominent settlement of Punic Sardinia. As in Ibiza, these colonial settlements developed increasingly intensive connections with Carthage from the mid-sixth century BC onwards, as is shown for instance by changes in mortuary practices involving Carthaginian-style rock-cut chamber tombs and the adoption of new types of domestic pottery and other items.[35]

While a few small sites had been established in the immediate vicinity of most of the larger settlements from the late seventh century BC onwards, it was not until two centuries later – again, like in Ibiza, from the end of the fifth century BC – that myriad small- to medium-sized rural sites of an evidently Punic nature were built throughout the inland areas of southern Sardinia to become a conspicuous feature of Punic Sardinia.

[35] See van Dommelen and Gómez Bellard 2008: 5–12 for Carthaginian influence in the central Mediterranean; Bartoloni 1981 and van Dommelen 1998a: 122–9 for the specific situation in Sardinia. For an overview of the earlier colonial history of Sardinia, see Bartoloni 2005 and Dyson and Rowland 2007: 102–26.

Part and parcel of this transformation of the Sardinian countryside was the appearance of a series of rural shrines that prominently featured ritual and votive elements associated with Demeter. In western and central Sardinia in particular, many of these small shrines were installed in *nuraghi*, the characteristically Sardinian prehistoric settlement towers, many of which by that time had lain abandoned for several centuries. The best documented example is that of *nuraghe* Genna Maria (Villanovaforru) in southern central Sardinia (Figure 9.4). Excavation of the site has shown that the courtyard of the *nuraghe* began to be used for ritual purposes from the late fourth century BC; by that time, both the tower and surrounding village had been abandoned for more than three centuries. The sanctuary remained in use until the fourth or fifth century AD.

When the *nuraghe* began to be used as a shrine, the original entry to the tower had already become blocked and the courtyard was by then only accessible from above. While it was open to the air, the former courtyard must have appeared as a deep and presumably quite dark cavity or underground chamber of up to three metres depth. It provided nevertheless the main ritual space for the Punic-period shrine and most if not all rituals were performed in this semi-underground area. These practices involved the regular lighting of a large open fire against one of the courtyard walls,

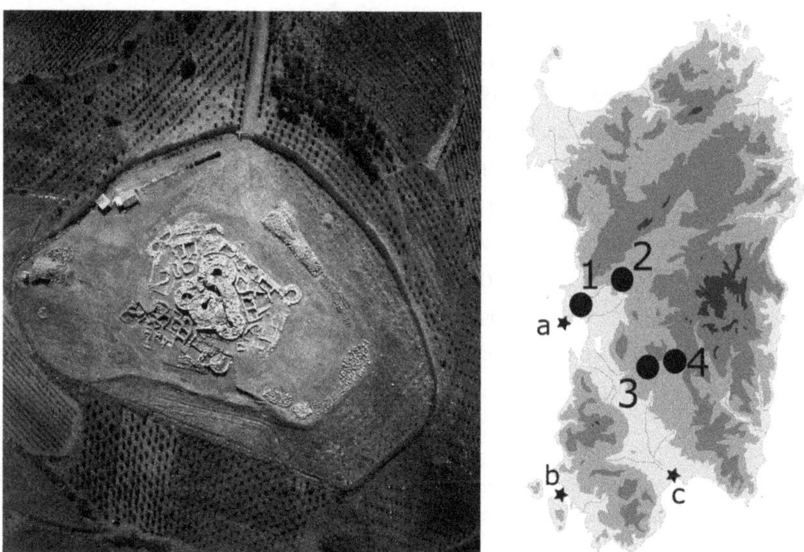

Figure 9.4 (a) Aerial photo of *nuraghe* Genna Maria (Villanovaforru). (b) Map of Sardinia showing the sites discussed; key: (1) Cuccuru s'Arriu; (2) *Nuraghe* Lugherras; (3) *Nuraghe* Genna Maria; (4) *Nuraghe* Su Mulinu; (a) Tharros; (b) Sulcis; (c) Cagliari.

presumably for burning offerings, although it would also have provided light. Animal offerings were an important feature of the rituals performed in the former courtyard, as is shown by the presence of a large number of burnt bones. The adjacent main tower of the *nuraghe*, the roof of which had remained intact and which could be entered through its original doorway from the courtyard area, was used for storage of the material offerings and other ritual items.[36]

The shrine at Genna Maria is generally identified as dedicated to Demeter because of the presence of at least sixteen incense burners, ten of which are in the shape of a female head wearing a *kalathos*. There are also several silver ears of grain, a gold mask and a small golden tiara that probably belonged to a ceramic figurine. Far more common, however, were coarse- and fine-ware ceramic vessels like bowls, plates and some amphorae, oil-lamps of various types (over 600), animal bones, mostly of sheep and goats, and coins (269). Both the lamps and incense burners show clear traces of use, suggesting that they had been lit and used during rituals in the courtyard before being stored in the adjacent chamber. The coins were primarily a later feature of the cult in Imperial Roman times, as no more than two Punic and twenty-five Roman Republican coins have been found. The oil-lamps are by contrast mostly Punic and Republican Roman types and their significance was therefore greatest in the earlier centuries of the cult.[37]

Similar contexts have been excavated at two other *nuraghi* in western and central Sardinia. The situation brought to light in 1906 at *nuraghe* Lugherras (Paulilatino) only differed from that of Genna Maria in specific details, such as the location of the main ritual space, which at Lugherras was not situated in the courtyard but in the first-floor room of the main tower. Unlike at Genna Maria, it possessed a modest altar. Like at Genna Maria, the lower room of the central tower was used as the votive deposit, despite the poor access through a steep and dark internal staircase. The deposit stands out in particular because of the large number of incense burners (520) and oil-lamps ('thousands') recovered. While the situation at *nuraghe* Su Mulinu (Villanovafranca)

[36] Although the excavations of the *nuraghe* and village have not been published, the Punic- and Roman-period sanctuary has been reported in good detail by Lilliu 1993b; see also van Dommelen 1997: 314–17. See Pala 1990 and Blake 1998 on reuse of *nuraghi* in the Iron Age and later.

[37] Only 17 per cent of the lamps are of Imperial date (Lilliu 1993a); the coins are presented by Guido 1993; Fonzo and Vigne 1993 discuss the bones, which amounted to 20 kg, of which 20 per cent was identifiable.

was again broadly comparable to that found at nearby Genna Maria, the crucial difference is that the Punic-period rituals were performed in a room that had already been the focus of cult activities during the Iron Age, possibly already since the Late Bronze Age (tenth or ninth century BC). The finds from this earlier context include, most significantly, a substantial number of Nuragic-style oil-lamps, including several bronze ones that show clear traces of use. Even if the *nuraghe* appears to have lain abandoned around the fifth and possibly part of the fourth century BC, the Iron Age ritual room was again used as a cult place from the fourth or third century BC onwards, and the continued use of the large Iron Age altar sculpted in the shape of a *nuraghe* suggests a certain degree of at least cultural continuity. While only a few fragments of incense burners in the shape of a female head were found, a significant (but unfortunately unspecified) number of oil-lamps of Punic and Roman types was recovered, alongside other items like silver ears of grain as known from Genna Maria.[38]

Elements associated with the Demeter cult have been found in other contexts as well, including in shrines installed in former Nuragic wells, most of which would have had a ritual function in the Late Bronze and Iron Ages. The best documented instance is that of Cuccuru s'Arriu, where a ritual area was created in front of the well by constructing a rectangular enclosure, which included a small altar. The finds from this site include fragments of incense burners in the shape of a female head as well as a range of ex-votos associated with healing. The faunal evidence that birds were the most common offerings is likely to be a local feature, because the site is situated in a large wetland between the Gulf of Oristano and a large lagoon.[39]

Surveying the evidence from Genna Maria, Lugherras and Su Mulinu in particular, it seems obvious that these rural cult places were far from conventional Demeter shrines and it is indeed questionable whether they may be interpreted as such at all. On the one hand, the people frequenting and worshipping at these sites were clearly familiar with at

[38] For Lugherras, see Taramelli 1910, whose report is summarised by Regoli 1991: 19–25; no further evidence is available for the lamps other than Taramelli's brief description. For Su Mulinu, see Ugas and Paderi 1990 and Ugas 1991; recent excavations (2005) as reported in *Fasti Online*, however, suggest continuous use of the ritual area: www.fastionline.org/record_view.php?fst_cd=AIAC_817 (accessed 30 May 2011).

[39] For Cuccuru s'Arriu, see Giorgetti 1982. For other relevant contexts, see Pirredda 1994; Garbati 2003: 128; van Dommelen and Finocchi 2008: 190–4; and Campanella and Garbati 2008: 15–23, 33–8.

least some aspects of the Demeter cult, including possibly her mythology, as is shown by the silver ears of grain and the small piglet from Genna Maria. On the other hand, the consistent presence of the female head-shaped incense burners points to a strong Punic cultural influence, as one might expect under Carthaginian rule. The picture is further complicated by the equally consistent and far more prominent presence of oil-lamps and the offering and consumption of sheep rather than pigs. While the oil-lamps might at first sight be explained in practical terms, as all three shrines were dark spaces, the careful storage of lamps at Genna Maria and Lugherras and the occurrence of oil-lamps in the Iron Age shrine of Su Mulinu suggest that they were of ritual significance. That suggestion is confirmed by the gradual replacement of the lamps with coins, as the latter could not replace the former in any practical role. No less pertinent is the evidence from Su Mulinu that the rituals involving oil-lamps predated the Punic-period activities, as this underscores their local significance.

The conventional interpretation of these rural shrines is that they represent the Demeter cult, which was introduced in the wake of the Carthaginian agrarian exploitation of the Sardinian countryside as if it were an 'ideology of agriculture'.[40] In a slightly different vein, it has also been represented as a popular cult brought to Sardinia by Punic immigrants from elsewhere in the Punic world, in particular North Africa. While the influence of local rituals and sites is underplayed in these views as merely facilitating the adoption of a new assumed 'Greek' cult, they are by contrast highlighted by others who propose that the innovations merely mask ritual and ideological continuities that may even be understood as 'ideological, religious and political resistance'.[41]

Both views, however, rely on the essentialist assumption that either the Demeter cult or the Nuragic rituals retained their 'original' meanings as they had been in Greek Sicily or during the Iron Age before the Carthaginian occupation. None of the proposed interpretations of the ritual sites therefore adequately address the questions of what the Punic-period rural cult sites and rituals meant in Sardinia and how we could understand their constitution in the context of the Sardinian countryside under Carthaginian domination.

[40] Xella 1969: 225 and Garbati 2003: 136–7, who emphasise the popular nature of the cult.

[41] Ugas and Paderi 1990: 482–3; they emphasise local continuity and resistance at Su Mulinu, while the significance of earlier cults at reused Nuragic sites is dismissed by Garbati 2003: 135–6.

Rural cult and ritual practice

Having discussed four Punic sites with evidence of an alleged Demeter cult in some detail, we hope to have demonstrated that interpretation of these contexts is less than straightforward and that their current representation is problematic; we would indeed say theoretically flawed. In the light of our theoretical discussion, the way forward to overcome the essentialist assumptions of most present views is to shift attention away from the deities that may or may not be identified at these cult places and to concentrate instead on the ritual practices that people engaged in when they frequented these sites.

In practical terms, this concerns the meaning of items and practices from different backgrounds in one and the same place. The question is not so much whether Demeter stayed Greek or how she became Punic, if not Ibizan or Sardinian; but rather how might those incense burners have been seen in Sardinia? Can we say anything about the people who were involved in their distribution? The starting-point has always been that the official introduction of the Demeter cult in 396 BC was the result of Carthaginian state and/or elite intervention and that its popularity in the Punic world was a direct result of state-sponsored promotion. But the Sardinian evidence has usually been interpreted otherwise, emphasising the popular or non-elite and less than 'regularly Punic' nature of the cult.

As an alternative starting-point, we go back to the local archaeological evidence from Ibiza and Sardinia and ask what these material remains can tell us about what people actually did at those sites between the fourth and second century BC.

Ritualisation

For a start, what do we mean when we speak of ritual activities? Traditionally, rituals have been presented as irrational and odd activities that are fundamentally different from daily domestic activities. Like culture, ritual has mostly been studied in isolation, as if it were a self-contained and well-defined entity. Ritual has indeed long been treated as a heading under which anything unusual or irrational could be grouped together and explained away. As a consequence, rituals often appear to be remarkably universal: as highly formal, repetitive, mechanical and instinctive actions they are mostly thought of as being outside regular time and space, which in turn is likely to have encouraged essentialist assumptions about ritual meanings.

Because such a perspective prevents us from seeing rituals as specific activities and as part of their social context, anthropologist Catherine Bell has proposed the concept of ritualisation to describe ritual in terms of contextualised practices. Following Bourdieu's 'theory of practice', she sees practice or human activities in general as strategies for reproducing and reformulating cultural settings and defines ritualisation as the process or social strategy by which certain activities or performances are set apart from regular everyday practice. As the concept also enables us to explore to what extent and how ritual practice is or has become different from other practices, daily practice in particular, ritualisation offers a conceptual tool for (re)contextualising ritual in its social context and reconnecting it to contemporary practices of everyday life.

According to Bell, ritualisation is in fact the only thing that rituals have in common and that sets them apart from everyday activities. In all other respects, rituals are related to everyday life and one could think of rituals as specific actions that for various reasons are exaggerated or highlighted. In the end, however, they still only make sense when considered in relation to their wider setting. A good example is food and eating, as many ritual contexts have yielded evidence of food processing and consumption, such as bones and cooking and eating vessels. Preparing and consuming food are some of the most basic human subsistence activities but in ritual contexts these normally very mundane acts are set apart by stressing and indeed exaggerating certain aspects such as ostentatiously sharing food with other people and divinities ('commensality') or preparing it in unusual ways.[42]

Rituals are therefore not odd experiences but on the contrary very concrete practices that people carry out in well-defined contexts. As they are performed by specific individuals or groups of people at a given time and place in a particular setting, a critical feature of ritualisation is constituted by the material culture involved, including the participants' bodies and the ritual spaces. People, for instance, perform rituals with and through their bodies by singing, praying, walking, or indeed lighting an oil-lamp, which are all highly visible ways of creating and maintaining rituals – hence Bell's emphasis on 'embodied

[42] See C. Bell 1992, 1997; in archaeological terms, Bradley 2003: 12–13; 2005: 1–120; Blake 2005: 104–6; and López-Bertran 2007; see also discussions in Kyriakidis 2007 and Fogelin 2007.

knowledge'.[43] At the same time, by walking along a given route or by lighting their lamps in a specific room, these spaces are ritualised and become cult places set aside but yet still part of the wider landscape.[44]

In the following section, we will use this concept to take a fresh look at the objects that have usually been taken as evidence of a 'Demeter cult', and to explore their significance as elements actively used by people in Ibiza and Sardinia to construct their rituals.

Contextualising rural cult

In terms of ritualisation and ritual practice, there are three elements that stand out at the four sites in Ibiza and Sardinia – in addition to the fact that items and rituals conventionally associated with Demeter have been found at all four of them. The oil-lamps are perhaps the most prominent feature, even though they are absent at Es Culleram. Shared by all four sites are the butchering, preparation and consumption of sheep and the physical setting of the sites themselves: not only are all sites an integral part of a rural landscape that was intensively inhabited and exploited for agricultural purposes, but they are also situated in the deep and dark spaces of a cave or something very similar like an abandoned *nuraghe*. The incense burners are less significant in this respect, because they are specialised items that are less often used outside ritual contexts, if at all.

The landscape setting is particularly noteworthy, as it is shared by all sites. The observation that the ritual sites were inaugurated roughly around the same time that the first Punic rural settlement sites were established is especially significant, as it demonstrates that these sites were fully integrated in the rural settlement system and, moreover, that their presence was important to the inhabitants of the first Punic-style farms in both Sardinia and Ibiza; in other words, inhabiting and working the land 'in the Punic way' apparently involved frequenting a ritual site that was situated beyond but still close to agricultural land (high up on a hill or mountain slope) and that was dark and penetrated deep into the land.

[43] C. Bell 1992: 107; see Garcia-Ventura and López-Bertran 2009 for an archaeological case-study.

[44] See López-Bertran 2011 for an archaeological case-study.

It remains nevertheless a fundamental difference between Sardinia and Ibiza that the inhabitants of the latter island's countryside were all newcomers who settled into a landscape that had hitherto remained empty, while the Sardinian countryside had been occupied for millennia; a substantial portion of the rural Sardinians are likely to have been of local descent and even if some of the rural inhabitants in Sardinia may have been new settlers, they encountered a landscape that was full of traces of earlier and contemporary occupation.[45]

The clear preference for a dark and underground space fits neatly in this context, as it sets the places for ritual activities clearly apart from the other sites in the rural settlement pattern. The use of *nuraghi* for such spaces is a uniquely Sardinian feature, if only because similar megalithic constructions are rare elsewhere and non-existent in Ibiza. In Sardinia, however, the reuse of internal rooms is particularly significant because *nuraghi* and some other types of Nuragic monuments did generally remain closely associated with Punic rural settlements in the interior of the island. The critical distinctive element is that neither the tower nor any of its minor rooms were normally reoccupied as domestic spaces, as, in all instances on record, Punic-period occupation of a *nuraghe* concerned structures built around the tower (the so-called 'village'). During the Punic period, there thus existed a notable preference in central Sardinia for settlements to be closely associated with a *nuraghe*. The towers themselves, however, were apparently not deemed suitable for habitation, as they had been for millennia, and they were exclusively reused for ritual purposes: this distinction suggests that their reuse may be seen as an instance of ritualisation, in this particular case of a rural site or place.[46]

Beyond Sardinia, the use of dark spaces for ritual practices may in itself also be regarded in terms of ritualisation, as moving underground everyday activities from the open air, such as preparing and consuming food, adds to setting them apart and making them special. Caves and similar deep, dark 'chthonic' spaces have indeed been used as cult places since early prehistory, presumably because of their liminal position between the upper world of the living and the lower world so often

[45] Gómez Bellard 2008b: 72–3 and van Dommelen and Finocchi 2008: 194–6 discuss the relevant archaeological evidence in detail. See van Dommelen *et al.* 2007: 61–2 for other cult places in relation to rural settlement sites in west central Sardinia.

[46] For an overview, see Pala 1990 and van Dommelen and Finocchi 2008: 194–6, while van Dommelen 1998b: 598–9 and Blake 1998: 62–3 discuss the reuse in the wider landscape context.

associated with death. The secretive nature of these secluded spaces is another element to consider.[47]

The animal bones are the only remains of the food-related activities carried out at the cult places and thus only give a partial view. A shift from everyday to ritual practices may nevertheless be discerned, as the animals butchered and consumed did not include pig at all, which otherwise featured regularly in people's diets, alongside sheep and goat. The cremation of certain parts of the animals, in particular the heads, as an offering to the god(s), is also a clearly distinctive activity. The absence of pig is particularly noteworthy, as it is in line with Phoenician-Punic ritual practices, in which pigs were taboo, but it contrasts explicitly with Greek rituals in honour of Demeter.[48]

The oil-lamps, finally, stand out as the most remarkable feature of the Sardinian sites. They provide a straightforward example of ritualisation, as a very common utilitarian object of everyday life was ritualised and transformed into a key feature of a prominent ritual practice; the objects themselves remained sacred as a consequence and could not simply be discarded once the ritual had taken place, but had to be carefully stored at the cult site. The latter fact confirms that the oil-lamps were not just functional objects for lighting up the rituals. It is on the contrary precisely because the darkness of the ritual places required oil-lamps and/or torches that they could become ritualised.

Reconceptualising Punic Demeter

The oil-lamps and absence of pig finally bring us back to Demeter and the question of the introduction of her cult in the Punic world, whether at the expense of local deities or not. Oil-lamps and torches are important and prominent features at Greek cult places dedicated to Demeter, as is abundantly clear from the *c.* 32,000 lamps recovered in the Malaphoros sanctuary of Selinunte in Sicily.[49] Their absence from

[47] See Whitehouse 1992 and Blake 2005 for a general discussion in relation to (central) Mediterranean prehistory. It is worth noting that there are at least two Sardinian caves with remains of Punic-period ritual activities involving oil-lamps; both are, however, poorly published: van Dommelen and Finocchi 2008: 192–3.

[48] The faunal evidence from Es Culleram has been analysed by Morales Pérez 2003, who also considers the evidence in a wider Mediterranean context, both ritual and domestic. On the consumption of pork, see Campanella 2008: 68; cf. Campanella and Zamora López 2010.

[49] Lamps are relatively unusual before the mid-sixth century BC at Selinunte and elsewhere in Sicily: Hermanns 2004: 102–12.

Ibiza is therefore remarkable. Equally worth noting, given the conspicuous presence of common types of oil-lamps, is the absence in Sardinia of the special multi-nozzle lamps which, as noted above, form a typical part of the ritual assemblage of Demeter cult in most parts of the Mediterranean. Since oil-lamps were already used in ritual practices in Sardinia, however, they may nevertheless have served as a *trait d'union* between the Sardinian and Sicilian cults and to have encouraged people familiar with both islands to introduce other elements associated with Demeter to the Sardinian sites, too.

That does not mean that 'Demeter took over Sardinia' – or Ibiza for that matter – as is quite clear from the absence of pig in the faunal evidence and the invariably much higher numbers of oil-lamps as compared to items associated with Demeter. Because meaning is not inherent in objects but constructed within its local context, as we argued above, this suggests that the Greek-style *thymiateria* in the shrines did not necessarily denote the Demeter cult and its mythology. One *thymiaterion* from Es Culleram, for instance, was made in the style of the winged figurines that represent Tanit rather than the typical Demeter shape.[50] The offering of birds in the Cuccurus' Arriu shrine underscores this point, as it offers yet another example of ritualisation in local terms: in the Cabras wetlands, birds were a common feature of everyday life and presumably of people's diet, and it is therefore no surprise that the preparation and consumption of these animals were ritualised.[51]

A final remark concerns the often-made comment that the rituals of the Sardinian sanctuaries point to a fertility cult. In reality, however, there is precious little evidence to support such a claim. This view is presumably based on the association made between Demeter and chthonic cult places and the generic assumption of an 'ideology of agriculture'. In the light of our arguments about locally constructed meanings and local ritualisation of practices, however, there is no good reason to maintain that point. While the rural character of the cult is beyond question, it is in the end only a small number of silver ears of grain that explicitly refer to agriculture, and their precise meaning remains difficult to ascertain. The faunal remains from Es Culleram, however, suggest that it may be possible to understand fertility in a

[50] Marín Ceballos *et al.* 2010: 147–8.

[51] A similar case is the Punic sanctuary at La Algaida near Cádiz (Sanlúcar de Barrameda, Andalusia), where mostly shellfish and fish were offered: Corzo 2000; López-Bertran 2007.

wider sense, as the teeth of the animals offered in the cave show that they were sacrificed during the months of February and March. It has been suggested that these sacrifices would have celebrated the rebirth of nature at the end of winter and the beginning of spring.[52]

The rural and local character of all four sites is key to understanding the nature of the distribution of these Demeter elements. Because all the Sardinian shrines and Es Culleram in Ibiza are small installations in remote places with modest offerings, they lend little support to the view that the Demeter cult was spread through the Punic world as a state-sponsored and coherent, let alone monolithic, cult. Its introduction in Carthage in 396 BC may well have been state- and elite-sponsored, as the written sources claim, but elsewhere the archaeological evidence is incompatible with such a formal dispersion beyond Carthage. Given the frequent presence in Sardinia of amphorae and perhaps fine-wares of Sicilian and South Italian production (especially Greco-Italic amphorae), it is quite likely that a direct 'Sicilian connection' rather than the 'state route' via Carthage represented the main way by which elements of the Demeter cult were distributed.[53]

To conclude, we contend that the Greek-style *thymiateria* and other items usually connected with the cult of Demeter and Kore do *not* imply the adoption of Greek traditions and rituals in Sardinia and Ibiza.[54] They do of course indicate contacts with the Greek world and leave no doubt that these may have been quite intensive at that, but our detailed analysis of four Punic contexts in Ibiza and Sardinia shows that it was only specific elements of the 'original' Demeter cult in Greece and Sicily that were adopted for particular local reasons. It is also evident that these new elements were subsumed in and integrated with locally existing traditions and that both were transformed in the process.

Conclusions: Hellenism as subaltern practice

If we lastly look beyond these four sites in Ibiza and Sardinia and consider the question of 'Greek influences' and Hellenism in the western

[52] Costa Ribas 2007: 18.

[53] See Garbati 2003: 136–7; Peri 2003: 145–7; and Campanella and Garbati 2008: 41–5 on Demeter worship as a popular cult.

[54] Bonnet 2006b: 374 goes so far as to call that view even 'abusif' and rightly refers to rituals 'à la mode grecque'.

Mediterranean at large, we suggest that there is good reason to reject the conventional view of a gradual but profound transformation of the Punic world into a homogeneous Hellenic culture. While Greek material culture was no doubt widely distributed across the Mediterranean and beyond and became increasingly widespread from the fourth century BC or so, the archaeological evidence does not support the conclusion that Greek culture became dominant; on the contrary, both theoretical arguments and detailed analysis of the archaeological remains lead to the conclusion that if economic and cultural interaction intensified from the fifth to fourth centuries BC onward, it did so within specific local and regional contexts on local terms and with the active involvement of local inhabitants.

In other words, many, if not most, of the allegedly 'Greek' objects found beyond the Greek heartlands were *not* strictly associated with Greek traditions and mythology in the perception of local inhabitants in most of the Mediterranean; that close association is by contrast a creation of modern Western scholarship. Instead, we argue, the meanings and significance of these objects may be found in the specific contexts in which the items were used by local people, because it was these people who created these contexts in line with their own local norms and customs and who constructed new meanings for new objects in new contexts. To return once more to Sardinia, it is therefore in our view not so much the female head-shaped incense burners that are critical for understanding the sites discussed but rather the oil-lamps and the ritual spaces, because these related to local customs of everyday life.

Given the rural nature of the ritual contexts in which these elements of the Demeter cult were adopted and adapted, it is surely significant to note the rural dimension of these shrines and to underline what we see as the peasant character of this instance of 'Greek-style' Punic culture. Precisely because of the local and rural nature of the ritualisation processes that we traced in Ibiza and Sardinia, including a likely direct 'Sicilian connection', we would like to present these rural shrines as evidence of peasant or, more appropriately, 'subaltern' practices. We use this term advisedly, as it brings out on the one hand the local and non-elite nature of these practices, but on the other hand also captures their connections and connotations within Sardinian society and indeed with the wider Punic and Greek worlds.[55]

[55] Borrowed from Antonio Gramsci's work, the term 'subaltern' has become a critical concept in post-colonial thinking to highlight alternative and non-elite perspectives and experiences and to

Taking into account local involvement and hybrid practices, as we have proposed, shifts attention away from debates about Hellenism and Hellenisation in generalising terms, cutting these terms down to size and exposing their lack of explanatory value. While our approach does not diminish the distribution and influence of Greek culture across the Mediterranean in the broadest sense of the term, it opens the way, we argue, for understanding the historical and archaeological contexts in which such influences worked, impacted and interacted.

explore the question 'Can the subaltern speak?' (Spivak 1985). See M. Green 2002 and Chattopadhyay and Sarkar 2005.

10 | Were the Iberians Hellenised?

SIMON KEAY

Both 'Hellenisation' and 'Romanisation' in the western Mediterranean have been the object of many key studies in recent years, with work moving on from the traditional focus on central and southern Italy[1] to considerations of the western Mediterranean as a whole.[2] The critical debate has centred upon the asymmetries implied in both terms, as well as the general argument that in the central and western Mediterranean at least 'Hellenisation' is more to do with changes in the cultural sphere, while 'Romanisation' during the middle and later Republican periods is primarily to do with conquest and political changes. Rather less attention has been directed towards relationships between Greek and Carthaginian and/or Punic cultures, and their impact upon local populations.[3]

In Spanish and Portuguese scholarship, the term 'Hellenisation' has been used to describe Greek influence as manifested in ceramics and metalwork, sculpture, architecture, burial rituals and monetary systems, primarily in eastern, but also in southern Iberia, primarily from the sixth to the third centuries BC.[4] The term 'Punic' is also used fairly loosely to refer to a range of cultural attributes in south-eastern and southern Spain from the fifth century BC onwards, having a particular relevance following the conquest of the region by Carthage in the late third century BC.[5] Since these 'Punic' attributes betray both Hellenised and North African traits, their significance is unclear, not least because they become especially visible after the sack of Carthage in 146 BC. By contrast, 'Romanisation' is often invoked by scholars to describe the gradual appearance of political, linguistic, architectural and artistic traits among the Iberian peoples following their conquest by Rome in the late third and earlier second centuries BC, becoming clearest

1 Zanker 1976a.

2 See for example Curti *et al.* 1996; Keay and Terrenato 2001 among many others.

3 See however Lancel 1995: 303–60.

4 Such as García y Bellido 1948; Almagro-Gorbea 1990; Jaeggi 1999; papers in Cabrera Bonet and Sánchez Fernández 2002, etc.

5 Bendala Galán 2000.

in eastern Iberia from the later second century onwards, and in the south somewhat later.[6]

The positivist tradition of seeking to ascribe elements of clearly non-local material culture, whether ceramics, sculpture or architecture, to 'Hellenised', 'Punic' or 'Roman' traditions, influence and settlement is deep-seated, but this article will question its validity in the context of the cultural *koine* that developed across the Mediterranean in the course of the fourth, third and second centuries BC. The approach will be to contrast the differing ways in which a range of peoples, who were already known to the Greek-speaking world, became familiar with aspects of a range of what are often considered 'Hellenised' cultural languages and chose to react to conquest and political integration, initially by a 'Hellenised' Carthage, and shortly afterwards by a 'Hellenised' Rome.[7] These complex cultural interrelationships are explored in the context of the urbanisation of the Iberian peoples of southern and eastern Spain between the later third and later second centuries BC, and of their contacts with the world beyond their shores. This horizon bridges the latter part of the so-called 'High Period' of Iberian culture and encompasses the immediate aftermath of the conquest of southern Iberia by the Barcids and the subsequent incorporation of all the Iberian peoples into the Roman Empire. The chapter concludes by arguing that the question as to whether or not the Iberians were 'Hellenised' is misplaced. While it cannot be denied that 'Hellenised', 'Punicised' and 'Romanised' cultural symbols and traits are present, one needs rather to ask why Iberian societies chose to adopt them, whether it was by means of individuals attempting to emulate power systems elsewhere in the Mediterranean, or as a reflection of state choices in the context of local and regional power strategies.[8]

The cultural context of the Iberians

The Mediterranean coast between the Hérault and Straits of Gibraltar (Figure 10.1) is generally understood as having been inhabited by peoples

[6] There have been numerous studies from a very broad range of archaeological, historical and artistic perspectives impossible to summarise here. However, Bendala Galán 2006 provides a useful starting point for understanding the background to contemporary Spanish attitudes to Romanisation: see also Keay 2001, and papers in Van Dommelen and Terrenato 2007.

[7] They are mentioned by Greek writers from the end of the sixth century BC onwards – see Domínguez Monedero 1983; Gómez Espelosín *et al.* 1995: 26–62; papers in Mangas and Plácido Suárez 1999; Plácido Suárez 2002; Moret 2006.

[8] I am grateful to Ricardo Olmos and Andrew Wallace-Hadrill for kindly reading and commenting upon on an earlier draft of this paper.

Figure 10.1 Map of principal cultural regions and peoples in eastern and southern Spain between the later sixth and later third centuries BC.

known collectively to the Greek writers as Iberians (οἱ Ἴβηρες) who had been exposed to direct and indirect Greek and east Mediterranean influences some 200 years before the creation of the Hellenistic kingdoms in the East.[9] Phoenician and Greek colonies in the south and north-east[10] were instrumental in the circulation of a complex blend of eastern Mediterranean ideas and imports among indigenous communities from at least the seventh century BC onwards,[11] which together with pre-existing indigenous Late Bronze Age traditions, formed the cultural context out of which the Iberians were to develop in the course of the sixth and fifth centuries BC onwards.[12] The

[9] See the works cited in n.7 (supra).

[10] On Phoenician and Greek colonies, see respectively Aubet 2001; Rouillard 1991.

[11] Traditionally ascribed to Semitic or Phoenician and Greek influence: see respectively the general works by Escacena and Belén Deamos 1998; Rouillard 1991; Cabrera Bonet 1986; Olmos 1986; Domínguez Monedero and Sánchez 2001.

[12] The cultural development of the Iberians is usually subdivided into a number of chronological periods. These are the result of attempts to systematise disparate data across large geographical areas and should only be regarded as notional, such as the Antiguo (Early), Pleno (High) and

principal focus of these 'orientalising' cultures in Iberia was Tartessos in the south-west, although there were also profound changes in the political, religious, social and artistic lives of the indigenous communities elsewhere.[13] Following the disintegration of Tartessos in the sixth century BC, markedly hierarchical societies emerged between the fifth and later third centuries BC.[14] Iberian communities in south-west, south-east and eastern Iberia,[15] and in the Balearic Islands[16] developed their own regional dynamics that drew differentially upon continued Greek influences as well as those from a growing Punic presence in the south-western Mediterranean. However, they shared elements of a common material culture with varying degrees of overseas cultural influence, as well as increasingly pronounced evidence of Greek ideas in urban layout and architecture in differentiated regional contexts. This is particularly clearly reflected in the various 'Iberian' scripts, ceramic types and decoration, and sculptures, which all embody complex balances between elements of similarity and regional differences.[17] In view of all these developments it is clear that a long-term perspective is crucial if we are to understand the relevance of Greek, 'Hellenising' and other influences to the Iberian peoples of the third and second centuries BC.

While the Iberians were peripheral to Italy and the principal arenas of 'Hellenisation' in the central Mediterranean, they played a crucial role as a cultural bridge between peoples of central Iberia, whose culture was more akin to the La Tène traditions of south-central France to the north, and peoples in the south who shared similarities with the peoples of Punic North Africa. Considerable fieldwork, historical analysis, artefactual studies and syntheses over the last forty years have transformed our understanding of the Iberians.[18]

By the later third century BC, Greek and Roman writers were loosely referring to the peoples of the Mediterranean coast as 'Iberians' (Figure 10.2).[19] Furthermore, Roman-period sources contemporary to, or writing about, the later third and second centuries BC, mention a range of

Baja (Low); see for example the schemes of Ruiz Rodríguez and Molinos 1998; Almagro-Gorbea 1996; Jaeggi 1999.

[13] For Tartessos see papers in Aubet 1989.

[14] The best introductions are to be found in Ruiz Rodríguez and Molinos 1985, 1998; Aranegui 1998.

[15] See specifically Almagro-Gorbea 1996 and regional studies of eastern Iberia in the Iron Age in Almagro-Gorbea and Ruiz Zapatero 1993.

[16] See particularly through the medium of the late seventh-century BC Punic colony at Ebussus (Eivissa): Costa Ribas *et al.* 1991; for Mallorca see Guerrero Ayuso *et al.* 2007.

[17] For scripts see J. De Hoz 1998a; for ceramics see Bonet Rosado and Mata 2008; for sculptures see León Alonso 1998.

[18] Arribas 1965; Ruiz Rodríguez and Molinos 1998.

[19] Gómez Espelosín *et al.* 1995: 26–65.

Figure 10.2 Map of the principal sites mentioned in the text.

distinct Iberian peoples such as the Contestani, Edetani, Ilergetes and Cossetani, whose precise location is uncertain and who cannot be readily reconciled with regional differences in archaeological evidence.[20] At one level, they provide us with clues about their social and political organisation at around that time. One wonders, however, the extent to which the names that have come down to us reflect the self-perception of the peoples concerned, perception by Rome, or somehow embody attempts by different groupings to distance themselves from each other and Rome within the context of Roman administrative control.

Notwithstanding this evidence, there has been a tendency to posit the existence of an Iberian 'culture' largely as a result of the work of the early twentieth century, such as Bosch Gimpera,[21] who drew upon philological, archaeological and artistic material, and which has come to dominate our understanding ever since.[22] However, detailed analyses of 'Iberian'

[20] See for example Tovar 1974, 1989. [21] Bosch Gimpera 1915.
[22] Olmos 1998a is a useful introduction to this issue.

settlement patterns and material culture make it clear that important regional differences belied some of these similarities.[23] At the very least these suggest that rather than seeing the 'Iberians' as a single people, there is much to be gained from understanding them to have been a range of peoples whose cultural characteristics embodied a tension between regionally specific traditions and cultural traits in which external Mediterranean influences played a key role.

The 'Hellenisation' of the Iberians between the later third and later second centuries BC

The Iberian communities came into direct contact with the broader Hellenised Mediterranean for the first time during the 'Low' or 'Late' Iberian horizon of the third to first centuries BC.[24] They were initially confronted by the expansion of Carthage into southern Spain in 237 BC and were subsequently drawn into the struggle between Carthaginians and Romans between 218 and 206 BC.[25] Details of this process are well known historically, and have been the subject of a number of important recent archaeological studies, and while it would be interesting to explore the relationship between cultural change and the establishment of military and political control by Carthage and Rome, this lies beyond the scope of this paper.[26] Instead, it attempts to gauge how far the Iberians could be considered to have been incorporated within the broader cultural *koine* of the Hellenised Mediterranean.

[23] Best exemplified by the range of papers in Almagro-Gorbea and Ruiz Zapatero 1993.

[24] While this horizon has not traditionally exercised the same degree of interest for scholars as earlier periods (see, however, AA. VV. 1979), the academic divide between protohistory and Roman studies has narrowed (see Abad Casal 2003a, for example).

[25] While the suggestion by Chaves Tristán (1990) that hoards of Carthaginian coinage at Iberian sites in southern Spain are evidence of Carthaginian garrisons is attractive, it has yet to be supported by other kinds of evidence.

[26] The best discussion of the broader context of Carthaginian imperialism remains Whittaker 1978. Bendala Galán 2000 provides a good introduction for the archaeological evidence for the Carthaginian conquest and impact. See J. Richardson 1986 for historical issues surrounding the struggle between Rome and Carthage in Iberia and the early stages of Roman occupation. Cadiou 2008 provides a good analysis of the Roman conquest in the context of the development of the Roman army itself; see also Cadiou 2003. East Mediterranean and Punic influences upon Iberian fortifications are discussed in Moret 1996: 189–222.

Commercial contacts

A traditional measure of this has been to consider the ceramic evidence. Analysis of material from a range of Iberian, Roman and some Carthaginian settlements on the one hand points to the continuation of many, but not all, pre-existing connections with parts of the central and eastern Mediterranean, while on the other there was a gradual reorientation of emphasis towards the Italian peninsula during the period that Roman hegemony was established throughout the western Mediterranean, as can be attested in Africa and elsewhere.[27] Evidence of the former can be found in the ceramics of Phoenicio-Punic tradition that were imported by communities in southern Iberia from Gadir, southern Spain and elsewhere in the central and south-western Mediterranean down until the end of the first century BC.[28] Ceramics of central Italian and Magna Graecian origin, by contrast, only began to be imported from the later fourth and third centuries BC onwards.[29] However they increased in volume throughout the later third and second centuries BC when black gloss and Megarian finewares, Greco-Italic and Dressel 1 amphorae and metalwork appeared at a range of sites along the whole of the Mediterranean coast of Iberia,[30] mediated by the presence of trading communities at Ebussus[31] and such major centres of Roman power as Emporion, Tarraco, Carthago Nova and Gades. The volume of Italic imports to communities in south-western Spain, however, may have been lower.[32] They are present, for example, at Córdoba[33] and a range of Iberian sites in the Guadalquivir valley.[34]

The proportion of these ceramics to other locally produced ceramics in these assemblages was small and it is important not to over-estimate their cultural significance. In time, however, they began to have an impact upon

[27] While the presence of Italic pottery is taken by some as implicit evidence for the 'Hellenisation' of the Iberians, there is a need to think also about it being used in the context of Iberian dining and other social rituals (Principal 2006); see van Dommelen and López-Bertran, Chapter 9 in this volume, for similar reflections on usages of 'Greek' cultural artefacts in the western Mediterranean islands.

[28] Pliego Vázquez 2003: 46–8. [29] Jaeggi 1999: Karte 2 and 3.

[30] Iberian sites: Sanmartí Grego 2000: 316–19; Molina Vidal 1997: 175–87; Cabrera Bonet 2004: 8; Mansel 2004.

[31] The discovery of coins from a range of mints along the Mediterranean coast of Iberia at Ebussus is further evidence for commercial contacts between these two areas during the second and first centuries BC (Campo 1976; Ripollès 1982: 460–9 and Mapa 42).

[32] M. Beltrán Lloris 1990: Figs. 6 and 7; Jaeggi 1999: Karte 8. [33] Ventura Martínez 1996.

[34] Ventura Martínez 2001; López Palomo 1999; Vaquerizo Gil *et al.* 2001: 71–8.

regional ceramic industries, which began to imitate Italian finewares, coarsewares and amphorae.[35]

Urban development

Large centralised towns with ample evidence for political and economic activity at the head of a marked settlement hierarchy are a hallmark of the Hellenistic period in the east and central Mediterranean from the fourth century BC onwards. In Iberia, few towns came anywhere near to this kind of cultural achievement prior to the widespread adoption of Roman building types that began[36] during the period of cultural renewal under Augustus.[37] Indeed most seem to have been instead unstructured interpretations by Iberian élites of Hellenised ideas in strongly regional cultural contexts.

Some of the best evidence comes from eastern Spain. Tarraco (Tarragona), for example, only gradually developed an urban identity. The initial late third-century BC hilltop settlement, which overlooked an Iberian coastal centre, was no more than a strategic base with fortifications (Figure 10.3) that can be paralleled in Latium Vetus and Sicily.[38] The two were not amalgamated into a single urban unit until the end of the second century BC.[39] Even then, however, Tarraco, like most towns in Citerior, did not issue coins bearing its Latin name until the Augustan period.[40] It was the Iberian element of the community that minted silver and bronze coins bearing fairly homogeneous obverse and reverse types depicting the head of a youth and galloping

[35] See for example Pérez Ballester 2008: 263–74.

[36] Note however the appearance of Italic-style buildings in newly founded settlements along the Catalan coast and the lower Ebro Valley in the late second and early first centuries BC and discussed by Keay 2007 among others.

[37] An issue which, in the context of Iberia, was first explored by a number of papers in Trillmich and Zanker 1990, many of whose chronological interpretations have been overtaken by the results of more recent excavations and analyses.

[38] Gros 1996: 43–4. The contemporary relief of Minerva (and short Latin dedication to Men(e)rva by M'. Vibius) which still adorns the Torre de Minerva is clearly Roman/Italian in style even though it has been suggested that there may be some Iberian influence in some of its decorative details (generally see Grünhagen 1976–7; Alföldy 1981; Rodà de Llanza 1998: 268–9).

[39] The clearest manifestation of this was the extension of the Roman wall on the hill to enclose the Iberian settlement (discussed by Ruiz de Arbulo 2007: 37–9), as well as the construction of a Roman temple within the Iberian settlement (Ruiz de Arbulo *et al.* 2006).

[40] Villaronga 1994 remains the most comprehensive treatment of these, and indeed coins issued elsewhere in the Iberian peninsula; Untermann 1995a provides a useful commentary. The situation in Citerior stands in contrast to the towns of Ulterior which had issued coins with Latin legends since the second century BC.

Figure 10.3 The third-century BC fortification at Tarraco showing a relief of the goddess Minerva.

Figure 10.4 Bronze coin of *KESE* issued by Tarraco (Villaronga 1994: 162 no. 34). Obv.: male head (r.), wearing cloak and fibula, club behind; rev.: horse and rider bearing palm branch (r.), below the legend *KESE*.

horseman, as well as the legends *TARAKONSALIR* and later *KESE* (Figure 10.4).[41] However, these images, like those on many issues minted by other Iberian and Celtiberian communities, were localised interpretations of widespread Hellenistic-period imagery that were acceptable to, or even indeed promoted by, Rome.

Little is known about the layout of the original mid-sixth-century BC town of Emporion, although recent research suggests that its later topography, with agora, temples and walls, which was Greek in inspiration,

[41] Villaronga 1983.

Figure 10.5 Aerial photo showing the main area of the Greek settlement at Emporion, known as the 'neapolis' to archaeologists, seen from the south-west. Although many of the visible structures date to the Roman Republican and Imperial periods, many of the street alignments follow the line of the Greek antecedents, and the area of the agora can be clearly seen as a grey area in the middle background. Beyond lies a mole belonging to the port area.

was the result of considerable rebuilding during the second century BC (Figure 10.5).[42] This strong Greek tradition is echoed by its coinage. Following a brief interval (late fourth to later third centuries BC) during which Emporion issued silver coinage with obverse (Persephone) and reverse (horse) types that shadow Carthaginian issues, there was a resumption of minting types that advertised the Greek symbols of Emporion, the head of Artemis (obverse) and winged Pegasus (reverse) down until the early second century BC.[43] These were subsequently replaced by bronze coins bearing the legend *UNTIKESKEN* in Iberian, rather than *EMPORITON* in Greek, presumably referring to the Iberians in the hinterland of the town, which continued well into the first century BC, even though the reverse still bore the characteristic winged Pegasus of Emporion.[44] Such interplay between Greek and Iberian cultural forms is echoed by burial rites from cemeteries bordering the town from the early second century BC onwards.[45]

[42] Aquilué *et al.* 2007: 21–4. [43] Villaronga 1994: 17–30. [44] Villaronga 1994: 140–51.
[45] López Borgoñoz 1998: 276–87.

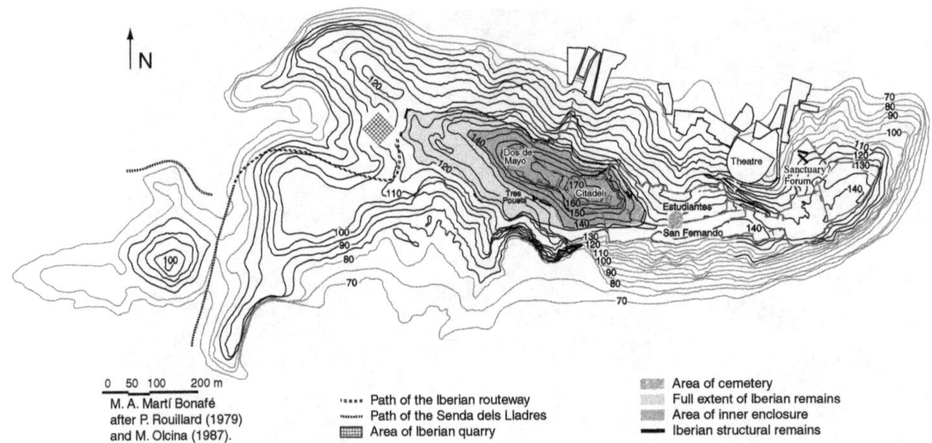

Figure 10.6 Plan of Roman buildings within the Iberian settlement at Saguntum.

Arse-Saguntum (Sagunto) comes closest to the Hellenised towns known from other parts of the Mediterranean. It was an Iberian centre of considerable antiquity with close links to Rome that had played a pivotal role in the struggle between Rome and Carthage in eastern Iberia from 219 BC onwards.[46] Following its capture from the Carthaginians by Scipio in 212 BC, the Iberian walled centre on the western summit of the prominent hill of El Castell was extended and rebuilt, rather than being moved on to lower-lying land as in the case of other Iberian settlements. Furthermore, the site of a small sanctuary on the eastern summit was obliterated with the construction of a suite of buildings that have been interpreted as a temple, possibly associated with a Hercules cult, and the forum of the town (Figure 10.6).[47]

This topographic transformation has been interpreted as commemorating the refoundation of a town that had been loyal to Rome as well as maintaining links with an historic past.[48] The latter may have been formalised in some kind of foundation legend. By the end of the Republic and beginning of the early Imperial period, Silius Italicus and Dionysius of Halicarnassus had written Saguntum into the broader mythology of the Graeco-Roman world, with Strabo suggesting that the Saguntines originated from the town of Zakynthos.[49] The voluminous issues of Saguntine silver and bronze coinage may be evidence of a conscious link to this Iberian past, with the name *ARSITKAR* in Iberian appearing down to the later second century BC, and only gradually giving way to the use of *ARSE*,

[46] Jacob 1989 discusses relevant texts. [47] Aranegui 2004.

[48] Aranegui 2004: 33–9, 95–111; 2007: 64–8.

[49] Sil. *Pun.* 1.273–753; Dion. Hal. *Ant. Rom.* 1.50.2–3; Strabo 4.6.

SAGUNT and the moneyers' names in Latin.[50] Inscriptions of late Augustan/Tiberian and late second-/third-century AD date that still commemorated Scipio Africanus' recapture of the town from the Carthaginians in the Second Punic War may be further evidence of this.[51]

At Carthago Nova, by contrast, the Punic town conditioned the layout of much of the city from the late third to first centuries BC. This is evident in its layout (Figure 10.7), with a casemate wall (Figure 10.8), citadel, agora, public buildings attested in recent excavations, as well as a shrine to the Syrian deity Atargartis,[52] and in descriptions by Appian and Livy.[53] Italic influence has also been detected in the decorated *opus signinum* pavements, and in the establishment of an extramural shrine to Iuppiter Stator, from the later second century BC onwards.[54] Following the sack of the town by Rome in 209 BC, coinage was not, however, issued until the later first century BC.[55] In contrast to all of these towns, Valentia (Valencia), which was founded in 136 BC,[56] offers the closest comparison with contemporary colonial establishments in Italy: late second-century BC baths, for example, bear similar comparison with those at Fregellae,[57] while the cremation burials from the Calle Quart stand close comparison with examples from Italian contexts.[58]

The character of the many other Iberian urban settlements in eastern Spain is harder to read. Archaeological evidence prior to the later second and early first century BC is elusive, and there are few settlements where one can do more than point to continued occupation, the existence of wall circuits, small areas of habitation or individual buildings. One index of the degree to which some settlements were monumentalised along 'Hellenised' lines can be gauged, however, by the monumentalisation of Iberian sanctuaries in the course of the second and earlier first centuries BC, particularly the well-documented examples at La Encarnación de Caravaca (Murcia)[59] and the Cerro de los Santos (Albacete).[60] Evidence for more generalised external influences in the treatment of the dead is rare. Exceptions include

[50] Villaronga 1994: 304–14. [51] *CIL* II^2.14, fasc. 1, nos. 327–8.

[52] Ramallo Asensio 2003; 2007; 2009; Ramallo Asensio *et al.* 2008.

[53] App. *Hisp.* 22; Livy 26.47.6.

[54] However, recent analysis of early examples from Sicily and Carthage (K. Dunbabin 1994) suggests that this kind of flooring may have been Punic in origin. This now seems to be the *communis opinio*: see A. Wilson (Chapter 5) and, to a lesser extent, Fentress (Chapter 6) and R. Wilson (Chapter 4) in this volume on *pavimenta punica.*

[55] Llorens Forcada 1994: 37–54.

[56] The archaeological evidence for Valentia is discussed in Ribera i Lacomba 2007.

[57] Marín Jordá and Ribera i Lacomba 2000; note Fentress, Chapter 6 in this volume, on baths in the central western Mediterranean.

[58] García Prosper and Guérin 2002. [59] Murcia: Ramallo Asensio 1992; 1993.

[60] Albacete: Sánchez Gómez 2002.

Figure 10.7 Plan of the Punic and Republican topography of Carthago Nova (Cartagena) (after Ramallo Asensio *et al.* 2008: Fig. 1) showing findspots of material and sites of primarily Barcid date. Key:

(1) Fragment of Attic red ware under the *porticus post scaenam* of the theatre.
(2) Wall of La Milagrosa.
(3) Sector A of Molinete.
(4) Pre-Barcid structure on the NW side of Despenaperros.
(5) Pre-Roman structures of the Plaza del Hospital.
(6) Plaza de San Ginés.
(7) Pre-Barcid and Barcid structures of Calle Palas.
(8) Possible stretch of Barcid Wall.
(9) Punic terracing-wall beneath a Roman temple platform.
(10) Stretch of Punic street in Calle Duque no. 2.
(11) Punic walls and street in Cuatro Santos no. 40.
(12) Punic structures in Calle Saura and San Cristobal la Larga 36.
(13) Punic street and structures in Calle Duque nos. 8–12.
(14) Roman Imperial forum.
(15) Punic structures in PERI CA-4.
(16) Metalworking furnaces on the north-western side of Despenaperros.
(17) Punic structures in La Serreta 8/12.
(18) Punic and Roman Republican remains in the Moreria.
(19) Grotto with altars.
(20) Possible warehouses.
(21) Remains of uncertain identification.
(22) Possible Punic sanctuary at the foot of Molinete.

Figure 10.8 Photograph of the Punic casemate wall at Carthago Nova.

second- and first-century BC burials at the cemeteries of El Tolmo de Minateda (Albacete) and Vilajoyosa (Alicante), which were aligned along roads close to the entrance to settlements, possibly imitating the Roman practice of situating burials along approach roads to towns.[61] The appearance of funerary stelae with Iberian inscriptions in southern Catalunya and northern Pais Valenciano during the second and first centuries BC may also be significant. They resemble similar monuments from lower Aragón[62] and seem to precede the generalised appearance of Roman stelae during the early Imperial period.[63]

Evidence for Hellenising influences in the layout of towns in southern Iberia is rare, even among the main centres of Roman power. The *colonia latina* of Carteia (171 BC) is the only Roman foundation with defined legal status, and even here the development of the town was comparatively late. An Italic-style temple was only built on a sacred site at the centre of a smaller Punic settlement by the late second century BC, a date that coincides roughly with the issue of bronze coins bearing the name of the town in Latin.[64] Little is known about Republican Corduba[65] and even less about Italica (206 BC) prior to the mid-first century BC,[66] apart from a later

[61] Abad Casal 2003b. [62] F. Beltrán Lloris 1999: 139–40.

[63] Izquierdo Peraile and Arasa 1999: 284–95; cf. Prag, Chapter 11 in this volume, on epigraphic practice more generally.

[64] Roldán Gámez *et al.* 2003.

[65] Stylow 1996; Ventura Martínez 1996; Ventura *et al.* 1998: 88–93. [66] Keay 1997.

Figure 10.9 Bronze coin issued by Gades (Villaronga 1994: 86 no. 35), showing the head of Melqart on the obverse and two fish on the reverse, with the letters *MP'L* and *'GDR* in Punic script.

inscription that may well commemorate the presentation of spoils from the captured city of Zakynthos to the town by L. Aemilius Paullus in 168 BC.[67]

Gadir can be distinguished from other centres by its Phoenician background, small size and distinctive offshore location.[68] While the evidence for its layout prior to the construction of the *neapolis* by Cornelius Balbus on the *kotinoussa* in the mid-first century BC is limited,[69] it hints at a strongly Phoenician or Punic flavour, and the town continued to act as both a major economic centre[70] and sanctuary to Hercules Gaditanus (Melqart)[71] down to the early imperial period. Both these aspects of the town, symbolised by a tuna fish and a bust of Hercules wearing a lionskin, as well as by the prevailing Punic script used by the community, were advertised on the silver and bronze coins (Figure 10.9) issued throughout the third, second and first centuries BC.[72]

For most towns, however, a full understanding of interplays between local traditions and eastern Mediterranean influences is hampered by lack of systematic fieldwork and publication; the major centre of Castulo (Linares) in the upper Guadalquivir valley is a good example of unrealised potential in this regard.[73] What evidence there is, however, does suggest that Punic influences prevailed, often in Hellenised form, over more obviously Roman

67 *CILA* 2.2.377.

68 Arteaga and Roos 2002 for the geomorphological constraints of its setting.

69 De Frutos Reyes and Muñoz Vicente 2004: 25–6.

70 Bernal Casasola (2004) discusses the amphora evidence, while Niveau de Villedary y Marinas (2003) suggests that the Kouass pottery found at sites along the southern coast of Iberia may have been manufactured at Gadir between the late fourth and second centuries BC; see also López Castro 2007: 106.

71 García y Bellido 1963; Sáez Romero *et al.* 2005; Sáez Romero 2009.

72 Alfaro 1988.

73 Blázquez and García-Gelabert 1994: 421–72; García-Bellido 1978.

Figure 10.10 Bronze coin issued by Carmo (Villaronga 1994: 382 no. 2), showing the helmeted head of a youth on the obverse, and legend *CARMO* between two ears of corn on the reverse.

ones, although their depth or extent is hard to gauge. Carmo (Carmona) is a case in point. It was a key centre that visibly dominated much of the lower Guadalquivir valley down into the Imperial period[74] and was itself dominated by substantial fortifications.[75] Excavations within the modern town suggest that the Turdetanian and Roman Republican town covered some forty-seven hectares and had been continuously and intensively occupied throughout the Republican period.[76] Since they are mostly scattered *sondages*, they are not able to tell us much about the layout or architecture of the town. However, some degree of Punic influence is evident in its coins that bear the symbol of Tanit (Figure 10.10),[77] and in the continued use of *hypogea* in the cemetery down to the end of the Republican period.[78] Occasional discoveries like the 'dolls' (*muñecos*) that accompany burials at the early Imperial cemetery at the port of Baelo (Bolonia)[79] and the small sanctuary outside the walls of Torreparedones (Baena, Córdoba) in the Córdoban *campina*, apparently dedicated to some form of Tanit-Caelestis, would seem to support this (Figure 10.11).[80]

A similar impression can be gained from other major centres from their bronze coinages, dateable in large measure to between the third and second centuries BC. They bear a range of obverse and reverse types that advertised specific aspects of the issuing community's identity; the

[74] Keay *et al.* 2001.

[75] The standing ashlar walls were initially identified as Carthaginian by Jiménez Martín (1989). Recently they have been redated to the Augustan period by Schattner (2005). There is, however, other evidence to suggest that the Turdetanian settlement was defended by walls which continued in use into the Republican period (Anglada Curada and Rodríguez Rodríguez 2007).

[76] Beltrán Fortes 2001; Lineros Romero 2007. [77] Coinage: Chaves Tristán 2001.

[78] Burial practice: Bendala Galán 1976; Belén Deamos *et al.* 1986.

[79] Sillières 1995: 198–202; Jiménez Díez 2008b: 212–37.

[80] Cunliffe and Fernández Castro 1999: 445–53.

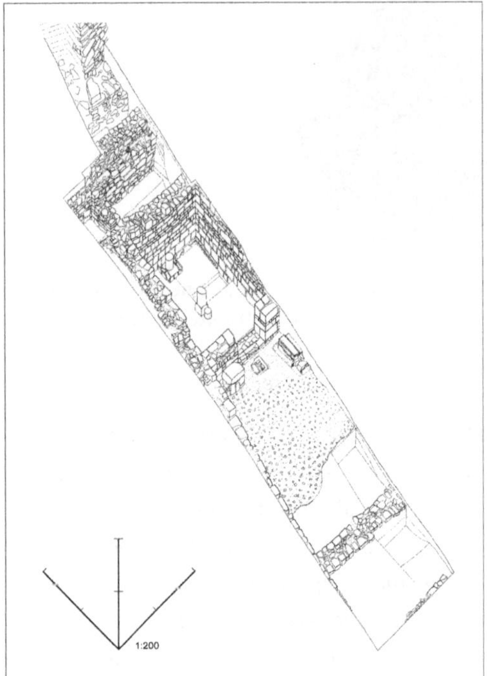

Figure 10.11 Plan of the Iberian sanctuary at Torreparedones (Córdoba).

Figure 10.12 Bronze coin issued by Ursone (Villaronga 1994: 368 no. 3), showing the head of a youth with laurel wreath on the obverse, with the legend *URSONE*, and on the reverse a sphinx above the legend *L.AP.DEC.*

former was usually the head of a male or female deity, while the latter was often a symbol such as an ear of corn or a tuna fish.[81] While the inspiration for many of these coin images is to be sought in iconography that originated in both the Greek and Punic worlds, current scholarship suggests that images were chosen to represent predominantly Punic deities and other mythological figures, as at Ursone (Sphinx) (Figure 10.12)

[81] Villaronga 1994; Chaves Tristán 1998.

and Ipolka-Obulco (Tanit and Baal-Hammon).[82] Furthermore, Olmos has suggested that some of these images may have expressed the foundation myths of individual communities.[83] The promotion of urban identities in this way could have been further reinforced by coin legends naming the issuing authority in the prevailing script used for official transactions.[84] Those issued in western Ulterior were in Latin, while Southern Iberian was used in the East, Punic along the south coast, and Libyo-Phoenician by communities inland to the east of Gades; Latin only came to be used by all mints in the course of the first century BC.[85]

Punic cultural influence would seem to have been key in southern Iberia as López Castro and Bendala have argued, but it should perhaps be understood in the context of long-standing regional Iberian social and cultural traditions.[86] There are also grounds to suggest that Iberian communities were open to influences from elsewhere in the Mediterranean. The recent stylistic analysis of stone funerary lions from Gades and centres in the Guadalquivir valley, for example, suggests that they originally adorned high-status tower burials between the second century BC and the mid-first century AD,[87] and that they are best understood in the context of contact between Iberians and Romans.[88]

Discussion

This paper suggests that Hellenistic and Carthaginian influence, whether direct or indirect, had long been a significant issue in the development of the Iberians. However, the conquest of the Iberians, initially by Carthage and later by Rome, led to an intensification of the integration of the Iberians into the prevalent cultural convergence that was taking place across the western Mediterranean. The Greek, Carthaginian or Italic ideas and material culture circulating in Iberian towns were the direct and indirect result of complex processes of adoption and reinterpretation across the Mediterranean. This means that it is hard to interpret their appearance in urban contexts as Greek, Carthaginian or Italic, and in this sense, 'Hellenisation', 'Punicisation' and 'Romanisation' were inextricably intertwined.[89] The fact that all the Iberian peoples are mentioned for the first time by Roman and Greek sources of the

[82] See respectively Chaves Tristán 1989; Arevalo González 1999: 63–72; García-Bellido 1987.
[83] Olmos 1998b: 152–4. [84] Burnett 2002. [85] Chaves Tristán 1998.
[86] López Castro 1995; Bendala Galán 1994. [87] Chapa Brunet 1985.
[88] Beltrán Fortes 2002: 238–56; *contra* Pérez López 1999.
[89] See Quinn, Chapter 7 in this volume, for a similar perspective on North Africa.

third and second centuries BC onwards is eloquent demonstration of this, as is the growing volume of ceramic imports originating in Italic contexts that are often described as 'Hellenised' for one reason or another.

While the establishment of Roman power in Iberia undoubtedly brought about significant changes, such as the creation of new towns and changes in settlement patterns, it is hard to see transformative cultural changes really beginning to take place before the late second/early first centuries BC,[90] or becoming widespread until at least the Augustan period.[91] 'Romanisation' at this period, therefore, is perhaps best understood more in terms of the subjugation and management of provincial communities. It is difficult, then, to see any of this in terms of a 'Hellenising', 'Punicising' or 'Romanising' cultural process distinct from the creeping cultural convergence of the western Mediterranean in general – a process that has traditionally been referred to as 'Hellenisation'.[92]

'Hellenisation', however, is an asymmetrical term that privileges the Greek over other traditions, such as Carthaginian and Iberian, in the history of the Mediterranean, on the implicit basis that Greek cultural traditions were somehow superior and, as a consequence, the cultural standard to which peoples around the Mediterranean aspired. It also wrongly decentralises dialogues about cultural changes away from key local and regional issues towards traditions germane to the eastern Mediterranean, converting peoples such as the Iberians into passive respondants at the western periphery of an eastern dominated *oikoumene.*

In so far as there was a 'Hellenisation' of the Iberians in the course of the later third and second centuries BC, it has to be understood primarily through a Roman filter and in terms of long-standing regional contexts, not least since it seems to have been predominantly a feature of the later second century BC onwards. The paradox is, of course, that the Roman filter itself was becoming 'Hellenised' to a degree by this time.[93] This take-up of new ideas, beliefs, traditions and political structures from areas across the

[90] Indeed, it would be interesting to establish how far the late second/early first centuries BC marked the start of the breakdown of long-standing ethnic groupings in the face of a growing social and cultural convergence that was contingent upon the municipalisation of Iberia within the Roman Empire.

[91] In architectural terms this is discussed in Trillmich and Zanker 1990; Ramallo Asensio 2004; Keay 2007.

[92] For central and southern Italy of the fourth and third centuries BC see Curti *et al.* 1996: 181–9.

[93] The ways in which the transformation of Roman élite culture at Rome through contact with the Greeks worked in the course of the third and second centuries BC is explored by Gruen 1992; see also Curti *et al.* 1996.

Mediterranean was partially grounded in power relations between a conquering power and its subject peoples, and partly driven by a range of local strategies and imperatives. Account needs to be taken of regional Iberian contexts and the ways in which Iberians might have chosen to interpret, deploy or use them, a complex series of processes which give rise to the emergence of new cultural forms that are neither Iberian, Greek, Carthaginian, Italic nor Roman – but hybrid and different.[94] The long cultural shadow cast by the cultural developments in pre-Hellenistic Iberia (i.e. fourth century BC and earlier) suggests instead that we need to think of these kinds of evidence in the context of the changing local and regional social strategies in which they were created. In this sense all of these cultural traits are symptomatic of a long and ongoing tradition of cultural accretion that gives rise to a patchwork of series of regionally based cultural amalgams.[95]

[94] Wallace-Hadrill 2008: 73–143 explores similar themes in the development of Roman Italy.
[95] Similar regional variation in Italy has been described by Terrenato (1998) as a form of 'cultural *bricolage*'.

11 Epigraphy in the western Mediterranean: a Hellenistic phenomenon?

JONATHAN R. W. PRAG

Preliminary remarks: contextualising epigraphic cultures in the West

The spread of writing in the West might seem to be reasonably treated, as it usually is, as just one aspect of the expansion of the classical world. But on closer examination, the history of non-classical writing is more complex. . . . The idea of a classical civilisation invented by Greeks and propagated by Romans, is in any case a myth, one that has effaced the contributions of groups like the Phoenicians and the Etruscans, and disguised cultural discontinuities that accompanied shifting configurations of power.[1]

The aim of this contribution is to undertake a survey of the epigraphic cultures in the western Mediterranean (Italy and further west) over approximately the last four centuries BC.[2] The purpose of so doing is to explore the value and significance of the concept of the 'Hellenistic' in relation both to the western and the wider Mediterranean. The central result of this survey will be the observation that a wide range of epigraphic cultures first develop and/or transform and expand in precisely this period across the western Mediterranean, and so that from an epigraphic perspective the Hellenistic *period*, loosely defined chronologically, has some real significance across the whole Mediterranean region. From this observation two principal lines of thought develop: firstly, that this substantial, new and widely attested level of activity, which in certain respects looks like that familiar from the

Versions of this chapter were presented in Vancouver, Oxford, and Cambridge, and I am most grateful to audiences at all three for their feedback. I am particularly grateful to Alex Mullen for an advance copy of Mullen 2008, a copy of the relevant sections of her PhD thesis (see now 2013), and detailed comments; she is of course not responsible for my interpretation of her work. Jo Quinn laboured far beyond the call of duty to try to improve this text; its failings are all my own.

1 Woolf 1994: 84–5.

2 To the best of my knowledge, no such survey currently exists; cf. F. Beltrán Lloris 1995b: 170 with n. 6 for its desirability. It is an unavoidable corollary of such a survey that I shall deal in broad generalisations, and risk infuriating those who work on the specific regions and languages in question; I beg their indulgence, while welcoming criticism.

traditional Hellenistic world, is not therefore specific to the traditionally defined Hellenistic world, but reflects an increased Mediterranean-wide connectivity; and secondly, that Roman imperialism, and by implication Romanisation as seen in the spread of Latin epigraphy, cannot be the explanation for this pattern in the West – rather, Latin epigraphy is itself just one instance of a wider set of developments.

The study of epigraphy in the western Mediterranean brings together two particular historiographical trends. In the first place, study of the western Mediterranean in the Hellenistic period is most commonly approached in terms of the 'Roman West', endlessly contrasted with the 'Greek East': regions of the West are studied individually in relation to the Roman conquest, and from the time of the Roman conquest onwards almost always in a Romanocentric fashion.[3] Secondly, an emphasis upon the concept of the Latin 'epigraphic habit' has reinforced one particular aspect of that Romanocentrism. The idea of the 'epigraphic habit' was coined by Ramsey MacMullen in his study of the Latin epigraphic culture of the High Empire.[4] MacMullen highlighted the visible and rapid spread of Latin epigraphy from the Augustan period through to the third century AD and, precisely because the Latin 'habit' is, superficially at least, so uniform, so extensive, and so monoglot, it has been both very visible and very easy to delineate, if not quite so easy to explain. Although attempts at explanation have moved well beyond the much-caricatured Romanisation debates, and tend instead to focus upon social relations, structures of power and moments or periods of connectivity, it remains the case that the study of Latin epigraphic culture is, in general, remarkably narrow in its focus.[5] Thus, for example, William Harris, in his major study of ancient literacy, in considering the (Latin) epigraphic evidence from across the provinces merely remarked, in a footnote, that '. . . some provinces . . . made considerable use of other languages'.[6] Harris' dataset, based upon *CIL*, illustrates a much deeper-seated problem (and one hardly of Harris' own making), which is that emphasised in the quotation from Woolf at the head of this

[3] This point is expanded in the Introduction to this volume.

[4] MacMullen 1982 and 1986, with imperial honorifics in Latin forming the starting point (although see already, e.g. Mrozek 1973).

[5] See esp. Woolf 1996, as well as e.g. E. Meyer 1990 on North Africa; Mann 1985 on Britain; compare the studies on transformations in epigraphic culture in late antiquity, e.g. Roueché 1997; Galvao Sobrinho 1995.

[6] Harris 1989: 267 n. 468; cf. the mapping of Harris' data by Woolf 1998: 82 Fig. 4.1 (after Harris 1989: 265–9, esp. Tab. 4). On the validity of this 'snapshot', see Edmondson 2002: 44, with Prag 2002: 15.

chapter: the study of classical civilisation has tended to prioritise Latin and Greek material, and in the West to prioritise Latin above all, to the detriment or even exclusion of other languages and material – the Roman West is simultaneously the Latin West. Consequently, the Latin epigraphic habit has become emblematic of Roman imperial expansion in a way that goes far beyond that habit's actual historical value.

In a somewhat parallel fashion, Greek epigraphy is commonly seen as a defining feature of the 'Hellenistic' period, in the eastern Mediterranean:

> It is [inscriptions], perhaps more than any other single artefact or activity, that define our period chronologically and geographically, for not only did they proliferate after the late fourth century in the older Greek-speaking regions, but they also came to be an invaluable trace element in the areas of conquest.[7]

Furthermore, 'Hellenistic epigraphy' has a broadly agreed content:

> ... far from negligible for the Archaic and Classical periods (especially the fourth century), [it] really comes to the forefront in the Hellenistic period (late fourth to late first century B.C.). Royal correspondence, official documents of the Greek cities (by far the largest category), honorific texts (statue bases and/or epigrams), religious ordinances, and funerary texts (epitaphs of varying elaboration) ...[8]

To take the most obvious example, what then should we make of the fact that Sicily, in the last three centuries BC, offers, in its Greek inscriptions, a perfectly good example of such 'Hellenistic epigraphy'?[9] The Hellenistic world is generally defined with reference to the *diadochoi*, the Successor kingdoms (whence the 'areas of conquest' in the first of the two quotations above).[10] On that basis, Sicily has no place within it, and indeed is commonly all but omitted from works on the Hellenistic world. On the basis of the epigraphic definition above, Sicily belongs firmly within such a world (as one of the 'older Greek-speaking regions'); indeed, given that Greek inscriptions, albeit often in small numbers, can be found in Italy, Sicily, Sardinia, southern Gaul, the Iberian peninsula and parts of North Africa, the above epigraphic definition might suggest that some attention be paid to the whole Mediterranean, except that these were never 'areas of conquest'. But, for precisely that reason, the western Mediterranean is, at best, treated as the periphery of a Greek-speaking Hellenistic world, an example of one

[7] Davies 2006: 75–6. [8] Ma 2000c: 95–6.

[9] Overviews in Prag 2003 and 2007a, and the 'Italy' section below.

[10] As in, e.g., Ogden 2002b: x–xi, and see further the Introduction to this volume.

further implication of the word 'Hellenistic', and so of the Hellenistic world, viz. Hellenisation (and the implicit priority of Greek culture).

Vice versa, if one focuses solely upon the Latin epigraphy of Sicily, the island looks typical of the Latin epigraphic habit, participating in the process of Romanisation.[11] Either, therefore, one concludes that the island is simply a curious exception, as the clichéd 'crossroads of the Mediterranean' tag implies; or one must question why in the realm of epigraphy it remains legitimate to prioritise individual languages, when in other areas such a checklist approach to culture has increasingly been rejected. Academic specialisation, and in particular linguistic specialisation, provides one, banal, explanation. The tradition of publishing monolingual epigraphic corpora only reinforces the problem.[12] In combination with the historiographic tendencies already noted, this means that local epigraphic cultures are frequently studied from the limited perspective of specific languages and the local response to, above all, the Roman conquest (or occasionally Carthage or Hellenism). In the survey that follows examples of this process will be illustrated.[13] The purpose of this survey, in setting the epigraphic cultures of the western Mediterranean side-by-side, is to move beyond the narrow confines of individual 'habits' or cultures, whether Latin, Greek, Iberian, or Punic, and so to begin to frame alternative models for the spread of epigraphic practice that are not, for example, language specific. The Hellenistic *period* is patently central to this development, but it is not at all clear that some of the other common boundaries of 'Hellenistic' (the Successor kingdoms or the specific use of Greek epigraphy) are helpful. But if, therefore, these broader constraints of 'Hellenistic' are not very helpful in the western Mediterranean, is there any good reason for so prioritising them in the East?[14]

[11] Prag 2002.

[12] Contrast now the multi-lingual *Corpus Inscriptionum Iudaeae/Palestinae*, of which vol. 1.1, ed. H. Cotton *et al.* was published in 2010 (Berlin, De Gruyter); cf. Cotton and Price 2007 (note the comment top of 330 and contrast still, e.g., Decourt 2004: viii on bilingual texts).

[13] I emphasise that it is not my intention to suggest that those who work on the epigraphies of the western Mediterranean (and who are the source of most of the material cited in what follows, and far better qualified to discuss it than I) are not fully aware of most or all of what is set out here. But the majority of published study is much narrower in its focus.

[14] As the opening quotation from Woolf illustrates, these concerns are hardly new. See also, e.g., J. De Hoz 1995: 68: 'The increase in the volume of writing [in Spain], however, is part of a much more wide-reaching process, which both precedes and is not limited to the Roman world but embraces the entire Mediterranean, and the manifestations of which have their closest chronological parallels in some of the Hellenistic centres of the third century, with repercussions that affected Italy as much as the Punic world or Iberian culture' (my transl.). Likewise *ibid.* 71; *idem* 2006; Berrendonner 2002 quoted below.

The epigraphic cultures of the western Mediterranean

Some cautionary remarks are necessary before proceeding. The material from antiquity does not lend itself to statistical study – the idea that epigraphic survivals might be in some way a representative sample is at the very least highly questionable, and in the West in particular the total numbers are almost certainly too small to be statistically significant.[15] But the problems of overly narrow concentration on (sub)sets of material hinted at above require that one attempts something broader; in the words of Moses Finley:

> What I seek is a shift in the still predominant concentration of research from individual, usually isolated documents to those that can be subjected to analysis collectively, and where possible in a series over time; an emancipation from the magnetism of the words in an individual text in favour of a *quasi-* (or even *pseudo-*) statistical study.[16]

The numbers employed below have, I suspect, no statistical validity; but a synthesis of the bigger picture and of the more readily available sets of material may have some subjective value, and at the least be suggestive, if only when set alongside the existing study of those individual datasets. The majority of the material considered consists of inscriptions on stone; some discussions do include *instrumentum domesticum*, and even coin legends, but 'statistics' on this sort of material are rarely available (on the other hand, as for example Javier De Hoz has suggested, at least some of this material may be of considerable significance for delineating the period in question).[17] The survey proceeds in a loosely anti-clockwise direction around the western Mediterranean, beginning with Italy and the Tyrrhenian islands, and ending with North Africa.

Italy, Sicily and Sardinia

As suggested in the Introduction, it is surely mistaken, or at least overly simplistic, to consider Latin as *the* driver of epigraphic practice in the West before the very late Republic. Even in Italy the Latin epigraphic culture is

[15] For discussions of survival rates and sampling of epigraphic data, see esp. Duncan-Jones 1982: 360; Saller and Shaw 1984.

[16] Finley 2000 (1982): 44, my emphasis.

[17] J. De Hoz 2006. It should be added that the 'statistics' quoted for different epigraphies in what follows are all collected according to different criteria and definitions, by different scholars, so they are only very loosely comparable.

slow to develop, and it is only from the fourth, and in particular the third century BC onwards that it develops in anything like significant numbers (*c.* 40 inscriptions down to the early fourth century, *c.* 600 in the fourth/third century, *c.* 3,600 in the second/first century; there is an apparent gap in the period *c.* 450–350 BC, to which only a single inscription is assigned).[18] Roman funerary epigraphy is a case in point, with barely twenty epitaphs from Rome itself pre-100 BC, and the development of epitaphic practice in mid-Republican Rome has been attributed to Etruscan or Hellenic influence.[19] In fact, the content of Republican Latin epigraphy looks similar in many ways to eastern 'Hellenistic' epigraphy as outlined in the Introduction – should it therefore be classed as a nascent 'Hellenistic' epigraphic culture, as much from its content as from its chronology, notwithstanding the fact that it is not Greek? But how useful is such an assessment? Latin epigraphy is commonly studied either in isolation, or else in relation to the dominant Mediterranean epigraphic language down to the end of this period, Greek. Merely by way of example, an important paper by Silvio Panciera (1997) discusses the increase in Latin euergetic epigraphy in Italy as a phenomenon illustrative of the spread of Roman imperialism, and considered otherwise solely in parallel with Greek epigraphic practice – but these were not the only two epigraphic cultures present in the region, and a wider range of explanations and interactions, at least at the local level, needs to be canvassed.

What then of the other epigraphic languages in Italy? The distribution of Greek material, present from the eighth century BC onwards, is difficult to quantify.[20] Some comments may be ventured on the principal islands, however, where (as with the rest of the West) Republican-period Latin epigraphy is minimal. In Sardinia, although epigraphic material is in general very limited, and the Latin material of the Imperial period dominates the landscape, it is noticeable that the Greek material, such as it is, appears only

[18] Following the survey in Solin 1999; see also Panciera 1995 on lapidary material. Harris 1989: 175 suggests that 100 BC marks the tipping point in Latin epigraphy; Panciera 1995: 321–2 that lapidary epigraphy at Rome shows 'a strong increase only in the second century and explodes in the first, following a quite sporadic use in the sixth and fifth centuries and a limited increase in the fourth to third centuries' (my transl.).

[19] Berrendonner 2009: 181 for numbers; 190–1 for suggested external influences for aristocratic epitaphs; cf. 196–7 for lack of obvious parallels for the rather different, seemingly distinctively Roman third-/second-century practices which develop at the level below the aristocracy. Michael Crawford points out to me that epitaphic practice across Italy and the Italic languages is very varied geographically with, for example, numerous examples among the Paeligni, none in Samnium.

[20] I am not aware of any published figures that attempt to quantify the phenomenon, but see, e.g. Lomas 1991 and the general remarks in Lomas 1993: 176–85 on Magna Graecia; overview of sorts in Lazzarini 2007 (noting the need for a replacement for *IG* XIV).

from the third century BC and, in the words of one recent discussion, reflects the island's 'opening up to the Mediterranean'.[21] Giovanni Marginesu notes that the production of this material coincides with the Roman conquest, something which he does not believe should be put down merely to chance; he proposes that 'Sardinian Hellenism, in reality, presents one of the many faces of that diverse phenomenon that was Romanisation' (my transl.). Punic material, by contrast, first appears on the island in the early Archaic period, in the form of the Nora stele (perhaps *c.* 800 BC), but with very few exceptions the other material from the island does not predate the fifth/fourth century BC. The third century appears to mark the peak in Punic epigraphic practice in Sardinia.[22]

Not dissimilar things can be said about Sicily although the numbers are larger.[23] Both Greek and Punic make a significant appearance in the Archaic period, alongside the evidence for several indigenous languages (Sikel, Sikan and Elymian), followed by what appears to be a marked gap in epigraphic practice in all languages at the end of the Classical period (esp. in the fourth century BC). In the Hellenistic period, Greek, Punic, Oscan and Latin are all visible, although only the first of these in large numbers: Oscan appears as a small pocket of material in third-century Messana; Punic shows a small resumption in activity in the third/second century BC (likewise in Malta, where the peak falls a little earlier in the fourth and third centuries); Latin pre-50 BC totals *c.* fifteen texts.[24] All of this material consists principally of official or civic texts, honorifics, dedications and funerary texts, but this is most marked in the flourishing Greek epigraphic culture of the last three centuries BC, which looks typical of 'Hellenistic epigraphy'.[25] This is followed by a major rise in Latin epigraphy in the later first century BC and the first two centuries AD, highly typical of the Latin 'epigraphic habit'; Greek epigraphy, however, does not diminish and overtakes Latin again in the third and fourth centuries. It has frequently been observed that Hellenistic-period Sicily shows few signs of Romanisation, epigraphic culture included.

[21] 'Apertura all'ambito mediterraneo' (Marginesu 2002: 1825, and for the following quotation also). For Latin epigraphy on Sardinia see Mastino 1993 and for the material down to 31 BC (mostly graffiti on ceramic, and otherwise almost all first-century BC) Zucca 1996: 1450–89; Greek epigraphy, Marginesu 2002.

[22] For Punic epigraphy in Sardinia, see the survey of Amadasi Guzzo 1990: 39–54, together with the texts in Amadasi Guzzo 1967.

[23] For a global quantitative survey of Sicilian epigraphy, see Prag 2002.

[24] For Oscan in Sicily, see Crawford 2011: 1511–23; 2006; Mastelloni 2005; for Punic see Prag 2002: Fig. 2 and Amadasi Guzzo 1999; details of most texts from Sicily and Malta in Amadasi Guzzo 1967; for Republican Latin texts Prag 2007a: 259–60. For languages in ancient Sicily, see now Tribulato 2012.

[25] Prag 2003, 2007a.

More recently, in relation to epigraphic culture (and other aspects of Sicilian cultural practice) it has been suggested that the Hellenistic (i.e. Greek) epigraphic culture of the island may be at least partially linked to the consequences of Roman imperialism.[26] But, whether on Sicily or Sardinia, it is difficult to see how this might usefully be called 'Romanisation'. However pleasing the oxymoron – Hellenistic behaviour is a product of Romanisation – it still begs the question of what creates and drives the broader epigraphic phenomenon being described, especially when, as in the third century BC, four languages are in play simultaneously, of which Latin the least and the last.[27]

Returning to the Italian peninsula, Etruscan material substantially outnumbers Latin. Furthermore, Etruscan, for which some 9,000 inscriptions survive down to the time of Augustus (as against *c.* 4,500 Latin), shows a substantial increase in survival after 400 BC (*c.* 900 pre-400 BC, as opposed to *c.* 4,000 in the period 400–200 BC).[28] Oscan, another of the more substantial epigraphic languages of Republican Italy, and which at least matches Latin numerically in the period pre-200 BC (the total number of recorded Oscan inscriptions is *c.* 1,150), also shows substantial growth in the surviving number of inscriptions in the period post-400 BC.[29] In an extended and detailed analysis of the shifts in practice in both Oscan and Etruscan in this period, Clara Berrendonner identifies not only significant quantitative increases in both epigraphies from the third century BC onwards, but also marked typological shifts in epigraphic practice. Although Berrendonner begins by observing the apparent paradox of such development following the Roman conquest – and this would be the 'typical' way of approaching the material, prioritising the role of Rome – her discussion goes on to complicate the issues by pointing out that some practices, such as stamps on building materials, begin in Etruscan or Oscan before they appear in Latin, and that it is to say the least difficult to give the Roman model priority.[30] The 'unification' of epigraphic practice in Italy subsequent to

[26] For links to Roman imperialism, Prag 2007b: 96–9; for the Imperial period, see also Salmeri 2004; Korhonen 2011.

[27] There are perhaps two Latin inscriptions from third-century Sicily – a milestone (*CIL* I^2.2877) and a dedication (*CIL* I^2.2219). Cf. Campagna 2011b for a nuanced account of public architecture on the island, suggesting (p. 180) that 'the Hellenistic appearance of the cities was one of the consequences of Roman government' (note, not 'Romanisation', but emphasising in particular economic considerations).

[28] Following the survey by Colonna 1999, who compares Etruscan with Latin; detailed tables of both Etruscan and Oscan, broken down by geographical region, are provided by Berrendonner 2002.

[29] For Oscan (and Umbrian and Picene) see now *Imagines Italicae* (= Crawford 2011).

[30] Berrendonner 2002: 819.

the Social War is a different development. Her conclusions are therefore of a rather different order, such as that:

> ... the epigraphic production testifies equally to a wish to demarcate public and private space, to the increasing complexity of administrative and juridical systems, and to the reinforcement of a sense of civic belonging – in sum, to the development of the public sphere.[31]

The same might no doubt be said about Latin epigraphy. Questions for the historian then become, why are such shifts taking place in this period, why do they manifest in these ways, and is it either helpful or meaningful to call this 'Hellenistic', beyond the term's use as a chronological marker? Berrendonner remarks in general that, 'the Hellenistic period coincides, across most of the Italian peninsula, with a notable development in the practice of epigraphy', and on occasion refers to 'documents hellénistiques'.[32] But is there something more substantial here than mere chronological coincidence? If so, we are at the least stretching our use of the word 'Hellenistic'. In a more widely ranging discussion of identity and cultural expression in southern Italy in the fourth century BC, Edward Herring has noted that, 'The increased use of writing, a skill acquired from the Greeks, is another possible expression of cultural identity' (he has in mind specifically Messapic and Oscan). He places this more broadly in the context of cultural threats and a sense of anxiety, driven no less by an increase in local and regional interaction than by the rise of Rome specifically. 'The use of strong visible symbols of identity [such as writing] can be seen as a positive response to these perceived threats.'[33] This is perhaps a more useful way of approaching the broader issues; if we fall back upon the traditionally prioritised model of eastern Greek epigraphy of the Hellenistic period as the means to classify epigraphic cultures of a particular type/

[31] Berrendonner 2002: 845 (my transl.). [32] Berrendonner 2002: 822–3 (my transl.).

[33] Herring 2007: 17. I do not here discuss the many other languages of the Italian peninsula which leave some trace in the epigraphic record. Bandinelli 2008, for example, discusses northern Italian practices (Cisalpina) in this period, describing among other things the existence of an Archaic epigraphic phase with Gallic, Venetic, Camunnic and Retic traditions (43–4); a partial epigraphical gap in the fourth century (45); and the presence from the third century of a combination of local continuity of practices (48), and Roman institutional epigraphy (49), alongside a growth in local epigraphy of institutional and epigraphic varieties (50–3). This last can of course readily be classed as 'Romanisation'; whether it should be is another matter. Kathryn Lomas points out to me that, based upon De Simone and Marchesini 2002 (*non vidi*), Messapic epigraphy appears to show its greatest period of output (or at least survival) in the third century BC. Rare examples of Punic epigraphy from the Italian mainland are largely limited to the Archaic/Classical periods (e.g. the famous Pyrgi tablets); the handful of Neo-Punic texts found at Pompeii (Jongeling 2008: 272–3) are all on Tripolitanian amphorae.

content, then we ultimately fail to escape that traditional Hellenocentric model and continue to treat the problem in a binary rather than a holistic fashion.

Southern Gaul and Hispania

Moving westwards around the northern side of the Mediterranean, southern Gaul and the Iberian peninsula provide good examples of the ways in which study of particular areas and traditions tends to be driven by metanarratives and ideology.[34] So, discussion of the development of epigraphy in southern Gaul has often been driven by a discourse of Hellenisation, focused around Massalia (Marseilles); vice versa, discussion of epigraphic development in the Iberian peninsula is more concerned with elucidating a process of Romanisation attendant upon the Roman military presence from 218 BC onwards. Modern national boundaries can also limit study in a way that is not reflective of the ancient practices.[35] In both cases this risks missing crucial alternative perspectives.

In southern Gaul, Gallo-Greek (i.e. Gaulish written in Greek script) is a 'Hellenistic' epigraphic culture, at least in date. Gallo-Greek texts are known from the area of the Rhone basin, as well as being found along the line of the principal river valleys well into central Gaul. The letters of Gallo-Greek are said to have the phonetic values of 'Hellenistic' Greek *koine* of *c.* 200 BC (note the absence of direct evidence for Massalia as the source).[36] In this instance, considerable debate exists over the exact moment when the phenomenon first develops, and consequently as to whether it should be classed as 'Hellenisation' (favoured by those arguing for an earlier beginning, *c.* 250 BC) or an indigenous development, reflecting, for instance, a need to assert identity in the face of Roman conquest (associated with assigning the material a later date, principally the later second and first centuries BC).[37]

[34] There are, needless to say, plenty of exceptions, and the wider shift in approach towards a discourse of Mediterranean interactions and a more 'Hellenistic' pattern, which Mullen 2008: 249 n.3 observes for southern Gaul, reflects the concerns of this volume (also Mullen 2013).

[35] Woolf 1994: 85; cf. Bats 1988.

[36] Mullen 2013: §4.2.1; cf. J. De Hoz 1998b: 124 for some evidence that Gallo-Iberic inscriptions of the Hellenistic period (i.e. Iberian written in a Greek script), in contrast to the earlier Greek material, show indications of influence from wider eastern *koine*, rather than being an isolated western development.

[37] Contrast Lambert 1997, arguing for 250–50 BC and Hellenisation, with Bats 2003, who argues that the first true examples of Gallo-Greek (as opposed to just Greek), especially on stone, only occur late in the second century BC, and who rejects 'Hellenisation' as an explanation. Cf. Mullen 2013: §4.2.2.

Somewhere over 300 documents are now recorded, of which over 73 are lapidary, over 223 are on ceramic and a small number are to be found on other materials. Of the lapidary inscriptions, *c.* 40 are funerary, *c.* 24 votive, with a small number of signatures or incomprehensible texts.[38] One notable feature of Gallo-Greek, from the perspective of 'Hellenistic' epigraphy, is the existence of public, or official documents. Examples include an inscription from Vitrolles which refers to a *praitor*, an inscription from Martigues referring to the construction of a road, a collective dedication, a number of inscriptions referring to tribal organisation, and one from Segomaros involving a sacred wood and refering collectively to the citizens of ancient Nîmes. By contrast, Gallo-Latin, which develops later and co-exists alongside Latin epigraphy, has only produced *c.* 17 lapidary inscriptions, most of which come instead from the Gallic interior, almost none from the south-east – it is not therefore something as simple as a mere chronological successor to Gallo-Greek, and cannot be used to support a blunt reading along the lines of Hellenisation followed by Romanisation.[39]

Two particular sets of observations are worth highlighting here. The first is Michel Bats' comments on the more general question of the adoption of language and writing (or at least, the practice of inscribing on durable materials). While Greek and Phoenician epigraphic practices can be traced back to the Archaic period in Gaul and Spain, and some very limited evidence exists for the development of local scripts and their use at such an early date, the majority of the local take-up of such practices belongs to the fourth century (in the case of Iberian, in both southern Gaul and Spain) or the third and second centuries (Gallo-Greek, Celtiberian). As Bats remarks: 'The adoption of an alphabet and of writing is not only the resolution of a technical problem but at the same time marks a moment in the internal evolution of a society and of the functions which that society assigns to writing.'[40] The very obvious time-lags involved, sometimes of several centuries, require explanation – either in terms of the delay, or in terms of the impulse when it comes. Put bluntly, why now, why in the 'Hellenistic' period? Bats himself repeatedly emphasises both the personal and the commercial/economic aspects of much of the material, but one could also highlight the existence of public documents from communities among this material and what that might suggest about local community identity in this period.

[38] After Lambert 1997. [39] See e.g. the cautions in Woolf 1994: 96–7.
[40] Bats 1988: 133 (my transl.).

The second consideration is both a more specific set of observations, and a partial follow-up to the first. In a study of a set of Gallo-Greek dedications, Alex Mullen has brought out the range of Italic linguistic influences to be found within the principal formula employed, thereby complicating the more traditional idea of primarily Greek linguistic influence (but, crucially, without invoking specifically Roman origins, Oscan being at least as significant as Latin). Mullen also highlights the implications of a distribution map of the Gallo-Greek material: Massalia is visibly on the periphery of this material's distribution, which is concentrated upon the confluence of the major rivers in the region, strongly suggesting that communication and trade were key elements in the use and diffusion of epigraphic practice.[41] If the delay of centuries in the take-up of writing/epigraphic culture is a point requiring explanation, then the local presence of Massalia is usually considered central to the issue, since it provides an obvious source for the adoption of such a practice; but if Massalia is in fact peripheral to the practice when it does develop, then the Greek colony appears peripheral to our possible explanations both for the non-take-up in the Archaic/Classical period and for the take-up in the Hellenistic period. Another motivation (and source) appears to be desirable. Throughout Mullen's discussion the emphasis is upon complexity and a range of both internal and external factors. Within the context of the broader, western Mediterranean picture the chronological parameters are once again striking.

Against all of this should be set the limited evidence provided by the Greek epigraphy of the region of ancient Gaul. Of the 169 inscriptions now collected in *Inscriptions Grecques de la France*, a mere four are dated earlier than the third/second century BC – although these include a striking fifth-century BC commercial document on lead from Pech Maho.[42] A significant body of material belongs to the later Hellenistic period, while the greatest proportion of the texts is Imperial in date. The lack of material highlights the relatively *a priori* nature of the debate regarding the process of Hellenisation in the development of Gallo-Greek. The chronology of the material itself, seeing its first significant developments in the third/second century, fits eminently well with the wider patterns observed in this paper, not simply in Gallo-Greek but across the western Mediterranean as a whole.

41 Mullen 2008 and 2013 (Map 3); see also on northern Italy/southern Gaul, Häussler 2002.

42 *Inscriptions Grecques de la France* (*IGF*) = Decourt 2004. *IGF* 2 (funerary or dedicatory text from Marseilles, C5 BC); *IGF* 84 ('le galet d'Antibes', C5/4 BC); *IGF* 130 (letter on lead plaque, C4/3 BC); *IGF* 135 (commercial document on lead from Pech Maho, second quarter C5 BC). Note also the third-century BC letter on lead from Marseilles, *IGF* 4. See now Mullen 2013: ch. 6 for a larger collection of non-lapidary Greek epigraphy from the region.

Turning to the Iberian peninsula, the principal scripts of interest are Iberian and Celtiberian.[43] The former has its origins in the South-West script which develops *c.* 700 BC from the Phoenician alphabet, used in turn by the Iberian peoples from perhaps the end of the fifth century BC, with modifications such as being written left–right generally assumed to develop under Greek influence. The most notable early (fourth-/third-century) texts are commercial documents on lead from Ampurias (compare that from Pech Maho, above), taken to be of Greek inspiration – although it is worth pointing out that the Pech Maho texts include Etruscan also, and the archaeological evidence from all these sites suggests a highly complex world of interaction between natives of the Iberian peninsula and southern Gaul, Greeks, Etruscans, Phoenicians/Punics and others.[44] A modest corpus of Phoenicio-Punic texts is attested for Spain, with some presence in the Archaic period, but which shows the greatest period of activity precisely in the period of the fourth to second centuries BC.[45] Greek material is present in the peninsula throughout antiquity, but in small numbers; almost half the material comes from Ampurias/Emporion alone.[46] The Archaic material is predominantly to be found on functional objects, on ceramic and metal, frequently associated with trade and commerce; documents on lead are notable in the fifth to third centuries BC, with funerary epigraphy developing principally from the first century BC onwards, more closely in tandem with the familiar later Latin 'habit'. Of the Iberian material itself, much is undated, but it is generally considered to cluster between the late third and late first centuries BC, from which period *c.* 1,750 Iberian inscriptions survive, ranging across coin legends, epitaphs on stone, inscriptions on mosaics and amphorae and graffiti on ceramics. Celtiberian is a later and smaller phenomenon, constituting a small sub-group of *c.* 100 inscriptions belonging to the second/first centuries BC, using either Iberian script or occasionally the Latin alphabet.[47]

[43] See the collection of papers in F. Beltrán Lloris 1995a; also F. Beltrán Lloris 1999; and see now the overview in Simkin 2012.

[44] See esp. the comments of Gailledrat and Solier 2004: 438–9, with further references.

[45] Fuentes Estañol 1986 provides the most complete corpus of the Spanish material, detailing 24 texts of C8-C5 BC, 60 of C4-C2, and 30 of C2-C1.

[46] M. P. De Hoz 1997 for a corpus (127 distinct texts, across all materials, between C7 BC and C4 AD; overview at 90–1); corrections in M. P. De Hoz 1998; cf. Ramírez Sádaba 2009 for an overview (comments at 59 on Archaic material).

[47] For a useful tabulation of Celtiberian inscriptions, see Villar *et al.* 2001: 87–101. Iberian and Celtiberian material as a whole is collected in *Monumenta Linguarum Hispanicarum* (Wiesbaden, 1975-), ed. J. Untermann, esp. vols 3 and 4.

The quantity of 'public' epigraphy in both Iberian and Celtiberian is very limited – but importantly it does exist. Particularly striking among the Celtiberian material are the Celtiberian texts on bronze from Botorrita, on which Beltrán Lloris observes: 'These two bronzes [now three], again leaving aside their exact meaning, have other points of interest. One of them is the use of writing to produce texts for public exhibition (perhaps in the monumental building of the acropolis) . . .' And, in the case of the second Celtiberian text (= Botorrita 3), with its list of names, he observes: 'What is striking is not so much the permanent exhibition of personal names (which is a normal feature of classical epigraphy), but the fact that they are exhibited not individually, but as a collective manifestation linked to an official act of the community, which surely expresses a remarkable collective instance of what the Germans call "Selbstdarstellung".'[48] Particularly in the case of Celtiberian, where all the material is dated to after the arrival of the Romans, it is inevitably tempting to attribute such activity to Roman influence. And yet, Latin material from the region before the late Republican period is very scarce indeed and largely restricted to official acts of Roman magistrates – a pattern that is repeated across the western Mediterranean (and should be placed alongside the slow growth of Latin epigraphy within Italy itself, noted above).[49] The need for caution is rightly recognised: 'the appearance of the first indigenous inscriptions, barely a generation after the conquest, comes therefore too soon for this first epigraphic flowering to be attributed exclusively to Roman influence.'[50] In the case of Iberian epigraphy it is instead a question of whether particular categories of epigraphic material are attested before the Roman arrival in 218 BC – the question matters within the existing debate because if Iberian epigraphy precedes the arrival of the Romans *en masse* then the role of

[48] F. Beltrán Lloris 1999: 146. There are altogether four Botoritta bronzes, nos. 1, 3, 4 being in Celtiberian, no. 2 in Latin (see respectively Beltrán and Tovar 1982; Beltrán Lloris *et al.* 1996; Villar *et al.* 2001; and J. Richardson 1983 for the Latin document).

[49] Díaz Ariño 2008 collects all Latin epigraphy down to 31 BC for the Iberian peninsula, with a survey at 35–44; the earliest Latin epigraphy (late third century BC) is graffiti and stamps on amphorae; the earliest inscribed text is Díaz Ariño 2008: C58 = *CIL* I^2.iv.3449.l (a graffito dedication to Minerva on stone) of *c.* 200 BC, and the first examples of the use of Latin by the local population belong to the second half of the second century BC or later; cf. Stylow 1998 for Hispania Ulterior (nothing pre-50 BC); cf. Prag 2007a: 259–60 for a similar picture in Sicily (*c.* 15 texts on stone, all by/for Romans/Italians); Quinn 2003: 16 for the same in North Africa (5 texts on stone all by/for Latin speakers); Zucca 1996 collects the full range of material for Africa, Sardinia, and Corsica to 31 BC.

[50] F. Beltrán Lloris 1995b: 174 (my transl.).

'Romanisation' in the phenomenon's development receives a seemingly clear (and negative) answer.[51]

As with other regions, the coincidence with the arrival of the Roman Empire is obvious – and may well not be merely coincidental – but whether it follows from that that the discernible developments in epigraphic practice have anything to do with anything that might be called 'Romanisation' is far less obvious. One might argue that the clash between Rome and Carthage in the later third century in the western Mediterranean basin is itself simply emblematic of the greatly increased levels of exchange and interaction, of connectivity and complexity in this region in this period.[52] The lack of precision in the available evidence, which inhibits clear answers regarding the chronology and priority of particular languages and practices, means that the debates about the growth of epigraphic practice in the Iberian peninsula provide a particularly clear example of the ideological issues at stake: put simply (too simply), should one prioritise indigenous practices, Romanisation, or even, as Javier de Hoz has come to argue more recently, 'Hellenistic' practices, detectable both in the occasional public presentation of magistrates, and in the presence of *instrumentum domesticum* and 'industrial epigraphy'?[53] The fact that it is not so simple is readily illustrated by the suggestions of both Jürgen Untermann and Francisco Beltrán Lloris that the use of Iberian script by the Celtiberians, in apparent preference to Latin, in the second/first centuries BC, was most likely a consequence of the Celtiberians having learned writing from the Iberians in the *emporia* of the Catalan and Valencian coast – which promptly turns most of the uni- or bidirectional models of influence on their heads; but then, the Ampurias texts of the fourth century probably implied as much already.[54]

One particular example of this development and the difficulties of assessing it may be seen in discussion of the phenomenon of the *tessera hospitalis* in the Spanish context.[55] Because the greatest concentration of such material is found in the Iberian peninsula, and because the Celtiberian examples

[51] See for instance J. De Hoz 1995: 60 on funerary epigraphy.

[52] For increased commercial activity in the Tyrrhenian basin in this period, and the steady rise in Roman involvement, see, e.g. Bechtold 2007, Tchernia 2007, Olcese 2004, Vandermersch 2001.

[53] 'Too simply', because of course many offer rather nuanced positions across and between these alternatives, e.g. F. Beltrán Lloris 1995b; for Iberian epigraphy as a Hellenistic phenomenon, J. De Hoz 1995 and 2006.

[54] Untermann 1995b: 197; F. Beltrán Lloris 1995b: 181–2.

[55] The Spanish material is variously surveyed in Abascal 2003: 249 Tab. 1 (28 Celtiberian examples, 8 Celtiberian written in Latin letters, 8 Latin); Díaz Ariño 2008: 56–8 (*c.* 50 Celtiberian *tesserae* written in 'paleohispanic' or Latin alphabet, alongside 9 Latin examples); and Balbín Chamorro 2006: 149–92 (45 examples).

all appear to post-date the Roman conquest – in contrast to the few Latin examples from Italy, some of which seem to precede the Celtiberian material – a very similar debate regarding directions of influence is found as in relation to other regions and epigraphic cultures in this period.[56] Explanatory hypotheses for this development range from the existence of an indigenous Celtiberian practice, to the complete rejection of any indigenous origin, alongside finely nuanced attempts to find a middle ground.[57] It is worth adding that the vast majority of this material is not susceptible of accurate dating; consequently the dates tend to be shifted by a century or so either way according to the hypothesis being presented, offering a further example of the way in which the narrative affects the interpretation.

Although the existence of similar material beyond Spain and Italy, and across a broader range of time, is frequently acknowledged, such material is all too often subordinated to the primary argument over the historical developments of the Iberian peninsula and specific problems internal to the Iberian material.[58] It is, however, possible to argue that enough aspects of the practices associated with *hospitium* (formal ties of hospitality) and *tesserae hospitales* (tokens of guest-friendship) are attested at other moments and in other places that the Celtiberian examples should not necessarily be prioritised for any other reason than their numerical preponderance (although that fact itself undoubtedly requires explanation). Ivory and bronze *tesserae*, of similar form but in diverse languages, are occasionally found elsewhere: Etruscan examples from Rome and Carthage in the Archaic period; Greek examples from Sicily and southern Gaul in the Hellenistic period.[59] An Athenian text of the 370s BC appears to imply a

[56] Italian examples include *CIL* I^2.23, 828, 1764.

[57] Respectively (illustrative examples only): Ramos Loscertales 1942 (indigenous); Dopico 1989 (non-indigenous); F. Beltrán Lloris 2004 (suggesting an indigenous tradition of *hospitium*, which in turn adopted a specifically Latin practice of using bronze *tesserae*; further developed – very speculatively – in *idem* 2010).

[58] I (over)simplify deliberately and leave aside, for instance, detailed consideration of specific *formulae* in the various *tesserae*, or the transition from *tesserae* to *tabulae* and the appearance of *patrocinium*; useful recent overviews of the problem in Díaz Ariño 2008: 56–8; Balbín Chamorro 2006: 13–15, 44–7; Abascal 2003: 247–57; cf. F. Beltrán Lloris 2004: 35–6; J. De Hoz 1999.

[59] *IG* XIV.2432 (excellent photographs in Barruol 1969: Pl. VIII, with pp. 372–3; also Guarducci 1967–78: II, 582–3 with Fig. 183; now *IGF* 1, albeit with no reference to the Iberian tradition), recording links between one of the Alpine peoples and another community; *IG* XIV.279 from Lilybaeum in Sicily, containing mixed Punic and Greek nomenclature (see C. Di Stefano 1984: no. 153 and Fig. 70). Neither can be more closely dated than the later Hellenistic. Etruscan *tessera* on ivory from S. Omobono (Rome), Pallottino 1979; Etruscan *tessera* from a sixth-century burial in Carthage, Rix 1991: *Af.* 3.1, with photographs in Peruzzi 1970: I, Tav. i-ii, discussion Prag 2006: 8 (nb *Puinel* is an Etruscan personal name, not an ethnic). Ve 221 = Crawford 2011: 209 is sometimes cited as a possible Oscan example on ivory.

very similar practice in use to facilitate relations between Athens and the king of Sidon, since the actions described there can only be understood through the employment of something like a *tessera hospitalis*.[60] Literary texts across a broad range in time and space, both Greek and Latin, reflect the same practice or something very similar.[61] Many of the general elements, such as the symbol of clasped right hands, likewise find a broader Mediterranean context – in other words, viewed from the outside, the Iberian examples look like one manifestation of a pan-Mediterranean phenomenon.[62]

Given the existence of wider evidence for *hospitium* practices in the ancient Mediterranean, a focus upon the question of whether Iberian *hospitium* reflects specifically indigenous customs or the adoption of Roman practices risks missing the point. An alternative strategy in this debate has been to examine the hypothesis that the use of bronze in particular (both in the *tesserae* and in other inscriptions) is a distinctively Roman practice in origin, taken up in the Iberian peninsula.[63] However, an emphasis upon bronze as a primarily Roman practice in this period seems no less open to question than other assumptions about directions of influence or choices in the prioritisation of cultural developments within a rather wider world.[64] Both Javier De Hoz and Paolo Poccetti observe the earlier use, especially in the Greek-speaking world, of metal as an epigraphic support.[65] Poccetti in turn observes a general expansion in the use of bronze

60 *Syll.*[3] 185, ll.18–25, discussed in Gauthier 1972: 81–2.

61 Especially Plaut. *Poen.* 1047–52 (NB based ultimately upon a Greek New Comedy original and with a Punic context, reworked for a Latin audience), but also *Cist.* 503; see the wide range of material collected in Lécrivain 1900: 297–9, and Gauthier 1972: ch. 2 *passim* and esp. 65–7 (on Plato, *Symp.* 191d, 193a and Arist. *Mete.* 360a 25–6 for use of the σύμβολον (*symbolon*, 'token') as a metaphor or simile, in a way which presumes the idea of a specific object, split in two with the intention of being able to be reunited for recognition purposes).

62 Knippschild 2004: esp. 299–302 puts this material in relation to Persian practice; Knippschild 2002: esp. 29, 40 links this material to wider Mediterranean practice; Herman 1987: 63–5 offers a distinctly Hellenocentric perspective instead. Messineo 1983 focuses on the four examples mentioned above (my n. 59) and takes them to be representative of 'un'antica consuetudine pan-mediterranea' (p. 4).

63 See in particular the very rich explorations of J. De Hoz 1999 and F. Beltrán Lloris 2004 (the latter now suggesting, in Beltrán Lloris 2010, that aspects of the practice originated in Punic North Africa, and reached Spain and Roman Italy via Sicily – a speculative hypothesis based primarily upon later evidence); also the more Italo-centric and wide-ranging survey of Poccetti 1999. A useful survey of specifically Roman use of bronze now in Mitchell 2005: 178–85; for Greek use of bronze see also the material cited in Crema 2007: esp. 249–52.

64 Note the remarks of Mayer and Velaza 1989: 667–8.

65 J. De Hoz 1999: 438–9; Poccetti 1999: esp. 555–6; also Crema above n. 63. For early Hellenistic examples (first half of the third century BC), clearly illustrative of a well-developed practice which can hardly be attributed to Roman influence (although the reverse might be true), note

among many Italic peoples (in particular in central and southern Italy, as well as among the Etruscans) from the third century onwards. Poccetti also observes that Latin epigraphic practice appears to be much slower to adopt another wider Mediterranean practice, that of lead *defixiones* (curse tablets), in contrast to other Italic peoples (Poccetti suggests Oscan mediation for the specific adoption by the Romans, while also noting a broader fourth-century climate for epigraphy on metal in the western Mediterranean, which extends to the Iberian coast). Interestingly, as De Hoz observes, it is the use of lead that is best attested in the Iberian peninsula in the same ('proto-Hellenistic'?) period, in contact with Greek, Etruscan, and perhaps Punic, elements.[66] Once again it is therefore the period around the third century BC which seems to be the key moment for the diffusion of epigraphic practice – and once again, it is by no means a development restricted to Rome or to Latin epigraphy (or to the Iberian peninsula), and Rome's own place in that expansion should hardly be considered in isolation.[67] Notwithstanding this broader picture, there remains a temptation to channel, for example, the use of bronze in Celtiberian inscriptions, through a primarily Roman filter.[68]

In other words, both the *tesserae hospitales* and the use of bronze could be argued to represent aspects of a much broader set of developments in epigraphic culture across a much broader region, in multiple languages, and in multiple different epigraphic genres. Specifically in relation to the spread of (bronze) *tesserae hospitales*, there may be considerable value in revisiting Philippe Gauthier's suggestion that levels of literacy are a key consideration in the use of such *symbola* or *tesserae*.[69] It is Gauthier's hypothesis that the increasing spread of literacy renders physical and visual tokens of this sort increasingly redundant (whence their apparent disappearance from mainland Greek culture in the course of the fourth century BC), with letters on papyrus and similarly ephemeral documents taking

purely *exempli gratia* the Entella tablets from Sicily (Ampolo 2001) and the Locri archive from Magna Graecia (De Franciscis 1972); western and southern Greece produces considerable amounts of such material also, and from an early date (for a fifth-century example from Argos, by no means unique, Charnoux 1953: 395–7).

66 Poccetti 1999: 555 (cf. Berrendonner 2002: 841–2 on Oscan use of epigraphy in public construction preceding that in Latin); J. De Hoz 1999: 442–8. The most obvious examples of texts on lead from the Iberian coast are the commercial documents from Ampurias (and Pech Maho on the Gallic coast), noted above.

67 Cf. Mullen 2008, above, on mixed influences on Gallo-Greek.

68 Thus, even in the excellent discussion of J. De Hoz (which goes far beyond what this paper attempts), while allowing that the use of writing may precede the Roman conquest, it is nonetheless by the second century a 'Roman' model that drives much of the *epigraphic* practice in the region (1999: 456–62); it is rather as if once the Romans arrive, the rest is forgotten.

69 Gauthier 1972: 86–9; compare the remarks of Woolf 1994.

their place. Such a hypothesis would in fact tie in rather nicely with the rise in the phenomenon of the *tessera* in the western Mediterranean at the same period in which a broad range of epigraphic practice begins to appear in the region – coincident, one assumes, with the first real steps forward in the spread of public literacy in the region.[70] The fact that the use of *tesserae* declines again as we move into the high Empire would also fit with Gauthier's hypothesis, in turn reflecting the moment when literacy arguably took a greater hold across the western Empire. The exact relationship between the spread of epigraphic culture, and more specific elements such as the use of bronze (or other metals), or specific practices such as recording *hospitium* still need to be teased apart, and some of the answers will of course be contingent upon local factors, but the wider context is, I suggest, at least as important, and answers of a more systemic nature also need to be sought.

North Africa

Within North Africa, Cyrenaica marks the traditional limit of Hellenistic studies and of Hellenistic epigraphy as traditionally defined.[71] There are, however, two other major epigraphic cultures of the Hellenistic period which belong within this survey: Punic and Libyco-Berber. Compared to most of the epigraphic cultures considered in this study, Phoenicio-Punic epigraphy is quantitatively significant, with surviving inscriptions totalling nearly 10,000 items. The material is, however, widely spread over time and space, spanning 1,000 years and the whole Mediterranean, and the major concentrations of material, such as at Carthage itself, tend to be of narrowly specific types. Although what follows will focus upon North Africa, and particularly Carthage, it is difficult to treat the Punic material without reference to the wider western Mediterranean basin (although the existence of Punic material in Sicily, Sardinia and Spain has already been noted above).[72] The Archaic material from the western Mediterranean, predominantly stelai from the *tophet* sanctuaries at Carthage and Motya in western Sicily, is small in quantity and mostly lacks the features that mark out the

[70] J. De Hoz 1999: 456 for the penetration of writing ahead of epigraphy among Celtiberians. As noted above, cf. Harris 1989: esp. 174–5, suggesting the major transition in literacy in the Roman world begins around 100 BC, although perhaps later in the western provinces (267–73).

[71] In the absence of a true corpus, the majority of the Hellenistic-period Cyrenaican material is presented and discussed within Laronde 1987.

[72] General survey in Amadasi Guzzo 1995, which is the basis for much of what follows.

later development of Punic (in terms of both script and language), suggesting essentially autonomous developments.[73] The distinctive traits which are associated with Punic, and which mark it out from Phoenician, emerge subsequently and in particular from the fourth century onwards: indeed one could very tentatively suggest that the diffusion in the western Mediterranean of Punic texts in the form typical of that to be found at Carthage is essentially a Hellenistic phenomenon, chronologically speaking. The great majority of Punic epigraphy is votive, or else funerary, and predominantly on stone; other types of text, such as honorifics, are rarely found in western Punic epigraphy (although they are found in small numbers in the Archaic eastern Phoenician material).[74] The material from Carthage, which far outweighs that from elsewhere (over 6,000 texts), dates principally to the period of the fourth to second centuries BC. Smaller but still substantial concentrations of similar material are found at other sites across Libya, Tunisia and Algeria, such as at Constantine (anc. Cirta with the sanctuary of El Hofra).[75] Even on this very limited basis, therefore, it might be possible to argue that the epigraphic culture of Punic sanctuaries, especially the *tophet*, is chronologically at least 'Hellenistic'.

Examples of what one might classify as typical Hellenistic epigraphy in terms of content are rare in the Punic corpus, and in particular in the North African material: a highly unusual example of a public dedication from *c.* 400 BC appears to commemorate a military expedition to Sicily, but in general Punic epigraphy contributes almost nothing to political/military history.[76] The formulation of votive texts shifts over time, and although most of this change relates to shifts in religious practice, Maria Giulia Amadasi notes that in the most complex texts of the Hellenistic period one finds details of sufets or other magistrates currently in office as well as those responsible for the actual work of the dedication. Additionally, a small but significant body of Punic texts of the Hellenistic period reflects some of the patterns associated more generally above with 'Hellenistic' epigraphy, and which do not feature otherwise in Phoenicio-Punic epigraphy. These include the several categories of inscription (mostly North African) gathered by Maurice Szyncer containing the term *'M* ('the people'), which reflect civic activity and identity: third-century BC inscriptions of Carthage recording manumission at the decree of the people; and a more dispersed set of texts, again mainly third-century,

[73] For the Motya material in detail, Amadasi Guzzo 1986.

[74] For categories of Punic material, Amadasi Guzzo 1989–90.

[75] The Carthage material is primarily collected in *CIS* I; for Constantine, see Bertrandy and Sznycer 1987.

[76] *CIS* I.5510 A–B, see now Amadasi Guzzo 2006 with earlier bibliography.

consisting of votives set up at sanctuaries in one city by members of another, recorded as 'belonging to the assembly of the people of *x*'.[77] This latter group finds a broader context in the multi-cultural, multi-lingual presence detectable at several western Mediterranean sanctuaries within the Punic sphere, such as that at Eryx in Sicily, Tas-Silġ in Malta, or of Sid/Sardus Pater at Antas in Sardinia.[78] Such sanctuaries themselves provide one very obvious channel through which the transmission of specific practices, such as writing, are disseminated and taken up. One interesting feature which emerges from the large quantity of onomastic data to be garnered from Punic epigraphy in the western Mediterranean is the gradual diffusion of non-Semitic names in the fourth/third centuries BC, interpreted by Amadasi to suggest 'una certa frammistione di popolazione', i.e. increased interaction and connectivity.[79]

In other words, although the North African Punic epigraphic habit of the fourth to second centuries BC is not typical of the Hellenistic world as traditionally defined, it is nonetheless the case that it is in precisely this period that a particular Punic epigraphic culture flourished, and one which shows some of those elements which elsewhere have attracted the label 'Hellenistic', such as the presence of magistrates in texts, acts of public epigraphy and the epigraphic representation of the civic community. Many other elements of Carthaginian culture accord with this – most obviously the relatively late introduction of coinage, adopted at the end of the fifth/beginning of the fourth century, which is in clear dialogue with material from Sicily and the Hellenistic East[80] – and the broader claim has been made that by the time of the Punic Wars the city was 'by now an integral part of a broadly unified Mediterranean reality'.[81] Such a view sits well with the preceding discussion about the priority or otherwise of Rome in relation to developments in the Iberian peninsula and elsewhere.

[77] Szyncer 1975; the latter group (pp. 59–66) are found in particular at Carthage, but also elsewhere in North Africa and in Sardinia; the Carthaginian texts attest to individuals from across the western Mediterranean, such as Cossura (Pantelleria, *CIS* I.265), Ebusus (Ibiza, *CIS* I.266), Heraclea Minoa (in Sicily, *CIS* I.3707), Sulcis (in Sardinia, *CIS* I.5606).

[78] Eryx, e.g. *CIS* I.135 (= *ICO Sic.* 1, Punic), *IG* XIV.282 (Greek), *CIL* I^2.2221–3 (Latin); dedications to the goddess of Eryx are attested well beyond Sicily, e.g. *ICO Sard.* 19, and the cult was also imported to Rome in the Second Punic War (see in general Schilling 1982: 233–66). Tas-Silġ, e.g. dedication in Punic by Massinissa (Cic. *Verr.* 4.103), a pair of Graeco-Punic bilingual baetyls (*ICO Malta* 1 / 1*bis* = *CIS* I.122 / 122*bis*, see Yarrow, Chapter 12 in this volume), and extensive ceramic graffiti dedications (*ICO Malta*). Antas, e.g. Amadasi Guzzo 1990: no. 17 (dedication by an individual describing himself as 'of the people of Cagliari'). Compare also the discussion of a Sardinian trilingual dedication to Eshmun/Asklapios (*ICO Sard.* 9) by Culasso Gastaldi 2000.

[79] Amadasi Guzzo 1990: 38; cf. Bourdin and Crouzet 2009 for a specific study.

[80] Cf. Yarrow, Chapter 12, this volume; Prag 2011b with bibliography on the Siculo-Punic material in particular.

[81] Bondì 2001: 400 (my transl.).

However, Punic is not the only epigraphic culture to be found in North Africa in this period: Libyan, or Libyco-Berber, is attested by a body of over 1,100 texts from antiquity, found mostly in Algeria, as well as Tunisia and Morocco (as well as a debated set of material from the Canary Islands).[82] The material presents considerable difficulties of interpretation, and is no less subject to the pull of ideologically driven narratives than many of the other epigraphic cultures here considered. Even the choice of name is not without implications, Libyco-Berber appearing to be the currently accepted 'compromise' – as the name indicates, the language, or languages, represented by the several related alphabets used in these inscriptions, is generally taken to have some relation to modern Berber. However, even the relationship between the variant versions of Libyco-Berber attested in the epigraphic record is highly uncertain.

As often, dating lies at the heart of the issue, since only a single Libyco-Berber text (*RIL* 2, from Dougga) contains secure internal evidence for a date (138 BC). Consequently, many scholars tend towards a date in the third or second century BC for the appearance of these inscriptions and the development of the script. However, a strong, but by no means watertight case has been made to date one major text to the sixth or fifth century BC,[83] and arguments have been offered to date some texts as early as the fourteenth or thirteenth century BC.[84] There is greater unanimity on dating the end of the practice to around the fifth century AD. Needless to say, those who argue for an early, or very early date, tend to be those who downplay the extent of Phoenician or Punic influence on the formation of the language and its written form(s), and place greater emphasis upon indigenous traditions.[85] Here too the problem lies in ambivalent evidence, since the alphabet is largely lacking in vowel phonemes, making a Semitic model highly likely, while some half-dozen characters have close correlates in Punic. By itself this does not suggest direct borrowing so much as some

[82] Recent discussion in Kerr 2010, cf. Chaker n.d., also Pichler 1970; the principal *corpus* is that of Chabot 1940–1 (= *RIL*), supplemented but not superceded.

[83] Camps 1978: 148–51, preceded by trenchant arguments against the *a priori* tendencies in the arguments over the relationship of the variant alphabets; but the case for the early date of this particular text depends wholly upon the dating of inscribed iconography in rock art, which is inevitably speculative. It is notable that with one exception the rest of the material collected in Camps 1978 (summary table p. 166) is dated to the third century BC or later.

[84] Chaker and Hachi 2000 (arguing for a two-stage process, where the underlying principles and many of the symbols evolve early in an indigenous context, but are then redeveloped in full as an alphabet in the course of contact with Phoenician/Punic practices – summary on p. 107).

[85] In part reacting against the earlier tendency to attribute a civilising role to Carthage, clearly visible in, e.g. Mommsen 1903: 674–6 and Meltzer 1879–1913: III, 594–608 (so e.g. Chaker n.d.: 10 n. 6 and Camps 1978: 143–5).

level of influence, and the chronology of that influence and its relationship to the language's origin is at the heart of the debate. One recent linguistic analysis by Robert Kerr has plausibly concluded that the best explanation of the various elements is to hypothesise the invention of the alphabet for epigraphic purposes, most probably to be placed in the time of the reign of Massinissa, in the first half of the second century BC.[86] As Kerr reasonably suggests, the use to which the alphabet can be seen to be put in the second century in a public setting makes eminently good sense in the context of a kingdom active on the international stage and seeking to distance itself from Carthage.[87] Viewed in this light, the hypothetical development of Libyco-Berber epigraphy at this point fits eminently well alongside the developments suggested by so-called 'Numidian Royal Architecture', as analysed in Chapter 7 in this volume by Josephine Quinn, who argues that this is all about 'the exploitation of real and symbolic sources of power', in ways that 'cut across lines of conventionally understood political, ethnic or cultural identities', and belong in a much wider set of Mediterranean interactions. From an epigraphic perspective, it is also noteworthy that the local kings of the region inscribe otherwise in Punic, and only begin to make use of Latin from the time of the Civil Wars onwards; Latin itself is almost non-existent in the region before 50 BC (five texts, all by/for Latin speakers).[88]

However, it must be acknowledged that this is only one interpretation, and the evidence is by no means conclusive. The uncertain relationship of the different variants of Libyco-Berber, and the potentially earlier date of some of the material, as well as the extensive presence of graffiti, not merely official or funerary texts, have encouraged some to suggest multiple lines of development and that the use of the script(s) extends some way below the elite.[89] From the perspective of this discussion, the interpretations are not mutually exclusive and both find a place in the picture I am seeking to

[86] Kerr 2010: esp. 54–62. This is of course an interesting return to the chronology of the earlier model of Massinissa the Carthaginian- and Roman-influenced 'civiliser', and specifically as responsible for the development of the Libyco-Berber script (e.g. Meltzer 1879–1913: I, 439, after Mommsen 1903: 674–6 (Meltzer of course citing an earlier edition of Mommsen)), but it is important to emphasise that Kerr does not express it in these terms, and develops a clearly linguistics-based argument (Chaker and Hachi 2000: 107–8 are conscious of similarly echoing earlier interpretations by Gsell and others, but likewise from a different starting point). It is tempting to draw a parallel with the creation of the Old Persian script under Darius, used on the Bisitun Inscription.

[87] Kerr 2010: 61–2.

[88] The point is made by Kerr 2010: 52, 52 n.33 and 62; in more detail Quinn 2003: 16; material in Zucca 1996: 1429–50.

[89] Neatly summed up in Mattingly and Hitchner 1995: 172.

develop. The potentially widespread adoption of writing, perhaps at a relatively early date but which only visibly comes into its own in the course of the third century, speaks of North African society participating in a broader set of western Mediterranean cultural developments. The specific use made of it in an official context in the second and first centuries BC speaks more directly to the use of writing in a public and official context, symbolic of power and authority, again within a wider stream of Mediterranean developments. The latter use, language and location aside, does not look out of place in a typical account of Hellenistic epigraphy; the wider adoption, besides being Hellenistic in date, looks to be no less representative than other Hellenistic epigraphy of the social and cultural developments and interactions of the period.

Epigraphy, connectivity and changing relations of power

It should be apparent from the preceding survey that the period from the fourth to the first centuries BC (i.e. the 'Hellenistic' period) in the western Mediterranean is distinctively rich and diverse from an epigraphic perspective. Not only that, but a number of patterns can be observed that repeat across the region. At a basic level, the spread and use of epigraphy in diverse languages becomes a visible and significant phenomenon. The Hellenistic period marks the moment when many of these regions and peoples experimented on a significant scale with such practices. This is true not only for those peoples who did not previously inscribe, but also for those who did so already, among whom both the scale and the nature of the practice underwent visible transformations, often loosely to be placed in the (long) third century BC. At a more specific level, but not confined to individual languages, particular types of epigraphic practice seem to gain greater prominence, whether commercial documents and *instrumentum domesticum*, or building inscriptions, or public documents and the formulae and content associated with such practices.

Two further elements are worth highlighting briefly, as possible avenues for further investigation. Firstly, I have several times noted that there are some suggestions of a 'gap' in epigraphic practice in various areas, broadly between the late Archaic and the early Hellenistic periods, often to be placed very approximately in the first half of the fourth century BC, whether in Sicily or the Iberian peninsula, in Latin or Punic epigraphy. I suspect that such a gap is itself an artifact of the narratives illustrated above that drive the interpretation of both epigraphic and material culture in the face of difficulties in dating; but whether this is the case requires further study. Secondly, if the discussion initiated here is to be developed further, it seems imperative to take the numismatic evidence more fully into consideration. Space (and lack of competence) precludes examination of this material, but the spread of local coinages in the western Mediterranean, and the diverse use of languages, legends and types shows some striking affinities with the trends in the epigraphic material.[90]

What is it therefore that is 'special' about this period? Two major themes suggest themselves, and they take their inspiration respectively from the principal pre-existing models of the Hellenistic period and Romanisation. As already suggested at the start of this chapter, calling such patterns of practice 'Hellenistic', other than by virtue of their chronology, does not seem particularly constructive, and hardly offers an explanation; frequently it only encourages the even more problematic application of the concept of 'Hellenisation'.[91] One theme, however, which recurs in many recent discussions of this epigraphic material is that of pan-Mediterranean interactions, of a Mediterranean (or Hellenistic) *koine*. So, for example, Javier De Hoz, discussing the Iberian material, remarks:

> we must remember that, regardless of wars and conquests, the Mediterranean had been, for centuries, a zone of contact and exchange in which technologies and skills, frequently involving writing, were transmitted, and that a whole series of epigraphic practices existed, which were linked to commerce and manufacture, of Hellenistic origin, and which, with adaptions and local peculiarities, were being taken up in Italy and Iberia prior to 218 [BC].[92]

As was noted at the very beginning, it is quite possible to draw parallels with epigraphic practice in, e.g. Asia Minor or the Aegean, traditionally described as Hellenistic. But how far the observation of such parallels should lead to a suggestion of 'Hellenistic origin' is another matter (compare the discussion of Andrew Wilson in Chapter 5 in this volume). Should we define or map the Hellenistic by, for example, the distribution of particular patterns of Greek epigraphic practice, or by the far more extensive web of economic (and human) connections across (and beyond) the Mediterranean in this period?[93] Perhaps we should be considering what, if anything, the West has

[90] Cf. Liv Yarrow's paper, Chapter 12, this volume. See for example Chaves Tristán 1998 on coinage of Baetica in this period, Frey-Kupper 2006 on Sicilian coinage, or the development of Siculo-Punic coinage (Manfredi 2000; Cutroni Tusa 2000, cf. Prag 2011b), or Punic coinage more generally (Manfredi 2006).

[91] Cf. Bats *et al.* 1992: 469 urging that the latter term be banned.

[92] J. De Hoz 1995: 71 (my transl.).

[93] The paradox internal to Davies 2006, noted at the start.

in common with the East in this period: rather than emphasising epigraphic practice or material culture *per se*, I would, therefore, prefer to emphasise the conditions which generate that material culture and the Mediterranean *koine*, and I take epigraphy to be particularly illustrative of those changing conditions.

The regional discussions cited earlier in this paper repeatedly place the emphasis on what can most easily be tagged as 'connectivity' and its consequences. Thus Sardinian epigraphy illustrated an 'opening up to the Mediterranean'; Etruscan and Oscan revealed increasing administrative and juridical complexity, civic identity, the growing public/private divide, 'in sum, the development of the public sphere', in other words, an effort to present an outward-facing identity; in southern Italy it was an assertion of identity in the face of increased regional interaction and perceived cultural threats; in southern Gaul it marked 'the internal evolution of a society', with a predominance in commercial and economic material, and repeated emphasis upon increasing complexity; in Spain, 'a remarkable collective instance' of self-representation; Carthage was 'an integral part of a broadly unified Mediterranean reality'. Increasing commercial interaction, human movement, social complexity and concern with collective and personal representation are constant themes of the Hellenistic period, all of which find one obvious outlet (among many) in epigraphic practice. Viewed in this light, the division between East and West is highly artificial (cf. Nicholas Purcell, Chapter 13 of this volume), since these are common themes across the Mediterranean. Calling any of this 'Hellenistic' begins to look increasingly counter-productive (and unnecessarily Hellenocentric), so-called 'Hellenistic epigraphy' of the East itself belonging within a wider world of contemporary development.

In the second place, as has been repeatedly highlighted in this chapter, many regional discussions of epigraphic practice, and indeed discussions of the western Mediterranean as a whole in this period, have taken the rise of the Roman Empire as central to any explanatory model. The coincidence with Roman expansion is indeed striking, but as many commentators have observed (those quoted above, and others), the relevance of that coincidence is far from immediately obvious. In Sicily, in Spain, in southern Gaul, almost the first visible *Latin* epigraphy, frequently in virtual isolation both spatially and chronologically, is a solitary surviving milestone, and Latin epigraphy in the West, outside Italy, is scarce in the extreme before 50 BC. This is hardly the material for such 'epigraphic revolutions' – although it is perhaps emblematic of the role of the inscribed word and the changing world of the western Mediterranean in this period. The Latin epigraphic habit suggests that Rome is no more than another example of the wider phenomenon.

In other words, on the basis of the picture of epigraphic development in the western Mediterranean from the fourth century BC onwards, I wish to suggest not only that Romanisation is not the relevant model, but also that the 'Hellenistic' world, as traditionally defined, is itself merely part of a broader set of developments. If that is the case, besides increased connectivity, what common factors might we observe? One repeating theme across these regional discussions, besides increasing interactions (economic, military, demographic), is that of clear shifts in regional power structures. In this respect, Roman imperialism is a major consideration, but hardly unique in the western Mediterranean. For Greg Woolf, looking at southern Gaul and Spain, the key lay in the significance of power relations:

> . . . as a context shaping the way that writing was adopted, adapted, used, and rejected. The punctuation of the history of the spread of writing [at least as witnessed in epigraphic practice] resulted from shifts in power . . . In this respect, then, writing seems no different from other aspects of culture, for example the potter's wheel, viticulture, or stone architecture.[94]

That being so, to prioritise writing in Latin (or Punic or Greek), as opposed to writing itself, risks missing the point. But use of the term Romanisation makes such prioritisation almost unavoidable, and the term 'Hellenistic' has a very similar effect. The world of Alexander and his Successors, the 'Hellenistic East', was itself an area of massively shifting power relations, and that is often cited as a major consideration in the development and understanding of 'Hellenistic culture'.[95] Rome and Carthage may not be Hellenistic kingdoms, Syracusan leaders mere pretenders to such a title, but these still lie at the heart of major shifts in the power relations of the West (and, indeed, of the East), to which communities and individuals felt the need to respond. In the struggles over Hellenisation and Romanisation, it should not be forgotten that Carthaginian hegemony in the western Mediterranean, however precisely it should be understood, took on new forms from the fourth century onwards.[96] The Hellenistic period, whether in the East, under the Successors, or in the West in the face of first Carthage, and then Rome, saw the rise of a new level of power relations, with supra-*polis* (i.e. city-state), indeed supra-regional powers emerging across the

[94] Woolf 1994: 98 (my insertion in square brackets).

[95] See Ma 2000b for an excellent discussion of one aspect of this.

[96] See e.g. Bondì 1990–1 on Sicily, and 2006: 134–5, 2009b: 462 on the developments in territorial control of Sicily and Sardinia in this period; Wagner 1989 on Spain.

Mediterranean. Alongside Nicholas Purcell's 'novel conditions of circulation' (Chapter 13), we should perhaps think about 'novel relations of power' across the Mediterranean from the fourth century onwards, and the ways in which communities and individuals can respond. The Hellenistic kings were just one part of this; Rome, Carthage, Syracusan tyrants, the Numidian kings and the Spaniards who called Scipio 'king' were some of the others.[97] Polybius was right, and for precisely that reason it is time we put the 'Hellenistic' behind us.[98]

97 Polyb. 10.38.3.

98 Polyb. 1.3.4: 'But ever since this date [220 BC–216 BC], history has been an organic whole (σωματοειδῆ), and the affairs of Italy and Libya have been interlinked with those of Greece and Asia . . .' (trans. Paton, revised Walbank and Habicht). Cf. Eckstein 2006 for an IR-theory-based analysis of the entire Mediterranean as a single system, placing the key moment of power-transition in the same period (explicitly with Polybius) – although still ultimately oriented around an approach that deals with Rome in the West, the Hellenistic states in the East.

12 | Heracles, coinage and the West: three Hellenistic case-studies

LIV MARIAH YARROW

Any pervasive socio-political phenomenon is made up of repeated individual acts. Each act is informed by broader trends and is yet simultaneously local and unique. It follows that socio-political phenomena should be identifiable through the presence of such iterations. As Barthes says, 'repetition of the concept through different forms is precious to the mythologist, it allows him to decipher the myth: it is the insistence of a kind of behaviour that reveals its intention'.[1] We can rephrase the beginning of the quotation and do little harm to the logic: 'repetition of a socio-political phenomenon through different actions is precious to the historian, it allows her to decipher the cultural construction: it is the insistence of a kind of behaviour that reveals its intention'.

The creation and reception of numismatic images are among the many acts which generated the socio-political phenomenon we label as the 'Hellenistic'. Reproduction and deployment of any image in diverse contexts disseminates the meaning, allowing its semantic field to broaden, shift and develop.[2] This is particularly true of numismatic imagery on account of the repetition and dispersal inherent in striking and circulation.[3]

One of the criticisms most often levelled at studies concerned with numismatic iconography is that coins are first and foremost units of monetary

I am indebted to J. Quinn and J. Prag for the opportunity to contribute to this project and their patience and encouragement throughout. J. Ma's response to my paper was invaluable. I also owe heartfelt thanks to R. Viscusi, M. Hashmi, D. Schur and C. Williams for their inspiration, advice and critique. All errors and omissions are my own. The American Numismatic Society and British Museum generously allowed me access to their collections and libraries during the preparation of this paper.

[1] Barthes 1972 [1957]: 120.

[2] On dissemination, see generally Derrida 1981 and more specifically 1982: xxiv and 1988; for analysis Bearn 1995: esp. 9. Also relevant here and worthy of further consideration for their theoretical application to the study of Greco-Roman antiquity are post-colonial studies of mimicry such as Bhabha 1984, and also anthropological investigations such as Toren 1988, a particularly careful reading of reproductions of Leonardo da Vinci's 'Last Supper' displayed in Fijian domestic contexts.

[3] Benjamin 1969: esp. 218 where there is passing reference to the striking of coins as one of the only means by which ancient peoples mass-produced images. Also, see Goux 1990; and Shell 1982, 1994 for theoretical approaches to numismatics.

exchange and that one should not inflate the significance of the images when we have little testimony for their impact on viewers or the intentions of those creating the images.[4] While at present many scholars seem positively disposed to interpreting coin imagery as politically significant, two arguments in particular for that point of view are worth emphasising.

Firstly, gender theory has taught us that an act may perpetuate a social construction without that being the conscious intention of the agent.[5] Most women do not get up in the morning, think 'I'm going to enact my gender' and then put on their make-up. This does not negate the fact that the wearing of eyeliner is a performance which has come to be naturalised as a 'feminine' act through collective repetition. In fact the banal pervasiveness of the action lends it greater power to naturalise the social construction. This is no less true of numismatic iconography: an image that becomes normative, even 'thoughtless' in its deployment, is more, not less, likely to be generating a social construction.

Secondly, that coinage has a primary monetary function does not mean that it cannot have secondary functions. 'Identity formation' is just one example of a secondary function of ancient coinage that has come to be widely accepted.[6] These secondary functions are directly analogous to linguistic connotations or Barthes' 'myth', i.e. to what is called the second order of signification in semiotics. The semiotic model reminds us that secondary orders of signification are no less real than the first. They are dependent on the first and consequently cannot negate or replace or overshadow it: the connotations of any word are inextricably linked to its denotation. Thus a coin has a monetary function, but it may also perform further socio-political functions. Notably both functions are dependent on iterability. Money only works as currency because it is recognised as such by its multiple iterations. The unique coin does not spend; the unique coin cannot disseminate the meaning of the image it bears.

The question of eastern influences on the western Mediterranean has been approached from a numismatic perspective before. Williams and Burnett have given full treatment to the question of the influence of Alexander's coinage on minting in the western Mediterranean.[7] They question the

[4] The debate has been most vocal in the study of Roman imperial coinage; see Levick 1999 with bibliographical references to earlier stages in the debate.

[5] Butler 1990, 2004.

[6] The best literature on this treats coinage of the Roman period, but the basic concept is equally applicable to earlier periods. For the use of numismatics in a historical approach to questions of identity, see Pobjoy 2000. For a variety of numismatic approaches, see Howgego *et al.* 2005.

[7] Williams and Burnett 1998.

assumptions which have often been made regarding both the quantity of Alexander coinage that circulated in the West and the political motivations behind any iconographic changes. Their systematic survey of published hoard material and broad coverage of the mints gives great weight to their largely negative conclusions. In short, they assert that there were few coins of Alexander in the West and that it is dangerous to assume particular political conditions lurk behind any shift in iconography. This landmark study is an invaluable anchor point. Whereas they were looking for specific links between Alexander's numismatic iconography and that of the western mints in the first generation after his death (that is in the first thirty years), I am considering how the shifts in western numismatic imagery over a wider time-span are part of the creation of the Hellenistic period.

The following three case-studies examine changes in the representation of the divinity know as Heracles on the coinage of different minting authorities from the late fourth to mid-third centuries in Italy, Sicily and North Africa. I argue that the deployment of such numismatic representations is not a reflection, that is to say a byproduct, of the emergence of the 'Hellenistic' in the western Mediterranean, but part of the means by which the period was made manifest. This shift in numismatic images is one of the many socio-political acts which, taken together, generated a broad cultural shift to what we call the Hellenistic period. The nature of these shifts helps illuminate some of what makes the Hellenistic West unique and distinctive. Above all, these three case-studies demonstrate a willingness to deploy iconography developed in the East in contexts which localise and resignify the representations of Heracles. This usage broadens, and does not limit, the underlying connotations of each image.

This emblematic versatility of representations of Heracles in the Hellenistic West can be tied to three underlying factors: (1) the elaborate narrative tradition of his western labours; (2) the patterns of religious syncretism with Melqart; and (3) how the Heracles mythology and iconography was radically developed by Alexander the Great, in no small part through his numismatic iconography and that of the *diadochoi*.[8] If a mythic figure is likely to help us

[8] Heracles has not suffered in recent years from a lack of scholarly attention, particularly in regard to his role in the western Mediterranean; of particular note are Bernardini and Zucca 2005; Massa Pairault 1999 (esp. the three articles in section one, 'Héraclès en Occident: Le «Visiteur», Le Héros «Ethnique» et Le Héros Gentilice'); Mastrocinque 1993; Bonnet and Jourdain-Annequin 1992 (esp. articles by Jourdain-Annequin, Le Glay, and Van Wonterghem); and especially the landmark work, Bonnet 1988. The current avenues of inquiry have been inspired largely by the techniques developed and refined by Malkin for looking at mythology as both a product and catalyst of social interaction, see his 1998: esp. 5–7; for methodology compare also Dench 1995: esp. 32 and Erskine 2001: esp. 2–6. There is still much value in Bickermann 1952.

Figure 12.1 AR stater, Heraclea Lucaniae. Obv.: head of Athena (r.) with Attic helmet; rev.: Heracles wrestling the Nemean lion, club to left. Image not to scale.

answer questions regarding the distinctive nature of the Hellenistic West, it will surely be the figure of Heracles.

Heraclea Lucaniae

At the end of the fourth century BC or, at the latest, at the beginning of the third, the mint of Heraclea Lucaniae changed its previously stable obverse and reverse designs. The mint had issued coins since the foundation of the city in 433/2 BC by colonists from both Tarentum and Thurii, and the dominant type seems to reflect these founding influences (Figure 12.1). The obverse shows the head of Athena in an Attic helmet, often found on the coinage of Thurii and thought to be inspired by that city's connections with Athens. The reverse shows Heracles wrestling the Nemean lion; a similar design periodically occurs on the coins of Tarentum. Van Keuren suggests that this is an appropriate choice of imagery because of Heracles' status as a 'Dorian Hero'.[9] Although there is some parallel iconography from the Peloponnesus from an early date, I am not convinced this is a particularly meaningful framework for thinking about the iconographic choices involved. More significant is how the image choice consciously reiterates the iconography of near neighbours (i.e. Thurii and Tarentum), communities of continuing importance to Heraclea's well-being.

At the end of the fourth century the designs suddenly shift, even though the basic subject matter stays the same. On the obverse Athena is represented with a Corinthian helmet and the reverse displays a standing Heracles with attributes.[10] In a city named for the hero, representations of Heracles are

[9] Van Keuren 1994: 14. On the coinage of this mint also see the entry by Johnston in Rutter 2001: 124–130.

[10] Most attention has been given to the Corinthian helmet which appears on the head of Athena. Even sceptical Williams and Burnett concede that this may be influenced by the gold stater design of Alexander the Great (1998: 383). Except for a short-lived experimentation with a

Figure 12.2 AR stater, Heraclea Lucaniae. Obv.: head of Athena (r.) with Corinthian helmet; rev.: Heracles standing, lion-skin pelt draped over his left arm, bow in left hand, club in right hand. Image not to scale.

likely to take on particular symbolic meaning, to be reflections of that city's self-constructed identity. In fact, the reverse design changes before the obverse helmet. There is a short-lived issue dated to the 330s BC which shows the standing Heracles with an Attic helmet on the obverse. From this point onwards the wrestling scene never reappears and the standing Heracles is consistently shown nude, the lion-skin pelt draped over his left arm, and usually with a club in or near his right hand (Figure 12.2). There are variations with owl and *nike* in the field, others in which Heracles holds a *skyphos*, cornucopia, or is crowning himself. I do not mean to minimise these variations, but the basic type of the standing Heracles emerges at the point we usually associate with the beginning of the Hellenistic age and remains consistent until the end of silver minting by the city, a debated date, but plausibly placed *c.* 250 BC. The end of minting is sometimes connected with Rome's growing political influence at Heraclea, beginning with the treaty signed during the Pyrrhic War.

Some still credit Lehmann's suggestion that the variations on the reverse 'standing Heracles' type correspond to two different cult statues at Heraclea and that both statues derive from Scopas' Sicyonian cult statue, with the important difference of the bow being substituted for the apples of the Hesperides.[11] Holloway, however, interprets the variations to indicate that the scene is pictorial, rather than sculptural.[12] In defence of Lehmann's hypothesis, van Keuren has drawn attention to a small unpublished statuette of Heracles in the Museo Nazionale della Siritide near the ancient site of Heraclea, which he says has 'the same weighting of the legs and the

three-quarter-facing Athena during the Pyrrhic Wars, the Corinthian helmet remains the obverse type for Heraclea Lucaniae until the end of its silver minting. As an aside, it seems perfectly plausible to me that the Corinthian helmet may have been derived directly from the Corinthian Pegasus staters which circulated in southern Italy at this time as well.

[11] Lehmann 1946: 53–62. [12] Holloway 1978: 56–7.

same position of the club and the right arm with elbow out'.[13] However, he acknowledges that the lion-skin is draped over the shoulder not the arm on the statuette. Even if we could establish that the image is intended to represent the local cult statue, would this bring us closer to understanding the iconographic switch? The inspiration for this representation is undoubtedly to be found in the art of the eastern Mediterranean, be it Scopas' Sicyonian cult statue or a similar composition; nevertheless determining a specific direct antecedent seems tenuous, even irrelevant, given the variations in the Lucanian types.

Perhaps we can approach the question from another direction. By setting aside the image of Heracles wrestling the Nemean lion, what in particular were they rejecting? What did that earlier image connote? One answer might be a close identification with their mother-cities which inspired the original types. The initial catalyst for the changes is likely to have been the arrival of Alexander the Molossian, who broke with the Tarentines by seizing Heraclea and trying to move the general assembly which met there to Thurian territory (Livy 8.24.4 and Strabo 6.3.4). The abandonment of the Tarentine reverse design, followed shortly by the discarding of the Thurian obverse design, seems to fit this narrative well. Thus we see a rejection not of an image for its primary meaning, but instead for its second order of signification, its connotations.

However, the consistency of the new types thereafter seems to me to argue against limiting our interpretation of the type to a single political impetus. The new types allowed Heraclea to develop their public iconography independent of the original influences, to explore what sort of Heracles was appropriate to symbolise their city in its own right. Unlike Heracles wrestling the lion, which was for all intents and purposes a borrowed type, the standing Heracles allowed Heraclea to represent their own Heracles on their coinage. By which I mean, not one limited to a single labour, the defeat of the Nemean lion, but one which through the use of accompanying attributes could reflect the appropriate characteristics of this divinity as a patron of the city. The standing figure was versatile enough to allow small symbolic changes of local meaning as they were felt desirable: winged victories, pious libations, cornucopiae and more. It would be futile for us to search for a specific stimulus behind each variation, but I do not doubt that each choice was symbolic and appropriate to the time in which it was minted. The Heracleans decided to utilise the symbolic potency of their patron divinity, leaving behind a static

[13] Van Keuren 1994: 31.

borrowed narrative. Each new attribute allowed the reiterated Heracles to disseminate further its meaning.

What does this change tell us about the Hellenistic West? First, eastern catalysts, whether political (Alexander the Molossian) or cultural (Scopas' Sicyonian cult statue), cannot fully account for the form or extent of the change. The new representation of Heracles at Heraclea Lucaniae may be simultaneously a response to local, regional and supra-regional influences, but this was not strictly a reactionary or momentary trend. The stability and endurance of the new image on the city coinage ensures that it came to be definitive of a period within the city's history. The statuette of Heracles in the Museo Nazionale della Siritide confirms that this new type of Heracles was adopted for personal as well as civic representations. The flexibility of the new image to respond with small design variations to local contemporary circumstances may well have added to its longevity and utility as a badge of civic identity. At the same time the overall character of the image – Heracles and his common attributes – is stable and readily identifiable, not just by a local audience, but anywhere within the Mediterranean basin. This Heracles is at once local and universal.

Siculo-Punic issues

The two remaining case-studies demonstrate both Greek and Punic influences and they are both short-lived issues produced for very specific military purposes. However, like the coins of Heraclea Lucaniae, these issues demonstrate a sharp stylistic break from earlier imagery and seem to interact with local, regional and supra-regional trends. In particular the new representations of Heracles can be read from both a local and universalising perspective.

Firstly, there are the Siculo-Punic issues with a lion-scalp covered head on the obverse and a horse head with palm tree on the reverse (Figure 12.3). For the moment I withhold judgement as to whether it would be more accurate to speak of the obverse head as Heracles or Melqart. These issues have been dated from hoard evidence to the period between 305 and 295 BC, after Agathocles' return from Africa. They come in a long series of silver coinage minted by the Carthaginians in Sicily, but break sharply in iconography from both preceding issues and the gold coinage minted at Carthage itself. The majority of earlier issues are of the Tanit (Demeter)/Horse type (Figure 12.4), and just before the issue in question there had been a type with Arethusa, borrowing the iconography of Syracuse. Jenkins has fully

Figure 12.3 AR tetradrachm, Carthage, Siculo-Punic issue. Obv.: lion-scalp covered male head (r.); rev.: horse head (l.) with palm tree to right. Image not to scale.

Figure 12.4 AR tetradrachm, Carthage, Siculo-Punic issue. Obv.: head of Tanit/Demeter (l.); rev.: standing horse (l.), palm tree behind. Image not to scale.

published and discussed these issues and I do not propose to revisit them in detail here.[14] For our purposes it is sufficient to note that there is a sharp break in obverse iconography.[15] The designers of these coins decided to copy relatively faithfully not just the image of Alexander's tetradrachms, but also carefully to imitate the artistic style, a reiteration in a wholly unprecedented context.

Jenkins wants to see the adoption of an Alexander-style coinage as a statement by Carthage itself that it is a major imperial power; he links this with Carthaginian consciousness of the fall of Tyre to Alexander. In his mind it is logical that Carthage would want to model itself on the coinage of the new eastern power. Williams and Burnett have questioned the likelihood of this logic primarily because of what they see as very little evidence of widespread familiarity with Alexander's coinage in the West at this time.

[14] G. Jenkins 1978. Cf. Jenkins and Lewis 1963: esp. discussion on 23–4, appendix 1, nos. 41–53, and Pl. 26.10. For broader contextualisation, see Mildenberg 1989: esp. 6–8 and Bondì 1990–1 and 2000.

[15] Camarina *c.* 425–405 BC struck tetradrachms with a head of Heracles wearing the lion-scalp (*SNG ANS* 1205); the dies are signed by the engraver Exakestidas. This representation provides an important artistic link between more classical representations of the same subject and those of the Hellenistic period.

I am concerned that it may be incorrect to see these Siculo-Punic issues, which so clearly assert that they are military issues not civic coinage, as evidence of general Carthaginian aspirations. We need to think of them in their Siculo-Punic context minted by and for men who lived in a world governed by particularly diverse cultural influences.[16]

Williams and Burnett may well be right that not all of the men originally paid in this coinage would have recognised the iconic obverse design like we do as emblematic of Alexander the Great. So if that is not what they would see, why is it there? And what would they have thought they were looking at? How does the meaning of the imagery disseminate in this new context? Here we come to the question of whether this head should, in this context, be called Heracles or Melqart and even whether this is a meaningful distinction. Syncretism between these two divinities began well before this period.[17] What the iconography of these obverses forces us to consider, when coupled with the clearly Punic reverse, is whether that syncretism underwent a change, a change generated in part by the iconography itself, perhaps even a change which we might label as Hellenistic.

The designers of the coins were conscious of the coinage of Alexander the Great, of that much we can be certain. They also knew that the Carthaginian population, or at least those serving in the Carthaginian army – we should not make too many assumptions regarding their ethnic identity given the extensive use of mercenaries – would be familiar with the god Melqart as an important Carthaginian deity.[18] The assimilation of Heracles' attributes to Melqart was such that even on funerary art we find Hellenising images of Melqart juxtaposed with more Punic iconography.[19] Artistic syncretism, the assimilation of imagery from one divinity to another, and the juxtaposition of artistic styles were already normative in the western Mediterranean.

For this instance of Heracles imagery to be generative of the new cultural phenomenon of 'the Hellenistic', its iteration must disseminate the meaning of Heracles in such a way as to naturalise the association of the image with the Hellenistic. That is to say, in this context the image must evoke something

[16] Bondì argues that it is precisely at this moment that Carthaginian territorial imperialism in Sicily begins fully to develop with supra-polis regional institutions (1990–1 and 2000) and we can also recall literary allusions to cultural exchange such as Dion's guest-friendship with a Carthaginian (Plut. *Dion* 25.5–6) and Agathocles' father in Thermae sending to Delphi via Carthaginian envoys (Diod. Sic. 19.2.2). J. Prag kindly drew my attention to these references.

[17] See n. 8 above for relevant bibliography.

[18] Diod. Sic. 20.14 records how Melqart had received special honours less than a decade earlier when the Carthaginians sent a special offering to Tyre in 310 BC after Agathocles' landing in Africa.

[19] E.g. the two razor hatchets from the Sainte-Monique cemetery, Bonnet 1988: 220–2.

which other images could not, and this iteration must evoke something which the same image could not in a different context.

Unlike previous obverse designs that borrowed from the surrounding western Greek communities, particularly Syracuse, the recipients of these coins would have immediately noted the strong stylistic difference, and perhaps even understood it to have been of eastern inspiration. Consider how the head fills the whole field of the flan, the strong modelling of the face, the deep-set eyes, the dynamic, well-defined hair on the lion-scalp. Contrast this with the general impression of both the preceding Arethusa and Tanit (Demeter) types, with soft, smooth, placid faces, and delicately arranged hair, all framed by a wide field. By introducing this radical new eastern iconography the minters were breaking with a Sicilian numismatic vocabulary. The Alexander prototype offered an opportunity to embrace a distinctively different type of Greek imagery from the western Greek models they had thus far been employing. Moreover, it allowed them to associate that powerful cultural precedent with a significant Phoenician divinity of timely relevance.

Our familiarity with the coinage of the *diadochoi* leaves us feeling relatively confident as we deduce what this particular image connotes, but in this western context ought we to be so confident regarding the denotations? If asked whether it is Melqart or Heracles being represented on these Siculo-Punic coins, I must answer that it is simultaneously both. The possibility of simultaneity is perhaps easier to conceptualise if we consider a pair of bilingual inscriptions from Malta, dating from the second century BC (*IG* XIV.600 = *CIS* I.122 and 122*bis*).[20] The Greek inscription reads:

Διονύσιος καὶ Σαραπίων οἱ Σαραπίωνος Τύριοι Ἡρακλεῖ ἀρχηγέτει.

The Tyrians Dionysius and Sarapion, sons of Sarapion, (dedicate these) to Heracles the Founder.

The Punic inscription:

L'DNN LMLQRT B'L ṢR 'Š NDR 'BDK 'BD'SR W'ḤY 'SRŠMR ŠN BN 'SRŠMR BN 'BD'SR K ŠM' QLM YBRKM.

To our Lord Melqart, Lord of Tyre, your servant Abdosir and his brother Osirshamar, both sons of Osirshamar, son of Abdosir dedicate these, because he heard their voice; let him bless them.

These betylic dedications each carry the same bilingual text. If we compare the two halves of the text, the first point to observe is that there are no direct

[20] For contextualisation one might compare Culasso Gastaldi 2000 (on a Sardinian trilingual).

parallels. As we might have suspected the name of the honoured divinity has changed, but note that the names of the dedicants also change. Abdosir refers to himself as Dionysius in Greek and his brother Osirshamar is Sarapion. The names Abdosir and Osirshamar are theophoric, based on the Egyptian god Osiris, respectively 'Servant of Osir' and 'Osir has guarded'.[21] Thus Osiris is 'translated' as Dionysus and Sarapis in the Greek names of the two brothers. When the language shifts so does the identity of the speaker, and likewise the identity of the divinity. Abdosir conceived of himself as having two identities and in this religious context he wanted to make an offering using both of his identities. Dionysius honours Heracles and Abdosir Melqart: the dual language inscription is required to express the totality of the benefaction. And yet just as Dionysius is Abdosir, so Heracles is Melqart. We can think about the identity of the head on the coin in the same way: it is an image chosen by Carthaginians to reach a partly Carthaginian audience, so hence it is Melqart, but that does not mean it has stopped being Heracles, specifically the Heracles whom Alexander the Great had infused with meaning, and it certainly does not preclude the Carthaginians also thinking of the image as Heracles. The one instantiation contains within it all possible iterations. There are only right answers to the question 'is it Heracles or Melqart?'.[22]

The role of iteration in this dissemination of meaning is made even more apparent when we contrast the Siculo-Punic tetradrachms with the lion-scalp head with a very rare specimen depicting a bearded male with an earring from earlier in the Siculo-Punic coin series (Figure 12.5).[23] This coin is usually dated to the last quarter of the fourth century BC along with the rest of the types bearing the legend RŠMLQRT. This legend translates, 'head of Melqart' and probably refers to a Carthaginian provincial institution,

Figure 12.5 AR tetradrachm, Carthage, Siculo-Punic issue. Obv.: head of a bearded male (r.) with an earring; rev.: quadriga (l.). Image not to scale.

[21] So Renan in *CIS* I.122 and 122*bis*.

[22] On bilingualism, see J. Adams 2003 and Amadasi Guzzo 1988.

[23] G. Jenkins 1971: 55.

perhaps an army unit, rather than a specific city or geographical place.[24] The legend has led most scholars reasonably to identify the head as Melqart. There are local parallels for a bearded male with an earring on the coins of Solus (Solunto) and Motya, as well as on Siculo-Punic bronzes. Thus the image is not unique, but of only local and limited resonance. We cannot even be wholly confident of our identification of the iconography. By contrast the later Siculo-Punic tetradrachms with the lion-scalp head are part of a Mediterranean-wide trend towards imitating the coinage of Alexander. The widespread dispersal of Alexander's coinage and its imitators brings the imagery into the common cultural framework of diverse viewers. Thus iteration of the image naturalises the association with Alexander, but also, through the diversity of the deployment, the image takes on innumerable local dimensions.

This is not necessarily an immediate result, but a development over time. Burnett and Williams are absolutely correct to emphasise the implausibility that the first recipients of these coins would have recognised them as imitating the coinage of Alexander – and consequently our inability to attribute to the minters any plausible hope of deriving immediate political benefit from evoking such a connection. However, the large-scale production of this imitative image juxtaposed with Punic imagery meant that the minters, probably unconsciously, were naturalising the association of this Heracles type with their own power as well as that of Alexander. Those who first encountered these Siculo-Punic issues and then later handled tetradrachms of Alexander or his successors would have come to recognise the Heracles type as associated with Hellenistic military-political structures regardless of whether or not this was one of the original motivations behind the choice of type.

Mercenary Revolt coinage

Although the widespread dispersal of Alexander's coinage and its imitators brought specific types of Heracles imagery into the common cultural framework of diverse viewers, this process took time. My final, later, case-study demonstrates how the reiteration of the imagery, and the consequent dissemination, naturalise the ideological underpinnings. The coinage in

[24] Mildenberg 1993, but also see Cutroni Tusa 1995. Manfredi 1985 hypothesises that the coins bearing this legend may be linked to an as yet unidentified sanctuary. See discussion and bibliography collected by Lipiński 1995: 237 n. 107.

question uses two different representations of Heracles in the same series: both are Hellenistic in character, both integrate eastern parallels with regional traditions in new local contexts.

This is an unusual issue of coinage attributed to the Mercenary Revolt (241–238 BC) which followed the First Punic War, and in this instance we have extensive literary testimony from Polybius regarding the context in which the objects were created (Polyb. 1.67). After the Romans defeated the Carthaginians in Sicily and imposed sharp punitive fines, the Carthaginians were faced with the dilemma of how to disband their very sizable, ethnically mixed mercenaries. Gisco, the governor of Lilybaeum, sent them back in small groups hoping that they could be dealt with piecemeal, but when delays caused them to group together in the city of Carthage and the first signs of trouble began, they were sent on to wait in Sicca. The Carthaginians needed to negotiate a reduced rate of pay because of their financial straits. Unsurprisingly, this was not acceptable to the mercenaries.

Polybius emphasises the mixed nationality of the forces: Iberians, Gauls, Ligurians, Balearics, part-Greeks and Africans. He attributes the difficulty of the payment negotiations to problems of communication; skilled oratory had no hope of working on this audience. In describing the leaders of the revolt he focuses on one man, Spendius, whom he identifies as an ex-Roman slave from Campania, largely motivated to make trouble by his fear of returning to a state of servitude. He is presented as an unscrupulous character with a talent for motivational speaking. He is said to have created a powerful partnership with Matho, the leader of the Libyan soldiers. They were able to convince the communities of North Africa under Carthaginian rule to revolt, creating a civil war. Although Polybius might have taken some liberties in his characterisation of Spendius, we should take seriously his comments on cultural interaction. The coins themselves reflect such interaction in the choice and juxtaposition of images and text.

The series is complex: multiple denominations, diverse iconography, unique metallurgical profile and uncertain chronology. Scholarly discussion has been equally complex.[25] Zimmermann identifies nine types, four silver in three denominations and six bronze ranging in size from *c.* 19.5 grams to *c.* 6.5 grams, all with the Greek ethnic, ΛIBYΩN. However, his system excludes anepigraphic coins usually attributed to the mercenaries. Crawford's older division of the coinage into 'Carthaginian types' and 'native types' covering five denominations (double-shekel, shekel, half-shekel, bronze

[25] E. Robinson 1943, 1953; Crawford 1985: 135–8; Carradice and La Niece 1988; Manganaro 1992; Vanni 1993: 123; Manfredi 1995: 155–7 and 260–3; Keyser 1995–6; Zimmermann 2001.

unit and bronze half) is still a useful overview of the entire coinage.[26] His 'Carthaginian types' all have Tanit on the obverse; the reverse designs include a standing horse, plough or corn-ear. His 'native types' include Zeus/bull charging, Heracles in lion-skin/lion prowling, diademed Heracles/lion prowling, Heracles in lion-skin/bull charging, Athena/bull charging. All the silver types are debased and contain less than 35 per cent silver; many specimens are obviously overstruck on Carthaginian coinage.[27] Our interpretation of the denominational structure is complicated by the use of an arsenical copper alloy as imitation silver.[28]

Taken together, the relatively sophisticated denomination system, the effort involved in restriking Carthaginian coins and the complex metallurgy all indicate the administrative sophistication of the revolt. This might be called crisis coinage because of its debasement, but in particular the overstriking of Carthaginian coins suggests that ideological motivations were also at play. The revolting mercenaries and their local allies clearly felt it was worth the time, energy and resources to remove Carthaginian imagery from the flans and replace it with iconography and inscriptions of their own. The symbolic change would not have made the coin more spendable or valuable (if anything, less so). The overstriking is an overt statement of autonomy, a rejection of the original mint authority. The language and iconography chosen for the overstriking is simultaneously part of that rejection and the establishment of a new authority.

The use of Greek script can be taken as a reflection of the mixed ethnic make-up of the group, even if Greekness is a characteristic Polybius tries to minimise in his description of the rebels. What one cannot say is that the Greek is a rejection of Punic. This coinage is in fact bilingual with a large prominent *mem* on nearly all specimens; some also have *alpha* or *zayin* or *mu*. The interpretation of the letters is much debated and still elusive; it cannot be just a mint mark given the size and consistence across the specimens.[29] Both the bilingual quality of the legends and the use of Tanit on many types suggest that the new authority sought to identify itself simultaneously with both Punic and Hellenic traditions.

The other iconography draws largely on regional precedents from the western Mediterranean. The bull on the reverse of the double shekel and the

26 Crawford 1985: 137–8 (table 5); his division builds on that first proposed by E.S.G. Robinson (1953) who divided the series into 'Carthaginian' and 'Libyan' types.

27 Carradice and La Niece 1988. 28 Carradice and La Niece 1988; Keyser 1995–6.

29 See Zimmermann 2001: 242 for survey of various proposals including an abbreviation for *machanat*, the word for camp which also appeared on the Siculo-Punic coinage, or the first initial of Matho, the revolt leader.

largest bronze units has been linked to the iconography of Campanian coinage, an interesting parallel to Polybius' assertion that one of the initial revolt leaders originated there.[30] Moreover, there was no shortage of Campanian mercenaries in Carthage's service generally.[31] However, charging bulls are well represented on Sicilian coinage as well, notably during Agathocles' reign in Syracuse. Manganaro juxtaposes Syracusan coins bearing Zeus' head with those of the Libyan revolt coinage in order to demonstrate the close iconographic link.[32] These other regional parallels help contextualise the two different representations of Heracles in this series.

The two representations of Heracles – an Alexander-style head in a lion-skin on the shekel (Figure 12.6) and the diademed beardless head on the half-shekel (Figure 12.7) – function primarily to distinguish denominations. Both have a prowling lion on the reverse; the half-shekel reverse also has a club in the upper field. The Alexander-style head also appears

Figure 12.6 AR shekel, Libya, 241–238 BC. Obv.: male head (l.) wearing a lion-skin; rev.: prowling lion (r.). Image not to scale.

Figure 12.7 AR fraction, Libya, 241–238 BC. Obv.: male head (l.), beardless and wearing a diadem; rev.: prowling lion (r.), club above. Image not to scale.

30 Acquaro 1974.

31 The significance of such Italian mercenaries is underlined by both the prohibition on recruiting included in the treaty of Lutatius and the waiving of these specific clauses in the context of the Mercenary Revolt (App. *Pun.* 5).

32 Manganaro 1992: Pl. XXV.

on the large bronzes but with a bull reverse. The inspiration for the half-shekel type clearly seems to be Syracusan bronze coins of Agathocles.[33] There are few differences between the two designs. The exergue of the revolt coins has a legend on some specimens whereas on the Syracusan coins the exergue contains a spear. The revolt coinage displays a rugged facial type, thick eyebrow ridge, textured forehead and prominent jaw – all commonplace within idealised Hellenistic royal portraiture. The Syracusan prototype has classical features: fine, smooth and youthful. Beardless diademed youths, while never common, are not unknown on the coinage of the western Mediterranean prior to the Hellenistic period; these are variously identified as Apollo or Heracles, often with little justification for either choice.[34] The revolt coinage depiction of a diademed Heracles bears stylistic resemblance to the diademed Heracles on the early wolf and twin didrachms bearing the legend *ROMANO*, which are usually dated to 269-266 BC and thought by many to have been struck at Neapolis.[35] From Robinson onwards, cataloguers of the Libyan revolt coinage have wanted to see a club laid across the neck of the head. If the club is present, this would bring the parallels with the *ROMANO* didrachms even closer.[36] That the Libyan revolt coinage should combine features familiar from Campania and Sicily is not surprising given the composition of the mercenary troops. That the stylistic execution of the facial type should reflect representations of regal power from the eastern Mediterranean is perhaps equally unsurprising. The pattern observed here and in the earlier case-studies could be summarised as follows: numismatic representations of Heracles in the western Mediterranean draw on eastern stylistic precedents while reacting to and interacting with regional representations in order to formulate images appropriate in very localised contexts. These images seem normative within the wider (even pan-Mediterranean) Hellenistic world, but simultaneously the meaning of the image has disseminated to take on time- and place-specific connotations.

This begins to contextualise the presence of the diademed Heracles on the revolt coinage, but does not adequately explain the simultaneous use of two different representations of Heracles. The need to distinguish between denominations is not sufficient explanation. Obviously, any two different

[33] *SNG ANS* 732–43. It is notable that the type, beardless diademed Heracles/prowling lion, recurs on bronze coinage of Capua during the Hannibalic War.

[34] One example from Croton: *SNG ANS* 421, *SNG München* 1464.

[35] *RRC* 20/1; Rutter 2001: 287.

[36] I cannot confirm the presence of the club on any of the specimens I have handled in London or New York. However, the condition of the coins is quite poor and the specimens may have further degraded since the initial cataloguing.

divinities could have been used; the repetition of Heracles must have deeper significance to those selecting the images and for those handling them immediately upon their manufacture. As a minimum, we can assume that Heracles was perceived as an auspicious, even strategic, deity with which to associate the revolt. Any more precise meaning may be too localised for us to decode, much like the variations of attributes of Heracles on the coinage of Heraclea Lucaniae. Since there is no clear or widely accepted iconographic differentiation between Melqart and Heracles at this time, the one thing we cannot say is that the two different representations on the revolt coinage show a desire to distinguish between the two. The shared reverse type of the prowling lion helps further to associate the two Heracles types with each other; in this series the prowling lion is only paired with Heracles obverse types. Given the bilingual character of the coinage as a whole, both of the representations of Heracles may be assumed to be equally culturally bilingual, in much the same way as was discussed in the second case-study.

Even if the precise reason behind the choice of two different representations is unrecoverable, we can say something about the implications of the choice of these specific images and their juxtaposition in the same series. Whereas it was reasonable to question if those handling the Siculo-Punic issues half a century earlier would have immediately recognised the echo of Alexander the Great's coinage, in this later context we can have little doubt the parallel would have been obvious. The revolting Libyans were invoking Heracles not just in his own right as a heroic divinity, but as an emblem of political power and conquest. Or, to put it another way, this particular image of Heracles was chosen in part because it seemed naturally to evoke the idea of political power and conquest. However, the anonymous designers of the series did not feel limited to a single Hellenistic Heracles. The same message of political power and conquest could be communicated through the diademed representation of Heracles: a representation with greater regional resonance because of the echoes of Agathocles' coinage, but also partaking in the new dramatic style used in the portraiture of the eastern *diadochoi* and thus associated with spear-won authority and wide-reaching power. The reiteration of multiple regional and supra-regional representations of Heracles ties the revolt coinage into a wider socio-political symbolic vocabulary. The coinage becomes iconographically intelligible not only to the diverse population of mercenaries and local peoples of North Africa, but also across the Mediterranean. The choice of two different Heracles demonstrates the complementary, non-competing nature of the different representations.

All three case-studies demonstrate the emblematic versatility of Heracles iconography and illustrate the role of coinage in the dissemination and naturalisation of such iconic images. This process of dissemination and naturalisation contributed to the generation of the socio-political phenomenon we label as 'Hellenistic'. We can observe how these types of iconographic choices help define a new period through reconsideration of what precedent is being rejected in each of the three case-studies. At Heraclea Lucaniae the mint rejected the regional precedents for a reverse type of Heracles wrestling the Nemean lion, in favour of a standing Heracles inspired by eastern statue types. The Siculo-Punic tetradrachms replaced placid imagery based on Syracusan coinage with the bold dynamic Alexander-type Heracles in lion scalp. The Libyan revolt coinage developed a new coinage for a new political authority, but one which drew not only on North African precedents, but also selected regional precedents which were themselves influenced by eastern artistic trends. There is a clear pattern of developing new imagery with antecedents in the eastern Mediterranean and the world of the *diadochoi*, while simultaneously setting aside traditional regional imagery.

Yet, all three cases studies exemplify how the meaning of the eastern antecedent was disseminated in local and regional contexts. The western iterations are rich with connotations impossible to attribute to eastern influence. The new standing Heracles type at Heraclea Lucaniae is augmented with numerous changing attributes (*nike*, cornucopiae, crowns, *skyphoi* and more), symbols which allow the figure to reflect local concerns on a brief temporal scale. The lion-scalp Heracles head of the Siculo-Punic issues is unlikely to have been recognised as an Alexander-type by the first recipients; instead, as was argued above, the new style is much more likely to have been interpreted as a rejection of Syracusan imagery and a new celebration of a deity, Melqart/Heracles, which resonated with both the Punic and Hellenic populations. The scale and dispersal of this issue is surely one of the factors that normalised this representation of Heracles in the West and allowed the image to be associated over time with regional military dominion, as well as the world of Alexander's Successors. Hence, when the image reappears on a different denomination in the Libyan revolt coinage, it partakes in a more generalised representation of power, instead of necessarily specifically evoking its Ur-eastern antecedents. Likewise, the diademed Heracles of this series, while undoubtedly drawing on eastern regal portraiture, draws primarily on Campanian and Syracusan precedents to make an image with strong regional resonance.

What can we say in the end about the generation of the Hellenistic period in the West? I started from the premise that repetition through different actions could allow the deciphering of a cultural construction, i.e. the Hellenistic, that the insistent reuse and reformulation of an image could reveal intention, the underlying assumption being that the peoples of the West actively participated in the socio-political changes of the time, drawing on local, regional and pan-Mediterranean precedents. No one symbolic vehicle can encompass the whole phenomenon, but the representation of Heracles in the preceding case-studies goes some way to illustrate that which is definitive of the Hellenistic West. All three case-studies demonstrate an interest in emblematic versatility. The borrowed types and stylistic choices partook in a wider iconographic vocabulary both eastern and regional, but each individual deployment had specific localised meaning as well. The repeated use of such numismatic imagery and the circulation of the coinage itself normalised types of representations across the region, leading not only to imitation, but also further experimentation.

13 On the significance of East and West in today's 'Hellenistic' history: reflections on symmetrical worlds, reflecting through world symmetries

NICHOLAS PURCELL

The problem of a Hellenistic West

Can the history of the peoples of the western Mediterranean basin between the fourth and first centuries B.C. be 'Hellenistic'?

The label Hellenistic, by common agreement, concerns that period, and it knows no thematic or ethnic limitations. The problem, then, is geography.[1] Since its invention, 'Hellenistic history' has been a sort of (usually unacknowledged) regional history. From Droysen's original interest in the fertile encounter of Asia and Europe, which gave the new subject a loose geographical definition around a Levantine centre of gravity, the subject has, oddly, become more regional, as the rich elaboration of historical understanding of Hellenistic West Asia in the last generation has shifted the original equipoise further eastward. Babylon is a very long way from Gades.

Scale did not prevent ancient observers integrating their understanding of their world. Polybius first eloquently expressed the difficulty of integrating the history of very many very different places.[2] But can Hellenistic history as it is currently studied have much to do with the ambit within which Carthage and Rome interacted with each other and with their neighbouring communities, great and small? Comparisons and links both offer ways forward: this essay combines the two, in proposing a way to build a comparative history on the historical study of the links, that is, the connectivities and interdependences between regions.

Its inevitable scale makes Mediterranean history a promising starting point. Since no-one would deny the label 'Hellenistic' to parts of the Mediterranean

[1] Dench 2003 does not hesitate to use Hellenistic themes in her splendid account of Italian history, but for a reviewer (Sullivan 2003) who speaks more conventionally in another context of 'the entry of the Romans into the Hellenistic arena', this 'pushes the boundaries of the term Hellenistic itself'. This is not an accusation that could be levelled against Bugh 2006a.

[2] Polyb. 1.4.6–11; 3.32. For theorists in the period itself, of course, the inclusion of the West in the *oikoumene* was not in doubt: Geus 2003, curiously brief on geography after Alexander.

coastlands, questions must follow about the difference between Mediterranean and non-Mediterranean segments of the Hellenistic world. The search for common or comparable environmental denominators for social and economic interaction in the Mediterranean basin, of the kind that were sketched for the Mediterranean in *The Corrupting Sea*, encourage the historian to situate the western basins of the sea in a larger Mediterranean context.[3] The historical character of the Mediterranean should not only illuminate the internal dynamics of its history, but also serve to make comparisons and contrasts with the zones which adjoin it: although different in character, some of these neighbouring regions may be equally extensive, and display similar levels of ecological distinctiveness.[4] So, one strategy for a Hellenistic history which includes the western Mediterranean is simply to compare the specific macroregional characteristics of the whole Mediterranean world with its equivalent to the east, backdrop to the remainder of the Hellenistic historian's usual concerns with the consequences of the aggressions of Alexander, positing a macroregional character for the West Asian heartlands, and asking what consequences follow from it. Moreover, the study of the edges of what can variously be perceived as Mediterranean is a potentially very fruitful strategy for the Mediterranean historian.[5] The more complicated the problem of modelling transitions away from 'the Mediterranean', the more interesting. No Mediterranean margin is more complex than the Levant. So the concerns of the Mediterranean historian and the Hellenistic historian converge: both are interested in macroregions, and the huge spaces which concern them actually meet.

But the most defensible common denominator of Mediterranean history is its distinctive regime of interdependence, the webs of communication on which social, cultural, economic relationships depended, and the character of the communications: in a word, the cluster of themes evoked by the term 'connectivity', which must be understood as encompassing extractive and redistributive systems as well as the dynamics of movement of materials, people and ideas which ultimately derived from them. The Mediterranean must be seen as a 'concatenation', in the literal sense of the word, a chain of interacting units, often very small, whose interaction is a central ingredient

[3] Horden and Purcell 2000, cf. 2005. This exploration foreshadows the themes of the forthcoming companion volume to *Corrupting Sea*, *Liquid Continents*: the continuing contributions of my co-author must thus be acknowledged here.

[4] Similar approaches to macroregions adjacent to the Mediterranean: Batty 2007 (the Danubian zone); Cunliffe 2001 (the Atlantic); Marfaing and Wippel 2004 (the Sahara, from a rather different perspective).

[5] Purcell 2004.

in the identity of the chain as a whole. At the same time, the geometries of the linkage – which starts, we must recall, with the miniature ecologies of the microregion – may be analysed on a much larger scale, up to a level of description which can only be described as macroregional, involving units of the size of the western or eastern Mediterranean basins – or beyond.[6]

In this analysis, differentiating the constituent parts itself becomes an interesting and instructive exercise: the historian is more interested in the connections which unite the links in the chain than in what keeps them discrete, and will for the most part interpret the transitions between these elements, which are the places where whole systems abut, not as barriers, but – in the terminology which I shall adopt in this paper – more as thresholds. The interpretation of the character of regions and thresholds will at the same time find much of heuristic value in the construction of regional geographies and histories by inhabitants and interpreters of the areas we are discussing in every period.

Boundaries within the Mediterranean and boundaries around Mediterranean space can be analysed comparatively, then, and the sequences of interaction and interdependence may extend far beyond the conventional boundaries of the Mediterranean basin. Instead of two spaces for history which might be compared, or two juxtaposed spaces whose contacts can be investigated, the Mediterranean and West Asian macroregions are entities whose definition depends on their place in sequences of interaction. The continuities which result go far to justify the study of both together. Since, moreover, the macroregions share an important boundary, the 'Levant', the exercise also raises particular questions about the comparison of the links within the regions which connectivity of different kinds binds together. This survey begins to enquire to what extent and by what means integration could be achieved between a Mediterranean world and a West Asia from which geography apparently formally divided it.

But in addition to the zone where they abutted, the study of comparative connectivity also encourages comparison of the outer edges of the Mediterranean and West Asian macroregions, the zones where connectivity decreases or changes its character.[7] Starting from the analysis of the relations of the west Mediterranean with its other neighbours, the whole Mediterranean (and those other neighbourly relationships) can be set in a context which will show what they have to do with Babylon and Bactria, and *their* neighbourly

[6] Shaw 2001: 447 for the analogy to the Mandelbrot series, the fractal geometry in which, the more one 'zooms in', the more complex and endlessly variable every outline seems.

[7] Purcell 2004 for the idea of the connectivity gradient.

relationships. The comparisons will prove easier and more fruitful than traditional schematic separations might suggest, supporting an integrated historical project for understanding the whole, for offering useful foundations for comparison, an inter-related history of the world between Lisbon and Kuwait, during broadly the period from the end of Achaemenid rule in Iran to the inception of the Roman imperial monarchy.

East and West Mediterraneans

Now Caesar and Antonius divided the whole Roman empire again between themselves, the boundary to be Scodra, a city of Illyria which seemed to be pretty well in the middle of the Ionian embayment (τοῦ Ἰονίου μυχοῦ). All provinces and islands east of this place, as far as the river Euphrates, were to belong to Antonius, and all west of it, to the Ocean, to Caesar (Appian, *B Civ.* 5.65).

The first step in exploring the interlocking of Mediterranean and West Asian histories must be to observe a basic fact of blinding simplicity – the shape and global disposition of their geographical setting, which orients the world of the ancient historian along global lines of latitude. The prominence of East–West thinking in Antiquity can hardly be over-emphasised: from the *Odyssey* through the mythology of Herakles and Dionysos to the investigations of Hekataios and Herodotus, it remained a central cultural *point-de-repère*: Tyrian Carthage, Trojan Rome, Asia versus Europe from Xerxes to Khusro.[8]

East/West differentiation is, of course, quite unlike North and South.[9] There are no east and west poles! The notion itself acquires a strong and easily intuited reality from experience of the apparent course of the sun through the heavens, but these orientation labels can only be meaningfully calibrated by the selection of a segment of a meridian according to very variable social, political and cultural horizons. Indeed, in the absence of the strong climatic factors which pattern North and South, embodied in the theory of the *klimata*, East and West can only be, in their entirety, culturally constructed concepts.[10] The construction was, however, importantly patterned by physical topography.

8 See further Erskine 'The view from the East', Chapter 1 in this volume.

9 'The distinction of east and west is arbitrary, and shifts around the globe', Gibbon 1782 (1896): xxxvi. Thus also, recently, Bowersock 2005: esp. 171.

10 Though, it is noteworthy that ancient geography hankered after meteorological definitions of East and West too. See Strabo 17.3.10 (830C) for Poseidonios on the sun's behaviour at its extreme 'turning-points', resulting in a well-watered East and an arid West. Strabo regards this as absurd, both as a general principle and as a description of the whole *oikoumene*, though allowing that it is *contingently* true that India is wet and Iberia dry.

The wholly haphazard layout of obstacles and lines of communication can be normal to latitude or contrary to it, with different effects on the development of East–West thinking. The Mediterranean, conceived either as a bundle of potential paths for voyages or as a set of coastlands, adds up, for all the local intricacies, to a notably long – and thinnish – geographical entity conspicuously aligned with latitude and, indeed, frequently adopted as a division between North and South.[11] The sea, from Gades to the Nile, strongly reinforced and patterned ancient notions of East and West, making it, for all its arbitrariness, a more familiar way of orienting than North and South.[12] The East–West alignment of the Mediterranean basin is, moreover, reinforced and continued by the regions which abut it to the east between the Taurus chains and the Arabian Desert, along the Persian Gulf, as far as the Bab el-Hormuz. The accident of global topography thus transcended the arbitrariness of East and West – the geophysical alignments of the Mediterranean and of the lowland of West Asia are heavily implicated, through their unremitting effect on the patterns of mobility, in the formation of all the cultural superstructures which articulate the differences between eastern and western worlds. On this view, geographical accident has played a major part in making possible ideologies such as those which are usually labelled Orientalist, not through any real geographical determinism, but by directing the axis with which people arrange their changing conceptual priorities.[13] Meanwhile, the essential relativism of longitude remains a major ingredient in the notorious complexity, instability and sensitivity of the terminology of modern cultural debate.

The long thin region which configured the practical geographical imagination of the ancients, then, certainly had the Mediterranean in it. But it clearly went much further east – further than the upper Euphrates, further than the mouths of the Two Rivers, it extended right to the Persian Gulf and its coastlands, as far as the Strait of Hormuz. The topographical continuity of this zone suggests a Corridor running from Atlantic to Indian Ocean, and that label will be used in what follows.

[11] Horden and Purcell 2000: 18–19, not however concerned with the way this concept constructs East and West.

[12] Climatic theories confined, defined and delineated the long thin world. For Agatharchides of Cnidos, 5.67 (Burstein 1989: 116–17), the narrowness of the temperate zone was a wonder: only twenty-four days' voyage, changing ships at Rhodes and Alexandria, separated coldest and hottest, the Don and Aithiopia.

[13] This is not the place for a full survey of this theme. Carrier 1995 applies it to Mediterranean history; cf. Abulafia 2005: 70. Elsewhere, as in areas where the grain of mountain chains obstruct east–west movement, the conceptual construction of East vs West has far less purchase: in India the term 'Southernisation' has had a certain recent vogue, Shaffer 2001.

This Corridor, rather satisfyingly, has a single, scientific, aetiology. It is laid out along the Greater Mediterranean of the middle Caenozoic, the narrow ocean or inland sea which geologists call Tethys – the sea in which the mountain ranges which define its steep northern edge were born, from west to east all along the tectonic zone where Africa and Arabia abut the plates and platelets which lie on the earth's crust to northward.[14] The tectonic structures of macro-topography, whose mutability was a prominent part of how the ancients too saw their world, have a vital role in patterning history. Within the Mediterranean, the landscape diversity and fragmentation which are such a feature of the ecological history of the region have their causes in the tectonics of Tethys, as, naturally, does the uniting Sea itself; and though it is now high (literally, at *c.* 500 m above sea-level) and dry, the eastern part of the Corridor shares in these characteristics (to the extent that northern Mesopotamia has been called Mediterranean in its fragmented archipelago of inhabited microregions).[15] Recent work on West Asia has, in an analogous way, sought to recognise the intuitive centrality of a western Asiatic lowland zone.[16] This lowland shares in certain climatic characteristics, being dominated by the semi-arid transitional landscapes between the mountains and the most rainfall-deprived tracts, whence its older description as part of a 'Fertile Crescent'. But rivers, and especially those of Mesopotamia, fulfil a crucial role in the ecology. At the same time, for all the diversity of local topographies, because of the relatively low relief of the region as a whole, it can also be defined through its relatively high internal connectivities, to which the larger rivers also make an important contribution.

In the applications of ancient geographical thought to political decision-making, this conceptualisation of how things are laid out entailed a special role for certain naturally determined, socially and economically influential, or politically convenient caesuras which could segment the long latitudinal sequence. In the nature of the imaginative geometry, these rare boundaries tend to run north-south. The Meridian of Scodra, described in the epigraph of this section, is a famous example. Such boundaries, drawing together practical, theoretical, administrative, cultural and environmental responses, form a special object of historical reflection. The demarcation of very large segments of the East–West unit can actually serve to reinforce a sense of its unity, by encouraging the notion that the segments respond to or mirror

[14] The origin of the nomenclature is Suess 1908: 19 (German original 1901).

[15] For the tectonic origins of Mediterranean diversity, Horden and Purcell 2000: 78; see also C. Robinson 2000: 34.

[16] E. Fowden 1999: 1–2 and G. Fowden 1993: 15–16, for instance, use the terminology of a 'mountain arena'.

each other, rather than being unrelated or disconnected. The Meridian of Scodra drew its significance from being the meeting point of two entities with no visible practical definition at all, in constant, problematic relationship with each other. Like other such division-markers, including the Levantine zone where the Mediterranean world itself abuts West Asia, it was not the barrier between immiscible regions.[17] This aspect of the Levant, and a further instance of these calibrations of the extended East–West region in the 'narrows' which divide eastern from western Mediterraneans, are explored further below.

The joined-up history of the Mediterranean and West Asia, propounded by the theme 'East and West' of my title, involves a sequence of questions. What is it that is laid out latitudinally which we are calibrating with these points of the compass? Does this strange, long thin zone have a distinctive history? How does its *imaginaire*, in so far as it has one, relate to environmental characteristics? How has it been conceptually and practically subdivided? What links and transitions are articulated at these division-points? What are its relations to what surrounds it, and what do these relationships in turn tell us about its nature? This paper sketches some answers, and argues that this last enquiry is particularly rewarding historically.

Mediterranean East–West-ness is generated by its linear, serial topography, an extended sequence of basins. Two narrows, at Sicily and between Malea and Cyrenaica, divide it into readily distinguishable segments. The western basin, the Ionian Sea, and the eastern basin, do have distinct oceanographic characters, derived above all from their own seasonal patterns of prevailing winds and currents: but it is the nature of the links which transcend the boundaries of the narrows that should interest the historian.[18]

A significant culprit is Fernand Braudel, whose *Méditerranée* had an arresting excursus on the East–West split:

> The two halves of the sea [West and East Mediterraneans], in spite of trading links and cultural exchanges, maintained their autonomy and their own spheres of influence. Genuine intermingling of populations was to be found only inside each region, and within these limits it defied all barriers of race, culture, or religion.[19]

17 Said 1978 was mistaken in thinking that a real dichotomy between West Asia and the Mediterranean went back to Antiquity: Hentsch 1988: 42–3.

18 Horden and Purcell 2000 have little to say on either the fissiparation of Mediterraneans, or the important effect of current-dominated circulation on maritime regionalism. For its consequences for navigation, see Arnaud 2005.

19 Braudel 1972: 133–8, at 135.

His proclamation of the essential impossibility of lasting political ties or important demographic transfers between the two Mediterraneans is hardly credible – indeed, with some *sang-froid*, Braudel himself ended the excursus with the conclusion that the insurmountable differences between the two regions set up a current between them, making interdependence unavoidable!

What led Braudel to perceive a 'finely meshed filter' preventing mass migration between East and West? He favoured the latently deterministic notion that the eastern and western seas were distinct 'vehicles' for the Spanish and Ottoman empires whose counterpointing was so important to his historical project.[20] But he also claimed that severing connections with the homeland was the common – and symmetrical – fate of easterners going west and westerners going east. The examples advanced are schematic and essentialised, groups of very different periods, whose changing social horizons and sense of community were actually very various: the Phocaeans, the Carthaginians and the Moslems of Spain, and the Latin adventurers of the Crusading Levant.[21]

Instead, we should make a virtue of the master's *volte-face*. The ambiguity between barrier and junction is helpful. Barriers are a special kind of contact-zone; places where contact is highly visible, reified, made into an object of reflection, serve as delimitations. The point is rather that the sill or threshold represented by the physical discontinuities of the central Mediterranean precisely lends itself to the maximum variety of interrelated-nesses, and the variability of connectivity in contexts of this kind is what makes them so 'good to think with', and so important to the historian.[22] Thus Sicily is capable of being interpreted as an axial centre, as in the Greek geographical tradition.[23] But equally, the same physical realities lend themselves to the construction of conceptual separations, and it was above all the Romans who played 'invent your own geography' with the Adriatic. Their choice was nicely partisan, though strikingly dressed up in the language of Hellenistic *geographia*.[24] It constructed an elongated world which was, importantly, a little different from the Mediterranean, being a latitudinal slice reaching from

[20] Braudel 1972: 134, 136. [21] Braudel 1972: 123.

[22] The interesting criterion of variable east–west linkage proposed, Harris 2005b: 9; Bresson 2005 sees the dual Mediterranean of two basins as two systems which sometimes intermesh (citing the controversial case of the Shardanes from Sardinia among the so-called sea peoples). Etruscan piracy makes a more robust example: Giuffrida Ientile 1983.

[23] Prontera 1998 for Sicily as axial point of the Mediterranean in Eratosthenes and Strabo.

[24] App. *B Civ.* 5.65, the epigraph to section II above.

the river of Ocean to the Euphrates.[25] Within it, the central Mediterranean divide was elaborated as a vital piece of world-geography, beyond which, on the other side of the quite undivisive Strait of Otranto, lay Overseas, or *to diapontion*, as Dionysius of Halicarnassus called it.[26]

When the dynasts settled the division of the world in autumn 40 BC at Brundisium, they too sought to essentialise a distinction between eastern and western seas. But they chose an explicitly arbitrary line, a meridian, to give a precise, scientific, air to a division which had earlier been loosely constructed out of maritime topography. They could hardly have done more to underline the arbitrariness of the boundaries of East–West space. The Meridian of Scodra has had a negative effect on Mediterranean historiography: it slices through the Ionian-Adriatic maritime hinterland, which has usually beaten with a single social and economic pulse, but, even worse, as a given of Roman diplomatic and administrative thinking for centuries, it has become fossilised. It is a prominent contributor to many a schematic historical separatism of East and West.[27] The contemporary consensus should, then, not favour the East–West divisions which Roman power had elaborated from the encounter with Pyrrhus to the crystallisation of the imperial monarchy.

In the Ionian Sea, the navigational difficulties posed by the Syrtis coast of Tripolitania and Cyrenaica compound the impression of separation, reinforced by the length and remoteness of the terrestrial route, backed by a desert interior to the south. On this view, the Ionian Sea prolonged the Libyan Desert, causing a general communications caesura.[28] Geographical determinism lingers longest where it is least explicit, and though the fashion for explanations of this kind has dwindled, the regional geography itself survives because it was taken up by highly influential authors who established it as a given which could outlive the deterministic reasoning in which it originated. In fact, the rarity of links across the Ionian Sea is belied by the evidence, new and old. Contact with the Maghreb is amply attested in the archaeology of Euesperides in Cyrenaica, a precursor of the integration

[25] The Euphrates makes an interesting but somewhat unexpected boundary-marker, huge though its impact on the environment is. Key ancient descriptions: Hdt. 1.193; Polyb. 9.43; and the magnificent excursus of Strabo 16.1.9–13 (739–43C).

[26] Dion. Hal. *Ant. Rom.* 1.90; for Adriatic connectivity and the unity of the basin, Abulafia 2005: 67. The Timavus was called into existence as a suitable *thauma* to mark the northern end of this divide, Strabo 5.1.8 (214–15C); for the construction in a rather similar manner of Arae Philaenorum to the south, see Quinn forthcoming.

[27] Thus Braudel 1972: 125–33, another classic essay within the great work.

[28] Braudel 1972: 133 following Philippson 1939, whose later work displayed geographical determinism.

along that coast thirteen centuries later in documents from the Cairo *geniza*.[29] There were important direct contacts between Algeria and the Peloponnese in the early modern period:

> all the people from Tripoli, Tunis and Algiers come here [Anavarin/Pylos] with their ships, and drop anchor in this harbour, bringing every sort of merchandise, as well as black African slaves. This is because ships making a run for it from the western lands pull up their steeds at this station and cast anchor here, for this castle of Anavarin stands with its chest bared toward the West. Ships coming from Algiers run north before a southwest wind for a full thousand miles to arrive at this Anavarin, and the business of these people is continually with the Algerians.[30]

How much should we labour the problems of cutting things up, whether it is periodisation or regionalism that we are tackling? In the end, arguing about how to slice the cake is pretty dull – though how others have justified their cutting is much more arresting. The reader can be forgiven a certain impatience with Braudel, in the passages cited above, first announcing divisions, and then tinkering with them. What kind of divisions between regions are robust enough to avoid this atmosphere of arbitrariness? The puzzle is a sorites. Take half the heap away and you still have a heap. Dividing it into quarters is no more revealing than dividing it into eighths. The nature of the linkages, of the *exceptions* to the divisions, is far more arresting. In all Braudel's little essay, by far the most challenging insight is the dazzling statement that it was not, after all, the Sicilian straits, important though they were, that mattered most in the sixteenth-century Mediterranean – it was overland traffic across peninsular Italy, from Ancona and Ferrara to Genoa or Livorno, that was 'decisive' in the sixteenth century for the unity of the Mediterranean and his project.[31]

Rather than a barrier or a filter, we have in the central Mediterranean, and around Sicily in particular, something much more interesting, which we can best portray as a threshold of a distinctive kind. It takes its highly various nature from the character of the zones which abut it, and mediates one to another in a large number of different ways. In doing so, it forms a link in that concatenation of which we have spoken, and must be understood as part of a zonal chain to the nature of which its own characteristics as they may be from time to time make an extremely influential contribution. That Sicily was the scene of the first great conflict between Carthage and Rome reminds us that in important ways, despite the western horizons for which

[29] A. Wilson, Chapter 5 in this volume.

[30] Evliya Çelebi, *Seyahatname* 267b, P. MacKay 2005: 220.

[31] Braudel 1972: 134.

Carthage is famous, and the opportunism with which Romans bounded their world from that east of the Adriatic, both polities took important aspects of their character in the third and second centuries from the articulation of this threshold in the heart of the extended Mediterranean.

In this threshold zone, we perceive the development of polities which derive their character and their dynamism from straddling peripheries, controlling the abutment of connectivities. These 'Janus states', are to be found around the edges of the Corridor itself, but, most interestingly of all, along the crucial cardinal zones within it such as the Sicilian bridge between Italy and Africa: but still more so, where the land and sea macroregions within the Corridor meet, and where the question of the edges of the Mediterranean becomes especially acute. The identification of the central Mediterranean threshold finds an important parallel on a much larger scale in an unexpected place. We turn our attention now to the eastern end of the Mediterranean basin itself.

The Mediterranean and its eastern mirror

In that day shall there be a highway out of Egypt to Assyria, and the Assyrian shall come into Egypt, and the Egyptian into Assyria; and the Egyptians shall serve with the Assyrians. In that day shall Israel be the third with Egypt and with Assyria, even a blessing in the midst of the land. (Isaiah 19: 23-4).

Turning next to the problem of the eastern boundary of a Mediterranean world (however defined), we must address the very singular cultural and social zone we call the Levant, running from the headwaters of the Euphrates to the Nile delta, but less than 150 kilometres wide.[32] If it is to be regarded as a threshold of the kind that can be seen between West and East Mediterraneans, but between two macroregional entities, one Mediterranean, and one West Asiatic, we must enquire what lies to the east, and turn from links to comparisons. How far can the West Asian part of the impressionistic Tethys Corridor outlined above be envisaged as a region comparable to the Mediterranean? Are there environmental common denominators like those which underlie the characteristic fragmentation and connectivity of the Mediterranean, the complex co-existence, and changing interrelationship, at different periods, between well-documented *Fernhandel* and the normal

[32] Indeed, the zone in question can be extended to the Caucasus or the Horn of Africa, but this is not the place to develop the idea on that scale.

Brownian motion of caboteurs, or the rhythms of normal interdependence?[33] Beginning such enquiries at the lowest level of texture of *la trame du monde* helps make sense of the nearly unimaginable problems of scale, in a way that works for the whole Mediterranean, but is also capable of still further extension.

For all the absence of sea-routes, connectivities unite the region from the Mediterranean to the Zagros more than might at first sight appear. Complex social reciprocities between settled and mobile communities are common to much of the zone. Within it, moreover, there is considerable interdependence. A characteristic regime of long-distance trade, centred on the caravan, is a third feature. And around the fringes of the 'Mountain Arena', comparable 'radial' exchanges across the boundaries to the adjacent mountain-zones are to be found in an arc from Palestine to Elam. Let us take these one by one.

In place of the contrast of 'the desert and the sown', the last generation has seen the formulation of a new approach to agro-pastoral societies and their choices, enabling the nature of these societies to be advanced as a principal common denominator of the West Asian basin. The theory of social dimorphism, and the secular pattern of shifting along an axis of changing balances between pastoral and agrarian strategies, have provided powerful tools for historical analysis.[34] The revolution in understanding these societies has ended the long domination of an essentially environmentally determined account which isolated West Asian 'nomadism' as a distinctive behaviour, and has made possible much richer comparisons with other histories. Prominent among these, indeed, is a Mediterranean world in which the agro-pastoral balance and its mutabilities have also acquired a central place in discussions of primary production.[35] In this respect, detailed Mediterranean–West Asian comparisons are long overdue. They will draw attention, especially, to the role of connectivity in shaping relations between more pastoral and more agrarian communities, and to the way in which the dynamics of interaction between pastoralists and farmers alters the overall connective frame of social and economic life.

The fortunes of agrarian-pastoral relations remind us that interdependence is a second common theme between an ecological Mediterranean history and

33 Horden and Purcell 2000: 142, the Mediterranean which 'hums and buzzes', in the (somewhat tendentious) phraseology of Fentress and Fentress 2001.

34 Rowton 1973, 1974; Golden 1998; Graf 1989; Dijkstra 1990. For the application of these ideas in the Classical period, Briant 1982b.

35 For Mediterranean pastoralism and history, Horden and Purcell 2000: 82–7, and recently Howe 2008.

its equivalent in West Asia. The distinction between the basin of the Euphrates and Tigris, its settlement-patterns, agrosystems, connectivity and complexity, and what happens in the intermontane plateaux to the east, is extremely sharp. In the latter region beyond the Corridor, some of the productive zones of the mountainous plateaux are large. But it is their interrelationship with one another that is quite different from the world of the Corridor. The great Arab geographer Ibn Hawqal said that although communities up to 100 miles apart might lend aid to each other in case of food shortage, that did not save them, as caravan trade was not sufficient to provide staples in case of crisis.[36] This 'index of famine-relief' is a helpful criterion of connectivity. If it marks out the lowland of the Two Rivers very plainly from the territories to the east, it can be equally revealing in Mediterranean history too.

As far as 'high commerce' goes, West Asia is of course a *univers caravanier*. And the caravan is a manifestation of long-distance, high-value exchange with which Mediterranean comparison is much easier than might at first be thought. It is revealing that Mediterranean traders have sometimes deliberately organised themselves on the model of the terrestrial caravan. At the top end, seaborne trade in the Mediterranean has certainly often had close analogies to the Palmyrene or Petraean cross-desert trade, to the trans-Sahara routes, or to the famous central Asian links, and these are paralleled by the Indian Ocean networks of the Periplous of the Erythraean Sea. The institutions of low-grade, small-scale interdependence, local and subregional marketing structures, redistribution of materials exacted in tribute or rent, and so on, are less well known. Here again, it is the fact of the co-existence of different registers of redistribution, and the probable importance of their interrelationship, that renders the regions comparable.[37] Over a major area, the river Euphrates, for instance, offers the same ease of communication as an arm of the sea (but with the provisos that its usefulness is more seasonal, and its connectivity, as with most rivers, made directional with the flow of the current). Explicitly linked with the prosperity of the networks of early Abbasid Baghdad, the river and its valley still await proper study as a central director of movements of people and materials. For reasons we have seen at work more than once, being such a hard-to-classify medium of communication made the Euphrates a long-lasting and potent conceptual boundary-marker.

[36] Ibn Hawqal 2.437, with Christensen 1993: 124–5.

[37] The consensus is riskily aprioristic: densely serried village landscapes 'must have' formed hierarchical structures of market orientation; Hallo 1964 claimed a marked distinction between local and inter-regional trade.

Boundary transactions, fourthly, unite the macroregions: links down the 'connectivity gradients' – the gradients, steep or gentle, by which the key Mediterranean conditions of connectivity and diversity shade off into less networked or more uniform areas elsewhere – into arid spaces or, especially, the mountainous tracts which fringe and interpenetrate so many parts of both great zones. Basic to the configurations of agro-pastoral exchange, these engagements are also of great importance for the movement of raw materials, and still more for their demographic implications, to which we shall return.

Connectivity and interdependence are both a guide to internal state-formation, as in the Sicilian narrows, and also serve to map the edges of the west Asiatic macroregion. The parallel with the boundary zones of the Mediterranean proper is therefore very tempting. The changing nature of arable–pastoral relations plays a vital role in these Mediterranean peripheries from Iberia or the Appennines to the Maghreb and the Balkans, and it appears to be of the greatest interest to compare how such differentials map the edges of the eastern Corridor.[38] These peripheral transitions, finally, are of great importance to understanding state-formation, and we shall return in the next section to the question of the historical importance in the genesis of states of these peripheries and zones of transition between densely inhabited, highly networked areas and more sparsely settled, much less well-connected, regions.

In all these ways, then, the West Asian basin can be seen to be situated in the Corridor in the manner of a 'terrestrial Mediterranean', united and defined from its neighbours to north, east and south by connectivity and by ecological interdependence. It is clearly better to identify it with an anodyne term such as 'Mountain Arena': though the old notion of a Fertile Crescent has the advantage of already positing an intrinsic unity extending from the Dead Sea to the mouths of the Two Rivers. In making 'fertility' a common denominator, the terminology certainly reaches in the direction of the search for environmental parameters which is advocated here. But 'Fertile Crescent' privileges a 'fertility' which is that of the old contrast between the Desert and the Sown, and which misunderstands much of the semi-arid steppe and its societies, and their relationship with the regions of settled agriculture.[39] While production remains basic to the pursuit of characterisation, we should give a similar place to the structures of connectivity.

[38] A. Greco 2003 gives a very stimulating view of Zagros transhumance in the Assyrian period. Christensen 1993 draws a sharp and important contrast between the ecological and demographic histories in the Middle Ages of the Iranian plateau and the Mesopotamian lowland.

[39] For the essentially constructed nature of fertility, Horden and Purcell 2000: 231.

Turning from comparison once again to linkages, from the Mediterranean, this West Asian region is distinguished by a contact zone, which in many respects resembles the threshold of the central Mediterranean narrows, a region of abutment between differently patterned connectivities. Where the Sicilian threshold divided two seas of different wind and current regimes, the Levantine threshold separates a terrestrial and a maritime world of connectivity. Two panels of a single connective diptych, the Tethys Corridor, these macroregions give the Levant a hinge-like character. Its societies participate – to varying extents, changing with time – in the lives of the two great zones to east and west, and draw much of their special character from their intermediate location. Ambiguities, elisions and imperfect separations mark the abutment of the zones.[40] A special type of gateway-settlement, an entrepôt in a new sense, is thus represented by certain of the cities of the hinge, drawing their character from their position at the interface between different *systems*, for which the apposite phrase is that of William of Tyre on twelfth-century Alexandria: 'forum publicum utrique orbi'.[41] Ugarit, Antioch, Palmyra, Aleppo, Jerusalem, Damascus, Beirut have all been shaped in different ways by their 'cardinal' macrogeographical setting, and through their far greater than regional role these cities of the hinge have patterned the economies, societies and cultures of the whole Corridor.

It is encouraging to find here confirmation that the diptychal layout of the Corridor which has been described has impinged on the consciousnesses of some of its inhabitants. The Mediterranean as a whole is notoriously absent from ancient thought-worlds, but Mediterranean *mentalités* are well attested. The Tethys Corridor, a modern formulation, is nonetheless reflected in sometimes well-known ancient texts.

Something a bit like the Corridor is the core concept in Greek and Roman thinking about the *oikoumene*. It is all too easy to be so interested in edges that you become unreflective about the nature of what is in the middle, and more has been said about the *eschatiai* of the civilised world than its own consistency: but an analysis of where you might find the things which were regarded as most characteristic of the civilised world would map something very like the Tethys Corridor.[42] The famous finale of Herodotus' histories, moreover, Cyrus' advice to the Persians about environmental determinism, is always taken very seriously as a piece of Herodotean *Weltanschauung* – but

40 Schwara 2003 is interesting on these aspects of the character of 'the Levant'.

41 William of Tyre, *Hist.* 19.26. For a similar approach to cities in a rather wider context in the early modern period, Eldem *et al.* 1999.

42 Romm 1992, in its focus on the *eschatiai* which surround the *oikoumene* is – not, perhaps, unreasonably – about the eggshell, not the egg, the feathers and not the bird.

the eastern terminus of the Corridor against the Iranian plateau is a major ecological transition prominent in the geographical history of other periods too.[43] The great dyadic theory of Land and Sea, which became so important to Hellenistic and Roman imperial ideology, also derives from the realities of the world patterned according to this topography.[44] We have an irremediably map-framed conceptualisation of continents. But an *epeiros* is half of a pair with a body of sea, a super-*peraia*, conceived as the space covered by an *anabasis* up from the sea. So the *epeiros* of Asia is not a gigantic sprawling space with Siberia and Tibet in it, but the eastern end of the Corridor and its adjacencies. Herodotus presented a complementarity between Asia and the Mediterranean, and his subject concerns the ways in which the inhabitants of either experience the others' world.[45]

From an unexpected and obscure quarter, lastly, comes an authentically Hellenistic vision of the *oikoumene*: the *Book of Eclipses of the Sun and Moon* attributed to Petosiris and Nechepso by Hephaistion, the astrologer.[46] The treatise sets out what different kinds of eclipse portended for specific localities, and a date around 100 BC is clear from the geographical repertoire. The news is mainly (though not exclusively) bad, and has a strikingly meteorological flavour. It includes disaster in Egypt and Syria, popular risings in Africa, shortage of wheat and popular unrest in Egypt, war in Media and Elymais, blight in Cyprus, festivals and demographic felicity in Asia, deaths in Syria. Again, a different eclipse-type heralds for Asia the death of a ruler, or the overthrow of leaders by mobs, want in Italy, Cilicia and Africa, and slaughters in Libya, Syria and Babylonia, while in Cilicia and at Rome there will be damage and cases of officials harmed by their superiors. Babylon, Thrace, Phrygia are all part of the world of this treatise, and so, more surprisingly, are Iberia and even Germany. From Elam to the Ebro – a more inclusive Hellenistic world, we might think, than *From Samarkand to Sardis* – this little work delineates the world of the Tethys Corridor.

[43] Hdt. 9.122, with Clarke 1999: 90–1, Thomas 2000: 106–8; one of several respects in which Herodotus prefigures this paper's argument.

[44] Momigliano 1942 is still classic.

[45] The famous Democedes-*logos* at Hdt. 3.129–37, focalising the Mediterranean from the Persian perspective as *parathalassia*, is a further instance: see Moyer 2006. In the celebrated dialogue between Aristagoras and Cleomenes at Sparta (5.49–51), the larger portrait of the king and the singularities of Herodotus' Spartans both suggest that the Milesian viewpoint, by which it is perfectly reasonable to ask the Spartans to go to the eastern end of the Tethys Corridor, might be a better guide to fifth-century Greek horizons than Cleomenes' horror.

[46] *CCAG* VII, 129–51, 12–19. Hephaistion's own horoscope gives his birthday as 26 November 380 AD.

The treatise was obviously composed in Alexandria. The hinge on which turned the terrestrial and maritime parts of the Corridor served as a conceptual centre for the whole *oikoumene*, a centrality which it would be otiose to document further. Ancient Alexandria and Antioch both derived their importance from their place at the binding of the two leaves of the Tethys diptych, as William of Tyre was to remark so much later. The prophetic vision which introduces this section already envisages the Jewish polity too as being sited at the conjunction of two worlds to east and west. The eastward and westward Jewish diasporas in their different chronological moments are thus a further instance of the circulatory networks shaped by the Corridor. So, in a quite different register of constructed geography, is the favourite Hellenistic parlour-game 'Alexander's last plans'. Diodorus' famous version presents the great road west towards Gibraltar and the blueprint for an Alexandrine thalassocracy, with the classic formulation of the wish for *epigamia* between the continents.[47] The symmetry of East and West, land and sea, Asia and the Mediterranean, is of course a tissue of commonplaces. But they are commonplaces which offer more to the historian than has usually been supposed.

The hinge, the diptych and inclusive Hellenistic history

Whatever else can be said about the Tethys Corridor, it is very big. A history which deals in entities of this size needs certain rules and methods of its own, and in the last decade those have been the object of systematic debate among historians of other periods, who have coined the phrase *histoire à très large échelle*.[48]

As ancient historians begin to break out of a tradition that has sometimes tended to exclusivism, we naturally ask what kind of units might we deal in, what would the edges of those units be like, and on what terms would the units interact, if our studies were to contribute to global history. The Mediterranean looks in principle an attractive starting-point. All comparison between the Roman world and other pre-modern hegemonial polities – such as Han China, or Mogul India – needs to recall the fact that the Roman dominion had a Mediterranean in it.[49] But it is not as the fiscal and political

[47] Diod. Sic. 18.4.

[48] Horden and Purcell 2006; Bayly 2003; G. Fowden 2002; Chartier 2001; Subrahmanyam 1998, 2001; Bin Wong 2001.

[49] These are the subjects of the ambitious research projects of Scheidel 2009 and Bang 2008. Woolf 2003, however, thinks that the Mediterranean is just the wrong size – either too large or too small – to be helpful.

foundation of a hegemony like Rome's or its Byzantine successor that the Mediterranean can be a tessera in the mosaic of a global history, a link in the concatenation of regions. The unit is not enough. The problem is not how to distinguish different segments of historical experience, how to break the world up into discrete units of investigation, but how to make the apparent units work together, how to model their boundaries, overlaps and interactions. Historical enquiry at the largest scale starts with the internal dynamics of coherent spaces, and then looks outside, at the interactions and negotiations between communities, economies and cultures rather than at the foundations of each, in a way which can only comfort the Hellenistic historian. The more dynamic formulation of interdependence in the term *histoires croisèes* may be fruitful.[50] Especially helpful is the analysis of the relations between the mobilities of social groups and the changing patterns of cultural history which has been called, with reference to the history of south Asia, 'circulation'.[51]

Concentrating on mobilities and interdependence will help make the sterile polarisations of the past obsolete. Doing without clear antinomies between Hellenistic and non-Hellenistic takes its place alongside other *désenclavements*: the replacement of the old thoughtworld of 'Orientalising' with new models for culture change in the first half of the first millennium BC; rethinking the encounter of Islam and the Mediterranean.[52] Underlying both schematisms is the form of Mediterranean exceptionalism which saw the sea as intimately connected to an essentialised Europe, sharply to be distinguished from an Asiatic alternative.[53] From the Asiatic Mode of Production to the characteristic but excessive firmness of Sir Moses Finley's complete differentiation of Ancient and Asian economies, polarisation has inhibited historical understanding.[54] If the Mediterranean and Asiatic universes were indeed so strongly differentiated, one might have thought, their comparison, and above all the investigation of how the zone where they abutted worked at different periods, would become proportionally *more*, not less, interesting to the historian.[55]

[50] Werner and Zimmermann 2006.

[51] Markovits *et al.* 2003. The 'circulatory regime' evoked here, patterned by ecology, explicitly shapes flows of ideas as well as people, and is fundamental to explaining culture change: see esp. 2–3 and 10–11.

[52] On the end of 'Orientalising', Purcell 2006; cf. Sommer 2004.

[53] East 1938: 85–6, 'A *Grenzraum* between Europe, Asia and Africa, it should be regarded in its entirety . . . as part of the continent of Europe, with which its relationships, physical and human, have been closest'. For the problem, Purcell 2004.

[54] Manning and Morris 2005: 2.

[55] G. Fowden 2002 makes a strong plea for the integrated study of Mediterranean and West Asia.

Overcoming the limitations of apparent boundaries is already a theme of modern Hellenistic history. The search for Hellenistic cores has been rightly abandoned, since all Hellenistic elite cultures experienced the social and cultural periphery on the inside.[56] Both West Asia and the Mediterranean, separately or interacting, best understood as spaces through circulation and connectivity, suit such a history admirably. The insights which Malkin has drawn from network theory to describe Mediterranean networks might be applied to the whole Corridor: 'distance creates a virtual centre', or 'the further you stretch it, the stronger it becomes'.[57] A Hellenistic Mediterranean, part of a much bigger continuum, would transcend oceanographical subdivisions.

Indeed, the character of the whole Corridor is importantly formed by the curious, basic and massive accident that it is part terrestrial and part maritime. The possibilities and characters of each of those zones make their contribution to the whole. But still more important than the consequences of Mediterranean-ness and Mesopotamian-ness is the fact that at the heart of the Corridor two such different macro-regions abut. That interaction has arguably done more to configure the character of the Corridor as a whole than has the distinctiveness of either the Mediterranean or of Mesopotamia taken on its own. This perception returns us to the original vision of Droysen, then, in which the Levantine meeting of East and West was the essential element in Hellenistic history, but by a very different route.[58]

The Corridor, then, functions as the frame for circulation and for our study of it. Our connected histories will need to begin with the comparison and interaction of the connectivity-based extractive systems of the macroregions. They will consider the balances of production, consumption and redistribution, and the economic imperatives imposed by part of the Corridor on other parts. For the Mediterranean world, the possibility of economic systems founded on the control of connectivity has been amply discussed in another place. For West Asia, we might adduce Larsen's memorable metaphor of the 'grand Assyrian vacuum-cleaner', hoovering up population and all other commodities through its tributary systems, and powering the dynamics of movement of people and things all over the Mediterranean as a consequence.[59] We have to consider what impact structures of this kind had at the level of buzzing and humming, of *histoire terre à terre* – once again, the macro depends on the micro – and how the terrestrial and maritime universes within the Corridor interacted.

[56] Thus, importantly, Shipley 1993. [57] Malkin 2004. [58] Thus Geus 2003.
[59] Larsen 1979: cf. Parpola 2003.

More specifically, there is a great deal of work to do on the circulatory regimes which united the two worlds within the Corridor. The global economic vision attributed to the founder of Abbasid Baghdad seems very far removed from the orthodoxies about the very restricted interdependence of Mesopotamia and the Mediterranean world in Antiquity:

This island between the Tigris in the east and the Euphrates in the west is the harbour of the world . . . goods brought . . . down the Euphrates from Diyār Muar, ar-Raqqah, Syria, the border regions, Egypt and al-Maghrib, these goods will be brought and unloaded here. Praise god who preserved it for me and caused all those who preceded me to neglect it! . . . It will indeed be the most flourishing city in the world.[60]

Even if the movements of people and materials and ideas which engaged the hinge-zone between the two macroregions involved relatively little reciprocal or symmetrical movement, the overlap zone at the centre drew its importance and interest from imbrication with both worlds. The interrupted trajectories, the problems, as well as the manifold opportunities, of interaction, make possible important historical deductions about both the worlds so strangely and strongly divided.[61]

Finally, movements and relations outwards from the major spaces of this large-scale history help determine the nature of macroregions themselves, and show how they fit into world-wide sequences or networks. Just as Mediterranean history needs to investigate the edges of possible Mediterranean worlds, which will ultimately be defined by the natures of these edges, so margins and contacts need to be investigated all along both edges of the thin, latitudinally extended strip in which the Mediterranean finds itself. Understanding the paroxysmic super-ecologies of the Mediterranean and West Asia aright poses urgent and revealing questions about their connections with different worlds, and the social, economic and cultural phenomena to which the routes outward and inward give rise.

Brent Shaw has written extremely interestingly on what he calls recursivity across such frontier zones, the differing and reversible polarities of power and complexity inside and outside the Mediterranean zone.[62] Across the edges of the Corridor, goods and ideas are put into circulation, mobilised. But still more important, and equally common to the fringes of the entire Corridor, is the mobilisation of people. Van der Mieroop recently identified a further transhistorical common denominator of the eastern

[60] Mansur: Yatqūbī, *Buldān* 237–8, quoted by Lassner 1970: 127.

[61] For Uruk's trade with the West around 550 BC, Oppenheim 1967. [62] Shaw 2006.

segment of the Corridor: its capacity, at many different periods, to make use of exogenous population resources. He cited the need for mercenaries, which is well known to historians of at least one of the Mediterranean regions which supplied this demand.[63] The forced movement of the unfree has perhaps been an even more important common denominator, whether it takes the form of a developed slave trade, or of the forced resettlements which are so prominent in the Asiatic record, and not wanting in that of the Mediterranean. Structures of supply and distribution of incoming people, and the institutions which could control and document the processes, became essential to the nature of the states which dominated the regions of demographic demand. Meanwhile, a superstructure of power and record was also built on the fringes of such hegemonies by those who controlled from time to time the channels of supply of population to the zones which deployed and consumed it. Where such conduits existed, from time to time, the movements of large numbers of the people who were so constantly sought in the heartlands of the West Asian corridor stimulated ethnogenesis, and perhaps even state-formation, patterning the edges of the more connective spaces within the Corridor with new polities, along the *piedmont* of the Taurus ranges, or among the mountain chains and basins of the Levant.

Likewise in the Mediterranean world, the deployment of demographic abundance was similarly a central foundation of hegemonial states occupying communications heartlands.[64] Around the zone of consumption, in the same way as happened around the West Asian corridor, the suppliers changed and grew in confidence, complexity and self-consciousness as a direct result of their involvement in these movements and the relationships with the hegemonial powers which patterned them, and sometimes challenged those powers, recursively, for supremacy. The idea that peripheral ethnogenesis is a transhistorical fact of the Mediterranean too, makes it possible to compare the effects of the geography of circulation along the whole length of the Corridor, juxtaposing the transformations of late La Tène Gaul, as it might be, not simply with those of Dacia or Numidia, but also adding Elam, Media or Commagene. The Persian ascendancy over the neighbouring lowlands about which Herodotus' Cyrus the Great was speaking becomes a comparandum for the Italic domination of the coastal

[63] Van der Mieroop 2005: 133–4. Antimenidas of Mitylene: Alcaeus frs. 48 and 350 LP, cf. Luraghi 2006. The mass deportations studied by Oded 1979 are a further important case: for the Hellenistic sequel, Cohen 1983.

[64] Horden and Purcell 2000: 377–91.

cities of the Tyrrhenian. Macedonian preoccupations with the Thracians find their parallel in Iranian concerns for the Scythians.[65]

Illustration could be drawn from many Mediterranean contexts, but few are richer or more suggestive for the macroregional analysis proposed than the cases of the rival hegemonies of the western basin of the sea. That both Rome and Carthage specialised in the control of population, in all its variety, is an obvious enough feature of the ways that their polities had developed from the fourth century onwards, and that this control had a geography which requires interpretation on a very large scale, are observations as Hellenistic in flavour as could be wished. And so we return from general observations about the grand framework of Hellenistic history to the western Mediterranean: and it is hard, as we move towards a conclusion, to deny, even by comparison with Rome's distinctive methods of controlling human resources, the particular interest of Carthage.

Carthage during the fourth and third centuries surpassed its western Mediterranean predecessors as a manager of the human resource. Sicily, in the heart of the narrow seas of the Tyrrhenian-Ionian threshold, sufficiently continent-like to have its own mountainous interior and demographic resources, provided a laboratory and a precedent.[66] Polybius' account of the War of the Mercenaries brightly illuminates the demographic reach of the Carthaginian state.[67] Maritime in its logic, this destabilising and violently integrative activity mirrors the terrestrial mobilisations and redeployments of the Mesopotamia-centred polities.

Carthage constructed itself historically on a Corridor-sized scale, between Tyre and Gades, as a sea-oriented, land-averse polity. East–West movement – a harbinger of the foreshortening of meridian distance in the perspective of the Cairo *geniza* – was present alike in *imaginaire* and in reality. From the first it was intimately entangled in the archaic webs of exchange between eastern and western Mediterranean basins.[68] At the same time, its site is defined in relation to the Tyrrhenian-Ionian threshold, 'opposite' Rome and

[65] Vogelsang 1992 for the perennial effects of the contact zone with the North on the government of the Iranian plateau.

[66] Thuc. 6.17.2–4 is the *locus classicus*. The Syracusan polity in its various incarnations also has an important place in the history of west Mediterranean demographic mobilisation. The Sardinian interventions of Carthage are also very relevant.

[67] Polyb. 1.67.7, a catalogue which rings the west Mediterranean, and puts a noteworthy emphasis on the ambiguities between slave, runaway, mercenary and deserter. Note also the regulation of recruitment in the Rome-Carthage treaties, Polyb. 3.22–7.

[68] Kourou 2002 has an interesting multi-cultural reappraisal of the origins of Carthage, advancing a case for a strong Cypriote link; cf. Boardman 2006. For later periods, Ramón Torres 1995; Berges 1998; Eiring and Lund 2004; Bechtold 2007.

central Italy in ancient conceptual geography in a way which seems counter-intuitive to modern map-based sensibilities. The patterns of behaviour which Greek tradition associated especially with Carthage, the attempt to control seaborne communications, and to create differential control of access in the routes of connectivity, is entirely right for a 'Janus-state', whose political economy is shaped by its location at a Mediterranean threshold.

Furthermore, new social and political formations came vigorously into being through the dialectic of the Carthaginian western Mediterranean with the areas which abutted it. Carthage, as a major deploying power, wielded a high degree of demographic influence, while its nodality in Corridor-scale networks of redistribution promoted economic intensification, which also conduced to rapid social change. The Hellenistic state-formation of the Celtiberian polities of Iberia and southern Gaul are the classic cases. It is of patent interest to compare these political geneses with those of the Mesopotamian and Syrian periphery.

As for Rome, we could tell a tale in which the Roman state, after the Latin settlement of 338 BC, took a similar trajectory, developing *pari passu* with Hellenistic Carthage as a deploying power and demographic organiser. The connectivities of Antiate, Etruscan, Roman or Brundisine pirates and traders might mirror the eastern networks of Carthage. The Romans continued Carthaginian patterns in Iberia through the second century, with similar effects on state-formation; and they arguably learned Carthaginian lessons about the imposition of limits and controlled zones on maritime topography. But perhaps their policies in Italy too, and their effects on their neighbours, were likewise indebted to Punic models. A Roman supremacist might insist on the primacy of Rome in pioneering these Hellenistic behaviours in the West. But it would also be possible to see Rome and its dominion as heavily indebted to Carthage and to explain the galvanising of the Roman system in the same way as the Celtiberian, as a response to the growth of Carthage, a phenomenon of the Carthaginian periphery.[69] Co-evolution of similar systems, however, remains a more appealing solution than allotting any prizes for primacy.

Taking stock, then, of what the method advocated here can offer, some final observations are in order. A Corridor-wide vision emancipates the historian from the essentialising notions of East and West. Attention shifts to the functioning of a linear system, to the articulation of the links in the chain, to its cohesiveness as a whole and the shifting definitions of its constituent parts. And we are enabled to study comparatively all the systems

[69] Palmer 1997 could be taken as a step in this direction.

of circulation and connectivity which lie beyond and around the linear system and which abut it. Not only, then, can we discern structural resemblances between the circles of societies around the communications heartlands of the west Mediterranean and West Asia, but the cultural contacts between the zones made it possible for those who ran the systems to exchange ideas and values configured by their essentially similar socio-political needs and experiences. The transfer of ideas is not, then, a cultural influence operating arbitrarily. Imitation and adaptation are less potent where there is no structural rationale – economic, social, ultimately political – for the transmission. Novel conditions of circulation made the extended Hellenistic world a new sort of cultural space.

In pursuing this larger analysis, we must not be fazed by the emphatic force with which the Romans situated themselves, for their own ideological convenience, in a West which they invented for the purpose, building on the convenient and equally forceful, but finally implausible, claim made historically by the Greeks that they occupied some sort of centre. Neither construction should shape our thinking. There was no great divide across the Mediterranean. The Mediterranean is the West, if you must have one, and the basin of West Asia lowland is the East. But recognising the nature of the Corridor helps avoid the more malignant constructions of the East, in the still continuing battle of at least ancient historians against Orientalism and the Orientalising. It is time to replace the Asia–Mediterranean dichotomy with models of abutting synergistic cultural systems, and this framework could further serve to transform the history of Roman–Parthian and Roman–Sassanian relations. Most relevantly to our discussion, it offers ways of making a constructive historical analysis of how the ecologies of the eastern Mediterranean and of its eastern neighbours in the Hellenistic period related to their equivalents to the west.

The homogenisation of cultural behaviours which has been seen in the abstract as the irradiation of receiver societies by richer or more sophisticated ones is a process of convergence based on certain closely shared ecological conditions – ecological conditions, moreover, which actually served, as we have seen, to facilitate the connections over long distances between hegemonial societies within the Corridor. It is this that should be seen, above all, as characteristic of Hellenistic history – and the western Mediterranean could hardly sensibly be excluded from it. The history of the mid-Mediterranean threshold and what met there is thus Hellenistic because it operated analogously to the greater threshold of the Levant, whose interactions have always been seen as central to the period.

Bibliography

Journal titles are abbreviated according to *L'Année philologique*

AA. VV. (1979) *La baja época de la cultura ibérica: actas de la mesa redonda celebrada en conmemoración del decimo aniversario de la Asociación Española de Amigos de la Arqueología*. Madrid.

Abad Casal, L. (ed.) (2003a) De Iberia in Hispaniam. *La adaptación de las ciudades ibéricas a los modelos romanos*. Alicante.

(2003b) 'El tránsito funerario. De las formas y los ritos ibéricos a la consolidación de los modelos romanos', in Abad Casal 2003a: 75–100.

Abad Casal, L., Keay, S. and Ramallo Asensio, S. (eds.) (2007) *Early Roman Towns in Hispania Tarraconensis*. JRA Suppl. 62. Portsmouth RI.

Abascal, J. M. (2003) 'La recepción de la cultura epigráfica romana en *Hispania*', in Abad Casal 2003a: 241–86.

Abulafia, D. (2005) 'Mediterraneans', in Harris 2005a: 64–93.

Acconcia, V. (2005) 'Iscrizioni puniche', in *Ardea, il deposito votivo di Casarinaccio*, ed. F. Di Mario. Rome: 126–7.

Acquaro, E. (1974) 'Il tipo del toro nelle monete puniche di Sardegna e la politica barcide in Occidente', *RStudFen* 2: 105–7.

Adam, J.-P. (1999) *Roman Building*. London.

Adams, J. (2003) *Bilingualism and the Latin Language*. Cambridge.

Adams, W. L. (2006) 'The Hellenistic kingdoms', in Bugh 2006a: 28–51.

Adriani, A. (1966) *Repertorio d'arte dell'Egitto greco-romano*, Serie C, vols. I–II. Rome.

Ager, S. L. (1996) *Interstate Arbitrations in the Greek World, 337–90 BC*. Berkeley, Los Angeles and London.

Alcock, S. E. (1994), 'Breaking up the Hellenistic world: survey and society', in *Classical Greece. Ancient Histories and Modern Archaeologies. New Directions in Archaeology*, ed. I. Morris. Cambridge: 171–90.

Alexandropoulos, J. (2000) *Les monnaies de l'Afrique antique, 400 av. J.-C. – 40 ap. J.-C.* Toulouse.

Alfaro, C. (1988) *Las monedas de Gadir/Gades*. Madrid.

Alföldy, G. (1981) 'Die alteste römische Inschrift der iberischen Halbinsel', *ZPE* 43: 1–12.

Allen, H. L. (1974) 'Excavations at Morgantina (Serra Orlando), 1970–2. Preliminary report XI', *AJA* 78: 361–83.

Allen, J. (2006) *Hostages and Hostage-Taking in the Roman Empire*. New York.

Allison, P. (2004) *Pompeian Households: An On-line Companion*. www.stoa.org/projects/ph/home. This site hosts materials to accompany Penelope M. Allison, *Pompeian Households: An Analysis of the Material Culture* (Cotsen Institute of Archaeology, Monograph 42); last accessed 25 April 2012.

Almagro-Gorbea, M. (1983a) 'Pozo Moro: El monumento orientalizante, su contexto socio-cultural y sus parallelos en la arquitectura funeraria ibérica', *MDAI(M)* 24: 177–293.

(1983b) 'Arquitectura y sociedad en la cultura iberica', in *Architecture et société de l'archaïsme grec à la fin de la république romaine*, ed. P. Gros. Rome: 387–414.

(1990) 'L'Hellénisme dans la culture ibérique', in *Akten des XIII. Internationalen Kongresses für Klassische Archäologie, Berlin 1988*. Mainz: 113–27.

(1996) *Ideología y poder en Tartessos y el mundo Ibérico*. Madrid.

Almagro-Gorbea, M. and Ruiz Zapatero, G. (1993) *La Palaeoetnología de la península ibérica*. Complutum Extra 2–3. Madrid.

Alvino, G. (1996) 'Alcune riflessioni sulla cultura equicola nella piana di Corvaro di Borgorose (RI)', in *Identità e civiltà dei Sabini*. Atti del XVIII Convegno di studi etruschi ed italici. Florence: 415–30.

(2004) 'Il tumulo di Corvaro di Borgorose', in Lapenna 2004: 60–76.

Amadasi Guzzo, M. G. (1967) *Le Iscrizioni fenicie e puniche delle colonie in Occidente*. Studi Semitici 28. Rome.

(1986) *Scavi a Mozia. Le iscrizioni*. Collezione di Studi Fenici 22. Rome.

(1988) 'Cultura punica e cultura latina in Tripolitania: osservazioni in base alla iscrizioni puniche e alle iscrizioni bilingui' in *Bilinguismo e biculturalismo nel mondo antico: atti del colloquio interdisciplinare tenuto a Pisa il 28 e 29 settembre 1987*, eds. E. Campanile, G. R. Cardona and R. Lazzarone. Pisa: 23–33.

(1989–90) 'Per una classificazione delle iscrizioni votive di dono', *Scienze dell'Antichità* 3–4: 825–43.

(1990) *Iscrizioni fenicie e puniche in Italia*. Rome.

(1995) 'Les inscriptions', in *La civilisation phénicienne et punique: manuel de recherche*, ed. V. Krings. Leiden: 19–30.

(1999) 'Epigrafia fenicia in Sicilia', in *Sicilia Epigraphica. Atti del convegno di studi, Erice, 15–18 ottobre 1998* (2 vols.), ed. M. I. Gulletta. ASNP ser. 4, quad. 1–2. Pisa: I, 33–45.

(2006) 'Epigrafia e storia politica fenicia e punica in Sicilia', in *Guerra e pace in Sicilia e nel Mediterraneo (VIII–III sec. a.C.). Arte, prassi e teoria della pace e della guerra* (2 vols.). Pisa: II, 693–702.

Ampolo, C. (ed.) (2001) *Da un'antica città di Sicilia. I decreti di Entella e Nakone*. Pisa.

(ed.) (2009) *Immagine e immagini della Sicilia e di altre isole del Mediterraneo antico. Atti delle seste giornate internazionali di studi sull'area elima e la Sicilia occidentale nel contesto mediterraneo, Erice, 12–16 ottobre 2006* (2 vols.). Pisa.

(ed.) (2010) *Relazioni preliminari degli scavi a Segesta (Calatafimi-Segesta, TP; 2007–08; Entella (Contessa Entellina, PA; 2007–08); Kaulonia (Monasterace, RC; 2006–08). Ricerche recenti a Roca (Melendugno, LE). Notizie degli scavi di antichità comunicate dalla Scuola Normale Superiore di Pisa. Rassegna archeologica del Laboratorio di Storia, Archeologia e Topografia del Mondo Antico. Annali della Scuola Normale Superiore di Pisa, Classe di Lettere e Filosofia,* series 5, 2/2, Supplemento. Pisa.

(ed.) (2012) Agora *greca e* agorai *di Sicilia*. Pisa.

Andreae, B. (2003) *Antike Bildmosaiken*. Mainz am Rhein.

Anello, P. (2002) 'Siracusa e Cartagine', in *La Sicilia dei due Dionisi*, eds. N. Bonacasa, L. Braccesi and E. De Miro. Rome: 343–60.

Anello, P. and Martínez-Pinna, J. (eds.) (2006) *Relaciones interculturales en el Mediterráneo antiguo: Sicilia e Iberia*. Malaga.

Aneziri, S. (2003) *Die Vereine der dionisischen Techniten im Kontext der hellenistischen Gesellschaft: Untersuchungen zur Geschichte, Organisation und Wirkung der hellenistischen Technitenvereine*. Historia Einzelschrift 163. Stuttgart.

Anglada Curada, R. and Rodríguez Rodríguez, I. (2007) 'Las defensas de la Carmona protohistórica', in *El nacimiento de la ciudad: Carmona protohistórica*, eds. M. Bendala Galán and M. Belén Deamos. Carmona: 455–78.

Antonaccio, C. (2003) 'Hybridity and the cultures within Greek culture', in Dougherty and Kurke 2003a: 57–74.

(2005) 'Excavating colonization', in *Ancient Colonisations: Analogy, Similarity and Difference*, eds. H. Hurst and S. Owen. London: 97–113.

Aquilué, X., Castanyer, P., Santos, M. and Tremoleda, J. (2007) 'Greek Emporion and Roman Republican Empúries', in Abad Casal *et al.* 2007: 18–31.

Aranegui, C. (ed.) (1998) *Los Iberos. Príncipes de Occidente. Estructuras de poder en la sociedad Ibérica. Actas del Congreso Internacional*. Barcelona.

(2004) *Sagunto. Oppidum, emporio y municipio romano*. Barcelona.

(2007) 'From Arse to Saguntum', in Abad Casal *et al.* 2007: 64–74.

Archibald, Z. H. (2001) 'Making the most of one's friends. Western Asia Minor in the early Hellenistic age', in *Hellenistic Economies*, eds. Z. H. Archibald, J. Davies, V. Gabrielsen and G. J. Oliver. London: 245–70.

Archibald, Z. H., Davies, J. K. and Gabrielsen, V. (eds.) (2011) *The Economies of Hellenistic Societies, Third to First Centuries BC*. Oxford.

Arevalo González, A. (1999) *La ciudad de Obulco: sus emisiones monetales*. Madrid.

Arnaud, P. (2005) *Les routes de la navigation antique: itinéraires en Méditerranée*. Paris.

Arnold, D. (2003) *The Encyclopedia of Ancient Egyptian Architecture*. Princeton, NJ.

Arribas, A. (1965) *The Iberians*. London.

Arteaga, O. and Roos, A.-M. (2002) 'El puerto fenicio-púnico de Gadir. Una nueva visión desde la geoarqueología urbana de Cádiz', *Spal* 11: 21–39.

Aubet, M. E. (1982) *El santuario púnico de Es Cuieram*. Trabajos del Museo Arqueológico de Ibiza 8. Ibiza.

(ed.) (1989) *Tartessos. Arqueología protohistórica del bajo-Guadalquivir*. Barcelona.

(2001) *The Phoenicians and the West: Politics, Colonies and Trade*, transl. M. Turton, 2nd edn. Cambridge.

Aureli, P. (2008) 'Il restauro del letto funerario in osso rinvenuto presso la necropoli di *Aquinum*', in Sapelli Ragni 2008a: 100–1.

Austin, M. M. (2006) *The Hellenistic World from Alexander to the Roman Conquest*, 2nd edn. Cambridge.

Bacci, G. M. and Coppolino, P. (2009) *La necropoli di Abakainon. Primi dati*. Messina.

Badian, E. (1958) *Foreign Clientelae (264–70 B.C.)*. Oxford.

Badisches Landesmuseum Karlsruhe (ed.) (2004) Hannibal ad portas. *Macht und Reichtum Karthagos*. Stuttgart.

Bagnall, R. S. and Derow, P. S. (2004) *The Hellenistic Period: Historical Sources in Translation*, 2nd edn. Oxford.

Baines, J. and Riggs, C. (2001) 'Archaism and kingship: a late royal statue and its Early Dynastic model', *JEA* 87: 103–18.

Balbín Chamorro, P. (2006) *Hospitalidad y patronato en la península ibérica durante la antiqüedad*. Salamanca.

Bandinelli, G. (2008) 'Epigrafie indigene ed epigrafia dominante nella romanizzazione della Cisalpina. Aspetti politici e istituzionali (283–89 a.C)', in *Epigrafia 2006*. Tituli 9. Rome: I, 43–66.

Bang, P. F. (2008) *The Roman Bazaar: A Comparative Study of Trade and Markets in a Tributary Empire*. Cambridge.

Baratte, F. (1986) *Le trésor d'orfèverie romaine de Boscoreale*. Paris.

Barceló, P. (1994) 'The perception of Carthage in Classical Greek historiography', *AClass* 37: 1–14.

Barker, G. and Rasmussen, T. (1998) *The Etruscans*. Peoples of Europe. Oxford.

Baron, C. A. (2013) *Timaeus of Tauromenium and Hellenistic Historiography*. Cambridge.

Barreca, F. (1986) *La civiltà fenicio-punica in Sardegna*. Sassari.

Barruol, G. (1969) *Les peuples préromains du sud-est de la Gaule. Étude de géographie historique*. Paris.

Barthes, R. (1972 [1957]) *Mythologies*, transl. Annette Lavers. New York.

Bartoloni, P. (1981) 'Contributo alla cronologia delle necropoli fenicie e puniche di Sardegna', *RStudFen* 9 (Supplement): 22–4.

(2005) 'La Sardegna fenicia e punica', in *Storia della Sardegna antica*, ed. A. Mastino. La Sardegna e la sua storia 2. Nuoro: 25–62.

Baslez, M.-F. (1981) 'Un monument numide à Délos', *REG* 94: 160–5.

Bats, M. (1988) 'La logique de l'écriture d'une société à l'autre en Gaule méridionale protohistorique', *RAN* 21: 121–48.

(2003) 'Les Gaulois et l'écriture aux IIe-Ier s. av. J.-C.', in *Les marges de l'Armorique à l'Âge du Fer. Archéologie et histoire: culture matérielle et sources écrites*, eds. B. Mandy and A. de Saulce. Revue archéologique de l'Ouest, suppl. 10. Nantes: 369–80.

Bats, M., Bertucchi, G., Conges, G. and Treziny, H. (eds.) (1992) *Marseille grecque et la Gaule*. Coll. Études Massaliètes 3. Aix-en-Provence.

Battistoni, F. (2010) *Parenti dei Romani. Mito troiano e diplomazia*. Bari.

Batty, R. (2007) *Rome and the Nomads: The Pontic-Danubian Realm in Antiquity*. Oxford.

Baxandall, M. (1985) *Patterns of Intention*. New Haven.

Bayly, C. A. (2003) *The Birth of the Modern World, 1780–1914: Global Connexions and Comparisons*. Oxford.

Beard, M., North, J. and Price, S. (1998) *Religions of Rome. Volume 1, A History*. Cambridge.

Bearn, G. C. F. (1995) 'Derrida dry: iterating iterability analytically', *Diacritics* 25(3): 2–25.

Bechtold, B. (1999) *La necropoli di Lilybaeum*. Palermo.

(2007) 'Alcune osservazione sui rapporti commerciali fra Cartagine, la Sicilia occidentale e la Campania (IV-metà del II sec. a.C.): nuovi dati basati sulla distribuzione di ceramiche campane e nordafricane/cartaginesi', *BABesch* 82(1): 51–76.

Beestman-Kruyshaar, C. (2003) 'Appendix 1. Catalogue of pottery', in *Housing in New Halos, a Hellenistic town in Thessaly, Greece*, eds. H. Reinder Reinders and W. Prummel. Lisse: 249–97.

Belén Deamos, M., Gil de los Reyes, S., Hernández, G., Lineros, R. and Puya, M. (1986) 'Rituals funeraris a la necròpolis romana de Carmona (Sevilla)', *Cota Zero* 2: 53–61.

Bell, C. (1992) *Ritual Theory, Ritual Practice*. Oxford.

(1997) *Ritual: Perspectives and Dimensions*. New York and Oxford.

Bell, M. (1981) *Morgantina Studies I: The Terracottas*. Princeton.

(1984–5) 'Recenti scavi nell'agora di Morgantina', *Kokalos* 30–31: 501–20.

(1993) 'Observations on western Greek stoas', in Eius Virtutis Studiosi: *Classical and Post-classical Studies in Memory of Frank Edward Brown*, eds. R. T. and A. R. Scott. Washington: 327–41.

(1995) 'The Motya Charioteer and Pindar's Isthmian 2', *MAAR* 40: 1–42.

(1999) 'Centro e periferia nel regno siracusano di Ierone II', in *La colonisation grecque en Méditerranée occidentale. Actes de la rencontre scientifique en hommage à Georges Vallet*. Rome: 257–77.

(2000) 'La provenienza ritrovata: cercando il contesto di antichità trafugate', in *Antichità senza provenienza II: atti del Colloquio Internazionale 17–18 ottobre 1997*, eds. P. Pelagatti and P. G. Guzzo. Supplement to *Bollettino d'Arte* 101–2. Rome: 31–41.

(2005) 'L'architettura civile di età ellenistica: le *stoai* e gli edifici con funzione politica', in Minà 2005: 159–64.

(2007a) 'An archaeologist's perspective on the *lex Hieronica*', in Dubouloz and Pittia 2007: 187–203.

(2007b) 'Apronius in the agora: Sicilian civil architecture and the *lex Hieronica*', in Sicilia nutrix plebis Romanae. *Rhetoric, Law & Taxation in Cicero's Verrines*, ed. J. R. W. Prag. Bulletin of the Institute of Classical Studies Supplement 97. London: 117–34.

(2010) 'Serra Orlando', in *Bibliografia Topografica della Colonizzazione Greca in Italia e nelle Isole Tirreniche*, XVIII. Pisa: 724–51.

(2011a) 'Recent news from central Sicily', in *American Excavations at Morgantina: Newsletter of the Friends of Morgantina. May 2011.* Charlottesville, VA: 1–3.

(2011b) 'Osservazioni sui mosaici greci della Casa di Ganimede a Morgantina', in La Torre and Torelli 2011: 105–23.

Bellini, G. R. (2008) 'Un nuovo rinvenimento da Aquinum: il letto in osso della tomba 6', in Sapelli Ragni 2008a: 38–48.

Beltrán, A. and Tovar, A. (1982) *Contrebia Belaisca (Botorrita, Zaragoza). I. El bronce con alfabeto 'Iberico' de Botorrita*. Zaragoza.

Beltrán Fortes, J. (2001) 'Arqueología de la Carmona romana: el esquema urbano', in Caballos Rufino 2001: 135–58.

(2002) 'La arquitectura funeraria en la Hispania meridional durante los siglos II a. C.–I d. C.', in *Espacios y usos funerarios en el Occidente Romano* (2 vols.), ed. D. Vaquerizo Gil. Córdoba: I, 233–58.

Beltrán Lloris, F. (ed.) (1995a) *Roma y el nacimiento de la cultura epigráfica en occidente*. Zaragoza.

(1995b) 'La escritura en la frontera. Inscripciones y cultura epigráfica en el valle medio del Ebro', in F. Beltrán Lloris 1995a: 169–95.

(1999) 'Writing, language and society: Iberians, Celts and Romans in northeastern Spain in the 2nd and 1st centuries BC', *BICS* 43: 131–51.

(2004) 'Una variante provincial del hospitium: pactos de hospitalidad y concesión de la ciudadanía local en la Hispania Tarraconense', in *Epigrafía y sociedad en Hispania durante el Alto Imperio: estructuras y relaciones sociales*, eds. S. Armani, B. Hurlet-Martineau and A. U. Stylow. Acta Antiqua Complutensia 4. Alcalá: 33–56.

(2010) 'El nacimiento de un tipo epigráfico provincial: Las tábulas de hospitalidad y patronato', *ZPE* 175: 273–86.

Beltrán Lloris, F., De Hoz, J. and Untermann, J. (1996) *El tercer bronce de Botorrita (Contrebia Belaisca)*. Zaragoza.

Beltrán Lloris, M. (1990) *Guía de la cerámica romana*. Zaragoza.

Ben Tahar, S. (2009) 'La céramique à vernis noir de Jerba' in *An Island through Time: Jerba Studies. Volume I. The Punic and Roman Periods*, eds. A. Drine, E. Fentress and R. Holod. *JRA* Suppl. 71. Portsmouth, RI: 244–56.

Ben Younès, H. (2007) 'Interculturality and the Punic funerary world', in *Mortuary Landscapes of North Africa*, eds. D. L. Stone and L. M. Stirling. Toronto: 32–42.

Bendala Galán, M. (1976) *La necrópolis romana de Carmona*. Sevilla.

(1994) 'El influjo cartaginés en el interior de Andalucía', in *Cartago, Gadir, Ebusus y la influencia púnica en los territorios hispanos. VIII Jornadas de*

Arqueología Fenicio-Púnica (Ibiza, 1993). Trabajos del Museo Arqueológico de Ibiza. Ibiza: 59–74.

(2000) 'Panorama arqueológico de la Hispania púnica a partir de la época Bárquida', in *Los Cartagineses y la monetización del Mediterraneo occidental*, eds. M. P. García-Bellido and L. Callegarin. Anejos de AEA 22. Madrid: 75–88.

(2006) 'Roma, la romanización de Hispania y nuestra generación científica', in *El concepto de la provincial en el mundo antigua. Homenaje a la Prof. Pilar León* (2 vols.), eds. D. Vaquerizo Gil and J. F. Murillo. Córdoba: I, 189–200.

Benelli, E. (2003) 'Le indagine archeologiche. Il costume funerario. Dai primi decenni del V secolo al terzo quarto del IV secolo a.C.', in D'Ercole and Copersino 2003: 322–3.

Beneventano del Bosco, P. (ed.) (1995) Siracusa urbs magnificentissima. *La collezione Beneventano di Monteclimiti*. Milan.

Bénichou-Safar, H. (1982) *Les tombes puniques de Carthage: topographie, structures, inscriptions et rites funéraires*. Paris.

Benjamin, W. (1969) 'The work of art in the age of mechanical reproduction' in *Illuminations*, trans. H. Zohn, ed. with intro. H. Arendt. New York: 217–52.

Benvenisti M. (2000) *Sacred Landscape: The Buried History of the Holy Land since 1948*. Berkeley.

Berges, D. (1998) 'Los sellos de arcilla del archivo del templo cartagines', in *Cartago fenicio-punica*, ed. M. Vegas. Barcelona: 111–132 (*MDAI(R)* 100 (1993): 245–68).

Bernabei, F. (1895) 'XIII. Trasacco – Di una rarissima "tessera hospitalis" con iscrizione latina', *NSA, anno 1895*: 85–93

Bernal, M. (1987) *Black Athena. The Afroasiatic Roots of Classical Civilization*, vol. I. New Brunswick NJ and London.

Bernal Casasola, D. (2004) 'Ánforas de transporte y contenidos, a propósito de la problemática de algunos envases de los ss. II y I a.C.', in *XVI Encuentros de Historia y Arqueología. "Las industrias alfareras y conserveras fenicio-púnicas de la Bahía de Cádiz"*. Córdoba: 321–78.

Bernard, P. (1967) 'Aï Khanum on the Oxus: a Hellenistic city in Central Asia', *PBA* 53: 71–95.

Bernardini, P. and Zucca, R. (eds.) (2005) *Il Mediterraneo di Herakles. Studi e ricerche*. Rome.

Berrendonner, C. (2002) 'Les cultures épigraphiques de l'Italie républicaine: les territoires de langue étrusque et les territoires de langue osque', *MEFRA* 114(2): 817–60.

(2009) 'L'invention des épitaphes dans la Rome médio-républicaine', in *Écritures, cultures, sociétés dans les nécropoles d'Italie ancienne*, ed. M.-L. Haack. Bordeaux: 181–201.

Berthier, A. (1980) 'Un habitat punique à Constantine', *AntAfr* 16: 57–76.

Berthold, R. (1984) *Rhodes in the Hellenistic Age*. Ithaca, NY.

Bertrandy, F. (1985) 'La communauté gréco-latine de *Cirta* (Constantine), capitale du royaume de Numidie, pendant le IIe siècle et la première moitié du Ier siècle av. J.C.', *Latomus* 44: 488–502.

Bertrandy, F. and Sznycer, M. (1987) *Les stèles puniques de Constantine.* Notes et documents des musées de France 14. Paris.

Bessi, B. (2003) 'Sabratha: la stratigrafia e i materiali delle fasi ellenistiche proto-romane dello scavo intorno al mausoleo B', *QAL* 18: 399–402.

Betancourt, P. (1977) *The Aeolic Style in Architecture: A Survey of its Development in Palestine, the Halikarnassos Peninsula, and Greece, 1000–500 B.C.* Princeton.

Betlyon, J. W. (1982) *The Coinage and Mints of Phoenicia: The Pre-Alexandrine Period.* Chico, CA.

Bhabha, H. (1984) 'Of mimicry and man: the ambivalence of colonial discourse', *October* 28: 125–33.

Bianchi, C. (2000) *I letti funerari in osso dalla necropoli di San Lorenzo.* Milan.

Bichler, R. (1983) *'Hellenismus': Geschichte und Problematik eines Epochenbegriffs.* Darmstadt.

Bickermann, E. J. (1932) 'Rom und Lampsakos', *Philologus* 87: 277–99.

(1952) 'Origines gentium', *CPh* 47: 65–81.

Bilde, P., Engberg-Pedersen, T., Hannestad, L., Zahle, J. and Randsborg, K. (eds.) (1993) *Centre and Periphery in the Hellenistic World.* Studies in Hellenistic Civilization 4. Aarhus.

Billows, R. A. (1995) *Kings and Colonists. Aspects of Macedonian Imperialism.* Leiden.

Bin Wong, R. (2001) 'Entre monde et nation: les régions braudéliennes en Asie', *Annales (HSS)* 56(1): 5–41.

Bing, P. (1988) *The Well-Read Muse.* Göttingen.

Biondi, G. (ed.) (2010) *Centuripe. Indagini archeologiche e prospettive di ricerca.* Monografie dell'Istituto per i Beni Archeologici e Monumentali – C.N.R. 4. Catania.

Bisi, A. M. (1983) 'Le commerce des amphores puniques en Tripolitaine. Quelques remarques à propos des découvertes de Mellita (Sabratha)', *BCTH* n.s. 19: 3–13.

Bisi, A. M. and Di Vita, A. (1969–70) 'Scoperta di due tombe puniche a Mellita (Sabratha)', *LibAnt* 6–7: 189–230.

Bispham, E. H. (2007) 'The Samnites', in *Ancient Italy. Regions without Boundaries*, eds. G. J. Bradley, E. Isayev and C. Riva. Exeter: 179–223.

Blackman, D. (1996) 'Archaeology in Greece 1996–97', *Archaeological Reports* 43: 1–125.

Blake, E. (1998) 'Sardinia's nuraghi: four millennia of becoming', *World Archaeology* 30: 59–71.

(2005) 'The material expression of cult, ritual, and feasting', in *The Archaeology of Mediterranean Prehistory*, eds. E. Blake and A. B. Knapp. Blackwell Studies in Global Archaeology. Malden, MA and Oxford: 102–29.

Blanck, H. (1983) 'Le pitture del 'sarcofago del sacerdote' nel Museo Nazionale di Tarquinia', *DArch*, ser. 3, 1: 79–84.

Blázquez, J. M. and García-Gelabert, M. P. (1994) *Cástulo, ciudad ibero-romana*. Madrid.

Boardman, J. (1988a) 'The trade figures', *OJA* 7(3): 371–3.

(1988b) 'Trade in Greek decorated pottery', *OJA* 7(1): 27–33.

(2006) 'Early Euboean settlements in the Carthage area', *OJA* 25(2): 195–200.

Bode, N. (2001) *Der Krieger von Milet und der Krieger von Mozia. Studien zur frühklassischen Plastik ostionischen Stils*. Diss. PhD, Ruhr-Universität Bochum. Online at www-brs.ub.ruhr-uni-bochum.de/netahtml/HSS/Diss/BodeNina (last accessed 27 April 2012).

Bodel, J. (1997) 'Monumental villas and villa monuments', *JRA* 10: 1–35.

(2001) 'Epigraphy and the Ancient Historian', in *Epigraphic Evidence. Ancient History from Inscriptions*, ed. J. Bodel. London and New York: 1–56.

Bonacasa, N. (1996) 'Sculpture and coroplastics in Sicily in the Hellenistic-Roman age', in *The Western Greeks: Classical Civilization in the Western Mediterranean*, ed. G. Pugliese Carratelli. London: 421–36.

(1999) 'Per una revisione della cultura figurativa ellenistica in Sicilia', in *Origine e culture nell'antichità. Magna Grecia e Sicilia. Stato degli studi e prospettive di ricerca*, eds. M. Barra Bagnasco, E. De Miro and A. Pinzone. Pelorias 4. Messina: 259–73.

(2008) 'Sicilia romana. Una questione di metodo', in *Sicilia. Arte e archeologia dalla preistoria all'Unità d'Italia*. Milan: 57–69.

Bonacasa, N. and Joly, E. (1985) 'L'ellenismo e la tradizione ellenistica', in *Sikanie. Storia e civiltà della Sicilia greca*, ed. G. Pugliese Carratelli. Milan: 277–358.

Bonacasa Carra, R. M. and Guidobaldi, F. (eds.) (1997) *Atti del IV Colloquio dell'associazione italiana per lo studio e la conservazione del mosaico (Palermo, 9–13 dicembre 1996)*. Ravenna.

Bonanno, A. (1992) *Roman Malta. The Archaeological Heritage of the Maltese Islands/Malta romana. Il patrimonio archeologico delle Isole Maltesi*. Rome.

(2005) *Malta. Phoenician, Punic and Roman*. Valletta.

Bond, R. C. and Swales, J. M. (1965) 'Surface finds of coins from the city of Euesperides', *LibAnt* 2: 91–101.

Bondì, S. F. (1990–1). 'L'eparchia punica in Sicilia. L'ordinamento giuridico', *Kokalos* 36–7: 215–31.

(2000) 'Nuove acquisizioni storiche e archeologiche sulla Sicilia fenicia e punica', in *Actas del IV Congreso Internacional de Estudios Fenicios y Púnicos (Cádiz 2–6 Octubre de 1995)* (3 vols.), eds. M. E. Aubet and M. Barthélemy. Cadiz: I, 83–9.

(2001) 'Interferenza fra culture nel Mediterraneo antico: Fenici, Punici, Greci', in *I Greci. Storia, cultura, arte, società. III. I Greci oltre la Grecia*, ed. S. Settis. Turin: 369–400.

(2006) 'Obiettivi e modalità dell'azione militare di Cartagine in Sicilia', in *Guerra e pace in Sicilia e nel Mediterraneo (VIII–III sec. a.C.). Arte, prassi e teoria della pace e della guerra* (2 vols.). Pisa: I, 131–8.

(ed.) (2009a) *Fenici e cartaginesi: una civiltà mediterranea*. Rome.

(2009b) 'Sicilia e Sardegna nel mondo punico: relazioni, funzioni, distinzioni', in Ampolo 2009: I, 457–65.

(forthcoming) 'Phoenicity, Punicities', in Quinn and Vella (forthcoming).

Bonet Rosado, H. (1995) 'Lugares de culto y ritos de influencia púnica en la edataria ibérica (Valencia, Spain)', in *Actes du IIIe congrès international des études phéniciennes et puniques, Tunis, 11–16 novembre 1991* (2 vols.), eds. M. H. Fantar and M. Ghaki. Tunis: I, 175–86.

Bonet Rosado, H. and Mata, C. (2008) 'Las cerámicas ibéricas. Estado de la cuestión', in *Cerámicas hispanorromanas. Un estado de la cuestión*, eds. D. Bernal and A. Ribera. Cádiz: 147–70.

Bonnell, F. (1915 [1916]) 'Monument gréco-punique de la Souma (près Constantine)', *Recueil des notices et mémoires de la Société archéologique du département de Constantine* 49: 167–78.

Bonnet, C. (1988) *Melqart: cultes et mythes de l'Héraclès Tyrien en Méditerranée*. Louvain.

(2005) 'Carthage, l' "autre nation" dans l'historiographie ancienne et moderne', *Anabases* 1: 139–60.

(2006a) 'La religione fenicia e punica in Sicilia', in *Ethne e religione nella Sicilia antica*, eds. P. Anello, G. Martorana and R. Sammartano. Supplementi a "Kókalos" 18. Rome: 205–16.

(2006b) 'Identité et altérité religieuses. A propos de l'hellénisation de Carthage', in *L'hellénisation en Méditerranée occidentale au temps des guerres puniques (260–180 av. J.C.). Actes du Colloque international de Toulouse 31 mars – 2 avril 2005*, ed. H. Guiraud. Pallas 70. Toulouse: 365–79.

Bonnet, C. and Jourdain-Annequin, C. (eds.) (1992) *Héraclès: d'une rive à l'autre de la Méditerranée. Bilan et perspectives*. Brussels.

Bosch Gimpera, P. (1915) *El problema de la cerámica ibérica*. Memorias de la Comisión de Investigaciones Paleontológicas y Prehistóricas 7. Madrid.

Bosworth, A. B. (2003) 'Plus ça change . . . Ancient Historians and their sources', *ClAnt* 22: 167–98.

(2006) 'Alexander the Great and the creation of the Hellenistic Age', in Bugh 2006a: 9–27.

Bouchenaki, M. (1991) *Le mausolée royal de Maurétanie*. Alger.

Bourdin, S. and Crouzet, S. (2009) 'Des Italiens à Carthage? Réflexions à partir de quelques inscriptions puniques de Carthage', in *L'onomastica dell'Italia antica: aspetti linguistici, storici, culturali, tipologici e classificatori*, ed. P. Poccetti. CEFR 413. Rome: 443–94.

Bowersock, G. (2005) 'The East–West orientation of Mediterranean studies and the meaning of north and south in Antiquity', in Harris 2005a: 167–78.

Bradley, R. (2003) 'A life less ordinary: the ritualization of the domestic sphere in later prehistoric Europe', *CArchJ* 13: 5–23.

(2005) *Ritual and Domestic Life in Prehistoric Europe*. London.

Bragantini, I. and Sampaolo, V. (2009) *La pittura pompeiana*. Naples.

Braudel, F. (1972) *The Mediterranean and the Mediterranean World in the Age of Philip II* (2 vols.), transl. S. Reynolds. London.

Braund, D. (1984) *Rome and the Friendly King: The Character of the Client Kingship*. London and New York.

(2002) 'Steppe and sea: the Hellenistic North in the Black Sea region before the first century B.C.', in Ogden 2002a: 199–219.

Bresson, A. (2005) 'Ecology and beyond: the Mediterranean paradigm', in Harris 2005a: 94–114.

Brett, M. and Fentress, E. (1996) *The Berbers*. Oxford.

Briant, P. (1982a) *Rois, tribus et paysans*. Paris.

(1982b) *État et pasteurs au Moyen-Orient ancien*. Paris.

Broise, H. and Lafon, X. (2001) *La villa Prato di Sperlonga*. CEFR 285. Rome: 70–89.

Brown, S. (1991) *Late Carthaginian Child Sacrifice and Sacrificial Monuments in their Mediterranean Context*. Sheffield.

Brumfield, A. (1981) *The Attic Festivals of Demeter and their Relation to the Agricultural Year*. Monographs in Classical Studies. New York.

Bruneau, P. (1970) *Recherches sur les cultes de Délos à l'époque hellénistique et à l'époque impériale*. Paris.

Bugh, G. R. (ed.) (2006a) *The Cambridge Companion to the Hellenistic World*. Cambridge.

(2006b) 'Introduction', in Bugh 2006a: 1–8.

(2006c) 'Hellenistic military developments', in Bugh 2006a: 265–94.

Buraselis, K. (2003) 'Considerations on symmachia and sympoliteia in the Hellenistic period', in *The Idea of European Community in History, II. Aspects of Connecting* Poleis *and* Ethne *in Ancient Greece*, eds. K. Buraselis and K. Zoumboulakis. Athens: 39–50.

Bürge, M. (2001) 'Das *laconicum* – eine Neubretrachtung nach dem Fund aus Monte Iato', in Buzzi *et al.* 2001: 57–66.

Burnett, A. (2002) 'Latin on the coins of the western empire' in *Becoming Roman, Writing Latin? Literacy and Epigraphy in the Roman West*, ed. A. E. Cooley. JRA Suppl. 48. Portsmouth, RI: 33–41.

Burstein, S. M. (1989) *Agatharchides of Cnidus On the Erythraean Sea*. London.

(1993) 'The Hellenistic fringe: the case of Meroë', in P. Green 1993a: 38–54.

Burton, P. J. (2003) '*Clientela* or *Amicitia*? Modeling Roman international behavior in the Middle Republic (264–146 B.C.)', *Klio* 85(2): 333–69.

Butler, J. (1990) *Gender Trouble: Feminism and the Subversion of Identity*. New York.

(2004) *Undoing Gender*. New York.

Buttrey, T. V. (1994) 'Coins and coinage at Euesperides', *LibStud* 25: 137–45.

Buzaian, A. M. and Lloyd, J. A. (1996) 'Early urbanism in Cyrenaica: new evidence from Euesperides (Benghazi)', *LibStud* 27: 129–52.

Buzzi, S., Käch, D., Kistler, E., Mango, E., Palaczyk, M. and Stefani, O. (eds.) (2001) *Zona archeologica. Festschrift für Hans Peter Isler zum 60. Geburtstag.* Bonn.

Caballos Rufino, A. (ed.) (2001) *Carmona Romana. Actas del II Congreso de Historia de Carmona.* Sevilla.

Cabrera Bonet, P. (1986) 'Los griegos en Huelva: Los materiales griegos', in *Homenaje a Luis Siret*, ed. O. Arteaga. Seville: 575–83.

(2004) 'Vasos cerámicos de importación del Mediterráneo oriental y central', in *La vajilla ibérica en época helenística (siglos IV–III al cambio de era)*, eds. R. Olmos and P. Rouillard. Madrid: 5–17.

Cabrera Bonet, P. and Sánchez Fernández, C. (eds.) (2002) *Els Grecs a Ibèria.* Barcelona.

Caccamo Caltabiano, M., Campagna, L. and Pinzone, A. (eds.) (2004) *Nuove prospettive della ricerca sulla Sicilia del III sec. a.C. Archeologia, numismatica, storia.* Pelorias 11. Messina.

Caccamo Caltabiano, M., Carroccio, B. and Oteri, E. (1997) *Siracusa ellenistica. Le monete 'regali' di Ierone II, della sua famiglia e dei Siracusani.* Pelorias 2. Messina.

Cadiou, F. (2003) 'Garnisons et camps permanents: un réseau défensif des territoires provinciaux dans l'Hispanie républicaine', in *Defensa y territorio en Hispania de los Escipiones a Augusto (Espacios urbanos y rurales, municipales y provinciales)*, eds. A. Morillo, F. Cadiou and D. Hourcade. Salamanca: 81–100.

(2008) Hibera in terra miles. *Les armées romaines et la conquête de l'Hispanie sous la république (218–45 av. J.-C.).* Bibliothèque de la Casa de Velázquez 38. Madrid.

Calascibetta, A. M. G. and Di Leonardo, L. (2012) 'Un nuovo documento epigrafico da Solunto', in *Sicilia occidentale. Studi, rassegne, ricerche*, ed. C. Ampolo. Pisa: 37–47.

Camerata Scovazzo, R. (1997) 'I pavimenti ellenistici di Segesta', in Bonacasa Carra and Guidobaldi 1997: 107–22.

Camp, J. M. (1986) *The Athenian Agora. Excavations in the Heart of Classical Athens.* London.

Camp, J. M., Ierardi, M., McInerney, J., Morgan, K. and Umholtz, G. (1992) 'A trophy from the battle of Chaironeia of 86 B.C.', *AJA* 96(3): 443–55.

Campagna, L. (1996) 'Una nuova abitazione a Eraclea Minoa: primi dati', in *Ricerche sulla casa in Magna Grecia e in Sicilia. Atti del Colloquio – Lecce, 23–24 giugno 1992*, eds. F. D'Andria and K. Mannino. Galatina: 111–22.

(1997) 'Note sulla decorazione architettonica della scena del teatro di Segesta', in *Seconde giornate internazionali di studi sull'area elima (Gibellina, 22–26 ottobre 1994). Atti* (3 vols.). Pisa and Gibellina: I, 227–49.

(2003a) 'Il capitello della cosidetta agorà di Siracusa e la cronologia dei più antichi capitelli corinzio-sicelioti', in *Studi classici in onore di Luigi Bernabò Brea*, eds. G. M. Bacci and M. C. Martinelli. Palermo: 149–68.

(2003b) 'Un capitello ionico a quattro facce nel Museo Regionale di Messina', in Fiorentini *et al.* 2003: 167–79.

(2003c) 'La Sicilia di età repubblicana nella storiografia degli ultimi cinquant'anni', *Ostraka* 12(1): 7–31.

(2004) 'Architettura e ideologia della *basileia* a Siracusa nell'età di Ierone II', in Caccamo Caltabiano *et al.* 2004: 151–89.

(2006) 'L'architettura di età ellenistica in Sicilia: per una rilettura del quadro generale', in Osanna and Torelli 2006: 15–34.

(2007) 'L'architettura pubblica ed evergetismo nella Sicilia di età repubblicana', in Micciché *et al.* 2007: 110–34.

(2011a) 'Sistemi decorativi parietali ellenistici in Sicilia: le cornici in stucco', in La Torre and Torelli 2011: 187–225.

(2011b) 'Exploring social and cultural changes in *provincia Sicilia*: reflections on the study of urban landscapes', in Colivicchi 2011: 161–83.

(forthcoming) 'The ancient agora of *Tauromenion* (Taormina, Sicily): new data from recent research', Proceedings of a conference on *The market in the Mediterranean from Homeric until the Roman period*, Kos, 14–17 April 2011.

Campagna, L. and La Torre, G. F. (2008) 'Ricerche sui monumenti e sulla topografia di Tauromenion: una stoà ellenistica nell'area della Naumachia', *Sicilia Antiqua* 5: 115–46.

Campanella, L. (2008) *Il cibo nel mondo fenicio e punico d'Occidente. Un'indagine sulle abitudini alimentari attraverso l'analisi di un deposito urbano di Sulky in Sardegna*. Collezione di Studi Fenici 43. Rome.

Campanella, L. and Garbati, G. (2008) 'Nuovi bruciaprofumi a testa femminile da Sulcis (Sardegna). Aspetti archeologici e storico-religiosi', *Daidalos. Studi e ricerche del dipartimento di scienze del mondo antico* 8: 11–48.

Campanella, L. and Zamora López, J. A. (2010) 'Il maiale presso le comunità fenicie e puniche di Sardegna: leggi, tabù e consuetudini alimentari tra culture a contatto, in 'La Sardegna dai Fenici ai Romani: incontri e relazioni tra culture', ed. C. Tronchetti: 48–57, in *Meetings between Cultures in the Ancient Mediterranean. Proceedings of the 17th International Congress of Classical Archaeology, Rome 22–6 September 2008*, eds. M. Dalla Riva and H. Di Giuseppe. Bollettino di Archeologia on line, I, volume speciale, A/A3/60. Rome. Online at: http://151.12.58.75/archeologia/bao_document/articoli/6_CAMPANELLA_ZAMORA.pdf (last accessed 8 May 2012).

Campo, M. (1976) *Las monedas de Ebusus*. Barcelona.

Camporeale, G. (2004) 'Greci a Veio e nell'agro Falisco-Capenate', in *I Greci in Etruria, Atti dell'XI Convegno Internazionale di Studi sulla Storia e l'Archeologia del'Etruria*, ed. G. M. Della Fina. Annali della fondazione per il museo 'Claudio Faina'. Rome: 42–68.

Camps, G. (1961a) *Aux origines de la Berbérie. Massinissa ou les débuts de l'histoire*. Alger.

(1961b) *Aux origines de la Berbérie. Monuments et rites funéraires protohistoriques*. Paris.

(1973) 'Nouvelles observations sur l'architecture et l'âge du Médracen, mausolée royal de Numidie', *CRAI*: 470–517.

(1978) 'Recherches sur les plus anciennes inscriptions libyques de l'Afrique du nord et du Sahara', *BCTH*, n.s. 10–11, fasc. b (1974–5): 143–66.

(1994) 'Afrique du Nord: les mausolées princiers de Numidie et Maurétanie', *Archéologia* 298: 50–8.

(1995) 'Modèle hellénistique ou modèle punique? Les destinées culturelles de la Numidie', in *Actes du IIIe congrès international des études phéniciennes et puniques, Tunis, 11–16 novembre 1991* (2 vols). Tunis: I, 235–48.

Camps, G., Chaker, S. and Laporte, J.-P. (1996) 'Deux nouvelles stèles au cavalier', *Bulletin Archéologique du comité des travaux historiques et scientifiques. Afrique du Nord*. n.s. B 25: 19–32.

Canfora, L. (1987) *Ellenismo*. Rome and Bari.

Capini, S. (1984) 'La ceramica ellenistica dello scarico A del santuario di Ercole a Campochiaro', *Conoscenze* 1: 9–58.

Carandini, A. (1983) 'Columella's vineyard and the rationality of the Roman economy', *Opus* 2: 177–203.

Carcieri, M. and Montanelli, E. (2008) 'Tracce di lavorazione sugli elementi in osso della tomba 6 di Aquinum', in Sapelli Ragni 2008a: 74–80.

Carradice, I. A. and La Niece, S. (1988) 'The Libyan War and coinage: a new hoard and the evidence of metal analysis', *NC* 148: 33–52.

Carrier, J. G. (1995) *Occidentalism: Images of the West*. Oxford.

Carter, J. C. (1980) 'A Classical landscape: rural archaeology at Metaponto', *Archaeology* 33(1): 23–32.

Cartledge, P. (1997) 'Introduction', in Cartledge *et al.* 1997: 1–19.

Cartledge, P., Garnsey, P. and Gruen, E. (eds.) (1997) *Hellenistic Constructs: Essays in Culture, History, and Historiography*. Hellenistic Culture and Society 26. Berkeley and Oxford.

Caruso, E. (2003) 'Lilibeo-Marsala: le fortificazioni puniche e medievali', in *Quarte giornate internazionali di studi sull'area elima (Erice, 1–4 dicembre 2000). Atti* (3 vols.). Pisa: I, 171–207.

(2005) 'L'insula di Capo Boeo nell'impianto urbanistico di Lilibeo', in Spanò Giammellaro 2005: 777–85.

Castagnino Berlinghieri, E. F. (2010) 'Archimede e Ierone II: dall'idea al progetto della più grande nave del mondo antico, la Syrakosia', in *Hesperìa*, 26. *Studi sulla grecità di Occidente*, eds. L. Braccesi, F. Raviola and G. Sassatelli. Rome: 169–88.

Catalano, P. (1996) 'La comunità di Corvaro (Rieti). Mutamenti delle condizioni di vita quotidiana in epoca arcaica e repubblicana: ipotesi antropologiche', in *Identità e civiltà dei Sabini. Atti del XVIII Convegno di studi etruschi ed italici, Rieti – Magliano Sabina, 30 maggio – 3 giugno 1993*, Istituto Nazionale di

Studi Etruschi ed Italici, eds. G. Maetzke and L. Tamagno Perna. Florence: 431–43.
Cataldi Dini, M. (1988) *Museo Archeologico Nazionale di Tarquinia. I sarcofagi delle famiglie Partunu, Camna e Pulena.* Rome.
Ceccarelli, L. (2010) 'Nuovi dati relativi all'area sacra extraurbana e al deposito votivo del Colle della Bantinella ad Ardea (Roma)', in *Lazio e Sabina* 6, ed. G. Ghini. Rome: 313–20.
Ceccarelli, P. (1996) 'L'Athènes de Periclès: "un pays de cocagne"? L'idéologie démocratique et l'αὐτόματος βίος dans la comedie ancienne', *QUCC* 54: 109–59.
Cerasetti, B. (2000) 'Punic Pantelleria. Preliminary report', *Rivista di Studi Punici* 1: 101–14.
Chabot, J.-B. (1940–1) *Recueil des inscriptions libyques.* Paris.
Chaker, S. (no date) 'L'écriture libyco-berbère. État des lieux et perspectives', online at: www.centrederechercheberbere.fr/lecriture-libyco-berbere.html (accessed 03 August 2011).
Chaker, S. and Hachi, S. (2000) 'À propos de l'origine et de l'âge de l'écriture libyco-berbère. Réflexions du linguiste et du préhistorien', in *Études berbères et chamito-sémitiques. Mélanges offerts à Karl-G. Prasse*, eds. S. Chaker and Z. Zaborski. SELAF 381, Maghreb-Sahara 15. Leuven: 95–111.
Chamoux, F. (2003) *Hellenistic Civilization.* Oxford.
Champion, C. (2004) *Cultural Politics in Polybius's* Histories. Berkeley.
Chapa Brunet, T. (1985) *La escultura ibérica zoomorfa.* Madrid.
Charnoux, P. (1953) 'Inscriptions d'Argos', *BCH* 77: 387–403.
Chartier, R. (2001) 'La conscience de la globalité', *Annales (HSS)* 56(1): 119–23.
Chattopadhyay, S. and Sarkar, B. (2005) 'Introduction: the subaltern and the popular', *Postcolonial Studies* 8: 357–63.
Chaves Tristán, F. (1989) 'La ceca de Urso: nuevos testimonios', in *Estudios sobre Urso. Colonia Iulia Genetiva*, ed. J. González. Sevilla: 113–32.
(1990) 'Los hallazgos numismáticos y el desarrollo de la Segunda Guerra Púnica en el Sur de la Península Ibérica', *Latomus* 49(3): 613–22.
(1998) 'The Iberian and early Roman coinage of Hispania Ulterior Baetica', in Keay 1998: 147–70.
(2001) 'La ceca de Carmo', in Caballos Rufino 2001: 339–68.
Chelbi, F. (1992) *Céramique à vernis noir de Carthage.* Tunis.
Christensen, P. (1993) *The Decline of Iranshahr: Irrigation and Environments in the History of the Middle East, 500 B.C. to A.D. 1500.* Copenhagen.
Ciurcina, C. (2006) *Siracusa in età ellenistica e romana. Museo Archeologico Regionale "Paolo Orsi" Siracusa.* Syracuse.
Clark, A. (2007) *Divine Qualities: Cult and Community in Republican Rome.* Oxford.
Clarke, K. J. (1999) *Between Geography and History: Hellenistic Constructions of the Roman World.* Oxford.
(2008) *Making Time for the Past. Local History and the Polis.* Oxford.

Clarysse, W. (1992) 'Some Greeks in Egypt', in *Life in a Multi-Cultural Society: Egypt from Cambyses to Constantine and Beyond*, ed. J. H. Johnson. Studies in Ancient Oriental Civilization 51. Chicago: 51–6.

Clinton, K. (2005) 'Pigs in Greek rituals', in *Greek Sacrificial Ritual, Olympian and Chthonian: Proceedings of the Sixth International Seminar on Ancient Greek Cult, Göteborg University, 25–7 April 1997*, eds. R. Hägg and B. Alroth. Acta Instituti Atheniensis Regni Sueciae, series 8, 18. Stockholm: 167–79.

Coarelli, F. (1983) 'Le pitture della tomba François a Vulci: una proposta di lettura', *DArch* ser. 3, 1(2): 43–69.

(1988). *Il foro Boario dalle origini alla fine della Repubblica*. Rome.

(1996a) 'La cultura artistica a Roma in età repubblicana. IV–II sec. a.C.', in *Revixit Ars. Arte e ideologia a Roma. Dai modelli ellenistici alla tradizione repubblicana*, ed. F. Coarelli. Rome: 15–84.

(1996b) 'Due rilievi fittili da Fregellae: un documento storico della prima guerra siriaca?', in *Revixit ars: arte e ideologia a Roma, dai modelli ellenistici alla tradizione repubblicana*, ed. F. Coarelli. Rome: 239–57.

Coarelli, F. and Pesando, F. (eds.) (2005) *Rileggere Pompei I. L'insula 10 della Regio VI*. Studi della Soprintendenza archeologica di Pompei 12. Rome.

Coarelli, F. and Thébert, Y. (1988) 'Architecture funéraire et pouvoir: réflections sur l'hellénisme en Numidie', *MEFRA* 100: 761–818.

Cobet, J. (1996) 'Europa und Asien – Griechen und Barbaren – Osten und Westen', *Geschichte in Wissenschaften und Unterricht* 47: 405–19.

Cohen, G. M. (1983) 'Colonization and population transfer in the Hellenistic world', in *Egypt and the Hellenistic world*, ed. E. Van't Dack. Leuven: 63–74.

(1995) *The Hellenistic Settlements in Europe, the Islands, and Asia Minor*. Berkeley and London.

(2006) *The Hellenistic Settlements in Syria, the Red Sea Basin, and North Africa*. Berkeley.

Cole, S. (1988) 'The uses of water in Greek sanctuaries', in *Early Greek Cult Practice: Proceedings of the Fifth International Symposium at the Swedish Institute in Athens, 26–29 June, 1986*, eds. R. Hägg, N. Marinatos and G. Nordquist. Acta Instituti Atheniensis Regni Sueciae, series 4, 38. Stockholm: 161–5.

(1994) 'Demeter in the ancient Greek city and its countryside', in *Placing the Gods. Sanctuaries and Sacred Space in Ancient Greece*, eds. S. Alcock and R. Osborne. Oxford: 199–216.

(2004) *Landscape, Gender and Ritual Space. The Ancient Greek Experience*. Berkeley.

Colivicchi, F. (2008) 'Hellenism and Romanization at Ancona: a case of invented tradition', *JRA* 21: 31–46.

(ed.) (2011) *Local Cultures of South Italy and Sicily in the Late Republican Period: Between Hellenism and Rome*. JRA Suppl. 83. Portsmouth, RI.

Colledge, M. (1987) 'Greek and non-Greek interaction in the art and architecture of the Hellenistic Age', in Kuhrt and Sherwin-White 1987: 134–62.

Colonna, G. (1977) 'Un aspetto oscuro del Lazio antico: le tombe del VI–V sec. a.C.', *PP* 32: 131–65.

(1999) 'Epigrafi etrusche e latine a confronto', in *XI Congresso Internazionale di Epigrafia Greca e Latina*. Rome: 435–50.

(2004) 'I Greci di Caere', in *I Greci in Etruria, Atti dell'XI Convegno Internazionale di Studi sulla Storia e l'Archeologia del'Etruria*, ed. G. M. Della Fina. Annali della fondazione per il museo 'Claudio Faina'. Rome: 69–94.

Coltelloni-Trannoy, M. (1997) *Le Royaume de Maurétanie sous Juba II et Ptolémée (25 av. J.-C.–40 ap. J.-C.)*. Paris.

Colvin, S. (2011) 'The Koine. A new language for a new world', in *Creating a Hellenistic World*, eds. A. Erskine and L. Llewellyn Jones. Swansea: 31–45.

Cook, J. M. (1959) 'Bath-tubs in ancient Greece', *G&R* 6: 31–41.

Cool, H. E. M. (2006) *Eating and Drinking in Roman Britain*. Cambridge.

Cooley, A. and Cooley, M. (2004) *Pompeii: A Sourcebook*. London and New York.

Copersino, M. R. (2003) 'Le indagine archeologiche. Letti funerari in osso: analasi e confronti', in D'Ercole and Copersino 2003: 307–19.

(2004) 'Le strutture architettoniche delle tombe a camera della necropoli di Fossa', in D'Ercole and Benelli 2004: 247–50.

Copersino, M. R. and D'Ercole, V. (2003) 'La necropoli di Fossa nel quadro dei costumi funerari di età ellenistica in Abruzzo', in D'Ercole and Copersino 2003: 333–78.

Cornell, T. J. (1989) 'The conquest of Italy', in *The Cambridge Ancient History, Second Edition, Volume VII, part 2. The Rise of Rome to 220 B.C.*, eds. F. W. Walbank, A. E. Astin, M. W. Frederiksen, R. M. Ogilvie and A. Drummond. Cambridge: 351–419.

(1995) *The Beginnings of Rome. Italy and Rome from the Bronze Age to the Punic Wars (c. 1000 – 264 B.C.)*. London and New York.

Correa Morales, I. (2000) 'Note sull'architettura templare del IV e III sec. a.C. in Sicilia', *NAC* 29: 191–234.

Corsten, T. (1992) 'Der Hilferuf des Akarnanischen Bundes an Rom: zum Beginn des römischen Eingreifens in Griechenland', *ZPE* 94: 195–210.

Corzo, R. (2000) 'El santuario de La Algaida (Sanlúcar de Barrameda, Cádiz) y la formación de sus talleres artesanales', in *Santuarios fenicio-púnicos en Iberia y su influencia en los cultos indígenas (XIV Jornadas de arqueología fenicio-púnica, Ibiza 1999)*, eds. B. Costa Ribas and J. H. Fernández Gómez. Treballs del Museu Arqueològic d'Eivissa i Formentera 46. Ibiza: 147–84.

Cosentino, S., D'Ercole, V. and Mieli, G. (2001) *La necropoli di Fossa I. Le testimonianze più antiche*. Pescara.

Cosentino, S. and Mieli, G. (2003) 'Il sito archeologico', in D'Ercole and Copersino 2003: 11–24.

Costa Ribas, B. (2007) *Es Culleram. 100 anys/años*. Ibiza.

Costa Ribas, B. and Fernández Gómez, J. H. (2000) 'El establecimiento de los fenicios en Ibiza. Algunas cuestiones actualmente en debate', in *Actas del IV*

Congreso Internacional de Estudios Fenicios y Púnicos, Cádiz, 2–6 octubre 1995 (3 vols.), eds. M. E. Aubet and M. Barthélemy. Cádiz: I, 91–101.

Costa Ribas, B., Fernández Gómez, J. H. and Gómez Bellard, C. (1991) 'Ibiza fenicia: La primera fase de la colonización de la Isla', in *Atti del II Congresso Internazionale di Studi Fenici e Punici. Roma, 9–14 novembre 1987* (3 vols.). Rome: II, 759–95.

Cotton, H. M. and Price, J. (2007) 'Corpus inscriptionum Iudaeae/Palestinae: a multilingual corpus of inscriptions', in *XII Congressus Internationalis Epigraphiae Graecae et Latinae. Provinciae imperii romani inscriptionibus descriptae. Barcelona, 3–8 Septembris 2002. Acta* (2 vols.), eds. M. Mayer i Olivé, G. Baratta, A. Guzmán Almagro. Monografies de la Secció Històrico-Arqueològica 10. Barcelona: I, 327–32.

Coulton, J. J. (1976) *The Architectural Development of the Greek Stoa*. Oxford.

Crawford, M. H. (1985) *Coinage and Money under the Roman Republic*. London.

(2006) 'The Oscan inscriptions of Messina', in *Guerra e pace in Sicilia e nel Mediterraneo (VIII–III sec. a.C.). Arte, prassi e teoria della pace e della guerra* (2 vols.). Pisa: II, 521–5.

(2011) *Imagines Italicae: A Corpus of Italic Inscriptions* (3 vols.). BICS Suppl. 110. London.

Crema, F. (2007) 'Dalla collezione Nani al Museo archeologico di Venezia: un chalkoma corcirese di prossenia', in *Studi in ricordo di Fulviomario Brolio*, eds. G. Cresci Marrone and A. Pistellato. Padova: 237–63.

Cristofani, M. (1989) 'Ripensando Pyrgi', in *Miscellanea Ceretana* I. Quaderni del Centro di Studio per l'Archeologia Etrusco-Italica. Rome: 85–94.

Crone, P. (1989) *Pre-Industrial Societies*. Oxford.

Crouzet, S. (2004) 'Les sarcophages du prêtre de Tarquinia et Carthage, témoignage des relations entre Carthage et l'Étrurie au IVe siècle', *AIACNews* 39–40: 15.

Culasso Gastaldi, E. (2000) 'L'iscrizione trilingue del Museo di Antichità di Torino (dedicante greco, ambito punico, età romana)', *Epigraphica* 62: 11–28.

Cultrera, G. (1938) 'Siracusa. Rovine di un'antico stabilimento idraulico in contrada Zappalà', *NSA* ser. 6, 14: 261–301.

(1940) 'Siracusa. Gli antichi ruderi di Via del Littorio', *NSA* ser. 7, 1: 199–224.

Cunliffe, B. W. (2001) *Facing the Ocean: the Atlantic and its Peoples, 8000 BC–AD 1500*. Oxford.

Cunliffe, B. W. and Fernández Castro, M. C. (1999) *The Guadajoz Project. Andalucía in the First Millennium BC. Volume 1. Torreparedones and its Hinterland*. OUCA Monograph No. 47. Oxford.

Curbera, J. B. (1997) 'The persons cursed on a *defixio* from Lilybaeum', *Mnemosyne*, ser. 4, 50: 219–25.

(1999) 'Defixiones', in *Sicilia Epigraphica. Atti del convegno di studi, Erice, 15–18 ottobre 1998* (2 vols.), ed. M. I. Gulletta. ASNP ser. 4, quad. 1–2. Pisa: I, 159–86.

Curti, E., Dench, E. and Patterson, J. R. (1996) 'The archaeology of central and southern Roman Italy: recent trends and approaches', *JRS* 86: 170–89.

Curtin, P. (1984) *Cross-Cultural Trade in World History*. Cambridge.
Curty, O. (1995) *Les parentés légendaires entre cités grecques*. Geneva.
Cutroni Tusa, A. (1995) 'Ršmlqrt è Selinunte?', *AIIN* 42: 235–9.
(2000) 'La monetazione punica in Sicilia', *AIIN* 47: 249–65.
Cutroni Tusa, A., Italia, A., Lima, D. and Tusa, V. (1994) *Solunto*. Itinerari XV. Rome.
Daehn, H. (1991) *Studia Ietina III. Die Gebäude an der Westseite der Agora von Iaitas*. Zürich.
D'Agostino, B. and Cerchiai, L. (2004) 'I Greci nell'Etruria Campana', in *I Greci in Etruria, Atti dell'XI Convegno Internazionale di Studi sulla Storia e l'Archeologia del'Etruria*, ed. G. M. Della Fina. Annali della fondazione per il museo 'Claudio Faina'. Rome: 278–83.
Dalcher, K. (1994) *Studia Ietina VI. Das Peristylhaus 1 von Iaitas: Architektur und Baugeschichte*. Zürich.
D'Andria, F. (1997) 'Ricerche archeologiche sul teatro di Segesta', in *Seconde giornate internazionali di studi sull'area elima (Gibellina, 22–26 ottobre 1994). Atti* (3 vols.). Pisa and Gibellina: I, 429–50.
(2005) 'Il teatro greco in Sicilia', in Minà 2005: 184–5.
D'Andria, F. and Campagna, L. (2002) 'L'area dei templi A ed O nell'abitato punico di Selinunte', in *Da Pyrgi a Mozia, studi sull'archeologia del Mediterraneo in memoria di Antonia Ciasca*, eds. M. G. Amadasi Guzzo, M. Liverani and P. Matthiae. Rome: 171–88.
Daniels, R. (1995) 'Punic influence in the domestic architecture of Roman Volubilis', *OJA* 14: 79–95.
Dany, O. (1999) *Akarnanien im Hellenismus: Geschichte und Volkerrecht in Nordwestgriechenland*. Munich.
D'Arms, J. (2003) 'The first coastal villas. The second century B.C.', in *Romans on the Bay of Naples and Other Essays on Roman Campania*, ed. F. Zevi with a preface by A. Tchernia. Bari: 15–29.
Daszewski, W. A. (1985) *Corpus of Mosaics from Egypt*, I. Mainz.
Daux, G. (1949) 'Listes delphiques de théarodoques', *REG* 62: 23–7.
Davies, J. K. (1984) 'Cultural, social and economic features of the Hellenistic world', in Walbank *et al.* 1984: 257–320.
(2002) 'The interpenetration of Hellenistic sovereignties', in Ogden 2002a: 1–21.
(2006) 'Hellenistic economies', in Bugh 2006a: 73–92.
De Franciscis, A. (1972) *Stato e società in Locri Epizefiri: L'archivio dell'Olympieion locrese*. Naples.
De Frutos Reyes, G. and Muñoz Vicente, A. (2004) 'La incidencia antrópica del poblamiento fenicio-púnico desde Cádiz a Sancti Petri', in *Gadir-Gades. Nueva perspectiva interdisciplinar*, eds. G. Chic García, G. De Frutos Reyes, A. Muñoz Vicente and A. Padilla Monge. Seville: 9–69.
De Hoz, J. (1995) 'Escrituras en contacto: ibérica y latina', in F. Beltrán Lloris 1995a: 57–84.
(1998a) 'La escritura ibérica', in Aranegui 1998: 191–203.

(1998b) 'Koiné sin Alejandro: griego y lenguas anhelénicas en el Mediterráneo occidental durante la época helenística', in *La koiné grecque antique. 3. Les contacts*, ed. C. Brixhe. Nancy: 119–36.

(1999) 'Los metales inscritos en el mundo griego y periférico y los documentos celtibéricos en bronce', in *Pueblos, lenguas y escrituras en la Hispania prerromana. Actas del VII Coloquio sobre lenguas y culturas paleohispánicas, Zaragoza 1997*, eds. F. Villar and F. Beltrán Lloris. Salamanca: 433–70.

(2006) 'La recepcíon de la epigrafia helenística en el extremo Occidente', in *L'hellénisation en Méditerranée Occidentale au temps des guerres puniques (260–180 av. J. C.). Actes du Colloque international de Toulouse 31 mars – 2 avril 2005*, ed. H. Guiraud. Pallas 70. Toulouse: 347–64.

De Hoz, M. P. (1997) 'Epigrafía Griega en Hispania', *Epigraphica* 59: 29–96.

(1998) 'Errata corrige a *Epigrafía Griega en Hispania*', *Epigraphica* 60: 295–6.

De Miro, E. (1980) 'La casa greca in Sicilia. Testimonianze nella Sicilia centrale dal VI al III sec. a.C.', in Φιλίας χάριν. *Miscellanea di studi classici in onore di Eugenio Manni* (6 vols.). Rome: II, 709–37.

(1988) 'Architettura civile in Agrigento ellenistico-romana e rapporti con l'Anatolia', *Quaderni dell'Istituto di Archeologia della Facoltà di Lettere e Filosofia della Università di Messina* 3: 63–72.

(1996a) 'Aspetti dell'urbanistica e dell'architettura civile in Agrigento', in *Sicilia e Anatolia dalla preistoria all'età ellenistica*, ed. G. Rizza. *CASA* 26–7 (1987–1988). Catania: 159–65.

(1996b) 'La casa greca in Sicilia', in *Ricerche sulla casa in Magna Grecia e in Sicilia*, eds. F. D'Andria and K. Mannino. Galatina: 17–40.

(2003) *Agrigento II. I santuari extraurbani. L'Asklepieion*. Soveria Mannelli.

(2009) *Agrigento IV. L'abitato antico. Il quartiere ellenistico-romano* (2 vols.). Rome.

De Rossi, G. (1979) *Bovillae*. Forma Italiae 26. Florence.

De Sensi Sestito, G. (1977) *Gerone II*. Palermo.

De Simone, C. and Marchesini, S. (2002) *Monumenta linguae messapicae* (2 vols.). Wiesbaden.

Decourt, J.-C. (2004) *Inscriptions Grecques de la France (IGF)*. Travaux de la Maison de l'Orient et de la Méditerranée 38. Lyon.

Delattre, A. L. (1898–9) *Carthage. La nécropole punique voisine de Sainte-Monique*. Paris.

(1890) *Musée Lavigerie de Saint-Louis de Carthage* I. Paris.

Delbrück, R. (1907–12) *Hellenistische Bauten in Latium*. Strasburg.

Delcor, M. (1976) 'Une inscription punique inédite trouvée à Carthage et conservée dans la region de Toulouse', in *Religion d'Israël et Proche Orient ancien: des Phéniciens aux Esséniens*. Leiden: 31–40.

Dench, E. (1995) *From Barbarians to New Men: Greek, Roman, and Modern Perceptions of Peoples from the Central Apennines*. Oxford.

(2003) 'Beyond Greeks and Barbarians: Italy and Sicily in the Hellenistic Age', in Erskine 2003a: 294–310.

(2005) *Romulus' Asylum. Roman Identities from the Age of Alexander to the Age of Hadrian*. Oxford.
D'Ercole, V. (1998) 'La protostoria nella piana dell'Aquila alla luce delle ultime scoperte', in *Archeologia in Abruzzo, storia di un metanodotto tra industria e cultura*, eds. V. D'Ercole and R. Cairoli. Montalto di Castro: 13–22.
D'Ercole, V. and Benelli, E. (2004) *La necropoli di Fossa II. I corredi orientalizzanti e arcaici*. Pescara.
D'Ercole, V. and Copersino, M. R. (eds.) (2003) *La necropoli di Fossa* IV. *L'età ellenistico-romana*. Documenti dell'Abruzzo Antico. Pescara.
D'Ercole, V. and Martellone, A. (2004) 'Commerci con Cartagine', in Lapenna 2004: 214–19.
(2005) *Il sonno degli avi. I letti funerari in osso di Collelongo e di Fossa*. L'Aquila.
(2007) *Regine d'Abruzzo. La ricchezza nelle sepolture del I millennio a.C.* L'Aquila.
(2008) 'Letti funerari in osso dall'Abruzzo alla luce delle ultime acquisizioni. Simboli delle aristocrazie italiche', in Sapelli Ragni 2008a: 59–68.
Derow, P. S. (2003) 'The arrival of Rome', in Erskine 2003a: 51–70.
Derrida, J. (1981) *Dissemination*, transl. B. Johnson. Chicago.
(1982) *Margins of Philosophy*, transl. A. Bass. Chicago.
(1988) *Limited Inc*. Evanston, Illinois.
Detienne, M. (1989) 'The violence of well-born ladies', in *The Cuisine of Sacrifice among the Greeks*, eds. M. Detienne and J. P. Vernant. Chicago: 129–47.
Deussen, P. W. (1994) 'The granaries of Morgantina and the *Lex Hieronica*', in *Le ravitaillement en blé de Rome et des centres urbains des débuts de la République jusqu'au haut empire*. Naples and Rome: 231–5.
Di Stefano, C. A. (ed.) (1984) *Lilibeo. Testimonianze archeologiche dal IV sec. a.C. al V sec. d.C.* Marsala and Palermo.
(1993) *Lilibeo Punica*. Marsala.
(1997) 'Nuove ricerche nell'edificio B di Piazza della Vittoria a Palermo e intervento di restauro del Mosaico della Caccia', in Bonacasa Carra and Guidobaldi 1997: 7–18.
Di Stefano, G. (2006) 'Aspetti urbanistici e topografici per la storia di Camarina', in *Camarina. 2600 anni dopo la fondazione. Nuovi studi sulla città e sul territorio. Atti del Convegno Internazionale, Ragusa, 7 dicembre 2002/7–9 aprile 2003*, eds. P. Pelagatti, G. Di Stefano and L. de Lachenal. Ragusa and Rome: 157–76.
Di Vita, A. (1976) 'Il mausoleo punico-ellenistico "B" di Sabratha', *MDAI(R)* 83: 273–85.
Díaz Ariño, B. (2008) *Epigrafía latina republicana de Hispania*. Collecció Instrumenta 26. Barcelona.
Die Numider (1979) = Horn, G. and Rüger, C. B. (eds.) (1979). *Die Numider: Reiter und Könige nördlich der Sahara. Rheinische Landesmuseum Bonn, Ausstellung 29.11.1979–29.2.1980*. Bonn and Cologne.
Dietler, M. (1998) 'Consumption, agency and cultural entanglement: theoretical implications of a Mediterranean colonial encounter', in *Studies in Culture*

Contact: Interaction, Culture Change and Archaeology, ed. J. H. Cosick. Carbondale: 288–315.

(2005) 'The archaeology of colonization and the colonization of archaeology: theoretical reflections on an ancient Mediterranean colonial encounter', in *The Archaeology of Colonial Encounters. Comparative Perspectives*, ed. G. Stein. School of American Research Advanced Seminars Series. Santa Fe and Oxford: 33–68.

(2010) *Archaeologies of Colonization*. Berkeley.

Dietz, S. (ed.) (2000) *Africa Proconsularis: Regional Studies in the Segermes Valley of Northern Tunisia*, vol. II. Copenhagen.

Dietz, S., Sebai, L. L. and Ben Hassen, H. (eds.) (1995) *Africa Proconsularis: Regional Studies in the Segermes Valley of Northern Tunisia*, vol. I. Copenhagen.

Dijkstra, K. (1990) 'State and steppe. The social and political implications of Hatra Inscription 79', *Journal of Semitic Studies* 35: 81–98.

Dillon, M. (1997) *Pilgrims and Pilgrimage in Ancient Greece*. London.

Dimartino, A. (2009) 'Ierone II, Filistide II e il teatro greco di Taormina. Una nota sul margine del *IG* XIV, 437', in Ampolo 2009: 721–6.

Domínguez Monedero, A. J. (1983) 'Los terminus "Iberia" y "Iberos" en las fuentes greco-latinas: estudios acerca de su origen y ámbito de aplicación', *Lucentum* 2: 203–24.

(2004) 'Greek identity in the Phocaean colonies', in *Greek Identity in the Western Mediterranean*, ed. K. Lomas. Leiden: 429–56.

(2006a) 'Greeks in Sicily', in *Greek Colonisation: An Account of Greek Colonies and Other Settlements Overseas*, vol. I., ed. G. R. Tsetskhladze. Leiden: 253–357.

(2006b) '¿Cartago en Iberia? Algunas observaciones sobre el papel de la Cartago pre-Bárquida en la Península Ibérica', *Boletín de la Asociación Española de Amigos de la Arqueología* 44 (2005–6): 181–99.

Domínguez Monedero, A. J. and Sanchez, C. (2001) *Greek Pottery from the Iberian Peninsula. Archaic and Classical Periods*. Leiden.

Dopico, D. (1989) 'El hospitium celtibérico un mito que se desvanece', *Latomus* 48: 19–35.

Dore, J. and Keay, N. (1989) *Excavations at Sabratha 1948–1951. II. The Finds, Part 1: The Amphorae, Coarse Pottery and Building Materials*, eds. M. Fulford and M. Hall. London.

Doublet, G. (1890) *Musée d'Alger*. Mus. et coll. arch. de l'Algérie et de la Tunisie. Paris.

Dougherty, C. and Kurke, L. (eds.) (2003a) *The Cultures within Ancient Greek Culture. Contact, Conflict, Collaboration*. Cambridge.

(2003b) 'Introduction. The cultures within Greek culture', in Dougherty and Kurke 2003a: 1–19.

Droysen, J. G. (1833) *Die Geschichte Alexanders des Grossen*. Gotha.

(1836) *Die Geschichte der Diadochen*. Gotha.

(1843) *Die Geschichte der Epigonen*. Gotha.

(1877–8) *Geschichte des Hellenismus* (3 vols.), 2nd edn. Gotha.

Dubouloz, J. and Pittia, S. (eds.) (2007) *La Sicile de Cicéron. Lectures des* Verrines. Besançon.

Dunbabin, K. M. D. (1979) 'Technique and materials of Hellenistic mosaics', *AJA* 83: 265–77.

(1994) 'Early pavement types and the invention of tessellation', in *Fifth International Colloquium on Ancient Mosaics, held at Bath, England on September 5–12, 1987*, eds. P. Johnson, R. Ling and D. J. Smith. JRA Suppl. 9. Ann Arbor, MI: 26–40.

(1999) *Mosaics of the Greek and Roman World.* Cambridge.

Dunbabin, T. J. (1948) *The Western Greeks: The History of Sicily and South Italy from the Foundation of the Greek Colonies to 480 B.C.* Oxford.

Duncan-Jones, R. P. (1982) *The Economy of the Roman Empire. Quantitative Studies*, 2nd edn. Cambridge.

Dyson, S. and Rowland, R. (2007) *Archaeology and History in Sardinia from the Stone Age to the Middle Ages. Shepherds, Sailors, and Conquerors.* Philadelphia.

East, W. G. (1938) 'The Mediterranean problem', *Geographical Review* 28: 83–101.

Eckstein, A. M. (1980) '*Unicum subsidium populi Romani*: Hiero II and Rome, 263–215 B.C.', *Chiron* 10: 183–203.

(1987) *Senate and General. Individual Decision-Making and Roman Foreign Relations, 264–194 B.C.* Berkeley, Los Angeles and London.

(1989) 'Hannibal at New Carthage: Polybius 3.15 and the power of irrationality', *CPh* 84: 1–15.

(1995) *Moral Vision in the Histories of Polybius.* Berkeley.

(2006) *Mediterranean Anarchy, Interstate War, and the Rise of Rome.* Berkeley, Los Angeles, London.

(2008) *Rome Enters the Greek East: From Anarchy to Hierarchy in the Hellenistic Mediterranean, 230–170 B.C.* Malden, MA and Oxford.

(2010) 'Polybius, "The treaty of Philinus", and Roman accusations against Carthage', *CQ* 60(2): 402–26.

Edmondson, J. (2002) 'Writing Latin in the Roman province of Lusitania', in *Becoming Roman, Writing Latin? Literacy and Epigraphy in the Roman West*, ed. A. E. Cooley. JRA suppl. 48. Portsmouth, RI: 41–60.

Edson, C. (1934) 'The Antigonids, Heracles, and Beroea', *HSPh* 45: 213–35.

Edwards, G. R. (1975) *Corinth VII.3. Corinthian Hellenistic Pottery.* Princeton, NJ.

Eilers, C. (ed.) (2009) *Diplomats and Diplomacy in the Roman World.* Mnemosyne Supplement 304. Leiden.

Eiring, J. and Lund, J. (eds.) (2004) *Transport Amphorae and Trade in the Eastern Mediterranean. Acts of the International Colloquium at the Danish Institute at Athens, 26–9 September 2002.* Athens.

Elayi J. and Elayi, A. G. (2004) *Le monnayage de la cité phénicienne de Sidon à l'époque perse (Ve-IVe s. av. J.-C.).* Transeuphratène Supplément 11. Paris.

Eldem, E., Goffman, D. and Masters, B. (1999) *The Ottoman City between East and West: Aleppo, Izmir, and Istanbul.* Cambridge.

Elia, O. (1934) 'Relazione sulla scavo dell'Insula X della Regio I (1)', *NSA, anno* 1934 (XII): 264–344.
(1955) 'La tradizione della morte di Cleopatra nella pittura pompeiana', *RAAN* 30: 153–7.
Errington, R. M. (1989) 'Rome and Greece to 205 BC', in *The Cambridge Ancient History. Second Edition. Volume VIII. Rome and the Mediterranean to 133 B.C.*, eds. A. E. Astin, F. W. Walbank, M. W. Frederiksen and R. M. Ogilvie. Cambridge: 81–106.
(2008) *A History of the Hellenistic World, 323–30 BC*. Oxford.
Erskine, A. (1996) 'Money-loving Romans', *Papers of the Leeds International Latin Seminar* 9: 1–11.
(2000) 'Polybios and barbarian Rome', *MediterrAnt* 3: 165–82.
(2001) *Troy between Greece and Rome. Local Tradition and Imperial Power*. Oxford.
(2002) 'O brother, where art thou? Tales of kinship and diplomacy', in Ogden 2002a: 97–115.
(ed.) (2003a) *A Companion to the Hellenistic World*. Blackwell Companions to the Ancient World. Malden, MA and Oxford.
(2003b) 'Approaching the Hellenistic world', in Erskine 2003a: 1–15.
(2005) 'Unity and identity: shaping the past in the Greek Mediterranean', in *Cultural Borrowings and Ethnic Appropriations in Antiquity*, ed. E. Gruen. Stuttgart: 121–36.
(2013) 'The view from the Old World: contemporary perspectives on Hellenistic culture', in *Shifting Social Imaginaries in the Hellenistic Period: Transforming Processes of Narrations, Practices and Images*, ed. E. Stavrianopoulou. Leiden: 339–63.
Escacena, J.-L. and Belén Deamos, M. (1998) 'Pre-Roman Turdetania', in Keay 1998: 23–37.
Famà, M. L. (1997) 'Il mosaico a ciotoli di Mozia dopo il restauro', in Bonacasa Carra and Guidobaldi 1997: 147–58.
Fantar, M. (1974) 'Stèles inédites de Carthage', *Semitica* 24: 13–24.
(1978) 'Présence punique au Cap Bon (Tunisie)', *Africa* 5–6: 54–70.
(1985) *Kerkouane. Cité punique du Cap Bon (Tunisie)*, II. Tunis.
(2002) 'Carthage et les Grecs', in *Da Pyrgi a Mozia, studi sull'archeologia del Mediterraneo in memoria di Antonia Ciasca*, eds. M. G. Amadasi Guzzo, M. Liverani, P. Matthiae. Rome: 227–31.
(2004) 'La présence Grecque dans le paysage funéraire de Carthage', *Reppal* 13: 113–19.
Farnsworth, M. (1964) 'Greek pottery: a minerological study', *AJA* 68: 221–8.
Faustoferri, A. (1997) 'L'area sacra di Fonte San Nicola: i votivi', in *I luoghi degli dei. Sacro e natura nell'Abruzzo italico*, eds. A. Campanelli and A. Faustoferri. Pescara: 99–116.
Fedak, J. (1990) *Monumental Tombs of the Hellenistic Age: A Study of Selected Tombs from the Pre-Classical to the Early Imperial Era*. Toronto.

(2006) 'Tombs and commemorative monuments', in Winter 2006: 71–95.

Feeney, D. (2007) *Caesar's Calendar: Ancient Time and the Beginnings of History*. Berkeley.

Feldherr, A. (1998) *Spectacle and Society in Livy's History*. Berkeley.

Fentress, E. (1979) *Numidia and the Roman Army: Social, Military and Economic Aspects of the Frontier Zone*. Oxford.

(1998) 'The House of the Sicilian Greeks' in *The Roman Villa. Villa Urbana*, ed. A. Frazer. Philadelphia: 29–42.

(2001) 'Villas, wine and kilns: the landscape of late Hellenistic Jerba', *JRA* 14: 249–68.

(2003a) *Cosa V: An Intermittent Town, Excavations 1991–1997*. Ann Arbor.

(2003b) 'Stately homes: recent work on Roman villas in Italy', *JRA* 16: 545–56.

(2006) 'Romanizing the Berbers', *P&P* 190(1): 3–33.

(2007) 'Where were North African Nundinae held?', in *Communities and Connections: Essays in Honour of Barry Cunliffe*, eds. C. Gosden, H. Hamerow, P. de Jersey and G. Lock. Oxford: 125–41.

Fentress, E. and Docter, R. F. (2008) 'North Africa: rural settlement and agricultural production', in van Dommelen and Gómez Bellard 2008: 101–28.

Fentress, E. and Fentress, J. (2001) 'The hole in the doughnut', *P&P* 173: 203–19.

Ferchiou, N. (1989) *L'évolution du décor architectonique en Afrique proconsulaire des derniers temps du Carthage aux Antonins*. Gap.

(1991) 'Le Kbor Klib (Tunisie)', *QAL* 14: 45–97.

(2008) 'Les trois tombeaux monumentaux puniques de l'Henchir Djaouf (région de Zagouan): le dessin du comte Borgia et les nouvelles données archéologiques', *CRAI*: 357–89.

(2009a) 'A Hellenistic cistern head', in *An Island Through Time: Jerba Studies. Volume I. The Punic and Roman Periods*, eds. E. Fentress, A. Drine and R. Holod. JRA Suppl. 71. Portsmouth, RI: 333–4.

(2009b) 'Recherches sur le mausolée hellénistique d'Hinshir Burgu', in *An Island Through Time: Jerba Studies. Vol I. The Punic and Roman Periods*, eds. E. Fentress, A. Drine and R. Holod. JRA Suppl. 71 Portsmouth, RI: 107–28.

Fernández, J. H., Mezquida, A. and Ramon, J. (2007) 'Pebeteros con representación leontocéfala de la calle Aragón, 33 (Eivissa)', in *Imagen y culto en la Iberia prerromana: los pebeteros en forma de cabeza femenin*, eds. M. C. Marín Ceballos and F. Horn. Spal Monografías 9. Seville: 85–107.

Ferrary, J.-L. (1988) *Philhellénisme et impérialisme. Aspects idéologiques de la conquête romaine du monde hellénistique*. BEFAR 271. Rome.

(2011) 'La géographie de l'hellénisme sous la domination romaine', *Phoenix* 65: 1–22.

Ferron, J. (1969–70) 'L'inscription du mausolée de Dougga', *Africa* 3–4: 83–98.

Ferruti, F. (2004) 'L'attività di Ierone II a favore dei ginnasi', in Caccamo Caltabiano *et al.* 2004: 191–212.

Février, J. G. (1957) 'La borne de Micipsa', *Cahiers de Byrsa* 7: 119–21.

(1959) 'L'inscription du Mausolée dit d'Atban (Dougga)', *Karthago* 10: 51–7.
Février, P. A. (1989) *Approches du Maghreb romain: pouvoirs, différences et conflits* (2 vols.). Aix-en-Provence.
Finley, M. I. (2000) 'Documents', in *Ancient History: Evidence and Models*. London: 27–46 (originally published in French in *Annales (ESC)* 37 (1982), 697–713).
Fiorentini, G. (1995) *Monte Adranone*. Itinerari 16. Rome.
(1998) *Monte Adranone: mostra archeologica*. Palermo, Agrigento and Sambuca di Sicilia.
(2002) 'L'età dionigiana a Gela e Agrigento', in *La Sicilia dei due Dionisi*, eds. N. Bonacasa, L. Braccesi, E. De Miro. Rome: 147–67.
(2009) 'Il ginnasio di Agrigento', *Sicilia Antiqua* 6: 71–109.
Fiorentini, G., Caccamo Caltabiano, M. and Calderone, A. (eds.) (2003) *Archeologia del Mediterraneo. Studi in onore di Ernesto De Miro*. Rome.
Fischer-Hansen, T. (ed.) (1995) *Ancient Sicily*. Acta Hyperborea 6. Copenhagen.
Flower, H. I. (ed.) (2004) *The Cambridge Companion to the Roman Republic*. Cambridge.
Fogelin, L. (2007) 'The archaeology of religious ritual', *Annual Review of Anthropology* 36: 55–71.
Fontana, S. (2009) 'Anfore in età punica', in *An Island Through Time: Jerba Studies. Vol I. The Punic and Roman Periods*, eds. E. Fentress, A. Drine and R. Holod. JRA Suppl. 71. Portsmouth, RI: 271–8.
Fonzo, O. and Vigne, J. D. (1993) 'Reperti osteologici', in *Genna Maria II,1: il deposito votivo del mastio e del cortile*. Cagliari: 163–73.
Fowden, E. K. (1999) *The Barbarian Plain: Saint Sergius between Rome and Iran*. Berkeley.
Fowden, G. (1993) *Empire to Commonwealth: Consequences of Monotheism in Late Antiquity*. Princeton.
(2002) 'Elefantiasi del tardoantico', *JRA* 15: 681–6.
Foxhall, L. (2007) *Olive Cultivation in Ancient Greece. Seeking the Ancient Economy*. Oxford.
Fraschetti, A. (1981a) 'Aristosseno, i Romani e la "barbarizzazione" di Poseidonia', *AION(archeol)* 3: 97–115.
(1981b) 'Per una prosopografia dello sfruttamento in Sicilia', in *Società romana e produzione schiavistica* (3 vols.), eds. A. Giardina and A. Schiavone. Bari: I, 51–77.
Fraser, P. M. (1951) 'An inscription from Euesperides', *Bulletin de la Société royale d'archéologie d'Alexandrie* 39: 132–43.
(1972) *Ptolemaic Alexandria* (2 vols.). Oxford.
(1977) *Rhodian Funerary Monuments*. Oxford.
(1996) *Cities of Alexander the Great*. Oxford.
Frey-Kupper, S. (2006) 'Aspects de la production et de la circulation monétaires en Sicile (300–180 av. J.-C.): continuités et ruptures', in *L'hellénisation en Méditerranée occidentale au temps des guerres puniques (260–180 av. J. C.).*

Actes du colloque international de Toulouse 31 mars – 2 avril 2005, ed. H. Guiraud. Pallas 70. Toulouse: 27–56.

Friedman, J. (1990) 'Notes on culture and identity in imperial worlds', in *Religion and Religious Practice in the Seleucid Kingdom*, eds. P. Bilde, T. Engberg-Pedersen, L. Hannestad and J. Zahle. Studies in Hellenistic Civilization 1. Aarhus: 14–39.

(1992) 'The past in the future: history and the politics of identity', *American Anthropologist* 94: 837–59.

(1995) 'Global system, globalization and the parameters of modernization', in *Global Modernities*, eds. M. Featherstone, L. Lash and R. Robertson. Theory, Culture and Society 36. London: 69–90.

Fuentes Estañol, M. J. (1986) *Corpus de las inscripciones fenicias, punicas y neopúnicas de España*. Barcelona.

Fulford, M. G. (1989) 'To East and West: the Mediterranean trade of Cyrenaica and Tripolitania in antiquity', *LibStud* 20: 169–91.

Fullerton, M. (1987) 'Archaistic statuary of the Hellenistic period', *MDAI(A)* 102: 259–78.

(1990) *The Archaistic Style in Roman Statuary*. Mnemosyne Suppl. 110. Leiden.

Gaebler, H. (1906) *Die antiken Münzen nord-Griechenlands. Band III. Makedonia und Paionia*. Berlin.

Gaggiotti, M. (1987) 'Pavimenta punica marmore numidico constrata', in *L'Africa romana 5. Atti del V convegno di studio, Sassari, 11–13 dicembre 1987*, ed. A. Mastino. Sassari: 215–21.

Gailledrat, E. and Solier, Y. (2004) *L'établissement côtier de Pech Maho (Sigean, Aude) aux VIe-Ve s. av. J.-C. (fouilles 1959–1979): Pech Maho I*. Lattes.

Gallini, C. (1973) 'Che cosa intendere per ellenizzazione. Problemi di metodo', *DArch* 7: 175–91.

Gallo, L. (1992) 'La Sicilia occidentale e l'approvvigionamento cerealicolo di Roma', *ASNP*, ser. 3, 22: 365–98.

Galvao-Sobrinho, C. R. (1995) 'Funerary epigraphy and the spread of Christianity in the West', *Athenaeum* 83: 431–62.

Garbati, G. (2003) 'Sul culto di Demetra nella Sardegna punica', in *Mutuare, interpretare, tradurre: storie di culture a confronto. Atti del 2° Incontro 'Orientalisti' (Roma, 11–13 dicembre 2002)*, ed. G. Regalzi. Rome: 127–43.

(2008) *Religione votiva. Per una interpretazione storico-religiosa delle terrecotte votive nella Sardegna punica e tardo-punica*. Pisa and Rome.

García Prosper, E. and Guérin, P. (2002) 'Nuevas aportaciones en torno a la necrópolis romana de la Calle Quart', in *Espacios y usos funerarios en el Occidente Romano* (2 vols.), ed. D. Vaquerizo Gil. Córdoba: I, 203–16.

García y Bellido, A. (1948) *Hispania Graeca* (2 vols.). Barcelona.

(1963) 'Hercules Gaditanus', *AEA* 36: 324–35.

Garcia-Bellido, Ma. P. (1978) 'La esfinge en las monedas de Cástulo', *Zephyrus* 27–29: 343–57.

(1987) 'Leyendas y imágenes púnicas en las monedas libio-fenices', in *Studia Paleohispanica. Actas del IV Coloquio sobre lenguas y culturas paleohispánicas = Veleia* 2–3: 512–6.

Garcia-Ventura, A. and López-Bertran, M. (2009) 'Music and sounds in Punic Ibiza (Balearic Islands, Spain)', in *SOMA 2007. Proceedings of the XI Symposium on Mediterranean Archaeology, Istanbul Technical University, 24 and 29 April 2007*, ed. Ç. Özkan Aygün. Oxford: 12–17.

Garland, R. (1982) 'A first catalogue of Attic peribolos tombs' *ABSA* 77: 125–76.

Gauthier, P. (1972) *Symbola. Les étrangers et la justice dans les cités grecques*. Nancy.

Gehrke, H-J. (2000) 'Myth, history, and collective identity: uses of the past in ancient Greece and beyond', in *The Historian's Craft in the Age of Herodotus*, ed. N. Luraghi. Oxford: 286–313.

Gell, W. (1832) *Pompeiana: The Topography, Edifices and Ornaments of Pompeii, the Result of Excavations since 1819*. London.

Gellner, E. (1983) *Nations and Nationalism. New Perspectives on the Past*. Oxford.

Geus, K. (2003) 'Space and geography', in Erskine 2003a: 231–45.

Ghaki, M. (1997) 'Epigraphique libyque et punique à Dougga', in *Dougga (Thugga): études épigraphiques*, eds. M. Khanoussi and L. Maurin. Paris: 27–43.

Ghedini, E. F. (2008) 'I letti in avorio e osso: tipologia e apparato decorativo', in Sapelli Ragni 2008a: 14–25.

Gibbon, E. (1896 [1782]) *The History of the Decline and Fall of the Roman Empire*, ed. J. B. Bury. London.

Gibson, S. (2004) *Aristoxenus of Tarentum and the Birth of Musicology*. London.

Gill, D. W. J. (1988) '"Trade in Greek decorated pottery": some corrections', *OJA* 7(3): 369–70.

(1991) 'Pots and trade: spacefillers or *objets d'art*', *JHS* 111: 29–47.

Ginouvès, R (1962) *Balaneutikè. Recherches sur le bain dans l'antiquité grecque*. BEFAR 200. Rome.

Giorgetti, S. (1982) 'Area cultuale annessa al tempio a pozzo nuragico', in V. Santoni (ed.) '1982, Cabras-Cuccuru s'Arriu. Nota preliminare di scavo (1978, 1979, 1980)', *RStudFen* 10: 103–27 (= *Tharros* VIII): 113–15.

Giovannini, A. (1993) 'Greek cities and Greek commonwealth', in *Images and Ideologies: Self-definition in the Hellenistic World*, eds. A. W. Bulloch, E. S. Gruen, A. A. Long and A. Stewart. Berkeley: 265–86.

Gisborne, M. (2005) 'A *curia* of kings. Sulla and royal imagery', in *Imaginary Kings: Royal Images in the Ancient Near East, Greece and Rome*, eds. R. Fowler and O. Hekster. Oriens et Occidens 11. Stuttgart: 105–23.

Giuffrida Ientile, M. (1983) *La pirateria tirrenica: momenti e fortuna*. Rome.

Golden, P. B. (1998) *Nomads and Sedentary Societies in Medieval Eurasia*. Washington DC.

Gómez Bellard, C. (1993) 'Die Phönizier auf Ibiza', *MDAI(M)* 34: 83–107.

(1996) 'Quelques réflexions sur les prémiers établissements phéniciens à Ibiza', in *Alle soglie della classicità. Il Mediterraneo tra tradizione e innovazione.*

Studi in onore di Sabatino Moscati (3 vols.), ed. E. Acquaro. Pisa and Rome: II, 763–79.

(2002) 'Ebusus', in *Valencia y las primeras ciudades romanas de Hispania*, eds. J. L. Jiménez Salvador and A. Ribera i Lacomba. Grandes temas arqueológicos 3. Valencia: 103–12.

(2008a) 'Espacios sagrados en la Ibiza púnica', in *Saturnia Tellus. Definizioni dello spazio consacrato in ambiente etrusco, italico, fenicio-punico, iberico e celtico (Convegno di studio, Roma 2004)*, eds. X. Dupré Raventós, S. Ribichini and S. Verger. Monografie Scientifiche. Rome: 119–32.

(2008b) 'Ibiza: the making of new landscapes', in van Dommelen and Gómez Bellard 2008: 44–76.

Gómez Bellard, C., Díes Cusí, E. and Marí i Costa, V. (2011) *Tres paisajes Ibicencos: un estudio arqueológico*. Saguntum Extra 10. Valencia.

Gómez Bellard, C., Marí i Costa, V. and Puig Moragón, R. (2005) 'Evolución del poblamiento rural en el NE de Ibiza en época púnica y romana (prospecciones sistemáticas 2001–2003)', *Saguntum* 37: 27–43.

Gómez Bellard, C. and Vidal González, P. (2000) 'Las cuevas-santuario fenicio-púnicas y la navegación en el Mediterráneo', in *Santuarios fenicio-púnicos en Iberia y su influencia en los cultos indígenas (XIV Jornadas de arqueología fenicio-púnica, Ibiza 1999)*, eds. B. Costa Ribas and J. H. Fernández Gómez. Treballs del Museu Arqueològic d'Eivissa i Formentera 46. Ibiza: 103–45.

Gómez Espelosín, F. J., Pérez Lagarcha, A. and Vallejo Girves, M. (1995) *La imagen de España en la Antigüedad Clásica*. Madrid.

Goodchild, R. G. (1952) 'Euesperides – a devastated city site', *Antiquity* 26(104): 208–12.

Göransson, K. (2004) 'Transport amphorae from Euesperides (Benghazi), Libya. A presentation of preliminary results', in Eiring and Lund 2004: 137–42.

(2007) *The Transport Amphorae from Euesperides. The Maritime Trade of a Cyrenaican City 400–250 BC*. Lund.

Gorman, R. V. (2007) 'The *tryphe* of the Sybarites: A historiographical problem in Athenaeus', *JHS* 127: 38–60.

Goux, J.-J. (1990) *Symbolic Economies: After Marx and Freud*, transl. J. Curtiss Gage. Ithaca, NY. (Contains selections from *Freud, Marx: Economie et symbolique* [1973] and *Les iconoclasts* [1978].)

Graf, D. F. (1989) 'Rome and the Saracens: reassessing the nomadic menace', in *L'Arabie préislamique et son environnement historique et culturel: actes du Colloque de Strasbourg, 24–27 juin 1987*, ed. T. Fahd. Leiden: 341–54.

Grandi Carletti, M. (2001) 'Opus signinum e cocciopesto: alcune osservazioni terminologiche', in *Atti dell VII Colloquio dell'AISCOM*. Ravenna: 183–97.

Grandjouan, C., Markson, E. and Rotroff, S. (1989) *Hellenistic Relief Molds from the Athenian Agora*. *Hesperia* Suppl. 23. Princeton.

Gras, M. (1985) *Trafics tyrrheniens archaiques*. Rome.

(2000) 'La Sicile, l'Afrique et les emporia', in *Damarato. Studi di antichità classiche offerte a Paola Pelagatti*. Rome: 130–4.

Greco, A. (2003) 'Zagros pastoralism and Assyrian imperial expansion: a methodological approach', in *Continuity of Empire: Assyria, Media, Persia*, eds. G. B. Lanfranchi, M. Roaf, R. Rollinger. Padua: 65–78.

Greco, C. (1997) 'Pavimenti in *opus signinum* e tessellati geometrici da Solunto: una messa a punto', in Bonacasa Carra and Guidobaldi 1997: 39–62.

(2005) *Solunto. Brief Guide.* Palermo.

Green, M. (2002) 'Gramsci cannot speak: presentations and interpretations of Gramsci's concept of the subaltern', *Rethinking Marxism* 14: 1–24.

Green, P. (1990) *Alexander to Actium: The Hellenistic Age.* London.

(ed.) (1993a) *Hellenistic History and Culture.* Hellenistic Culture and Society 9. Berkeley.

(1993b) 'Introduction: new approaches to the Hellenistic world', in P. Green 1993a: 1–11.

Greene, J. and Kehoe, D. (1995) 'Mago the Carthaginian', in *Actes du III congrès international des études phéniciennes et puniques* (2 vols.). Tunis: II, 110–17.

Grimal, P., with Bengston, H., Caskel, W., Derchain, P., Meuleau, M. and Smith, M. (1968) *Hellenism and the Rise of Rome*, transl. A. M. Sheridan Smith and C. Wartenburg. London.

Gringeri Pantano, F. (ed.) (2003) *Jean Hoüel: voyage a Siracusa.* Palermo.

Gros, P. (1996) *L'Architecture romaine. I. Les monuments publics.* Paris.

Gruen, E. S. (1984) *The Hellenistic World and the Coming of Rome* (2 vols.). Berkeley.

(1990) *Studies in Greek Culture and Roman Policy.* Leiden.

(1992) *Culture and National Identity in Republican Rome.* Ithaca, NY and London.

(1993) 'Hellenism and persecution: Antiochus IV and the Jews', in P. Green 1993a: 238–64.

(2011) *Rethinking the Other in Antiquity.* Princeton.

Grünhagen, W. (1976–7) 'Notas sobre el relieve de Minerva de la muralla de Tarragona', *Boletín Arqueológico de Tarragona*, ep. IV, fasc. 133–40: 75–94.

Gsell, St. (1914–28) *Histoire ancienne de l'Afrique du Nord* (8 vols.). Paris.

Guarducci, M. (1967–78). *Epigrafia greca* (4 vols.). Rome.

Guerrero Ayuso, V. M., Calvo Trias, M. and Salvà Simonet, B. (2007) 'Insularity and the indigenous world on the periphery of the system: the Balearic Islands (Majorca and Minorca) between the 6th and 1st centuries BC', in van Dommelen and Terrenato 2007: 71–83.

Guido, F. (1993) 'Monete', in *Genna Maria II,1: il deposito votivo del mastio e del cortile.* Cagliari: 123–44.

Guidobaldi, F. (1995) 'Per la strutturazione di una nuova terminologia convenzionale per la individuazione tipologica dei pavimenti antichi', in *Bollettino AISCOM* 2: 2–3.

Guidobaldi, M. P. (1995) *La romanizzazione dell'ager Praetuttianus (secoli III-I a.C.).* Perugia.

(1996) 'Articolazione cronologica della necropoli di Campovalano: la terza fase (IV-II secolo a.C.) – Piceno VI', in *Le valli della Vibrata e del Salinello.* Documenti dell'Abruzzo Teramano IV. Pescara: 194–212.

Guimier-Sorbets, A.-M. (2001) 'Les ateliers de mosaïques à Alexandrie à l'époque hellénistique et au début de l'époque impériale : continuité et innovation', in *La mosaïque gréco-romaine VIII. Actes du VIIIe colloque international pour l'étude de la mosaïque antique et médiévale, Lausanne, 6–11 octobre 1997* (2 vols.), eds. D. Paunier and C. Schmidt. Cahiers d'archéologie romande de la Bibliothèque historique vaudoise 85–6. Lausanne: I, 282–97.

Guzzardi, L. (2004) 'Montagna di Marzo. Nuovi dati sulla storia e sulla topografia del sito', *Kokalos* 45 (1999): 535–51.

Guzzo, P. G. (2003) 'A group of Hellenistic silver objects in the Metropolitan Museum', *MMJ* 38: 45–94.

(2007) *Pompei. Storia e paesaggi della città antica.* Milan.

Guzzo, P. G. and Guidobaldi, M. P. (eds.) (2005) *Nuove ricerche archeologiche a Pompei ed Ercolano.* Naples.

(eds.) (2008) *Nuove ricerche nell'area vesuviana (scavi 2003–2006).* Rome.

Habicht, C. (1976) *Jüdische Schriften aus hellenistich-römischer Zeit I: Historische und legendarische Erzählungen, 2. Makkabäerbuch.* Gütersloh.

Hafner, G. (1989) 'Zu den vermeintlich sullanischen Waffenreliefs von S. Omobono', *RdA* 13: 46–54.

Hales, S. (2002) 'How the *Venus de Milo* lost her arms', in Ogden 2002a: 253–73.

Haley, S. (1989) 'Livy, passion, and cultural stereotypes', *Historia* 39: 375–81.

Hall, E. (1993) 'Asia unmanned: images of victory in classical Athens', in *War and Society in the Greek World*, eds. J. Rich and G. Shipley. London: 108–33.

Hall, J. (2002) *Hellenicity. Between Ethnicity and Culture.* Chicago.

(2003) '"Culture" or "cultures"? Hellenism in the late sixth century', in Dougherty and Kurke 2003a: 23–34.

Hallo, W. W. (1964) 'The road to Emar', *JCS* 18: 57–88.

Hannestad, L. (1983) *The Hellenistic Pottery from Falaika.* Aarhus.

Hans, L.-M. (1983) *Karthago und Sizilien.* Hildesheim.

Harris, W. V. (1989) *Ancient Literacy.* Harvard.

(ed.) (2005a) *Rethinking the Mediterranean.* Oxford.

(2005b) 'The Mediterranean and ancient history', in Harris 2005a: 1–42.

Hatzopoulos, M. (1991) 'Une prêtre d'Amphipolis dans la grande liste de théarodoques', *BCH* 115: 345–7.

Häussler, R. (2002) 'Writing Latin – from resistance to assimilation: language, culture and society in N. Italy and S. Gaul', in *Becoming Roman, Writing Latin? Literacy and Epigraphy in the Roman West*, ed. A. E. Cooley. JRA Suppl. 48. Portsmouth, RI: 61–76.

Hay, D. and Law, J. (1989) *Italy in the Age of the Renaissance, 1380–1530.* Longman History of Italy. Harlow.

Hayes, P. P. and Mattingly, D. J. (1995) 'Preliminary report on fieldwork at Euesperides (Benghazi) in October 1994', *LibStud* 26: 83–96.

Haynes, S. (2000) *Etruscan Civilization. A Cultural History*. London.

Head, B. (1887) *Historia Numorum*. Oxford. Online in annotated form at www.snible.org/coins/hn and downloadable from www.archive.org/details/historianumorumm00headrich (last accessed 25 April 2012).

Hentsch, T. (1988) *L'Orient imaginaire. La vision politique occidentale de l'Est méditerranéen*. Paris.

Herbig, R. (1952) *Die jungeretruskishen Steinsarkophage*. Berlin.

Herman, G. (1987) *Ritualised Friendship and the Greek City*. Cambridge.

Hermanns, M. H. (2004) *Licht und Lampen im westgriechischen Alltag. Beleuchtungsgerät des 6.-3. Jhs. v.Chr. in Selinunt*. Internationale Archäologie 87. Rahden.

Herring, E. (2007) 'Identity crises in SE Italy in the 4th c. B.C.: Greek and native perceptions of the threat to their cultural identities', in *Roman by Integration: Dimensions of Group Identity in Material Culture and Text*, eds. R. Roth and J. Keller. JRA Suppl. 66. Portsmouth, RI: 11–25.

Herzog, R. and Klaffenbach, G. (1952) *Asylieurkunden aus Kos*. Berlin.

Higgins, R. A. (1967) *Greek Terracottas*. London.

Hinard, F. (2008) *Sullana varia: aux sources de la première guerre civile romaine*. Paris.

Hinz, V. (1998) *Der Kult von Demeter und Kore auf Sizilien und in der Magna Grecia*. Palilia 4. Wiesbaden.

Hodos, T. (2006) *Local Responses to Colonisation in the Iron Age Mediterranean*. London.

Holleaux, M. (1921) *Rome, la Grèce et les monarchies hellénistiques au IIIe siècle avant J.-C. (273–205)*. BEFAR 124. Paris.

Hollegaard Olsen, C., Rathje, A., Trier, C. and Winther, H. C. (1995) 'The Roman *domus* of the early Empire. A case study: Sicily', in Fischer-Hansen 1995: 209–61.

Holliday, P. (1997) 'Roman triumphal painting: its function, development, and reception', *ABull* 79(1): 130–47.

(2002) *The Origins of Roman Historical Commemoration in the Visual Arts*. Cambridge.

Holloway, R. R. (1978) *Art and Coinage in Magna Graecia*. Bellinzona.

(1991) *The Archaeology of Ancient Sicily*. London.

Hölscher, T. (1980) 'Römische Siegesdenkmäler der späten Republik', in *Tainia: Roland Hampe zum 70. Geburtstag am 2. Dezember 1978*, eds. H. Cahn and E. Simon. Mainz am Rhein: 351–71.

Holt, F. (1993) 'Response' to Burstein 1993, in P. Green 1993a: 54–64.

Horden, P. and Purcell, N. (2000) *The Corrupting Sea. A Study of Mediterranean History*. Malden, MA and Oxford.

(2005) 'Four years of corruption', in Harris 2005a: 348–75.

(2006) 'The Mediterranean and "the New Thalassology"', *AHR* 111(3): 722–40.

Houby-Nielsen, S. (1997) 'Grave gifts, women and conventional values in Hellenistic Athens', in *Conventional Values of the Hellenistic Greeks*, eds. P. Bilde, T. Engberg-Pedersen, L. Hannestad and J. Zahle. Studies in Hellenistic Civilisation 8. Aarhus: 220–62.

Howe, T. (2008) *Pastoral Politics: Animals, Agriculture and Society in Ancient Greece*. Claremont.

Howgego, C., Heuchert, V. and Burnett, A. (eds.) (2005) *Coinage and Identity in the Roman Provinces*. Oxford.

Hübner, G. (1993) *Die Applikenkeramik von Pergamon: eine Bildersprache im Dienst des Herrscherkultes. Pergamenische Forschungen* VII. New York.

Humbert, M. (1978) Municipium et civitas sine suffragio. *L'Organisation de la conquête jusqu'à la guerre sociale*. CEFR 36. Rome.

Iannello, A. (1994) 'I bouleuteria in Sicilia. Fonti e monumenti', *Quaderni dell'Istituto di Archeologia della Facoltà di Lettere e Filosofia della Università di Messina* 9: 63–99.

Isaac, B. 2004. *The Invention of Racism in Classical Antiquity*. Princeton.

Isler, H. P. (1996) 'Einflüsse der Makedonischen Palastarchitektur in Sizilien?', in *Basileia. Die Paläste der hellenistischen Könige. Internationales Symposion in Berlin vom 16.12.1992 bis 20.12.1992*, eds. W. Hoepfner and G. Brands. Mainz am Rhein: 252–7.

(1997) 'Monte Iato. Mosaici e pavimenti', in Bonacasa Carra and Guidobaldi 1997: 19–32.

(2000a) *Monte Iato. Guida archeologica*, 2nd edn. Palermo.

(2000b) 'Il teatro greco di Iaitas', *Sicilia Archeologica* 33(98): 201–20.

(2001) 'Monte Iato: Neues zur hellenistischen Wohnarchitektur', in *Recherches récentes sur le monde hellénistique. Actes du colloque international organisé à l'occasion du 60ᵉ anniversaire de Pierre Ducrey (Lausanne, 20–21 novembre 1998)*, eds. R. Frei-Stolba and K. Gex. Bern: 259–68.

(2003) '*Bouleuteria* di Sicilia', in Fiorentini *et al.* 2003: 429–33.

(2005) 'L'architettura domestica in Sicilia nel IV–III sec. a.C.', in Minà 2005: 153–5.

(2011) 'La data di costruzione dell'agorà e di altri monumenti architettonici di Iaitas: un contributo alla cronologia dell'architettura ellenistica della Sicilia Occidentale', *MEFRA* 123: 107–44.

Isler, H. P. and Käch, D. (eds.) (1997) *Wohnbauforschung in Zentral- und Westsizilien/Sicilia occidentale e centro-meridionale: ricerche archeologiche nell'abitato. Akten–Atti*. Zürich.

Isler Kerenyi, C. (1976) 'Die Stützfiguren der griechischen Theaters von Iaitas', in *Studia Ietina I*, eds. H. Bloesch and H. P. Isler. Zürich: 13–48.

Izquierdo Peraile, M. I. and Arasa, F. (1999) 'La imagen de la memoria. Antecedentes, tipología e iconografía de las estelas de época ibérica', *APL* 23: 259–300.

Jacob, P. (1989) 'Textes concernant Sagonte', in *Homenatge A. Chabret, 1888–1988*. Valencia: 13–28.

Jaeger, M. (1997) *Livy's Written Rome*. Ann Arbor.

Jaeggi, O. (1999) *Der Hellenismus auf der iberischen Halbinsel. Studien zur iberischen Kunst und Kultur: Das Beispiel eines Rezeptionsvorgangs*. Mainz.

Jeffery, L. H. (1990) *The Local Scripts of Archaic Greece*, revised edn with supplement by A. W. Johnston. Oxford.

Jenkins, G. K. (1971) 'Coins of Punic Sicily, Part 1', *SNR* 50: 25–78, Pl. 1–22.

(1978) 'Coins of Punic Sicily, Part 4', *SNR* 57: 5–68, Pl. 1–24.

Jenkins, G. K. and Lewis, R. B. (1963) *Carthaginian Gold and Electrum Coins*. London.

Jenkins, I. (2006) *Greek Architecture and its Sculpture*. London.

Jiménez Martín, A. (1989) *La puerta de Sevilla en Carmona*. Seville.

Jiménez Díez, A. (2008a) 'A critical approach to the concept of resistance: new "traditional" rituals and objects in funerary contexts of Roman Baetica', in *TRAC 2007. Proceedings of the Seventeenth Annual Theoretical Roman Archaeology Conference, London 2007*, eds. C. Fenwick, M. Wiggins and D. Wythe. Oxford: 15–30.

(2008b) *Imagines Hibridae. Una aproximación postcolonialista al estudio de las necrópolis de la Bética*. Anejos de AEA 43. Madrid.

Joly, E. (1997) 'Il signino in Sicilia: una revisione', in Bonacasa Carra and Guidobaldi 1997: 33–8.

Jones, C. P. (1999) *Kinship Diplomacy in the Ancient World*. Cambridge, MA.

Jones, G. D. B. (1983) 'Excavations at Tocra and Euhesperides, Cyrenaica 1968–1969', *LibStud* 14: 109–21.

(1985) 'Beginnings and endings in Cyrenaican cities', in *Cyrenaica in Antiquity*, eds. G. W. W. Barker, J. A. Lloyd and J. M. Reynolds. Oxford: 27–41.

Jongeling, K. (2008) *Handbook of Neo-Punic Inscriptions*. Tübingen.

Jonnes, L. and Ricl, M. (1998) 'A new royal inscription from Phrygia Paroreios: Eumenes II grants Tyriaion the status of a *polis*', *EA* 29: 1–30.

Kaiser Augustus 1988 = Hofter, M. R. (ed.) (1988) *Kaiser Augustus und die verlorene Republik: eine Ausstellung im Martin-Gropius-Bau, Berlin, 7. Juni-14. August 1988*. Mainz am Rhein.

Kallala, N., Sanmartí, J., Carme Belarte, M., Ramon, J. *et al.* (2008) 'Recherches sur l'occupation d'Althiburos (région du Kef, Tunisie) et de ses environs à l'époque numide', *Pyrenae. Revista de prehistorìa de la Mediterrania occidental* 39(1): 67–113. Available online at www.ub.edu/gracpe/documentsonline/Kallala_et_alii.pdf (last accessed 25 April 2012).

Karlsson, L. (1996) 'The altar of Hieron at Syracuse', *ORom* 21: 83–7.

Kbiri Alaoui, M. (2007) *Revisando Kuass (Asilah, Marruecos)*. Saguntum extra 7. Valencia.

Keaveney, A. (2005) *Sulla, the Last Republican*, 2nd edn. London.

Keay, S. (1997) 'Early Roman Italica and the romanization of western Baetica', in *Italica MMCC*, eds. A. Caballos Rufino and P. León Alonso. Seville: 21–47.

(ed.) (1998) *The Archaeology of Early Roman Baetica*. JRA Suppl. 29. Portsmouth, RI.

(2001) 'Rome and the Hispaniae', in Keay and Terrenato 2001: 117–44.
(2007) 'Discussion' in Abad Casal *et al.* 2007: 223–37.

Keay, S. and Terrenato, N. (eds.) (2001) *Italy and the West. Comparative Issues in Romanization*. Oxford.

Keay, S., Wheatley, D. and Poppy, S. (2001) 'The territory of Carmona during the Turdetanian and Roman periods: some preliminary notes about visibility and urban location', in Caballos Rufino 2001: 381–96.

Kerr, R. (2010) 'Some thoughts on the origins of the Libyco-Berber alphabet', in *Études berbères V. Essais sur des variations dialectales et autres articles*, eds. H. Stroomer, M. Kossmann, D. Ibriszimow and R. Vossen. Cologne: 41–68.

Keyser, P. T. (1995–6) 'Greco-Roman alchemy and coins of imitation silver', *AJN* 7–8: 209–34.

Kim, H. S. (2002) 'Small change and the moneyed economy', in *Money, Labour and Land. Approaches to the Economies of Ancient Greece*, eds. P. Cartledge, E. E. Cohen and L. Foxhall. London and New York: 44–51.

King, M. (2003) *The Penguin History of New Zealand*. Auckland and London.

Kleiner, D. (1992) *Roman Sculpture*. New Haven, CT.

Kleiner, F. S. (2007) *A History of Roman Art*. Boston, MA.

Knapp, A. B. (2008) *Prehistoric and Protohistoric Cyprus. Identity, Insularity, and Connectivity*. Oxford.

Knippschild, S. (2002) *«Drum bietet zum Bunde die Hände»: Rechtssymbolische Akte in zwischenstaatlichen Beziehungen im orientalischen und griechisch-römischen Altertum*. Potsdamer Altertumswissenschaftliche Beiträge 5. Stuttgart.
(2004) 'Im Namen des Königs: Identifikationsmarken zur Autorisierung königlicher Befehle im Perserreich', *Klio* 86: 293–304.

Knoepfler, D. (1993) 'Le temple du Métrôon de Sardes et ses inscriptions', *MH* 50: 26–43.

Koortbojian, M. (2002) 'A painted *exemplum* at Rome's temple of Liberty', *JRS* 92: 33–48.

Korhonen, K. (2011) 'Language and identity in the Roman colonies of Sicily', in *Roman Colonies in the First Century of their Foundation*, ed. R. J. Sweetman. Oxford: 7–31.

Kosmetatou, E. and Waelkens, M. (1997) 'The "Macedonian" shields of Sagalassos', in *Sagalassos* IV. Leuven: 277–91.

Kottaridi, A. (2011) 'Appendix: the palace of Philip II at Aegae', in *Heracles to Alexander the Great. Treasures from the Royal Capital of Macedon, a Hellenic Kingdom in the Age of Democracy*, eds. A. Kottaridi and S. Walker. Oxford and Athens: 233–6.

Kourou, N. (2002) 'Phéniciens, Chypriotes, Eubéens et la fondation de Carthage', *CCEC* 32: 89–114.

Krandel-Ben Younès, A. (2002) *La présence punique en pays numide*. Tunis.

Kreeb, M. (1988) *Untersuchungen zur figürlichen Ausstattung delischer Privathäuser*. Chicago.

Krevans, N. and Sens, A. (2006) 'Language and literature', in Bugh 2006a: 186–207.
Krings, V. (ed.) (1995) *La civilisation phénicienne et punique. Manuel de recherche.* Leiden.
Kuhrt, A. and Sherwin-White, S. (1987) *Hellenism in the East.* London.
Kurtz, D. C. and Boardman, J. (1971) *Greek Burial Customs.* Aspects of Greek and Roman Life. London.
Kuttner, A. (1993) 'Some new grounds for narrative: Marcus Antonius' base (the Altar of Domitius Ahenobarbus) and Republican biographies', in *Narrative and Event in Ancient Art*, ed. P. Holliday. Cambridge: 198–229.
(1995) *Dynasty and Empire in the Age of Augustus: The Case of the Boscoreale Cups.* Berkeley.
(1997) 'Republican Rome looks at Pergamon', *HSPh* 97: 157–78.
(2001) '"Do you look like you belong here?" Asianism at Pergamon and the Makedonian diaspora', in *Cultural Borrowings and Ethnic Appropriations in Antiquity*, ed. E. Gruen. *Oriens et Occidens* 8. Stuttgart: 137–87.
(2003) 'Delight and danger in the Roman water garden: Sperlonga and Tivoli', in *Landscape Design and the Experience of Motion*, ed. M. Conan. Dumbarton Oaks Colloquium on the History of Landscape Architecture 24. Washington DC: 103–56. Available online at www.doaks.org/resources/publications/doaks-online-publications/garden-and-landscape-studies/motion/04motion.pdf (last accessed 30 May 2012).
(2005) 'Cabinet fit for a queen: the Lithika as Posidippus' Gem Museum', in *The New Posidippus: A Hellenistic Poetry Book*, ed. K. Gutzwiller. New York: 141–63.
Kyriakidis, E. (ed.) (2007) *The Archaeology of Ritual.* Cotsen Advanced Seminars 3. Los Angeles.
La Regina, A. (1968) 'Ricerche sugli insediamenti vestini', *MAL* VIII, 13: 361–446.
(1976) 'Il Sannio', in Zanker 1976a: 219–44.
La Torre, G. F. (2004) 'Il processo di "Romanizzazione" della Sicilia: il caso di Tindari', *Sicilia Antiqua* 1: 111–46.
(2005) 'I recenti scavi sul Monte Sant'Angelo di Licata', in *Licata tra Gela e Finziada*, ed. C. Carità. Ragusa: 167–93.
La Torre, G. F. and Torelli, M. (eds.) (2011) *Pittura ellenistica in Italia e in Sicilia. Linguaggi e tradizioni. Atti di Convegno di Studi (Messina, 24–25 settembre 2009).* Rome.
Lacerenza, G. (2002) 'Masgaba dilectus Augusti', in *Lo Specchio d'Oriente: eredità afroasiatiche in Capri antica*, eds. M. C. Casaburi and G. Lacerenza. Naples: 73–92.
La'da, C. A. (2002) *Foreign Ethnics in Hellenistic Egypt.* Leuven.
Lambert, P.-Y. (1997) 'L'épigraphie gallo-grecque', in *Actes du Xe Congrès International d'Épigraphie grecque et latine, Nimes, 4–9 octobre 1992*, eds. M. Christol and O. Masson. Paris: 35–50.
Lancel, S. (1995) *Carthage: A History*, transl. A. Nevill. Oxford.
(1998) *Hannibal*, transl. A. Nevill. Oxford.

Lane Fox, R. (2011) 'The first Hellenistic man', in *Creating a Hellenistic World*, eds. A. Erskine and L. Llewellyn-Jones. Swansea: 1–29.

Lange, C. H. (2009) Res publica constituta. *Actium, Apollo and the Accomplishment of the Triumviral Assignment*. Leiden.

Langlotz, E. and Himer, M. (1965) *The Art of Magna Graecia*. London.

Lapenna, S. (ed.) (2004) *Gli Equi, tra Abruzzo e Lazio*. Catalogo della Mostra. Sulmona.

Laporte, J.-P. (1992) 'Datation des stèles libyques figurées de Grande Kabylie', in *L'Africa romana 9. Atti del IX convegno di studio, Nuoro, 13–15 dicembre 1991* (2 vols.), ed. A. Mastino. Sassari: I, 389–423.

Larner, J. (1980) *Italy in the Age of Dante and Petrarch, 1216–1380*. Longman History of Italy. Harlow.

Laronde, A. (1987) *Cyrène et la Libye hellénistique. 'Libykai Historiai': de l'époque républicaine au principat d'Auguste*. Paris.

(1990) 'Les Phéniciens et la Cyrénaïque jusqu'au IVe siècle avant J. C', *Semitica* 39: 7–12.

Larsen, M. T. (1979) *Power and Propaganda*. Copenhagen.

Lassner, J. (1970) *The Topography of Baghdad in the Early Middle Ages*. Detroit.

Lauter, H. (1975) 'Zur Siedlungsstruktur Pompejis in samnitischer Zeit', in *Neue Forschungen in Pompeji und den anderen vom Vesuvausbruch 79 n. Chr. verschütteten Städten*, eds. B. Andreae and H. Kyrieleis. Recklinghausen: 147–52.

(1986) *Die Architektur des Hellenismus*. Darmstadt.

Lauter-Bufe, H. (1987) *Die Geschichte des sikeliotisch-korinthischen Kapitells. Der sogenannte italisch-republikanische Typus*. Mainz am Rhein.

Lazzarini, M. L. (2007) 'Epigrafia greca d'Occidente', in *XII Congressus Internationalis Epigraphiae Graecae et Latinae. Provinciae imperii romani inscriptionibus descriptae. Barcelona, 3–8 Septembris 2002. Acta* (2 vols.), eds. M. Mayer i Olivé, G. Baratta, A. Guzmán Almagro. Monografies de la Secció Històrico-Arqueològica 10. Barcelona: II, 831–40.

Le Guen, B. (2001) *Les Associations de Technites dionysiaques à l'époque hellénistique* (2 vols.). Études d'Archéologie Classique, XI-XII. Paris.

Lécrivain, C. (1900) s.v. 'hospitium', in *Dictionnaire des antiquités grecques et romaines*, vol. III, eds. C. Daremberg and E. Saglio. Paris: 294–302.

Lehmann, P. W. (1946) *Statues on Coins of Southern Italy and Sicily in the Classical Period*. New York.

Lehmler, C. (2005) *Syrakus unter Agathokles und Hieron II. Die Verbindung von Kultur und Macht in einer hellenistischen Metropole*. Frankfurt-am-Main.

Leighton, R. (2004) *Tarquinia, an Etruscan City*. London.

León Alonso, P. (ed.) (1996) *Colonia Patricia Corduba. Una reflexión arqueológica. Coloquio internacional. Córdoba 1993*. Seville.

(1998) 'La escultura', in Aranegui 1998: 153–69.

Leone, R. and Spigo, U. (2008) *Tyndaris 1. Ricerche nel settore occidentale: campagne di scavo 1993–2004*. Palermo.

L'età della conquista 2010 = La Rocca, E. and Parisi Presicce, C. (eds.) (2010) *I giorni di Roma: l'età della conquista*. Milan (Catalogue of the exhibition *L'età della conquista: il fascino dell'arte greca a Roma*, 13 March–26 September 2010, Musei Capitolini, Rome).

Letta, C. (1984) 'Due letti funerari in osso dal centro italico-romano della Valle d'Amplero (Abruzzo)', *MonAL* 52. Rome: 67–115.

(1994) 'Una popolazione italica: i Marsi dalla formazione dell'ethnos alla romanizzazione', in *Miscellanea archeologica in onore di A. M. Radmilli*, ed. P. Stoduti. Pisa: 153–70.

(2003a) 'Presentazione', in D'Ercole and Copersino 2003: 7–8.

(2003b) 'Le iscrizioni della tomba 469', in D'Ercole and Copersino 2003: 320–1.

Levi, D. (1947) *Antioch Mosaic Pavements*. Princeton.

Levick, B. (1999) 'Messages on the Roman coinage: types and inscriptions' in *Roman Coins and Public Life under the Empire*, ed. G. M. Paul. Ann Arbor, MI: 41–60.

Lewis, N. (1974) *Papyrus in Classical Antiquity*. Oxford.

Lézine, A. (1959) *Architecture punique: recueil de documents*. Paris.

Liampi, K. (1998) *Der makedonische Schild*. Bonn.

Libertini, G. (1926) *Centuripe*. Catania.

Lightfoot, J. (2002) 'Nothing to do with the *Technitai* of Dionysus?', in *Greek and Roman Actors: Aspects of an Ancient Profession*, eds. P. Easterling and E. Hall. Cambridge: 209–24.

Lilliu, C. (1993a) 'Lucerne tardo-ellenistiche e tardo-repubblicane', in *Genna Maria II,1: il deposito votivo del mastio e del cortile*. Cagliari: 43–105.

(1993b) 'Un culto di età punico-romana al nuraghe Genna Maria di Villanovaforru', in *Genna Maria II,1: il deposito votivo del mastio e del cortile*. Cagliari: 11–39.

Lineros Romero, R. (2007) 'La arquitectura y la forma urbana de Carmona Protohistórica', in *El nacimiento de la ciudad: Carmona Protohistórica*, eds. M. Bendala Galán and M. Belén Deamos. Carmona: 425–54.

Ling, R. and Ling, L. (2004) *The Insula of the Menander at Pompeii*, vol. II. *The Decorations*. Oxford and New York.

Lipiñski, E. (ed.) (1992) *Dictionnaire de la civilisation phénicienne et punique*. Turnhout.

(1995) *Dieux et déesses de l'univers phénicien et punique*. Studia Phoenicia 14. Leuven.

Liverani, M. (1998) 'L'immagine dei fenici nella storiografia occidentale', *StudStor* 39: 5–22.

Llorens Forcada, M. M. (1994) *La ciudad de Carthago Nova: Las emisiones romanas*. La ciudad romana de Carthago Nova: Fuentes y materiales para su estudio No. 6. Murcia.

Lloyd, A. B. (2002) 'The Egyptian elite in the Early Ptolemaic Period: some hieroglyphic evidence', in Ogden 2002a: 117–36.

Lloyd, J. A., Bennett, P., Buttrey, T. V., Buzaian, A., El Amin, H., Fell, V., Kashbar, G., Morgan, G., Ben Nasser, Y., Roberts, P. C., Wilson, A. I. and Zimi, E. (1998) 'Excavations at Euesperides (Benghazi): an interim report on the 1998 season', *LibStud* 29: 145–68.

Lloyd, J. A., Buzaian, A. M. and Coulton, J. J. (1995) 'Excavations at Euesperides (Benghazi), 1995', *LibStud* 26: 97–100.

Loerke, W. (1990) 'A rereading of the interior elevation of Hadrian's rotunda', *JSAH* 49(1): 22–43.

Lomas, K. (1991) 'Local identity and cultural imperialism: epigraphy and the diffusion of Romanisation in Italy', in *The Archaeology of Power, Part 1. Papers of the Fourth Conference of Italian Archaeology*, eds. E. Herring, R. Whitehouse and J. Wilkins. London: 231–9.

(1993) *Rome and the Western Greeks, 350 BC–AD 200: Conquest and Acculturation in Southern Italy*. London.

(1997) 'Constructing "the Greek": ethnic identity in Magna Graecia', in *Gender and Ethnicity in Ancient Italy*, eds. T. Cornell and K. Lomas. London: 31–41.

Long, L. (2004) 'Les épaves protohistoriques de la côte gauloise et de la Corse (VIe–IIIe siècles avant J.-C.)', in *La circulació d'àmfores al Mediterrani occidental duran la Protohistòria (segles VIII–III) aC); aspectes quantitatius i anàlisi de continguts*, eds. J. Sanmartí, D. Ugolini, J. Ramon and D. Asensio. Arqueo Mediterrània 8: 127–57.

Longerstay, M. (1993) 'Les répresentations picturales de mausolées dans les haouanet du N-O de la Tunisie', *AntAfr* 29: 17–51.

López Borgoñoz, A. (1998) 'Distribución espacial y cronológica de las necrópolis emporitanas', in *De les estructures indígenes a l'organització provincial romana de la Hispània Citerior. Homenatge a Josep Estrada i Garriga*, eds. M. Mayer, J. M. Nolla and J. Pardo. Ítaca Annexos 1. Girona: 275–98.

López Castro, J. L. (1991) 'Cartago y la Península Ibérica: imperialismo o hegemonía?', in *La caída de Tiro y el auge de Cartago (V Jornadas de arqueología fenicio-púnica, Ibiza 1990)*. Trabajos del Museo Arqueológico de Ibiza 25. Ibiza: 73–86.

(1995) *Hispania Poena. Los fenicios en la Hispania romana*. Barcelona.

(2007) 'The western Phoenicians under the Roman Republic: integration and persistence', in van Dommelen and Terrenato 2007: 103–24.

López Palomo, L. A. (1999) *El poblamiento protohistórico en el valle medio del Genil*, vol. I. Écija.

López Pardo, F. (2006) *La torre de las almas: un recorrido por los mitos y creencias del mundo fenicio y orientalizante a través del monumento de Pozo Moro*. Madrid.

López-Bertran, M. (2007) *Ritualizando cuerpos y paisajes. Un análisis antropológico de los ritos fenicio-púnicos*. Ph.D. thesis, Universitat Pompeu Fabra. Barcelona. Available online at: http://hdl.handle.net/10803/7438 (accessed 31 May 2011).

(2011) 'Practical movements: kinetic rituals in the ancient Western Mediterranean', *JMA* 24(1): 85–109.

Lucore, S. K. (2009) 'Archimedes, the North Baths at Morgantina and early developments in vaulted construction', in *The Nature and Function of Water, Baths, Bathing and Hygiene from Antiquity through the Renaissance*, eds. C. Kosso and A. Scott. Technology and Change in History 11. Leiden and Boston: 43–59.

(2011) 'The North Baths, 2010', *American Excavations at Morgantina: Newsletter of the Friends of Morgantina. May 2011*, Charlottesville, VA: 4–5.

Lulof, P. S. (2005) 'Una bottega-tettoia ionica a Caere', in *Dinamiche di sviluppo delle città nell'Etruria meridionale. Veio, Caere, Tarquinia, Vulci. Atti del XXIII convegno di studi etruschi ed italici, 1–6 ottobre 2001* (2 vols.). Pisa and Rome: I, 209–12.

Lund, J. and Gabrielsen, V. (2005) 'A fishy business: transport amphorae of the Black Sea region as a source for the trade in fish and fish products in the Classical and Hellenistic periods', in *Ancient Fishing and Fish-processing in the Black Sea Region*, ed. T. Bekker-Nielsen. Aarhus: 160–9.

Luraghi, N. (2006) 'Traders, pirates, warriors: the proto-history of Greek mercenary soldiers in the Eastern Mediterranean', *Phoenix* 60: 21–47.

Lyons, C. L., Bennett, M. and Marconi, C. (eds.) (2012) *Sicily: Art and Invention between Greece and Rome*. Malibu.

Ma, J. (2000a) *Antiochus III and the Cities of Western Asia Minor*. Oxford.

(2000b) 'Fighting *poleis* of the Hellenistic world', in *War and Violence in Ancient Greece*, ed. H. van Wees. London and Swansea: 337–76.

(2000c) 'The epigraphy of Hellenistic Asia Minor: a survey of recent research (1992–1999)', *AJA* 104: 95–121.

(2003a) 'Kings', in Erskine 2003a: 177–95.

(2003b) 'Peer polity interaction in the Hellenistic age', *P&P* 180: 9–39.

MacIntosh Turfa, J. and Steinmayer, A. J. (1999) 'The *Syracosia* as a giant cargo vessel', *IJNA* 28: 105–25.

Mackay, C. S. (2000) 'Sulla and the monuments', *Historia* 49: 161–210.

MacKay, P. A. (2005) 'Evliya Çelebi's account of Anavarin', in *A Historical and Economic Geography of Ottoman Greece: The Southwestern Morea in the Eighteenth Century*, eds. F. Zarinebaf, J. Bennet and J. L. Davis. Princeton: 215–21.

MacKendrick, P. (1980) *The North African Stones Speak*. Chapel Hill, NC.

MacMullen, R. (1982) 'The epigraphic habit in the Roman Empire', *AJPh* 103: 233–46.

(1986) 'The frequency of inscriptions in Roman Lydia', *ZPE* 65: 237–8.

Mafodda, G. (2004) 'Transazioni economiche e relazioni diplomatiche tra Roma e Gela al tempo della tirannide di Gelone', *Kokalos* 46(1): 253–9.

Magie, D. (1950) *Roman Rule in Asia Minor* (2 vols.). Princeton.

Maiuri, A. (1939) *Le pitture delle case di 'M Fabius Amandio', del 'Sacerdos Amandus', e di 'P. Cornelius Teges' (Reg. I, Ins. 7) = Monumenti della pittura antica scoperti in Italia, III: La pittura ellenistico-romana, Pompei*, fasc. 2. Rome.

Malfitana, D. (2011) 'The view from the material culture assemblage of Late Republican Sicily', in Colivicchi 2011: 185–201.

Malkin, I. (1998) *The Returns of Odysseus: Colonization and Ethnicity*. Berkeley.
(2004) 'Networks and the emergence of Greek identity', *MHR* 18: 56–75.
(ed.) (2005) *Mediterranean Paradigms and Classical Antiquity*. London.
Manfredi, L.-I. (1985) 'Rsmlqrt, R'smlqrt: nota sulla numismatica punica di Sicilia', *RIN* 87: 3–8.
(1995) *Monete puniche: repertorio epigrafico e numismatico delle leggende puniche*. Rome.
(2000) 'Produzione e circolazione delle monete puniche nel sud dell'Italia e nelle isole del Mediterraneo occidentale (Sicilia e Sardegna)', in *Los Cartaginenses y la monetización del Mediterráneo occidental*, eds. M. P. García-Bellido and L. Callegarin. Anejos de AEA 22. Madrid: 11–22.
(2006) 'Le monete puniche nel Mediterraneo antico: produzione, coniazione, circolazione', *Mediterranea* 3: 257–98.
Manganaro, G. (1964) 'Città della Sicilia e santuari panellenici nel III e II sec. a. C.', *Historia* 13: 413–39.
(1992) 'Cronologia della emissioni a leggenda ΛΙΒΥΩΝ' in *Numismatique et histoire économique phéniciennes et puniques: actes du colloque tenu à Louvain-la-Neuve, 13–16 mai 1987*, eds. T. Hackens and G. Moucharte. Studia Phoenicia 9. Leuven: 93–106.
(1996) 'Alla ricerca di *poleis mikrai* della Sicilia centro-orientale', *Orbis Terrarum* 2: 129–44.
Mangas, J. and Plácido Suárez, D. (1999) *La peninsula ibérica prerromana de Eforo a Eustacio. Testimonia Hispaniae Antiqua* II B. Barcelona.
Mango, E. (2009) 'Il ginnasio in Sicilia: un caso particolare?', in Ampolo 2009: 763–72.
Mann, J. C. (1985) 'Epigraphic consciousness', *JRS* 75: 204–6.
Manning, J. and Morris, I. (2005) *The Ancient Economy: Evidence and Models*. Stanford.
Mansel, K. (2004) 'Vajilla de bronce en la Hispania republicana', in *La vajilla ibérica en época helenística (siglos iv-iii al cambio de era)*, eds. R. Olmos and P. Rouillard. Collection de la Casa de Velázquez 89. Madrid: 19–30.
Marconi, C. (2012) 'Le attività dell'Institute of Fine Arts – NYU sull'Acropoli di Selinunte (2006–10)', in *Sicilia occidentale. Studi, rassegne, ricerche*, ed. C. Ampolo. Pisa: 279–86.
Marconi, P. (1929) *Agrigento. Topografia ed arte*. Florence.
Marfaing, L. and Wippel, S. (eds.) (2004) *Les relations transsahariennes à l'époque contemporaine: un espace en constante mutation*. Paris.
Marginesu, G. (2002) 'Le iscrizioni greche della Sardegna: iscrizioni lapidarie e bronzee', in *L'Africa romana 14. Lo spazio marittimo del Mediterraneo occidentale: geografia storica ed economia. Atti del XIV convegno di studio, Sassari, 7–10 dicembre 2000* (3 vols.), eds. M. Khanoussi, P. Ruggeri and C. Vismara. Sassari: III, 1807–27.
Marín Ceballos, M. C. (2004) 'Observaciones en torno a los pebeteros en forma de cabeza femenina', in *El mundo púnico. Religión, antropología y cultura*

material, eds. A. González Blanco, G. Matilla Séiquer and A. Egea Vivancos. Estudios Orientales 5–6 (2001–2). Murcia: 319–35.

Marín Ceballos, M. C, Belén Deamos, M. and Jiménez Flores, A. M. (2010) 'El proyecto de estudio de los materiales de la cueva es Culleram', in *Los Púnicos de Iberia: proyectos, revisiones, síntesis*, ed. E. Ferrer Albelda. Mainake 32(1). Malaga: 133–57.

Marín Jordá, C. and Ribera i Lacomba, A. (2000) 'Un caso precoz de edificio termal: los baños republicanos de Valentia', in *II coloquio internacional de arqueología en Gijón. Termas romanas en el occidente romano*, ed. C. Fernández Ochoa. Serie Patrimonio 5. Gijón: 151–6.

Markle, M. (1977) 'The Macedonian sarissa, spear, and related armor', *AJA* 81(3): 323–39.

(1999) 'A shield monument from Veria and the chronology of Macedonian shield types', *Hesperia* 68(2): 219–54.

Markovits, C., Subrahmanyam, S. and Pouchepadass, J. (2003) 'Introduction', in *Society and Circulation: Mobile People and Itinerant Cultures in South Asia, 1750–1950*, eds. C. Markovits, S. Subrahmanyam, and J. Pouchepadass. New Delhi: 1–22.

Martelli, A. (2002) 'Per una nuova lettura dell'inscrizione Vetter 61 nel contesto del santuario di Apollo a Pompei', *Eutopia: Rivista di studi sull'Europa antica* II, 2: 71–81.

Martellone, A. (2008a) 'Letto funerario. Tomba 520, necropolis di Fossa', in Sapelli Ragni 2008a: 112–13.

(2008b) 'Letto funerario. Tomba 1140, necropolis di Bazzano', in Sapelli Ragni 2008a: 114–15.

(2008c) 'Letto funerario in osso dal territorio Vestino Cismontano', in Sapelli Ragni 2008a: 116–17.

Martin, R. (1970) 'Intervento', in *La Magna Graecia nel mondo ellenistico. Atti del nono convegno di studi sulla Magna Graecia*. Naples: 127–31.

Massa Pairault, F.-H. (1991) 'Strigiles féminins et ideologie funéraire (IVe-IIIe siècles av. N. È.)', *Nikephoros* 4: 197–209.

(1997) *Iconologia e politica nell'Italia antica. Roma, Lazio, Etruria dal VII al I secolo a.C.* Milan. (NB published under the name F.-H. Pairault Massa.)

(ed.) (1999) *Le mythe grec dans l'Italie antique. Fonction et image.* Paris and Rome.

Mastelloni, M. A. (2004a) 'Figli di Marte devoti ad Apollo/Children of Mars devoted to Apollo', in *Il profilo degli dei a Rhegion e Zancle Messana / The Profile of the Gods in Rhegion and Zancle Messana.* Messina: 44–5.

(2004b) 'Tra Cartaginesi, Romani e Sesto Pompeio / Of Carthaginians, Romans and Sextus Pompeius', in *Il profilo degli dei a Rhegion e Zancle Messana / The Profile of the Gods in Rhegion and Zancle Messana.* Messina: 50–1.

(2005) 'Messana e i Mamertini', in *Lo Stretto di Messina nell'antichità*, eds. F. Ghedini, J. Bonetto, A. R. Ghiotto and F. Rinaldi. Rome: 275–92.

Mastino, A. (1993) 'Analfabetismo e resistenza: geografia epigrafica della Sargegna', in *L'epigrafia del villaggio*, eds. A. Calbi, A. Donati, G. Poma. Bologna: 457–516.

Mastrocinque, A. (ed.) (1993) *Ercole in Occidente*. Trento.

Mattingly, D. J. (1992) 'War and peace in Roman North Africa', in *War in the Tribal Zone*, eds. R. B. Ferguson and N. L. Whitehead. Santa Fe: 31–60.

(2004) 'Being Roman: expressing identity in a provincial setting', *JRA* 17: 5–25.

(2007) 'The African way of death: burial rituals beyond the Roman Empire', in *Mortuary Landscapes of North Africa*, eds. D. L. Stone and L. M. Stirling. Toronto: 138–63.

Mattingly, D. J. and Hitchner, R. B. (1995) 'Roman Africa: an archaeological review', *JRS* 85: 165–213.

Mau, A. (1908) *Pompeji in Leben und Kunst*. Leipzig.

Mayer, M. and Velaza, J. (1989) 'Epigrafía ibérica sobre soportes típicamente romanos', in *Lengua y cultura en la Hispania prerromana*, eds. J. Untermann and F. Villar. Salamanca: 667–82.

Mazard, J. (1955) *Corpus nummorum Numidiae Mauretaniaeque*. Paris.

Mazois, F. (1824–38) *Les ruines de Pompéi* (4 vols.). Paris. Online at gallica.bnf.fr/ark:/12148/bpt6k106868d (last accessed 26 April 2012).

McKenzie, J. (2007) *The Architecture of Alexandria and Egypt, c.300 B.C. to A.D. 700*. New Haven.

Meltzer, O. (1879–1913) *Geschichte der Karthager* (3 vols.). Berlin.

Mercando, L. (1976) 'L'ellenismo nel Piceno', in Zanker 1976a: 160–76.

Mertens, D. (1997) 'Griechen und Punier. Selinunt nach 409 v. Chr.', *MDAI(R)* 104: 301–20.

Mertens, D. and De Siena, A. (1982) 'Metaponto: il teatro-ekklesiasterion', *BA* 67(16): 1–60.

Messineo, G. (1983) 'Tesserae hospitales?', *Xenia. Semestrale di Antichità* 5: 3–4.

Meyboom, F. (1995) *The Nile Mosaic of Palestrina. Early Evidence of Egyptian Religion in Italy*. Leiden, New York, Cologne.

Meyer, E. A. (1990) 'Explaining the epigraphic habit in the Roman Empire: the evidence of epitaphs', *JRS* 80: 74–96.

Meyer, H. (1991–2), 'Rom, Pergamon und Antiochos III: zu den Siegesreliefs von Sant'Omobono', *Bullettino della Commissione Archeologica Comunale di Roma* 94(1): 17–32.

Miccichè, C., Modeo, S. and Santagati, L. (eds.) (2007) *La Sicilia romana tra Repubblica e Alto Impero. Atti del convegno di studi*. Caltanissetta.

Mikalson, J. D. (2006) 'Greek religion. Continuity and change in the Hellenistic Period', in Bugh 2006a: 208–22.

Mildenberg, L. (1989) 'Punic coinage on the eve of the first war against Rome', in *Punic Wars: Proceedings of the Conference held in Antwerp from the 23rd to the 26th of November 1988 in Cooperation with the Department of History of the Universiteit Antwerpen*, eds. H. Devijver and E. Lipiñski. Studia Phoenicia 10. Leuven: 5–14.

(1993) 'RŠMLQRT', in *Essays in Honour of Robert Carson and Kenneth Jenkins*, eds. M. Price, A. Burnett, and R. Bland. London: 7–8.
Mileta, C. (2002) 'The king and his land: some remarks on the royal area (*basilikē chōra*) of Hellenistic Asia Minor', in Ogden 2002a: 157–75.
Miller, S. (1993) *The Tomb of Lyson and Kallikles: A Painted Macedonian Tomb.* Mainz am Rhein.
Millett, M. (1979) 'How much pottery?', in *Pottery and the Archaeologist*, ed. M. Millett. London: 77–80.
(1990) *The Romanization of Britain: An Essay in Archaeological Interpretation.* Cambridge.
Minà, P. (ed.) (2005) *Urbanistica e architettura nella Sicilia greca.* Palermo.
Mitchell, S. (2003) 'The Galatians: representation and reality', in Erskine 2003a: 280–93.
(2005) 'The treaty between Rome and Lycia of 46 BC (MS 2070)', in *Papyri graecae Schøyen*, ed. R. Pintaudi. Florence: 165–258.
Molina Vidal, J. (1997) *La dinámica comercial romana entre Italia e Hispania Citerior.* Alicante.
Momigliano, A. (1942) 'Terra Marique', *JRS* 32: 53–64.
(1970) 'J. G. Droysen between Greeks and Jews', in *History and Theory. Studies in the Philosophy of History* 9(2): 139–53 (reprinted in Momigliano, A. (1977) *Essays in Ancient and Modern Historiography.* Oxford: 307–32).
(1975) *Alien Wisdom: The Limits of Hellenization.* Cambridge.
Mommsen, T. (1903) *Römische Geschichte*, vol. I, 9th edn. Berlin.
Moore, J. (2007) 'The 'Mausoleum Culture' of Africa Proconsularis', in *Mortuary Landscapes of North Africa*, eds. D. L. Stone and L. M. Stirling. Toronto: 75–109.
Morales Pérez, J. (2003) 'Estudio de fauna de la cueva-santuario púnica de es Culleram (Sant Joan, Eivissa)', *Saguntum* 35: 113–22.
Moreau, Ph. (1983) 'Structures de parenté et d'alliance à Larinum d'aprés le pro Cluentio', in *Les bourgeoisies municipales italiennes au IIe et Ier siècles av. J.-C.*, ed. M. Cébeillac-Gervasoni. Naples: 99–123.
Moreno, P. (1994) *Scultura ellenistica.* Rome.
Moret, P. (1996) *Les fortifications ibériques. De la fin de l'Âge du Bronze à la conquête romaine.* Collection de la Casa de Velázquez 56. Madrid.
(2006) 'La formation d'une toponymie et d'une ethnonymie grecques de l'Ibérie: étapes et acteurs', in *La invención de una geografía de la peninsula ibérica. I. La época republicana. Actas*, eds. G. Cruz Andreotti, P. Le Roux and P. Moret. Málaga: 39–76.
Mørkholm, O. (1991) *Early Hellenistic Coinage from the Accession of Alexander to the Peace of Apamaea (336–188 BC)*, eds. P. Grierson and U. Westermark. Cambridge and New York.
Morris, I. (1992) *Death-Ritual and Social Structure in Classical Antiquity.* Key Themes in Ancient History. Cambridge.
Moscati, S. (ed.) (1988a) *The Phoenicians.* Milan.

(1988b) 'Fenicio o punico o Cartaginese', *RStudFen* 16: 3–13.
Moscovich, M. (1997) 'Cassius Dio on the death of Sophonisba', *AHB* 11(1): 25–9.
Moyer, I. S. (2006) 'Golden fetters and economies of cultural exchange', *Journal of Ancient Near Eastern Religions* 6(1): 225–36.
Mrozek, S. (1973) 'À propos de la répartition chronologique des inscriptions latines dans le Haut-Empire', *Epigraphica* 35: 113–18.
Mullen, A. (2008) 'Rethinking 'Hellenization' in South-eastern Gaul: the Gallo-Greek epigraphic record', in *Romanisation et épigraphie. Etudes interdisciplinaires sur l'acculturation et l'identité dans l'Empire romain*, ed. R. Häussler. Collection «Archéologie et Histoire Romaine» 17. Montagnac: 249–66.
(2013) *Southern Gaul and the Mediterranean. Multilingualism and Multiple Identities in the Iron Age and Roman Periods*. Cambridge.
Müller, P (1976) 'Die gestempelte Ziegel', in *Studia Ietina I: Die Stützfiguren des greichischen Theaters. Gestempelte Ziegel. Rezepte vom Monte Iato*, eds. H. Bloesch and H. P. Isler. Zürich: 49–77.
Muscolino, F. (2006) '*Kalathoi* iberici da Taormina. Aggiornamento sulla diffusione della ceramica iberica dipinta in Sicilia', *AEA* 79: 217–24.
Musomeci, A. (2010) 'Le terracotte figurate della necropoli in contrada Cassino in Centuripe', in Biondi 2010: 39–114.
Musti, D. (1963) 'Sull'idea di *suggeneia* in iscrizioni greche', *ASNP* 32: 225–39.
(1980) 'Il commercio degli schiavi e del grano: il caso di Puteoli. Sui rapporti tra l'economia italiana della tarda repubblica e le economie ellenistiche', in *The Seaborne Commerce of Ancient Rome: Studies in Archaeology and History*, ed. J. H. D'Arms. MAAR XXVI. Rome: 197–216.
Nappo, S. C. (1997) 'Urban transformation at Pompeii in the late third and early second centuries BC', in *Domestic Space in the Roman World: Pompeii and Beyond*, eds. R. Laurence and A. Wallace-Hadrill. JRA Suppl. 22. Portsmouth, RI: 91–120.
Negroni Catacchio, N. (1989) 'L'ambra: produzione e commercio in Italia preromana', in *Italia. Omnium terrarum parens*, ed. G. Pugliese Caratelli. Milan: 659–96.
Nicholls, R. V. (1979) 'A Roman couch in Cambridge', in *Archaeologia* 106: 1–32.
(1991) 'More bone couches', *AntJ* 71: 36–45.
Nielsen, M. (1989) 'Women and family in a changing society: a quantitative approach to late Etruscan burials', *ARID* 17–18: 53–98.
Niveau de Villedary y Marinas, A. M. (2003) *Cerámicas Gaditanas "Tipo Kouass"*. Real Academia de la Historia. Bibliotheca Archaeologica Hispana 21, Studia Hispano-Phoenicia 4. Madrid.
Oded, B. (1979) *Mass Deportations and Deportees in the Neo-Assyrian Empire*. Wiesbaden.
Ogden, D. (ed.) (2002a) *The Hellenistic World. New Perspectives*. Swansea and London.
(2002b) 'Introduction. From chaos to Cleopatra', in Ogden 2002a: ix–xxv.

Olcese, G. (2004) 'Anfore greco-italiche antiche', in *Metodi e approci archeologici: l'industria e il commercio nell'Italia antica*, eds. E. C. De Sena and H. Dessales. Oxford: 173–92.

Oleson, J. P. (ed.) (2008) *The Oxford Handbook of Engineering and Technology in the Classical World*. Oxford.

Olmos, R. (1986) 'Los griegos en Tarteso: replanteamiento arqueológico-histórico del problema', in *Homenaje a Luis Siret*, ed. O. Arteaga. Seville: 584–611.

(1998a) 'La invención de la cultura ibérica', in Aranegui 1998: 59–65.

(1998b) 'Naturaleza y poder en la imagen ibérica', in Aranegui 1998: 142–57.

Onians, J. (1979) *Art and Thought in the Hellenistic Age: The Greek World View, 350–50 BC*. London.

Oppenheim, A. L. (1967) 'Essay on overland trade in the first millennium B.C.', *JCS* 21: 236–54.

Orioles, V. (1992) 'Bilingualismo e biculturalismo nella Messana mamertina', in *Studi linguistici e filologici offerti a Giralamo Caracausi*. Palermo: 331–45.

Orlandini, P. (1968) 'Diffusione del culto di Demetra e Kore in Sicilia', *Kokalos* 14–15: 334–8.

Orton, C. (1993) 'How many pots make five? An historical review of pottery quantification', *Archaeometry* 35(2): 169.

Orton, C. and Tyers, P. (1990) 'Statistical analysis of ceramic assemblages', *Archeologia e Calcolatori* 1: 81–110.

Orton, C., Tyers, P. and Vince, A. (1993) *Pottery in Archaeology*. Cambridge.

Osanna, M. (2006) 'Architettura pubblica e privata a Kossyra', in Osanna and Torelli 2006: 35–50.

Osanna, M., Riethmüller, J. W., Schäfer, T. and Tusa, S. (2003) 'Ricerche a Pantelleria', *Siris: studi e ricerche della Scuola di Specializzazione in Archeologia di Matera* 4: 63–97.

Osanna, M. and Torelli, M. (eds.) (2006) *Sicilia ellenistica, consuetudo italica. Alle origini dell'architettura ellenistica d'Occidente*. Biblioteca di Sicilia Antiqua 1. Rome and Pisa.

Ouhlen, J. (1992) *Les théarodoques de Delphes*. Doctoral dissertation, Université de Paris X.

Pace, B. (1945) *Arte e civiltà della Sicilia antica. Volume terzo. Cultura e vita religiosa*. Genoa, Rome, Naples and Città di Castello.

Pala, P. (1990) 'Osservazioni preliminari per uno studio della riutilizzazione dei nuraghi in epoca romana', in *L'Africa romana 7. Atti del VII convegno di studio, Sassari, 15–17 dicembre 1989* (2 vols.), ed. A. Mastino. Sassari: II, 549–56.

Palagia, O. (2000) 'Hephaestion's pyre and the royal hunt of Alexander', in *Alexander the Great in Fact and Fiction*, eds. A. B. Bosworth and E. J. Baynham. Oxford: 167–206.

Pallottino, M. (1979 [1966]) 'Rapporti tra Greci, Fenici, Etruschi ed altre popolazioni italiche alle luce delle nuove scoperte', in *Saggi di Antichità* I. *Alle origini dell'Italia antica*. Rome: 392–7. (Originally published in *Problemi attuali di scienza e di cultura* 87 (1966): 11–16.)

(1979) 'Roma no. 29', in M. Cristofani (ed.), 'Rivista di epigrafia etrusca', *SE* 47: 319–25.

Palmer, R. E. A. (1997) *Rome and Carthage at Peace*. Historia Einzelschriften 113. Stuttgart.

Palmieri, C. (1983) 'L'opus signinum in Sicilia', in *Beni culturali e ambientali. Sicilia* 4: 171–6.

Panciera, S. (1995) 'La produzione epigrafica di Roma in età repubblicana. Le officine lapidarie', in *Acta Colloquii epigraphici Latini (Helsingiae 1991)*, eds. H. Solin, O. Salomies, and U.-M. Liertz. Helsinki: 319–42.

(1997) 'L'evergetismo civico nelle iscrizioni latine d'età repubblicana', in *Actes du Xe Congrès International d'Epigraphie Grecque et Latine*, eds. M. Christol and O. Masson. Paris: 249–90.

Parca, M. (2001) 'Local languages and native cultures', in *Epigraphic Evidence. Ancient History from Inscriptions*, ed. J. Bodel. London and New York: 57–72.

Parisi Presicce, C. (2004) 'Ecatombi nell'area del'altare di Ierone II a Siracusa', in Caccamo Caltabiano *et al.* 2004: 213–28.

Parisinou, E. (2000) *The Light of the Gods. The Role of Light in Archaic and Classical Greek Cult*. London.

Parker, R. (2004) 'New "Panhellenic" festivals in Hellenistic Greece', in *Mobility and Travel in the Mediterranean from Antiquity to Middle Ages*, eds. R. Schlesier and U. Zellmann. Münster: 9–22.

Parpola, S. (2003) 'Assyria's expansion in the eighth and seventh centuries and its long-term repercussions in the west', in *Symbiosis, Symbolism, and the Power of the Past: Canaan, Ancient Israel, and their Neighbors from the Late Bronze Age through Roman Palaestina*, eds. W. G. Dever and S. Gitin. Winona Lake: 99–111.

Parra, M. C. (2006) 'Note di architettura ellenistica a Segesta. Intorno all'*agora*', in Osanna and Torelli 2006: 107–22.

Patterson, L. E. (2010) *Kinship Myth in Ancient Greece*. Austin.

Pédech, P. (1964) *La méthode historique de Polybe*. Paris.

Pedley, J. G. (1990) *Paestum. Greeks and Romans in Southern Italy*. London.

Pelling, C. (2000) 'Fun with fragments: Athenaeus and the historians', in *Athenaeus and his World: Reading Greek Culture in the Roman Empire*, eds. D. Braund and J. Wilkins. Exeter: 171–90.

Pena, M. J. (2000) 'Sobre el origen y difusión de los *thymiateria* en forma de cabeza femenina', in *Actas del IV Congreso Internacional de Estudios Fenicios y Púnicos, Cádiz, 2–6 octubre 1995* (3 vols.), eds. M. E. Aubet and M. Barthélemy. Cádiz: II, 649–59.

(2007) 'Reflexiones sobre los pebeteros en forma de cabeza femenina', in *Imagen y culto en la Iberia prerromana: los pebeteros en forma de cabeza femenina*, eds. M. C. Marín Ceballos and F. Horn. Spal Monografías 9. Sevilla: 17–40.

Pérez Ballester, J. (2008) 'La cerámica de barniz negro', in *Cerámicas hispanorromanas. Un estado de la cuestión*, eds. D. Bernal Casasola and A. Ribera i Lacomba. Cadiz: 263–74.

Pérez López, I. (1999) *Leones romanos en Hispania*. Madrid.

Peri, C. (2003) 'Demetra e Core nella religione punica', in *Mutuare, interpretare, tradurre: storie di culture a confronto. Atti del 2° Incontro 'Orientalisti' (Roma, 11–13 dicembre 2002)*, ed. G. Regalzi. Rome: 145–54.

Perkins, P. (1999) *Etruscan Settlement, Society and Material Culture in Central Coastal Etruria*. BAR International Series 788. Oxford.

(2007) '*Aliud in Sicilia*? Cultural development in Rome's first province', in van Dommelen and Terrenato 2007: 33–53.

Perlman, P. (2000) *City and Sanctuary in Ancient Greece: The Theorodokia in the Peloponnese*. Göttingen.

Pernice, E. (1925–38) *Die hellenistische Kunst in Pompeij im Auftrage des Archäologischen Instituts des deutschen Reiches*. Berlin.

Peruzzi, E. (1970) *Origini di Roma* (2 vols.). Florence.

Pesando, F. (1996) 'Autocelebrazione aristocratica e propaganda politica in ambiente privato: la casa del Fauno a Pompei', *CCG* 7: 189–228.

(2008) 'Case di età medio-sannitica nella *Regio* VI: tipologia edilizia e apparati decorativi' in Guzzo and Guidobaldi 2008: 159–72.

Pesce, G. (1952–4) 'Un 'Ma'abed' a Nora', *SS* 12–13(1): 475–82.

Peterse, K. (1999) *Steinfachwerk in Pompeji: Bautechnik und Architektur*. Amsterdam.

Pfrommer, M. (1999) *Alexandria: im Schatten der Pyramiden*. Mainz am Rhein.

Philipp, H. (2004) *Archaische Silhouettenbleche und Schildzeichen in Olympia*. Berlin.

Philippson, A. (1939) *Das byzantinische Reich als geographische Erscheinung*. Leiden.

Phillips, K. M. (1960) 'Subject and technique in Hellenistic-Roman mosaics: a Ganymede mosaic from Sicily', *ABull* 42: 243–62.

Picard, C. (1984) 'Demeter et Kore à Carthage – Problèmes d'iconographie', *Kokalos* 28–9 (1982–3): 187–94.

Picard, G.-C. (1957) *Les trophées romains: contribution à l'histoire de la religion et de l'art triomphal de Rome*. Paris.

(1973) 'Recherches sur la composition héraldique dans l'art du Ier siècle av. J.-C.', *MEFRA* 85: 163–95.

(1988) 'Basilique et palais de Juba I de Numidie', *BCTH* 18: 165–7.

Pichler, W. (1970) *Origin and Development of the Libyco-Berber Script*. Berber Studies 15. Cologne.

Pilo, C. (2006) 'La villa di Capo Soprano a Gela', in Osanna and Torelli 2006: 153–66.

Pinzone, A. (2002) 'Elementi di novità e legami con la tradizione a Messina tra tarda repubblica e inizi impero', in *Messina e Reggio nell'antichità: storia, società, cultura*, eds. B. Gentili and A. Pinzone. Pelorias 9. Messina: 111–25.

Pirredda, S. (1994) 'Per uno studio delle aree sacre di tradizione punica della Sardegna romana', in *L'Africa romana 10. Atti del X convegno di studio, Oristano, 11–13 dicembre 1992* (4 vols.), eds. A. Mastino and P. Ruggeri. Sassari: II, 831–41.

Plácido Suárez, D. (2002) 'La peninsula ibérica: arqueología e imagen mítica', *AEA* 75: 123–36.

Plassart, A. (1921) 'Inscriptions de Delphes, la liste des Théorodoques', *BCH* 45: 1–85.

Platner, S. B. (1929) *A Topographical Dictionary of Ancient Rome*, rev. T. Ashby. London. Available online with ancient texts hyperlinked at penelope.uchicago.edu/Thayer/E/Gazetteer/Places/Europe/Italy/Lazio/Roma/Rome/_Texts/PLATOP*/home*.html (last accessed 26 April 2012).

Pliego Vázquez, R. (2003) 'Sobre el reclutamiento de mercenarios Turdetanos: El campamento cartaginés de El Gandul (Alcalá de Guadaira, Sevilla)', *Habis* 34: 39–56.

Pobjoy, M. (2000) 'The first Italia', in *The Emergence of State Identities in Italy in the First Millennium BC*, eds. K. Lomas and E. Herring. Accordia Specialist Studies on Italy 8. London: 187–211.

Poccetti, P. (1999) 'Il metallo come supporto di iscrizioni nell'Italia antica: aree, lingue e tipologia testuale', in *Pueblos, lenguas y escrituras en la Hispania prerromana. Actas del VII Coloquio sobre lenguas y culturas paleohispánicas, Zaragoza 1997*, eds. F. Villar and F. Beltrán Lloris. Salamanca: 545–61.

Poinssot, C. (1958) *Les ruines de Dougga*. Tunis.

Poinssot, C. and Salomonson, J. W. (1959 [1960]) 'Le mausolée libyco-punique de Dougga et les papiers du comte Borgia', *CRAI* 1959: 141–7 (published 1960).

(1963) 'Un monument punique inconnu: le mausolée d'Henchir Djaouf', *OMRL* 44: 57–88.

Poinssot, L. (1910) 'La restauration du mausolée de Dougga', *CRAI*: 780–7.

Polacco, L. (1977) 'Il teatro greco di Siracusa: modello al teatro romano', *NAC* 6: 107–17.

Polacco, L. and Anti, C. (1981) *Il teatro antico di Siracusa*. Rimini.

Polacco, L. and Mirisola, R. (1998–9) 'L'acropoli e il palazzo dei tiranni nell'antica Siracusa', *AIV* 157: 167–214.

Polito, E. (1998) Fulgentibus armis. *Introduzione allo studio dei fregi d'armi antichi*. Rome.

Pollitt, J. J. (1986) *Art in the Hellenistic Age*. Cambridge and New York.

(1993) 'Response', in P. Green 1993a: 90–103.

Portale, E. C. (2001–2) 'Per una rilettura delle arti figurative nella *Provincia Sicilia*: pittura e mosaico tra continuità e discontinuità', *Seia* n.s. 6–7: 43–90.

(2002) 'Un nuovo capitello "corinzio-italico" da Creta: osservazioni al margine del problema dei rapporti tra Gortina e Siracusa in età ellenistica', *Creta antica* 3: 279–99.

(2004) '*Euergetikotatos . . . kai philodoxotatos eis tous Hellenas*. Riflessioni sui rapporti fra Ierone II e il mondo greco', in Caccamo Caltabiano *et al.* 2004: 229–64.

(2006) 'Problemi dell'archeologia della Sicilia ellenistico-romana: il caso di Solunto', *ArchClass* 57: 49–114.

(2007a) 'Per una rilettura del II stile a Solunto', in *Villas, maisons, sanctuaries et tombeaux tardo-républicains: découvertes et relectures récentes*, ed. B. Perrier. Rome: 281–311.

(2007b) 'A proposito di "romanizzazione" della Sicilia. Reflessioni sulla cultura figurativa', in Miccichè *et al.* 2007: 150–69.

(2011) 'Un "fenomeno strano e inatteso": riflessioni sulla ceramica di Centuripe', in La Torre and Torelli 2011: 157–82.

Portale, E. C., Angiolillo, S. and Vismara, C. (2005) *Le grande isole del Mediterraneo occidentale: Sicilia, Sardinia, Corsica*. Rome.

Potter, D. (2003) 'Hellenistic religion', in Erskine 2003a: 407–30.

Pracchia, S. and Carcieri, M. (2008) 'Elementi in osso dalla tomba 6 della necropoli di Aquinum. Dal contesto alla ricostruzione', in Sapelli Ragni 2008a: 49–58.

Prados Martínez, F. (2008) *Arquitectura púnica. Los monumentos funerarios*. Anejos de AEA 44. Madrid.

Prag, J. R. W. (2002) 'Epigraphy by numbers: Latin and the epigraphic culture in Sicily', in *Becoming Roman, Writing Latin? Literacy and Epigraphy in the Roman West*, ed. A. E. Cooley. JRA Suppl. 48. Portsmouth, RI: 15–31.

(2003) 'Nouveaux regards sur les élites locales de la Sicile républicaine', *Histoire et Sociétés Rurales* 19: 121–32.

(2006) '*Poenus plane est* – but who were the 'Punickes'?', *PBSR* 74: 1–37.

(2007a) 'Ciceronian Sicily: the epigraphic dimension', in Dubouloz and Pittia 2007: 245–71.

(2007b) '*Auxilia* and *gymnasia*: a Sicilian model of Roman imperialism', *JRS* 97: 68–100.

(2009a) 'Republican Sicily at the start of the 21st century: the rise of the optimists?', *Pallas* 79: 131–44.

(2009b) 'Identità siciliana in età romano-repubblicana', in Ampolo 2009: 87–99.

(2010a) 'Tyrannizing Sicily: the despots who cried "Carthage!"', in *Private and Public Lies: The Discourse of Despotism and Deceit in the Graeco-Roman World*, eds. A. Turner, K. O. Chong-Gossard and F. Vervaet. Impact of Empire 11. Leiden: 51–71.

(2010b) '*Sicilia Romana tributim descripta*' in *Le tribù romane. Atti della XVIe rencontre sur l'épigraphie (Bari 8–10 ottobre 2009)*, ed. M. Silvestrini. Bari: 305–11.

(2011a) 'Kinship diplomacy between Sicily and Rome', in *Alleanze e parentele: Le "affinità elettive" nella storiografia sulla Sicilia antica. Convegno internazionale, Palermo 14–15 aprile 2010*, eds. C. Bonnet, D. Bonnano, N. Cusumano and S. Péré-Noguès. Caltanissetta: 179–206.

(2011b) 'Siculo-Punic coinage and Siculo-Punic interactions', in *Meetings between Cultures in the Ancient Mediterranean. Proceedings of the 17th International Congress of Classical Archaeology, Rome 22–26 Sept. 2008*, ed.

M. Dalla Riva. Bollettino di Archeologia online, I, 2010, Volume speciale. Online at: http://151.12.58.75/archeologia/bao_document/articoli/2_PRAG.pdf (last accessed 6 July 2012).

Préaux, C. (1978) *Le monde hellénistique: la Grèce et l'Orient de la mort d'Alexandre à la conquête romaine de la Grèce (323–146 av. J.-C.)* (2 vols.). Paris.

Price, S. and Nixon, L. (2005) 'Ancient Greek agricultural terraces: evidence from texts and archaeological survey', *AJA* 109: 665–94.

Principal, J. (2006) 'Late Hellenistic black gloss wares in the northeastern Iberian Peninsula: production traditions and social practices', in *Old Pottery in a New Century. Innovating Perspectives on Roman Pottery Studies. Atti del Convegno Internazionale di Studi Catania, 22–24 aprile 2004*, eds. D. Malfitana, J. Poblome and J. Lund. Rome: 41–56.

Prontera, F. (1998) 'La Sicilia nella tradizione della geografia greca', in *Geographica Historica*, eds. P. Arnaud and P. Counillon. Bordeaux and Nice: 97–107.

Pucci, G. (2001) 'Inscribed instrumentum and the ancient economy', in *Epigraphic Evidence. Ancient History from Inscriptions*, ed. J. Bodel. London and New York: 137–52.

Purcell, N. (1995) 'The Roman villa and the landscape of production', in *Urban Society in Roman Italy*, eds. T. J. Cornell and K. Lomas. London: 151–80.

(2004) 'The boundless sea of unlikeness? On defining the Mediterranean', *MHR* 18: 9–29 (reprinted in Malkin 2005: 9–29).

(2006) 'Orientalizing: five historical questions', in Riva and Vella 2006: 21–30.

Py, M. (1995) 'Les Etrusques, les Grecs et la foundation de Lattes', *Études Massaliètes* 4: 261–76.

Quinn, J. C. (2003) 'Roman Africa?', in *Romanization?*, eds. A. Merryweather and J. Prag. Digressus Supplement 1: 7–34. Published online at: www.digressus.org/articles/romanizationpp007-034-crawleyquinn.pdf (accessed 25 May 2011).

(2004) 'The role of the settlement of 146 in the provincialization of Africa', in *L'Africa romana 15. Ai confini dell'Impero: contatti, scambi, conflitti. Atti del XV convegno di studio, Tozeur, 11–15 dicembre 2002* (3 vols.), eds. M. Khanoussi, P. Ruggeri, and C. Vismara. Sassari: III, 1593–601.

(2009) 'North Africa', in *Blackwell Companion to Ancient History*, ed. A. Erskine. Oxford: 260–72.

(2011a) 'The Syrtes between East and West' in *Money and Trade Routes in Ancient North Africa*, eds. A. Dowler and L. Galvin. London: 11–20.

(2011b) 'The cultures of the tophet: identification and identity in the Phoenician diaspora', in *Cultural Identity in the Ancient Mediterranean*, ed. E. S. Gruen. Los Angeles: 388–413.

(2013) 'Imagining the imperial Mediterranean', in *Polybius and his World*, eds. B. Gibson and T. Harrison. Oxford: 337–52.

(forthcoming) 'A Carthaginian perspective on the Altars of the Philaeni', in Quinn and Vella (forthcoming).

Quinn, J. C. and Vella, N. (eds.) (forthcoming), *The Punic Mediterranean*. Cambridge.

Rakob, F. (1979) 'Numidische Königsarchitektur in Nordafrika', in *Die Numider* 1979: 119–71.

(1983) 'Architecture royale numide', in *Architecture et société de l'archaïsme grec à la fin de la république romaine. Actes du Colloque international organisé par le Centre national de la recherche scientifique et l'École française de Rome* (Rome 2–4 décembre 1980). CEFR 66. Rome: 325–48.

(ed.) (1991a) *Die deutschen Ausgrabungen in Karthago*. Mainz.

(1991b) 'Ein punisches Heiligtum in Karthago und sein römischer Nachfolgebau', *MDAI(R)* 98: 33–80.

(1998) 'Cartago. La topografía de la ciudad púnica. Neuvas investigaciones', in *Cartago fenicio-púnico: las excavaciones alemanas en Cartago 1975–1997*, ed. M. Vegas. Cuardernos de Arqueología Mediterránea 4. Barcelona: 14–46.

Ramallo Asensio, S. (1992) 'Un santuario de época tardo-republicana en La Encarnación, Caravaca, Murcia', in *Cuadernos de arquitectura romana I. Templos romanos de Hispania*, ed. S. Ramallo Asensio. Murcia: 67–82.

(1993) 'Terracotas arquitectónicas del santuario de La Encarnación (Caravaca de la Cruz, Murcia)', *AEA* 66: 71–86.

(2003) 'Carthago Nova: Arqueología y epigrafía de la muralla urbana', in *Defensa y territorio en Hispania de los Escipiones a Augusto (Espacios urbanos y rurales, municipales y provinciales)*, eds. A. Morillo, F. Cadiou and D. Hourcade. Salamanca: 325–62.

(ed.) (2004) *La decoración arquitectónica en las ciudades romanas de occidente*. Murcia.

(2007) 'Carthago Nova: urbs opulentissima omnium in Hispania', in Abad Casal *et al.* 2007: 91–104.

(2009) 'El diseño de una gran ciudad del sureste de Iberia: Qart Hadasht', in *Phönizisches und punisches Städtewesen. Akten der internationalen Tagung in Rom, vom 21 bis 23 februar 2007*, eds. S. Helas and D. Marzoli. Iberia Archaeologica 13. Mainz: 529–44.

Ramallo Asensio, S., Fernández Díaz, A., Madrid Balanza, M. J. and Ruiz Valderas, E. (2008) 'Carthago nova en los dos últimos siglos de la república: una approximación desde el registro arqueológico', in *Iberia e Italia: modelos romanos de integración territorial. Actas del IV congreso internacional hispano-italiano histórico-arqueológico*, eds. J. Uroz, J. Miguel Noguera and F. Coarelli. Murcia: 573–604.

Ramírez Sádaba, J. L. (2009) 'La epigrafía griega hallada en la península Ibérica', in *Estudios de Epigrafía Griega*, ed. A. Martínez Fernández. La Laguna: 57–77.

Ramón Torres, J. (1985) 'Es Cuieram 1981', *Noticiario Arqueológico Hispánico* 20: 227–56.

(1995) *Las ánforas fenicio-púnicas del Mediterráneo central y occidental*. Barcelona.

Ramos Loscertales, J. M. (1942) 'Hospicio y clientela en la España céltica', *Emerita* 10: 308–37.

Rawson, E. (1990) 'The antiquarian tradition: spoils and representations of foreign armour', in *Staat und Staatlichkeit in der frühen römischen Republik*, ed. W. Eder. Stuttgart: 158–73.

Reger, G. (1994) *Regionalism and Change in the Economy of Independent Delos*. Berkeley, Los Angeles, Oxford.

Reggiani, A. M. (2008) 'Archeologia medioitalica. Il senso di una mostra fra Lazio e Abruzzo', in Sapelli Ragni 2008a: 26–37.

Regoli, P. (1991) *I bruciaprofumi a testa femminile dal nuraghe Lugherras (Paulilatino)*. Studia Punica 8. Rome.

Reinach, S. (1922) *Répertoire de peintures grecques et romaines*. Paris. US public-domain copy at babel.hathitrust.org/cgi/pt?id=uc1.32106001459244.

Reusser, C. (1993) *Der Fidestempel auf dem Kapitol in Rom und seine Ausstattung. Ein Beitrag zu den Ausgrabungen an der Via del Mare und um das Kapitol 1926–1943*. BCAR Suppl. 2. Rome.

Ribera i Lacomba, A. (2007) 'The Roman foundation of Valentia and the Republican town', in Abad Casal *et al*. 2007: 75–89.

Ricci, C. (2005) *Orbe in Urbe, Fenomeni migratori nella Roma imperiale*. Vita e Costumi nel Mondo Romano Antico 26. Rome.

Richardson, J. S. (1983) 'The Tabula Contrebiensis: Roman law in Spain in the early first century B.C.', *JRS* 73: 33–41.

(1986) *Hispaniae. Spain and the Development of Roman Imperialism 218–82 BC*. Cambridge.

Richardson, L. (1992) *A New Topographical Dictionary of Ancient Rome*. Baltimore.

Rickman, G. E. (1971) *Roman Granaries and Store Buildings*. Cambridge.

Ridgway, B. (1990) *Hellenistic Sculpture I: The Styles of ca. 331–200 B.C.* Madison, WI.

(2000) *Hellenistic Sculpture II: The Styles of ca. 200–100 B.C.* Madison, WI.

(2002) *Hellenistic Sculpture III: The Styles of ca. 100–31 B.C.* Madison, WI.

Ridgway, D. and F. (1994) 'Demaratus and the archaeologists', in *Murlo and the Etruscans: Art and Society in Ancient Etruria*. Madison, WI: 6–15.

Rigsby, K. J. (1996) *Asylia. Territorial Inviolability in the Hellenistic World*. Hellenistic Culture and Society 22. Berkeley and London.

Riley, J. A. (1979) 'The coarse pottery from Berenice', in *Excavations at Sidi Khrebish Benghazi (Berenice), II*, ed. J. A. Lloyd. Tripoli: 91–467.

Ripollès, P. P. (1982) *La circulación monetaria en la Tarraconense mediterránea*. Servicio de Investigación Prehistórica, Serie de Trabajos Varios, núm. 77. Valencia.

Ritter, H. W. (1965) *Diadem und Königsherrschaft*. Munich.

Riva, C. and Vella, N. (eds.) (2006) *Debating Orientalization. Multidisciplinary Approaches to Processes of Change in the Ancient Mediterranean*. Monographs in Mediterranean Archaeology 10. London.

Rix, H. (1991) *Etruskische Texte. Editio minor* (2 vols.). Tubingen.

Rizza, G. (ed.) (2002) *Scavi e ricerche a Centuripe*. Catania.

Rizzitelli, C. (2003a) 'Le indagine archeologiche. Tipologia e cronologia dei materiali', in D'Ercole and Copersino 2003: 285–306.

(2003b) 'Le indagine archeologiche. Il costume funerario. L'inizio della fase ellenistica', in D'Ercole and Copersino 2003: 323–5.

(2003c) 'Le indagine archeologiche. Il costume funerario. Il III secolo a.C.', in D'Ercole and Copersino 2003: 325–7.

(2003d) 'Le indagine archeologiche. Il costume funerario. Dalla fine del III al I secolo a.C.', in D'Ercole and Copersino 2003: 327–31.

(2003e) 'Le indagine archeologiche. Il costume funerario. Le tombe a camera', in D'Ercole and Copersino 2003: 331.

(2003f) 'Le indagine archeologiche. Il costume funerario. La fine della necropoli. Considerazioni conclusive', in D'Ercole and Copersino 2003: 331–2.

Rizzo, G. E. (1923) *Il teatro greco di Siracusa*. Milan and Rome.

Robertson, C. M. (1965) 'Greek mosaics', *JHS* 85: 72–89.

Robinson, C. F. (2000) *Empire and Elites after the Muslim Conquest: The Transformation of Northern Mesopotamia*. Cambridge.

Robinson, D. and Graham, J. W. (1938) *Excavations at Olynthus VIII. The Hellenic House. A Study of the Houses found at Olynthus with a Detailed Account of those Excavated in 1931 and 1934*. Baltimore.

Robinson, E. S. G. (1943) 'The Coinage of the Libyans and kindred Sardinian issues', *NC* 3: 1–13.

(1953) 'A hoard of the Libyans', *NC* 13: 27–32.

Rodà de Llanza, I. (1998) 'La dificil frontiera entre escultura ibérica y escultura romana', in Aranegui 1998: 265–74.

Röder, G. (1988) 'Numidian marble and some of its specialities', in *Classical Marble: Geochemistry, Technology, Trade*, eds. N. Herz and M. Waelkens. Dordrecht and Boston: 91–6.

Roldán Gómez, L., Bendala Galán, M., Blánquez Pérez, J., Martínez Lillo, S. and Bernal Casasola, D. (2003) *Carteia III*. Seville.

Roller, D. W. (2002) 'A note on the Berber head in London', *JHS* 122: 144–6.

(2003) *The World of Juba II and Kleopatra Selene: Royal Scholarship on Rome's African Frontier*. New York.

Roller, M. (1996) *Dining Posture in Ancient Rome: Bodies, Values, and Status*. Princeton, NJ.

Romm, J. S. (1992) *The Ends of the Earth in Ancient Thought*. Princeton, NJ.

Ross, D. (2005) *Kbor Klib and the Battle of Zama*. *BAR* International Series 1399. Oxford.

Rostovtzeff, M. (1946) 'Numidian horsemen on Canosa vases', *AJA* 50: 263–7.

Rotroff, S. I. (1997) *The Athenian Agora*, XXIX, *Athenian and Imported Wheelmade Tableware and Related Material* (2 vols.). Princeton, NJ.

(2005) 'Four centuries of Athenian pottery', in *Chronologies of the Black Sea Area in the Period c. 400–100 BC*, eds. V. F. Stolba and L. Hannestad. Aarhus: 11–30.

(2006a) 'Material culture', in Bugh 2006a: 136–57.

(2006b) *The Athenian Agora*, XXXIII, *Hellenistic Pottery: the Plain Wares*. Princeton, NJ.

Roueché, C. (1997) 'Benefactors in the late Roman period: the eastern empire', in *Actes du X*[e] *Congrès International d'Epigraphie Grecque et Latine*, eds. M. Christol and O. Masson. Paris: 353–68.

Roueché, C. and Sherwin-White, S. (1985) 'Some aspects of the Seleukid Empire: the Greek inscriptions from Falaika, in the Arabian Gulf', *Chiron* 15: 1–39.

Rouillard, P. (1991) *Les Grecs et la péninsule ibérique du VIIIe au IVe siècle avant Jésus Christ*. Publications du Centre Pierre Paris 21. Bordeaux.

Roussel, P. and Hatzfeld, J. (1909) 'Fouilles de Délos', *BCH* 33: 472–522.

Rowe, A. and Healy, J. F. (1959) *Cyrenaican Expeditions of the University of Manchester 1955, 1956, 1957. The Excavated Areas of the Cemeteries at Cyrene. Descriptions of the Coins*. Manchester.

Rowton, M. B. (1973) 'Autonomy and nomadism in Western Asia', *Orientalia* 42: 247–258.

(1974) 'Enclosed nomadism', *JESHO* 17: 1–30.

Ruiz de Arbulo, J. (2007) '*Scipionum opus* and something more: an Iberian reading of the provincial capital', in Abad Casal *et al.* 2007: 33–43.

Ruiz de Arbulo, J., Vivo, D. and Mar, R. (2006) 'El capitolio de Tàrraco. Identificación y primeras observciones', in *El concepto de lo provincial en el mundo antiguo. Homenaje a la Prof. Pilar León* (2 vols.), eds. D. Vaquerizo Gil and J. F. Murillo Redondo. Córdoba: I, 391–418.

Ruiz Rodríguez, A. and Molinos, M. (eds.) (1985) *Iberos. Actas de las I Jornadas sobre el Mundo Ibérico. Jaén, 1985*. Jaén.

(1998) *The Archaeology of the Iberians*, transl. M. Turton. Cambridge.

Russo, A. (ed.) (2006) *Con il fuso e la conocchia*. Lavello.

Rutter, K. (2001) *Historia Numorum, Italy*. London.

Sáez Romero, A. (2009) 'El templo de Melqart de Gadir: hito religioso-económico y marítimo. Consideraciones sobre su relación con la industria conservera', in *Santuarios, oppida y ciudades: arquitectura, sacra y el origen y desarrollo urbano en el mediterráneo occidental*, eds. P. Mateos, S. Celestino, A. Pizzo and T. Tortosa. Anejos de AEA 45. Madrid: 115–27.

Sáez Romero, A., Montero, A. I. and Diaz, J. J. (2005) 'Nuevos vestigios del santuario gaditana de Melqart en Sancti Petri (San Fernando, Cádiz)', in *El periodo orientalizante. Actas del III simposio internacional de arqueología en Mérida: Protohistoria del mediterráneo occidental* (2 vols.), eds. S. Celestino Pérez and J. Jiménez Avila. Anejos de AEA 35. Madrid: II, 873–8.

Sahlins, M. (1999) 'Two or three things I know about culture', *Journal of the Royal Anthropological Institute* (NS) 5: 399–421.

Said, E. W. (1978) *Orientalism*. London.

Saller, R. and Shaw, B. D. (1984) 'Tombstones and Roman family relations in the Principate: civilians, soldiers and slaves', *JRS* 74: 124–56.

Salmeri, G. (2004) 'I caratteri della grecità di Sicilia e la colonizzazione romana', in *Colonie romane nel mondo greco*, eds. G. Salmeri, A. Raggi and A. Baroni. Rome: 255–308.

Salzmann, D. (1982) *Untersuchungen zu den antiken Kieselmosaiken: von den Anfangen bis zum Beginn der Tesseratechnik*. Berlin.

Sammartano, R. (2003) 'Riflessioni sulla 'Troianità' degli Elimi', in *Quarte giornate internazionali di studi sull'area elima (Erice, 1–4 dicembre 2000). Atti* (3 vols.). Pisa: III, 1115–48.

(2008–9) 'Magnesia sul Meandro e la "diplomazia della parentela"', *ὅρμος: Ricerche di Storia Antica*, n.s. 1: 111–39.

San Nicolás Pedraz, M. P. (2000) 'Interpretación de los santuarios fenicios y púnicos de Ibiza', in *Actas del IV Congreso Internacional de Estudios Fenicios y Púnicos, Cádiz, 2–6 Octubre 1995* (3 vols.), eds. M. E. Aubet and M. Barthélemy. Cádiz: II, 675–89.

Sánchez Gómez, M. L. (2002) *El santuario de El Cerro de los Santos (Montealegre del Castillo, Albacete). Nuevas aportaciones arqueológicas*. Albacete.

Sanders, D. H. (1996) *Nemrud Daği: The* Hierothesion *of Antiochus I of Commagene*. Winona Lake, Indiana.

Sanmartí Grego, J. (2000) 'Les relacions commercials en el món Ibèric', *III Reunió sobre economia en el Món Ibèric. Saguntum: Papeles del Laboratorio de Arqueología de Valencia*. Extra 3: 307–28.

Santangelo, F. (2008) 'Review of Anna J. Clark, *Divine Qualities. Cult and Community in Republican Rome*. Oxford: Oxford University Press, 2007', in *BMCRev* 18 April 2008. Online at bmcr.brynmawr.edu/2008/2008-04-18.html (last accessed 26 April 2012).

Sapelli Ragni, M. (ed.) (2008a), *Tra luce e tenebre. Letti funerari in osso da Lazio e Abruzzo*. Milan.

(2008b) 'Introduzione', in Sapelli Ragni 2008a: 11–13.

Sassi, M. M. (2001) *The Science of Man in Ancient Greece*, transl. P. Tucker. Chicago (originally published as (1988) *La scienza dell'uomo nella Grecia antica*, Turin).

Savalli, I. (1985) 'I neocittadini nelle città ellenistiche. Note sulla concessione e l'acquisizione della *politeia*', *Historia* 34: 387–41.

Scardigli, B. (1991) *I trattati romano-cartaginesi: relazioni interstatali nel mondo antico*. Fonti e Studi 5. Pisa.

Schäfer, T. (1979) 'Das Siegesdenkmal vom Kapitol', in *Die Numider* 1979: 243–50.

(1989) *Imperii insignia, sella curulis und fasces: zur Repräsentation römischer Magistrate*. MDAI(R) Ergänzungsheft 29. Mainz.

Schattner, T. (2005) 'La puerta de Sevilla en Carmona y otras puertas romanas en la Península Ibérica', *Romula* 4: 67–98.

Schaus, G. P. (1985) *The Extramural Sanctuary of Demeter and Persephone at Cyrene, Libya. Final Reports, 2. The East Greek, Island and Laconian Pottery*. Philadelphia.

Scheidel, W. (2009) *Rome and China: Comparative Perspectives on Ancient World Empires*. Oxford.

Scheidel, W., Morris, I. and Saller, R. (eds.) (2007) *The Cambridge Economic History of the Greco-Roman World*. Cambridge.

Schilling, R. (1982) *La religion romaine de Venus depuis les origines jusqu'aux temps d'Auguste*, 2nd edn. Paris.

Schmitt, H. H. (1957–8) 'Hellenen, Römer und Barbaren: eine Studie zu Polybios', *Wissenschaftliche Beilage zum Jahresbericht 1957/8 des humanistischen Gymnasiums Aschaffenburg*: 38–48.

Schwara, D. (2003) 'Rediscovering the Levant: a heterogeneous structure as a homogeneous historical region', *European Review of History / Revue Européenne d'Histoire*, 10(2): 233–51.

Scibona, G. and Tigano, G. (eds.) (2009) *Alaisa-Halaesa. Scavi e ricerche (1970–2007)*. Messina.

Scott, R. T. (1993) *Cosa IV: The Houses*. Michigan.

Sear, F. (2006a) *Roman Theatres. An Architectural Study*. Oxford.

(2006b) 'Cisterns, drainage and lavatories II,' *PBSR* 74: 163–201.

Sereni, E. (1970) 'Città e campagna nell'Italia preromana', in *Studi sulla città antica. Atti del convegno di studi sulla città etrusca e italica preromana*. Convegni e colloqui 1. Bologna: 109–28.

Serrati, J. (2000) 'Garrisons and grain: Sicily between the Punic wars', in Smith and Serrati 2000: 115–60.

(2007) 'Warfare and the state', in *The Cambridge History of Greek and Roman Warfare: Volume 1, Greece, The Hellenistic World and the Rise of Rome*, eds. P. Sabin, H. van Wees and M. Whitby. Cambridge: 461–97.

Shaffer, L. N. (2001) 'Southernization', in *Agricultural and Pastoral Societies in Ancient and Classical History*, ed. M. Adas. Philadelphia: 308–24.

Shaw, B. D. (2001) 'Challenging Braudel: a new vision of the Mediterranean', *JRA* 14: 419–53.

(2005) 'A peculiar island: Maghrib and Mediterranean', in Malkin 2005: 93–125.

(2006) *At the Edge of the Corrupting Sea*. Oxford.

Shell, M. (1982) *Money, Language, and Thought: Literary and Philosophical Economies from the Medieval to the Modern Era*. Berkeley.

(1994) *Art and Money*. Chicago.

Sherwin-White, S. (1978) *Ancient Cos: An Historical Study from the Dorian Settlement to the Imperial Period*. Göttingen.

Shipley, D. G. J. (1993) 'World-systems analysis and the "Hellenistic" world', in Bilde *et al.* 1993: 271–84.

(2000) *The Greek World after Alexander*. London and New York.

Shipley, D. G. J. and Hansen, M. H. (2006) 'The *Polis* and federalism', in Bugh 2006a: 52–72.

Sillières, P. (1995) *Baelo Claudia. Une cité romaine de la Bétique*. Madrid.

Simkin, O. (2012) 'Language contact in the pre-Roman and Roman Iberian peninsula: direct and indirect evidence', in *Multilingualism in the Graeco-Roman Worlds*, eds. A. Mullen and P. James. Cambridge: 77–105.

Sironen, T. (1995) 'Position of minority languages in Sicily: Oscan and Elymian', in Fischer-Hansen 1995: 185–94.

Sjöqvist, E. (1962) 'Excavations at Morgantina (Serra Orlando) 1961. Preliminary Report VI', *AJA* 66: 135–43.

Smith, C. and Serrati, J. (eds.) (2000) *Sicily from Aeneas to Augustus: New Approaches in Archaeology and History*. Edinburgh.

Smith, R. R. R. (1986) *Hellenistic Royal Portraits*. Oxford.

(1991) *Hellenistic Sculpture*. London.

Solin, H. (1999) 'Epigrafia repubblicana: bilancio, novità, prospettive', in *XI Congresso Internazionale di Epigrafia Greca e Latina*. Rome: 379–403.

Sommer, M. (2004) 'Die Peripherie als Zentrum: die Phönizier und der interkontinentale Fernhandel im Weltsystem der Eisenzeit', in *Commerce and Monetary Systems in the Ancient World: Means of Transmission and Cultural Interaction*, eds. R. Rollinger and C. Ulf. Stuttgart: 233–44.

Sordi, M. (1980) 'I rapporti fra Dionigi I e Cartagine fra la pace del 405/404 e quella del 392/391', *Aevum* 54: 22–34.

Spannagel, M. (2003) 'Die Tropaea des Marius und ihre Rolle in den inneren Auseinandersetzungen der späten römischen Republik', in O tempora, o mores! *Römische Werte und römische Literatur in den letzten Jahrzehnten der Republik*, eds. A. Haltenhoff, A. Heil and F.-H. Mutschler. Munich: 323–54.

Spanò Giammellaro, A. (ed.) (2005) *Atti del V Congresso Internazionale di studi fenici e punici: Marsala–Palermo, 2–8 ottobre 2000* (3 vols.). Palermo.

Spanò Giammellaro, A., Spatafora, F. and van Dommelen, P. (2008) 'Sicily and Malta: between sea and countryside', in van Dommelen and Gómez Bellard 2008: 129–58.

Sparkes, B. A. and Talcott, L. (1970) *The Athenian Agora*, XII, *Black and Plain Pottery of the 6th, 5th and 4th Centuries B.C.* (2 vols.). Princeton, NJ.

Spatafora, F. (2005) *Da Panormos a Balam. Nuove ricerche di archeologia urbana*. Palermo.

Spataro, M. and Villing, A. (2009) 'Scientific investigation of pottery grinding bowls in the Archaic and Classical Eastern Mediterranean', *British Museum Technical Research Bulletin* 3: 89–100.

Spigo, U. (ed.) (2005) *Tindari. L'area archeologica e l'*antiquarium. Milazzo.

Spivak, G. (1985) 'Can the subaltern speak? Speculations on widow sacrifice', *Wedge* 7/8: 120–30 (revised version in: Spivak, G. (1999) *A Critique of Postcolonial Reason*. Cambridge, MA: ch. 3).

Sposito, A. (ed.) (1995) *Morgantina. Architettura e città ellenistiche*. Palermo.

(2011) *Morgantina. Il teatro ellenistico. Storia e restauri*. Rome.

Stamper, J. (2005) *The Architecture of Roman Temples: The Republic to the Middle Empire*. Cambridge and New York.

Stannard, C. (2005) 'The monetary stock at Pompeii at the turn of the second and first centuries B.C.: Pseudo-Ebusus and Pseudo-Massilia', in Guzzo and Guidobaldi 2005: 120–43.

Staub Gierow, M. (1994) *Casa del Granduca (VII, 4, 56) und Casa dei Capitelli figurati (VII, 4, 57)*. Häuser in Pompeji vol. 7. Munich.

Stein G. J. (ed.) (2005) *The Archaeology of Colonial Encounters. Comparative Perspectives*. School of American Research Advanced Seminar Series. Santa Fe.

Stek, T. (2009) *Cult Places and Cultural Change in Republican Italy. A Contextual Approach to Religious Aspects of Rural Society after the Roman Conquest*. Amsterdam Archaeological Studies 14. Amsterdam.

Stephanidou-Tiberiou, T. (1998) *Anaskaphi Diou = Fouilles de Dion*, vol. I. Thessaloniki.

Stewart, A. F. (1993) *Faces of Power: Alexander's Image and Hellenistic Politics*. Hellenistic Culture and Society 11. Berkeley and Oxford.

(2006) 'Hellenistic art. Two dozen innovations', in Bugh 2006a: 158–85.

Stewart, A. F. and Korres, M. (2004) *Attalos, Athens, and the Akropolis: The Pergamene "Little Barbarians" and their Roman and Renaissance Legacy*. Cambridge.

Stillwell, R. (1961) 'Excavations at Morgantina (Serra Orlando) 1960. Preliminary Report V', *AJA* 65: 277–81.

Stone, D. L. (2007a) 'Monuments on the margins: interpreting the first millennium B.C.E. rock-cut tombs (haouanet) of North Africa', in *Mortuary Landscapes of North Africa*, eds. D. L. Stone and L. M. Stirling. Toronto: 43–74.

(2007b) 'Burial, identity and local culture in North Africa', in van Dommelen and Terrenato 2007: 126–44.

Stone, D. L. and Stirling, L. M. (2007) 'Funerary monuments and mortuary practices in the landscapes of North Africa', in *Mortuary Landscapes of North Africa*, eds. D. L. Stone and L. M. Stirling. Toronto: 3–31.

Storm, E. (2001) *Massinissa: Numidien im Aufbruch*. Stuttgart.

Storz, S. (1994) *Tonröhren im antiken Gewölbebau*. Mainz am Rhein.

Strong, D. (1988) *Roman Art*, 2nd edn, ed. R. Ling. Harmondsworth and New York.

Stucchi, S. (1976) 'Il Giardino delle Esperidi e le tappe della conoscenza greca della costa cirenaica', *QAL* 8: 19–73.

(1987) 'L'archittetura funeraria suburbana cirenaica', *QAL* 12: 249–377.

Stylow, A. U. (1996) 'De Corduba a Colonia Patricia. La fundación de la Corduba romana', in León Alonso 1996: 77–86.

(1998). 'The beginnings of Latin epigraphy in the Baetica. The case of the funerary inscriptions', in Keay 1998: 109–22.

Subrahmanyam, S. (1998) 'Notes on circulation and asymmetry in two Mediterraneans, c. 1400–1800', in *From the Mediterranean to the China Sea*, eds. C. Guillot, D. Lombard and R. Ptak. Wiesbaden: 21–43.

(2001) 'Du Tage au Gange au XVIe siècle: une conjoncture millénariste à l'échelle eurasiatique', *Annales (HSS)* 56(1): 51–84.

Suess, E. (1908) *The Face of the Earth*, Volume III. Oxford.

Sullivan, J. (2003) review of Erskine 2003a. *BMCRev* 2003.12.04, online at bmcr.brynmawr.edu/2003/2003-12-04.html (last accessed 30 July 2012).

Sumi, G. (2009) 'Monuments and memory: the Aedes Castoris in the formation of Augustan ideology', *CQ* 59: 167–86.

Swift, K. (2006) *Classical and Hellenistic Coarse Pottery from Euesperides (Benghazi, Libya): Archaeological and Petrological Approaches to Production and Interregional Distribution*, D.Phil. Thesis, School of Archaeology, University of Oxford.

Sznycer, M. (1975) 'L'"assemblée du peuple" dans les cités puniques', *Semitica* 25: 47–68.

Tagliamonte, G. (1996) *I Sanniti*. Milan.

(2002) 'Mercenari italici ad Agrigento', in *La Sicilia dei due Dionisi*, eds. N. Bonacasa, L. Braccesi, E. De Miro. Rome: 501–17.

Talamo, E, (2008) 'Un letto funerario da una tomba dell'Esquilino', in Sapelli Ragni 2008a: 69–73.

Tamburello, I. (1966) 'Punici e Greci a Palermo nell'età arcaica?', *Kokalos* 12: 234–9.

Taramelli, A. (1910) 'Il Nuraghe Lugherras presso Paulilatino', *MonAL* 20: 153–237 (reprinted in A. Moravetti (ed.) (1982) *Antonio Taramelli. Scavi e scoperti 1903–1910*. Sardegna Archeologica reprints. Sassari: 485–525. Available online at www.sardegnadigitallibrary.it/index.php?xsl=626&id=66451 (last accessed 30 July 2012).

Tarn, W. W. and Griffith, G. T. (1952) *Hellenistic Civilisation*, 3rd edn. London.

Tchernia, A. (2007) 'La plebiscitum Claudianum', in *Vocabulaire et expression de l'économie dans le monde antique*, eds. J. Andreau and V. Chankowski. Bordeaux: 253–78.

Terrenato, N. (1998) 'The Romanization of Italy: global acculturation or cultural *bricolage*?', in TRAC 97. *Proceedings of the Seventh Annual Theoretical Roman Archaeology Conference. Nottingham 1997*, eds. C. Forcey, J. Hawthorne and R. Witcher. Oxford: 20–7.

Testa, A. (1989) *Candelabri e thymiateria*. Rome.

Thein, A. (2002) *Sulla's Public Image and the Politics of Civic Renewal*. Diss. PhD, University of Pennsylvania.

Thiersch, H. (1910) 'Die alexandrinische Königsnekropole', *JDAI* 25: 55–97.

Thomas, R. (2000) *Herodotus in Context: Ethnography, Science and the Art of Persuasion*. Cambridge.

Thompson, D. J. (1984) 'The Idumaeans of Memphis and the Ptolemaic politeumata', in *Atti del XVII congresso internazionale di papirologia* (3 vols.). Naples: III, 1069–75.

(2001) 'Hellenistic Hellenes: the case of Ptolemaic Egypt', in *Ancient Perceptions of Greek Ethnicity*, ed. I. Malkin. Cambridge, MA: 301–22.

(2002) 'Families in early Ptolemiac Egypt', in Ogden 2002a: 137–56.

(2006) 'The Hellenistic family', in Bugh 2006a: 93–112.

Tocco, G. (1992) 'La villa ellenistica di monte Moltone', in *Testimonianze archeologiche nel territorio di Tolve*. Matera: 25–42.

Tölle-Kastenbein, R. (1994) *Das archaische Wasserleitungsnetz für Athen*. Mainz am Rhein.

Toppani, I. (1977–8) 'Una regina da ritrovare. Sofonisba e il suo tragico destino', *AIV* 136: 561–78.

Torelli, M. (1977) 'Il santuario greco di Gravisca', *PP* 32: 398–458.

(1982) 'Per la definizione del commercio greco-oriental: il caso di Gravisca', *PP* 37: 304–25.

(1993) 'Riflessi in Etruria del mondo fenicio e greco d'occidente', in *Magna Grecia, Etruschi, Fenici: Atti del trentatreesimo convegno di studi sulla Magna Grecia*. Taranto: 295–319.

(1995) *Studies in the Romanization of Italy*, edited and translated by H. Fracchia and M. Gualtieri. Edmonton, Alberta.

(1996) 'La romanizzazione del Sannio', in *La Tavola di Agnone nel contesto italico, Convegno di Studio, Agnone, 13–15 aprile, 1994*, ed. L. Del Tutto Palma. Florence: 27–44.

(2004) 'Quali Grecia a Gravisca?', in *I Greci in Etruria, Atti dell'XI convegno internazionale di studi sulla storia e l'archeologia del'Etruria*, ed. G. M. Della Fina. Annali della fondazione per il museo 'Claudio Faina'. Rome: 119–47.

(2008) 'Un italico nel regno di Ierone II: Cn. Modius e il suo *balneum* di Megara Iblea', *Sicilia Antiqua* 4: 99–104.

(2011) 'The early villa: Roman contributions to the development of a Greek prototype', in *Roman Republican Villas: Architecture, Context, and Ideology*, eds. J. A. Becker and N. Terrenato. Ann Arbor: 8–31.

Toren, C. (1988) 'Making the present, revealing the past: the mutability and continuity of tradition as process', *Man* 23(4): 696–717.

Tovar, A. (1974) *Iberische Landeskunde. Zweiter Teil. Die völker un die Städte des antiken Hispanien. Band 1. Baetica*. Baden-Baden.

(1989) *Iberische Landeskunde 2. Las tribus y las ciudades de la antigua Hispania 3. Tarraconensis*. Baden-Baden.

Toynbee, A. J. (1965) *Hannibal's Legacy* (2 vols.). London.

Treister, M. Y. (2001) *Hammering Techniques in Greek and Roman Jewellery and Toreutics*, ed. J. Hargrave. Leiden and Boston.

(2004) 'The theme of Amazonomachy in late Classical toreutics: on the phalerae from Bolshaya Bliznitsa', in *Pontus and the Outside World: Studies in Black Sea History, Historiography, and Archaeology*, ed. C. Tuplin. Colloquia Pontica 9. Leiden: 195–224.

Trell, B. (1979) 'Ancient coins: new light on North African architecture', in *Actes du premier congrès d'histoire et de la civilisation du Maghreb* I. Tunis: 81–97.

Tribulato, O. (ed.) (2012) *Language and Linguistic Contact in Ancient Sicily*. Cambridge.

Trigona, S. L. (2008) 'La necropoli occidentale di *Aquinum*. La tomba 6. I corredi', in Sapelli Ragni 2008a: 98–9.

Trillmich, W. and Zanker, P. (eds.) (1990) *Stadtbild und Ideologie: Die Monumentaliserung hispanischer Stadte zwischen Republik und Kaiserzeit*, Bayerische Akademie der Wissenschaften, philosphisch-historische Klasse, Abhandlungen, n.F. ciii. Munich.

Tsakirgis, B. (1984) *The Domestic Architecture of Morgantina in the Hellenistic and Roman Periods*, PhD dissertation. Michigan.

(1989) 'The decorated pavements of Morgantina I: the mosaics', *AJA* 93: 395–416.

(1990) 'The decorated pavements of Morgantina II: the *opus signinum*', *AJA* 94: 425–43.

(1995) 'Morgantina: a Greek town in central Sicily', in Fischer-Hansen 1995: 123–47.

(2009) 'The Greek house in Sicily. Influence and innovation in the Hellenistic period', in Koine. *Mediterranean Studies in Honor of R. Ross Holloway*, eds. D. B. Counts and A. S. Tuck. Oxford and Oakville: 109–21.

Tsiolis, V. (2006) 'Fregellae: il complesso termale e le origini degli edifici balneari urbani nel mondo romano', in Osanna and Torelli 2006: 243–55.

Tullio, A. (1984) 'Due sarcofagi tardo ellenistiche da Cefalù', in *Alessandria e il mondo ellenistico-romano: studi in onore di A. Adriani* (3 vols.), eds. N. Bonacasa and A. Di Vita. Rome: III, 598–610.

(1988–9) 'Scavi e ricerche a Cefalù (1984–1985)', *Kokalos* 34–5: 679–95.

(2005) 'Presenze puniche nella necropoli ellenistico-romana di Cefalù', in Spanò Giammellaro 2005: II, 551–65.

(2009) *Cefalù. La necropoli ellenistica I*. Studi e Materiali 13. Rome.

Tusa, V. (1966) 'Aree sacrificiali a Selinunte e a Solunto', in *Mozia II*. Rome: 143–53.

(1983) 'La statua di Mozia', *PP* 38(213): 445–56.

(1997) 'I mosaici di Mozia', in Bonacasa Carra and Guidobaldi 1997: 137–46.

(2001) 'La statua del c. d. Zeus da Solunto', in Buzzi *et al.* 2001: 433–8.

Ugas, G. (1991) 'Il sacello del vano e nella fortezza nuragica di Su Mulinu-Villanovafranca (CA)', in *Anathema. Regime delle offerte e vita dei santuari nel Mediterraneo antico. Atti del convegno internazionale, Roma, 15–18 giugno 1989*, eds. G. Bartoloni, C. Colonna and C. Grottanelli. Scienze dell'Antichità. Storia, Archeologia, Antropologia 3/4 (1989/1990). Rome: 551–73.

Ugas, G. and Paderi, M. C. (1990) 'Persistenze rituali e culturali in età punica e romana nel sacello nuragico del vano e della fortezza di Su Mulinu-Villanovafranca (Cagliari)', in *L'Africa romana 7. Atti del VII convegno di studio, Sassari, 15–17 dicembre 1989* (2 vols.), ed. A. Mastino. Sassari: I, 475–86.

Untermann, J. (1995a) 'La latinización de Hispania a través del documento monetal', in *La moneda hispánica ciudad y territorio*, eds. M. P. García-Bellido and R. M. Sobral Centeno. Anejos de AEA 14. Madrid: 305–16.

(1995b) 'Epigrafía indígena y romanización en la Celtibera', in F. Beltrán Lloris 1995a: 197–208.

Vallet, G., Villard, F. and Auberson, P. (1983) *Mégara Hyblaea 3. Guide des fouilles*. CEFR 185. Rome.

Van der Mieroop, M. (2005) 'The Eastern Mediterranean in Early Antiquity', in Harris 2005a: 117–40.

Van Dommelen, P. (1997) 'Colonial constructs: colonialism and archaeology in the Mediterranean', *World Archaeology* 28: 305–23.

(1998a) *On Colonial Grounds. A Comparative Study of Colonialism and Rural Settlement in 1st Millennium B.C. West Central Sardinia*. Archaeological Studies Leiden University 2. Leiden.

(1998b) 'Spazi rurali fra costa e colline in età punico-romana: Arborèa e Marmilla a confronto', in *L'Africa romana 12. Atti del XII convegno di studio, Olbia, 12–15 dicembre 1996* (3 vols.), eds. M. Khanoussi, P. Ruggeri and C. Vismara. Sassari: II, 589–601.

(2002) 'Ambiguous matters: colonialism and local identities in Punic Sardinia', in *The Archaeology of Colonialism*, eds. C. Lyons and J. Papadopoulos. Issues & Debates. Los Angeles: 121–47.

(2006a) 'The orientalizing phenomenon: hybridity and material culture in the western Mediterranean', in Riva and Vella 2006: 135–52.

(2006b) 'Colonial matters. Material culture and postcolonial theory in colonial situations', in *Handbook of Material Culture*, eds. C. Tilley, W. Keane, S. Kuechler, M. Rowlands and P. Spyer. London: 104–24.

Van Dommelen, P. and Finocchi, S. (2008) 'Sardinia: divergent landscapes', in van Dommelen and Gómez Bellard 2008: 159–201.

Van Dommelen, P. and Gómez Bellard, C. (eds.) (2008) *Rural Landscapes of the Punic World*. Monographs in Mediterranean Archaeology 11. London and Oakville, CT.

Van Dommelen, P. and Knapp, B. A. (eds.) (2010) *Material Connections in the Ancient Mediterranean: Mobility, Materiality, and Mediterranean Identities*. London.

Van Dommelen, P., Kostoglou, M. and Sharpe, L. (2007) 'Fattorie puniche e l'economia rurale della Sardegna punica: il progetto Terralba', in *Sítios e Paisagens rurais no Mediterrâneo Púnico*, eds. A. M. Arruda, C. Gómez Bellard and P. van Dommelen. Caderns da Uniarq 3; 6° Congresso Internacional de Estudos Fenícios e Púnicos. Lisbon: 51–67.

Van Dommelen, P. and Terrenato, N. (eds.) (2007) *Articulating Local Cultures. Power and Identity under the Expanding Roman Republic*. JRA Suppl. 63. Portsmouth, RI.

Van Keuren, F. (1994) *The Coinage of Heraclea Lucaniae*. Rome.

Vandermersch, C. (2001) 'Aux sources du vin romain, dans le Latium e la Campania à l'époque médio-républicaine', *Ostraka* 10(1–2): 157–206.

Vanni, F. M. (1993) 'L'iconografia di Ercole nelle monete di zecca africana' in *Ercole in Occidente*, ed. A. Mastrocinque. Trento: 119–23.

Vaquerizo Gil, D., Quesada Sanz, F. and Murillo Redondo, J. F. (eds.) (2001) *Protohistoria y romanización en la subbética cordobesa. Una aproximación al desarrollo de la cultura ibérica en el sur de la actual provincia de Córdoba*. Seville.

Vassal, V. (2006) *Les pavements d'*opus signinum. *Technique, décor, fonction architecturale. BAR* International Series 1472. Oxford: 24–6.

Vecchio, L. (2003) *Le iscrizioni greche di Velia*. Vienna.

Veit, C. (2009) 'Zur Kulturpolitik Hierons II. in Syrakus', in *Stadtbilder in Hellenismus*, eds. A. Matthaei and M. Zimmermann. Berlin: 365–79.

Vella, N. (1996) 'Elusive Phoenicians', *Antiquity* 70: 245–50.

(2001) 'Defining Phoenician religious space: Oumm el-'Amed reconsidered', *Ancient Near Eastern Studies* 37: 27–55.

Venit, M. (2002) *Monumental Tombs of Ancient Alexandria: The Theatre of the Dead*. Cambridge.

Vento, M. (2000) *Le stele dipinte di Lilibeo*. Marsala.

Ventura Martínez, J. J. (1996) 'El origen de la Córdoba romana a través del estudio de las cerámicas de barniz negro', in León Alonso 1996: 49–62.

(2001) 'Cerámicas de barniz negro en Carmona', in Caballos Rufino 2001: 321–38.

Ventura, A., León, P. and Márquez, C. (1998) 'Roman Córdoba in the light of recent archaeological research', in Keay 1998: 87–107.

Veyne, P. (1979) 'The hellenization of Rome and the question of acculturations', *Diogenes* 27: 1–27.

Vickers, M. (1985) 'Artful crafts. The influence of metalwork on Athenian painted pottery', *JHS* 105: 108–28.

Vickers, M., Gill, D. W. J. and Economou, M. (1994) 'Euesperides. The rescue of an excavation', *LibStud* 25: 125–36.

Villa, A. (1988) *I capitelli di Solunto*. Rome.

Villar, F., Díaz, M. A., Medrano, M. M. and Jordán, C. (2001) *El IV bronce de Botorrita (Contrebia Belaisca): arqueología y lingüística*. Salamanca.

Villaronga, L. (1983) *Les monedes ibèriques de Tàrraco*. Tarragona.

(1994) *Corpus nummorum Hispaniae ante Augusti aetatem*. Madrid.

Villing, A. and Pemberton, E. G. (2010) 'Mortaria from ancient Corinth: form and function', *Hesperia* 79: 555–638.

Vitali, D. (1987) 'Monte Bibele tra Etruschi e Celti: dati archeologichi e interpretazione storica', in *Celti ed Etruschi nell'Italia centro-settentrionale dal V sec. a.C. alla romanizzazione, atti del colloquio internazionale*, ed. D. Vitali. Imola: 309–80.

Vogelsang, W. J. (1992) *The Rise and Organisation of the Achaemenid Empire: The Eastern Iranian Evidence*. Leiden.

Von Boeselager, D. (1983) *Antike Mosaiken in Sizilien*. Rome.

Von Hase, F.-W. (1993) 'Il bucchero etrusco a Cartagine', in *Produzione artigianale ed esportazione nel mondo antico: il bucchero Etrusco*, ed. M. Bonghi Jovino. Milan: 187–94.

Von Sydow, W. (1984) 'Die hellenistischen Gebälke in Sizilien', *MDAI(R)* 91: 239–358.

Voza, G. (1999) *Nel segno dell'antico. Archeologia nel territorio di Siracusa*. Palermo.

Vuillemot, G. (1964) 'Fouilles du mausolée de Beni Rhénane', *CRAI*: 71–95.

Wagner, C. G. (1986) 'Critical remarks concerning a supposed hellenisation of Carthage', *Reppal* 2: 357–75.

(1989) 'The Carthaginians in ancient Spain: from administrative trade to territorial annexation', in *Punic Wars*, eds. H. Devijver and E. Lipiński. Studia Phoenicia 10. Leuven: 145–56.

Walbank, F. W. (1957–79) *A Historical Commentary on Polybius* (3 vols.). Oxford.

(1972) *Polybius*. Berkeley.

(1975) '*SYMPLOKE*: its role in Polybius' *Histories*', *YClS* 24: 197–212 (reprinted in Walbank 1985: 313–24).

(1984a) 'Sources for the period', in Walbank *et al.* 1984: 1–22.

(1984b) 'Monarchies and monarchic ideas', in Walbank *et al.* 1984: 62–100.

(1985) *Selected Papers: Studies in Greek and Roman History and Historiography*. Cambridge.

(1992) *The Hellenistic World*, 2nd edn. Fontana History of the Ancient World. London.

(1993) 'Η ΤΩΝ ΟΛΩΝ ΕΛΠΙΣ and the Antigonids', in *Ancient Macedonia* 3: 1721–30 (reprinted in Walbank 2002: 127–36).

(2002) *Polybius, Rome and the Hellenistic World: Essays and Reflections*. Cambridge.

Walbank, F. W., Astin, A. E., Frederiksen, M. W. and Ogilvie, R. M. (eds.) (1984) *The Cambridge Ancient History, 2nd edn, Volume VII, part 1, The Hellenistic World*. Cambridge.

Wallace-Hadrill, A. (1998) 'The villa as a cultural symbol', in *The Roman Villa, Villa Urbana*, ed. A. Frazer. Philadelphia: 43–54.

(2005) 'Excavation and standing structures in Pompeii Insula I.9', in Guzzo and Guidobaldi 2005: 101–8.

(2008) *Rome's Cultural Revolution*. Cambridge.

(2011) 'Pompeian identities: between Oscan, Samnite, Greek, Roman, and Punic', in *Cultural Identity in the Ancient Mediterranean*, ed. E. S. Gruen. Los Angeles: 415–27.

Webb, P. (1996) *Hellenistic Architectural Sculpture: Figural Motifs in Western Anatolia and the Aegean Islands*. Madison, WI.

Weinstock, S. (1971) *Divus Julius*. Oxford.

Welles, C. B. (1934) *Royal Correspondence in the Hellenistic Period*. New Haven.

Weriemmi-Akkari, J. (1985) 'Un témoinage spectaculaire sur la presence libyco-punique dans l'ile de Jerba: le mausolée de Henchir Bourgou', *Reppal* 1: 189–96.

Werner, M. and Zimmermann, B. (2006) 'Beyond comparison: *histoire croisée* and the challenge of reflexivity', *History and Theory* 45: 30–50.

Westgate, R. (2002) 'Hellenistic mosaics', in Ogden 2002a: 221–51.

Whitaker, J. (1921) *Motya, a Phoenician Colony in Sicily*. London.

Whitbread, I. (1995) *Greek Transport Amphorae: A Petrological and Archaeological Study*. Athens.

Whitehouse, R. (1992) *Underground Religion. Cult and Culture in Prehistoric Italy.* Accordia Specialist Studies on Italy 1. London.

Whittaker, C. R. (1978) 'Carthaginian imperialism in the fifth and fourth centuries', in *Imperialism in the Ancient World*, eds. P. Garnsey and C. R. Whittaker. Cambridge: 59–90.

Wiegand, A. (1991) 'Zwei Beiträge zur Topographie Soluntś', *MDAI(R)* 98: 121–30.

(1997) *Das Theater von Solunt. Ein besonderer Skenentyp des Späthellenismus auf Sizilien.* Deutsches Archäologisches Institut Rom, Sonderschriften 12. Mainz am Rhein.

Will, E. (1984) 'The succession to Alexander', in Walbank *et al.* 1984: 23–61.

Williams, J. H. C. (2001) *Beyond the Rubicon: Romans and Gauls in Republican Italy.* Oxford.

Williams, J. H. C. and Burnett, A. (1998) 'Alexander the Great and the coinages of western Greece', in *Studies in Greek Numismatics in Memory of Martin Jessop Price*, eds. R. Ashton, S. Hurter with G. Le Rider and R. Bland. London: 379–93.

Wilson, A. I. (2005) 'Une cité grecque de Libye: fouilles d'Euesperides (Benghazi)', *CRAI* 2003: 1648–75.

Wilson, A. I. *et al.* (1999) = Wilson, A. I., Bennett, P., Buzaian, A. M., Ebbinghaus, S., Halliwell, M., Hamilton, K., Kattenberg, A. and Zimi, E. (1999) 'Urbanism and economy at Euesperides (Benghazi): a preliminary report on the 1999 season', *LibStud* 30: 147–68.

Wilson, A. I. *et al.* (2001) = Wilson, A. I., Bennett, P., Buzaian, A. M., Fell, V., Göransson, K., Green, C., Hall, C., Helm, R., Kattenberg, A., Swift, K. and Zimi, E. (2001) 'Euesperides (Benghazi): preliminary report on the spring 2001 season', *LibStud* 32: 155–77.

Wilson, A. I. *et al.* (2002) = Wilson, A. I., Bennett, P., Buzaian, A. M., Buttrey, T., Göransson, K., Hall, C., Kattenberg, A., Scott, R., Swift, K. and Zimi, E. (2002) 'Euesperides (Benghazi): preliminary report on the spring 2002 season', *LibStud* 33: 85–123.

Wilson, A. I. *et al.* (2003) = Wilson, A. I., Bennett, P., Buzaian, A. M., Buttrey, T., Fell, V., Found, B., Göransson, K., Guinness, A., Hardy, J., Harris, K., Helm, R., Kattenberg, A., Morley, G., Swift, K., Wootton, W. and Zimi, E. (2003) 'Euesperides (Benghazi): preliminary report on the spring 2003 season', *LibStud* 34: 191–228.

Wilson, A. I. *et al.* (2004) = Wilson, A. I., Bennett, P., Buzaian, A. M., Buttrey, T., Fell, V., Found, B., Göransson, K., Guinness, A., Hardy, J., Harris, K., Helm, R., Kattenberg, A., Tébar Megias, E., Morley, G., Murphy, A., Swift, K., Twyman, J., Wootton, W. and Zimi, E. (2004) 'Euesperides (Benghazi): preliminary report on the spring 2004 season', *LibStud* 35: 149–90.

Wilson, A. I. *et al.* (2005) = Wilson, A. I., Bennett, P., Buzaian, A. M., Found, B., Göransson, K., Guinness, A., Hardy, J., Holman, J., Kattenberg, A., Morley, G., al-Mugasbi, M., Swift, K., Vaughan-Williams, A., Wootton, W. and Zimi, E.

(2005 [2006]) 'Euesperides 2005: preliminary report on the spring 2005 season', *LibStud* 36: 135–82.

Wilson, A. I. *et al.* (2006) = Wilson, A. I., Bennett, P., Buzaian, A. M., Cherstich, L., Found, B., Göransson, K., Holman, J., Lane, R., Morley, G., Russell, B., Swift, K., Vaughan-Williams, A. and Zimi, E. (2006) 'Euesperides 2006: preliminary report on the spring 2006 season', *LibStud* 37: 117–57.

Wilson, A. I. and Tébar Megías, E. (2008) 'Purple dye production at Hellenistic Euesperides (Benghazi, Libya)', in *Ressources et activités maritimes des peuples de l'antiquité*, ed. J. Napoli. Boulogne-sur-Mer: 231–8.

Wilson, R. J. A. (1985) 'Changes in the pattern of urban settlement in Roman, Byzantine and Arab Sicily', in *Papers in Italian Archaeology IV.1*, eds. C. Malone and S. Stoddart. BAR International Series 243. Oxford: 313–44.

(1990a) *Sicily under the Roman Empire: the Archaeology of a Roman Province, 36 B.C. - A.D. 535*. Warminster.

(1990b) 'Roman architecture in a Greek world: the example of Sicily', in *Architecture and Architectural Sculpture in the Roman Empire*, ed. M. Henig. Oxford: 67–90.

(1992) '*Tubi fittili* (vaulting tubes): on their origin and distribution', *JRA* 5: 97–129.

(2000a) 'Aqueducts and water supply in Greek and Roman Sicily: the present *status quaestionis*', in *Cura aquarum in Sicilia*, ed. G. C. M. Jansen. Leiden: 5–36.

(2000b) 'Ciceronian Sicily: an archaeological perspective', in Smith and Serrati 2000: 134–60.

(2000c) 'Rural settlement in Hellenistic and Roman Sicily: excavations at Campanaio (AG), 1994–1998', *PBSR* 68: 337–69.

(2005) 'La sopravivenza dell'influenza punica in Sicilia durante il dominio romano', in Spanò Giammellaro 2005: 907–17.

(2012) 'Agorai and fora in Hellenistic and Roman Sicily: an overview of the current *status quaestionis*', in *Ampolo* 2012: 245–67.

(2013) 'Sicily, c. 300 BC–133 BC', in *The Cambridge Ancient History, New Edition: Plates to Volumes VII.2 to IX (500–133 BC)*, ed. C. Smith. Cambridge: 156–96.

Winter, F. E. (2006) *Studies in Hellenistic Architecture*. Toronto, Buffalo and London.

Wintermeyer, U. (1975) 'Die polychrome Reliefkeramik aus Centuripe', *JDAI* 90: 136–241.

Wiseman, T. P. (1987) 'Conspicui postes tectaque digna deo: the public image of aristocratic houses in the Late Republic and Early Empire', in *L'Urbs: espace urbain et histoire (1er siècle av. J.C–IIIe siècle ap. J.C.)*. CEFR 98. Rome: 393–413.

(1998) *Roman Drama and Roman History*. Exeter.

(2004) *The Myths of Rome*. Exeter.

Wolf, M. (2003) *Die Häuser von Solunt und die hellenistische Wohnarchitektur*. Deutsches Archäologisches Institut Rom, Sonderschriften 14. Mainz am Rhein.

Wolff, S. R. (1986) 'Carthage and the Mediterranean: imported amphoras from the Punic commercial harbor', *CEA* 9: 135–53.

(2004) 'Punic amphoras in the Eastern Mediterranean', in Eiring and Lund 2004: 451–7.

Wonder, J. (2002) 'What happened to the Greeks in Lucanian-occupied Paestum? Multiculturalism in Southern Italy', *Phoenix* 56: 40–55.

Woolf, G. (1994) 'Power and the spread of writing in the west', in *Literacy and Power in the Ancient World*, eds. A. K. Bowman and G. Woolf. Cambridge: 84–98.

(1996) 'Monumental writing and the expansion of Roman society in the early empire', *JRS* 86: 22–39.

(1998) *Becoming Roman: The Origins of Provincial Civilization in Gaul*. Cambridge.

(2003) 'A sea of faith', *MHR* 18.2: 126–43 (reprinted in Malkin 2005: 126–43).

Wootton, W. (2002) 'Another Alexander mosaic. Reconstructing the Hunt mosaic from Palermo', *JRA* 15: 264–74.

(2006) *The Techniques of Production of Hellenistic and Roman Mosaics*. D. Phil. thesis, School of Archaeology, University of Oxford.

Xella, P. (1969) 'Sull'introduzione del culto di Demetra e Kore a Cartagine', *SMSR* 40: 215–28.

Yarrow, L. (2006) 'Lucius Mummius and the spoils of Corinth', *SCI* 25: 57–70.

Zachos, K. L. (2003) 'The tropaeum of the sea-battle of Actium at Nikopolis: interim report', *JRA* 16: 84–85.

Zambon, E. (2006) 'From Agathocles to Hieron II: the birth and development of *basileia* in Hellenistic Sicily', in *Ancient Tyranny*, ed. S. Lewis. Edinburgh: 77–91.

(2008) *Tradition and Innovation. Sicily between Hellenism and Rome*. Historia Einzelschriften 205. Stuttgart.

Zanker, P. (ed.) (1976a) *Hellenismus in Mittelitalien, Kolloquium in Gottingen vom 5. bis 9. Juni 1974*. Abhandlungen der Akademie der Wissenschaften in Gottingen, Philologisch-Historische Klasse 3.97. Gottingen.

(1976b) 'Einleitung', in Zanker 1976a: 11–20.

(1988a) *The Power of Images in the Age of Augustus*, transl. A. Shapiro. Ann Arbor.

(1988b) *Pompeji. Stadtbilder als Spiegel von Gesellschaft und Herrschaftsform*. Mainz.

(1993a) *Pompei. Società, immagini urbane e forme dell'abitare*, transl. A. Zambrini. Turin.

(1993b) 'The Hellenistic grave stelai from Smyrna: identity and self-image in the polis', in *Images and Ideologies. Self-Definition in the Hellenistic World*, eds. A. W. Bulloch, E. S. Gruen, A. A. Long and A. Stewart. Berkeley: 212–30.

(1998) *Pompeii: Public and Private Life*, transl. D. Lucas Schneider. Cambridge, MA.

Zevi, F. (1998) 'Die Casa del Fauno in Pompeji und das Alexandermosaik', *MDAI(R)* 105: 21–65.

Zimmerman Munn, M. L. (2003) 'Corinthian trade with the Punic West in the Classical Period', in *Corinth* XX. *The Centenary 1896–1996*, eds. C. K. Williams II and N. Bookidis. Athens: 195–218.

Zimmermann, K. (2001) 'Zur münzprägung "der Libyer" während des Söldnerkrieges', in *Punica – Libyca – Ptolemaica, Festschrift für Werner Huß, zum 65. Geburtstag dargebracht von Schülern, Freunden und Kollegen*, eds. K. Geus and K. Zimmermann. Louvain-La Neuve: 235–52.

Zucca, R. (1996) 'Inscriptiones latinae liberae rei publicae Africae, Sardiniae et Corsicae', in *L'Africa romana* 11. *Atti dell'XI convegno di studio, Cartagine, 15–18 dicembre 1994* (3 vols.), eds. M. Khanoussi, P. Ruggeri and C. Vismara. Sassari: III, 1425–89.

Zuckerman, L. (2000) *The Potato*. London.

Index

Plate I Reconstruction of the funerary bed from chamber tomb t. 520 (Fossa), with the *corredo* in the foreground.

Plate II Syracuse, Altar of Hieron seen from the north-west.

Plate III Morgantina, North Baths, vaulting tubes from the roofing as found in its collapsed state.

Plate IV Segesta, the Hellenistic theatre.

Plate V Segesta, the limestone stoa bordering the east side of the agora, reconstruction view.

Plate VI Pre-Campana Italian black glaze small bowl.

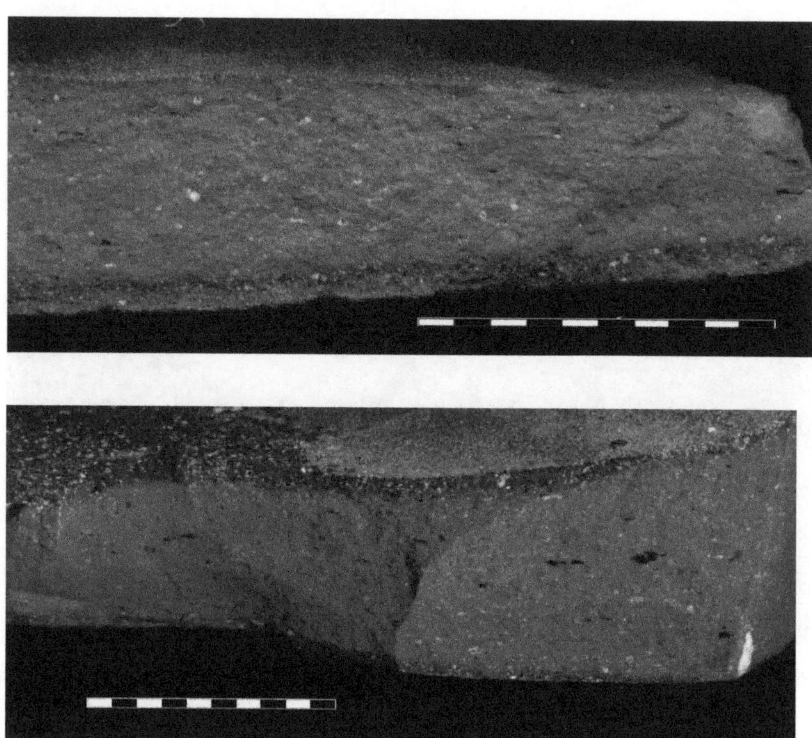

Plate VII Punic fabrics found at Euesperides. Scales in mm.

Plate VIII General view of final phase floors in Area P, Euesperides. Scale: 1m.

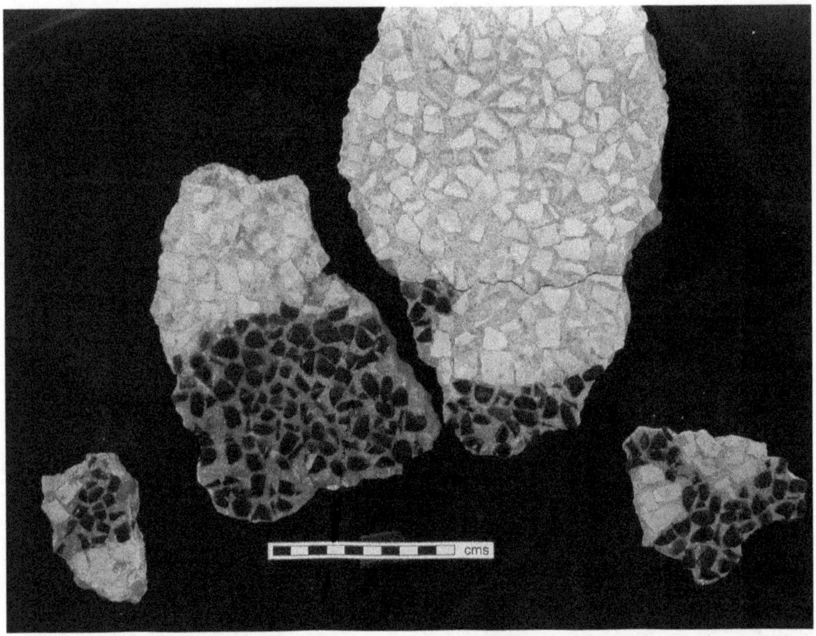

Plate IX Pebble mosaic fragments representing two dolphins (the tail belongs to a second dolphin), from the destroyed mosaic floor of the final phase in Area P, Euesperides.

Plate X The Hellenistic baths in Area Q, Euesperides.

Plate XI Detail of floor of terracotta sherds set in cement, from the Hellenistic baths, Euesperides. Scale: 10cm in cm units.

Plate XII The Thugga mausoleum.

Plate XIII The Medracen.

Plate XIV The Kbor er Roumia.

Plate XV 'Death of Sophonisba', Third Style, from Pompeii, Casa di Giuseppe II.

Plate XVI 'Death of Sophonisba', Third Style, at Pompeii, Casa del Fabbro.

Lightning Source UK Ltd.
Milton Keynes UK
UKHW051643051222
413253UK00005BA/16